Implementing Cisco IP Routing (ROUTE) Foundation Learning Guide

Diane Teare

Bob Vachon

Rick Graziani

Cisco Press

800 East 96th Street

Indianapolis, IN 46240 USA

Implementing Cisco IP Routing (ROUTE) Foundation Learning Guide

Diane Teare, Bob Vachon, Rick Graziani

Copyright © 2015 Cisco Systems, Inc.

Published by:
Cisco Press
800 East 96th Street
Indianapolis, IN 46240 USA

Printed in the United States of America

Third Printing: February 2016

Library of Congress Control Number: 2014957555

ISBN-13: 978-1-58720-456-2

ISBN-10: 1-58720-456-8

Warning and Disclaimer

This book is designed to provide information about Cisco CCNP routing. Every effort has been made to make this book as complete and as accurate as possible, but no warranty or fitness is implied.

The information is provided on an "as is" basis. The authors, Cisco Press, and Cisco Systems, Inc. shall have neither liability nor responsibility to any person or entity with respect to any loss or damages arising from the information contained in this book or from the use of the discs or programs that may accompany it.

The opinions expressed in this book belong to the author and are not necessarily those of Cisco Systems, Inc.

Trademark Acknowledgments

All terms mentioned in this book that are known to be trademarks or service marks have been appropriately capitalized. Cisco Press or Cisco Systems, Inc., cannot attest to the accuracy of this information. Use of a term in this book should not be regarded as affecting the validity of any trademark or service mark.

Special Sales

For information about buying this title in bulk quantities, or for special sales opportunities (which may include electronic versions; custom cover designs; and content particular to your business, training goals, marketing focus, or branding interests), please contact our corporate sales department at corpsales@pearsoned.com or (800) 382-3419.

For government sales inquiries, please contact governmentsales@pearsoned.com.

For questions about sales outside the U.S., please contact international@pearsoned.com.

Feedback Information

At Cisco Press, our goal is to create in-depth technical books of the highest quality and value. Each book is crafted with care and precision, undergoing rigorous development that involves the unique expertise of members from the professional technical community.

Readers' feedback is a natural continuation of this process. If you have any comments regarding how we could improve the quality of this book, or otherwise alter it to better suit your needs, you can contact us through email at feedback@ciscopress.com. Please make sure to include the book title and ISBN in your message.

We greatly appreciate your assistance.

Publisher: Paul Boger	**Associate Publisher:** Dave Dusthimer
Business Operation Manager, Cisco Press: Jan Cornelssen	**Executive Editor:** Mary Beth Ray
Managing Editor: Sandra Schroeder	**Senior Development Editor:** Christopher Cleveland
Project Editor: Mandie Frank	**Copy Editor:** Keith Cline
Technical Editor: Denise Donahue	**Team Coordinator:** Vanessa Evans
Designer: Mark Shirar	**Composition:** Trina Wurst
Indexer: Tim Wright	**Proofreader:** Paula Lowell

About the Authors

Diane Teare, P.Eng, CCNP, CCDP, CCSI, PMP, is a professional in the networking, training, project management, and e-learning fields. She has more than 25 years of experience in designing, implementing, and troubleshooting network hardware and software, and has been involved in teaching, course design, and project management. She has extensive knowledge of network design and routing technologies. Diane is a Cisco Certified Systems Instructor (CCSI), and holds her Cisco Certified Network Professional (CCNP), Cisco Certified Design Professional (CCDP), and Project Management Professional (PMP) certifications. She is an instructor, and the Course Director for the CCNA and CCNP Routing and Switching curriculum, with one of the largest authorized Cisco Learning Partners. She was the director of e-learning for the same company, where she was responsible for planning and supporting all the company's e-learning offerings in Canada, including Cisco courses. Diane has a bachelor's degree in applied science in electrical engineering and a master's degree in applied science in management science. She authored or co-authored the following Cisco Press titles: the first edition of this book; the second edition of *Designing Cisco Network Service Architectures (ARCH)*; *Campus Network Design Fundamentals*; the three editions of *Authorized Self-Study Guide Building Scalable Cisco Internetworks (BSCI)*; and *Building Scalable Cisco Networks*. Diane edited the first two editions of the *Authorized Self-Study Guide Designing for Cisco Internetwork Solutions (DESGN)*, and *Designing Cisco Networks*.

Bob Vachon, is a professor at Cambrian College in Sudbury, Ontario, Canada, where he teaches Cisco networking infrastructure courses. He has more than 30 years of work and teaching experience in the computer networking and information technology field. Since 2001, Bob has collaborated as team lead, lead author, and subject matter expert on various CCNA, CCNA-S, and CCNP projects for Cisco and the Cisco Networking Academy. He also was a contributing author for the *Routing Protocols Companion Guide*, *Connecting Networks Companion Guide*, and authored the *CCNA Security (640-554) Portable Command Guide*. In his downtime, Bob enjoys playing the guitar, playing pool, and either working in his gardens or white-water canoe tripping.

Rick Graziani teaches computer science and computer networking courses at Cabrillo College in Aptos, California. Rick has worked and taught in the computer networking and information technology field for almost 30 years. Before teaching, Rick worked in IT for various companies, including Santa Cruz Operation, Tandem Computers, and Lockheed Missiles and Space Corporation. He holds a Master of Arts degree in computer science and systems theory from California State University Monterey Bay. Rick also works for the Cisco Networking Academy Curriculum Engineering team and has written other books for Cisco Press, including *IPv6 Fundamentals*. When Rick is not working, he is most likely surfing. Rick is an avid surfer who enjoys surfing at his favorite Santa Cruz breaks.

About the Technical Reviewer

Denise Donohue, CCIE No. 9566 (Routing and Switching), is a senior solutions architect with Chesapeake NetCraftsmen. Denise has worked with computer systems since the mid-1990s, focusing on network design since 2004. During that time, she has designed for a wide range of networks, private and public, of all sizes, across most industries. Denise has also authored or co-authored many Cisco Press books covering data and voice networking technologies and spoken at Cisco Live and other industry events.

Dedications

From Diane: This book is dedicated to my husband, Allan Mertin—thank you for your love, encouragement, and patience; to our extraordinary son, Nicholas—thank you for your love and for sharing as you discover the world; and to my parents, Syd and Beryl, for their inspiration.

From Rick: This book is dedicated to the Cabrillo College CIS/CS faculty, staff, administration, and especially students for giving me the privilege and honor to teach computer networking courses at such a wonderful institution. I would also like to thank all my family and friends for their love and support.

From Bob: This book is dedicated to my beautiful wife, Judy, and my girls, Lee-Anne, Joëlle, Brigitte, and Lilly. Thank you for your encouragement and for putting up with me while working on this project. I also dedicate this book to my students at Cambrian College and to my dean, Joan Campbell, for your continued support.

Acknowledgments

We want to thank many people for helping to put this book together:

The Cisco Press team: Mary Beth Ray, the executive editor, coordinated the whole project, steered the book through the necessary processes, and understood when the inevitable snags appeared. Sandra Schroeder, the managing editor, brought the book to production. Vanessa Evans was once again wonderful at organizing the logistics and administration. Chris Cleveland, the development editor, has been invaluable in coordinating and ensuring we all focused on producing the best manuscript.

We also want to thank Mandie Frank, the project editor, and Keith Cline, the copy editor, for their excellent work in getting this book through the editorial process.

The Cisco ROUTE course development team: Many thanks to the members of the team who developed the ROUTE course.

The technical reviewer: We want to thank the technical reviewer of this book, Denise Donahue, for her thorough review and valuable input.

Our families: Of course, this book would not have been possible without the endless understanding and patience of our families. They have always been there to motivate and inspire us and we are forever grateful.

From Diane: A few special thank yous are in order. First, to Brett Bartow (who invited me to first write with Cisco Press many years ago) and Mary Beth Ray, for the very warm welcome when I finally met you both in person and for continuing to involve me in your projects. Second, to Rick and Bob for including me in this book; it has been a great pleasure to work with you both!

From Rick: A special thank you to Mary Beth Ray for giving me the opportunity years ago to begin writing for Cisco Press, and for being such a wonderful friend. Also, thank you to my two good friends Diane and Bob for letting me work with you on this book.

From Bob: A special thank you to Mary Beth Ray and her team at Cisco Press for your continued support, your professionalism, and skills to make us look good. Also, a big thank you to my fellow co-authors, Diane and my good friend Rick, whom I've had the honor and pleasure to work with on numerous projects.

Contents at a Glance

Contents

Icons Used in This Book

Router

Switch

Multilayer Switch

Cisco IOS Firewall

Route/Switch Processor

Access Server

PIX Firewall

Laptop

Server

PC

Authentication Server

Camera PC/Video

Ethernet Connection

Serial Line Connection

Network Cloud

IP Phone

Analog Phone

Command Syntax Conventions

The conventions used to present command syntax in this book are the same conventions used in the IOS Command Reference. The Command Reference describes these conventions as follows:

- **Boldface** indicates commands and keywords that are entered literally as shown. In actual configuration examples and output (not general command syntax), boldface indicates commands that are manually input by the user (such as a **show command**).

- *Italic* indicates arguments for which you supply actual values.

- Vertical bars (|) separate alternative, mutually exclusive elements.

- Square brackets ([ ]) indicate an optional element.

- Braces ({ }) indicate a required choice.

- Braces within brackets ([{ }]) indicate a required choice within an optional element.

Configuration and Verification Examples

Most of the configuration and verification examples in this book were done using Cisco IOS over Linux (IOL) virtual environment (the same environment used in the ROUTE course). This environment runs the IOS software on Linux instead of on actual router and switch hardware. As a result, there are a few things to note for these configuration examples:

- All Ethernet-type interfaces on the devices are "Ethernet" (rather than "FastEthernet" or "GigabitEthernet").

- All PCs used in the examples are actually running the IOL, so testing is done with IOS commands such as ping and traceroute.

- An interface always indicates that it is up/up unless it is shutdown. For example, if an interface on device 1 is shutdown, the interface on device 2, connected to that down interface on device 1, will indicate up/up (it does not reflect the true state).

Introduction

Networks continue to grow, becoming more complex as they support more protocols and more users. This book teaches you how to plan, implement, and monitor a scalable routing network. It focuses on using Cisco routers connected in LANs and WANs typically found at medium to large network sites.

In this book, you study a broad range of technical details on topics related to routing. First, basic network and routing protocol principles are examined in detail before the following IP Version 4 (IPv4) and IP Version 6 (IPv6) routing protocols are studied: Enhanced Interior Gateway Routing Protocol (EIGRP), Open Shortest Path First (OSPF), and Border Gateway Protocol (BGP). Enterprise Internet connectivity is explored. Manipulating routing updates and controlling the path that traffic takes are examined. Best practices for securing Cisco routers are described.

Configuration examples and sample verification outputs demonstrate troubleshooting techniques and illustrate critical issues surrounding network operation. Chapter-ending review questions illustrate and help solidify the concepts presented in this book.

This book starts you down the path toward attaining your CCNP or CCDP certification, providing in-depth information to help you prepare for the ROUTE exam (300-101).

The commands and configuration examples presented in this book are based on Cisco IOS Release 15.1 and 15.2.

Who Should Read This Book?

This book is intended for network architects, network designers, systems engineers, network managers, and network administrators who are responsible for implementing and troubleshooting growing routed networks.

If you are planning to take the ROUTE exam toward your CCNP or CCDP certification, this book provides you with in-depth study material. To fully benefit from this book, you should have your CCNA Routing and Switching certification or possess the same level of knowledge, including an understanding of the following topics:

- A working knowledge of the OSI reference model and networking fundamentals.

- The ability to operate and configure a Cisco router, including:

    - Displaying and interpreting a router's routing table

    - Configuring static and default routes

    - Enabling a WAN serial connection using High-Level Data Link Control (HDLC) or Point-to-Point Protocol (PPP), and configuring Frame Relay permanent virtual circuits (PVCs) on interfaces and subinterfaces

    - Configuring IP standard and extended access lists

    - Managing network device security

- Configuring network management protocols and managing device configurations and IOS images and licenses

- Verifying router configurations with available tools, such as **show** and **debug** commands

- Working knowledge of the TCP/IP stack, for both IPv4 and IPv6, and the ability to establish and troubleshoot Internet and WAN connectivity with both protocols

- The ability to configure, verify, and troubleshoot basic EIGRP and OSPF routing protocols, for both IPv4 and IPv6

If you lack this knowledge and these skills, you can gain them by completing the Interconnecting Cisco Network Devices Part 1 (ICND1) and Interconnecting Cisco Network Devices Part 2 (ICND2) courses or by reading the related Cisco Press books.

ROUTE Exam Topic Coverage

Cisco.com has the following information on the exam topics page for the ROUTE exam, exam number 300-101 (available at http://www.cisco.com/web/learning/exams/list/route2.html#~Topics):

"The following topics are general guidelines for the content that is likely to be included on the practical exam. However, other related topics may also appear on any specific delivery of the exam. In order to better reflect the contents of the exam and for clarity purposes, the following guidelines may change at any time without notice."

The referenced list of exam topics available at the time of writing of this book is provided in Table I-1.

The Cisco ROUTE course does not cover all the listed exam topics, and may not cover other topics to the extent needed by the exam because of classroom time constraints. The Cisco ROUTE course is not created by the same group that created the exam.

This book does provide information on each of these exam topics (except when the topic is covered by prerequisite material as noted), as identified in the "Where Topic Is Covered" column in Table I-1. This book's authors provided information related to all the exam topics to a depth that they believe should be adequate for the exam. Do note, though, that because the wording of the topics is quite general in nature and the exam itself is Cisco proprietary and subject to change, the authors of this book cannot guarantee that all the details on the exam are covered.

As mentioned, some of the listed ROUTE exam topics are actually covered by the prerequisite material. The authors believe that readers would already be familiar with this material and so have provided pointers to the relevant chapters of the ICND1 and ICND2 Foundation Learning Guide (ISBN 978-1587143762 and 978-1587143779) Cisco Press books for these topics.

Table I-1 *ROUTE Exam Topic Coverage*

Topic #	Topic	Where Topic Is Covered
1.0	Network Principles	
1.1	Identify Cisco Express Forwarding concepts	
	FIB	Chapter 5
	Adjacency table	Chapter 5
1.2	Explain general network challenges	
	Unicast	ICND1 Chapter 5
	Out-of-order packets	ICND1 Chapter 9 (sequencing)
	Asymmetric routing	Chapter 1
1.3	Describe IP operations	
	ICMP unreachable and redirects	Chapter 1, and IPv6 in ICND1 Chapter 20
	IPv4 and IPv6 fragmentation	IPv4 in Chapter 1, IPv6 in Chapter 6 and ICND1 Chapter 20
	TTL	ICND1 Chapter 7 and Glossary
1.4	Explain TCP operations	
	IPv4 and IPv6 (P)MTU	IPv4 in Chapter 1, IPv6 in Chapter 6
	MSS	Chapter 1
	Latency	ICND1 Chapter 1
	Windowing	ICND1 Chapter 9
	Bandwidth-delay product	Chapter 1
	Global synchronization	ICND1 Chapter 9
1.5	Describe UDP operations	
	Starvation	Chapter 1
	Latency	Chapter 1
1.6	Recognize proposed changes to the network	
	Changes to routing protocol parameters	Chapter 4
	Migrate parts of a network to IPv6	Chapter 6
	Routing protocol migration	Chapter 4
2.0	Layer 2 Technologies	
2.1	Configure and verify PPP	
	Authentication (PAP, CHAP)	Chapter 1
	PPPoE (client side only)	Chapter 1

Topic #	Topic	Where Topic Is Covered
2.2	Explain Frame Relay	
	Operations	Chapter 1
	Point-to-point	Chapters 1, 2, and 3
	Multipoint	Chapters 1, 2, and 3
3.0	Layer 3 Technologies	
3.1	Identify, configure, and verify IPv4 addressing and sub-netting	
	Address types (unicast, broadcast, multicast, and VLSM)	Appendix B
	ARP	Appendix B
	DHCP relay and server	Chapter 6
	DHCP protocol operations	Chapters 6 and ICND1 Chapter 16
3.2	Identify IPv6 addressing and subnetting	
	Unicast	Chapter 1
	EUI-64	Chapters 6 and ICND1 Chapter 20
	ND, RS/RA	Chapter 1
	Autoconfig (SLAAC)	Chapter 6
	DHCP relay and server	Chapter 6
	DHCP protocol operations	Chapter 6
3.3	Configure and verify static routing	Chapter 1
3.4	Configure and verify default routing	Chapter 1
3.5	Evaluate routing protocol types	
	Distance vector	Chapter 1
	Link state	Chapter 1
	Path vector	Chapter 1
3.6	Describe administrative distance	Chapter 4
3.7	Troubleshoot passive interfaces	Chapters 2 and 3
3.8	Configure and verify VRF-lite	Chapter 8
3.9	Configure and verify filtering with any protocol	Chapter 4
3.10	Configure and verify redistribution between any routing protocols or routing sources	Chapter 4
3.11	Configure and verify manual and autosummarization with any routing protocol	Chapters 1, 2, and 3
3.12	Configure and verify policy-based routing	Chapter 5
3.13	Identify suboptimal routing	Chapter 4

Topic #	Topic	Where Topic Is Covered
3.14	Explain route maps	Chapter 4
3.15	Configure and verify loop prevention mechanisms	
	Route tagging and filtering	Chapter 4
	Split horizon	Chapters 1 and 2
	Route poisoning	Chapter 1
3.16	Configure and verify RIPv2	Chapter 1
3.17	Describe RIPng	Chapter 1
3.18	Describe EIGRP packet types	Chapter 2
3.19	Configure and verify EIGRP neighbor relationship and authentication	Chapters 2 and 8
3.20	Configure and verify EIGRP stubs	Chapter 2
3.21	Configure and verify EIGRP load balancing	
	Equal cost	Chapter 2
	Unequal cost	Chapter 2
3.22	Describe and optimize EIGRP metrics	Chapter 2
3.23	Configure and verify EIGRP for IPv6	Chapter 2
3.24	Describe OSPF packet types	Chapter 3
3.25	Configure and verify OSPF neighbor relationship and authentication	Chapters 3 and 8
3.26	Configure and verify OSPF network types, area types, and router types	
	Point-to-point, multipoint, broadcast, nonbroadcast	Chapter 3
	LSA types, area type: backbone, normal, transit, stub, NSSA, totally stub	Chapter 3
	Internal router, backbone router, ABR, ASBR	Chapter 3
	Virtual link	Chapter 3
3.27	Configure and verify OSPF path preference	Chapter 3
3.28	Configure and verify OSPF operations	Chapter 3
3.29	Configure and verify OSPF for IPv6	Chapter 3
3.30	Describe, configure, and verify BGP peer relationships and authentication	
	Peer group	Chapter 7
	Active, passive	Chapter 7 (But there is no "passive" in BGP; it's "established.")
	States and timers	Chapter 7

Topic #	Topic	Where Topic Is Covered
3.31	Configure and verify eBGP (IPv4 and IPv6 address families)	
	eBGP	Chapter 7
	4-byte AS number	Chapter 6
	Private AS	Chapter 6
3.32	Explain BGP attributes and best-path selection	Chapter 7
4.0	VPN Technologies	
4.1	Configure and verify GRE	Chapter 1 for GRE tunnels; configuration and verification in ICND2 Chapter 5.
4.2	Describe DMVPN (single hub)	Chapter 1
4.3	Describe Easy Virtual Networking (EVN)	Chapter 8
5.0	Infrastructure Security	
5.1	Describe IOS AAA using local database	Chapter 8
5.2	Describe device security using IOS AAA with TACACS+ and RADIUS	
	AAA with TACACS+ and RADIUS	Chapter 8
	Local privilege authorization fallback	Chapter 8
5.3	Configure and verify device access control	
	Lines (VTY, AUX, console)	Chapter 8
	Management plane protection	Chapter 8
	Password encryption	Chapter 8
5.4	Configure and verify router security features	
	IPv4 access control lists (standard, extended, time-based)	Appendix B
	IPv6 traffic filter	Chapter 6
	Unicast reverse path forwarding	Chapter 8
6.0	Infrastructure Services	
6.1	Configure and verify device management	
	Console and vty	Chapter 8
	Telnet, HTTP, HTTPS, SSH, SCP	Chapter 8
	(T)FTP	Chapter 8

Topic #	Topic	Where Topic Is Covered
6.2	Configure and verify SNMP	
	v2	Chapter 8 and ICND2 Chapter 6
	v3	Chapter 8 and ICND2 Chapter 6
6.3	Configure and verify logging	
	Local logging, syslog, debugs, conditional debugs	Chapter 8 and ICND2 Chapter 6
	Timestamps	ICND2 Chapter 6
6.4	Configure and verify Network Time Protocol	
	NTP master, client, version 3, version 4	Chapter 8
	NTP authentication	Chapter 8
6.5	Configure and verify IPv4 and IPv6 DHCP	
	DHCP Client, IOS DHCP server, DHCP relay	Chapter 6
	DHCP options (describe)	Chapter 6
6.6	Configure and verify IPv4 Network Address Translation	
	Static NAT, dynamic NAT, PAT	Chapter 6
6.7	Describe IPv6 NAT	
	NAT64	Chapter 6
	NPTv6	Chapter 6
6.8	Describe SLA architecture	Chapter 5
6.9	Configure and verify IP SLA	
	ICMP	Chapter 5
6.10	Configure and verify tracking objects	
	Tracking object	Chapter 5
	Tracking different entities (for example, interfaces, IP SLA results)	Chapter 5
6.11	Configure and verify Cisco NetFlow	
	NetFlow v5, v9	ICND2 Chapter 6
	Local retrieval	ICND2 Chapter 6
	Export (configuration only)	ICND2 Chapter 6

How This Book Is Organized

The chapters and appendixes in this book are as follows:

■ Chapter 1, "Basic Network and Routing Concepts," begins with an overview of routing protocols that focuses on characteristics that describe their differences. It describes how limitations of different underlying technologies affect routing protocols, followed by a closer look at how Layer 2 and Layer 3 VPNs, including Dynamic Multipoint Virtual Private Network (DMVPN), affect routing protocols. RIPv2 and RIPng configuration are covered.

■ Chapter 2, "EIGRP Implementation," explains EIGRP neighbor relationships and how EIGRP chooses the best path through the network. Configuration of stub routing, route summarization, and load balancing with EIGRP are covered. Basic EIGRP for IPv6, including with route summarization is covered. The chapter concludes with a discussion of a new way of configuring EIGRP for both IPv4 and IPv6: named EIGRP.

■ Chapter 3, "OSPF Implementation," introduces basic OSPF and OSPF adjacencies, and explains how OSPF builds the routing table. OSPF summarization and stub areas are covered. The chapter concludes with the configuration of OSPFv3 using address families for IPv6 and IPv4.

■ Chapter 4, "Manipulating Routing Updates," discusses network performance issues related to routing and using multiple IP routing protocols on a network. Implementing route redistribution between different routing protocols is described, and methods of controlling the routing information sent between these routing protocols are explored, including using distribute lists, prefix lists, and route maps.

■ Chapter 5, "Path Control Implementation," starts by discussing the Cisco Express Forwarding (CEF) switching method. Path control fundamentals are explored, and two path control tools are detailed: policy-based routing (PBR) and Cisco IOS IP service-level agreements (SLAs).

■ Chapter 6, "Enterprise Internet Connectivity," describes how enterprises can connect to the Internet, which has become a vital resource for most organizations. Planning for a single connection to an Internet service provider (ISP), or redundant connections to multiple ISPs, is a very important task, and is covered first in the chapter. The details of single connections for IPv4 and IPv6 are then described. The chapter concludes with a discussion of using multiple ISP connections to improve Internet connectivity resilience.

■ Chapter 7, "BGP Implementation," describes how enterprises can use BGP when connecting to the Internet. This chapter introduces BGP terminology, concepts, and operation, and provides BGP configuration, verification, and troubleshooting techniques. The chapter describes BGP attributes and how they are used in the path selection process, and also introduces route maps for manipulating BGP path attributes and filters for BGP routing updates. The chapter concludes with a section on how BGP is used for IPv6 Internet connectivity.

- Chapter 8, "Routers and Routing Protocol Hardening," discusses how to secure the management plane of Cisco routers using recommended practices. The benefits of routing protocol authentication are described and configuration of routing authentication for EIGRP, OSPF, and BGP is presented. The chapter concludes with Cisco VRF-lite and Easy Virtual Networking (EVN).

- Appendix A, "Answers to End of Chapter Review Questions," contains the answers to the review questions that appear at the end of each chapter.

- Appendix B, "IPv4 Supplement," provides job aids and supplementary information that are intended for your use when working with IPv4 addresses. Topics include a subnetting job aid, a decimal-to-binary conversion chart, an IPv4 addressing review, an IPv4 access lists review, IP address planning, hierarchical addressing using variable-length subnet masks (VLSMs), route summarization, and classless interdomain routing (CIDR).

- Appendix C, "BGP Supplement," provides supplementary information on BGP covering the following topics: BGP route summarization, redistribution with interior gateway protocols (IGPs), communities, route reflectors, advertising a default route, and not advertising private autonomous system numbers.

- Appendix D, "Acronyms and Abbreviations" identifies abbreviations, acronyms, and initialisms used in this book.

Chapter 1

Basic Network and Routing Concepts

This chapter discusses:

- Differentiating Between Dynamic Routing Protocols

- How Different Traffic Types, Network Types, and Overlaying Network Technologies Influence Routing

- Differentiating Between the Various Branch Connectivity Options and Describing Their Impact on Routing Protocols

- How to Configure Routing Information Protocol Next Generation (RIPng)

This chapter begins with an overview of routing protocols that focuses on characteristics that describe their differences. It describes how limitations of different underlying technologies affect routing protocols, followed by a closer look at how Layer 2 and Layer 3 VPNs affect routing protocols. Dynamic Multipoint Virtual Private Network (DMVPN) is introduced as a scalable VPN solution, followed by the configuration of a simple routing protocol RIPng, which supports Internet Protocol version 6 (IPv6).

Differentiating Routing Protocols

Dynamic routing protocols play an important role in the enterprise networks of today. There are several different protocols available, with each having its advantages and limitations. Protocols can be described and compared in regard to where they operate and how they operate. Three important characteristics that also influence routing protocol selection are convergence, support for summarization, and the ability to scale in larger environments.

Upon completing this section, you will be able to:

- Identify general enterprise network infrastructure
- Describe the role of dynamic routing protocols within the enterprise network infrastructure
- Identify the major areas of differences among routing protocols
- Describe the differences between IGP and EGP routing protocols
- Describe the different types of routing protocols
- Identify the importance of convergence
- Describe route summarization
- Describe what influences routing protocol scalability

Note   The term *IP* is used for generic IP and applies to both IPv4 and IPv6. Otherwise, the terms *IPv4* and *IPv6* are used for the specific protocols.

Enterprise Network Infrastructure

Examining the network infrastructure of enterprises today can be complicated at first glance. A large number of interconnected devices and differences between physical and logical topologies are just two reasons for this complexity. To help with the analysis, most of these devices can be mapped into different areas according to the functionality that they provide in the network infrastructure. Figure 1-1 shows an example of an enterprise network infrastructure.

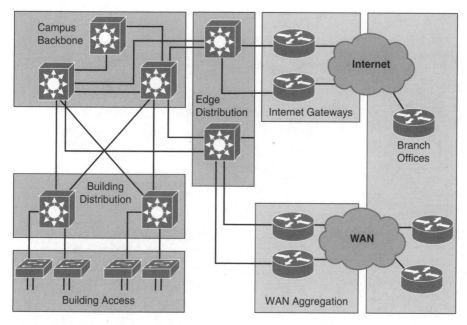

Figure 1-1 *Enterprise Network Infrastructure*

To better understand a high-level overview of a typical enterprise network, it helps if you divide it into two major areas:

- **Enterprise Campus:** An enterprise campus provides access to the network communications services and resources to end users and devices. It is spread over a single geographic location, spanning a single floor, building, or several buildings in the same locality. In networks with a single campus, it can act as the core or backbone of the network and also provide interconnectivity between other portions of the overall network infrastructure. The campus is commonly designed using a hierarchical model—comprising the core, distribution, and access layers—creating a scalable infrastructure.

- **Enterprise Edge:** An enterprise edge provides users at geographically disperse, remote sites with access to the same network services as users at the main site. Enabled access to services is achieved by aggregating connectivity from various devices and technologies at the edge of the enterprise network. The network edge aggregates private WAN links that are rented from service providers, and it enables individual users to establish VPN connections. In addition, the network edge also provides Internet connectivity for campus and branch users.

Role of Dynamic Routing Protocols

Routing protocols play an important role in networks today. They are used heavily in all network segments from the enterprise campus to branch offices to the enterprise edge. Figure 1-2 shows an example of the role of dynamic routing protocols.

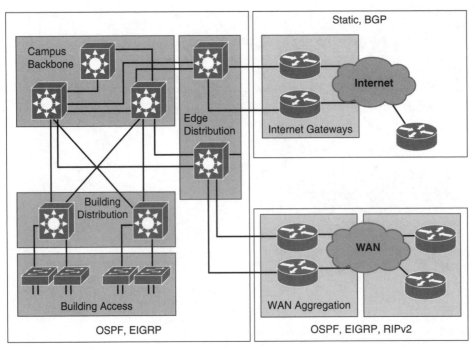

Figure 1-2   *Role of Dynamic Routing Protocols*

The basic objective of routing protocols is to exchange network reachability information between routers and dynamically adapt to network changes. These protocols use routing algorithms to determine the optimal path between different segments in the network and update routing tables with the best paths.

It is a best practice that you use one IP routing protocol throughout the enterprise, if possible. In many cases, you will manage network infrastructures where several routing protocols will coexist. One common example of when multiple routing protocols are used is when the organization is multihomed to two or more Internet service providers (ISPs) for Internet connectivity. In this scenario, the most commonly used protocol to exchange routes with the service provider is Border Gateway Protocol (BGP), whereas within the organization, Open Shortest Path First (OSPF) or Enhanced Interior Gateway Routing Protocol (EIGRP) is typically used. In smaller networks, you can also find RIPv2. In a single-homed environment where the enterprise is connected to a single ISP, static routes are commonly used between the customer and the ISP.

The choice of routing protocol or routing protocols used in a network is one factor in defining how paths are selected; for example, different administrative distances, metrics, and convergence times may result in different paths being selected.

Asymmetric routing or asymmetric traffic is traffic flows that use a different path for the return path than the original path. Asymmetric routing occurs in many networks that have redundant paths. Asymmetry, far from being a negative trait, is often a desirable network trait because it uses available bandwidth effectively, such as on an Internet connection on which downstream traffic may require higher bandwidth than upstream traffic. BGP includes a good set of tools to control traffic in both directions on an Internet connection. However, most routing protocols have no specific tools to control traffic direction.

Optimal routing in terms of network utilization within specific requirements is usually a design goal. Those requirements should be considered within the context of the applications in use, the user experience, and a comprehensive set of performance parameters.

Choosing a of Dynamic Routing Protocols

When choosing the optimal routing protocol for an organization, several different possibilities exist. There is no easy answer to what is the most optimal selection, so it is important to understand the benefits and drawbacks of each protocol. The following is a list of input requirements and protocol characteristics for choosing a dynamic routing protocol.

- **Input requirements:**
  - Size of network
  - Multivendor support
  - Knowledge level of specific protocol
- **Protocol characteristics:**
  - Type of routing algorithm
  - Speed of convergence
  - Scalability

The preceding list shows the most common input requirements that are specific to each organization. You may have to consider the network size as per your requirement, multivendor products being used, expertise level for specific protocols, and so on. You will also need to consider the common protocol characteristics that are specific to each routing protocol.

In addition to the organization having different routing protocol needs, so too do the different parts of the network. In the enterprise campus, the routing protocol must support high-availability requirements and provide very fast convergence. On the enterprise edge, between the headquarters and branch locations, it is important for routing protocols to determine optimal paths and sometimes also support the simultaneous use of multiple, unequal WAN links. If your small offices are connected over 3G or 4G mobile networks, where the amount of exchanged data is charged, very low overhead of the routing protocol can be a top priority.

IGP versus EGP

Before analyzing the behavior of individual routing protocols, you can group similar protocols together. Routing protocols can be grouped in several different ways. One option is to group them based on whether protocols operate within or between autonomous systems.

An autonomous system (AS) represents a collection of network devices under a common administrator. Typical examples of an AS are an internal network of an enterprise or a network infrastructure of an ISP.

Routing protocols can be divided based on whether they exchange routes within an AS or between different autonomous systems:

- **Interior Gateway Protocols (IGP):** These are used within the organization, and they exchange the routes within an AS. They can support small, medium-sized, and large organizations, but their scalability has its limits. The protocols can offer very fast convergence, and basic functionality is not complex to configure. The most commonly used IGPs in enterprises are Enhanced Interior Gateway Routing Protocol (EIGRP) and Open Shortest Path First (OSPF) as well as Routing Information Protocol (RIP) (rarely). Within the service provider internal network, the routing protocol named Intermediate System-to-Intermediate System (IS-IS) is also commonly found.

- **Exterior Gateway Protocols (EGP):** These take care of exchanging routes between different autonomous systems. Border Gateway Protocol (BGP) is the only EGP that is used today. The main function of BGP is to exchange a huge number of routes between different autonomous systems that are part of the largest network (the Internet).

Figure 1-3 illustrates the differences between an IGP and an EGP.

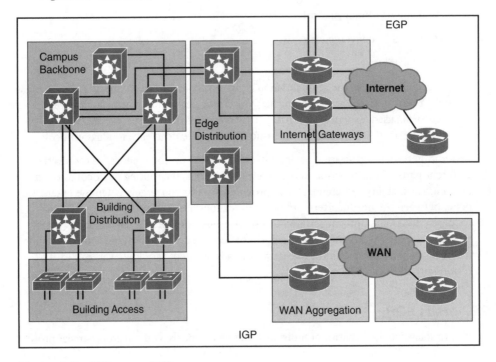

Figure 1-3 *IGP versus EGP*

Types of Routing Protocols

Routing protocols can also be divided based on which kind of information about network reachability is exchanged between the routers, distance vector, link-state or path vector. Table 1-1 shows how RIP, EIGRP, OSPF, IS-IS, and BGP routing protocols are categorized by type of routing protocol.

Table 1-1 *Routing Protocol Classification*

	Interior Gateway Protocols				Exterior Gateway Protocols
	Distance Vector		**Link-State**		**Path Vector**
IPv4	RIPv2	EIGRP	OSPFv2	IS-IS	BGP-4
IPv6	RIPng	EIGRP for IPv6	OSPFv3	IS-IS for IPv6	MBGP

Routing protocols can be divided into the following groups:

- **Distance vector protocols:** The distance vector routing approach determines the direction (vector) and distance (such as link cost or number of hops) to any link in the network. Distance vector protocols use routers as signposts along the path to the final destination. The signpost only indicates direction and distance, but gives no indication of what the path is like. The only information that a router knows about a remote network is the distance or metric to reach this network and which path or interface to use to get there. Distance vector routing protocols do not have an actual map of the network topology. Early distance vector protocols, such as RIPv1 and IGRP, used only the periodic exchange of routing information for a topology change. Later versions of these distance vector protocols (EIGRP and RIPv2) implemented triggered updates to respond to topology changes.

- **Link-state protocols:** The link-state approach uses the Shortest Path First (SPF) algorithm to create an abstract of the exact topology of the entire network or at least within its area. A link-state routing protocol is like having a complete map of the network topology. The map is used to determine best path to a destination instead of using signposts. The signposts along the way from the source to the destination are not necessary because all link-state routers have an identical "map" of the network. A link-state router uses the link-state information to create a topology map and to select the best path to all destination networks in the topology. The OSPF and IS-IS protocols are examples of link-state routing protocols.

- **Path vector protocols:** The path vector routing approach not only exchanges information about the existence of destination networks but also exchanges the path on how to reach the destination. Path information is used to determine the best paths and to prevent routing loops. Similar to distance vector protocols, path vector protocols do not have an abstract of the network topology. Using the signpost analogy, path vector protocols use signposts indicating direction and distance, but also include additional information about the specific path of the destination. The only widely used path vector protocol is BGP.

Convergence

Convergence describes the process of when routers notice change in the network, exchange the information about the change, and perform necessary calculations to re-evaluate the best routes.

A converged network describes the state of the network in which all routers have the same view on the network topology. Convergence is the normal and desired state of the network, and it is achieved when all routing information is exchanged between routers participating in the routing protocol. Any topology change in the network temporarily breaks the convergence until the change is propagated to all routers and best paths are recalculated.

As shown in Figure 1-4, a broken primary method of connectivity for Branch B introduces a topology change and breaks the convergence state. When information about the unavailable WAN link is propagated to routers, the routing protocol determines the new best path to reach affected destination networks.

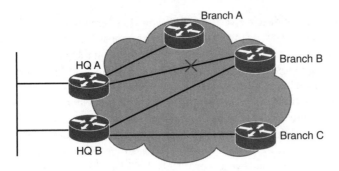

Figure 1-4   *Convergence*

Convergence time describes how fast network devices can reach the state of convergence after a topology change. Business continuity requires high availability of the network services. To minimize downtime and quickly respond to network changes, a fast convergence time is desired. Speed of convergence can be influenced by several factors. One of the determining factors is the choice of routing protocol. Each protocol uses a different mechanism to exchange information, trigger updates, and calculate the best path. While IGPs achieve acceptable convergence times using default settings, BGP as an EGP, by default, reacts to network changes in a slower manner.

There are several ways that you can influence convergence time. The first common option is to fine-tune timers that are used by routing protocols. Tuning timers enables you to instruct the routing protocol to exchange information more frequently. With faster timers, network change is detected more quickly, and information about the change can be sent sooner. Keep in mind, however, that faster timers also introduce greater protocol overhead or higher utilization on less powerful platforms.

The second common option to influence convergence time is to configure route summarization. Route summarization reduces the amount of information that needs to be exchanged between the routers and lowers the number of routers that need to receive topology change information. Both of these conditions help lower the needed convergence time, regardless of the protocol that is used.

Route Summarization

Route summarization enables you to reduce routing overhead and improve stability and scalability of routing by reducing the amount of routing information that is maintained and exchanged between routers. This results in smaller routing tables and improves convergence.

The purpose of route summarization is to squeeze several subnets into one aggregate entry that describes all of them. As shown in Figure 1-5, route summarization reduces the size of routing tables because only one summary route is received by Router B, instead of eight more detailed routes.

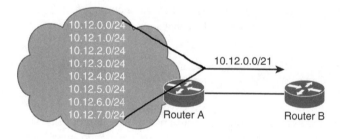

Figure 1-5 *Route Summarization on Router A*

In addition, route summarization also reduces the number of updates that needs to be exchanged between these two routers. For example, examine the event of network change, when network 10.12.6.0/24 becomes unreachable. Router A does not need to inform the neighbor about an unreachable prefix because the summary route is not affected by the network change.

Less frequent and smaller updates, as a result of route summarization, also lower convergence time. For this reason, route summarization is heavily used in larger networks where convergence time can be a limiting factor for further network growth.

Different routing protocols support different route summarization options. While distance vector protocols support route summarization configuration on each outbound interface, link-state protocols support summarization only at area boundaries.

When planning for route summarization, also keep in mind that in order to implement route summarization efficiently, IP addresses must be hierarchically assigned in contiguous blocks across the network.

Route Protocol Scalability

As a network grows and becomes larger, the risk of routing protocol instability or long convergence times becomes greater. Scalability describes the ability of a routing protocol to support further network growth.

Scalability factors include:

- Number of routes

- Number of adjacent neighbors

- Number of routers in the network

- Network design

- Frequency of changes

- Available resources (CPU and memory)

The ability to scale the network depends on the overall network structure and addressing scheme. The number of adjacent neighbors, number of routes, and number of routers along with their utilization and frequency of network changes are the impacting factors that affect protocol scalability the most.

Hierarchical addressing, structured address assignment, and route summarization improve the overall scalability regardless of routing protocol type.

Each routing protocol also implements additional protocol-specific features to improve the overall scalability. OSPF, for example, supports the use of hierarchical areas that divide one large network into several subdomains. EIGRP, on the other hand, supports the configuration of stub routers to optimize information exchange process and improve scalability.

The scalability of the routing protocol and its configuration options to support a larger network can play an important role when evaluating routing protocols against each other.

Understanding Network Technologies

You can establish routing protocols over a variety of different network technologies. It is important to consider the limitations of a specific solution and how it affects routing protocol deployments and operation.

Upon completing this section, you will be able to:

- Differentiate traffic types

- Differentiate IPv6 address types

- Describe ICMPv6 neighbor discovery

- Differentiate network types

- Describe the impact of NBMA (Nonbroadcast Multiaccess) on routing protocols

- Describe how the Internet breaks enterprise routing

Traffic Types

By using a specific destination IP address type, the device can send traffic to one recipient, to selected recipients, or to all devices within a subnet at the same time. Routing protocols use different traffic types to control how routing information is exchanged.

Selecting a destination IP according to different address types enables a device to send different types of traffic:

- **Unicast:** Unicast addresses are used in a one-to-one context. Unicast traffic is exchanged only between one sender and one receiver. Source addresses can only be a unicast address.

- **Multicast:** Multicast addresses identify a group of interfaces across different devices. Traffic that is sent to a multicast address is sent to multiple destinations at the same time. An interface may belong to any number of multicast groups. In IPv4, the reserved address space range for multicast addresses is 224.0.0.0–239.255.255.255. IPv6 reserved multicast addresses have the prefix FF00::/8.

- **Anycast:** An anycast address is assigned to an interface on more than one node. When a packet is sent to an anycast address, it is routed to the nearest interface that has this address. The nearest interface is found according to the measure of distance of the particular routing protocol. All nodes that share the same address should behave the same way so that the service is offered similarly regardless of the node that services the request. A common use case for anycast is the Internet DNS server. There are several instances of the same server across the world, and anycast enables you to reach the nearest one by simply using the anycast destination address. The arrows in the figure for anycast indicate that one destination is closer than the other.

- **Broadcast:** IPv4 broadcast addresses are used when sending traffic to all devices in the subnet. Information is transmitted from one sender to all connected receivers. Local broadcast address 255.255.255.255 is used when you wish to communicate with all devices on the local network. The directed broadcast address, which is the last IPv4 address in each subnet, allows a device to reach all devices in a remote network. IPv6 does not use a broadcast address, but uses multicast addresses instead, as discussed in the next section, "IPv6 Address Types."

Figure 1-6 illustrates the four different traffic types.

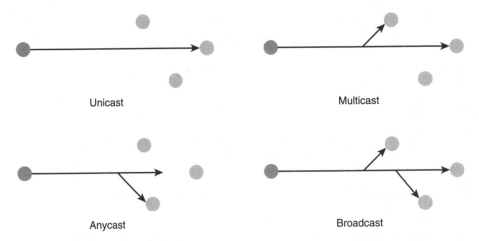

Figure 1-6 *Traffic Types*

Early routing protocols used only broadcasts to exchange routing information. Broadcast messages containing routing updates unnecessarily utilized other devices that were connected to the same network because each device needed to process broadcast packets when they were received. All modern IGPs use multicast addresses to perform neighbor discovery, exchange routing information, and send updates.

Table 1-2 lists some of the well-known IPv4 and IPv6 multicast addresses used by routing protocols. Notice that the low-order values in the multicast addresses are the same for both IPv4 and IPv6.

Table 1-2 *Well-known IPv4 and Assigned IPv6 Multicast Addresses Used by Routing Protocols*

IPv4 Multicast Address	Description
224.0.0.5	Used by OSPFv2: All OSPF Routers
224.0.0.6	Used by OSPFv2: All Designated Routers
224.0.0.9	Used by RIPv2
224.0.0.10	Used by EIGRP
IPv6 Multicast Address	**Description**
FF02::5	Used by OSPFv3: All OSPF Routers
FF02::6	Used by OSPFv3: All Designated Routers
FF02::9	Used by RIPng
FF02::A	Used by EIGRP for IPv6

IPv6 Address Types

There are several different basic types of IPv6 addresses as shown in Figure 1-7. It is important that you are familiar with them, since some of them are also used by routing protocols.

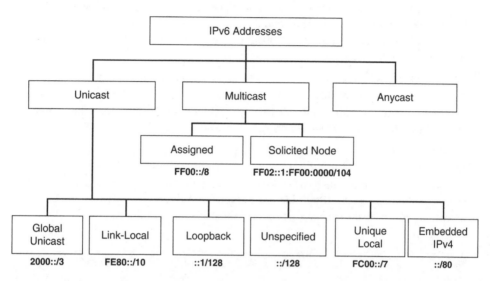

Figure 1-7 *IPv6 Address Types*

RFC 3587 specifies 2000::/3 to be global unicast address space that the IANA may allocate to the Regional Internet Registries (RIRs). A global unicast address is an IPv6 address from the global unicast prefix, equivalent to a public IPv4 address. These addresses are unique and globally routable. The allocation and structure of global unicast addresses enables the aggregation of routing prefixes, which limits the number of routing table entries in the global routing table. Global unicast addresses that are used on links are aggregated upward through organizations and eventually to the ISPs.

IPv6 link-local addresses use the prefix FE80::/10 (1111 1110 10). Any device that is an IPv6 device must at least have a link-local address, which is automatically configured by default using EUI-64 or the privacy extension, although the link-local address can be statically configured. Routers typically have statically configured link-local addresses to make the address more easily recognizable when looking at IPv6 routing tables and examining IPv6 routing protocol information. Nodes on a local link can use link-local addresses to communicate; the nodes do not need globally unique addresses to communicate. Link-local addresses are not routable, therefore only stay on the link or network.

Multicast addresses are heavily used in IPv6 as there are no broadcast addresses. You can recognize them as part of the prefix FF00::/8. There are both assigned and solicited node multicast addresses. Routing protocols make extensive use of the assigned multicast addresses. Assigned multicast addresses are similar to well-known multicast addresses in IPv4 used by routing protocols such as EIGRP and OSPF. Solicited node multicast addresses are used by ICMPv6 Neighbor Discovery (ND) address resolution. Similar to ARP for IPv4, ND address resolution is used to map a Layer 2 MAC address to a Layer 3 IPv6 address.

Unique local addresses are IPv6 unicast addresses that are globally unique and are intended for local communications. It is not expected to be routable on the global Internet and is routable inside of a limited area, such as a site. It may also be routed between a limited set of sites. The FC00::/7 prefix is used to identify the unique local IPv6 unicast addresses.

Just as in IPv4, a provision has been made for a special loopback IPv6 address for testing; datagrams that are sent to this address "loop back" to the sending device. In IPv6, however, there is just one address rather than a whole block for this function. The loopback address is 0:0:0:0:0:0:0:1, which is normally expressed as "::1".

In IPv4, an address of all zeroes has a special meaning in that it refers to the host itself and is used when a device does not know its own address. In IPv6, this concept has been formalized, and the all-zeroes address is named the "unspecified" address, "::". This address is used as a source IPv6 address and typically indicates the absence of a global unicast address or that the source address of the packet is insignificant.

Note   For more information about IPv6 addressing, see *IPv6 Fundamentals*, by Rick Graziani (Cisco Press, 2013).

ICMPv6 Neighbor Discovery

Internet Control Message Protocol for IPv6 (ICMPv6) is similar to ICMP for IPv4 (ICMPv4). Like ICMPv4, ICMPv6 uses informational and error messages for testing Layer 3 connectivity and to inform the source of any issues such as the network is unreachable.

ICMPv6 is also a much more robust protocol than its IPv4 counterpart as it includes ICMPv6 Neighbor Discovery Protocol as described in RFC 4861. ICMPv6 Neighbor Discovery is used for automatic address allocation, address resolution, and duplicate address detection in IPv6. ICMPv6 Neighbor Discovery includes five messages:

- **Router Solicitation (RS):** Sent by a device to the all IPv6 routers multicast to request a Router Advertisement message from the router.

- **Router Advertisement (RA):** Sent by an IPv6 router to the all IPv6 devices multicast. Includes link information such as prefix, prefix-length, and the default gateway address. The RA also indicates to the host whether it needs to use a stateless or stateful DHCPv6 server.

- **Neighbor Solicitation (NS):** Sent by a device to the solicited node multicast address when it knows the IPv6 address of a device but not its Ethernet MAC address. This is similar to Address Resolution Protocol (ARP) for IPv4.

- **Neighbor Advertisement (NA):** Sent by a device usually in response to a Neighbor Solicitation message. Sent as a unicast, it informs the recipient of its Ethernet MAC address associated with the IPv6 address in the NS message.

- **Redirect:** This has similar functionality as in IPv4. Sent by a router to inform the source of a packet of a better next-hop router on the link that is closer to the destination.

Network Types

Not all Layer 2 network topologies support all traffic types. Because unsupported traffic types influence the operation of routing protocols, it is important to be aware of the limitations of specific network topologies. As shown in Figure 1-8, there are three general network types, described further in the list that follows.

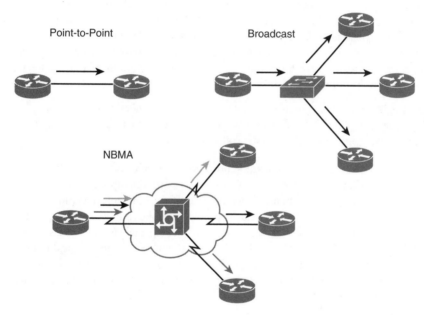

Figure 1-8   *Network Types*

- **Point-to-point network:** A network that connects a single pair of routers. A packet that is sent from one end is received exactly by one recipient on the other end of the link. A serial link is an example of a point-to-point connection.

- **Broadcast network:** A network that can connect many routers along with the capability to address a single message to all of the attached routers. Ethernet is an example of a broadcast network.

- **Nonbroadcast Multiaccess (NBMA) network:** A network that can support many routers but does not have broadcast capability. The sender needs to create an individual copy of the same packet for each recipient if it wishes to inform all connected neighbors. Also, the sender must know the recipient address before the packet can be transmitted. Frame Relay and Asynchronous Transfer Mode (ATM) are examples of an NBMA network type.

While point-to-point and broadcast networks do not present any difficulties for routing protocols, NBMA networks introduce several challenges. Routing protocols need to be adapted through configuration in how they perform neighbor discovery. Distance vector protocols need additional configuration, which also changes the default behavior of how routing information is exchanged between neighbors. This is due to the loop prevention mechanism split horizon that prevents the transmitting of information that is received on a specific interface from going out of that same interface.

NBMA Networks

NBMA networks can use a variety of topologies. The most common are hub-and-spoke or partial-mesh topologies. This is because full-mesh topologies do not scale well and can become very expensive with a greater number of interconnected locations. Frame Relay technology is the most common example of an NBMA network. There are several options for how you can adapt routing protocols to support operations in a Frame Relay NBMA, hub-and-spoke network.

If you use a single Frame Relay, multipoint interface to interconnect multiple sites, reachability issues may be a problem because of the NBMA nature of Frame Relay. The Frame Relay NBMA topology can cause the following issues:

- **Split horizon:** For distance vector routing protocols, the split-horizon rule reduces routing loops. As illustrated in Figure 1-9, it prevents a routing update that is received on an interface from being forwarded out of the same interface. In a scenario using a hub-and-spoke Frame Relay topology, a spoke router sends an update to the hub router that is connecting multiple permanent virtual circuits (PVCs) over a single physical interface. The hub router receives the update on its physical interface but cannot forward it through the same interface to other spoke routers. Split horizon is not a problem if there is a single PVC on a physical interface because this type of connection would be point-to-point.

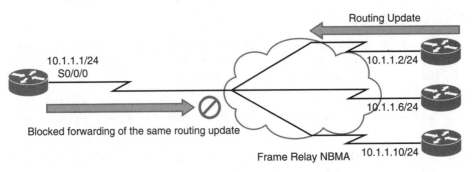

Figure 1-9 *Split Horizon*

■ **Neighbor discovery:** OSPF over NBMA networks works in a nonbroadcast network mode by default, and neighbors are not automatically discovered. You can statically configure neighbors, but an additional configuration is required to manually configure the hub as a Designated Router (DR). OSPF treats an NBMA network like Ethernet by default, and on Ethernet, a DR is needed to exchange routing information between all routers on a segment. Therefore, only the hub router can act as a DR because it is the only router that has PVCs with all other routers.

■ **Broadcast replication:** With routers that support multipoint connections over a single interface that terminates at multiple PVCs, the router must replicate broadcast packets, such as routing update broadcasts, on each PVC to the remote routers. These replicated broadcast packets consume bandwidth and cause significant latency variations in user traffic.

When a router is connected to multiple physical locations over a WAN NBMA link, you can use the logical subinterfaces to terminate multiple virtual circuits on one physical interface. Subinterfaces also overcome some limitations of NBMA networks. You can choose between two different types of subinterfaces:

■ **Point-to-point subinterfaces:** Each subinterface, which provides connectivity between two routers, uses its own subnet for addressing. From a perspective of routing protocol, connectivity looks just like several physical point-to-point links, which means there are no issues with neighbor discovery and the split-horizon rule. Figure 1-10 shows an example of point-to-point subinterfaces.

■ **Point-to-multipoint subinterfaces:** One subnet is shared between all virtual circuits. Because private address space is normally used for addressing, saving address space is not a significant benefit. Because both EIGRP and OSPF need additional configuration to support this underlying technology, point-to-point subinterfaces are the preferred and recommended choice.

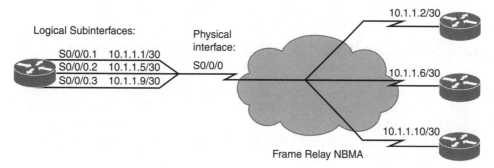

Figure 1-10 *Point-to-Point Subinterfaces*

Routing Over the Internet

You can select among several different options and technologies when choosing how to interconnect remote locations with a central location such as a headquarters site. One of the options is to rent Internet connectivity, which is usually a less expensive alternative.

There are several reasons why IGP routing protocols are not used to establish connections over the Internet:

- All IGPs establish adjacency only between directly connected neighbors. Routers that are connected over the Internet are several hops apart.

- Typically within an organization, you use private IPv4 addressing while packets that are sent to the Internet get routed only if public IPv4 addressing is used. If you would wish to route internal traffic between remote locations over the Internet, you would need to use NATs extensively. Relying on NAT in this scenario introduces great complexity as both the sender and receiver IPv4 addresses need to be translated to public IPv4 addresses.

- The Internet as a transport medium cannot be trusted. Anyone who is part of the transport path can eavesdrop or modify data. Without additional security mechanisms, the Internet is not suitable to exchange private data.

To overcome the described obstacles, different tunneling mechanisms can be used that extend a private network across the Internet. Although there are several different technologies involved, they are generally named virtual private networks (VPNs), which enable the exchange of information as if remote hosts would be connected to the same private network. The majority of VPN technologies also support routing protocols. Neighbor adjacencies between routers are established over tunnel interfaces, which are created when VPNs are established.

VPN technologies are well integrated with additional security mechanisms, which provide suitable authentication, encryption, and antireplay protection.

Connecting Remote Locations with Headquarters

To connect remote locations with the headquarters, there is no longer a need to use only traditional solutions such as leased lines or Frame Relay connections. Newer technologies, such as Multiprotocol Label Switching (MPLS) VPNs and DMVPNs, are now widespread because they offer more flexibility at a lower cost compared to traditional solutions. It is important to be aware of these new VPN types because they also influence deployments and the configuration of routing protocols.

Upon completing this lesson, you will be able to:

- Identify options for connecting branch offices and remote locations

- Describe the use of static and default static routes

- Describe basic PPP configuration on point-to-point serial links

- Describe basic Frame Relay on point-to-point serial links

- Explain VRF Lite

- Describe the interaction of routing protocols over MPLS VPNs

- Explain the use of GRE for branch connectivity

- Describe Dynamic Multipoint virtual private networks

- Describe multipoint GRE tunnels

- Describe the Next Hop Resolution Protocol

- Identify the role of IPsec in DMVPN solutions

Principles of Static Routing

This section explains the situations in which static routes are the most appropriate to use.

A static route can be used in the following circumstances:

- When it is undesirable to have dynamic routing updates forwarded across slow bandwidth links, such as a dialup link.

- When the administrator needs total control over the routes used by the router.

- When a backup to a dynamically recognized route is necessary.

- When it is necessary to reach a network accessible by only one path (a stub network). For example, in Figure 1-11, there is only one way for Router A to reach the 10.2.0.0/16 network on Router B. The administrator can configure a static route on Router A to reach the 10.2.0.0/16 network via its Serial 0/0/0 interface.

- When a router connects to its ISP and needs to have only a default route pointing toward the ISP router, rather than learning many routes from the ISP.

- When a router is underpowered and does not have the CPU or memory resources necessary to handle a dynamic routing protocol.

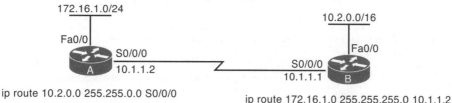

Figure 1-11 *Configuring Static Routing*

A perfect use for static routing is a hub-and-spoke design, with all remote sites defaulting back to the central site (the hub) and the one or two routers at the central site having a static route for all subnets at each remote site. The caveat is that without proper design, as the network grows into hundreds of routers, with each router having numerous subnets, the number of static routes on each router also increases. Each time a new subnet or router is added, an administrator must add a static route to the new networks on several routers. The administrative burden to maintain this network can become excessive, making dynamic routing a better choice.

Another drawback of static routing is that when a topology change occurs on the internetwork, an administrator might have to reroute traffic by configuring new static routes around the problem area. In contrast, with dynamic routing, the routers must learn the new topology. The routers share information with each other and their routing processes automatically discover whether any alternative routes exist and reroute without administrator intervention. Because the routers mutually develop an independent agreement of what the new topology is, they are said to converge on what the new routes should be. Dynamic routing provides faster convergence than statically configured routes.

Configuring an IPv4 Static Route

Use the **ip route** *prefix mask* {*address* | *interface* [*address*]} [**dhcp**] [*distance*] [**name** *next-hop-name*] [**permanent**| **track** *number*] [**tag** *tag*] global configuration command to create IPv4 static routes. Table 1-3 explains the parameters of this command.

Table 1-3   ip route *Command*

ip route **Command**	**Description**
prefix mask	The IPv4 network and subnet mask for the remote network to be entered into the IPv4 routing table.
address	The IPv4 address of the next hop that can be used to reach the destination network.
interface	The local router outbound interface to be used to reach the destination network.
dhcp	(Optional) Enables a Dynamic Host Configuration Protocol (DHCP) server to assign a static route to a default gateway (option 3).
distance	(Optional) The administrative distance to be assigned to this route. Must 1 or greater.
name *next-hop-name*	(Optional) Applies a name to the specified route.
permanent	(Optional) Specifies that the route will not be removed from the routing table even if the interface associated with the route goes down.
track *number*	(Optional) Associates a track object with this route. Valid values for the number argument range from 1 to 500.
tag *tag*	(Optional) A value that can be used as a match value in route maps.

If no dynamic routing protocol is used on a link connecting two routers, such as in Figure 1-11, a static route must be configured on the routers on both sides of the link; otherwise, the remote router will not know how to return the packet to its originator located on the other network—there will be only one-way communication.

While configuring a static route, you must specify either a next-hop IP address or an exit interface to notify the router which direction to send traffic. Figure 1-11 shows both configurations. Router A recognizes the directly connected networks 172.16.1.0 and 10.1.1.0. It needs a route to the remote network 10.2.0.0. Router B knows about the directly connected networks 10.2.0.0 and 10.1.1.0; it needs a route to the remote network 172.16.1.0. Notice that on Router B, the next-hop IP address of the Router A serial interface has been used. On Router A, however, the **ip route** command specifies its own Serial 0/0/0 interface as the exit interface. If a next-hop IP address is used, it should be the IP address of the interface of the router on the other end of the link. If an exit interface is used, the local router sends data out of the specified interface to the router on the other end of its attached link. When an exit interface is specified, although the entry in the routing table indicates "directly connected," it is still a static route with an administrative distance of 1 and not a directly connected network with an administrative distance of 0.

Note   This section describes the use and configuration of IPv4 static routes. The same practices and similar configuration also applies to IPv6 static routes.

Cisco Express Forwarding (CEF) is enabled by default on most Cisco platforms running Cisco IOS Software Release 12.0 or later. Prior to IOS 12.0 it was more efficient to use an exit interface instead of a next-hop IP address on point-to-point links. Using an exit interface meant the router didn't have to perform a recursive lookup in the routing table to find the exit interface. With CEF now being the default on IOS, however, it is recommended that the next-hop IP address is used.

Note   CEF provides optimized lookup for efficient packet forwarding by using two main data structures stored in the data plane: a Forwarding Information Base (FIB), which is a copy of the routing table, and an adjacency table that includes Layer 2 addressing information. The information combined in both of these tables work together so there is no recursive lookup needed for next-hop IP address lookups. In other words, a static route using a next-hop IP requires only a single lookup when CEF is enabled on the router.

Configuring a Static Default Route

In some circumstances, a router does not need to recognize the details of remote networks. The router is configured to send all traffic, or all traffic for which there is not a more specific entry in the routing table, in a particular direction; this is known as a default route. Default routes are either dynamically advertised using routing protocols or statically configured.

To create a static default route, use the normal **ip route** command, but with the destination network (the *prefix* in the command syntax) and its subnet mask (the *mask* in the command syntax) both set to 0.0.0.0. This address is a type of wildcard designation; any destination network will match. Because the router tries to match the longest common bit pattern, a network listed in the routing table is used before the default route. If the destination network is not listed in the routing table, the default route is used.

In Figure 1-12, on Router A, the static route to the 10.2.0.0 network has been replaced with a static default route pointing to Router B. On Router B, a static default route has been added, pointing to its ISP. Traffic from a device on the Router A 172.16.1.0 network bound for a network on the Internet is sent to Router B. Router B recognizes that the destination network does not match any specific entries in its routing table and sends that traffic to the ISP. It is then the ISP's responsibility to route that traffic to its destination.

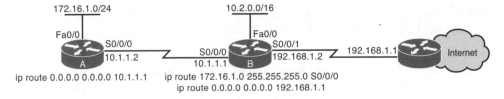

Figure 1-12 *Configuring the Static Default Route*

In Figure 1-12, to reach the 172.16.1.0/24 network, Router B still needs a static route pointing out its S0/0/0 interface.

Entering the **show ip route** command on Router A in Figure 1-12 returns the information shown in Example 1-1.

Example 1-1 show ip route *Command*

```
RouterA# show ip route
<Output omitted>
Gateway of last resort is not set
C    172.16.1.0 is directly connected, FastEthernet0/0
C    10.1.1.0 is directly connected, Serial0/0/0
S*   0.0.0.0/0 [1/0] via 10.1.1.1
```

Basic PPP Overview

Point-to-Point Protocol (PPP) has several advantages over its predecessor High-Level Data Link Control (HDLC). This section introduces PPP as well as examines the benefits of PPP. Recall that HDLC is the default serial encapsulation method when connecting two Cisco routers. With an added protocol type field, the Cisco version of HDLC is proprietary. Thus, Cisco HDLC can work only with other Cisco devices; however, when there is a need to connect to a non-Cisco router, PPP encapsulation can be used.

Basic PPP configuration is very straightforward. After PPP is configured on an interface the network administrator can then apply one or more PPP options.

To set PPP as the encapsulation method used by a serial interface, use the **encapsulation ppp** interface configuration command.

The following example enables PPP encapsulation on interface serial 0/0/0:

```
R1# configure terminal
R1(config)# interface serial 0/0/0
R1(config-if)# encapsulation ppp
```

The **encapsulation ppp** interface command has no arguments. Remember that if PPP is not configured on a Cisco router, the default encapsulation for serial interfaces is HDLC. Other PPP configuration options include PPP compression, PPP quality link monitoring, PPP multilink, and PPP authentication.

The abbreviated listing that follows shows that router R1 has been configured with both an IPv4 and an IPv6 address on the serial interface. PPP is a Layer2 encapsulation that supports various Layer 3 protocols including IPv4 and IPv6.

```
hostname R1
!
interface Serial 0/0/0
ip address 10.0.1.1 255.255.255.252
ipv6 address 2001:db8:cafe:1::1/64
encapsulation ppp
```

PPP Authentication Overview

RFC 1334 defines two protocols for authentication, PAP and CHAP. PAP is a very basic two-way process. There is no encryption. The username and password are sent in plaintext. If it is accepted, the connection is allowed. CHAP is more secure than PAP. It involves a three-way exchange of a shared secret.

The authentication phase of a PPP session is optional. If used, the peer is authenticated after LCP (Link Control Protocol) establishes the link and chooses the authentication protocol. If it is used, authentication takes place before the network layer protocol configuration phase begins.

The authentication options require that the calling side of the link enter authentication information. This helps to ensure that the user has the permission of the network administrator to make the call. Peer routers exchange authentication messages.

To specify the order in which the CHAP or PAP protocols are requested on the interface, use the **ppp authentication** interface configuration command.

```
Router(config-if)# ppp authentication {chap | chap pap | pap chap | pap} [if-needed]
[list-name | default] [callin]
```

Use the **no** form of the command to disable this authentication.

Table 1-4 explains the syntax for the **ppp authentication** interface configuration command.

Table 1-4   *PPP Command Syntax*

ip route **Command**	Description
chap	Enables CHAP on serial interface.
pap	Enables PAP on serial interface.
chap pap	Enables both CHAP and PAP on serial interface, and performs CHAP authentication before PAP.
pap chap	Enables both CHAP and PAP on serial interface, and performs PAP authentication before CHAP.
if-needed (Optional)	Used with TACACS and XTACACS. Do not perform CHAP or PAP authentication if the user has already provided authentication. This option is available only on asynchronous interfaces.
list-name (Optional)	Used with AAA/TACACS+. Specifies the name of a list of TACACS+ methods of authentication to use. If no list name is specified, the system uses the default. Lists are created with the **aaa authentication ppp** command.
default (Optional)	Used with AAA/TACACS+. Created with the **aaa authentication ppp** command.
callin	Specifies authentication on incoming (received) calls only.

After you have enabled CHAP or PAP authentication, or both, the local router requires the remote device to prove its identity before allowing data traffic to flow. This is done as follows:

- PAP authentication requires the remote device to send a name and password to be checked against a matching entry in the local username database or in the remote *TACACS/TACACS+* database.

- CHAP authentication sends a challenge to the remote device. The remote device must encrypt the challenge value with a shared secret and return the encrypted value and its name to the local router in a response message. The local router uses the name of the remote device to look up the appropriate secret in the local username or remote TACACS/TACACS+ database. It uses the looked-up secret to encrypt the original challenge and verify that the encrypted values match.

Both routers authenticate and are authenticated, so the PAP authentication commands mirror each other. The PAP username and password that each router sends must match those specified with the **username** *name* **password** *password* command of the other router.

PAP provides a simple method for a remote node to establish its identity using a two-way handshake. This is done only on initial link establishment. The hostname on one router must match the username the other router has configured for PPP. The passwords must also match. Specify the username and password parameters, use the following command: **ppp pap sent-username** *name* **password** *password*.

Partial running-config for R1:

```
hostname R1
username R2 password sameone
!
interface Serial0/0/0
 ip address 10.0.1.1 255.255.255.252
 ipv6 address 2001:DB8:CAFE:1::1/64
 encapsulation ppp
 ppp authentication pap
 ppp pap sent-username R1 password sameone
```

Partial running-config for R2:

```
hostname R2
username R1 password 0 sameone
!
interface Serial 0/0/0
 ip address 10.0.1.2 255.255.255.252
 ipv6 address 2001:db8:cafe:1::2/64
 encapsulation ppp
 ppp authentication pap
 ppp pap sent-username R2 password sameone
```

CHAP periodically verifies the identity of the remote node using a three-way handshake. The hostname on one router must match the username the other router has configured. The passwords must also match. This occurs on initial link establishment and can be repeated any time after the link has been established. The following is an example of a CHAP configuration.

Partial running-config for R1:

```
hostname R1
username R2 password sameone
!
interface Serial0/0/0
 ip address 10.0.1.1 255.255.255.252
 ipv6 address 2001:DB8:CAFE:1::1/64
 encapsulation ppp
 ppp authentication chap
```

Partial running-config for R2:

```
hostname R2
username R1 password 0 sameone
!
interface Serial 0/0/0
 ip address 10.0.1.2 255.255.255.252
 ipv6 address 2001:db8:cafe:1::2/64
 encapsulation ppp
 ppp authentication chap
```

PPPoE

PPP can be used on all serial links including those links created with older dialup analog and ISDN modems. In addition, ISPs often use PPP as the data-link protocol over broad-band connections. There are several reasons for this. First, PPP supports the ability to assign IP addresses to remote ends of a PPP link. With PPP enabled, ISPs can use PPP to assign each customer one public IPv4 address. More important, PPP supports CHAP authentication. ISPs often want to use CHAP to authenticate customers because during authentication ISPs can check accounting records to determine whether the customer's bill is paid, prior to letting the customer connect to the Internet.

ISPs value PPP because of the authentication, accounting, and link management features. Customers appreciate the ease and availability of the Ethernet connection. However, Ethernet links do not natively support PPP. A solution to this problem was created: PPP over Ethernet (PPPoE). As shown in Figure 1-13, PPPoE allows the sending of PPP frames encapsulated inside Ethernet frames.

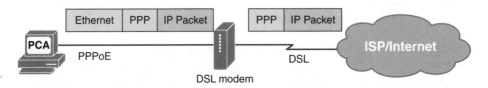

Figure 1-13 *PPP Frames over an Ethernet Connection (PPPoE)*

PPPoE creates a PPP tunnel over an Ethernet connection. This allows PPP frames to be sent across the Ethernet cable to the ISP from the customer's router. The modem converts the Ethernet frames to PPP frames by stripping the Ethernet headers. The modem then transmits these PPP frames on the ISP's digital subscriber line (DSL) network.

With the ability to send and receive PPP frames between the routers, the ISP could continue to use the same authentication model as with analog and ISDN. To make it all work, the client and ISP routers need additional configuration, including PPP configuration. Example 1-2 shows the PPPoE client configuration. To understand the configuration, consider the following:

1. To create a PPP tunnel, the configuration uses a dialer interface. A dialer interface is a virtual interface. The PPP configuration is placed on the dialer interface, not on the physical interface. The dialer interface is created using the **interface dialer number** command. The client can configure a static IP address, but will more likely be automatically assigned a public IP address by the ISP.

2. The PPP CHAP configuration usually defines one-way authentication; therefore, the ISP authenticates the customer. The hostname and password configured on the customer router must match the hostname and password configured on the ISP router.

3. The physical Ethernet interface that connects to the DSL modem is then enabled with the command **pppoe enable** that enables PPPoE and links the physical interface to the dialer interface. The dialer interface is linked to the Ethernet interface with the **dialer pool** and **pppoe-client** commands, using the same number. The dialer interface number does not have to match the dialer pool number.

4. The maximum transmission unit (MTU) should be reduced to 1492, versus the default of 1500, to accommodate the PPPoE headers. The default maximum data field of an Ethernet frame is 1500 bytes. However, in PPPoE the Ethernet frame payload includes a PPP frame which also has a header. This reduces the available data MTU to 1492 bytes.

Example 1-2 *PPPoE Client Configuration*

```
interface Dialer 2
 encapsulation ppp         !  1. PPP and IP on the Dialer
 ip address negotiated


_ppp chap hostname Bob      !  2. Authenticate inbound only
 ppp chap password D1@ne


 ip mtu 1492
 dialer pool 1                        !  3. Dialer pool must match


interface Ethernet0/1
 no ip address
 pppoe enable
 pppoe-client dial-pool-number 1    !  3. Dialer pool must match
```

Note For more information about PPP, see the *Connecting Networks Companion Guide* (Cisco Press, 2014).

Basic Frame Relay Overview

Frame Relay provides several benefits over traditional point-to-point leased lines depending on the needs of the organization.

Leased lines provide permanent dedicated capacity and are used extensively for building WANs. Leased lines have been the traditional connection of choice, but have a number of disadvantages, one of which is that customers pay for leased lines with a fixed capacity. This is a disadvantage because WAN traffic is often variable and leaves some of the capacity unused. In addition, each endpoint needs a separate physical interface on the router, which increases equipment costs. Any change to the leased line generally requires a site visit by the carrier personnel. Frame Relay is a high-performance WAN protocol that operates at the physical and data link layers of the OSI reference model. Unlike leased lines, Frame Relay requires only a single access circuit to the Frame Relay provider to communicate with other sites connected to the same provider, as shown in Figure 1-14. The capacity between any two sites can vary.

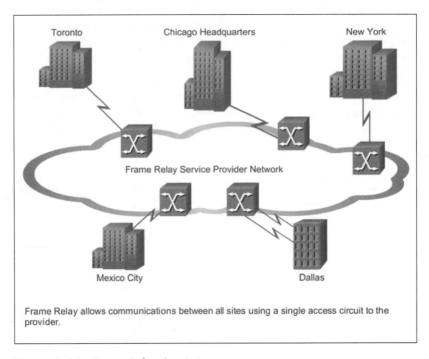

Figure 1-14 *Frame Relay Service*

Frame Relay is a switched WAN technology where virtual circuits (VCs) are created by a service provider (SP) through the network. Frame Relay allows multiple logical VCs to be multiplexed over a single physical interface. The VCs are typically PVCs that are identified by a data-link connection identifier (DLCI). DLCIs are locally significant between the local router and the Frame Relay switch to which the router is connected. Therefore, each end of the PVC may have a different DLCI. The SP's network takes care of sending the data through the PVC. To provide IP layer connectivity, a mapping between IP addresses and DLCIs must be defined, either dynamically or statically.

By default, a Frame Relay network is an NBMA network. In an NBMA environment all routers are on the same subnet, but broadcast (and multicast) packets cannot be sent just once as they are in a broadcast environment such as Ethernet.

To emulate the LAN broadcast capability that is required by IP routing protocols (for example, to send EIGRP hello or update packets to all neighbors reachable over an IP subnet), Cisco IOS implements pseudo-broadcasting, in which the router creates a copy of the broadcast or multicast packet for each neighbor reachable through the WAN media, and sends it over the appropriate PVC for that neighbor.

In environments where a router has a large number of neighbors reachable through a single WAN interface, pseudo-broadcasting has to be tightly controlled because it could increase the CPU resources and WAN bandwidth used. Pseudo-broadcasting can be controlled with the **broadcast** option on static maps in a Frame Relay configuration. However, pseudo-broadcasting cannot be controlled for neighbors reachable through dynamic maps created via Frame Relay Inverse Address Resolution Protocol (INARP) for IPv4 or Frame Relay Inverse Neighbor Discovery (IND) for IPv6. Dynamic maps always allow pseudo-broadcasting.

Frame Relay neighbor loss is detected only after the routing protocol hold time expires or if the interface goes down. An interface is considered to be up as long as at least one PVC is active.

Frame Relay allows remote sites to be interconnected using full-mesh, partial-mesh, and hub-and-spoke (also called star) topologies, as shown in Figure 1-15.

For example, to deploy EIGRP for IPv4 over a physical interface using Inverse ARP dynamic mapping is easy because it is the default. Figure 1-16 illustrates an example network. Example 1-3 is the configuration of Router R1 in the figure. The physical interface Serial 0/0 is configured for Frame Relay encapsulation and an IP address is assigned. Inverse ARP is on by default and will automatically map the IP addresses of the devices at the other ends of the PVCs to the local DLCI number. EIGRP is enabled using autonomous system number 110, and the proper interfaces and networks are included in EIGRP using the **network** commands under the EIGRP routing process.

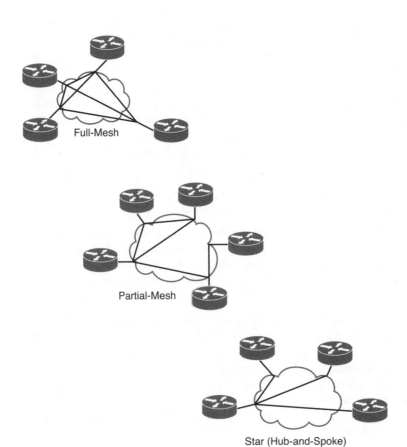

Figure 1-15   *Frame Relay Topologies*

Note   EIGRP is discussed in more detail in Chapter 2, "EIGRP Implementation."

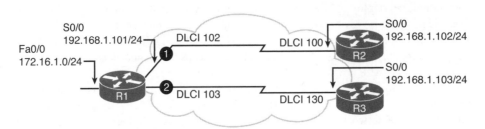

Figure 1-16   *EIGRP on a Physical Frame Relay Interface*

Example 1-3 *Configuration of Router R1 in Figure 1-16 with Dynamic Mapping*

```
interface Serial0/0
 encapsulation frame-relay
 ip address 192.168.1.101 255.255.255.0
!
router eigrp 110
 network 172.16.1.0 0.0.0.255
 network 192.168.1.0
```

Split horizon is disabled by default on Frame Relay physical interfaces. Therefore, routes from Router R2 can be sent to Router R3, and vice versa. Note that Inverse ARP does not provide dynamic mapping for the communication between Routers R2 and R3 because they are not connected with a PVC. You must configure this mapping manually.

Note For more information about Frame Relay, see the *Connecting Networks Companion Guide*, (Cisco Press, 2014. ISBN: 978-1-58713-332-9).

VPN Connectivity Overview

The requirements of modern businesses dictate new trends in connecting remote and branch offices. Traditional solutions, such as leased lines or Frame Relay, are not sufficient in terms of capacity, number of deployed services, WAN bandwidth, and cost. The next generation of VPNs needs to support quick and easy provisioning of full-mesh connectivity between hub and spoke without compromising scalability and security.

MPLS-based VPNs

A service provider uses the MPLS technology to build tunnels through the service provider core network. Traffic forwarding through the MPLS backbone is based on labels that are previously distributed among the core routers. With a Layer 3 MPLS VPN, the service provider participates in customer routing. The service provider establishes routing peering between the PE and CE routers. Then customer routes that are received on the PE router are redistributed into MP-BGP and conveyed over the MPLS backbone to the remote PE router. On the remote PE, these customer routes are redistributed back from MP-BGP into a remote PE-CE routing protocol. Routing protocols between PE-CE routers on the local and remote sites may be totally different.

A Layer 2 MPLS VPN CE router interconnects with the PE router at Layer 2 using any Layer 2 protocol with Ethernet being the most common. Layer 2 traffic is sent between PE routers, over a pre-established pseudowire. Pseudowire emulates a wire between PE routers that carries Layer 2 frames across the IP-MPLS backbone. There are two basic Layer 2 MPLS VPN service architectures. Virtual Private Wire Service (VPWS) is a point-to-point technology that allows the transport of any Layer 2 protocol at the PE.

The second type of Layer 2 MPLS VPN is Virtual Private LAN Service (VPLS), which emulates an Ethernet multiaccess LAN segment over the MPLS core and provides multi-point-to-multipoint service.

Tunneling VPNs

Several tunneling VPN options exist, with Generic Routing Encapsulation (GRE), IPsec, and DMVPN being the most widely deployed.

- GRE is a tunneling protocol developed by Cisco that enables encapsulation of arbitrary Layer 3 protocols inside a point-to-point, tunnel-over-IP network. Traffic that is transported over the GRE tunnel is not encrypted, and it therefore may be a target of different security attacks. Because of this circumstance, GRE traffic is usually encapsulated within IPsec to form a GRE-over-IPsec tunnel.

- IPsec is a framework that uses a set of cryptographic protocols to secure traffic at Layer 3. It also secures any network application or communication that uses IP as a transport protocol.

- The DMVPN solution architecture is primarily used to better scale IPsec hub-to-spoke and spoke-to-spoke designs in large networks. This solution offers the capability to dynamically establish hub-to-spoke and spoke-to-spoke IPsec tunnels, thus reducing latency and optimizing network performance. DMVPN supports dynamic routing protocols between hub and spokes as well as IP multicast. It is also suitable for environments with dynamic IP addresses on physical interfaces such as DSL or cable connections.

Hybrid VPNs

MPLS-based VPNs and tunnel VPNs are not mutually exclusive; they may exist on the same IP infrastructure. In some situations, the customer wants to tunnel traffic across the service provider network, but due to legal regulations, this traffic must be encrypted. The customer combines the best characteristics of both VPNs to create new, hybrid VPN types. Examples of these services are Layer 3 MPLS VPN over GRE or Layer 3 MPLS VPN over DMVPN. Common for both types is that you create your own private IP-MPLS network over public IP infrastructure. The first solution does not include traffic encryption. The second option is much more secure because DMVPN includes the possibility of using IPsec. It also offers an end-to-end path testing possibility, and optimal traffic flows across the network. The main drawback of the hybrid VPN is that several layers of encapsulation lead to a lower effective MTU as well as increased latency and complexity.

Routing Across MPLS VPNs

Initially, branch offices were connected using leased lines. Later, service providers offered Layer 2 VPNs based on point-to-point data link layer connectivity, using ATM or Frame Relay VCs. Customers built their own Layer 3 networks to accommodate IP traffic. As a result, separate networks existed for the Layer 2 and Layer 3 traffic. To optimize operational expenses and to offer additional services, service providers wanted a single IP-based network to provide both Layer 2 and Layer 3 VPN solutions as shown in Figure 1-17.

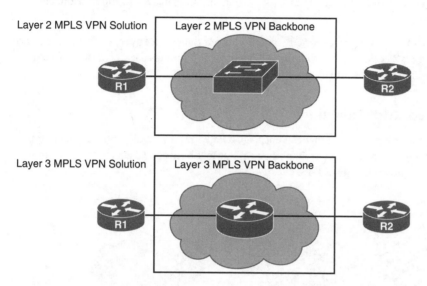

Figure 1-17 *MPLS VPN Solutions*

MPLS is a transport mechanism that is developed to carry data over the packet-switched network. It was designed to offer a great level of flexibility to operate seamlessly with any Layer 3 or Layer 2 technology. MPLS VPN is a service extension of the MPLS that is intended to provide VPN service that enables service providers and large enterprises to build flexible, scalable, and secure VPNs. Two types of MPLS VPNs have been developed: Layer 2 MPLS VPN and Layer 3 MPLS VPN.

Figure 1-17 presents the basic difference between a Layer 2 MPLS VPN and a Layer 3 MPLS VPN backbone solution. Customer routers (R1 and R2 in this example) are connected across the MPLS VPN backbone, and it is important to define the difference.

The Layer 2 MPLS VPN backbone solution is providing the Layer 2 service across the backbone, where R1 and R2 are connected together directly using the same IP subnet. If you deploy a routing protocol over the Layer 2 MPLS VPN, neighbor adjacency is established between your R1 and R2 routers. The figure presents the connectivity through the backbone, which can be illustrated as one big switch.

The Layer 3 MPLS VPN backbone solution is providing the Layer 3 service across the backbone, where R1 and R2 are connected to ISP edge routers. A separate IP subnet is used on each side. If you deploy a routing protocol over this VPN, service providers need to participate in it. Neighbor adjacency is established between your R1 and the closest PE router and between your R2 and it's closest PE router. The figure presents the connectivity through the backbone, which can be illustrated as one big router.

From the customer perspective, selecting a Layer 3 or Layer 2 MPLS VPN will largely depend on customer requirements:

Layer 3 MPLS VPN is appropriate for customers who prefer to outsource their routing to a service provider. The service provider maintains and manages routing for the customer sites.

Layer 2 MPLS VPN is useful for customers who run their own Layer 3 infrastructure and require Layer 2 connectivity from the service provider. In this case, the customer manages its own routing information.

Routing Over GRE Tunnel

GRE is a tunneling protocol that can encapsulate a wide variety of protocol packet types inside IP tunnels, creating a virtual point-to-point link between Cisco routers over an IP network, as shown in Figure 1-18.

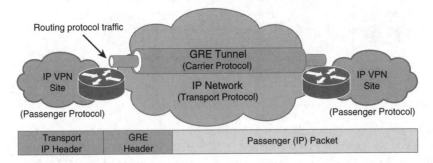

Figure 1-18 *GRE Tunnel*

Generally speaking, a tunnel is a logical interface that provides a way to encapsulate passenger packets inside a transport protocol. A GRE tunnel is a point-to-point tunnel developed by Cisco that allows a wide variety of passenger protocols to be transported over the IP network. It comprises three main components:

- A passenger protocol or encapsulated protocol, such as IPv4 or IPv6 that is being encapsulated.

- A carrier protocol, GRE in this example, that is defined by Cisco as a multiprotocol carrier protocol and described in RFC 2784.

- A transport protocol, such as IP, that carries the encapsulated protocol.

GRE has the following characteristics:

- GRE uses a protocol-type field in the GRE header to support the encapsulation of any OSI Layer 3 protocol. GRE is IP protocol 47.

- GRE itself is stateless. It does not include any flow-control mechanisms, by default.

- GRE does not include any strong security mechanisms to protect its payload.

- The GRE header, along with the tunneling IP header, creates at least 24 bytes of additional overhead for tunneled packets.

GRE tunnels offer the possibility to connect branch offices across the Internet or WAN. The main benefit of the GRE tunnel is that it supports IP multicast and therefore is appropriate for tunneling routing protocols. However, there are a few things that you should take into consideration when using the GRE tunnel as a connectivity option. Traffic that is sent through the tunnel is not encrypted and so is susceptible to man-in-the-middle attacks. To tackle this issue, you should combine GRE with IPsec. GRE encapsulates the plaintext packet, and then IPsec cryptographically encapsulates the packet to form the GRE-over-IPsec tunnel.

Dynamic Multipoint Virtual Private Network

With a generic hub-and-spoke topology, you can typically implement static tunnels (typically GRE with IPsec) between central hub and remote spokes, as shown in Figure 1-19 When a new spoke needs to be added to the network, it requires configuration on the hub router. In addition, traffic between spokes has to traverse the hub, where it must exit one tunnel and enter another. Static tunnels may be an appropriate solution for small networks, but this solution becomes unacceptable as the number of spokes grows larger and larger.

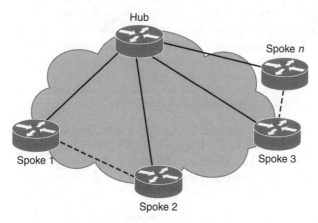

Figure 1-19 *Hub-and-Spoke Topology*

The Cisco DMVPN feature enables better scaling for large and small IPsec VPNs. The Cisco DMVPN feature combines mGRE tunnels, IPsec encryption, and Next Hop Resolution Protocol (NHRP) to provide simple provisioning of many VPN peers. DMVPN also easily supports dynamically addressed spoke routers by its design, if an appropriate peer authentication method is used, such as PKI-enabled peer authentication.

The primary benefits of DMVPNs follow:

- **Hub router configuration reduction:** Traditionally, the individual configuration of a GRE tunnel and IPsec would need to be defined for each individual spoke router. The DMPVN feature enables the configuration of a single mGRE tunnel interface and a single IPsec profile on the hub router to manage all spoke routers. Thus, the size of the configuration on the hub router remains constant even if additional spoke routers are added to the network.

■ **Automatic IPsec initiation:** GRE uses NHRP to configure and resolve the peer destination address. This feature allows IPsec to be immediately triggered to create point-to-point GRE tunnels without any IPsec peering configuration.

■ **Support for dynamically addressed spoke routers:** When using point-to-point GRE and IPsec hub-and-spoke VPN networks, it is important to know the physical interface IP address of the spoke routers when configuring the hub router. The spoke IP address must be configured as the GRE and IPsec tunnel destination address. DMVPN enables spoke routers to have dynamic physical interface IP addresses and uses NHRP to register the dynamic physical interface IP addresses of the spoke routers with the hub router. This process also enables the support of spoke routers that are connected with dynamic public IPv4 addresses to the Internet.

Multipoint GRE

An important characteristic of the DMVPN solution is scalability, which is enabled by deploying Multipoint GRE (mGRE). mGRE technology enables a single GRE interface to support multiple GRE tunnels and simplifies the complexity of the configuration. GRE tunnels also provide support for IP multicast and non-IP protocols. IP multicast, in turn, enables the designer to use routing protocols to distribute routing information and detect changes in the VPN. All DMVPN members use GRE or mGRE interfaces to build tunnels between devices.

The main characteristics of the mGRE configuration are as follows:

■ Only one tunnel interface needs to be configured on a router to support multiple remote GRE peers. In a hub-and-spoke network, a single mGRE tunnel interface on the hub accommodates many spoke GRE peers. This greatly simplifies the management of the hub device because new spokes can be added without the need to reconfigure the hub.

■ In order to learn about the IP addresses of other peer, devices using mGRE require NHRP to build dynamic GRE tunnels. Peers can also use dynamically assigned addresses that will then be used by NHRP when registering with the hub.

■ mGRE interfaces also support unicast, multicast, and broadcast traffic.

Figure 1-20 shows two options for implementing mGRE functionality:

■ The left diagram shows the hub that is optimized with an mGRE interface. In this setup, only a single interface is required on the hub. However, you must deploy NHRP for the hub to learn spoke addresses and correctly provision the spoke-to-hub GRE tunnels.

■ In the right diagram, all devices in a hub-and-spoke network use the mGRE interface. Using NHRP, these devices can establish a partial mesh or full mesh of GRE
tunnels. By only configuring a single mGRE interface on each device, the configuration is greatly simplified and manageability improved.

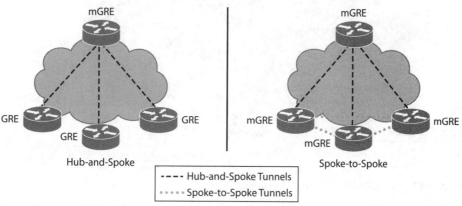

Figure 1-20   *GRE Options*

NHRP

DMVPN supports dynamic physical IP addresses on the spoke routers. When the
spoke is connected to the network, a dynamic mutual discovery of spokes is initiated.
Discovery is enabled by the use of NHRP (Next Hop Resolution Protocol).

NHRP is a client-server protocol, as illustrated in Figure 1-21. The hub acts as the server,
and the spokes are clients. NHRP is used by routers to determine the IP address of the
next hop in IP tunneling networks. When a spoke router initially connects to a DMVPN
network, it registers its inner (tunnel) and outer (physical interface) address with the hub
router (NHRP server). This registration enables the mGRE interface on the hub router to
build a dynamic GRE tunnel back to the registering spoke router without having to know
the branch tunnel destination in advance. Therefore, NHRP creates a mapping for a tunnel IP address to the physical interface IP address for each spoke at the hub.

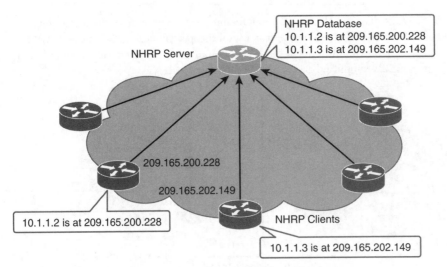

Figure 1-21   *NHRP Client-Server Protocol*

From the routing protocol perspective, the NHRP domain operates similarly to an NBMA network, such as a multipoint Frame Relay network.

Using NHRP in mGRE networks maps inner tunnel IP addresses to the outer transport IP addresses. In a hub-and-spoke DMVPN deployment, no GRE or IPsec information about a spoke is configured on the hub router. The spoke router for the GRE tunnel is configured (via NHRP commands) with information about the hub router as the next-hop server. When the spoke router starts up, it automatically initiates the IPsec tunnel with the hub router. It then uses NHRP to notify the hub router of its current physical interface IP address. This notification is useful for the following reasons:

- Configuration of the hub router is shortened and simplified because it does not need to have GRE or IPsec information about the peer routers. All of this information is learned dynamically via NHRP.

- When you add a new spoke router to the DMVPN network, you do not need to change the configuration on the hub or on any of the current spoke routers. The new spoke router is configured with the hub information, and when it starts up, it dynamically registers with the hub router. The dynamic routing protocol propagates the routing information from the spoke to the hub. The hub propagates new routing information to the other spokes, and it also propagates the routing information from the other spokes to the new spoke.

- In Figure 1-22, one spoke wants to send IP traffic to another spoke, which has a tunnel interface that is configured with the IP address of 10.1.1.3. The originating router sends an NHRP query for the 10.1.1.3 IP address to the hub, which is configured as an NHRP server. The hub responds with information that IP address 10.1.1.3 is mapped to the physical interface (209.165.202.149) of the receiving spoke router.

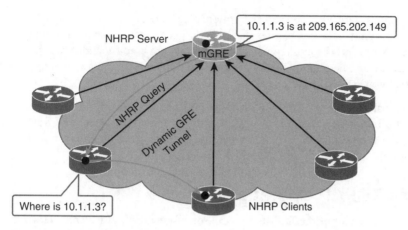

Figure 1-22 *NHRP Example*

IPsec

Security is also an important part of the DMVPN solution. Security services are enabled by the use of the IPsec framework. IPsec is a framework of open standards that define how to provide secure communications. It relies on existing algorithms to implement the encryption, authentication, and key exchange.

IPsec provides four important security services:

- **Confidentiality (encryption):** The sender can encrypt the packets before transmitting them across a network. By doing so, no one can eavesdrop on the communication. If the communication is intercepted, it cannot be read.

- **Data integrity:** The receiver can verify that the data was transmitted through the path without being changed or altered in any way. IPsec ensures data integrity by using checksums, which is a simple redundancy check.

- **Authentication:** Authentication ensures that the connection is made with the desired communication partner. The receiver can authenticate the source of the packet by guaranteeing and certifying the source of the information. IPsec uses Internet Key Exchange (IKE) to authenticate users and devices that can carry out communication independently. IKE uses several types of authentication including username and password, one-time password, biometrics, Pre-Shared Keys (PSKs), and digital certificates.

- **Antireplay protection:** Antireplay protection verifies that each packet is unique and not duplicated. IPsec packets are protected by comparing the sequence number of the received packets with a sliding window on the destination host. A packet that has a sequence number that is before the sliding window is considered either late or a duplicate packet. Late and duplicate packets are dropped.

Two IPsec functions, authentication and encryption, play an important role in the DMVPN solution. Authentication ensures that only desired peers can establish communication with other peers. The most common methods that are used for authentication are PSKs or certificates. Because one PSK must be shared among all locations, it is recommended that you use certificates.

You would normally enable encryption when DMVPN connects remote locations over the Internet. It is becoming a common practice to also use encryption when spokes are connected to the hub over leased WAN links because the service provider infrastructure cannot be trusted.

Routing and TCP/IP Operations

Routing protocols are part of the TCP/IP protocol suite, specifically at Layer 3. Network communications requires a wide range of protocols responsible for a wide variety of tasks to ensure communications between devices.

MSS, Fragmentation, and PMTUD

The IP protocol was designed for use over a wide variety of transmission mediums. An IPv4 packet has a maximum size of 65,535 bytes. An IPv6 packet with a hop-by-hop extension header and the jumbo payload option can support up to 4,294,967,295 bytes. However, most transmission links enforce as smaller maximum packet length called the *maximum transmission unit* (MTU).

When a router receives an IPv4 packet larger than the MTU of the egress or outgoing interface, it must fragment the packet unless the DF (Don't Fragment) bit is set in the IPv4 header. Reassembly of the packet is the responsibility of the destination device, the device associated with the destination IPv4 address. Fragmentation causes several issues including the following:

- CPU and memory overhead in fragmentation of the packet

- CPU and memory overhead in destination devices during reassembly of packets

- Retransmission of the entire packet when one fragment is dropped

- Firewalls that do Layer 4 through Layer 7 filtering may have trouble processing IPv4 fragments correctly

To avoid fragmentation, the TCP Maximum Segment Size (MSS) defines the largest amount of data that the receiving device is able to accept in a single TCP segment. The TCP segment may be sent in a single IPv4 packet or fragmented using multiple IPv4 packets. The MSS is not negotiated between sender and receiver. The sending device is required to limit the size of the TCP segment equal to or less than the MSS reported by the receiving device.

To avoid fragmentation of an IPv4 packet, the selection of the TCP MSS is the minimum buffer size and MTU of the outgoing interface minus 40 bytes. The 40 bytes take into account the 20-byte IPv4 header and the 20-byte TCP header. For example, the default Ethernet MTU is 1500 bytes. A TCP segment over IPv4 sent out an Ethernet interface will have a TCP MSS of 1460, which is 1500 bytes for the Ethernet MTU, minus 20 bytes for the IPv4 header, and minus 20 bytes for the TCP header.

The TCP MSS helps avoid fragmentation at the two ends of the TCP connection but it does not prevent fragmentation due to a smaller MTU on a link along the path. Path MTU Discovery (PMTUD) was developed for the purpose of determining the lowest MTU along a path from the packet's source to destination. PMTUD is only supported by TCP.

PMTUD is performed by a host using the full MSS determined by the outgoing interface and setting the TCP DF bit so that packets cannot be fragmented. If a router along the path needs to fragment the packet because of a lower MTU link on the egress interface, it will drop the packet due to the DF bit being set and send an ICMP Destination Unreachable message back to the originator of the packet. The ICMP Destination Unreachable message contains the code indicating "fragmentation needed and DF set" and the MTU for the egress interface that caused the packet to be dropped. The source receives the ICMP message, reduces the size of the MSS to be within the MTU, and retransmits the message.

Problems with PMTUD can occur when a router sends the ICMP Destination Unreachable message but the messages are blocked by other routers, firewalls, or the source device itself. PMTUD relies on ICMP messages, so it is important when implementing ICMP packet filtering on devices to make an exception to those that are "unreachable" or "time exceeded."

IPv6 Fragmentation and PMTUD

IPv6 routers do not fragment a packet unless it is the source of the packet. If an IPv6 router receives a packet larger than the MTU of the outgoing interface, it will drop the packet and send an ICMPv6 Packet Too Big message back to the source including the smaller MTU.

The PMTUD operations for IPv6 are similar to that of PMTUD for IPv4. RFC 1981, *Path MTU Discovery for IP version 6*, suggests that IPv6 devices should perform PMTUD.

Bandwidth Delay Product

TCP can experience bottlenecks on paths with high bandwidth and long round-trip delays. These networks are known as a *long fat pipe* or *long fat network*, LFN (pronounced "elephan [t])." The key parameter is the Bandwidth Delay Product (BDP), which is the product of the bandwidth (bps) times the round-trip delay (RTT in seconds). The BDP is the number of bits it takes to "fill the pipe" (in other words, the amount of unacknowledged data that TCP must handle to keep the pipeline full). BDP is used to optimize the TCP window size to fully utilize the link. The result is the maximum of data that can be transmitted on the link at any given time. The TCP window size should then use the BDP. The TCP window size indicates the amount of data that can be sent before expecting an acknowledgment, usually several times the MSS.

TCP Starvation

TCP incorporates mechanisms for reliability, flow control, and congestion avoidance. However, UDP is a lightweight protocol for faster and simpler data transmissions and does not include these features.

When there is a combination of TCP and UDP flows during a period of congestion, TCP tries to do its part by backing off on bandwidth, called *slow start*. However, UDP without any flow control mechanisms continues, potentially using up the available bandwidth given up by TCP. This is known as *TCP starvation/UDP dominance*.

It is not always possible to separate TCP- and UDP-based flows, but it is important to be aware of this behavior when mixing applications that use both transport layer protocols.

Latency

Latency is the amount of time for a message to go from point to another. Network latency is the amount of time for the packet to travel the network from the original source to the final destination. Several factors can cause latency, including propagation delay, serialization, data protocols, routing, switching, queuing, and buffering.

The flow control and reliability features of TCP have an effect on end-to-end latency. TCP requires an established virtual connection, and bidirectional communications for acknowledgments, window sizes, congestion control, and other TCP mechanisms, all of which has an effect on latency.

UDP is a protocol that does not include reliability or flow control. A device simply sends packets with UDP segments with the assumption that they will reach their destination. UDP is typically used for applications such as streaming media that require minimal delay and can tolerate occasional packet loss. UDP has very low latency, better than most TCP connections.

ICMP Redirect

ICMP Redirect messages are used by routers to notify the sender of a packet that there is a better route available for a particular destination.

For example, in Figure 1-23, two routers, R1 and R2, are connected to the same Ethernet segment as host PCA. The IPv4 default gateway of PCA is the IPv4 address of router R1. PCA sends a packet for PCX to its default gateway R1. R1 examines its routing table and determines the next hop as router R2, on the same Ethernet segment as PCA. R1 forwards the packet out the same interface used to receive the packet from PCA. R1 also sends an ICMP Redirect message informing PCA of a better route to PCX by way of R2. PCA can now forward subsequent packets more directly using R2 as the next-hop router.

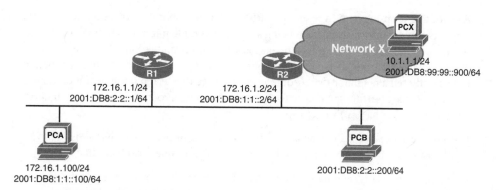

Figure 1-23 *ICMP Redirect*

The ICMPv6 (ICMP for IP version 6) Redirect message functions the same way as the Redirect message for ICMPv4, with one additional feature. In Figure 1-23, PCA and PCB are on separate IPv6 networks. R1 is the IPv6 default gateway for PCA. When sending an IPv6 packet to PCB, a device on the same Ethernet segment but different IPv6 networks, PCA will forward that packet to R1, its default gateway. Similar to IPv4, R1 will forward the IPv6 packet to PCB, but unlike ICMP for IPv4, it will send an ICMPv6 redirect message to PCA informing the source of the better route. PCA can now send subsequent IPv6 packets directly to PCB even though it is on a different IPv6 network.

Implementing RIPng

RIP is an IGP that is used in smaller networks. It is a distance vector routing protocol that uses hop count as a routing metric. There are three versions of RIP: RIPv1, RIPv2, and RIPng. RIPv1 and RIPv2 route in IPv4 networks. RIPng routes in IPv6 networks.

Upon completing this section, you will be able to:

■ Describe general RIP characteristics

■ Describe how to configure and verify basic RIPng

■ Describe how to configure RIPng to share default routes

■ Analyze the RIPng database

RIP Overview

RIP is one of the oldest routing protocols. RIP is a standardized IGP routing protocol that works in a mixed-vendor router environment. It is one of the easiest routing protocols to configure, making it a good choice for small networks.

RIP is a distance vector protocol that uses hop count, the number of routers, as the metric. If a device has two paths to the destination network, the path with fewer hops will be chosen as the path to forward traffic. If a network is 16 or more hops away, the router considers it unreachable.

As a routing loop-prevention technique, RIP implements split horizon. Split horizon prevents routing information from being sent out the same interface from which it was received. Split horizon with poison reverse is a similar technique but sends the update with a metric of 16, which is considered unreachable by RIP. The idea is that it is better to explicitly tell a neighbor that a route is inaccessible than not tell the neighbor at all. Route poisoning (setting the metric to 16) is also used by a router to inform a neighbor when it no longer has a route to a specific network.

RIP is also capable of load balancing traffic over equal-cost paths. The default is four equal-cost paths. If the maximum number of paths is set to one, load balancing is disabled.

In Figure 1-24, PC1 is sending traffic to PC2. Which path will be chosen for the packets? RIP will choose the direct path—the one over the 100-Mbps link—because the destination is only 2 hops away. The hop count over the three 1-Gbps links is 4. So, in this case, RIP will choose the worse path. A more advanced protocol, such as OSPF or EIGRP, would not choose the path over the weak, 100-Mbps link. Traffic would be forwarded over the 1-Gbps links.

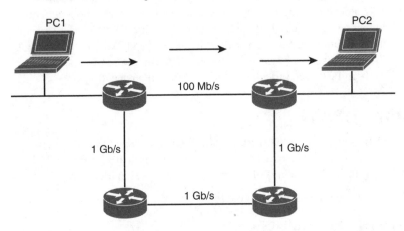

Figure 1-24 *RIP Uses Hop Count as its Metric*

RIP exists in three versions: RIPv1, RIPv2, and RIPng. Table 1-5 provides a comparison of RIPv2 and RIPng.

Table 1-5 *Comparing Features in RIPv2 and RIPng*

Feature	RIPv2	RIPng
Advertise routes	IPv4	IPv6
Transport protocol	UDP (port 520)	UDP (port 521)
Multicast address used	224.0.0.9	FF02::9
VLSM support	Yes	Yes
Metric	Hop count (maximum of 15)	Hop count (maximum of 15)

Feature	RIPv2	RIPng
Administrative Distance	120	120
Routing updates	Every 30 seconds and with topology change	Every 30 seconds and with topology change
Authentication support	Yes	Yes

RIPv1 is a classful routing protocol that was replaced by RIPv2, which is a classless routing protocol. Classless routing protocols can be considered second generation because they are designed to address some of the limitations of the earlier classful routing protocols. A serious limitation in a classful network environment is that the subnet mask is not exchanged during the routing update process, thus requiring that the same subnet mask be used on all subnetworks within the same major network. RIPv1 is considered a legacy, obsolete protocol.

RIPng operates much like RIPv2. Both protocols use UDP as the transport layer protocol, and both use multicast address to exchange updates (RIPv1 uses broadcast). Because both protocols are classless, this means that they support VLSM. Both protocols use hop count as the metric. The administrative distance (trustworthiness of the routing source) is 120 in both cases. With both protocols, updates are propagated throughout the network every 30 seconds and when a change occurs in the network. Also, both protocols support authentication.

There are two major differences between RIPv2 and RIPng:

- RIPv2 advertises routes for IPv4 and uses IPv4 for transport, while RIPng advertises routes for IPv6 and uses IPv6 for transport.

- The configuration of RIPng is quite different when compared to RIPv2 configuration.

RIPv2 Overview

This section shows a simple example of configuring RIPv2 for those who may not be familiar with configuring RIP. Configuring RIPv2 is similar to configuring EIGRP.

In Figure 1-25, all routers have been configured with basic management features and all interfaces identified in the reference topology are configured and enabled. There are no static routes configured and no routing protocols enabled; therefore, remote network access is currently impossible. RIPv2 is used as the dynamic routing protocol.

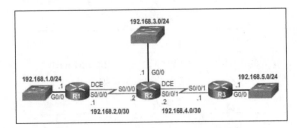

Figure 1-25   *RIPv2 Topology*

To enable RIP, use the **router rip** command to enter router configuration mode. To enable RIP routing for a network, use the **network** *network-address* router configuration mode command. Enter the classful network address for each directly connected network. The **version 2** command is used to enable RIPv2.

Example 1-4 shows the RIPv2 configuration on router R1.

Example 1-4   *Configuration of RIPv2 on R1*

```
R1(config)# router rip
R1(config-router)# network 192.168.1.0
R1(config-router)# network 192.168.2.0
R1(config-router)# version 2
R1(config-router)#
```

By default, RIPv2 automatically summarizes networks at major network boundaries, summarizing routes to the classful network address. If you have disconnected or discontiguous subnets, it is necessary to disable automatic route summarization to advertise the subnets to ensure reachability all networks. When route summarization is disabled, the software sends subnet routing information across classful network boundaries.

To modify the default RIPv2 behavior of automatic summarization, use the **no auto-summary** router configuration mode command:

```
Router(config-router)# no auto-summary
```

The **ip summary-address rip** *ip-address network-mask* interface command is used to summarize an address or subnet under a specific interface. This is known as *manual summarization*. Only one summary address can be configured for each classful subnet. Here is an example specifying the IP address and network mask that identifies the routes to be summarized:

```
Router(config-if)# ip summary-address rip 10.2.0.0 255.255.0.0
```

You can use the **show ip protocols** command to verify whether automatic or manual summarization is used.

Note Supernet advertisement (advertising any network prefix less than its classful major network) is not allowed in RIP route summarization, other than advertising a supernet learned in the routing tables.

Configuring RIPng

We will begin by configuring basic RIPng on R2 using the topology in Figure 1-26. RIPng is already preconfigured on R1. On R1, there is a static default route that is already configured, which routes all the unknown traffic toward the Internet. Later in this section, R1 will be configured to share this default route with R2 using RIPng.

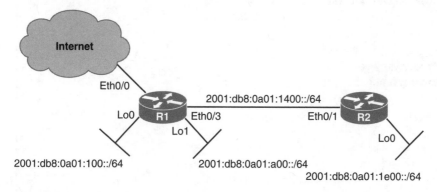

Figure 1-26 *RIPng Topology*

Basic RIPng Configuration

Next, IPv6 routing is enabled using the **ipv6 unicast-routing** command, as shown in Example 1-5. While IPv4 routing is enabled by default on Cisco routers, IPv6 routing is not.

Example 1-5 ipv6 unicast-routing *Command*

```
R2> enable
R2# configure terminal
Enter configuration commands, one per line.  End with CNTL/Z.
R2(config)# ipv6 unicast-routing
```

On R2, enable RIPng using the **ipv6 router rip** *name* command. Set the name of the process to "CCNP_RIP."

The routing process name does not need to match between neighbor routers.

```
R2(config)# ipv6 router rip CCNP_RIP
```

When trying to configure the RIPng routing process, if IPv6 routing has not been enabled the **ipv6 router rip** *name* command will be rejected.

On R2, use the **show ipv6 interface brief** command and verify that Ethernet0/1 (connects to R1) and Loopback0 (simulates the R2 LAN) are configured with IPv6 addresses.

Notice in Example 1-6 that each of the two interfaces has two IPv6 addresses configured. The addresses that start with "2001" are global IPv6 addresses that were configured using the **ipv6 address** *ipv6_address/prefix* command. "FE80" are link-local addresses and are derived automatically when you configure a global IPv6 address, or if you just enable the interface for IPv6 using the **ipv6 enable** command in interface configuration mode. Link-local addresses are used for the exchange of routing information.

Example 1-6   show ipv6 interface brief *Command*

```
R2# show ipv6 interface brief
Ethernet0/0            [administratively down/down]
    unassigned
Ethernet0/1            [up/up]
    FE80::A8BB:CCFF:FE00:2010
    2001:DB8:A01:1400::2
Ethernet0/2            [administratively down/down]
    unassigned

<Output omitted>

Ethernet3/3            [administratively down/down]
    unassigned
Loopback0              [up/up]
    FE80::A8BB:CCFF:FE00:2000
    2001:DB8:A01:1E00::1
```

On R2, enable RIPng on interfaces Ethernet 0/1 and Loopback0 with the **ipv6 rip** *name* **enable** interface subcommand, as shown in Example 1-7. If IPv6 is not enabled on the interface and you are trying to enable this same interface for RIPng, the **ipv6 rip** *name* **enable** command will be rejected.

Example 1-7   *Enable RIPng on the Interfaces*

```
R2(config)# interface ethernet 0/1
R2(config-if)# ipv6 rip CCNP_RIP enable
R2(config-if)# interface loopback 0
R2(config-if)# ipv6 rip CCNP_RIP enable
```

If you forgot to create a routing process using the **ipv6 router rip** *name* command and you enable RIPng on an interface, the command will be accepted. In this case, the RIPng process will be automatically created by Cisco IOS Software.

Suppose that you created a RIPng routing process called "CCNP_RIP" in the second step of configuring RIPng. But then in the fourth step, you made a mistake and enabled RIPng on an interface using the process name "CCNP_PIR." The command will not be rejected.

Cisco IOS Software will create a new RIPng process called "CCNP_PIR." You will end up with two routing processes, one that was created by you directly and the second that Cisco IOS Software created on your behalf. As RIPng process name has local significance, and as both interfaces will be included in the same routing process, RIPng configuration will be operations, even though two processes with different names has been defined.

On R2, enter the **show ipv6 protocols** command, as demonstrated in Example 1-8. The **show ipv6 protocols** command will show you information on all IPv6 protocols that are configured. In this case, because you only have RIPng configured, the command will tell you interfaces that you have enabled for RIPng.

Example 1-8   show ipv6 protocols *Command*

```
R2# show ipv6 protocols
IPv6 Routing Protocol is "connected"
IPv6 Routing Protocol is "ND"
IPv6 Routing Protocol is "rip CCNP_RIP"
  Interfaces:
    Loopback0
    Ethernet0/1
  Redistribution:
    None
```

As shown in Example 1-9, on R2, verify the IPv6 routing table using the **show ipv6 route** command. Notice that R2 learned about the two LAN networks from R1.

Example 1-9   *R2's IPv6 Routing Table*

```
R2# show ipv6 route
IPv6 Routing Table - default - 7 entries
Codes: C - Connected, L - Local, S - Static, U - Per-user Static route
       B - BGP, R - RIP, I1 - ISIS L1, I2 - ISIS L2
       IA - ISIS interarea, IS - ISIS summary, D - EIGRP, EX - EIGRP external
       ND - ND Default, NDp - ND Prefix, DCE - Destination, NDr - Redirect
       O - OSPF Intra, OI - OSPF Inter, OE1 - OSPF ext 1, OE2 - OSPF ext 2
       ON1 - OSPF NSSA ext 1, ON2 - OSPF NSSA ext 2
R   2001:DB8:A01:100::/64 [120/2]
     via FE80::A8BB:CCFF:FE00:130, Ethernet0/1
R   2001:DB8:A01:A00::/64 [120/2]
     via FE80::A8BB:CCFF:FE00:130, Ethernet0/1
C   2001:DB8:A01:1400::/64 [0/0]
     via Ethernet0/1, directly connected
L   2001:DB8:A01:1400::2/128 [0/0]
     via Ethernet0/1, receive
C   2001:DB8:A01:1E00::/64 [0/0]
     via Loopback0, directly connected
L   2001:DB8:A01:1E00::1/128 [0/0]
```

```
        via Loopback0, receive
L   FF00::/8 [0/0]
        via Null0, receive
```

The metric for RIPng routes in the routing table is shown as 2. In RIPng, the sending router already considers itself to be one hop away; therefore, R1 advertises its LANs with a metric of 1. When R2 receives the update, it adds another hop count of 1 to the metric. Therefore, R2 considers the R1 LANs to be two hops away.

Note   There is a significant difference in how RIPv2 and RIPng calculate the number of hops for a remote network. In RIPng, the routers adds one hop to the metric when it receives the RIPng update and then includes that metric in its IPv6 routing table for that network. In RIPv1 and RIPv2, the router receives the RIP update, uses that metric for its IPv4 routing table and then increments the metric by one before sending the update to other routers. The effect of all of this is that RIPng will show a metric, a hop count of one more than RIPv1 or RIPv2.

The concept of classful networks doesn't exist in IPv6, so there isn't any automatic route summarization in RIPng. To configure RIPng to advertise summarized IPv6 addresses on an interface, manual summarization, use the **ipv6 rip summary-address** command in interface configuration mode.

In Example 1-10, the two loopback interfaces on R1 are summarized out the Ethernet 0/3 interface for the RIPng process CCNP_RIP.

Example 1-10   ipv6 rip summary-address *Command*

```
R1(config)# interface Ethernet 0/3
R1(config-router)# ipv6 rip CCNP_RIP summary-address 2001:db8:A01::/52
```

The same process for summarizing IPv4 networks is used for summarizing IPv6 prefixes. The 2001:DB8:A01:100::/64 and 2001:DB8:A01:A00::/64 prefixes have the first 52 bits in common, represented as 2001:DB8:A01::/52.

Propagating a Default Route

In Figure 1-27, R1 has a configured static default route that that sends all the unknown traffic toward the Internet.

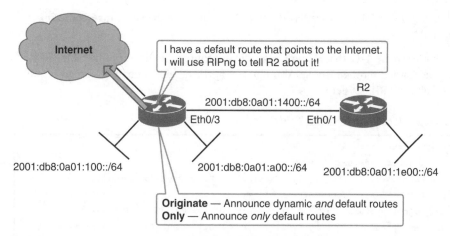

Figure 1-27 *RIPng Topology with Default Route*

If you want R1 to share this default route with R2, use the following command:

```
R1(config-if)# ipv6 rip name default-information originate | only
```

You need to enter this command in the interface configuration mode. In this example, you need to be in Ethernet 0/3 interface configuration mode because R1 connects to R2 through this interface.

There are two ways of sharing information about default routes through RIPng:

- The first way is specified through the **originate** keyword. In this case, R1 shares the default route information alongside the information about every other route (for example, the R1 LAN networks).

- The second way of sharing default route information is to use the **only** keyword. With **only**, R1 will only share the default route with R2.

Note that the **default-information originate** command announces the default route to the neighboring routers even if there is no local default route present in the router's routing table.

R1 has a preconfigured IPv6 route. The default route routes traffic toward the Internet. On R1, share the default route to R2 using the **ipv6 rip** *name* **default-information origi-nate** command. The name of the RIPng process is CCNP_RIP. Enter this command while in Ethernet 0/3 interface configuration mode.

In Example 1-11, R1 takes its default route and shares it with R2 through the RIPng routing process along with all the other RIPng routes.

Example 1-11 *Propagating the Default Route on R1*

```
R1(config)# interface Ethernet 0/3
R1(config-if)# ipv6 rip CCNP_RIP default-information originate
```

On R2, verify that R1 has shared its default IPv6 route. Use the **show ipv6 route rip** command.

Notice in Example 1-12 that R2 now has a default route in its IPv6 routing table. This route was learned through RIPng. Also notice that the default route was learned in addition to all other RIPng routes.

Example 1-12 *R2's IPv6 Routing Table*

```
R2# show ipv6 route rip
IPv6 Routing Table - default - 9 entries
Codes: C - Connected, L - Local, S - Static, U - Per-user Static route
       B - BGP, R - RIP, I1 - ISIS L1, I2 - ISIS L2
       IA - ISIS interarea, IS - ISIS summary, D - EIGRP, EX - EIGRP external
       ND - ND Default, NDp - ND Prefix, DCE - Destination, NDr - Redirect
       O - OSPF Intra, OI - OSPF Inter, OE1 - OSPF ext 1, OE2 - OSPF ext 2
       ON1 - OSPF NSSA ext 1, ON2 - OSPF NSSA ext 2
R   ::/0 [120/2]
     via FE80::A8BB:CCFF:FE00:130, Ethernet0/1
R   2001:DB8:A01:100::/64 [120/2]
     via FE80::A8BB:CCFF:FE00:130, Ethernet0/1
R   2001:DB8:A01:A00::/64 [120/2]
     via FE80::A8BB:CCFF:FE00:130, Ethernet0/1
```

On R1's Ethernet 0/3 interface, enter the **ipv6 rip** *name* **default-information only** command, as shown in Example 1-13. With this configuration, R1 shares only its default route with R2 through the RIPng routing process.

Example 1-13 *Propagating the Default Route on R1 Using the* **only** *Option*

```
R1(config)# interface Ethernet 0/3
R1(config-if)# ipv6 rip CCNP_RIP default-information only
```

The **ipv6 rip** *name* **default-information only** command will override the **ipv6 rip** *name* **default-information originate** command. Only one of these two commands can take effect at a time.

On R2, verify that RIPng now only receives default routes from R1. Use the **show ipv6 route rip** command.

Notice the change in behavior in Example 1-14. R1 now only tells R2 about the default routes through RIPng. There are no other RIPng routes included in the updates or in R2's routing table.

Example 1-14 *Verifying the Default Route on R1*

```
R2# show ipv6 route rip
IPv6 Routing Table - default - 6 entries
Codes: C - Connected, L - Local, S - Static, U - Per-user Static route
```

```
        B - BGP, R - RIP, I1 - ISIS L1, I2 - ISIS L2
        IA - ISIS interarea, IS - ISIS summary, D - EIGRP, EX - EIGRP external
        ND - ND Default, NDp - ND Prefix, DCE - Destination, NDr - Redirect
        O - OSPF Intra, OI - OSPF Inter, OE1 - OSPF ext 1, OE2 - OSPF ext 2
        ON1 - OSPF NSSA ext 1, ON2 - OSPF NSSA ext 2
R   ::/0 [120/2]
    via FE80::A8BB:CCFF:FE00:130, Ethernet0/1
```

The change in behavior is not instantaneous. After changing the sharing of default routes from "originate" to "only," R2 stopped sharing information about nondefault routes. However, R1 will still have nondefault routes in its routing table from before, and these will expire in 180 seconds and be moved out of the routing table. You can speed up this process by clearing the RIPng process on R2 using the **clear ipv6 rip** command. The router will flush its RIPng routes and relearn them. Note that you would never do this on a production network.

Investigating the RIPng Database

The **show ipv6 protocols** command shows you that RIPng is enabled and which interfaces are RIPng-enabled. The **show ipv6 route rip** command shows you routes that are learned through RIPng. However, there is one more command that can be very useful to investigate RIPng behavior: **show ipv6 rip**.

The **show ipv6 rip** command in Example 1-15 shows you information about all RIPng routing processes on the router. In the bottom of the output, interfaces that are enabled for RIPng are shown—similarly as with the **show ipv6 protocols** command.

Example 1-15 *Verifying the RIPng Process on R2*

```
R2#show ipv6 rip
RIP process "CCNP_RIP", port 521, multicast-group FF02::9, pid 138
     Administrative distance is 120. Maximum paths is 16
     Updates every 30 seconds, expire after 180
     Holddown lasts 0 seconds, garbage collect after 120
     Split horizon is on; poison reverse is off
     Default routes are not generated
     Periodic updates 308, trigger updates 1
     Full Advertisement 0, Delayed Events 0
  Interfaces:
    Loopback0
    Ethernet0/1
  Redistribution:
    None
R2#
```

However, in contrast to **show ipv6 protocols**, **show ipv6 rip** will tell you other information such as the port number used, hello timer, and dead timer. All settings that are shown in the example are system-default.

The **show ipv6 rip database** output in Example 1-16 lists the following:

- The RIP process (there can be multiple RIPng processes on a single router).

- The route prefix.

- The route metric, in which RIPng uses hop count as a metric. In the example, all three routes have a metric of 2. This means the destination network is 2 hops away, counting itself as a hop.

- Installed and expired, in which the keyword "installed" means the route is in the routing table. If a network becomes unavailable, the route will become "expired" after the dead timer expires. An expired route value (in seconds), during which the route will be advertised as expired, is listed.

- Expires in, in which if the countdown timer reaches 0, the route is removed from the routing table and marked expired. This timer, the dead timer, is by default three times the hello timer—180 seconds.

Example 1-16 *Verifying the RIPng Database on R2*

```
R2# show ipv6 rip database
RIP process "CCNP_RIP", local RIB
 2001:DB8:A01:100::/64, metric 2, installed
     Ethernet0/1/FE80::A8BB:CCFF:FE00:7430, expires in 155 secs
 2001:DB8:A01:A00::/64, metric 2, installed
     Ethernet0/1/FE80::A8BB:CCFF:FE00:7430, expires in 155 secs
 2001:DB8:A01:1400::/64, metric 2
     Ethernet0/1/FE80::A8BB:CCFF:FE00:7430, expires in 155 secs
R2#
```

The **show ipv6 rip next-hops** output in Example 1-17 lists RIPng processes and under each process all next-hop addresses. Each next-hop address also has an interface that is listed through which it was learned. Next hops are either the addresses of IPv6 RIP neighbors from which you have learned routes or explicit next hops that are received in IPv6 RIP advertisements. An IPv6 RIP neighbor may choose to advertise all of its routes with an explicit next hop. In this case, the address of the neighbor would not appear in the next-hop display. Lastly, in brackets, the number of routes in the IPv6 RIP routing table using the specified next hop is shown.

Example 1-17 *Verifying the RIPng Next-Hop Addresses on R2*

```
R2# show ipv6 rip next-hops
 RIP process "CCNP_RIP", Next Hops
  FE80::A8BB:CCFF:FE00:7430/Ethernet0/1 [3 paths]
R2#
```

Summary

In this chapter, you learned about differentiating routing protocols, various network technologies, connecting remote locations to a central location and RIPng. The chapter focused on the following topics:

- The role of static routes and dynamic routing protocols in enterprise networks.

- The differences between IGP and EGP routing protocols.

- The three types of routing protocols: distance vector, link-state and path vector.

- The importance of convergence time and how route summarization reduced convergence time and improves scalability.

- The four traffic types: unicast, multicast, anycast, and broadcast.

- The differences between point-to-point, broadcast, and NBMA networks.

- How point-to-point subinterfaces are used to overcome the limitations of NBMA networks.

- How VPNs are used to provide security of a public Internet.

- Common types of VPNs: MPLS-based VPNs, GRE+IPsec, and DMVPN.

- How a customer establishes connectivity with a service provider using a routing protocol and a layer 3 MPLS VPN.

- How static GRE tunnels can establish virtual point-to-point links and support dynamic routing protocols.

- Using DMVPN to provide fully meshed VPN connectivity with a simple hub-and-spoke configuration.

- How DMVPN relies on NHRP, mGRE, and IPsec.

- The differences and similarities between RIPv2 and RIPng.

- How to configure RIPng.

- How to propagate a default route in RIPng.

- Some key points in this chapter are that convergence time, support for summarization, and ability to scale impact selection of a suitable routing protocol. It is recommended that you use point-to-point subinterfaces when establishing routing protocols over NBMA networks. DMVPN can be used as a scalable solution. RIPng is a simple IGP protocol that supports IPv6.

Review Questions

Answer the following questions, and then see Appendix A, "Answers to Review Questions," for the answers.

1. What is a converged network?

2. What are two drawbacks of static routes?

   a. Reconfiguring to reflect topology changes
   b. Complex metrics
   c. Involved convergence
   d. Absence of dynamic route discovery

3. The **show ip route** and **show ipv6 route** commands usually provides information on which of the following two items?

   a. Next hop
   b. Metric
   c. CDP
   d. Hostname

4. Which of the following is not a dynamic routing protocol?

   a. RIPv1
   b. CDP
   c. EIGRP
   d. BGP
   e. RIPv2

5. What is a metric?

   a. A standard of measurement used by routing algorithms
   b. The set of techniques used to manage network resources
   c. Interdomain routing in TCP/IP networks
   d. Services limiting the input or output transmission rate

6. Which of the following is not a classification of routing protocols?

   a. Link state
   b. Default
   c. Path vector
   d. Distance vector

7. What is autosummarization?

8. What is the default administrative distance value of RIPng?

   a. 90
   b. 100
   c. 110
   d. 120

9. Match each routing protocol characteristic to its description.

___ distance-vector protocols
___ link-state protocols
___ convergence time
___ scalability
___ EGP
___ IGP

a. Operates within an autonomous system
b. Operates between autonomous systems
c. Describes the time that is needed for routing protocol to respond to change
d. Describes the ability to support network growth
e. Exchanges only the best route with neighbors
f. Each router determines the best path on its own

10. Which three benefits are a result of route summarization? (Choose three.)

a. Smaller routing table
b. Lower use of IP addresses
c. More accurate path selection
d. Fewer routing updates
e. Improved convergence

11. IPv6 supports which three address types? (Choose three.)

a. Unicast
b. Multicast
c. Anycast
d. Broadcast

12. Modern IGP routing protocols use which traffic type for sending advertisements, by default?

a. Unicast
b. Multicast
c. Anycast
d. Broadcast

13. A GRE tunnel connecting two remote locations over the Internet supports encapsulation of dynamic routing protocols.

a. True
b. False

14. Match each DMVPN component with its function.

___ IPsec   ___ mGRE   ___ NHRP

a. Provides a scalable tunneling framework
b. Provides dynamic mutual discovery of spokes
c. Provides key management and transmission protection

15. Which statement is true about RIPng?

    a. It can only route in IPv4 networks.

    b. It uses hop count as the metric.

    c. It is a link-state protocol.

    d. It can route for networks up to 17 hops away.

Chapter 2

EIGRP Implementation

This chapter covers the following topics:

- Establishing EIGRP Neighbor Relationships

- Building the EIGRP Topology Table

- Optimizing EIGRP Behavior

- Configuring EIGRP for IPv6

- Named EIGRP Configuration

Enhanced Interior Gateway Routing Protocol (EIGRP) is an advanced distance vector routing protocol designed by Cisco. The basic configuration is simple and easy to understand, so it is commonly used in smaller networks. Its advanced features, which provide rapid convergence, higher scalability, and support for multiple routed protocols, fulfill requirements in complex network environments.

EIGRP supports both IPv4 and IPv6. Although standard EIGRP configuration between IPv4 and IPv6 differs, it can be unified using newly introduced named EIGRP configuration mode.

Upon completing this chapter, you will be able to do the following:

- Explain EIGRP neighbor relationships

- Explain how EIGRP chooses the best path through the network

- Configure stub routing, route summarization, and load balancing with EIGRP

- Configure basic EIGRP for IPv6 and optimize it with route summarization

- Configure EIGRP through named configuration

Establishing EIGRP Neighbor Relationships

EIGRP was developed as an enhanced version of the older Interior Gateway Routing Protocol (IGRP) protocol and has many of the same characteristics of an advanced Interior Gateway Protocol, such as high-speed convergence, partial updates, and the possibility to support multiple network layer protocols. The first step in configuring EIGRP is to establish EIGRP neighbor relationships over the various interface types. It is important to know how to verify these have been properly formed and how parameters like hello and hold timers and different WAN technologies influence session establishment.

Upon completion of this section, you will be able to do the following:

- Describe EIGRP characteristics

- Describe how EIGRP ensures reliable transport

- Describe the steps that EIGRP follows to add routes to the routing table

- Change EIGRP timers

- Describe where EIGRP adjacencies are formed in a Frame Relay network

- Describe where EIGRP adjacencies are formed in a Layer 3 MPLS VPN network

- Describe where EIGRP adjacencies are formed in a Layer 2 MPLS VPN Ethernet network

EIGRP Features

Key capabilities that distinguish EIGRP from other routing protocols include fast convergence, support for variable-length subnet masking (VLSM), partial updates, and support for multiple network layer protocols. Basic description of protocol design and architecture has been published as an Informational RFC that allows Cisco to retain control of EIGRP and customer experience while opening it to other vendors to promote interoperability.

EIGRP is a Cisco proprietary protocol that combines the advantages of link-state and distance vector routing protocols. However, EIGRP is a distance vector routing protocol. EIGRP includes advanced features not found in other distance vector protocols, like RIP, which is why it is referred to as an advanced distance vector routing protocol.

Like its predecessor IGRP, EIGRP is easy to configure and is adaptable to a wide variety of network topologies. What makes EIGRP an *advanced* distance vector protocol is the addition of several features found in link-state protocols, such as dynamic neighbor discovery. EIGRP is an *enhanced* IGRP because of its rapid convergence and the guarantee of a loop-free topology at all times. Features of this protocol include the following:

- **Fast convergence:** EIGRP uses the diffusing update algorithm (DUAL) to achieve rapid convergence. A router running EIGRP stores its neighbors' routing tables so that it can quickly adapt to changes in the network. If no appropriate route exists in the local routing table and no appropriate backup route exists in the topology table, EIGRP queries its neighbors to discover an alternative route. These queries are propagated until an alternative route is found or until it is determined that no alternative route exists.

- **Partial updates:** EIGRP sends partial triggered updates rather than periodic updates. These updates are sent only when the path or the metric for a route changes. They contain information about only that changed link rather than the entire routing table. Propagation of these partial updates is automatically bounded so that only those routers that require the information are updated. As a result, EIGRP consumes significantly less bandwidth than IGRP. This behavior also differs from link-state protocol operation, which sends a change update to all routers within an area.

- **Multiple network layer support:** EIGRP supports IP Version 4 (IPv4) and IP Version 6 (IPv6) using protocol-dependent modules that are responsible for protocol requirements specific to the network layer. EIGRP's rapid convergence and sophisticated metric offer superior performance and stability when implemented in IPv4 and IPv6 networks.

- **Use of multicast and unicast:** For communication between routers, EIGRP uses multicast and unicast rather than broadcast. As a result, end stations are unaffected by routing updates or queries. The multicast address used for EIGRP for IPv4 is 224.0.0.10, and the multicast address for EIGRP for IPv6 is FF00::A.

Note   EIGRP previously was called a hybrid protocol, which is not accurate and so it is no longer used. EIGRP is not a combination of a distance vector and link-state routing protocol, but a distance vector routing protocol with features found in a link-state protocol. Therefore, currently the term *advanced distance vector* is typically used to describe EIGRP.

Other EIGRP features include the following:

- **VLSM support:** EIGRP is a classless routing protocol, which means that it advertises a subnet mask for each destination network. This enables EIGRP to support discontinuous subnetworks and VLSM.

- **Seamless connectivity across all data link layer protocols and topologies:** EIGRP does not require special configuration to work across any Layer 2 protocols. Other routing protocols, such as Open Shortest Path First (OSPF) Protocol, require different configurations for different Layer 2 protocols, such as Ethernet and Frame Relay. EIGRP was designed to operate effectively in both LAN and WAN environments. WAN support for dedicated point-to-point links and nonbroadcast multiaccess (NBMA) topologies is standard for EIGRP. EIGRP accommodates differences in media types and speeds when neighbor adjacencies form across WAN links and can be configured to limit the amount of bandwidth that the protocol uses on WAN links.

■ **Sophisticated metric:** EIGRP represents metric values in a 32-bit format to provide enough granularity. EIGRP supports unequal metric load balancing, which allows administrators to distribute traffic flow more efficiently in their networks.

Note   The term *IP* is used for generic IP and applies to both IPv4 and IPv6. Otherwise, the terms *IPv4* and *IPv6* are used for the specific protocols.

Note   Although there is some review, this chapter assumes the reader has basic CCNA knowledge of EIGRP. If you need a more thorough review of EIGRP or other routing protocols, see *Routing Protocols Companion Guide* (Cisco Press, 2014).

EIGRP Features

One of the key technologies used in EIGRP is RTP (Reliable Transport Protocol), which is used for the reliable exchange of information.

As shown in Figure 2-1, EIGRP runs directly above the IP layer as its own protocol, numbered 88. RTP is the component of the EIGRP responsible for guaranteed, ordered delivery of EIGRP packets to all neighbors. It supports intermixed transmission of multicast or unicast packets. When using multicast on the segment, packets are sent to EIGRP's reserved multicast address 224.0.0.10 for IPv4 and FF02::A for IPv6.

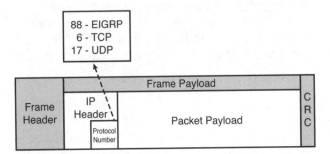

Figure 2-1   *EIGRP Encapsulation*

For efficiency reasons, RTP sends only certain EIGRP packets reliably, which means the recipient is required to send an EIGRP acknowledgment. For example, on a multiaccess network that has multicast capabilities, such as Ethernet, it is not necessary to send hello packets reliably to all neighbors individually. In this case, EIGRP sends a single multicast hello packet containing an indicator that informs the receivers that the packet does not need to be acknowledged. Other types of packets, such as updates, contain an indicator in the packet that an acknowledgment is required. Reliable transport protocol can send multicast packets quickly, even when unacknowledged packets are pending. This characteristic of the protocol helps to ensure that convergence time remains low in the presence of varying link speeds.

EIGRP Operation Overview

Operation of the EIGRP protocol is based on the information stored in three tables: neighbor table, topology table, and the routing table.

The main information stored in the neighbor table is a set of neighbors with which EIGRP router has established adjacencies. Neighbors are characterized by their primary IP address and the directly connected interface that leads to them.

The topology table contains all destination routes advertised by the neighbor routers. Each entry in the topology table is associated with a list of neighbors that have advertised the destination. For each neighbor, an advertised metric is recorded. This is the metric that a neighbor stores in its routing table to reach a particular destination. Another important information is the metric that a router uses to reach the same destination. This is the sum of the advertised metric from the neighbor plus link cost to the neighbor. The route with the best metric to the destination is called the successor and is placed in the routing table and advertised to the other neighbors.

The process to establish and discover neighbor routes occurs simultaneously with EIGRP. A high-level description of the process follows, using the topology in Figure 2-2 as an example.

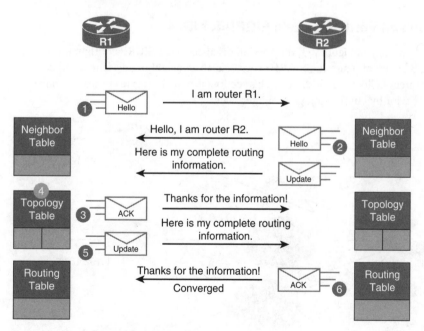

Figure 2-2 *EIGRP Operation Overview*

1. A new router (router R1 in this example) comes up on the link and sends a hello packet through all its EIGRP-configured interfaces.

2. Routers that are receiving the hello packet (R2) on one interface reply with update packets that contain all the routes that they have in their routing tables, except

those that are learned through that interface (split horizon). R2 sends an update packet to R1, but a neighbor relationship is not established until R2 sends a hello packet to R1. The update packet from R2 has the initialization bit set, indicating that this is the initialization process. The update packet includes information about the routes that the neighbor (R2) is aware of, including the metric that the neighbor is advertising for each destination.

3. After both routers have exchanged hellos and the neighbor adjacency is established, R1 replies to R2 with an ACK packet, indicating that it received the update information.

4. R1 assimilates all the update packets in its topology table. The topology table includes all destinations that are advertised by neighboring adjacent routers. It lists each destination, all the neighbors that can reach the destination, and their associated metric.

5. R1 sends an update packet to R2.

6. Upon receiving the update packet, R2 sends an ACK packet to R1.

After R1 and R2 successfully exchange update packets, they are ready to update their routing tables with the successor routes from the topology table.

Configuring and Verifying Basic EIGRP for IPv4

Using the topology in Figure 2-3, this section discusses basic EIGRP configuration, including how to configure the EIGRP process, analyze neighbor adjacency, and configure different hello and hold timers. This section also demonstrates how to optimize EIGRP behavior by configuring passive interfaces.

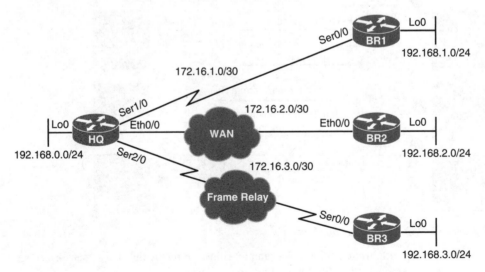

Figure 2-3 *Basic EIGRP Topology*

Example 2-1 shows EIGRP enabled on both interfaces using the **network** command and autonomous system number 100.

Example 2-1 *Configuration of EIGRP on BR1*

```
BR1> enable
BR1# configure terminal
Enter configuration commands, one per line.  End with CNTL/Z.
BR1(config)# router eigrp 100
BR1(config-router)# network 172.16.0.0
BR1(config-router)# network 192.168.1.0
```

To establish EIGRP neighbor relationship between the two routers, both routers must belong to the same autonomous system. The autonomous system number uniquely identifies the EIGRP process on the router and is used to define the EIGRP routing domain. Routers from the same routing domain will exchange EIGRP routes and those routes will be marked as EIGRP internal routes. Routers with different autonomous system numbers will not exchange routing information. Routers in two separate EIGRP domains, having different autonomous system numbers, must have redistribution configured to share routing information.

To start the EIGRP routing process on the router, configure it using the **router eigrp** *autonomous-system-number* command.

To include one or more local interfaces in the EIGRP process use the **network** *ip-address* [*wildcard-mask*] command. Interfaces matched by the network command will be enabled with EIGRP and will start to send and receive EIGRP packets.

The wildcard mask is optional and if omitted the EIGRP process assumes that all directly connected networks that are part of the major class network will participate in the routing process. EIGRP will attempt to establish neighbor relationships from each interface that is part of that Class A, B, or C major network. For example, if there are two Class B subnets 172.16.1.0/30 and 172.16.2.0/30 on interfaces and the network 172.16.0.0 is configured without the wildcard mask, you will include both interfaces in the EIGRP process. EIGRP will assume the default wildcard mask for the Class B network (0.0.255.255) when determining which interfaces to include in EIGRP.

Next, EIGRP on BR2 is configured, shown in Example 2-2. The wildcard mask parameter is used to limit which interfaces will be included in the EIGRP process. If you want to include only the 172.16.2.0/30 subnet in the EIGRP process, you must issue the network 172.16.2.0 0.0.0.3 command. With all 0s in the third wildcard mask octet, you state that the third octet of the network IPv4 address must match value of 2. With the last octet set to 3, the last 3 bits are not verified, and other bits must match values defined in the network IP address.

> **Note**   The wildcard mask can also be thought of as the inverse of a subnet mask. In a
> wildcard mask, the network bits are represented by 0s, and the host bits are represented
> by 1s. The inverse of subnet mask 255.255.255.252 is 0.0.0.3.

Example 2-2   *Configuration of EIGRP on BR2*

```
BR2(config)# router eigrp 100
BR2(config-router)# network 172.16.2.0 0.0.0.3
BR2(config-router)# network 192.168.2.1 0.0.0.0
```

To enable only a specific interface on the router, the wildcard mask 0.0.0.0 can be used
to specifically match all four octets of the interface address. To enable all interfaces on
the router for routing protocol, the address and wildcard mask combination of 0.0.0.0
255.255.255.255 is used to match all interfaces.

Next, the BR3 router is enabled for EIGRP in autonomous system 100 on all interfaces
in Example 2-3. Each router in an EIGRP routing domain is identified by its router ID. It
is used by a router each time it is communicating with its EIGRP neighbors. EIGRP router ID is also used for validating origin of external routes. If an external route is received
with a local router ID, the route is discarded. You can set the router ID manually using
the **eigrp router-id** *router-id* command. The router ID is a 32-bit value and is configured
as any IPv4 address except 0.0.0.0 and 255.255.255.255. A unique 32-bit value should be
configured for each router. If the router ID is not explicitly configured, the router will
select the highest address of its loopback interfaces. If there is no loopback interface on
the router, it will select the highest IPv4 address of any other active local interface. The
router ID is not changed unless the EIGRP process is cleared or if the router ID is manually configured.

Example 2-3   *Configuration of EIGRP on BR3*

```
BR3(config)# router eigrp 100
BR3(config-router)# eigrp router-id 192.168.3.255
BR3(config-router)# network 0.0.0.0 255.255.255.255
```

On BR1, verify EIGRP neighbor relationships using the **show ip eigrp neighbors** command with the optional **detail** keyword at the end, as shown in Example 2-4.

Example 2-4   *Verifying EIGRP Neighbor Relationships on BR1*

```
BR1# show ip eigrp neighbors
EIGRP-IPv4 Neighbors for AS(100)
H   Address        Interface    Hold  Uptime     SRTT  RTO  Q    Seq
                                (sec)  (ms)             Cnt  Num
0   172.16.1.1     Se0/0        13    01:29:20   17    102  0    11
BR1# show ip eigrp neighbors detail
EIGRP-IPv4 Neighbors for AS(100)
```

```
H   Address        Interface     Hold  Uptime     SRTT  RTO   Q    Seq
                                 (sec) (ms)                   Cnt  Num
0   172.16.1.1     Se0/0          14   01:40:47   17    102   0    11
    Version 7.0/3.0, Retrans: 0, Retries: 0, Prefixes: 5
    Topology-ids from peer - 0
```

The command output shows you neighbor relationships established within an autonomous system:

- **H** column shows you the order in which peering sessions were formed.

- **Address** column shows you the IP address of the EIGRP peer.

- **Interface** column shows you the interface to which the peer is connected.

- **Hold** and **Uptime** columns show you the amount of time, in seconds, that the router will wait to hear from its EIGRP peer before declaring it unreachable and the amount time since the neighbor relationship formed, respectively.

- **SRTT** column shows the amount of time, in milliseconds, required for the router to send an EIGRP packet to its neighbor and receive an acknowledgment for that packet.

- **RTO** or Retransmission timeout column shows you the amount of time the router waits before sending a packet from the retransmission queue.

- **Q** or Queue count column shows you the number of packets that the software is waiting to send. In case of network congestion, this number becomes greater than zero.

Additional information is displayed if you use the **detail** keyword:

- **Retrans** shows you the number of times that a packet has been retransmitted.

- **Retries** shows you the number of times an attempt was made to retransmit the packet.

- **Prefixes** is the number of prefixes received from the peer.

In Example 2-5, the active EIGRP interfaces are displayed on BR1 using the **show ip eigrp interfaces** command.

Example 2-5 *Verifying the EIGRP Interfaces on BR1*

```
BR1# show ip eigrp interfaces
EIGRP-IPv4 Interfaces for AS(100)
                   Xmit Queue    PeerQ         Mean  Pacing Time  Multicast  Pending
Interface   Peers  Un/Reliable   Un/Reliable   SRTT  Un/Reliable  Flow Timer Routes
Se0/0         1       0/0           0/0          17     0/16          88         0
Lo0           0       0/0           0/0           0     0/0            0         0
```

The Interface column in the output describes which interfaces are included in the EIGRP process, and the Peers column indicates the number of directly connected EIGRP neighbors over a specified interface. For more details, use the **show ip eigrp interfaces detail** command in Example 2-6, which shows additional information like number of sent packets, number of retransmits, and the values of hello interval and hold-time timers.

Example 2-6 *Verifying the EIGRP Interfaces' Details on BR1*

```
BR1# show ip eigrp interfaces detail
EIGRP-IPv4 Interfaces for AS(100)
                    Xmit Queue   PeerQ       Mean  Pacing Time  Multicast  Pending
Interface Peers  Un/Reliable  Un/Reliable  SRTT  Un/Reliable  Flow Timer Routes
Se0/0       1       0/0          0/0         17    0/16          88         0
Hello-interval is 5, Hold-time is 15
Split-horizon is enabled
Next xmit serial <none>
Packetized sent/expedited: 5/1
Hello's sent/expedited: 16200/2
Un/reliable mcasts: 0/0  Un/reliable ucasts: 4/5
Mcast exceptions: 0  CR packets: 0  ACKs suppressed: 0
Retransmissions sent: 0  Out-of-sequence rcvd: 0
<Output omitted>
```

The EIGRP configuration on the preconfigured HQ router is examined next using the **show ip protocols** and **show ip eigrp interfaces** commands.

Output of the **show ip protocols** command in Example 2-7 shows which networks were included in the EIGRP process and which routing information sources exist—in this case, those sources corresponding to WAN IP addresses belonging to BR1, BR2, and BR3.

Example 2-7 *Verifying the EIGRP Networks on HQ*

```
HQ# show ip protocols
*** IP Routing is NSF aware ***

Routing Protocol is "eigrp 100"
  <Output omitted>
  Routing for Networks:
    0.0.0.0
  Routing Information Sources:
    Gateway         Distance      Last Update
    172.16.2.2          90        23:04:13
    172.16.3.2          90        23:04:13
    172.16.1.2          90        23:04:13
  Distance: internal 90 external 170
```

The output of the **show ip eigrp interfaces** command in Example 2-8 shows the working interfaces on which EIGRP is enabled. Notice that Loopback 0 does not peer with any router. In other words, on the Loopback 0 interface, EIGRP packets will not be received. The same would be true for LAN interface where there are no additional routers attach. To preserve some resources and instruct routers to stop sending and receiving packets on the specific interface, you can configure such interfaces as passive.

Example 2-8   *Verifying the EIGRP Interfaces' Details on HQ*

```
HQ# show ip eigrp interfaces
EIGRP-IPv4 Interfaces for AS(100)

              Xmit     Queue       PeerQ       Mean   Pacing Time   Multicast    Pending
Interface    Peers  Un/Reliable  Un/Reliable  SRTT   Un/Reliable   Flow Timer   Routes
Et0/0          1       0/0          0/0          1       0/2          50           0
Se1/0          1       0/0          0/0         19       0/16         96           0
Se2/0          1       0/0          0/0         24       0/16        120           0
Lo0            0       0/0          0/0          0       0/0           0           0
```

Example 2-9 shows configure interfaces as passive using the **passive-interface default** command.

Example 2-9   *Configuring Passive Interfaces as the Default*

```
HQ(config)# router eigrp 100
HQ(config-router)# passive-interface default
*Sep 24 03:27:31.719: %DUAL-5-NBRCHANGE: EIGRP-IPv4 100: Neighbor 172.16.3.2
  (Serial2/0) is down: interface passive
*Sep 24 03:27:31.719: %DUAL-5-NBRCHANGE: EIGRP-IPv4 100: Neighbor 172.16.1.2
  (Serial1/0) is down: interface passive
*Sep 24 03:27:31.720: %DUAL-5-NBRCHANGE: EIGRP-IPv4 100: Neighbor 172.16.2.2
  (Ethernet0/0) is down: interface passive
```

When the **passive-interface default** command is used under the EIGRP process, the router immediately stops sending and receiving hello packets and routing updates on all interfaces. When configured, all existing neighbor relationships are terminated.

To disable passive interface for selected interfaces connecting HQ to BR routers, use the **no passive-interface** *interface-name* command, as shown in Example 2-10.

Example 2-10   *Disabling Passive Interfaces on HQ*

```
HQ(config-router)# no passive-interface ethernet 0/0
*Sep 24 03:31:16.376: %DUAL-5-NBRCHANGE: EIGRP-IPv4 100: Neighbor 172.16.2.2
  (Ethernet0/0) is up: new adjacency
HQ(config-router)# no passive-interface serial 1/0
*Sep 24 03:31:42.184: %DUAL-5-NBRCHANGE: EIGRP-IPv4 100: Neighbor 172.16.1.2
  (Serial1/0) is up: new adjacency
HQ(config-router)# no passive-interface serial 2/0
*Sep 24 03:31:56.265: %DUAL-5-NBRCHANGE: EIGRP-IPv4 100: Neighbor 172.16.3.2
  (Serial2/0) is up: new adjacency
```

After you configure the **no passive-interface** *interface-name* on all interfaces leading to the BR routers, the router starts sending EIGRP hellos and updates, and the EIGRP neighbor relationships get reestablished.

The **show ip protocols** command in Example 2-11 verifies the configuration of passive interfaces on HQ. As indicated in the output, only interface Loopback 0 remained configured as passive.

Example 2-11   *Verifying the Passive Interface on HQ*

```
HQ# show ip protocols
*** IP Routing is NSF aware ***
  <Output omitted>
  Routing for Networks:
    0.0.0.0
Passive Interface(s):
Passive Interface(s):
    Loopback0
Routing Information Sources:
    Gateway          Distance        Last Update
    172.16.2.2             90        00:29:44
    172.16.3.2             90        00:29:44
    172.16.1.2             90        00:29:44
  Distance: internal 90 external 170
```

To dynamically observe the sending and receiving of hello packets in real time, you can enable debugging of EIGRP hello packets with the **debug eigrp packets hello** command. In Example 2-12, debugging of EIGRP hello packets using the **debug eigrp packets hello** command is enabled on BR1. After 20 seconds, debugging is disabled by issuing the **no debug all** command.

Example 2-12   *Observing EIGRP Hello Packets on BR1*

```
BR1# debug eigrp packets hello
    (HELLO)
EIGRP Packet debugging is on
BR1#
*Sep 24 04:19:50.535: EIGRP: Sending HELLO on Serial0/0
*Sep 24 04:19:50.535:    AS 100, Flags 0x0:(NULL), Seq 0/0 interfaceQ 0/0 iidbQ un/
rely 0/0
*Sep 24 04:19:50.877: EIGRP: Received HELLO on Serial0/0 nbr 172.16.1.1
*Sep 24 04:19:50.877:    AS 100, Flags 0x0:(NULL), Seq 0/0 interfaceQ 0/0 iidbQ un/
rely 0/0 peerQ un/rely 0/0
BR1#
*Sep 24 04:19:55.232: EIGRP: Sending HELLO on Serial0/0
*Sep 24 04:19:55.232:    AS 100, Flags 0x0:(NULL), Seq 0/0 interfaceQ 0/0 iidbQ un/
rely 0/0
```

```
*Sep 24 04:19:55.264: EIGRP: Received HELLO on Serial0/0 nbr 172.16.1.1
*Sep 24 04:19:55.264:   AS 100, Flags 0x0:(NULL), Seq 0/0 interfaceQ 0/0 iidbQ un/
rely 0/0 peerQ un/rely 0/0
BR1# no debug all
All possible debugging has been turned off
```

To dynamically learn about other devices on the directly attached networks and thus establish and maintain EIGRP neighbor relationships, EIGRP uses small hello packets. These are sent periodically approximately every 5 seconds on all kind of interfaces except low-speed (T1 or slower) NBMA networks, where they are sent by default every 60 seconds. The time interval is called a hello timer.

Hello packets are used by EIGRP to determine whether the neighbor is alive and functioning. These packets also contain the hold-time parameter, which is used by EIGRP-enabled routers to determine the length of time after which the neighbor relationship becomes declared dead if the neighbor stops sending hello packets. Should this happen, EIGRP will start looking for alterative routing paths. Hold time defaults to three times the hello interval (15 or 180 seconds, depending on the underlying network).

Example 2-13 shows the verification of hello and hold timers on HQ using the **show ip eigrp interfaces detail** command.

Example 2-13 *Verifying Hello and Hold Timers on HQ*

```
HQ# show ip eigrp interfaces detail
EIGRP-IPv4 Interfaces for AS(100)
                 Xmit   Queue        PeerQ        Mean   Pacing Time  Multicast   Pending
Interface        Peers  Un/Reliable  Un/Reliable  SRTT   Un/Reliable  Flow Timer  Routes
Et0/0              1      0/0          0/0          5       0/2          50          0
  Hello-interval is 5, Hold-time is 15
  <Output omitted>
Se1/0              1      0/0          0/0          13      0/15         71          0
  Hello-interval is 5, Hold-time is 15
  <Output omitted>
Se2/0              1      0/0          0/0          1008    10/400       4432        0
  Hello-interval is 60, Hold-time is 180
  <Output omitted>
```

Hello interval defaults to 5 seconds on all interfaces except on the low-speed NBMA links. Because Serial 2/0 uses Frame Relay with a default speed of 1544 Kbps, which is not greater than T1 speed, the hello timer defaults to 60 seconds. On NBMA links that are faster than T1, the hello timer defaults to 5 seconds.

Note that the loopback interface is not included in the output, because it is still configured as a passive interface.

Hello and hold timers can be observed using the **debug eigrp packets hello** command on BR1, as shown in Example 2-14. After debugging is enabled on BR1, the Serial 1/0 interface on HQ is disabled, and results of the debug are shown on BR1.

When the Serial 1/0 interface is shut down on HQ, it will stop sending EIGRP hello packets to BR1 and immediately declare the EIGRP neighbor relationship down due to fact that the interface is down. However, BR1 will still believe that the EIGRP neighbor relationship is up until the hold-down timer on BR1 expires. After 15 seconds without receiving hello packets, BR1 will terminate the EIGRP neighbor relationship.

Example 2-14   *Observing EIGRP Hello Packets When an Interface Is Disabled*

```
BR1# debug eigrp packets hello
    (HELLO)
EIGRP Packet debugging is on


--------------------------------------------------------------------------------

HQ(config)# interface Serial 1/0
HQ(config-if)# shutdown
HQ(config-if)#
*Apr  9 12:09:53.485: %DUAL-5-NBRCHANGE: EIGRP-IPv4 100: Neighbor 172.16.3.2
(Serial2/0) is down: interface down
HQ(config-if)#
*Apr  9 12:09:55.483: %LINK-5-CHANGED: Interface Serial2/0, changed state to admin-
istratively down
*Apr  9 12:09:56.483: %LINEPROTO-5-UPDOWN: Line protocol on Interface Serial2/0,
changed state to down
```

```
BR1#
*Oct 10 13:47:03.981: EIGRP: Received HELLO on Serial0/0 nbr 172.16.1.1
*Oct 10 13:47:03.981:   AS 100, Flags 0x0:(NULL), Seq 0/0 interfaceQ 0/0 iidbQ un/
rely 0/0 peerQ un/rely 0/0
*Oct 10 13:47:08.953: EIGRP: Sending HELLO on Serial0/0
*Oct 10 13:47:08.953:   AS 100, Flags 0x0:(NULL), Seq 0/0 interfaceQ 0/0 iidbQ un/
rely 0/0
*Oct 10 13:47:13.833: EIGRP: Sending HELLO on Serial0/0
*Oct 10 13:47:13.833:   AS 100, Flags 0x0:(NULL), Seq 0/0 interfaceQ 0/0 iidbQ un/
rely 0/0
*Oct 10 13:47:18.457: EIGRP: Sending HELLO on Serial0/0
*Oct 10 13:47:18.457:   AS 100, Flags 0x0:(NULL), Seq 0/0 interfaceQ 0/0 iidbQ un/
rely 0/0
*Oct 10 13:47:18.982: %DUAL-5-NBRCHANGE: EIGRP-IPv4 100: Neighbor 172.16.1.1
(Serial0/0) is down: holding time expired
BR1# no debug all
All possible debugging has been turned off
```

Be sure to disable debugging on BR1 using the **no debug all** command after the neighbor relationship goes down.

Note that EIGRP would detect neighbor failure quicker if the Layer 2 status of the WAN link immediately reflected the failure of end-to-end connectivity.

Manipulating EIGRP Timers

EIGRP determines default timer values based on link type. If default values are not suitable for a specific network topology, you can manipulate values of hello and hold timers.

The main reason for considering the changing of hello and hold timers is to improve convergence time. This may appear particularly attractive on the low-speed NBMA links where default hello and hold timers default to a relatively long 60 and 180 seconds, respectively. However, you need to consider a few caveats before you decide to change default timer values.

In comparison with other IGPs, such as OSPF, EIGRP hello and hold timers between neighbors do not need to be identical to successfully establish EIGRP neighbor relationship; however, asymmetrical timers may lead to flapping EIGRP neighbor relationships and network instability.

For example, if one side of the link has hello interval set to 5 seconds with default hold time set to 15 seconds and the other side has hello interval set to 30 seconds, the routers will establish neighbor relationship for 15 seconds, and then it will be down for the next 15 seconds.

If you increase the hello interval on the link, it may lead to a situation where the network needs more time to detect potential failure with longer convergence time. In contrast, decreasing the hello timer to extremely small values may lead to high utilization of the link with routing traffic.

To change the EIGRP timers, you can use the interface configuration commands **ip hello-interval eigrp** *as-number hello-time-interval* and **ip hold-time eigrp** *as-number hold-time-interval*. The autonomous system number used in these commands must match the autonomous system number of the EIGRP process. The value of the interval is specified in seconds. Example 2-15 shows an example of modifying these timers on BR3.

Example 2-15 *Modifying and Verifying EIGRP Hello and Hold Time Timers on BR3*

```
BR3(config)# interface serial 0/0
BR3(config-if)# ip hello-interval eigrp 100 10
BR3(config-if)# ip hold-time eigrp 100 30
BR3# show ip eigrp interface detail serial 0/0
EIGRP-IPv4 Interfaces for AS(100)
            Xmit    Queue        PeerQ         Mean    Pacing Time  Multicast    Pending
Interface   Peers   Un/Reliable  Un/Reliable   SRTT    Un/Reliable  Flow Timer   Routes
Se0/0         1       0/0          0/0          1268      0/16         6340         0
  Hello-interval is 10, Hold-time is 30
<Output omitted>
```

EIGRP Neighbor Relationship over Frame Relay

Frame Relay supports two different interface types:

- Multipoint logical interfaces emulating a multiaccess network

- Point-to-point physical interfaces or logical point-to-point subinterfaces

When configuring EIGRP over point-to-multipoint subinterfaces, a single IP subnet is used. To emulate broadcast multiaccess network and enable EIGRP to send multicast packets over Frame Relay virtual circuits (VCs), you must add the broadcast keyword in the Frame Relay static mapping statement using the **frame-relay map ip** *ip-address dlci* **broadcast** interface configuration command.

Frame Relay multipoint subinterfaces are applicable to partial-mesh and full-mesh topologies. Partial-mesh Frame Relay networks must deal with the possibility of the split horizon, which prevents routing updates from being retransmitted on the same interface on which they were received.

When configuring EIGRP over point-to-point subinterfaces, a different IP subnet is used for each subinterface. Several point-to-point subinterfaces can be created over a single Frame Relay physical interface. These are logical interfaces that are emulating a leased-line network and are a routing equivalent to point-to-point physical interfaces. Because there is a single data-link connection identifier (DLCI) attached to the point-to-point subinterface, there is no need for static mappings here. Multicast traffic will be transmitted without need for any additional configuration. In addition, EIGRP considers point-to-point subinterfaces from the topology perspective as separate physical interfaces, and there is no possibility of the split-horizon issues. Frame Relay point-to point subinterfaces are applicable to hub-and-spoke topologies.

Note   For more information about configuring Frame Relay, see *Connecting Networks* (Cisco Press, 2014).

Establishing EIGRP over Layer 3 MPLS VPN

When you connect branch offices over Layer 3 Multiprotocol Label Switching (MPLS) virtual private network (VPN), you can establish EIGRP routing protocol directly with the service provider.

Shown in Figure 2-4, Layer 3 MPLS VPN provides the Internet service providers (ISPs) with a peer-to-peer VPN architecture the following characteristics:

- Provider-edge (PE) routers participate in customer routing, guaranteeing optimum routing between customer sites.

- PE routers carry a separate set of routes for each customer, resulting in perfect isolation between the customers.

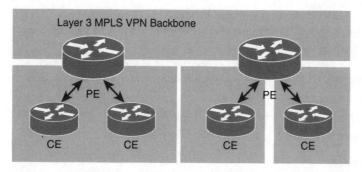

Figure 2-4 *Layer 3 MPLS VPN*

The Layer 3 MPLS VPN terminology divides the overall network into the customer-controlled part (customer network, or C network) and the provider-controlled part (provider network, or P network). Contiguous portions of the C network are called sites and are linked with the P network via customer-edge (CE) routers. The CE routers are connected to the PE routers, which serve as the edge devices of the provider network. The core devices in the provider network (provider routers, or P routers) provide the transit transport across the provider backbone and do not carry customer routes.

The Layer 3 MPLS VPN backbone provides a Layer 3 backbone in which the CE routers see PE routers as additional customer routers in the path. The PE routers maintain separate routing tables for each customer, to keep customer information isolated.

The Layer 3 MPLS VPN backbone looks like a standard corporate backbone to the CE routers. The CE routers run standard IP routing software and exchange routing updates with the PE routers that appear to them as normal routers in the customer network. The backbone routers in SP network are hidden from the view of the customer, and CE routers are unaware of the Layer 3 MPLS VPN. Therefore, the internal topology of the MPLS backbone is transparent to the customer.

Establishing EIGRP over Layer 2 MPLS VPN

In general, there are three different types of Layer 2 MPLS VPN solution from the customer perspective:

- Customer routers are located within single metropolitan area and they may be connected over the local Layer 2 MPLS VPN switch network. Customer traffic never passes through the SP backbone.

- Customer routers are located between several geographically distant areas that need to be connected over L2 MPLS VPN with point-to-point links through the SP backbone.

- Customer routers are located between several geographically distant areas that need to be connected over L2 MPLS VPN with multipoint links through the SP core. From the customer perspective SP network looks like a LAN switch.

A point-to-point MPLS L2 VPN solution is where an MPLS backbone provides a Layer 2 Ethernet point-to-point connection between the customer routers. When establishing EIGRP neighbor relationships over point-to-point WAN Ethernet links, every point-to-point connection will be in its own IP subnet. This solution is not very scalable as the number of your branch offices rises and you want to ensure direct communication between branches.

In the case of the multipoint MPLS L2 VPN solution, all routers belong to the same shared L2 broadcast domain. Figure 2-5 shows a logical network scheme.

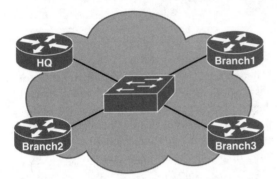

Figure 2-5   *Layer 2 MPLS VPN*

When you establish EIGRP neighbor relationships on the shared segment, every router on the segment will be neighbor with all other routers. In this topology, you will typically want to configure EIGRP authentication between neighbors to prevent unauthorized persons to add routers to your WAN network.

Building the EIGRP Topology Table

Once EIGRP neighbor relationships are established, the exchange of routing information begins. EIGRP uses update packets to exchange this information. All the routing information received from neighbors is stored in an EIGRP topology table.

EIGRP uses DUAL to calculate best routes to remote networks. For a route to be inserted into the routing table, it must satisfy the feasibility condition, which is used to prevent loops in the EIGRP networks. The route with the lowest metric to the destination becomes a candidate to be inserted into the routing table. If any routes remain, they must satisfy the feasibility condition to become a backup route to the destination network, should the primary route become unavailable.

To calculate the cost for each destination network, EIGRP uses a sophisticated metric, which is by default composed of bandwidth and delay.

Upon completing this lesson, you will be able to do the following:

- Describe how EIGRP neighbors exchange routing information

- Describe how EIGRP chooses the best path through the network

■ Describe how EIGRP metric gets calculated

■ Calculate EIGRP metric

■ Describe how the feasibility condition prevents loops in EIGRP networks

■ Understand EIGRP path selection process

Building and Examining the EIGRP Topology Table

This section examines different EIGRP packet types, explores the EIGRP topology table, and examines how EIGRP elects the best path to the destination.

This section begins with a discussion of EIGRP packet type as we configure EIGRP in the topology shown in Figure 2-6.

Before configuring EIGRP on the BR router, EIGRP debugging is enabled using the **debug eigrp packets** command shown in Example 2-16.

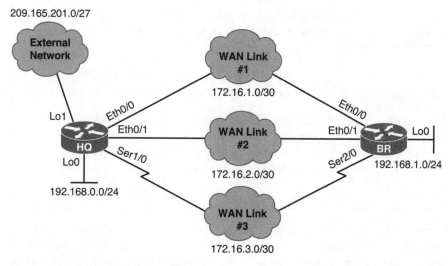

Figure 2-6 *EIGRP Topology*

Example 2-16 *Observing EIGRP on BR*

```
BR# debug eigrp packet
    (UPDATE, REQUEST, QUERY, REPLY, HELLO, IPXSAP, PROBE, ACK, STUB, SIAQUERY,
SIAREPLY)
EIGRP Packet debugging is on
```

Next, in Example 2-17, EIGRP is enabled on BR with an autonomous system of 100 but only on Loopback 0 and Ethernet 0/0 interfaces. After observing the hello packet in the debug process, debugging is disabled.

Example 2-17   *Observing EIGRP Hello Packets on BR*

```
BR(config)# router eigrp 100
BR(config-router)# network 192.168.1.0 0.0.0.255
BR(config-router)# network 172.16.1.0 0.0.0.3
*Oct  8 15:20:19.227: EIGRP: Sending HELLO on Ethernet0/0
*Oct  8 15:20:19.227:   AS 100, Flags 0x0:(NULL), Seq 0/0 interfaceQ 0/0 iidbQ un/
rely 0/0
*Oct  8 15:20:19.235: EIGRP: Received HELLO on Ethernet0/0 nbr 172.16.1.1
*Oct  8 15:20:19.235:   AS 100, Flags 0x0:(NULL), Seq 0/0 interfaceQ 0/0
*Oct  8 15:20:19.235: %DUAL-5-NBRCHANGE: EIGRP-IPv4 100: Neighbor 172.16.1.1
(Ethernet0/0) is up: new adjacency

*Oct  8 15:20:19.261: EIGRP: Enqueueing UPDATE on Ethernet0/0 tid 0 iidbQ un/rely
0/1 serno 1-2
*Oct  8 15:20:19.266: EIGRP: Sending UPDATE on Ethernet0/0 tid 0
*Oct  8 15:20:19.266:   AS 100, Flags 0x0:(NULL), Seq 2/0 interfaceQ 0/0 iidbQ un/
rely 0/0 serno 1-2
*Oct  8 15:20:19.274: EIGRP: Received ACK on Ethernet0/0 nbr 172.16.1.1
*Oct  8 15:20:19.275:   AS 100, Flags 0x0:(NULL), Seq 0/2 interfaceQ 0/0 iidbQ un/
rely 0/0 peerQ un/rely 0/1
<Output omitted>
*Oct  8 15:20:19.253: EIGRP: Received UPDATE on Ethernet0/0 nbr 172.16.1.1
*Oct  8 15:20:19.253:   AS 100, Flags 0x0:(NULL), Seq 2/0 interfaceQ 0/0 iidbQ un/
rely 0/0 peerQ un/rely 0/1
*Oct  8 15:20:19.360: EIGRP: Enqueueing ACK on Ethernet0/0 nbr 172.16.1.1 tid 0
*Oct  8 15:20:19.360:   Ack seq 2 iidbQ un/rely 0/0 peerQ un/rely 1/0
*Oct  8 15:20:19.364: EIGRP: Sending ACK on Ethernet0/0 nbr 172.16.1.1 tid 0
*Oct  8 15:20:19.364:   AS 100, Flags 0x0:(NULL), Seq 0/2 interfaceQ 0/0 iidbQ un/
rely 0/0 peerQ un/rely 1/0
BR# no debug all
```

Immediately after the EIGRP process is enabled on the WAN link 172.16.1.0/30, EIGRP begins sending and receiving hello packets. The process of sending and receiving hello packets is unidirectional, meaning that the router sends the hello packets unreliably using multicast and expects no acknowledgment from the other side. When the BR router receives a hello packet from the HQ neighbor, it dynamically forms a new EIGRP adjacency. Hello packets are sent out periodically to check the neighbor availability.

In contrast to the process of sending and receiving hello packets, routing updates are sent and received bidirectionally. Update packets contain routing information and are always sent reliably, meaning that an acknowledgment packet is expected for every sent update packet. Vice versa, every update packet received must be acknowledged. The process of transmitting reliable packets is composed of two steps: enqueuing and bundling routing updates on the interface and sending the reliable packet to the neighbor. Output of the **debug** command shows the two separate processes of sending and receiving update and acknowledge packet pairs.

The numbers after the "Seq..." part of the debug output represent sequence and acknowledgment numbers. Looking at the debug output carefully, notice that each packet that is sent out reliably has a sequence number. Acknowledgment that confirms a successful receipt of the packet must carry the same number as the received packet.

Next, using the **show ip eigrp traffic** command, EIGRP packet traffic statistics are verified, as shown in Example 2-18.

Example 2-18 *Verifying EIGRP Packet Traffic on BR*

```
BR# show ip eigrp traffic
EIGRP-IPv4 Traffic Statistics for AS(100)
  Hellos sent/received: 65/67
  Updates sent/received: 9/7
  Queries sent/received: 0/0
  Replies sent/received: 0/0
  Acks sent/received: 5/5
  SIA-Queries sent/received: 0/0
  SIA-Replies sent/received: 0/0
  Hello Process ID: 101
  PDM Process ID: 63
  Socket Queue: 0/10000/2/0 (current/max/highest/drops)
  Input Queue: 0/2000/2/0 (current/max/highest/drops)
```

The **show ip eigrp traffic** command displays information about which type of EIGRP packets were sent and received. This command may prove extremely useful when troubleshooting, especially in combination with other EIGRP **show** and **debug** commands. The command output displays statistics for hellos, updates and acknowledgment packets, as well as for queries and replies.

Query packets are sent out when a router performs a route computation and does not have an alternative path to the destination network. The packet is sent reliably as multicast to the neighbors to determine whether they have an alternative path for the destination.

Reply packets are sent in response to a query packet. They are sent reliably as unicasts.

EIGRP routes on the BR router are verified using the **show ip route eigrp** command, as demonstrated in Example 2-19.

Example 2-19 *Verifying the EIGRP Routes on BR*

```
BR# show ip route eigrp
Codes: L - local, C - connected, S - static, R - RIP, M - mobile, B - BGP
       D - EIGRP, EX - EIGRP external, O - OSPF, IA - OSPF inter area
       N1 - OSPF NSSA external type 1, N2 - OSPF NSSA external type 2
       E1 - OSPF external type 1, E2 - OSPF external type 2
       i - IS-IS, su - IS-IS summary, L1 - IS-IS level-1, L2 - IS-IS level-2
```

```
ia - IS-IS inter area, * - candidate default, U - per-user static route
o - ODR, P - periodic downloaded static route, H - NHRP, l - LISP
+ - replicated route, % - next hop override

Gateway of last resort is not set

D     192.168.0.0/24 [90/409600] via 172.16.1.1, 18:20:16, Ethernet0/0
D EX  209.165.201.0/27 [170/537600] via 172.16.1.1, 18:20:16, Ethernet0/0
```

Output of the **show ip route eigrp** command shows the EIGRP routes present in the routing table. In the output, you can see two EIGRP routes, one marked with the code D and the other with the code D EX. Code D represents EIGRP internal routes.

An internal route originated within an EIGRP autonomous system, meaning that a directly attached network that is configured in EIGRP is considered internal and is propagated through the EIGRP autonomous system. External routes, however, were learned by another routing protocol and redistributed to EIGRP. They are represented with code D EX.

The numbers in square brackets represent AD and the EIGRP metric, respectively. IPv4 addresses after "via" represent the next-hop IPv4 addresses (in this case, 172.16.1.1), and at the end you can see the exit interface for that route.

To complete the configuration on BR, the two remaining interfaces Ethernet 0/1 and Serial 0/2 are configured to be a part of the EIGRP process, as shown in Example 2-20.

Example 2-20   *Configuring* network *Commands on BR*

```
BR(config)# router eigrp 100
BR(config-router)# network 172.16.2.0 0.0.0.3
BR(config-router)# network 172.16.3.0 0.0.0.3
```

The configuration and verification of EIGRP in this topology will be continued in the next section.

Choosing the Best Path

EIGRP uses DUAL to calculate the best path to a destination network. It uses the distance information, also known as a composite metrics to select efficient, loop-free paths.

DUAL calculates this composite metric by adding two values. The first value is the metric from neighboring router to the destination network. This value is reported to the router and is called the reported distance (RD). In many books, you will also find the term *advertised distance*. The second value is the metric from the local router to the router that reported the first value. Among all metrics from the local router to the destination network, the router will choose the one with the smallest composite metric and consider it the best path to the given destination. The selected value is called feasible distance (FD).

The route with the smallest metric is called the successor route and the next-hop router is called the successor. Multiple successors may exist if they have the same FD to the destination network. In this case, EIGRP tries to insert all the successor routes into the routing table. Up to four successor routes may be added to the routing table by default.

A feasible successor is a next-hop router with a loop-free path that has a larger cost to the destination than the successor. When more than one route exists for the given prefix in the topology table, the router verifies whether the route is a part of a loop-free topology. To do this, the router uses a simple rule that requires that the RD of an alternative backup route is always smaller than the FD of the best path. This is called the feasibility condition. Routes that satisfy this condition are considered as backup routes and are called feasible successor routes. Next hop routers are called feasible successors.

Continuing with the configuration from the previous section, the content of BR's EIGRP topology table using the **show ip eigrp topology** command is displayed in Example 2-21. Observe the information about HQ LAN 192.168.0.0/24.

Example 2-21   *Verifying the EIGRP Topology Table on BR*

```
BR# show ip eigrp topology
EIGRP-IPv4 Topology Table for AS(100)/ID(192.168.1.1)
Codes: P - Passive, A - Active, U - Update, Q - Query, R - Reply,
       r - reply Status, s - sia Status


P 172.16.2.0/30, 1 successors, FD is 1536000
        via Connected, Ethernet0/1
P 192.168.0.0/24, 1 successors, FD is 409600
       via 172.16.1.1 (409600/128256), Ethernet0/0
       via 172.16.2.1 (1664000/128256), Ethernet0/1
P 192.168.1.0/24, 1 successors, FD is 128256
       via Connected, Loopback0
P 172.16.3.0/30, 1 successors, FD is 2169856
       via Connected, Serial2/0
P 172.16.1.0/30, 1 successors, FD is 281600
       via Connected, Ethernet0/0
P 209.165.201.0/27, 1 successors, FD is 537600
        via 172.16.1.1 (537600/426496), Ethernet0/0
        via 172.16.2.1 (1792000/426496), Ethernet0/1
```

EIGRP topology table is a data structure that contains all the prefixes learned from all EIGRP neighbors. Code P in front of the prefix means that the prefix is in passive state. A route is considered passive when DUAL is not executing any computation to discover the possible alternative paths. Passive state is the normal and desirable state for all routes. When all routes are in a passive state, the network is fully converged.

The route will stay in the passive state as long as there is at least one valid path to the destination that satisfies FC. The feasibility condition is a fundamental way of how EIGRP internally resolves the problem of routing loops. *To fully understand FC you must first understand two other important concepts: reported distance and feasible distance.*

The distance or composite metric in EIGRP is an integer number used to compare different paths toward the same destination network. Each received route includes reported distance and is stored in the EIGRP topology table. You can find it in the output in the parentheses as the second number. For path to the network 192.168.0.0/24, it has a value of 128256 for both path options.

The total cost to the destination is the first number in the parentheses and reflects the reported distance plus the cost to get to the neighbor. Total cost for the network 192.168.0.0/24 is 409600 via interface Ethernet 0/0 and 1664000 via interface Ethernet 0/1.

The best path to the destination is based on the lowest total cost to the destination. The best path is selected as the successor route, and the value of total cost for the successor path is selected as FD.

The remaining paths become candidates for feasible successor routes. For a path to become a feasible successor, it must satisfy the feasibility condition. Path's reported distance must be lower that the value of feasible distance.

Note   For a thorough review of DUAL, see *Routing Protocols Companion Guide* (Cisco Press, 2014).

Continuing with previous scenario, Example 2-22 shows the EIGRP routes in the routing table of BR using the **show ip route eigrp** command.

Example 2-22   *Verifying the EIGRP Routes on BR*

```
BR# show ip route eigrp
Codes: L - local, C - connected, S - static, R - RIP, M - mobile, B - BGP
       D - EIGRP, EX - EIGRP external, O - OSPF, IA - OSPF inter area
       N1 - OSPF NSSA external type 1, N2 - OSPF NSSA external type 2
       E1 - OSPF external type 1, E2 - OSPF external type 2
       i - IS-IS, su - IS-IS summary, L1 - IS-IS level-1, L2 - IS-IS level-2
       ia - IS-IS inter area, * - candidate default, U - per-user static route
       o - ODR, P - periodic downloaded static route, H - NHRP, l - LISP
       + - replicated route, % - next hop override

Gateway of last resort is not set

D     192.168.0.0/24 [90/409600] via 172.16.1.1, 02:32:24, Ethernet0/0
D EX  209.165.201.0/27 [170/537600] via 172.16.1.1, 02:32:24, Ethernet0/0
```

Examining all the routes present in the topology table, EIGRP will try to insert only the successor routes into the routing table. If the router learns the same destination networks from other more-trusted routing sources, EIGRP successor routes will not be inserted into the routing table. Feasible successor routes stay in the topology table in case the successor route fails.

All the received routes in the BR topology table are displayed using the **show ip eigrp topology all-links** command, shown in Example 2-23.

Example 2-23 *Verifying All Networks in the EIGRP Topology Table on BR*

```
BR# show ip eigrp topology all-links
EIGRP-IPv4 Topology Table for AS(100)/ID(192.168.1.1)
Codes: P - Passive, A - Active, U - Update, Q - Query, R - Reply,
       r - reply Status, s - sia Status

P 172.16.2.0/30, 1 successors, FD is 1536000, serno 4
        via Connected, Ethernet0/1
        via 172.16.3.1 (3449856/1536000), Serial2/0
        via 172.16.1.1 (1561600/1536000), Ethernet0/0
P 192.168.0.0/24, 1 successors, FD is 409600, serno 2
        via 172.16.1.1 (409600/128256), Ethernet0/0
        via 172.16.3.1 (256512000/256000000), Serial2/0
        via 172.16.2.1 (1664000/128256), Ethernet0/1
P 192.168.1.0/24, 1 successors, FD is 128256, serno 6
        via Connected, Loopback0
P 172.16.3.0/30, 1 successors, FD is 2169856, serno 5
        via Connected, Serial2/0
        via 172.16.1.1 (2195456/2169856), Ethernet0/0
        via 172.16.2.1 (3449856/2169856), Ethernet0/1
P 172.16.1.0/30, 1 successors, FD is 281600, serno 1
        via Connected, Ethernet0/0
        via 172.16.3.1 (2195456/281600), Serial2/0
        via 172.16.2.1 (1561600/281600), Ethernet0/1
P 209.165.201.0/27, 1 successors, FD is 537600, serno 3
        via 172.16.1.1 (537600/426496), Ethernet0/0
        via 172.16.3.1 (256512000/256000000), Serial2/0
        via 172.16.2.1 (1792000/426496), Ethernet0/1
```

The **show ip eigrp topology all-links** command displays all possible paths to the destination. In addition to the successor and feasible successor routes, the topology table may also contain nonsuccessor routes. A nonsuccessor route is a route that does not satisfy the feasibility condition. The output shows the route to the network 192.168.0.0/24 now with three possible paths. Path via next hop 172.16.3.1 has a reported distance of 256000000, which is greater than the feasible distance for the route 409600. Because the feasibility condition is not satisfied, the path via 172.16.3.1 will not be a candidate for the successor role. When the router stays without routes that satisfy the FC, and a new path calculation for the prefix must be performed; the route will transit into the active state, and the router will start querying neighbors for alternative routes.

Next, Example 2-24 shows a continuous ping from the BR router to the IP address 192.168.0.1 on HQ.

Example 2-24   *Continuous Ping from BR to 192.168.0.1*

```
BR# ping 192.168.0.1 repeat 100000 size 1000
Type escape sequence to abort.
Sending 100000, 1000-byte ICMP Echos to 192.168.0.1, timeout is 2 seconds:
!!!!!!!!!!!!!!!!!!!!!!!!!!!!!!!!!!!!!!!!!!!!!!!!!!!!!!!!!!!!!!!!!!!!!!!!!!!!!
<Output omitted>
```

Because there is only one successor route in the routing table and two routes that satisfy feasibility condition in the topology table, Internet Control Message Protocol (ICMP) traffic will use the path over the 172.16.1.0/24 link.

In Example 2-25, HQ's Ethernet 0/0 interface is disabled, and the ongoing ping process behavior on BR is observed.

Example 2-25   *HQ Ethernet 0/0 Interface Shutdown and Results Observed on BR*

```
HQ(config)# interface Ethernet 0/0
HQ(config-if)# shutdown
*Oct 10 18:47:09.312: %DUAL-5-NBRCHANGE: EIGRP-IPv4 100: Neighbor 172.16.1.2
(Ethernet0/0) is down: interface down
*Oct 10 18:47:11.313: %LINK-5-CHANGED: Interface Ethernet0/0, changed state to
administratively down
*Oct 10 18:47:12.313: %LINEPROTO-5-UPDOWN: Line protocol on Interface Ethernet0/0,
changed state to down


BR#
!!!!!!!!!!!!!!!!!!!!!!!!!!!!!!!!!!!!!!!!!!!!!!!!!!!!!!!!!!!!!!!!!!!!!!!!!!!!!
!.....
*Oct 9 22:04:24.088: %DUAL-5-NBRCHANGE: EIGRP-IPv4 100: Neighbor 172.16.1.1
(Ethernet0/0) is down: holding time expired.
!!!!!!!!!!!!!!!!!!!!!!!!!!!!!!!!!!!!!!!!!!!!!!!!!!!!!!!!!!!!!!!!!!!!!!!!!!
!!!!!!!!!!!!!!!!!!!!!!!!!!!!!!!!!!!!!!!!!!!!!!!!!!!!!!!!!!!!!!!!!!!!!!!!!!
<Output omitted>
```

After the shutdown of the Ethernet 0/0 interface on HQ, the line protocol on the interface instantly changes the state to down, and EIGRP on HQ cancels its neighbor relationship over this interface. However, the status of the interface on the HQ side is not signalized to the corresponding BR interface. Therefore, the EIGRP process on the BR router will not immediately declare the EIGRP neighbor relationship over Ethernet 0/0 dead. BR realizes that there is no live peer on the other side of the link after the hold timer expires due to no hello packets being received.

By default, it takes 15 seconds on the Ethernet interfaces for EIGRP to converge. During this time frame, ICMP packets are dropped. When BR realizes that the neighbor is down, it starts forwarding ICMP packets using the feasible successor route over the 172.16.2.0/30 link.

Situations when Layer 2 status of the link does not reflect the operation status of the neighboring devices are common in real-world situations. If you need to speed up the convergence, the EIGRP timer can be adjusted, or other status detection mechanisms can be deployed.

If the continuous ping has not yet completed, end it by pressing **Ctrl+Shift+6**.

Example 2-26 shows the routing table on BR.

Example 2-26 *EIGRP Routes on BR*

```
BR# show ip route eigrp
Codes: L - local, C - connected, S - static, R - RIP, M - mobile, B - BGP
       D - EIGRP, EX - EIGRP external, O - OSPF, IA - OSPF inter area
       N1 - OSPF NSSA external type 1, N2 - OSPF NSSA external type 2
       E1 - OSPF external type 1, E2 - OSPF external type 2
       i - IS-IS, su - IS-IS summary, L1 - IS-IS level-1, L2 - IS-IS level-2
       ia - IS-IS inter area, * - candidate default, U - per-user static route
       o - ODR, P - periodic downloaded static route, H - NHRP, l - LISP
       + - replicated route, % - next hop override


Gateway of last resort is not set


D    192.168.0.0/24 [90/1664000] via 172.16.2.1, 00:33:49, Ethernet0/1
D EX 209.165.201.0/27 [170/1792000] via 172.16.2.1, 00:33:49, Ethernet0/1
```

The former feasible successor route that points over the 172.16.2.0/30 link has now become the successor route and is installed in the routing table.

The topology table on the BR is verified using the **show ip eigrp topology** command in Example 2-27.

Example 2-27 *EIGRP Topology Table on BR with New Successor*

```
BR# show ip eigrp topology
EIGRP-IPv4 Topology Table for AS(100)/ID(192.168.1.1)
Codes: P - Passive, A - Active, U - Update, Q - Query, R - Reply,
       r - reply Status, s - sia Status


P 172.16.2.0/30, 1 successors, FD is 1536000
      via Connected, Ethernet0/1
```

```
P 192.168.0.0/24, 1 successors, FD is 409600
        via 172.16.2.1 (1664000/128256), Ethernet0/1
P 192.168.1.0/24, 1 successors, FD is 128256
        via Connected, Loopback0
P 172.16.3.0/30, 1 successors, FD is 2169856
        via Connected, Serial2/0
P 172.16.1.0/30, 1 successors, FD is 281600
        via Connected, Ethernet0/0
P 209.165.201.0/27, 1 successors, FD is 537600
        via 172.16.2.1 (1792000/426496), Ethernet0/1
```

After the failure of the successor route, only the route over the Ethernet 0/1 interface satisfies the feasibility condition. This former feasible successor route has now become a successor and is present in both the topology and the routing table. The third route over 172.16.3.0/24 does not satisfy the feasibility condition and is not displayed in the output of the **show ip eigrp topology** command.

In Example 2-28, a continuous ping is done on BR toward HQ and during the ping, HQ's Ethernet 0/1 interface is disabled.

Example 2-28   *Continuous Ping on BR with HQ Interface Disabled*

```
BR# ping 192.168.0.1 repeat 100000 size 1000
Type escape sequence to abort.
Sending 100000, 1000-byte ICMP Echos to 192.168.0.1, timeout is 2 seconds:
!!!!!!!!!!!!!!!!!!!!!!!!!!!!!!!!!!!!!!!!!!!!!!!!!!!!!!!!!!!!!!!!!!!!!!!!!!
<Output omitted>
--------------------------------------------------------------------
HQ(config)# interface ethernet 0/1
HQ(config-if)# shutdown
*Oct 10 20:42:45.548: %DUAL-5-NBRCHANGE: EIGRP-IPv4 100: Neighbor 172.16.2.2
(Ethernet0/1) is down: interface down
*Oct 10 20:42:47.543: %LINK-5-CHANGED: Interface Ethernet0/1, changed state to
administratively down
*Oct 10 20:42:48.543: %LINEPROTO-5-UPDOWN: Line protocol on Interface Ethernet0/1,
changed state to down
--------------------------------------------------------------------
BR#
!!!!!!!!!!!!!!!!!!!!!!!!!!!!!!!!!!!!!!!!!!!!!!!!!!!!!!!!!!!!!!!!!!!!!!!!!!!
!!!!!!!!!!!!!!!!!!!!!!
*Oct 10 20:42:56.443: %DUAL-5-NBRCHANGE: EIGRP-IPv4 100: Neighbor 172.16.2.1
(Ethernet0/1) is down: holding time expired
!!!!!!!!!!!!
<Output omitted>
```

After the shutdown of the Ethernet 0/1 interface on the HQ router, the EIGRP neighbor relationship using the current successor route is canceled. The last remaining route that satisfies the feasible condition is gone from the topology and routing table. The DUAL calculation starts, and destination 192.168.0.0/24 goes into the active state. The BR router sends a special packet called a query, which is used to ask neighboring routers if they have any alternative paths for the lost prefix. The packet reaches router HQ over the only remaining active path, 172.16.3.0/30. HQ responds to the query with the reply packet, which confirms that it has a path to reach the lost network. When BR receives the reply packet, the process of the new path calculation ends.

During the DUAL calculation, 192.168.0.0/24 will be in the active state. Dropped packets during the convergence phase result because the hold timer on the BR must expire for the EIGRP neighbor over the 172.16.2.0/30 link and then the DUAL calculation must be executed.

ICMP packets are dropped before BR detects the unreachable neighbor over the successor path and while EIGRP determines a new valid path toward the destination network. Although the selected route in the topology table in previous examples did not satisfy the feasibility condition, in the absence of the other two routes from the topology table, this route is now the only route available. It is chosen as the successor and installed in the routing table.

If a continuous ping has not completed, you can cancel it by pressing **Ctrl+Shift+6**.

Example 2-29 shows the examination of the content of the routing table on BR using the **show ip route eigrp** command.

Example 2-29   *BR Routing Table with New Successor*

```
BR# show ip route eigrp
Codes: L - local, C - connected, S - static, R - RIP, M - mobile, B - BGP
       D - EIGRP, EX - EIGRP external, O - OSPF, IA - OSPF inter area
       N1 - OSPF NSSA external type 1, N2 - OSPF NSSA external type 2
       E1 - OSPF external type 1, E2 - OSPF external type 2
       i - IS-IS, su - IS-IS summary, L1 - IS-IS level-1, L2 - IS-IS level-2
       ia - IS-IS inter area, * - candidate default, U - per-user static route
       o - ODR, P - periodic downloaded static route, H - NHRP, l - LISP
       + - replicated route, % - next hop override


Gateway of last resort is not set

D     192.168.0.0/24 [90/256512000] via 172.16.3.1, 00:32:19, Serial2/0
D EX  209.165.201.0/27 [170/256512000] via 172.16.3.1, 00:32:19, Serial2/0
```

The only remaining available path toward between HQ and BR is now active and present in both topology and routing tables.

Exchange of Routing Knowledge in EIGRP

Before routers exchange their routing information, they must establish the EIGRP neighbor relationship. Session establishment is followed by an immediate exchange of update packets, which advertise the routing information from the EIGRP topology table. Keep in mind that only the best routes are advertised to the neighbors. So, only the routes that are used by EIGRP, the successor routes, get advertised.

In addition to the received routing information, the topology table has two other local sources:

- Subnets of directly connected interfaces on which EIGRP has been enabled using the **network** command

- Subnets learned by redistribution of routes into EIGRP from other routing protocols or routing information sources

Redistribution is a method of taking routing information from one source and advertising it into another routing protocol. Redistribution is used in situations when multiple routing protocols are used in the same autonomous system. Another common case is when you want to include already-defined static routes into the selected routing protocol.

EIGRP Metric

EIGRP uses a composite metric to determine the best path to the destination. The metric's value derives from a formula that can use the following parameters:

- **Bandwidth:** Least value of the bandwidth for all links between the local router and the destination.

- **Delay:** Cumulative delay obtained as sum of values of all delays for all links between the source and destination.

- **Reliability:** This value represents the worst reliability between source and destination (based on keepalives).

- **Load:** This value represents the worst load on the link between the source and the destination (based on the packet rate and the configured bandwidth of the interface).

You might find it in many books or online articles that maximum transmission unit (MTU) is also used in EIGRP metric calculations. Although it is true that MTU value is exchanged in the routing updates together with other metric components, it is never used for the metric calculation. It is only used as a tie-breaker, when the router needs to ignore some equal-cost paths to the same destination, because of too many equal-cost paths. In such cases, the route with the highest minimum MTU is preferred.

By default, EIGRP uses only bandwidth and delay to calculate the metric. Optionally, the computation may include interface load and reliability, although Cisco does not recommend using them. All routers in routing domain must use the same components for metric calculation, and changing the metric calculation on only one router can introduce connectivity issues in inconsistent environments.

The components used for the metric calculation are determined by the metric weights, or K values. Default K values are: K1=1, K2=0, K3=1, K4=0, K5=0. If the K values are set to default, the metric is based on only bandwidth and delay values.

Use the **show ip protocols** command to verify K values.

EIGRP Metric Calculation

To calculate composite metric to the given destination, EIGRP uses the following formula:

Metric = [(K1 * Bandwidth + [(K2 * Bandwidth) / (256 − Load)] + K3 * Delay) * K5/ (K4 + Reliability)] * 256

If K4 and K5 values are set to default values, which are 0, the quotient K5 / (K4 + Reliability) is not used; that is, it is set to 1. The formula thus effectively reduces to the following:

Metric = (K1 * Bandwidth +[(K2 * Bandwidth) / (256 − Load)] + K3 * Delay) * 256

If you take into account default K1–K3 values, K1=K3=1, and K2=0, the formula reduces EIGRP metric computation to the following:

Metric = (Bandwidth + Delay) * 256

Note that changing the K values is not recommended.

The format of the delay and bandwidth values that are used for EIGRP metric calculations is different from those that are displayed by the **show interface** command. The EIGRP delay value is the sum of the delays in the path, in tens of microseconds, whereas the **show interface** output displays the delay in microseconds. The EIGRP bandwidth is calculated using the minimum bandwidth link along the path, in kilobits per second. The value 10^7 is divided by this value. Sum of bandwidth and delay is multiplied by 256 to ensure backward compatibility with the EIGRP predecessor IGRP.

Note   Values of delay displayed in the **show interface** output are not measured but calculated. Cisco IOS calculates them based on the negotiated or configured interface bandwidth.

Note   For a thorough review of the EIGRP metric calculation, see *Routing Protocols Companion Guide* (Cisco Press, 2014).

EIGRP Wide Metrics

The EIGRP composite cost metric does not scale correctly for high-bandwidth interfaces or Ethernet channels, resulting in incorrect or inconsistent routing behavior. The lowest delay that can be configured for an interface is 10 microseconds. As a result, high-speed interfaces, such as 10 Gigabit Ethernet (GE) interfaces, or high-speed interfaces channeled together (GE ether channel) will appear to EIGRP as a single GE interface. This may cause undesirable equal-cost load balancing.

To resolve this issue, the EIGRP Wide Metrics feature supports 64-bit metric calculations and Routing Information Base (RIB) scaling that provides the ability to support interfaces (either directly or via channeling techniques like port channels or EtherChannels) up to approximately 4.2 terabits.

The 64-bit metric calculations work only in EIGRP named mode configurations. EIGRP classic mode uses 32-bit metric calculations. EIGPR named mode configuration is discussed later in this chapter.

The EIGRP Wide Metric is beyond the scope of this book. For more information, see the Cisco.com document "EIGRP Wide Metrics," at http://www.cisco.com/c/en/us/td/docs/ios-xml/ios/iproute_eigrp/configuration/15-mt/ire-15-mt-book/ire-wid-met.pdf.

EIGRP Metric Calculation Example

In Figure 2-7, R1 has two paths to reach networks behind R4. The bandwidths (Mbps) and the delays (in milliseconds) of the various links are shown in the figure. Let's determine EIGRP metric for both paths.

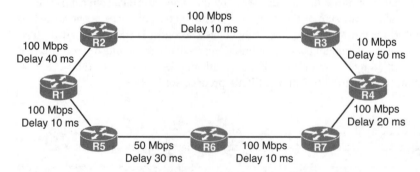

Figure 2-7   *R1 Has Two Paths to Networks Behind R4*

The calculation of the top path is as follows:

1. The lowest bandwidth along the top path (R1 - R2 - R3 - R4) is 10 Mbps (10000 Kbps). The EIGRP bandwidth calculation for this path is as follows:

   ■ Bandwidth = (10^7 / Least bandwidth in kilobits per second)

   ■ Bandwidth = (10,000,000 / 10,000) = 1,000

2. The delay through the top path is as follows:

- Delay = [(Delay R1 → R2) + (Delay R2 → R3) + (Delay R3 → R4)]

- Delay = [4000 + 1000 + 5000] = 10000 [tens of microseconds]

3. Therefore, the EIGRP metric calculation for the top path is as follows:

- Metric = (Bandwidth + Delay) * 256

- Metric = (1000 + 10,000) * 256 = 2,816,000

The calculation of the bottom path is as follows.

1. The lowest bandwidth along the lower path (R1 - R5 - R6 - R7 - R4) is 50000 kbps. The EIGRP bandwidth calculation for this path is as follows:

- Bandwidth = (10^7 / Least bandwidth in kilobits per second)

- Bandwidth = (10,000,000 / 50,000) = 200

2. The delay through the bottom path is as follows:

- Delay = [(Delay R1 → R5) + (Delay R5 → R6) + (Delay R6 → R7) + (Delay R7 → R4)]

- Delay = [1000 + 3000 + 1000 + 2000] = 7000 [tens of microseconds]

3. Therefore, the EIGRP metric calculation for the bottom path is as follows:

- Metric = (Bandwidth + Delay) * 256

- Metric = (200 + 7000) * 256 = 1,843,200

Therefore, R1 chooses the bottom path, with a lower metric of 1,843,200, over the top path, with a higher metric of 2,816,000. R1 installs the lower path, with R5 as the next-hop router, and a metric of 1,843,200 in the IP routing table. The bottlenecks along the top path are 10-Mbps links, and that explains why the router takes the lower path. This link means that the rate of transfer to R4 can be at a maximum 10 Mbps. Along the lower path, the lowest speed is 50 Mbps, meaning that the throughput rate can be as high as that speed. Therefore, the lower path represents a better choice—for example, for moving large files at greater speeds.

Feasibility Condition

Feasibility condition ensures EIGRP domain remains loop free. To be considered as a feasible successor route, the prefix must satisfy the feasibility condition, and its reported distance must be lower than the feasible distance of the successor route. This is the primary way how EIGRP ensures loop-free topology through the network.

To illustrate the importance of the feasibility condition, see Figure 2-8. Router D advertises its LAN network to routers B and C with the metric of 5. Routers B and C add their respective metrics of 5 and 10 to calculate their distances to the router D LAN network and then advertise these distances to router A. Router A adds a link metric of 3 to the advertisement from B and a link metric of 2 to the advertisement from C. Therefore, the best path from A to D goes over B because the metric of the A-B-D path is 13 and the metric of the A-C-D path is 17.

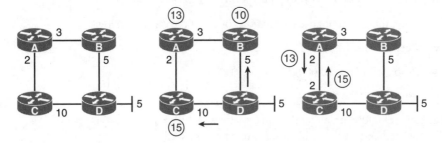

Figure 2-8   *R1 Has Two Paths to Networks Behind R4*

Assume for a moment that the split horizon has been disabled on router C on the link between router A and C. When router A advertises a best path metric of 13 from router A to C, router C may advertise the same route back to router A with an increased metric of 15. In this case, router A will not know whether router C has an alternate path to the LAN network of router D or whether it is advertising the route for the best path just back to router A. Because RD over router C is greater than FD of the best path, router A will not rely on the RD from router C. This is how router A ensures that the EIGRP domain stays loop free.

EIGRP Path Calculation Example

Figure 2-9 shows an example of how the RD is calculated. R1 has several options that are available to reach network 10.0.0.0/8. R2, R4, and R8 each send an update to R1. Each update contains a RD, which is the cost determined by the neighboring router toward the announced network 10.0.0.0/8.

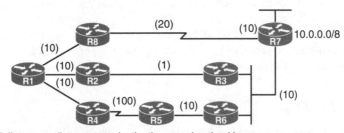

- Reported distance = distance to a destination as advertised by an upstream neighbor

Destination	RD	Neighbor
10.0.0.0/8	20+10=30	R8
10.0.0.0/8	1+10+10=21	R2
10.0.0.0/8	100+10+10+10=130	R4

Figure 2-9   *Reported Distance Calculations for R1*

Figure 2-10 shows an example of how the FD is calculated. R1 has several options that are available to reach network 10.0.0.0/8. Each update from the three neighbors has a different RD. By adding the cost of the local link to R2, R4, and R8 to the RD of each path, R1 calculates the distances for each path to the network 10.0.0.0/8. The lowest metric to the destination is over R2. The FD for the 10.0.0.0/8 network therefore equals 31.

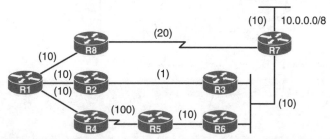

- Lowest metric = Feasible distance

Destination	RD	Metric	Neighbor
10.0.0.0/8	30	30+10=40	R8
10.0.0.0/8	21	21+10=31 (FD)	R2
10.0.0.0/8	130	130+10=140	R4

Figure 2-10 *Feasible Distance Calculations for R1*

Figure 2-11 shows the successor and feasible successor on R1 to network 10.0.0.0/8. Three paths exist for network 10.0.0.0/8. The distances (metrics) and RD values are calculated for all three paths—the three candidates for the routing table. The candidate with the lowest distance (metric) value over R2 becomes the successor route. The route with the second best metric (and if the RD for this route is lower than the FD on the successor route) becomes a feasible successor route. The route via R8 fulfills this criteria and becomes the feasible successor route. The route via R4 does not satisfy the feasibility condition and is therefore considered as a nonsuccessor route. Only the successor route is a candidate to be placed into the routing table.

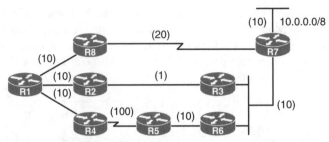

- Route over R2 becomes successor.
- Alternative route over R8 becomes feasible successor.

Destination	RD	Metric	Neighbor	Status
10.0.0.0/8	30	40	R8	FS
10.0.0.0/8	21	31 (FD)	R2	S
10.0.0.0/8	130	140	R4	Non-S

Figure 2-11   *Successor and Feasible Successor for R1*

Note   For a thorough review of the EIGRP metric calculation and examples, see the *Routing Protocols Companion Guide* (Cisco Press, 2014).

Optimizing EIGRP Behavior

When EIGRP is deployed in larger networks, you need to optimize the default EIGRP behavior to achieve the desired scalability. By implementing EIGRP stub configuration, you can limit the EIGRP query range, making EIGRP more scalable with fewer complications. By using summarization, you can reduce the size of the routing tables and optimize the exchange of routing information between the routers.

To utilize available redundant links, EIGRP by default supports load balancing across multiple links. To improve network utilization, you can also configure EIGRP to utilize unequal-cost load balancing.

Upon completion of this section, you will be able to do the following:

- Understand EIGRP queries

- Describe how stub routing can be used to reduce the amount of queries when EIGRP goes active

- Describe the EIGRP stuck-in-active issue

- Explain how using summary routes lessen the impact of query scope when EIGRP goes active

- Describe load-balancing options with EIGRP

EIGRP Queries

EIGRP relies on neighboring routers to provide routing information. When a router loses a route and does not have a feasible successor in its topology table, it looks for an alternative path to the destination. This is known as *going active* on a route.

When the route is lost, the router sends query packets to all neighbors on interfaces other than the one that is used to reach the previous successor (split-horizon behavior). These packets query whether each of the neighbors has a route to the given destination. If a neighbor router has an alternate route, it answers the query and does not propagate it further. If a neighbor does not have an alternate route, it queries each of its own neighbors for an alternate path. The queries then propagate through the network, creating an expanding tree of queries. When a router answers a query, it stops the spread of the query through that branch of the network.

In the Figure 2-12, you can see a network example in which a single lost route might result in an enormous number of queries that are sent throughout the EIGRP domain. When the route to network 192.168.14.0 on router R1 is lost, R1 sends a query to all neighboring routers and to all interfaces except the interface of the successor (split horizon). The query is propagated to R2. Because it has no information about the lost route, R2 cascades the query to its neighbors, which cascade it to their neighbors, and so on. Each query requires a reply from the neighbor, and the amount of traffic increases. The network topology in the figure shows that there is no available redundant path to network 192.168.14.0.

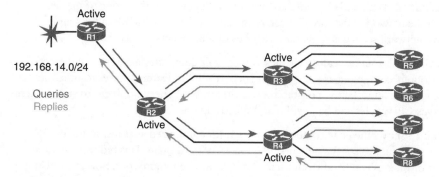

Figure 2-12 *EIGRP Queries and Replies*

The route in the active state can be observed using the **show ip eigrp topology** command in Example 2-30. They are marked with the letter *A*, and *P* indicates normal passive state.

Example 2-30 *Observing the Active Route on R1*

```
R1# show ip eigrp topology
EIGRP-IPv4 Topology Table for AS(1)/ID(172.16.1.2)
Codes: P - Passive, A - Active, U - Update, Q - Query, R - Reply,
       r - reply Status, s - sia Status
```

```
P 192.168.12.0/24, 1 successors, FD is 281600
        via Connected, GigabitEthernet0/1
A 192.168.14.0/24, 0 successors, FD is 409600, Q
    1 replies, active 00:00:02, query-origin: Local origin
      Remaining replies:
          via 172.16.1.1, r, GigabitEthernet0/0
P 172.16.1.0/30, 1 successors, FD is 281600
        via Connected, GigabitEthernet0/0
```

The EIGRP query propagation process is far from efficient. Many queries are sent, and each query is followed by a reply. Two major solutions exist to optimize the query propagation process and to limit the amount of unnecessary EIGRP load on the links. You can either use route summarization or the EIGRP stub routing feature to optimize how queries are exchanged.

Note   For a thorough review of the EIGRP DUAL and examples, see the *Routing Protocols Companion Guide* (Cisco Press, 2014).

EIGRP Stub Routers

The stability of large-scale EIGRP networks often depends on the scope of queries through the network. One way you can reduce the number of EIGRP queries and improve network scaling is to mark the spokes of a large network as stubs.

The EIGRP stub routing feature enables you to limit query message scope in the network. Routers configured as stubs do not forward EIGRP learned routes to other neighbors, and more importantly, nonstub routers do not send query messages to stub routers. This saves CPU cycles and bandwidth and speeds up convergence.

Figure 2-13 shows the edge routers R5 through R8 configured as stubs, so R3 and R4 will not send queries for the network 192.168.14.0/24 to them. This reduces the total number of queries and bandwidth used. Configuring the remote routers as stubs also reduces the complexity of the topology and simplifies the configuration, especially in hub-and-spoke topologies, where stub routing is enabled on dual-homed remote routers or spokes. This means that you do not have to configure route filtering on remote routers to prevent them from appearing as transit paths to hub routers.

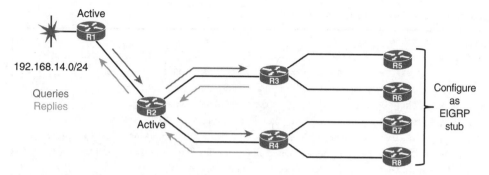

Figure 2-13 *EIGRP Stub Routers*

Configuring EIGRP Stub Routing

The EIGRP query propagation process is not very efficient. Many queries are sent, and each query is followed by a reply. The EIGRP stub configuration option enables you to mark the routers as stubs and thus reduce the number of exchanged EIGRP queries. This section illustrates the commands to configure and verify EIGRP stubs.

Using the topology in Figure 2-14, notice that there are three routers: HQ, BR1A, and BR1B. All routers are already preconfigured with EIGRP. BR1A announces the summary network 192.168.16.0/23 (which summarizes prefixes 192.168.16.0/24 and 192.168.17.0/24) to HQ. BR1A redistributes its static route to 192.168.18.0/24 into EIGRP (so it is an external EIGRP route). BR1A is running EIGRP on all of its directly connected networks.

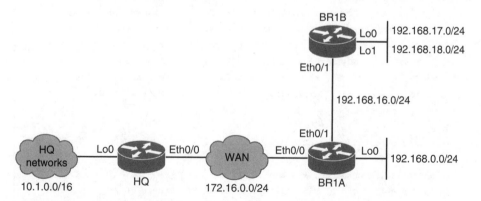

Figure 2-14 *EIGRP Topology for Configuring Stub Routers*

Example 2-31 shows the examination of the routing tables on routers HQ and BR1A with specific routes highlighted, which will be discussed.

Example 2-31   *R1 and BR Routing Tables*

```
HQ# show ip route
Codes: L - local, C - connected, S - static, R - RIP, M - mobile, B - BGP
       D - EIGRP, EX - EIGRP external, O - OSPF, IA - OSPF inter area
       N1 - OSPF NSSA external type 1, N2 - OSPF NSSA external type 2
       E1 - OSPF external type 1, E2 - OSPF external type 2
       i - IS-IS, su - IS-IS summary, L1 - IS-IS level-1, L2 - IS-IS level-2
       ia - IS-IS inter area, * - candidate default, U - per-user static route
       o - ODR, P - periodic downloaded static route, H - NHRP, l - LISP
       + - replicated route, % - next hop override


Gateway of last resort is not set


      10.0.0.0/8 is variably subnetted, 2 subnets, 2 masks
C        10.1.0.0/16 is directly connected, Loopback0
L        10.1.0.1/32 is directly connected, Loopback0
      172.16.0.0/16 is variably subnetted, 2 subnets, 2 masks
C        172.16.1.0/30 is directly connected, Ethernet0/0
L        172.16.1.1/32 is directly connected, Ethernet0/0
D        192.168.0.0/24 [90/409600] via 172.16.1.2, 00:12:07, Ethernet0/0
D        192.168.16.0/23 [90/307200] via 172.16.1.2, 00:12:07, Ethernet0/0
D EX     192.168.18.0/24 [170/307200] via 172.16.1.2, 00:12:07, Ethernet0/0
```

```
BR1A# show ip route
Codes: L - local, C - connected, S - static, R - RIP, M - mobile, B - BGP
       D - EIGRP, EX - EIGRP external, O - OSPF, IA - OSPF inter area
       N1 - OSPF NSSA external type 1, N2 - OSPF NSSA external type 2
       E1 - OSPF external type 1, E2 - OSPF external type 2
       i - IS-IS, su - IS-IS summary, L1 - IS-IS level-1, L2 - IS-IS level-2
       ia - IS-IS inter area, * - candidate default, U - per-user static route
       o - ODR, P - periodic downloaded static route, H - NHRP, l - LISP
       + - replicated route, % - next hop override


Gateway of last resort is not set


      10.0.0.0/16 is subnetted, 1 subnets
D        10.1.0.0 [90/409600] via 172.16.1.1, 00:34:56, Ethernet0/0
      172.16.0.0/16 is variably subnetted, 2 subnets, 2 masks
C        172.16.1.0/30 is directly connected, Ethernet0/0
L        172.16.1.2/32 is directly connected, Ethernet0/0
      192.168.0.0/24 is variably subnetted, 2 subnets, 2 masks
C        192.168.0.0/24 is directly connected, Loopback0
L        192.168.0.1/32 is directly connected, Loopback0
D        192.168.16.0/23 is a summary, 03:05:24, Null0
```

```
         192.168.16.0/24 is variably subnetted, 2 subnets, 2 masks
C          192.168.16.0/24 is directly connected, Ethernet0/1
L          192.168.16.1/32 is directly connected, Ethernet0/1
S       192.168.17.0/24 [1/0] via 192.168.16.2
S       192.168.18.0/24 [1/0] via 192.168.16.2
```

Notice that HQ learns about networks 192.168.0.0/24, 192.168.16.0/23, and 192.168.18.0/24 via EIGRP. The first route represents the LAN on BR1A, the second is a summary route, and the last one is a redistributed static route.

The **show ip eigrp neighbors details** command is used to verify HQ's neighbors, as shown in Example 2-32.

Example 2-32   *Verifying HQ's neighbors*

```
HQ# show ip eigrp neighbors detail
EIGRP-IPv4 Neighbors for AS(1)
H   Address      Interface          Hold  Uptime   SRTT   RTO  Q   Seq
                                    (sec) (ms)                 Cnt Num
0   172.16.1.2  Et0/0              13    02:14:33  12    100  0   20
    Version 7.0/3.0, Retrans: 0, Retries: 0, Prefixes: 3
    Topology-ids from peer - 0


BFD sessions
 NeighAddr          Interface
```

Notice that BR1A is the only neighbor visible to HQ. All learned EIGRP routes were received from it. Note also that BR1A and HQ are configured in EIGRP autonomous system 1.

Next, in Example 2-33, EIGRP packet debugging is enabled on HQ with the **debug eigrp packet terse** command, and the Loopback 0 interface is shut down.

Example 2-33   *Debugging EIGRP Query and Reply Packets on HQ*

```
HQ# debug eigrp packets terse
    (UPDATE, REQUEST, QUERY, REPLY, IPXSAP, PROBE, ACK, STUB, SIAQUERY, SIAREPLY)
EIGRP Packet debugging is on


HQ# configure terminal
Enter configuration commands, one per line.  End with CNTL/Z.
HQ(config)# interface Loopback 0
HQ(config-if)# shutdown
*Oct  8 13:11:18.173: EIGRP: Enqueueing QUERY on Ethernet0/0 tid 0 iidbQ un/rely 0/1
serno 21-21
*Oct  8 13:11:18.177: EIGRP: Sending QUERY on Ethernet0/0 tid 0
*Oct  8 13:11:18.177:   AS 1, Flags 0x0:(NULL), Seq 19/0 interfaceQ 0/0 iidbQ un/
rely 0/0 serno 21-21
```

```
*Oct  8 13:11:18.178: EIGRP: Received ACK on Ethernet0/0 nbr 172.16.1.2
*Oct  8 13:11:18.178:   AS 1, Flags 0x0:(NULL), Seq 0/19 interfaceQ 0/0 iidbQ un/
rely 0/0 peerQ un/rely 0/1
*Oct  8 13:11:18.178: EIGRP: Ethernet0/0 multicast flow blocking cleared
*Oct  8 13:11:18.207: EIGRP: Received REPLY on Ethernet0/0 nbr 172.16.1.2
*Oct  8 13:11:18.207:   AS 1, Flags 0x0:(NULL), Seq 21/19 interfaceQ 0/0 iidbQ un/
rely 0/0 peerQ un/rely 0/0
*Oct  8 13:11:18.207: EIGRP: Enqueueing ACK on Ethernet0/0 nbr 172.16.1.2 tid 0
*Oct  8 13:11:18.207:   Ack seq 21 iidbQ un/rely 0/0 peerQ un/rely 1/0
*Oct  8 13:11:18.207:    Handling TLV: 242 41 for 0 route: 10.1.0.0/16
*Oct  8 13:11:18.215: EIGRP: Sending ACK on Ethernet0/0 nbr 172.16.1.2 tid 0
*Oct  8 13:11:18.215:   AS 1, Flags 0x0:(NULL), Seq 0/21 interfaceQ 0/0 iidbQ un/
rely 0/0 peerQ un/rely 1/0
HQ(config-if)#
*Oct  8 13:11:20.155: %LINK-5-CHANGED: Interface Loopback0, changed state to
  administratively down
*Oct  8 13:11:21.159: %LINEPROTO-5-UPDOWN: Line protocol on Interface Loopback0,
changed state to down
```

Notice that HQ sends a query message to neighbor BR1A over the Ethernet 0/0 interface. EIGRP routers use query packets to ask neighbors about the path to the recently lost routes. BR1A first confirms the receipt of the query message with an ack message, followed by a reply packet that responds to the received query. The reply packet contains information that BR1A has no alternative route toward lost network 10.1.0.0/16. HQ responds to a reply packet by sending acknowledgment.

When router HQ loses the path to the network 10.1.0.0/16, EIGRP goes into the active state for the lost route. The routing process stays in the active state until it finds an alternative path or receives responses to all sent queries from its neighbors.

EIGRP Stub Options

Several different EIGRP stub options allow you to precisely specify which routes the EIGRP stub should advertise, as shown in Table 2-1.

To configure a router as a stub using Enhanced Interior Gateway Routing Protocol (EIGRP), use the **eigrp stub** command in router configuration mode or address family configuration mode. To disable the EIGRP stub routing feature, use the **no** form of this command.

Table 2-1   *Parameters for the* eigrp stub *Global Configuration Command*

Parameter	Description
receive-only	(Optional) Sets the router as a receive-only neighbor
leak-map *name*	(Optional) Allows dynamic prefixes based on a leak map
connected	(Optional) Advertises connected routes

Parameter	Description
static	(Optional) Advertises static routes
summary	(Optional) Advertises summary routes
redistributed	(Optional) Advertises redistributed routes from other protocols and autonomous systems

A router that is configured as a stub shares information about connected and summary routes with all neighboring routers by default. You can combine all stub options except for **receive-only** to achieve desired combination of advertised routes.

The **connected** option permits the EIGRP stub router to advertise all connected routes for interfaces that are matched with an EIGRP network command. This option is enabled by default and is the most widely practical stub option.

The **summary** option permits the EIGRP stub router to send summary routes. You can create summary routes manually, or you can create them automatically by enabling **auto-summary** at a major network boundary router. The **summary** option is enabled by default.

The **static** option permits the EIGRP stub router to advertise static routes. You still need to redistribute static routes into EIGRP using the **redistribute static** command.

The **redistribute** option permits the EIGRP stub router to advertise all redistributed routes, as long as redistribution is configured on the stub router using the **redistribute** command.

The **receive-only** option restricts the stub router from sharing any of its routes with any other router within an EIGRP autonomous system. This option does not permit any other option to be specified because it prevents any type of route from being sent. This option is rarely used. Two examples are when a router has a single interface or if Network Address Translation (NAT) with Port Address Translation (PAT) is configured, so all hosts are hidden behind a single WAN interface.

In Example 2-34, HQ's Loopback 0 interface is reenabled. In Example 2-35, BR1A is configured as an EIGRP stub using the **eigrp stub** command, and the output on HQ indicates that the adjacency is reestablished.

Example 2-34   *Reenabling the HQ's Loopback 0 Interface*

```
HQ(config)# interface loopback 0
HQ(config-if)# no shutdown
```

Example 2-35   *BR1A Configured as an EIGRP Stub Router*

```
BR1A(config)# router eigrp 1
BR1A(config-router)# eigrp stub
*Oct 18 11:51:16.232: %DUAL-5-NBRCHANGE: EIGRP-IPv4 1: Neighbor 172.16.1.1
(Ethernet0/0) is down: peer info changed
BR1A(config-router)#
```

```
*Oct 18 11:51:20.495: %DUAL-5-NBRCHANGE: EIGRP-IPv4 1: Neighbor 172.16.1.1
(Ethernet0/0) is up: new adjacency


-----------------------------------------------------------------
*Oct 18 11:51:16.228: %DUAL-5-NBRCHANGE: EIGRP-IPv4 1: Neighbor 172.16.1.2
(Ethernet0/0) is down: Interface PEER-TERMINATION received
HQ#
*Oct 18 11:51:20.503: EIGRP: Adding stub (1 Peers, 1 Stubs)
*Oct 18 11:51:20.503: %DUAL-5-NBRCHANGE: EIGRP-IPv4 1: Neighbor 172.16.1.2
(Ethernet0/0) is up: new adjacency
*Oct 18 11:51:20.503: EIGRP: Enqueueing UPDATE on Ethernet0/0 nbr 172.16.1.2 tid 0
iidbQ un/rely 0/1 peerQ un/rely 0/0
*Oct 18 11:51:20.508: EIGRP: Received UPDATE on Ethernet0/0 nbr 172.16.1.2
<Output omitted>
```

When the BR1A router is configured as a stub, the EIGRP adjacency needs to be reestablished.

EIGRP stub routers announce their new status in EIGRP hello packets. This informs neighbors that the router on the other end of the link is a stub router and that they must stop sending query packets to that router. This results in improved convergence time because the central routers do not have to wait for query responses from the remote offices.

Next, we will verify how HQ detects that BR1A is now configured as a stub router. All debugging is disabled on HQ using the **undebug all** command, shown in Example 2-36.

Example 2-36 *Disabling Debug on HQ*

```
HQ# undebug all
All possible debugging has been turned off
```

In Example 2-37, EIGRP neighbors on HQ are verified using the **show ip eigrp neighbors details** command.

Example 2-37 *Neighbor BR1A Verified as an EIGRP Stub on HQ*

```
HQ# show ip eigrp neighbors detail
EIGRP-IPv4 Neighbors for AS(1)
H   Address                 Interface          Hold Uptime   SRTT   RTO  Q   Seq
                                               (sec)         (ms)       Cnt  Num
0   172.16.1.2              Et0/0               11 00:39:00    7    100  0   13
    Version 7.0/3.0, Retrans: 0, Retries: 0, Prefixes: 2
    Topology-ids from peer - 0
    Stub Peer Advertising (CONNECTED SUMMARY ) Routes
    Suppressing queries


BFD sessions
 NeighAddr          Interface
```

Notice in Example 2-37 that router HQ sees router BR1A a stub router. By default, stub routers advertise only connected and summary routes to their neighbors; all other routes are filtered. Also notice the information about the queries. HQ is now suppressing them because BR1A is configured as stub.

In Example 2-38, the routing table on BR1A is verified using the **show ip route** command.

Example 2-38   *Verifying the Routing Table on BR1A*

```
BR1A# show ip route
Codes: L - local, C - connected, S - static, R - RIP, M - mobile, B - BGP
       D - EIGRP, EX - EIGRP external, O - OSPF, IA - OSPF inter area
       N1 - OSPF NSSA external type 1, N2 - OSPF NSSA external type 2
       E1 - OSPF external type 1, E2 - OSPF external type 2
       i - IS-IS, su - IS-IS summary, L1 - IS-IS level-1, L2 - IS-IS level-2
       ia - IS-IS inter area, * - candidate default, U - per-user static route
       o - ODR, P - periodic downloaded static route, H - NHRP, l - LISP
       + - replicated route, % - next hop override

Gateway of last resort is not set

      10.0.0.0/16 is subnetted, 1 subnets
D        10.1.0.0 [90/409600] via 172.16.1.1, 00:18:52, Ethernet0/0
      172.16.0.0/16 is variably subnetted, 2 subnets, 2 masks
C        172.16.1.0/30 is directly connected, Ethernet0/0
L        172.16.1.2/32 is directly connected, Ethernet0/0
      192.168.0.0/24 is variably subnetted, 2 subnets, 2 masks
C        192.168.0.0/24 is directly connected, Loopback0
L        192.168.0.1/32 is directly connected, Loopback0
D     192.168.16.0/23 is a summary, 00:22:21, Null0
      192.168.16.0/24 is variably subnetted, 2 subnets, 2 masks
C        192.168.16.0/24 is directly connected, Ethernet0/1
L        192.168.16.1/32 is directly connected, Ethernet0/1
S     192.168.17.0/24 [1/0] via 192.168.16.2
S     192.168.18.0/24 [1/0] via 192.168.16.2
```

Notice how the routing table on BR1A did not change after it was configured as a stub. Configuring a router as a stub does not change or limit the information that it receives from its neighbors, but rather limits what information it shares with its neighbors.

Now, examine the routing table on HQ using the **show ip route** command in Example 2-39.

By default, EIGRP stub router announces only connected and summary routes. Notice in the output how the external EIGRP route 192.168.18.0/24 is no longer present in the routing table on HQ.

Example 2-39   *Verifying the Routing Table on HQ with BR1A as a Stub*

```
HQ# show ip route
Codes: L - local, C - connected, S - static, R - RIP, M - mobile, B - BGP
       D - EIGRP, EX - EIGRP external, O - OSPF, IA - OSPF inter area
       N1 - OSPF NSSA external type 1, N2 - OSPF NSSA external type 2
       E1 - OSPF external type 1, E2 - OSPF external type 2
       i - IS-IS, su - IS-IS summary, L1 - IS-IS level-1, L2 - IS-IS level-2
       ia - IS-IS inter area, * - candidate default, U - per-user static route
       o - ODR, P - periodic downloaded static route, H - NHRP, l - LISP
       + - replicated route, % - next hop override

Gateway of last resort is not set

      10.0.0.0/8 is variably subnetted, 2 subnets, 2 masks
C        10.1.0.0/16 is directly connected, Loopback0
L        10.1.0.1/32 is directly connected, Loopback0
      172.16.0.0/16 is variably subnetted, 2 subnets, 2 masks
C        172.16.1.0/30 is directly connected, Ethernet0/0
L        172.16.1.1/32 is directly connected, Ethernet0/0
D     192.168.0.0/24 [90/409600] via 172.16.1.2, 00:09:07, Ethernet0/0
D     192.168.16.0/23 [90/307200] via 172.16.1.2, 00:09:07, Ethernet0/0
```

In Example 2-40, BR1A is configured as an EIGRP stub advertising only connected routers using the **eigrp stub connected** command.

Example 2-40   *BR1A Configured as a EIGRP Connected Stub*

```
BR1A(config)# router eigrp 1
BR1A(config-router)# eigrp stub connected
*Oct 20 18:46:50.137: %DUAL-5-NBRCHANGE: EIGRP-IPv4 1: Neighbor 172.16.1.1
(Ethernet0/0) is down: peer info changed
*Oct 20 18:46:50.419: %DUAL-5-NBRCHANGE: EIGRP-IPv4 1: Neighbor 172.16.1.1
(Ethernet0/0) is up: new adjacency
```

When you change the EIGRP stub options, any neighboring session needs to be torn down and reestablished.

Next, the EIGRP neighbor stub setting on HQ is verified using the **show ip eigrp neighbors detail** command in Example 2-41.

Example 2-41   *Neighbor BR1A Verified as an EIGRP Connected Stub on HQ*

```
HQ# show ip eigrp neighbors detail
EIGRP-IPv4 Neighbors for AS(1)
H   Address               Interface        Hold Uptime    SRTT   RTO  Q   Seq
                                           (sec)          (ms)        Cnt Num

0   172.16.1.2            Et0/0            14 00:10:25    12     100  0   8
```

```
     Version 7.0/3.0, Retrans: 0, Retries: 0, Prefixes: 2
     Topology-ids from peer - 0
     Stub Peer Advertising (CONNECTED ) Routes
     Suppressing queries

BFD sessions
  NeighAddr          Interface
```

On the HQ router, the routing table is verified using the **show ip route** command in
Example 2-42.

Example 2-42 *Verifying the Routing Table HQ*

```
HQ# show ip route
Codes: L - local, C - connected, S - static, R - RIP, M - mobile, B - BGP
       D - EIGRP, EX - EIGRP external, O - OSPF, IA - OSPF inter area
       N1 - OSPF NSSA external type 1, N2 - OSPF NSSA external type 2
       E1 - OSPF external type 1, E2 - OSPF external type 2
       i - IS-IS, su - IS-IS summary, L1 - IS-IS level-1, L2 - IS-IS level-2
       ia - IS-IS inter area, * - candidate default, U - per-user static route
       o - ODR, P - periodic downloaded static route, H - NHRP, l - LISP
       + - replicated route, % - next hop override


Gateway of last resort is not set

      10.0.0.0/8 is variably subnetted, 2 subnets, 2 masks
C        10.1.0.0/16 is directly connected, Loopback0
L        10.1.0.1/32 is directly connected, Loopback0
      172.16.0.0/16 is variably subnetted, 2 subnets, 2 masks
C        172.16.1.0/30 is directly connected, Ethernet0/0
L        172.16.1.1/32 is directly connected, Ethernet0/0
D     192.168.0.0/24 [90/409600] via 172.16.1.2, 00:14:52, Ethernet0/0
D     192.168.16.0/24 [90/307200] via 172.16.1.2, 00:14:52, Ethernet0/0
```

Notice that BR1A now advertises only connected networks 192.168.0.0/24 and
192.168.16.0/24. The summary route 192.168.16.0/23 and the redistributed static route
pointing to network 192.168.18.0/24 are no longer received by HQ.

Next, Example 2-43 shows the BR1A router configured as an EIGRP receive-only stub
using the **eigrp stub receive-only** command.

Example 2-43 *BR1A Configured as an EIGRP Receive-Only Stub*

```
BR1A(config)# router eigrp 1
BR1A(config-router)# eigrp stub receive-only
*Oct 20 19:06:42.909: %DUAL-5-NBRCHANGE: EIGRP-IPv4 1: Neighbor 172.16.1.1
(Ethernet0/0) is down: peer info changed
```

```
BR1A(config-router)#
*Oct 20 19:06:46.356: %DUAL-5-NBRCHANGE: EIGRP-IPv4 1: Neighbor 172.16.1.1
(Ethernet0/0) is up: new adjacency
```

With each change of EIGRP stub settings, reestablishment of the EIGRP neighboring session is required.

The EIGRP neighbor stub setting on HQ is verified using the **show ip eigrp neighbors detail** command in Example 2-44.

Example 2-44   *Neighbor BR1A Verified as an EIGRP Receive-Only Stub on HQ*

```
HQ# show ip eigrp neighbors detail
EIGRP-IPv4 Neighbors for AS(1)
H   Address                 Interface           Hold Uptime   SRTT   RTO  Q   Seq
                                                (sec)         (ms)        Cnt Num
0   172.16.1.2              Et0/0               10 00:03:03  1999   5000  0   10
    Version 7.0/3.0, Retrans: 1, Retries: 0
    Topology-ids from peer - 0
    Receive-Only Peer Advertising (No) Routes
    Suppressing queries


BFD sessions
 NeighAddr        Interface
```

Neighboring router BR1A is now configured as a receive-only stub. HQ will still suppress query packets, but router BR1A is not announcing any routes, even though the EIGRP session is established.

This is verified in HQ's routing table using the **show ip route** command in Example 2-45.

Example 2-45   *Verifying the Routing Table on HQ*

```
HQ# show ip route
Codes: L - local, C - connected, S - static, R - RIP, M - mobile, B - BGP
       D - EIGRP, EX - EIGRP external, O - OSPF, IA - OSPF inter area
       N1 - OSPF NSSA external type 1, N2 - OSPF NSSA external type 2
       E1 - OSPF external type 1, E2 - OSPF external type 2
       i - IS-IS, su - IS-IS summary, L1 - IS-IS level-1, L2 - IS-IS level-2
       ia - IS-IS inter area, * - candidate default, U - per-user static route
       o - ODR, P - periodic downloaded static route, H - NHRP, l - LISP
       + - replicated route, % - next hop override

Gateway of last resort is not set

      10.0.0.0/8 is variably subnetted, 2 subnets, 2 masks
C        10.1.0.0/16 is directly connected, Loopback0
```

```
L        10.1.0.1/32 is directly connected, Loopback0
      172.16.0.0/16 is variably subnetted, 2 subnets, 2 masks
C        172.16.1.0/30 is directly connected, Ethernet0/0
L        172.16.1.1/32 is directly connected, Ethernet0/0
```

Notice that all dynamic EIGRP routes have disappeared from the HQ's routing table. Router BR1A is configured as receive-only stub and is not advertising any routes to HQ. This stub option can be useful in cases when all hosts behind router BR1A would be translated using NAT with PAT. In a scenario like this, HQ has no need to be aware of networks behind router BR1A because all outgoing traffic would be destined for the BR1A WAN interface, where NAT would be performed.

In Example 2-46, BR1A's routing table is shown using the **show ip route** command.

Example 2-46 *Routing Table of BR1A Configured as a Receive-Only Stub*

```
BR1A# show ip route
Codes: L - local, C - connected, S - static, R - RIP, M - mobile, B - BGP
       D - EIGRP, EX - EIGRP external, O - OSPF, IA - OSPF inter area
       N1 - OSPF NSSA external type 1, N2 - OSPF NSSA external type 2
       E1 - OSPF external type 1, E2 - OSPF external type 2
       i - IS-IS, su - IS-IS summary, L1 - IS-IS level-1, L2 - IS-IS level-2
       ia - IS-IS inter area, * - candidate default, U - per-user static route
       o - ODR, P - periodic downloaded static route, H - NHRP, l - LISP
       + - replicated route, % - next hop override

Gateway of last resort is not set

      10.0.0.0/16 is subnetted, 1 subnets
D        10.1.0.0 [90/409600] via 172.16.1.1, 00:05:57, Ethernet0/0
      172.16.0.0/16 is variably subnetted, 2 subnets, 2 masks
C        172.16.1.0/30 is directly connected, Ethernet0/0
L        172.16.1.2/32 is directly connected, Ethernet0/0
      192.168.0.0/24 is variably subnetted, 2 subnets, 2 masks
C        192.168.0.0/24 is directly connected, Loopback0
L        192.168.0.1/32 is directly connected, Loopback0
D     192.168.16.0/23 is a summary, 01:20:33, Null0
      192.168.16.0/24 is variably subnetted, 2 subnets, 2 masks
C        192.168.16.0/24 is directly connected, Ethernet0/1
L        192.168.16.1/32 is directly connected, Ethernet0/1
S     192.168.17.0/24 [1/0] via 192.168.16.2
S     192.168.18.0/24 [1/0] via 192.168.16.2
```

Notice that even the receive-only stub option does not influence which routes are received by the stub router. The routing table on BR1A remains the same regardless of EIGRP stub configuration on the BR1A router.

Stuck in Active

When a router loses a route and sends a query message to its neighbors, it is expecting a response to that query message in a form of a reply packet. Failure to receive a response to a query message can lead to session termination.

EIGRP uses a reliable multicast approach to search for an alternative route. Therefore, it is imperative that EIGRP receives a reply for each query that it generates in the network.

Once a route goes active and the query sequence is initiated, it can only come out of the active state and transition to the passive state when it receives a reply for every generated query. If the router does not receive a reply to all the outstanding queries within 3 minutes (the default time), the route goes into the stuck-in-active (SIA) state. This timer is called the active timer. Once the active timer expires, the neighbor relationship is reset. This setting causes the router to go active on all routes that were known through the lost neighbor and to re-advertise all the routes that it knows to the lost neighbor.

Shown in Figure 2-15, the most common reason for lost reply messages is an unreliable link between the two routers, on which some packets might get lost. Although the routers receive enough packets to maintain the neighbor relationship, the router does not receive all the queries or replies. When this condition occurs, the effected devices will generate EIGRP DUAL-3-SIA error messages.

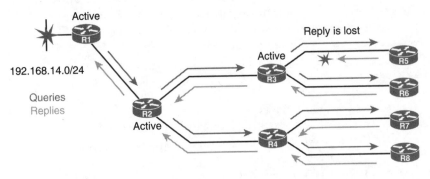

Figure 2-15   *EIGRP Lost Reply*

Resetting a neighbor relationship due to a lost reply message is very aggressive behavior. In large environments with slower links, it can cause long convergence times and network instability.

Two new additional EIGRP packets were introduced to overcome the described limitation. When no reply to a query is received, EIGRP sends an SIA query packet when the active timer is halfway through (after 90 seconds). This enables the neighboring router to respond with a SIA reply and confirm to the upstream router that it is still searching for a replacement route.

Figure 2-16   *EIGRP Stuck in Active*

Packets illustrated in the Figure 2-16 are exchanged in the following order:

- R1 queries downstream R2 (with an SIA query) at the midway point of the active timer (one and a half minutes by default) about the status of the route.

- R2 responds (with an SIA reply) that it still is searching for a replacement route.

- Upon receiving this SIA reply response packet, R1 validates the status of R2 and does not terminate the neighbor relationship.

- Meanwhile, R2 will send up to three SIA queries to R3. If they go unanswered, R2 will terminate the neighbor relationship with R3. R2 will then update R1 with an SIA reply indicating that the network 192.168.14.0/24 is unreachable.

- R1 and R2 will remove the active route from their topology tables. The neighbor relationship between R1 and R2 remains intact.

Reducing Query Scope by Using Summary Routes

Another way you can reduce the number of query messages is to implement route summarization. When a router receives an EIGRP query for a specific network, which is included in a summary route present in the router's routing table, it immediately sends a reply message without further forwarding the query packet. This reduces the number of queries sent and improves convergence time.

In the Figure 2-17 scenario example, router HQ performs summarization for all remote networks. A summary route is announced to other routers, like router GW. When connectivity to the remote location fails and HQ is left without any feasible successors to reach the lost network, it sends a query to its neighbors. When router GW receives a query for a network 192.168.12.0/24, it immediately responds with a reply message without further forwarding the query because it has a summary route 192.168.0.0/16, which also describes 192.168.12.0/24 prefix. However, because this route was learned from router HQ, router GW will respond that it does not have an alternative path for 192.168.12.0/24.

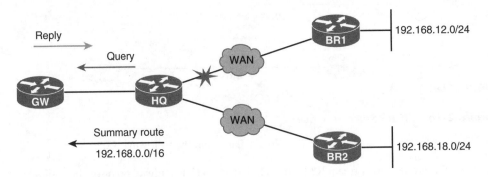

Figure 2-17   *Reducing Queries Using a Summary Route*

Configuring EIGRP Summarization

Implementing EIGRP summarization provides several benefits. Not only does it reduce the size of routing tables on the routers, but it also limits the query scope. In this section, we will configure EIGRP summarization using the topology in Figure 2-18.

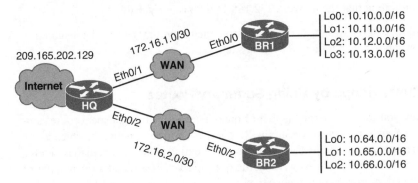

Figure 2-18   *EIGRP Topology for Summarization*

Prior to any summarization, Example 2-47 shows the routing table on HQ using the **show ip route** command.

Example 2-47   *Verifying HQ's Routing Table Prior to Summarization*

```
HQ# show ip route
Codes: L - local, C - connected, S - static, R - RIP, M - mobile, B - BGP
       D - EIGRP, EX - EIGRP external, O - OSPF, IA - OSPF inter area
       N1 - OSPF NSSA external type 1, N2 - OSPF NSSA external type 2
       E1 - OSPF external type 1, E2 - OSPF external type 2
       i - IS-IS, su - IS-IS summary, L1 - IS-IS level-1, L2 - IS-IS level-2
       ia - IS-IS inter area, * - candidate default, U - per-user static route
       o - ODR, P - periodic downloaded static route, H - NHRP, l - LISP
       + - replicated route, % - next hop override
```

```
Gateway of last resort is 209.165.200.226 to network 0.0.0.0

S*     0.0.0.0/0 [1/0] via 209.165.200.226
       10.0.0.0/16 is subnetted, 7 subnets
D          10.10.0.0 [90/409600] via 172.16.1.2, 00:18:16, Ethernet0/1
D          10.11.0.0 [90/409600] via 172.16.1.2, 00:18:16, Ethernet0/1
D          10.12.0.0 [90/409600] via 172.16.1.2, 00:18:16, Ethernet0/1
D          10.13.0.0 [90/409600] via 172.16.1.2, 00:18:16, Ethernet0/1
D          10.64.0.0 [90/409600] via 172.16.2.2, 00:16:55, Ethernet0/2
D          10.65.0.0 [90/409600] via 172.16.2.2, 00:16:55, Ethernet0/2
D          10.66.0.0 [90/409600] via 172.16.2.2, 00:16:55, Ethernet0/2
       172.16.0.0/16 is variably subnetted, 4 subnets, 2 masks
C          172.16.1.0/30 is directly connected, Ethernet0/1
L          172.16.1.1/32 is directly connected, Ethernet0/1
C          172.16.2.0/30 is directly connected, Ethernet0/2
L          172.16.2.1/32 is directly connected, Ethernet0/2
       209.165.200.0/24 is variably subnetted, 2 subnets, 2 masks
C          209.165.200.224/27 is directly connected, Ethernet0/0
L          209.165.200.225/32 is directly connected, Ethernet0/0
```

Notice in the output that HQ received seven different internal networks from routers BR1 and BR2. Reducing the number of routes in the routing table by using summarization improves network convergence and also reduces the number of queries. EIGRP supports both automatic and manual summarization.

In Example 2-48, automatic EIGRP summarization is configured on BR1 using the **auto-summary** EIGRP configuration command.

Example 2-48 *Configuring Automatic Summarization on BR1*

```
BR1(config)# router eigrp 1
BR1(config-router)# auto-summary
*Oct 26 08:56:42.288: %DUAL-5-NBRCHANGE: EIGRP-IPv4 1: Neighbor 172.16.1.1
(Ethernet0/0) is resync: summary configured
*Oct 26 08:56:42.292: %DUAL-5-NBRCHANGE: EIGRP-IPv4 1: Neighbor 172.16.1.1
(Ethernet0/0) is resync: summary up, remove components
```

When automatic summarization is enabled, the neighboring adjacency does not terminate; only routing information is synchronized. The **auto-summary** EIGRP command enables automatic summarization of routes to classful network boundaries. This EIGRP behavior was enabled by default on devices running older software, before Cisco IOS 15.

In Example 2-49, the summarized route on HQ is verified using the **show ip route** command.

Example 2-49 *Verifying BR1's Summarized Routes on HQ*

```
HQ# show ip route
Codes: L - local, C - connected, S - static, R - RIP, M - mobile, B - BGP
       D - EIGRP, EX - EIGRP external, O - OSPF, IA - OSPF inter area
       N1 - OSPF NSSA external type 1, N2 - OSPF NSSA external type 2
       E1 - OSPF external type 1, E2 - OSPF external type 2
       i - IS-IS, su - IS-IS summary, L1 - IS-IS level-1, L2 - IS-IS level-2
       ia - IS-IS inter area, * - candidate default, U - per-user static route
       o - ODR, P - periodic downloaded static route, H - NHRP, l - LISP
       + - replicated route, % - next hop override

Gateway of last resort is 209.165.200.226 to network 0.0.0.0

S*     0.0.0.0/0 [1/0] via 209.165.200.226
       10.0.0.0/8 is variably subnetted, 4 subnets, 2 masks
D         10.0.0.0/8 [90/409600] via 172.16.1.2, 00:17:23, Ethernet0/1
D         10.64.0.0/16 [90/409600] via 172.16.2.2, 00:32:36, Ethernet0/2
D         10.65.0.0/16 [90/409600] via 172.16.2.2, 00:32:36, Ethernet0/2
D         10.66.0.0/16 [90/409600] via 172.16.2.2, 00:32:36, Ethernet0/2
       172.16.0.0/16 is variably subnetted, 4 subnets, 2 masks
C         172.16.1.0/30 is directly connected, Ethernet0/1
L         172.16.1.1/32 is directly connected, Ethernet0/1
C         172.16.2.0/30 is directly connected, Ethernet0/2
L         172.16.2.1/32 is directly connected, Ethernet0/2
       209.165.200.0/24 is variably subnetted, 2 subnets, 2 masks
C         209.165.200.224/27 is directly connected, Ethernet0/0
L         209.165.200.225/32 is directly connected, Ethernet0/0
```

The routes 10.10.0.0/16 to 10.13.0.0/16 are no longer in the HQ routing table. Instead, they are replaced by the auto summary route 10.0.0.0/8.

Next, in Example 2-50, view the routing table on BR1 using the **show ip route** command.

Example 2-50 *Null0 Summary Route on BR1*

```
BR1# show ip route
Codes: L - local, C - connected, S - static, R - RIP, M - mobile, B - BGP
       D - EIGRP, EX - EIGRP external, O - OSPF, IA - OSPF inter area
       N1 - OSPF NSSA external type 1, N2 - OSPF NSSA external type 2
       E1 - OSPF external type 1, E2 - OSPF external type 2
       i - IS-IS, su - IS-IS summary, L1 - IS-IS level-1, L2 - IS-IS level-2
       ia - IS-IS inter area, * - candidate default, U - per-user static route
       o - ODR, P - periodic downloaded static route, H - NHRP, l - LISP
       + - replicated route, % - next hop override
```

```
Gateway of last resort is not set


      10.0.0.0/8 is variably subnetted, 12 subnets, 3 masks
D        10.0.0.0/8 is a summary, 00:15:53, Null0
C        10.10.0.0/16 is directly connected, Loopback0
L        10.10.0.1/32 is directly connected, Loopback0
C        10.11.0.0/16 is directly connected, Loopback1
L        10.11.0.1/32 is directly connected, Loopback1
C        10.12.0.0/16 is directly connected, Loopback2
L        10.12.0.1/32 is directly connected, Loopback2
C        10.13.0.0/16 is directly connected, Loopback3
L        10.13.0.1/32 is directly connected, Loopback3
D        10.64.0.0/16 [90/435200] via 172.16.1.1, 00:31:01, Ethernet0/0
D        10.65.0.0/16 [90/435200] via 172.16.1.1, 00:31:01, Ethernet0/0
D        10.66.0.0/16 [90/435200] via 172.16.1.1, 00:31:01, Ethernet0/0
      172.16.0.0/16 is variably subnetted, 4 subnets, 3 masks
D        172.16.0.0/16 is a summary, 00:15:53, Null0
C        172.16.1.0/30 is directly connected, Ethernet0/0
L        172.16.1.2/32 is directly connected, Ethernet0/0
D        172.16.2.0/30 [90/307200] via 172.16.1.1, 00:31:06, Ethernet0/0
      209.165.200.0/27 is subnetted, 1 subnets
D        209.165.200.224 [90/307200] via 172.16.1.1, 00:31:06, Ethernet0/0
```

Note the additional route in BR1's routing table describing network 10.0.0.0/8 and pointing to the Null0 interface. This route is installed automatically when route summarization is configured, to prevent routing loops. Imagine that BR1 receives a packet for a network that is described with the summary route 10.0.0.0/8 and is not present in BR1's routing table. If BR1 had a default route pointing to HQ, it would send this packet back to HQ, and HQ would bounce it back to BR1. This packet would be stuck in a routing loop until the Time To Live (TTL) field expired. A summary route pointing to the Null0 interface on a router that announces the summary route to other neighbors therefore prevents potential routing loops.

In Example 2-51, automatic EIGRP summarization is also enabled on BR2 using the auto-summary EIGRP configuration command on BR2.

Example 2-51 *Configuring Automatic Summarization on BR2*

```
BR2(config)# router eigrp 1
BR2(config-router)# auto-summary
BR2(config-router)#
*Oct 26 09:30:45.251: %DUAL-5-NBRCHANGE: EIGRP-IPv4 1: Neighbor 172.16.2.1
(Ethernet0/0) is resync: summary configured
*Oct 26 09:30:45.255: %DUAL-5-NBRCHANGE: EIGRP-IPv4 1: Neighbor 172.16.2.1
(Ethernet0/0) is resync: summary up, remove components
```

The summary route on HQ is verified by viewing HQ's routing table on HQ using the **show ip route** command, as shown in Example 2-52.

Example 2-52   *Verifying BR2's Summarized Routes on HQ*

```
HQ# show ip route
Codes: L - local, C - connected, S - static, R - RIP, M - mobile, B - BGP
       D - EIGRP, EX - EIGRP external, O - OSPF, IA - OSPF inter area
       N1 - OSPF NSSA external type 1, N2 - OSPF NSSA external type 2
       E1 - OSPF external type 1, E2 - OSPF external type 2
       i - IS-IS, su - IS-IS summary, L1 - IS-IS level-1, L2 - IS-IS level-2
       ia - IS-IS inter area, * - candidate default, U - per-user static route
       o - ODR, P - periodic downloaded static route, H - NHRP, l - LISP
       + - replicated route, % - next hop override

Gateway of last resort is 209.165.200.226 to network 0.0.0.0

S*    0.0.0.0/0 [1/0] via 209.165.200.226
D     10.0.0.0/8 [90/409600] via 172.16.2.2, 00:51:02, Ethernet0/2
                 [90/409600] via 172.16.1.2, 00:51:02, Ethernet0/1
      172.16.0.0/16 is variably subnetted, 4 subnets, 2 masks
C        172.16.1.0/30 is directly connected, Ethernet0/1
L        172.16.1.1/32 is directly connected, Ethernet0/1
C        172.16.2.0/30 is directly connected, Ethernet0/2
L        172.16.2.1/32 is directly connected, Ethernet0/2
      209.165.200.0/24 is variably subnetted, 2 subnets, 2 masks
C        209.165.200.224/27 is directly connected, Ethernet0/0
L        209.165.200.225/32 is directly connected, Ethernet0/0
```

Notice that HQ received the same summary route from BR2 as it did from BR1. This is because both BR1 and BR2 sit on a major network boundary and therefore advertise the same summary route. Because both routes have the same cost, HQ will load balance between these two routes.

Connectivity is tested using the **ping** command from HQ to IP address 10.10.0.1, which belongs to the summarized network on router BR1. Example 2-53 shows the results of the ping.

Example 2-53   *Testing Connectivity from HQ to the Summarized Network*

```
HQ# ping 10.10.0.1
Type escape sequence to abort.
Sending 5, 100-byte ICMP Echos to 10.10.0.1, timeout is 2 seconds:
U.U.U
Success rate is 0 percent (0/5)
```

There is a good chance that this connectivity test will fail. If you received successful ICMP replies, try to test connectivity to IPs from other summarized networks, such as 10.11.0.1, 10.12.0.1, or 10.13.0.1.

The output U.U.U indicates that HQ received ICMP destination unreachable replies. Because HQ thinks that both routers have access to all networks within 10.0.0.0/8 prefix, it can easily forward traffic to the incorrect neighbor.

Automatic summarization causes connectivity issues in networks where classless networks are discontiguous. Network 10.0.0.0/8 represents one large classful network, but in our scenario, portions of this network are used in different locations. Because a vast majority of networks today use small subnets of classless addresses, automatic summarization becomes useful only in rare cases and therefore is not a recommended way to optimize EIGRP.

To disable EIGRP automatic summarization on both BR1 and BR2 the **no auto-summary** command is used on both routers, as shown in Example 2-54.

Example 2-54   *Disabling Automatic Summarization on BR1 and BR2*

```
BR1(config)# router eigrp 1
BR1(config-router)# no auto-summary
*Oct 26 12:59:46.864: %DUAL-5-NBRCHANGE: EIGRP-IPv4 1: Neighbor 172.16.1.1
(Ethernet0/0) is resync: summary configured
-------------------------------------------------------------------------
BR2(config)# router eigrp 1
BR2(config-router)# no auto-summary
*Oct 26 13:01:07.169: %DUAL-5-NBRCHANGE: EIGRP-IPv4 1: Neighbor 172.16.2.1
(Ethernet0/0) is resync: summary configured
```

The output in Example 2-55 verifies that automatic summarization has been disabled on both routers, by using the **show ip route** command on HQ.

Example 2-55   *HQ's Routing Table Verifying Automatic Summarization Has Been Disabled*

```
HQ# show ip route
Codes: L - local, C - connected, S - static, R - RIP, M - mobile, B - BGP
       D - EIGRP, EX - EIGRP external, O - OSPF, IA - OSPF inter area
       N1 - OSPF NSSA external type 1, N2 - OSPF NSSA external type 2
       E1 - OSPF external type 1, E2 - OSPF external type 2
       i - IS-IS, su - IS-IS summary, L1 - IS-IS level-1, L2 - IS-IS level-2
       ia - IS-IS inter area, * - candidate default, U - per-user static route
       o - ODR, P - periodic downloaded static route, H - NHRP, l - LISP
       + - replicated route, % - next hop override

Gateway of last resort is 209.165.200.226 to network 0.0.0.0
```

```
S*      0.0.0.0/0 [1/0] via 209.165.200.226
        10.0.0.0/16 is subnetted, 7 subnets
D          10.10.0.0 [90/409600] via 172.16.1.2, 00:23:26, Ethernet0/1
D          10.11.0.0 [90/409600] via 172.16.1.2, 00:23:26, Ethernet0/1
D          10.12.0.0 [90/409600] via 172.16.1.2, 00:23:26, Ethernet0/1
D          10.13.0.0 [90/409600] via 172.16.1.2, 00:23:26, Ethernet0/1
D          10.64.0.0 [90/409600] via 172.16.2.2, 00:22:05, Ethernet0/2
D          10.65.0.0 [90/409600] via 172.16.2.2, 00:22:05, Ethernet0/2
D          10.66.0.0 [90/409600] via 172.16.2.2, 00:22:05, Ethernet0/2
        172.16.0.0/16 is variably subnetted, 4 subnets, 2 masks
C          172.16.1.0/30 is directly connected, Ethernet0/1
L          172.16.1.1/32 is directly connected, Ethernet0/1
C          172.16.2.0/30 is directly connected, Ethernet0/2
L          172.16.2.1/32 is directly connected, Ethernet0/2
        209.165.200.0/24 is variably subnetted, 2 subnets, 2 masks
C          209.165.200.224/27 is directly connected, Ethernet0/0
L          209.165.200.225/32 is directly connected, Ethernet0/0
```

The HQ router now has all announced EIGRP networks.

Determining the Summary Route

To determine the summary route, you need to analyze the subnets you want to summarize. You need to determine the highest-order bits that match in all of the addresses. By converting the IP addresses to the binary format, you can identify the common bits shared among the subnets.

In the example in Table 2-2, the first 13 bits are common among the subnets. Therefore, the best summary route is 10.8.0.0/13.

Table 2-2   *Calculating an IPv4 Summary Route*

Prefix	Binary Format
10.10.0.0/16	00001010 . 00001010 . 00000000 . 00000000
10.11.0.0/16	00001010 . 00001011 . 00000000 . 00000000
10.12.0.0/16	00001010 . 00001110 . 00000000 . 00000000
10.13.0.0/16	00001010 . 00001111 . 00000000 . 00000000
Summary route	
10.8.0.0/13	00001010 . 00001000 . 00000000 . 00000000

Keep in mind that the summary route 10.8.0.0/13 also describes some unlisted networks beside the four subnets in the table. Two such examples are network 10.9.0.0/16 and 10.14.0.0/16. If these subnets are used in a different part of the network, the determined summary route would cause connectivity issues. In this example, two separate summary routes would need to be defined. Summary route 10.10.0.0/15 would describe only networks 10.10.0.0/16 and 10.11.0.0/16, and summary route 10.12.0.0/15 would describe only the 10.12.0.0/16 and 10.13.0.0/16 subnets.

If a router has two routes to the same destination (for example, a summary route and a more specific route with a longer matching prefix length), the routing table process will choose the more specific match.

Continuing with the prior topology, Example 2-56 shows BR1 configured for manual summarization on interface Ethernet 0/0 using the **ip summary-address eigrp 1 10.8.0.0/13** interface command.

Example 2-56 *Configuring Manual Summarization on BR1*

```
BR1(config)# interface Ethernet 0/0
BR1(config-if)# ip summary-address eigrp 1 10.8.0.0/13
*Dec  3 13:22:53.406: %DUAL-5-NBRCHANGE: EIGRP-IPv4 1: Neighbor 172.16.1.1
(Ethernet0/0) is resync: summary configured
```

To configure manual route summarization, it is necessary to select the correct interface to propagate the summary route, the correct autonomous system number, the summary address, and its mask. Beginning with Cisco IOS 15, the **ip summary-address** command can use either the subnet mask in dotted-decimal format or use the prefix length, as indicated in the example.

You can determine what kind of summary route you need to specify by analyzing common bits in IP address of all subnets that you want to summarize to one network. All bits that are common between addresses define the summary address and its mask.

Note that the summary route is advertised only if a more specific component (a more specific entry) of the summary route is present in the routing table.

Examine BR1's routing table using the **show ip route** command, as shown in Example 2-57.

Example 2-57 *Null0 Route in BR1's Routing Table*

```
BR1# show ip route
Codes: L - local, C - connected, S - static, R - RIP, M - mobile, B - BGP
       D - EIGRP, EX - EIGRP external, O - OSPF, IA - OSPF inter area
       N1 - OSPF NSSA external type 1, N2 - OSPF NSSA external type 2
       E1 - OSPF external type 1, E2 - OSPF external type 2
       i - IS-IS, su - IS-IS summary, L1 - IS-IS level-1, L2 - IS-IS level-2
       ia - IS-IS inter area, * - candidate default, U - per-user static route
       o - ODR, P - periodic downloaded static route, H - NHRP, l - LISP
       + - replicated route, % - next hop override

Gateway of last resort is not set
```

```
         10.0.0.0/8 is variably subnetted, 10 subnets, 4 masks
D           10.8.0.0/13 is a summary, 00:43:25, Null0
C           10.10.0.0/16 is directly connected, Loopback0
L           10.10.0.1/32 is directly connected, Loopback0
C           10.11.0.0/16 is directly connected, Loopback1
L           10.11.0.1/32 is directly connected, Loopback1
C           10.12.0.0/16 is directly connected, Loopback2
L           10.12.0.1/32 is directly connected, Loopback2
C           10.13.0.0/16 is directly connected, Loopback3
L           10.13.0.1/32 is directly connected, Loopback3
D           10.64.0.0/14 [90/435200] via 172.16.1.1, 00:24:06, Ethernet0/0
         172.16.0.0/16 is variably subnetted, 3 subnets, 2 masks
C           172.16.1.0/30 is directly connected, Ethernet0/0
L           172.16.1.2/32 is directly connected, Ethernet0/0
D           172.16.2.0/30 [90/307200] via 172.16.1.1, 05:09:11, Ethernet0/0
         209.165.200.0/27 is subnetted, 1 subnets
D           209.165.200.224 [90/307200] via 172.16.1.1, 05:09:11, Ethernet0/0
```

When configuring a router to announce a summary route, it also adds this route to its routing table and points it at the Null interface to prevent routing loops. A packet forwarded to the Null interface is simply dropped, which prevents the router from forwarding the packet to a default route and possibly creating a routing loop.

For example, if BR1 receives a packet destined for network 10.8.0.0/24, the route 10.8.0.0/13 pointing to the Null interface is identified as the best match. This packet gets discarded because a more specific route is not known to the router.

As shown in Example 2-58, BR2 is also configured with manual summarization on interface Ethernet 0/0 using the **ip summary-address eigrp 1 10.64.0.0/14** interface command.

Example 2-58 *Configuring Manual Summarization on BR2*

```
BR2(config)# interface Ethernet 0/0
BR2(config-if)# ip summary-address eigrp 1 10.64.0.0/14
*Dec  3 13:31:55.741: %DUAL-5-NBRCHANGE: EIGRP-IPv4 1: Neighbor 172.16.2.1
(Ethernet0/0) is resync: summary configured
```

The summary address 10.64.0.0/14 is determined by analyzing the common bits among the subnets that are present on router BR2.

Verify that the summary routes are advertised by examining the routing table on HQ using the **show ip route** command, shown in Example 2-59.

Example 2-59 *Verifying Summary Routes Received on HQ*

```
HQ# show ip route
Codes: L - local, C - connected, S - static, R - RIP, M - mobile, B - BGP
       D - EIGRP, EX - EIGRP external, O - OSPF, IA - OSPF inter area
```

```
            N1 - OSPF NSSA external type 1, N2 - OSPF NSSA external type 2
            E1 - OSPF external type 1, E2 - OSPF external type 2
            i - IS-IS, su - IS-IS summary, L1 - IS-IS level-1, L2 - IS-IS level-2
            ia - IS-IS inter area, * - candidate default, U - per-user static route
            o - ODR, P - periodic downloaded static route, H - NHRP, l - LISP
            + - replicated route, % - next hop override

Gateway of last resort is 209.165.200.226 to network 0.0.0.0

S*    0.0.0.0/0 [1/0] via 209.165.200.226
      10.0.0.0/8 is variably subnetted, 2 subnets, 2 masks
D        10.8.0.0/13 [90/409600] via 172.16.1.2, 01:30:05, Ethernet0/1
D        10.64.0.0/14 [90/409600] via 172.16.2.2, 01:10:46, Ethernet0/2
      172.16.0.0/16 is variably subnetted, 4 subnets, 2 masks
C        172.16.1.0/30 is directly connected, Ethernet0/1
L        172.16.1.1/32 is directly connected, Ethernet0/1
C        172.16.2.0/30 is directly connected, Ethernet0/2
L        172.16.2.1/32 is directly connected, Ethernet0/2
      209.165.200.0/24 is variably subnetted, 2 subnets, 2 masks
C        209.165.200.224/27 is directly connected, Ethernet0/0
L        209.165.200.225/32 is directly connected, Ethernet0/0
```

All branch subnets are now summarized by two summary routes. The metric of the summary route equals to the minimum metric of more specific routes, which are aggregated in the summary route.

Notice also the default route, pointing to the next hop IP address 209.165.200.226, which is reachable over the Ethernet 0/0 interface.

Test whether HQ has connectivity to external network reachable over the Internet by using the **ping 209.165.202.129** command, shown in Example 2-60.

Example 2-60 *Testing Connectivity to the External Network on HQ*

```
HQ# ping 209.165.202.129
Type escape sequence to abort.
Sending 5, 100-byte ICMP Echos to 209.165.202.129, timeout is 2 seconds:
!!!!!
Success rate is 100 percent (5/5), round-trip min/avg/max = 1/1/1 ms
```

Connectivity to the external IP address is successful because HQ has a default route pointing toward the Internet network.

Next, in Example 2-61, test to determine whether BR1 has connectivity to the external network by using the **ping 209.165.202.129** command. Verify also the routing table using the **show ip route 209.165.202.129** command.

Example 2-61   *Testing Connectivity to the External Network on BR1*

```
BR1# ping 209.165.202.129
Type escape sequence to abort.
Sending 5, 100-byte ICMP Echos to 209.165.202.129, timeout is 2 seconds:
.....
Success rate is 0 percent (0/5)
BR1# show ip route 209.165.202.129
% Network not in table
```

Connectivity to external IP address 209.165.202.129 fails because BR1 has no information on how to reach 209.165.202.129 IP address.

Connectivity to external networks is normally provided by the use of the default route, because describing all individual external networks, like those present on the Internet, would be time- and resource-consuming.

Obtaining Default Route

A router can obtain a default route in several different ways.

The main purpose of using a default route is to decrease the size of the routing table. This especially applies to the stub networks, where it is preferred to optimize the number of routes.

Before a router installs the default route, it examines default route candidates:

- The candidate can be a statically configured default route defined locally with the command **ip route 0.0.0.0 0.0.0.0** *next-hop | interface*. In this command, *interface* is the outgoing interface through which all packets with unknown destinations will be forwarded, and *next-hop* is the IP address to which packets with unknown destinations will be forwarded.

- The candidate is also a default route announced by the dynamic routing protocol. EIGRP can redistribute statically defined default routes by using the **redistribute static** configuration command.

- In addition, any classful network residing in the local routing table can become a default candidate when used with the **ip default-network** configuration command. The command attaches an exterior flag to any classful EIGRP route, thus making it a candidate for a default route.

> **Note**   In EIGRP, default routes cannot be directly injected as in OSPF, for example, where you can use the **default-information originate** command; however, you can summarize to 0.0.0.0/0 on an interface.

The router examines all default candidates and selects the best one based on the AD and route metric.

When selected, the router sets the gateway of last resort to the next hop of the selected candidate. This does not apply when the best candidate happens to be one of the directly connected routes.

In Example 2-62, the routing table is verified, and a static default route is redistributed on HQ into EIGRP using the redistribute static EIGRP configuration command.

Example 2-62 *Verifying HQ's Routing Table and Redistributing a Static Default Route*

```
HQ# show ip route
Codes: L - local, C - connected, S - static, R - RIP, M - mobile, B - BGP
       D - EIGRP, EX - EIGRP external, O - OSPF, IA - OSPF inter area
       N1 - OSPF NSSA external type 1, N2 - OSPF NSSA external type 2
       E1 - OSPF external type 1, E2 - OSPF external type 2
       i - IS-IS, su - IS-IS summary, L1 - IS-IS level-1, L2 - IS-IS level-2
       ia - IS-IS inter area, * - candidate default, U - per-user static route
       o - ODR, P - periodic downloaded static route, H - NHRP, l - LISP
       + - replicated route, % - next hop override

Gateway of last resort is 209.165.200.226 to network 0.0.0.0

S*    0.0.0.0/0 [1/0] via 209.165.200.226
      10.0.0.0/8 is variably subnetted, 2 subnets, 2 masks
D        10.8.0.0/13 [90/409600] via 172.16.1.2, 23:00:26, Ethernet0/1
D        10.64.0.0/14 [90/409600] via 172.16.2.2, 22:41:07, Ethernet0/2
      172.16.0.0/16 is variably subnetted, 4 subnets, 2 masks
C        172.16.1.0/30 is directly connected, Ethernet0/1
L        172.16.1.1/32 is directly connected, Ethernet0/1
C        172.16.2.0/30 is directly connected, Ethernet0/2
L        172.16.2.1/32 is directly connected, Ethernet0/2
      209.165.200.0/24 is variably subnetted, 2 subnets, 2 masks
C        209.165.200.224/27 is directly connected, Ethernet0/0
L        209.165.200.225/32 is directly connected, Ethernet0/0
HQ# configure terminal
HQ(config)# router eigrp 1
HQ(config-router)# redistribute static
```

Notice the static default route present in HQ's routing table. The **redistribute static** command redistributes all statically defined routes on HQ into the EIGRP process. Because the default route is the only static route defined on HQ, only this route will be redistributed.

In Example 2-63, the routing table on BR1 is verified using the **show ip route** command.

Example 2-63   *Verifying the Redistributed Static Default Route Is Received on BR1*

```
BR1# show ip route
Codes: L - local, C - connected, S - static, R - RIP, M - mobile, B - BGP
       D - EIGRP, EX - EIGRP external, O - OSPF, IA - OSPF inter area
       N1 - OSPF NSSA external type 1, N2 - OSPF NSSA external type 2
       E1 - OSPF external type 1, E2 - OSPF external type 2
       i - IS-IS, su - IS-IS summary, L1 - IS-IS level-1, L2 - IS-IS level-2
       ia - IS-IS inter area, * - candidate default, U - per-user static route
       o - ODR, P - periodic downloaded static route, H - NHRP, l - LISP
       + - replicated route, % - next hop override

Gateway of last resort is 172.16.1.1 to network 0.0.0.0

D*EX  0.0.0.0/0 [170/307200] via 172.16.1.1, 00:17:06, Ethernet0/0
      10.0.0.0/8 is variably subnetted, 10 subnets, 4 masks
D        10.8.0.0/13 is a summary, 23:10:22, Null0
C        10.10.0.0/16 is directly connected, Loopback0
L        10.10.0.1/32 is directly connected, Loopback0
C        10.11.0.0/16 is directly connected, Loopback1
L        10.11.0.1/32 is directly connected, Loopback1
C        10.12.0.0/16 is directly connected, Loopback2
L        10.12.0.1/32 is directly connected, Loopback2
C        10.13.0.0/16 is directly connected, Loopback3
L        10.13.0.1/32 is directly connected, Loopback3
D        10.64.0.0/14 [90/435200] via 172.16.1.1, 22:51:03, Ethernet0/0
      172.16.0.0/16 is variably subnetted, 3 subnets, 2 masks
C        172.16.1.0/30 is directly connected, Ethernet0/0
L        172.16.1.2/32 is directly connected, Ethernet0/0
D        172.16.2.0/30 [90/307200] via 172.16.1.1, 1d03h, Ethernet0/0
      209.165.200.0/27 is subnetted, 1 subnets
D        209.165.200.224 [90/307200] via 172.16.1.1, 1d03h, Ethernet0/0
```

You can see that BR1 received a default route over EIGRP. The neighboring router, HQ, which announced the default route, was selected as a gateway of last resort. BR1 will now send all packets with unknown destinations toward HQ.

Route 0.0.0.0 is marked with an asterisk (*), which indicates that it is a candidate default route. It is also labeled with D EX, which indicates that route is an external EIGRP route. EIGRP marks all routes that have been learned by another routing protocol or that reside in the routing table as static routes as external routes.

Connectivity on BR1 to external network is verified using the **ping 209.165.202.129** command, as shown in Example 2-64.

Example 2-64 *Verifying Connectivity from BR1 to an External Network*

```
BR1# ping 209.165.202.129
Type escape sequence to abort.
Sending 5, 100-byte ICMP Echos to 209.165.202.129, timeout is 2 seconds:
!!!!!
Success rate is 100 percent (5/5), round-trip min/avg/max = 1/1/1 ms
```

Connectivity from BR1 to external network is now successful. Because BR1 has no specific information about the destination IP address 209.165.202.129, it uses the received default network to forward packets toward the HQ router.

Load Balancing with EIGRP

EIGRP can distribute traffic over multiple links leading to the same destination to increase the effective network bandwidth. It supports load balancing over equal-metric paths and also over unequal-metric paths.

EIGRP enables load balancing between a maximum of four equal-metric paths by default. You can configure the maximum number of parallel routes that an IP routing protocol can support using the **maximum-paths** router configuration command. The maximum number of equally good routes that can be kept in the routing table is IOS version-dependent; testing results typically found 32 as the maximum.

When a packet is process switched, load balancing over equal-metric paths occurs on a per-packet basis. When packets are fast switched, load balancing over equal-metric paths occurs on a per-destination basis. Cisco Express Forwarding (CEF) switching, enabled by default, supports both per-packet and per-destination load balancing.

Load balancing over unequal-metric links is disabled by default. Only feasible successor paths can be included in the EIGRP load-balancing, to ensure the topology stays loop free.

Configuring EIGRP Load Balancing

In this section, we will configure EIGRP unequal-cost load balancing. The topology in Figure 2-19 includes two routers, which are interconnected with three links. The first two Ethernet links are equal, but the third serial link is slower. EIGRP has already been configured on both routers.

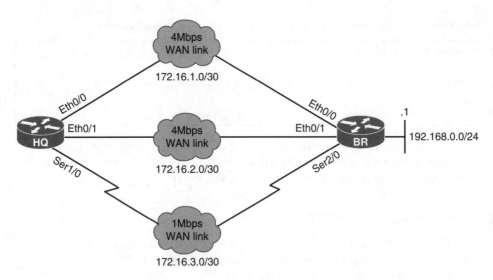

Figure 2-19   *EIGRP Topology for Load Balancing*

EIGRP Load Balancing

First, in Example 2-65, we verify connectivity from HQ to IP address 192.168.0.1 on the BR router.

Example 2-65   *Verifying Connectivity from HQ to BR*

```
HQ# ping 192.168.0.1
Type escape sequence to abort.
Sending 5, 100-byte ICMP Echos to 192.168.0.1, timeout is 2 seconds:
!!!!!
```

The routing table on HQ is verified in Example 2-66.

Example 2-66   *Verifying the Routing Table on HQ*

```
HQ# show ip route
Codes: L - local, C - connected, S - static, R - RIP, M - mobile, B - BGP
       D - EIGRP, EX - EIGRP external, O - OSPF, IA - OSPF inter area
       N1 - OSPF NSSA external type 1, N2 - OSPF NSSA external type 2
       E1 - OSPF external type 1, E2 - OSPF external type 2
       i - IS-IS, su - IS-IS summary, L1 - IS-IS level-1, L2 - IS-IS level-2
       ia - IS-IS inter area, * - candidate default, U - per-user static route
       o - ODR, P - periodic downloaded static route, H - NHRP, l - LISP
       + - replicated route, % - next hop override

Gateway of last resort is not set
```

```
         172.16.0.0/16 is variably subnetted, 6 subnets, 2 masks
C        172.16.1.0/30 is directly connected, Ethernet0/0
L        172.16.1.1/32 is directly connected, Ethernet0/0
C        172.16.2.0/30 is directly connected, Ethernet0/1
L        172.16.2.1/32 is directly connected, Ethernet0/1
C        172.16.3.0/30 is directly connected, Serial1/0
L        172.16.3.1/32 is directly connected, Serial1/0
D     192.168.0.0/24 [90/409600] via 172.16.2.2, 00:26:18, Ethernet0/1
                     [90/409600] via 172.16.1.2, 00:26:18, Ethernet0/0
```

Even though three links are established between the routers, HQ has inserted only two equal-cost EIGRP routes into the route table for the destination network 192.168.0.0/24. Traffic for this destination will be load balanced across interfaces Ethernet 0/0 and Ethernet 0/1.

HQ's routing table has two paths for the 192.168.0.0/24 network, but it is helpful to see what is stored in HQ's EIGRP topology table. In Example 2-67, we examine the EIGRP topology table on HQ.

Example 2-67 *Viewing HQ's Topology Table with Equal-Cost Routes*

```
HQ# show ip eigrp topology
EIGRP-IPv4 Topology Table for AS(1)/ID(172.16.3.1)
Codes: P - Passive, A - Active, U - Update, Q - Query, R - Reply,
       r - reply Status, s - sia Status

P 172.16.2.0/30, 1 successors, FD is 281600
        via Connected, Ethernet0/1
P 192.168.0.0/24, 2 successors, FD is 409600
        via 172.16.1.2 (409600/128256), Ethernet0/0
        via 172.16.2.2 (409600/128256), Ethernet0/1
        via 172.16.3.2 (2297856/128256), Serial1/0
P 172.16.3.0/30, 1 successors, FD is 2169856
        via Connected, Serial1/0
P 172.16.1.0/30, 1 successors, FD is 281600
        via Connected, Ethernet0/0
```

The EIGRP topology table reveals that HQ received information about the destination network 192.168.0.0/24 over all three interfaces. Both routes over Ethernet interfaces have the lowest cost and are both selected as successor routes. The third route received over the serial interface has a higher cost because of the lower bandwidth on the serial link.

By default, only equal-cost load balancing is enabled. For utilization of unequal-cost links, additional configuration is required.

EIGRP Load Balancing Across Unequal-Metric Paths

EIGRP can balance traffic across multiple routes that have different metrics, which is called unequal-metric load balancing. The degree to which EIGRP performs load balancing is controlled by the **variance** parameter. Setting a variance value enables EIGRP to install multiple loop-free routes with unequal metric in a local routing table. EIGRP will always install a successor into the local routing table. Additional feasible successors are candidates for the local routing table. Additional entries through EIGRP must meet two criteria to be installed in the local routing table:

- The route must be loop free. This condition is satisfied when the route is a feasible successor, such that its reported distance is less than the feasible distance of the successor route.

- The metric of the route must be lower than the metric of the best route (the successor) multiplied by the variance that is configured on the router.

The default value for the **variance** command is 1, which indicates equal-cost load balancing; only routes with the same metric as the successor are installed in the local routing table. The **variance** command is not limiting the maximum number of paths; it is the multiplier that defines the range of metric values that are accepted for load balancing by the EIGRP process. If the variance is set to 2, any EIGRP-learned route with a metric that is less than two times the successor metric will be installed in the local routing table. The EIGRP **variance** command has a single parameter, *multiplier*, which is the metric value used for load balancing. It can be a value from 1 to 128. The default is 1, which means equal-cost load balancing.

Note   EIGRP does not load-share between multiple routes; it only installs the routes in the local routing table. The local routing table then enables switching hardware or software to load share between the multiple paths.

On HQ, modifying the **variance** *multiplier*, as shown in Example 2-68, enables EIGRP unequal load balancing.

Example 2-68   *Verifying Connectivity from BR1 to an External Network*

```
HQ(config)# router eigrp 1
HQ(config-router)# variance 6
```

The cost of the path over the serial link equals 2297856, and the best path has a cost of 409600. You need to define the variance value as at least 6 or higher if you want to include the path over the serial link into the routing table. When variance is set to 6 or higher, the cost of the path over the serial link (2297856) is lower than the best path cost multiplied by the variance multiplier.

Example 2-69 shows the change in HQ's routing table.

Example 2-69 *Verifying Connectivity from HQ to an External Network*

```
HQ# show ip route
Codes: L - local, C - connected, S - static, R - RIP, M - mobile, B - BGP
       D - EIGRP, EX - EIGRP external, O - OSPF, IA - OSPF inter area
       N1 - OSPF NSSA external type 1, N2 - OSPF NSSA external type 2
       E1 - OSPF external type 1, E2 - OSPF external type 2
       i - IS-IS, su - IS-IS summary, L1 - IS-IS level-1, L2 - IS-IS level-2
       ia - IS-IS inter area, * - candidate default, U - per-user static route
       o - ODR, P - periodic downloaded static route, H - NHRP, l - LISP
       + - replicated route, % - next hop override

Gateway of last resort is not set

      172.16.0.0/16 is variably subnetted, 6 subnets, 2 masks
C        172.16.1.0/30 is directly connected, Ethernet0/0
L        172.16.1.1/32 is directly connected, Ethernet0/0
C        172.16.2.0/30 is directly connected, Ethernet0/1
L        172.16.2.1/32 is directly connected, Ethernet0/1
C        172.16.3.0/30 is directly connected, Serial1/0
L        172.16.3.1/32 is directly connected, Serial1/0
D     192.168.0.0/24 [90/2297856] via 172.16.3.2, 00:02:03, Serial1/0
                     [90/409600] via 172.16.2.2, 00:02:03, Ethernet0/1
                     [90/409600] via 172.16.1.2, 00:02:03, Ethernet0/0
```

After configuring the variance multiplier, router HQ installs all three routes for destination 192.168.0.0/24 into the routing table.

The variance value can be verified by displaying the IP protocols settings shown in Example 2-70.

Example 2-70 *Verifying Variance Setting on HQ*

```
HQ# show ip protocols
*** IP Routing is NSF aware ***

Routing Protocol is "eigrp 1"
  Outgoing update filter list for all interfaces is not set
  Incoming update filter list for all interfaces is not set
  Default networks flagged in outgoing updates
  Default networks accepted from incoming updates
  EIGRP-IPv4 Protocol for AS(1)
    Metric weight K1=1, K2=0, K3=1, K4=0, K5=0
    NSF-aware route hold timer is 240
    Router-ID: 172.16.3.1
    Topology : 0 (base)
```

```
    Active Timer: 3 min
    Distance: internal 90 external 170
    Maximum path: 4
    Maximum hopcount 100
    Maximum metric variance 6

Automatic Summarization: disabled
Maximum path: 4
Routing for Networks:
  0.0.0.0
Routing Information Sources:
  Gateway          Distance        Last Update
  172.16.2.2             90        00:02:21
  172.16.3.2             90        00:02:21
  172.16.1.2             90        00:02:21
Distance: internal 90 external 170
```

The command output shows you the current variance settings on the router, in addition to the maximum number of paths that can be used for load balancing. You can change the latter by using the **maximum-path** EIGRP configuration command. By setting this value to 1, you effectively disable EIGRP load balancing.

Configuring EIGRP for IPv6

Originally created to route for IPv4, IPX, and AppleTalk, EIGRP was easily extended to advertise IPv6 routes. Although EIGRP for IPv6 shares much of the characteristics of the EIGRP for IPv4, it also has some unique specifics.

One of the major differences between IPv4 and IPv6 EIGRP versions is the fact that you must explicitly enable EIGRP for IPv6 on each IPv6-enabled interface.

Upon completing this section, you will be able to do the following:

■ Describe differences and similarities of EIGRP for IPv4 and IPv6

■ Configure basic EIGRP for IPv6 settings

■ Configure and verify EIGRP for IPv6 summarization

■ Verify basic EIGRP for IPv6 settings

Overview of EIGRP for IPv6

EIGRP for IPv6 is a version of EIGRP intended to send IPv6 prefixes/lengths rather than IPv4 subnet/mask values. It is sometime referred in the Cisco documentation as EIGRPv6 to emphasize that it is used with the IPv6. EIGRP for IPv6 has much in common with EIGRP for IPv4, but the following differences between the two exist:

- EIGRP for IPv6 uses IPv6 prefixes and lengths rather than IPv4 subnets and masks.

- To establish EIGRP for IPv6 neighbor relationship, it uses IPv6 link-local addresses. EIGRP for IPv4 does not have the concept of link-local address.

- EIGRP uses built-in authentication features of the IPv6 protocol rather than protocol-specific authentication implemented with IPv4 to guarantee message authentication.

- To transport routing information, EIGRP for IPv6 encapsulates IPv6 prefixes in the IPv6 messages, not in the IPv4 packets.

- IPv6 has no concept of the classful network; so when you use EIGRP for IPv6, there is no automatic summarization at the class boundaries. The only way to summarize IPv6-advertised prefixes is through manual summarization.

- If IPv4 address is not configured on the router, EIGRP for IPv6 requires an EIGRP router ID before it can start running. In IPv4, if you do not configure the EIGRP router ID, the router will automatically assign it using the highest loopback or the highest active interface IPv4 address.

- You configure EIGRP for IPv6 under a specific interface intended to send and receive routing protocol messages. In EIGRP for IPv4, you configure interfaces under the routing protocol configuration mode.

- EIGRP for IPv6 uses assigned dedicated multicast address FF02::A, whereas EIGRP for IPv4 uses dedicated multicast address 224.0.0.10.

Configuring and Verifying EIGRP for IPv6

In this section, we configure, establish, and verify EIGRP for IPv6. The topology in Figure 2-20 has three router: HQ, BR1, and BR2. The branch routers are connected to the headquarters using Ethernet links. HQ and BR1 have already been configured for EIGRP for IPv6, but BR2 has not been. IPv6 addresses on all routers have also already been configured.

Besides the IPv6 global unicast addresses shown Figure 2-20, each router has been manually configured with the following IPv6 link-local addresses:

- **HQ - Ethernet 0/0:** FE80:100::1

- **HQ - Ethernet 0/1:** FE80:200::1

- **BR1 - Ethernet 0/0:** FE80:100::2

- **BR2 - Ethernet 0/0:** FE80:200::2

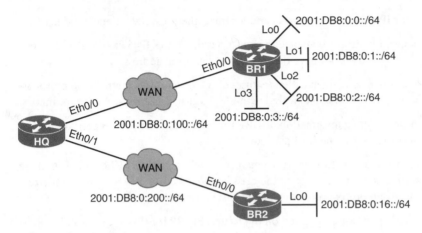

Figure 2-20 *EIGRP for IPv6 Topology*

EIGRP for IPv6 Configuration

Before configuring EIGRP for IPv6, IPv6 unicast routing must be enabled on the router. Example 2-71 shows IPv6 routing enabled on the BR2 router using the **ipv6 unicast-routing** global configuration command.

Example 2-71 *Enabling IPv6 Routing on BR2*

```
BR2# configure terminal
Enter configuration commands, one per line.  End with CNTL/Z.
BR2(config)# ipv6 unicast-routing
```

The essential command to enable routing of the IPv6 datagrams is **ipv6 unicast-routing** in global configuration mode. In the absence of this command, the router can still be configured with IPv6 addresses on its interfaces but will not be an IPv6 router.

The **ipv6 unicast-routing** command enables the router:

- To be configured for static and dynamic IPv6 routing

- To forward IPv6 packets

- To send ICMPv6 router advertisement messages

If you have configured IPv6 routing protocols on the router, the command **no ipv6 unicast-routing** will remove all IPv6 routing protocol entries from the IPv6 routing table. Example 2-72 shows the configuration of EIGRP for IPv6 on BR2 using autonomous system 100 and IP address 192.168.2.1 for the router ID.

Example 2-72 *Configuring the EIGRP Router ID on BR2*

```
BR2(config)# ipv6 router eigrp 100
BR2(config-rtr)# eigrp router-id 192.168.2.1
```

Note EIGRP for IPv6 has a shutdown feature. The routing process must be in "no shutdown" mode for EIGRP for IPv6 processing. No shutdown is the default on later IOSs. If necessary, you might have to issue the **no shutdown** command in EIGRP for IPv6 configuration mode.

Configuring EIGRP for IPv6 consists of two steps. The initial step is to configure EIGRP for the IPv6 routing process using the **ipv6 router eigrp** command. When entering the command, you must specify the autonomous system number, which has the same meaning as it does in EIGRP for IPv4. It defines autonomous systems under the control of a single administrator, and it must match between all neighboring routers that intend to establish an EIGRP adjacency.

Another important parameter is the EIGRP router ID. Like EIGRP for IPv4, EIGRP for IPv6 uses a 32-bit router ID. If no IPv4 active address is configured on the router, the router will not be able to choose the EIGRP router ID. In this case, you must configure the router ID manually under the EIGRP routing process.

Each router participating in EIGRP for IPv4 and IPv6 is identified by a 32-bit router ID. Routers will try to determine the router ID based on the highest configured IPv4 address on a loopback interface or, if no loopback is configured, based on the highest configured IPv4 address on an active physical interface. If no IPv4 interface is configured on the router, the router ID must be manually defined to make EIGRP for IPv6 operational.

Example 2-73 shows the configuration of EIGRP for IPv6 on Ethernet 0/0 and Loopback 0 interfaces on BR2.

Example 2-73 *Configuring EIGRP for IPv6 on BR2 Interfaces*

```
BR2(config)# interface ethernet 0/0
BR2(config-if)# ipv6 eigrp 100
*Oct 23 19:57:55.933: %DUAL-5-NBRCHANGE: EIGRP-IPv6 100: Neighbor
FE80:200::1 (Ethernet0/0) is up: new adjacency
BR2(config-if)# exit
BR2(config)# interface loopback 0
BR2(config-if)# ipv6 eigrp 100
```

The second step in the EIGRP for IPv6 configuration process is to enable the protocol on the interface. Before you enable EIGRP for IPv6 on the interface, it must have a valid IPv6 link-local address. This is because EIGRP for IPv6 uses link-local addresses to form EIGRP neighbor relationships.

The link-local address is automatically created on an interface when the interface obtains a global IPv6 address, either manually or dynamically. Cisco IOS uses EUI-64 to create the link-local address's interface ID.

IPv6 can also be enabled on an interface without assigning a global unicast address using the interface mode command **ipv6 enable**. In this case, IPv6 link-local address will be assigned automatically to the interface, again using EUI-64 for the interface ID.

However, automatically created EUI-64 link-local addresses are difficult to remember or recognize because or the nondescriptive 64-bit interface ID. It is common practice to manually assign easily recognizable IPv6 link-local addresses on the router using the command **ipv6 address** *link-local-address* **link-local**. A router can be configured with the same link-local address on all of its links as long as the link-local address is unique on each of its links.

Example 2-74 verifies that the EIGRP for IPv6 neighbor adjacency is established with router HQ.

Example 2-74 *Verifying EIGRP for IPv6 Neighbor Adjacency on BR2*

```
BR2# show ipv6 eigrp neighbors
EIGRP-IPv6 Neighbors for AS(100)
H   Address                    Interface         Hold Uptime    SRTT   RTO  Q  Seq
                                                 (sec)          (ms)        Cnt Num
0   Link-local address:        Et0/0             13 08:25:34       9   100  0  16
    FE80:200::1
```

Output of the **show ipv6 eigrp neighbors** command is similar to the output of the **show ip eigrp neighbors** command. You can notice the difference in the Address Format field, because link-local IPv6 addresses are used to establish EIGRP neighbor relationship. The meaning of other fields are identical to the IPv4 verification command.

Example 2-75 shows the EIGRP for IPv6 topology table on BR2.

Example 2-75 *Verifying the EIGRP for IPV6 Topology Table on BR2*

```
BR2# show ipv6 eigrp topology
EIGRP-IPv6 Topology Table for AS(100)/ID(192.168.2.1)
Codes: P - Passive, A - Active, U - Update, Q - Query, R - Reply,
       r - reply Status, s - sia Status


P 2001:DB8:0:2::/64, 1 successors, FD is 435200
        via FE80:200::1 (435200/409600), Ethernet0/0
P 2001:DB8:0:200::/64, 1 successors, FD is 281600
        via Connected, Ethernet0/0
P 2001:DB8::/64, 1 successors, FD is 435200
        via FE80:200::1 (435200/409600), Ethernet0/0
P 2001:DB8:0:1::/64, 1 successors, FD is 435200
        via FE80:200::1 (435200/409600), Ethernet0/0
P 2001:DB8:0:3::/64, 1 successors, FD is 435200
        via FE80:200::1 (435200/409600), Ethernet0/0
P 2001:DB8:0:100::/64, 1 successors, FD is 307200
        via FE80:200::1 (307200/281600), Ethernet0/0
```

Output of the **show ipv6 eigrp topology** command again shows the similarities between EIGRP for IPv4 and IPv6. Both protocols use a composite metric, which is an integer number calculated by using default interface bandwidth and delay parameters. To send packets to the destination, the router chooses the route with the smallest (best) metric. This route, called the successor route, will be placed in the routing table. Other routes that satisfy the feasibility condition will be candidates for the feasible successor routes.

EIGRP for IPv6 uses link-local addresses to establish neighbor relationship, and these addresses are also shown in the topology table as sources of learned routes.

Example 2-76 displays the IPv6 routing table for EIGRP routes on BR2.

Example 2-76 *Displaying the IPv6 Routing Table on BR2*

```
BR2# show ipv6 route eigrp
IPv6 Routing Table - default - 10 entries
Codes: C - Connected, L - Local, S - Static, U - Per-user Static route
       B - BGP, R - RIP, I1 - ISIS L1, I2 - ISIS L2
       IA - ISIS interarea, IS - ISIS summary, D - EIGRP, EX - EIGRP external
       ND - ND Default, NDp - ND Prefix, DCE - Destination, NDr - Redirect
       O - OSPF Intra, OI - OSPF Inter, OE1 - OSPF ext 1, OE2 - OSPF ext 2
       ON1 - OSPF NSSA ext 1, ON2 - OSPF NSSA ext 2
D   2001:DB8::/64 [90/435200]
     via FE80:200::1, Ethernet0/0
D   2001:DB8:0:1::/64 [90/435200]
     via FE80:200::1, Ethernet0/0
D   2001:DB8:0:2::/64 [90/435200]
     via FE80:200::1, Ethernet0/0
D   2001:DB8:0:3::/64 [90/435200]
     via FE80:200::1, Ethernet0/0
D   2001:DB8:0:100::/64 [90/307200]
     via FE80:200::1, Ethernet0/0
```

The successor routes from the topology table are candidates to be inserted in the routing table. Administrative distance, shown as the first number in squared parentheses, is by default the same as it is for IPv4 EIGRP. For internal EIGRP routes, it is set to 90. The second number in the brackets represents the feasible distance, which is an EIGRP composite metric of the best path.

Example 2-77 shows a ping from the BR2 LAN interface to the BR1 LAN address.

Example 2-77 *Verifying Connectivity to BR1 LAN*

```
BR2# ping 2001:DB8:0:1::1 source loopback 0
Type escape sequence to abort.
Sending 5, 100-byte ICMP Echos to 2001:DB8:0:1::1, timeout is 2 seconds:
Packet sent with a source address of 2001:DB8:0:16::1
!!!!!
Success rate is 100 percent (5/5), round-trip min/avg/max = 1/1/1 ms
```

If you have configured LAN and WAN interfaces on the BR2 router to be advertised using EIGRP for IPv6, the stream of ICMP echo and reply packets between LAN interfaces will be sent and received successfully.

Determining the IPv6 Summary Route

To determine the IPv6 summary route, you need to analyze the subnets you want to summarize. You need to determine the highest-order bits that match in all of the addresses. By converting the IP addresses to the partial binary format, you can identify the common bits shared among the subnets.

In Table 2-3, the first 62 bits are common among all four subnets. Therefore, the best summary route is 2001:DB8:0:0::/62.

Table 2-3   *Calculating an IPv6 Summary Route*

Prefix	Binary Format
2001:DB8:0:0::64	2001:DB8:0:0000000000000000::/64
2001:DB8:0:1::64	2001:DB8:0:0000000000000001::/64
2001:DB8:0:2::64	2001:DB8:0:0000000000000010::/64
2001:DB8:0:3::64	2001:DB8:0:0000000000000011::/64
Summary route	
2001:DB8:0:0::62	2001:DB8:0:0000000000000000::/62

Example 2-78 shows router BR1 summarizing all local prefixes by using the **ipv6 summary-address eigrp** configuration command.

Example 2-78   *Configuring EIGRP for IPv6 Summary Route*

```
BR1(config)# interface Ethernet0/0
BR1(config-if)# ipv6 summary-address eigrp 100 2001:DB8:0:0::/62
*Oct 24 18:14:31.222: %DUAL-5-NBRCHANGE: EIGRP-IPv6 100: Neighbor
FE80:100::1 (Ethernet0/0) is resync: summary configured
```

Summarization is a method of replacing several longer prefixes with one shorter prefix. Your only option to summarize routes in EIGRP for IPv6 is manual summarization. EIGRP for IPv6 does not support automatic summarization. Similar to EIGRP for IPv4, manual summarization can be configured in the interface configuration mode using the **ipv6 summary-address eigrp** command. When a summary route is configured for EIGRP for IPv6, the router will resynchronize its neighbor relationship on the interface where summarization was configured. The BR1 router will send only one aggregated route to the HQ router instead of sending several prefixes.

Summarization reduces the number of routing table entries and improves network stability by eliminating unnecessary routing updates after the part of network fails. It also reduces processor workload and memory requirements.

Example 2-79 displays BR2's IPv6 routing table.

Example 2-79   *Verifying Summary Route Received on BR2*

```
BR2# show ipv6 route eigrp
IPv6 Routing Table - default - 7 entries
Codes: C - Connected, L - Local, S - Static, U - Per-user Static route
       B - BGP, R - RIP, I1 - ISIS L1, I2 - ISIS L2
       IA - ISIS interarea, IS - ISIS summary, D - EIGRP, EX - EIGRP external
       ND - ND Default, NDp - ND Prefix, DCE - Destination, NDr - Redirect
       O - OSPF Intra, OI - OSPF Inter, OE1 - OSPF ext 1, OE2 - OSPF ext 2
       ON1 - OSPF NSSA ext 1, ON2 - OSPF NSSA ext 2
D  2001:DB8::/62 [90/435200]
     via FE80:200::1, Ethernet0/0
D  2001:DB8:0:100::/64 [90/307200]
     via FE80:200::1, Ethernet0/0
```

The content of the IPv6 routing table on the router BR2 shows that instead of four LAN prefixes there is only one aggregated prefix with the shorter prefix length of /62.

Another very useful command for the EIGRP for IPv6 verification is **show ipv6 protocols**, shown in Example 2-80. Included in the output from this command are the interfaces that participate in the EIGRP for IPv6 routing, the K values, and the router ID. The default ADs for the IPv6 EIGRP internal and external routes are the same as for the IPv4 EIGRP: 90 and 170. This command also reveals the distance vector side of the EIGRP for IPv6; it has a relatively large maximum hop count of 100.

Example 2-80   *Verifying EIGRP for IPv6 on BR1*

```
BR2# show ipv6 protocols
IPv6 Routing Protocol is "connected"
IPv6 Routing Protocol is "ND"
IPv6 Routing Protocol is "eigrp 100"
EIGRP-IPv6 Protocol for AS(100)
  Metric weight K1=1, K2=0, K3=1, K4=0, K5=0 K6=0
  NSF-aware route hold timer is 240
  Router-ID: 192.168.2.1
  Topology : 0 (base)
    Active Timer: 3 min
    Distance: internal 90 external 170
    Maximum path: 16
    Maximum hopcount 100
    Maximum metric variance 1
    Total Prefix Count: 0
    Total Redist Count: 0

  Interfaces:
```

```
      Ethernet0/0
      Loopback0
 Redistribution:
    None
```

Named EIGRP Configuration

Even though basic EIGRP configuration is pretty simple, configuring additional parameters can increase configuration complexity. Some parameters are configured in global configuration mode, others under specific interfaces. When you enable EIGRP configuration for IPv6, things can become overwhelming. You must use similar, slightly different commands and configuration procedures to enable EIGRP for IPv6.

Cisco introduced a new way of configuring EIGRP, which is called named EIGRP. It enables you to gather all EIGRP configurations in one place, using unified configuration commands for all underlying network protocols.

Upon completion of this section, you will be able to do the following:

- Describe how EIGRP named configuration is different from the classic EIGRP configuration

- Explain what is configured under different address family configuration modes

- Compare examples of classic and named EIGRP configuration

- Configuring and verifying EIGRP for IPv6

Introduction to Named EIGRP Configuration

Configuring EIGRP for both IPv4 and IPv6 on the same router can become a complex task because configuration takes place using different router configuration modes: **router eigrp** and **ipv6 router eigrp**. A newer configuration option is available that enables the configuration of EIGRP for both IPv4 and IPv6 under a single configuration mode.

EIGRP named configuration helps eliminate configuration complexity that occurs when configuring EIGRP for both IPv4 and IPv6. For example, enabling interfaces for EIGRP for IPv4 is done in EIGRP router configuration mode. However, in EIGRP for IPv6, interfaces are enabled on the specific interface. This discrepancy leads to confusion, and it is this reason that EIGRP named configuration tries to unify EIGRP configuration and simplify configuration tasks, reducing the chances of configuration mistakes.

EIGRP named configuration is available in Cisco IOS Release 15.0(1)M and later releases.

Configuring Named EIGRP

Figure 2-21 shows the topology used in this section for configuring named EIGRP. Notice that the all three routers have been configured with both IPv4 and IPv6 addresses. Basic EIGRP for IPv4 and IPv6 has also been configured on HQ, BR1, and BR2.

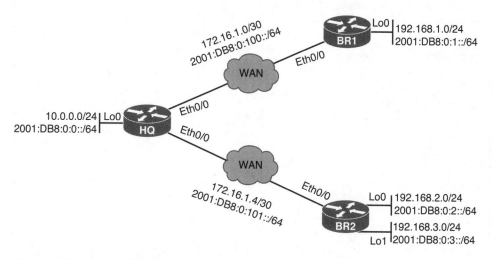

Figure 2-21 *Named EIGRP Topology*

To verify complete IPv4 and IPv6 connectivity in the topology, pings are sent from BR2 to BR1, as shown in Example 2-81.

Example 2-81 *Verifying IPv4 and IPv6 Connectivity*

```
BR2# ping 192.168.1.1 source Loopback0
Type escape sequence to abort.
Sending 5, 100-byte ICMP Echos to 192.168.1.1, timeout is 2 seconds:
Packet sent with a source address of 192.168.2.1
!!!!!
Success rate is 100 percent (5/5), round-trip min/avg/max = 1/1/1 ms
BR2# ping 2001:DB8:0:1::1 source Loopback0
Type escape sequence to abort.
Sending 5, 100-byte ICMP Echos to 2001:DB8:0:1::1, timeout is 2 seconds:
Packet sent with a source address of 2001:DB8:0:2::1
!!!!!
Success rate is 100 percent (5/5), round-trip min/avg/max = 1/1/1 ms
```

Because all three routers in the topology are preconfigured with EIGRP for IPv4 and IPv6, connectivity tests should be successful.

The existing EIGRP configuration on BR2 is shown in Example 2-82.

Example 2-82 *Current EIGRP for IPv4 and IPv6 Configuration*

```
BR2# show running-config
<Output omitted>
interface Loopback0
 ip address 192.168.2.1 255.255.255.0
 ipv6 address 2001:DB8:0:2::1/64
 ipv6 enable
 ipv6 eigrp 1
!
interface Loopback1
 ip address 192.168.3.1 255.255.255.0
 ipv6 address 2001:DB8:0:3::1/64
 ipv6 enable
 ipv6 eigrp 1
!
interface Ethernet0/0
 ip address 172.16.1.6 255.255.255.252
 ipv6 address 2001:DB8:0:101::2/64
 ipv6 enable
 ipv6 eigrp 1
<Output omitted>
router eigrp 1
 network 0.0.0.0
<Output omitted>
ipv6 router eigrp 1
<Output omitted>
```

Notice that EIGRP is configured with an autonomous system of 1 for both IPv4 and IPv6.
All present IPv4 configuration is gathered under router configuration mode, and IPv6
EIGRP configuration is present in router configuration mode and with each interface.

Before configuring named EIGRP for IPv4 and IPv6 on BR2, the basic EIGRP configurations are removed, as shown in Example 2-83.

Example 2-83 *Removing EIGRP for IPv4 and IPv6 Configuration on BR2*

```
BR2# configure terminal
Enter configuration commands, one per line.  End with CNTL/Z.
BR2(config)# no router eigrp 1
BR2(config)# no ipv6 router eigrp 1
BR2(config)#
*Dec 27 09:50:05.585: %DUAL-5-NBRCHANGE: EIGRP-IPv6 1: Neighbor
FE80::A8BB:CCFF:FE00:3310 (Ethernet0/0) is down: procinfo free
BR2(config)# interface Ethernet0/0
BR2(config-if)# no ipv6 eigrp 1
```

```
BR2(config-if)# interface Loopback0
BR2(config-if)# no ipv6 eigrp 1
BR2(config-if)# interface Loopback1
BR2(config-if)# no ipv6 eigrp 1
```

Basic EIGRP must be removed from interface configuration mode for IPv6 and from global configuration mode from both IPv4 and IPv6.

Address Families

Classic or basic EIGRP uses the global configuration command **router eigrp** *as-number* for IPv4 and **ipv6 router eigrp** *as-number* for IPv6. In both cases, the autonomous system number is used to identify the individual EIGRP process.

EIGRP named configuration mode uses the global configuration command **router eigrp** *virtual-instance-name*. Both EIGRP for IPv4 and IPv6 can be configured within this same mode.

EIGRP supports multiple protocols and can carry information about many different route types. Named EIGRP configuration is organized in a hierarchical manner, where configuration for specific route type is grouped under the same address family.

IPv4 unicast and IPv6 unicast are two of the most commonly used address families.

EIGRP for IPv4 Address Family

Using the same topology in Figure 2-21, Example 2-84 shows the configuration of BR2's named EIGRP virtual instance called LAB. Named EIGRP is configured in global configuration mode using the **router eigrp** command followed by the name of the EIGRP virtual instance. The name has local significance and does not need to match between neighboring routers. The **router eigrp** *virtual-instance-name* command defines a single EIGRP instance that can be used for all address families. At this point, the routing protocol is not yet enabled. At least one address family must be defined first.

Example 2-84 shows BR2 entering the IPv4 address family configuration mode using the existing autonomous system number 1. The autonomous system number must be the same in all routers in the EIGRP routing domain.

Example 2-84 *IPv4 Address Family Added to the EIGRP Named Configuration on BR2*

```
BR2(config)# router eigrp LAB
BR2(config-router)# address-family ipv4 autonomous-system 1
BR2(config-router-af)#
```

The EIGRP **ipv4 address-family** command is configured in EIGRP name mode using the syntax and the parameters in Table 2-4:

```
address-family ipv4 [multicast] [unicast] [vrf vrf-name] autonomous-system
autonomous-system-number
```

Table 2-4   *Parameters for the EIGRP* **address-family ipv4** *Command*

Parameter	Description
ipv4	Selects the IPV4 protocol address family.
multicast	(Optional) Specifies the multicast address family. This keyword is available only in EIGRP named IPv4 configurations.
unicast	(Optional) Specifies the unicast address family. This is the default.
vrf *vrf-name*	(Optional) Specifies the name of the VRF.
autonomous-system *autonomous-system-number*	Specifies the autonomous system number.

The **address-family** command enables the IPv4 address family and starts EIGRP for the defined autonomous system. The command puts you in the address family configuration mode, which is also reflected by the change of the prompt.

In IPv4 address family configuration mode, you can enable EIGRP for specific interfaces by using the **network** command, and you can define some other general parameters such as **router-id** or **eigrp stub**.

Unless specified otherwise, address family is by default defined as unicast address family. Unicast address families are used for exchange of unicast routes.

Note   The EIGRP **address-family** command is also available under classic or basic EIGRP for both IPv4 and IPv6. Configuration is similar to named EIGRP.

Next, in address family configuration mode, EIGRP is enabled on BR2 all IPv4 interfaces, as shown in Example 2-85.

Example 2-85   *Enabling All Interfaces in IPv4 Address Family Configuration Mode*

```
BR2(config-router-af)# network 0.0.0.0
*Dec 27 14:15:53.944: %DUAL-5-NBRCHANGE: EIGRP-IPv4 1: Neighbor 172.16.1.5
(Ethernet0/0) is up: new adjacency
```

You can enable EIGRP for IPv4 on interfaces in named configuration with the **network** command, the same way as with normal EIGRP configuration. You can be specific and use a wildcard mask to select only individual interfaces, or you can use **0.0.0.0**, which enables EIGRP on all IPv4-enabled interfaces.

To verify the named configuration of EIGRP for IPv4, EIGRP neighbors, the EIGRP topology table, and the routing table for EIGRP routes are verified on BR2, as shown in Example 2-86.

Example 2-86 *Verifying Named Configuration of EIGRP for IPv4 BR2*

```
BR2# show ip eigrp neighbors
EIGRP-IPv4 VR(LAB) Address-Family Neighbors for AS(1)
H   Address                 Interface                Hold Uptime    SRTT   RTO  Q  Seq
                                                     (sec)          (ms)        Cnt Num
0   172.16.1.5              Et0/0                    14 00:21:56    10    100   0  12


BR2# show ip eigrp topology
EIGRP-IPv4 VR(LAB) Topology Table for AS(1)/ID(192.168.3.1)
Codes: P - Passive, A - Active, U - Update, Q - Query, R - Reply,
       r - reply Status, s - sia Status


P 192.168.3.0/24, 1 successors, FD is 163840
        via Connected, Loopback1
P 192.168.2.0/24, 1 successors, FD is 163840
        via Connected, Loopback0
P 10.0.0.0/24, 1 successors, FD is 458752000
        via 172.16.1.5 (458752000/327761920), Ethernet0/0
P 192.168.1.0/24, 1 successors, FD is 524288000
        via 172.16.1.5 (524288000/458752000), Ethernet0/0
P 172.16.1.4/30, 1 successors, FD is 131072000
        via Connected, Ethernet0/0
P 172.16.1.0/30, 1 successors, FD is 196608000
        via 172.16.1.5 (196608000/131072000), Ethernet0/0


BR2# show ip route eigrp
Codes: L - local, C - connected, S - static, R - RIP, M - mobile, B - BGP
       D - EIGRP, EX - EIGRP external, O - OSPF, IA - OSPF inter area
       N1 - OSPF NSSA external type 1, N2 - OSPF NSSA external type 2
       E1 - OSPF external type 1, E2 - OSPF external type 2
       i - IS-IS, su - IS-IS summary, L1 - IS-IS level-1, L2 - IS-IS level-2
       ia - IS-IS inter area, * - candidate default, U - per-user static route
       o - ODR, P - periodic downloaded static route, H - NHRP, l - LISP
       + - replicated route, % - next hop override


Gateway of last resort is not set


      10.0.0.0/24 is subnetted, 1 subnets
D        10.0.0.0 [90/3584000] via 172.16.1.5, 00:36:57, Ethernet0/0
      172.16.0.0/16 is variably subnetted, 3 subnets, 2 masks
D        172.16.1.0/30 [90/1536000] via 172.16.1.5, 00:36:57, Ethernet0/0
D     192.168.1.0/24 [90/4096000] via 172.16.1.5, 00:36:57, Ethernet0/0
```

Even though you have configured EIGRP in named configuration mode, how EIGRP operates and interacts with neighbors does not really change. You can use the same verification commands to analyze and verify EIGRP status.

Individual interfaces can be configured or removed from the EIGRP for IPv4 and IPv6 process using the **af-interface** *interface-type interface number* command in address family configuration mode. This command is used to configure EIGRP parameters on the interfaces such as manual summarization and authentication. An example of this command is discussed in the next, using the EIGRP for IPv6 address family.

EIGRP for IPv6 Address Family

Example 2-87 shows the IPv6 address family for autonomous system 1 added to the EIGRP named configuration on BR2.

Example 2-87 *IPv6 Address Family Added to the Named EIGRP Configuration on BR2*

```
BR2(config)# router eigrp LAB
BR2(config-router)# address-family ipv6 autonomous-system 1
BR2(config-router-af)#
*Dec 30 09:37:23.652: %DUAL-5-NBRCHANGE: EIGRP-IPv6 1: Neighbor
FE80::A8BB:CCFF:FE00:3310 (Ethernet0/0) is up: new adjacency
```

The EIGRP **address-family ipv6** command is configured in router configuration mode using the syntax and the parameters in Table 2-5:

```
address-family ipv6 [unicast] [vrf vrf-name] autonomous-system autonomous-system-
number
```

Table 2-5 *Parameters for the EIGRP **address-family ipv6** Command*

Parameter	Description
Ipv6	Selects the IPv6 protocol address family.
unicast	(Optional) Specifies the unicast address family. This is the default.
vrf *vrf-name*	(Optional) Specifies the name of the VRF.
autonomous-system *autonomous-system- number*	Specifies the autonomous system number.

When defining the IPv6 address family, it is important to use the correct autonomous system number. All three routers in the topology were configured with IPv6 autonomous system 1 in the beginning, so it is necessary that you use the same autonomous system if you do not want to reconfigure HQ and BR1 as well. Keep in mind that there is no requirement for an autonomous system number to match between IPv4 and IPv6 address families; it must only match between neighbors within the same address family.

Note The EIGRP autonomous system numbers for the IPv4 and IPv6 address families do not have to be the same. The only requirement is that the same autonomous system number for IPv4 and the same autonomous system number for IPv6 be used by all routers in the same EIGRP routing domain.

Notice how an IPv6 EIGRP neighbor relationship gets established as soon as you define the IPv6 address family. EIGRP for IPv6 does not need to be enabled on the interface. All IPv6-enabled interfaces are automatically included in the EIGRP for IPv6 process.

The IPv6 address family configuration will show up in the running configuration as a unicast address family by default.

You can configure or remove individual interfaces from the EIGRP for IPv6 process by using the **af-interface** *interface-type interface number* command in address family configuration mode, as described in Table 2-6:

```
af-interface {default | interface-type interface number}
```

Table 2-6 *Parameters for the* **af-interface** *Address Family Configuration Mode Command*

Parameter	Description
default	Specifies the default address family interface configuration mode. Commands applied under this mode affect all interfaces used by this address family instance.
interface-type interface number	Interface type and number of the interface that the address family submode commands will affect.

Using an interface not actually on BR2, Ethernet 0/1 (so we do not affect our configuration), is shown in Example 2-88. The **shutdown** command is used in address family interface configuration mode to remove this interface from EIGRP for IPv6, which was included by default. However, for all other IPv6 purposes, the interface is still in the up/up state. The interface can still be pinged from another device on the network.

The **af-interface** command is also used to configure other specific EIGRP interface options such as authentication, bandwidth percent, and manual summarization. A complete listing of these options is shown later in this chapter, in Example 2-95.

Example 2-88 *Disabling EIGRP for IPv6 on an Interface*

```
BR2(config)# router eigrp LAB
BR2(config-router)# address-family ipv6 autonomous-system 1
BR2(config-router-af)# af-interface ethernet 0/1
BR2(config-router-af-interface)# shutdown
```

Example 2-89 verifies the EIGRP neighbors, IPv6 EIGRP topology table, and IPv6 routing table for EIGRP routes on BR2. The same commands are used to verify EIGRP for IPv6 in basic and named configuration modes.

Example 2-89 *Verifying EIGRP for IPv6 on BR2*

```
BR2# show ipv6 eigrp neighbors
EIGRP-IPv6 VR(LAB) Address-Family Neighbors for AS(1)
H   Address                Interface        Hold Uptime   SRTT   RTO  Q   Seq
                                            (sec)         (ms)        Cnt Num
0   Link-local address:    Et0/0            10 02:03:36 1594   5000 0   11
    FE80::A8BB:CCFF:FE00:3310

BR2# show ipv6 eigrp topology
EIGRP-IPv6 VR(LAB) Topology Table for AS(1)/ID(192.168.3.1)
Codes: P - Passive, A - Active, U - Update, Q - Query, R - Reply,
       r - reply Status, s - sia Status

P 2001:DB8:0:2::/64, 1 successors, FD is 163840
        via Connected, Loopback0
P 2001:DB8::/64, 1 successors, FD is 458752000
        via FE80::A8BB:CCFF:FE00:3310 (458752000/327761920), Ethernet0/0
P 2001:DB8:0:1::/64, 1 successors, FD is 524288000
        via FE80::A8BB:CCFF:FE00:3310 (524288000/458752000), Ethernet0/0
P 2001:DB8:0:3::/64, 1 successors, FD is 163840
        via Connected, Loopback1
P 2001:DB8:0:100::/64, 1 successors, FD is 196608000
        via FE80::A8BB:CCFF:FE00:3310 (196608000/131072000), Ethernet0/0
P 2001:DB8:0:101::/64, 1 successors, FD is 131072000
        via Connected, Ethernet0/0


BR2# show ipv6 route eigrp
IPv6 Routing Table - default - 10 entries
Codes: C - Connected, L - Local, S - Static, U - Per-user Static route
       B - BGP, HA - Home Agent, MR - Mobile Router, R - RIP
       H - NHRP, I1 - ISIS L1, I2 - ISIS L2, IA - ISIS interarea
       IS - ISIS summary, D - EIGRP, EX - EIGRP external, NM - NEMO
       ND - ND Default, NDp - ND Prefix, DCE - Destination, NDr - Redirect
       O - OSPF Intra, OI - OSPF Inter, OE1 - OSPF ext 1, OE2 - OSPF ext 2
       ON1 - OSPF NSSA ext 1, ON2 - OSPF NSSA ext 2, l - LISP
D   2001:DB8::/64 [90/3584000]
     via FE80::A8BB:CCFF:FE00:3310, Ethernet0/0
D   2001:DB8:0:1::/64 [90/4096000]
     via FE80::A8BB:CCFF:FE00:3310, Ethernet0/0
D   2001:DB8:0:100::/64 [90/1536000]
     via FE80::A8BB:CCFF:FE00:3310, Ethernet0/0
```

Example 2-90 shows the running configuration, which illustrates the structure of named EIGRP on BR2.

Example 2-90 *Displaying BR2's Running Configuration*

```
BR2# show running config | section router eigrp
router eigrp LAB
 !
 address-family ipv4 unicast autonomous-system 1
  !
  topology base
  exit-af-topology
  network 0.0.0.0
 exit-address-family
 !
 address-family ipv6 unicast autonomous-system 1
  !
  topology base
  exit-af-topology
 exit-address-family
```

Notice that the configuration is structured around address families in a hierarchical format. Configuration is also unified among address families, meaning that additional parameters such as authentication and summarization are configured in the same manner.

The Topology Base section of the configuration refers to the topology base configuration mode. Within the topology base is where general EIGRP settings are configured that relate to the topology table. For example, you can define **variance** and **maximum-paths** parameters for load balancing or redistribute routes from other routing sources within the topology base. This is discussed later in this chapter, in Example 2-97.

Example 2-91 shows how manual summarization is configured in named EIGRP configuration mode. Within the EIGRP IPv4 address family, the address family interface configuration mode is entered, and BR2's loopback prefixes are summarized.

Example 2-91 *EIGRP Summarization in Named Configuration Mode*

```
BR2(config)# router eigrp LAB
BR2(config-router)# address-family ipv4 autonomous-system 1
BR2(config-router-af)# af-interface ethernet 0/0
BR2(config-router-af-interface)# summary-address 192.168.2.0/23
BR2(config-router-af-interface)#
*Dec 30 13:36:07.935: %DUAL-5-NBRCHANGE: EIGRP-IPv4 1: Neighbor
172.16.1.5 (Ethernet0/0) is resync: summary configured
```

To enter the address family interface configuration mode, use the **af-interface** command. All interface-specific EIGRP commands are configured within the address family interface configuration mode. Summarization, hello and dead timers, and passive interface settings are a few examples of available options.

When in the IPv4 address family interface configuration mode, you can summarize IPv4 prefixes using the **summary-address** command. You can specify subnet mask either in decimal format or prefix length format, as shown in the example.

The summary route is verified by examining the routing table on BR1, as shown in Example 2-92.

Example 2-92 *Displaying BR1's Routing Table with the Summary Route*

```
BR1# show ip route
Codes: L - local, C - connected, S - static, R - RIP, M - mobile, B - BGP
       D - EIGRP, EX - EIGRP external, O - OSPF, IA - OSPF inter area
       N1 - OSPF NSSA external type 1, N2 - OSPF NSSA external type 2
       E1 - OSPF external type 1, E2 - OSPF external type 2
       i - IS-IS, su - IS-IS summary, L1 - IS-IS level-1, L2 - IS-IS level-2
       ia - IS-IS inter area, * - candidate default, U - per-user static route
       o - ODR, P - periodic downloaded static route, H - NHRP, l - LISP
       + - replicated route, % - next hop override

Gateway of last resort is not set

      10.0.0.0/24 is subnetted, 1 subnets
D        10.0.0.0 [90/409600] via 172.16.1.1, 3d05h, Ethernet0/0
      172.16.0.0/16 is variably subnetted, 3 subnets, 2 masks
C        172.16.1.0/30 is directly connected, Ethernet0/0
L        172.16.1.2/32 is directly connected, Ethernet0/0
D        172.16.1.4/30 [90/307200] via 172.16.1.1, 3d05h, Ethernet0/0
      192.168.1.0/24 is variably subnetted, 2 subnets, 2 masks
C        192.168.1.0/24 is directly connected, Loopback0
L        192.168.1.1/32 is directly connected, Loopback0
D        192.168.2.0/23 [90/307200] via 172.16.1.1, 00:34:21, Ethernet0/0
```

Notice BR1 now receives only summarized route describing both loopbacks on BR2.

Example 2-93 shows all of BR2's IPv6 interfaces configured as passive except for Ethernet 0/0.

Example 2-93 *Configuring All IPv6 Interfaces as Passive Except for Ethernet 0/0*

```
BR2(config)# router eigrp LAB
BR2(config-router)# address-family ipv6 autonomous-system 1
BR2(config-router-af)# af-interface default
BR2(config-router-af-interface)# passive-interface
```

```
*Dec 31 08:42:40.864: %DUAL-5-NBRCHANGE: EIGRP-IPv6 1: Neighbor
FE80::A8BB:CCFF: FE00:F010 (Ethernet0/0) is down: interface passive
BR2(config-router-af-interface)# exit
BR2(config-router-af)# af-interface ethernet0/0
BR2(config-router-af-interface)# no passive-interface
*Dec 31 08:42:57.111: %DUAL-5-NBRCHANGE: EIGRP-IPv6 1: Neighbor
FE80::A8BB:CCFF: FE00:F010 (Ethernet0/0) is up: new adjacency
```

The **af-interface default** command is useful for defining user defaults to apply to EIGRP interfaces that belong to an address family when EIGRP is configured using the named method. For example, authentication mode is disabled by default, and you can enable message digest 5 (MD5) authentication for all EIGRP interfaces in the address family by using address family interface configuration mode and then selectively overriding the new default setting using different address family interface configuration commands.

The output in Example 2-93 shows how using the **passive-interface** command applies to all interfaces, including Ethernet 0/0, that connect BR2 to the rest of the network.

To edit a single interface, enter **af-interface** configuration mode and specify the appropriate interface. Once Ethernet 0/0 interface is configured with the **no passive-interface** command, EIGRP neighbor adjacency gets reestablished.

Use the **af-interface default** command with caution because some default settings can be different depending on the interface type. For example, the default hello interval is 5 seconds for most interfaces, but is 60 seconds for slow NBMA interfaces, and changing the hello interval in address family interface configuration mode will affect *all* interfaces.

Using the **show ip protocols** command in Example 2-94, we can verify which interfaces are marked as passive.

Example 2-94 *Verifying Passive Interfaces on BR2*

```
BR2# show ipv6 protocols
IPv6 Routing Protocol is "connected"
IPv6 Routing Protocol is "ND"
IPv6 Routing Protocol is "eigrp 1"
EIGRP-IPv6 VR(lab) Address-Family Protocol for AS(1)
  Metric weight K1=1, K2=0, K3=1, K4=0, K5=0 K6=0
  Metric rib-scale 128
  Metric version 64bit
  NSF-aware route hold timer is 240
  Router-ID: 192.168.3.1
  Topology : 0 (base)
    Active Timer: 3 min
    Distance: internal 90 external 170
    Maximum path: 16
    Maximum hopcount 100
    Maximum metric variance 1
```

```
    Total Prefix Count: 6
    Total Redist Count: 0


Interfaces:
  Ethernet0/0
  Loopback1 (passive)
  Loopback0 (passive)
Redistribution:
  None
```

Named EIGRP Configuration Modes

Named EIGRP configuration mode gathers all EIGRP configurations in one place. It uses three different configuration modes to structure different configuration options.

- **Address family configuration mode:** General EIGRP configuration commands for selected address family are entered under address family configuration mode. Here you can configure the router ID and define network statements, which are required for IPv4 EIGRP configuration. You can also configure router as an EIGRP stub.

  Address family configuration mode gives you access to two additional configuration modes: address family interface configuration mode and address family topology configuration mode.

  Example 2-95 is showing address family configuration mode, not address family interface configuration mode. Example 2-95 shows the commands on BR1 available in address family interface configuration mode.

- **Address family configuration mode:** You should use address family interface configuration mode for all those commands that you have previously configured directly under interfaces. Most common options are setting summarization with the **summary-address** command or marking interfaces as passive using **passive-interface** command. You can also modify default hello and hold-time timers.

  Example 2-96 shows the commands on BR1 available in address-family interface configuration mode.

- **Address family topology configuration mode:** Address family topology configuration mode gathers all configuration options that directly impact the EIGRP topology table. Here you can set load-balancing parameters such as **variance** and **maximum-paths,** or you can redistribute static routes using the **redistribute** command.

  Example 2-97 shows the commands on BR1 available in address family topology configuration mode.

Example 2-95 *Address Family Configuration Mode*

```
BR1(config)# router eigrp LAB
BR1(config-router)# address-family ipv6 unicast autonomous-system 1
BR1(config-router-af)# ?
Address Family configuration commands:
```

```
   af-interface         Enter Address Family interface configuration
   default              Set a command to its defaults
   eigrp                EIGRP Address Family specific commands
   exit-address-family  Exit Address Family configuration mode
   help                 Description of the interactive help system
   maximum-prefix       Maximum number of prefixes acceptable in aggregate
   metric               Modify metrics and parameters for address advertisement
   neighbor             Specify an IPv6 neighbor router
   no                   Negate a command or set its defaults
   shutdown             Shutdown address family
   timers               Adjust peering based timers
   topology             Topology configuration mode

BR1(config-router-af)#
```

Example 2-96 *Address Family Interface Configuration Mode*

```
BR1(config)# router eigrp LAB
BR1(config-router)# address-family ipv6 unicast autonomous-system 1
BR1(config-router-af)# af-interface ethernet 0/0
BR1(config-router-af-interface)# ?
Address Family Interfaces configuration commands:
   authentication       authentication subcommands
   bandwidth-percent    Set percentage of bandwidth percentage limit
   bfd                  Enable Bidirectional Forwarding Detection
   dampening-change     Percent interface metric must change to cause update
   dampening-interval   Time in seconds to check interface metrics
   default              Set a command to its defaults
   exit-af-interface    Exit from Address Family Interface configuration mode
   hello-interval       Configures hello interval
   hold-time            Configures hold time
   next-hop-self        Configures EIGRP next-hop-self
   no                   Negate a command or set its defaults
   passive-interface    Suppress address updates on an interface
   shutdown             Disable Address-Family on interface
   split-horizon        Perform split horizon
   summary-address      Perform address summarization

BR1(config-router-af-interface)#
```

Example 2-97 *Address Family Topology Configuration Mode*

```
BR1(config)# router eigrp LAB
BR1(config-router)# address-family ipv6 unicast autonomous-system 1
BR1(config-router-af)# topology base
```

```
BR1(config-router-af-topology)# ?
Address Family Topology configuration commands:
  default            Set a command to its defaults
  default-information  Control distribution of default information
  default-metric     Set metric of redistributed routes
  distance           Define an administrative distance
  distribute-list    Filter entries in eigrp updates
  eigrp              EIGRP specific commands
  exit-af-topology   Exit from Address Family Topology configuration mode
  maximum-paths      Forward packets over multiple paths
  metric             Modify metrics and parameters for advertisement
  no                 Negate a command or set its defaults
  redistribute       Redistribute IPv6 prefixes from another routing protocol
  summary-metric     Specify summary to apply metric/filtering
  timers             Adjust topology specific timers
  traffic-share      How to compute traffic share over alternate paths
  variance           Control load balancing variance

BR1(config-router-af-topology)#
```

Classic Versus Named EIGRP Configuration

The easiest way to compare classic EIGRP configuration to named EIGRP configuration mode is to show configuration examples side by side.

As you can see in Example 2-98, named EIGRP puts all configurations in one place. IPv4 and IPv6 EIGRP configuration commands are structured within corresponding address families. All commands previously configured under interfaces are now set within EIGRP address family interface configuration mode. Not only is configuration easier, clear hierarchical structure also simplifies analysis and troubleshooting process.

Example 2-98 *Classic Versus Named EIGRP Configuration*

```
interface Loopback1
 ip address 192.168.3.1 255.255.255.0
 ipv6 address 2001:DB8:0:3::1/64
 ipv6 eigrp 1
!
interface Ethernet0/0
 ip address 172.16.1.6 255.255.255.252
 ip summary-address eigrp 1 192.168.2.0 255.255.254.0
 ipv6 address 2001:DB8:0:101::2/64
 ipv6 eigrp 1
!
router eigrp 1
 network 0.0.0.0
```

```
 passive-interface default
 no passive-interface Ethernet0/0
!
ipv6 router eigrp 1
!

_____

router eigrp LAB
 !
 address-family ipv4 unicast autonomous-system 1
  !
  af-interface default
   passive-interface
  exit-af-interface
  !
  af-interface Ethernet0/0
   summary address 192.168.2.0/23
   no passive-interface
  exit-af-interface
  !
  topology base
  exit-af-topology
  network 0.0.0.0
 exit-address-family
 !
 address-family ipv6 unicast autonomous-system 1
 !
  topology base
  exit-af-topology
 exit-address-family
```

Summary

In this chapter, you learned about establishing EIGRP neighbor relationships, building the EIGRP topology table, optimizing EIGRP behavior, configuring EIGRP for IPv6, and implementing name EIGRP configuration. Key points in this chapter include the following:

- EIGRP is an advanced distance vector protocol.

- EIGRP uses RTP for reliable, guaranteed delivery of packets.

- Hello and hold timers can be adapted to influence network convergence.

- EIGRP adapts well to various technologies such as Frame Relay, Layer 3 MPLS VPN, and Layer 2 MPLS VPN.

- EIGRP uses hello, update, query, reply, and acknowledgment packets.

- EIGRP uses a composite metric that is by default based on bandwidth and delay.

- Reported distance is the metric value reported by the neighboring router.

- Feasible distance is the lowest distance to a destination from the perspective of the local router.

- Alternative path must satisfy the feasibility condition to become a feasible successor. The reported distance of an alternate path must be less than the feasible distance.

- When a route is lost and no feasible successor is available, queries are sent to all neighboring routers on all interfaces.

- EIGRP stub configuration improves network stability and reduces resource utilization.

- Summarization decreases the size of the IP routing table and optimizes exchange of routing information.

- EIGRP performs equal-cost load balancing.

- To support unequal-cost load balancing, a **variance** parameter must be configured.

- EIGRP for IPv6 uses IPv6 link-local addresses to form neighbor relationships.

- EIGRP for IPv6 supports only manual prefix summarization.

- To configure EIGRP for IPv6, you must define the routing process and configure interfaces participating in EIGRP routing.

- EIGRP for IPv6 verification commands have similar syntax to EIGRP for IPv4 commands.

- Classic EIGRP configuration is divided over different configuration modes.

- Named EIGRP configuration gathers EIGRP configuration in one place.

- Named EIGRP configuration unifies configuration commands for different address families.

- Named EIGRP configuration is hierarchically organized using three address family configuration modes.

- The same verification commands for classic EIGRP are used to verify named EIGRP configuration.

Review Questions

Answer the following questions, and then see Appendix A, "Answers to Review Questions," for the answers.

1. Which transport layer protocol is used for exchange of EIGRP messages?

   a. TCP
   b. UDP
   c. RSVP
   d. RTP
   e. EIGRP runs directly above the network layer and does not use additional transport protocols.

2. Which packet type establishes neighbor relationships?

   a. Ack

   b. Hello

   c. Query

   d. Reply

   e. Update

3. What is used in EIGRP metric calculations by default? (Choose two.)

   a. Bandwidth

   b. MTU

   c. Reliability

   d. Load

   e. Delay

   f. Hop count

4. What is the formula for selecting a feasible successor?

   a. The RD of the current successor route is less than the FD of the feasible successor route.

   b. The FD of the current successor route is less than the RD of the feasible successor route.

   c. The FD of the feasible successor route is less than the RD of the current successor route.

   d. The RD of the feasible successor route is less than the FD of the current successor route.

5. What does the passive state in the EIGRP topology table signify?

   a. There are outstanding queries for this network.

   b. The network is unreachable.

   c. The network is up and operational, and this state signifies normal conditions.

   d. A feasible successor has been selected.

6. EIGRP for IPv6 uses which multicast address?

   a. FF01::2

   b. FF01::10

   c. FF02::5

   d. FF02::A

   e. EIGRP for IPv6 does not use multicast addressing

7. Which verification command shows you reported distance of received EIGRP IPv6 routes?

   a. show ipv6 route

   b. show ipv6 route eigrp

   c. show ipv6 eigrp

   d. show ip eigrp neighbors

   e. show ipv6 eigrp topology

   f. show ip protocols

8. What are two benefits of using named EIGRP configuration?

   a. Improved scalability
   b. Faster convergence
   c. Unifying IPv4 and IPv6 configuration commands
   d. Support for multiple areas
   e. Gathering all EIGRP configuration in once place

9. Is EIGRP operational traffic multicast or broadcast?

10. What are the four key technologies employed by EIGRP?

11. Which of the following best describes the EIGRP topology table?

   a. It is populated as a result of receiving hello packets.
   b. It contains all learned routes to a destination.
   c. It contains only the best routes to a destination.

12. Describe the five types of EIGRP packets.

13. How often are EIGRP hello packets sent on LAN links?

14. What is the difference between the hold time and the hello interval?

15. Which of the following statements are true? (Choose three.)

   a. A route is considered passive when the router is not performing recomputation on that route.
   b. A route is passive when it is undergoing recomputation.
   c. A route is active when it is undergoing recomputation.
   d. A route is considered active when the router is not performing recomputation on that route.
   e. Passive is the operational state for a route.
   f. Active is the operational state for a route.

16. Which of the following statements are true about reported distance (RD) and feasible distance (FD)? (Choose two.)

   a. The RD is the EIGRP metric for a neighbor router to reach a particular network.
   b. The RD is the EIGRP metric for this router to reach a particular network.
   c. The FD is the EIGRP metric for this router to reach a particular network.
   d. The FD is the EIGRP metric for the neighbor router to reach a particular network.

17. Router A has three interfaces with IP addresses 172.16.1.1/24, 172.16.2.3/24, and 172.16.5.1/24. What commands enable you to configure EIGRP to run in autonomous system 100 on only the interfaces with addresses 172.16.2.3/24 and 172.16.5.1/24?

18. What does the **passive-interface** command do when configured with EIGRP?

19. How does the EIGRP stub feature limit the query range?

20. What does the **eigrp stub receive-only** command do?

Chapter 3

OSPF Implementation

This chapter covers the following topics:

- Basic OSPF Configuration and OSPF Adjacencies

- How OSPF Builds the Routing Table

- Configuration of Summarization and Stub Areas in OSPF

- Configuration of OSPFv3 for IPv6 and IPv4

This chapter examines the Open Shortest Path First (OSPF) Protocol, one of the most commonly used interior gateway protocols in IP networking. OSPFv2 is an open-standard protocol that provides routing for IPv4. OSPFv3 offers some enhancements for IP Version 6 (IPv6). OSPF is a complex protocol that is made up of several protocol handshakes, database advertisements, and packet types.

OSPF is an interior gateway routing protocol that uses link-states rather than distance vectors for path selection. OSPF propagates link-state advertisements (LSAs) rather than routing table updates. Because only LSAs are exchanged instead of the entire routing tables, OSPF networks converge in a timely manner.

OSPF uses a link-state algorithm to build and calculate the shortest path to all known destinations. Each router in an OSPF area contains an identical link-state database, which is a list of each of the router-usable interfaces and reachable neighbors.

Establishing OSPF Neighbor Relationships

OSPF is a link-state protocol based on the open standard. At a high level, OSPF operation consists of three main elements: neighbor discovery, link-state information exchange, and best-path calculation.

To calculate the best path, OSPF uses the shortest path first (SPF) or Dijkstra's algorithm. The input information for SPF calculation is link-state information, which is exchanged between routers using several different OSPF message types. These message types help improve convergence and scalability in multi-area OSPF deployments.

OSPF also supports several different network types, which enables you to configure OSPF over a variety of different underlying network technologies.

Upon completion of this section, you will be able to describe the main operational characteristics of the OSPF protocol and configure its basic features. You will also be able to meet following objectives:

- Explain why would you choose OSPF over other routing protocols

- Describe basic operation steps with link-state protocols

- Describe area and router types in OSPF

- Explain what the design limitations of OSPF are

- List and describe OSPF message types

- Describe OSPF neighbor relationship over point-to-point link

- Describe OSPF neighbor relationship behavior on MPLS VPN

- Describe OSPF neighbor relationship behavior over L2 MPLS VPN

- List and describe OSPF neighbor states

- List and describe OSPF network types

- Configure passive interfaces

OSPF Features

OSPF was developed by the Internet Engineering Task Force (IETF) to overcome the limitations of distance vector routing protocols. One of the main reasons why OSPF is largely deployed in today's enterprise networks is the fact that it is an open standard; OSPF is not proprietary. Version 1 of the protocol is described in the RFC 1131. The current version used for IPv4, Version 2, is specified in RFCs 1247 and 2328. OSPF Version 3, which is used in IPv6 networks, is specified in RFC 5340.

OSPF offers a large level of scalability and fast convergence. Despite its relatively simple configuration in small and medium-size networks, OSPF implementation and troubleshooting in large-scale networks can at times be challenging.

The key features of the OSPF protocol are as follows:

- **Independent transport:** OSPF works on top of IP and uses protocol number 89. It does not rely on the functions of the transport layer protocols TCP or UDP.

- **Efficient use of updates:** When an OSPF router first discovers a new neighbor, it sends a full update with all known link-state information. All routers within an OSPF area must have identical and synchronized link-state information in their OSPF link-state databases. When an OSPF network is in a converged state and a new link comes up or a link becomes unavailable, an OSPF router sends only a partial update to all its neighbors. This update will then be flooded to all OSPF routers within an area.

■ **Metric:** OSPF uses a metric that is based on the cumulative costs of all outgoing interfaces from source to destination. The interface cost is inversely proportional to the interface bandwidth and can be also set up explicitly.

■ **Update destination address:** OSPF uses multicast and unicast, rather than broadcast, for sending messages. The IPv4 multicast addresses used for OSPF are 224.0.0.5 to send information to all OSPF routers and 224.0.0.6 to send information to DR/BDR routers. The IPv6 multicast addresses are FF02::5 for all OSPFv3 routers and FF02::6 for all DR/BDR routers. If the underlying network does not have broadcast capabilities, you must establish OSPF neighbor relationships using a unicast address. For IPv6, this address will be a link-local IPv6 address.

■ **VLSM support:** OSPF is a classless routing protocol. It supports variable-length subnet masking (VLSM) and discontiguous networks. It carries subnet mask information in the routing updates.

■ **Manual route summarization:** You can manually summarize OSPF interarea routes at the Area Border Router (ABR), and you have the possibility to summarize OSPF external routes at the Autonomous System Boundary Router (ASBR). OSPF does not know the concept of autosummarization.

■ **Authentication:** OSPF supports clear-text, MD5, and SHA authentication.

Note The term *IP* is used for generic IP and applies to both IPv4 and IPv6. Otherwise, the terms *IPv4* and *IPv6* are used for the specific protocols.

Note Although there is some review, this chapter assumes that you have basic CCNA knowledge of OSPF. If you need a more thorough review of OSPF or other routing protocols, see the *Routing Protocols Companion Guide* (Cisco Press, 2014).

OSPF Operation Overview

To create and maintain routing information, OSPF routers complete the following generic link-state routing process, shown in Figure 3-1, to reach a state of convergence:

1. **Establish neighbor adjacencies:** OSPF-enabled routers must form adjacencies with their neighbor before they can share information with that neighbor. An OSPF-enabled router sends Hello packets out all OSPF-enabled interfaces to determine whether neighbors are present on those links. If a neighbor is present, the OSPF-enabled router attempts to establish a neighbor adjacency with that neighbor.

2. **Exchange link-state advertisements:** After adjacencies are established, routers then exchange link-state advertisements (LSAs). LSAs contain the state and cost of each directly connected link. Routers flood their LSAs to adjacent neighbors. Adjacent neighbors receiving the LSA immediately flood the LSA to other directly connected neighbors, until all routers in the area have all LSAs.

3. **Build the topology table:** After the LSAs are received, OSPF-enabled routers build the topology table (LSDB) based on the received LSAs. This database eventually holds all the information about the topology of the network. It is important that all routers in the area have the same information in their LSDBs.

4. **Execute the SPF algorithm:** Routers then execute the SPF algorithm. The SPF algorithm creates the SPF tree.

5. **Build the routing table:** From the SPF tree, the best paths are inserted into the routing table. Routing decisions are made based on the entries in the routing table.

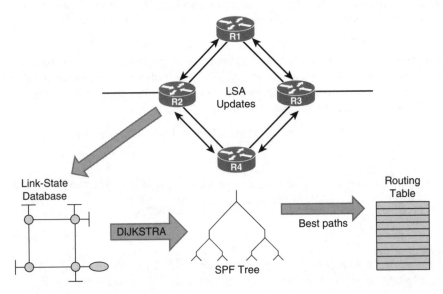

Figure 3-1   *OSPF Operation*

Hierarchical Structure of OSPF

If you run OSPF in a simple network, the number of routers and links are relatively small, and best paths to all destinations are easily deduced. However, the information necessary to describe larger networks with many routers and links can become quite complex. SPF calculations that compare all possible paths for routes can easily turn into a complex and time-consuming calculation for the router.

One of the main methods to reduce this complexity and the size of the link-state information database is to partition the OSPF routing domain into smaller units called *areas*, shown in Figure 3-2. This also reduces the time it takes for the SPF algorithm to execute. All OSPF routers within an area must have identical entries within their respective LSDBs. Inside an area, routers exchange detailed link-state information. However, information transmitted from one area into another contains only summary details of the LSDB entries and not topology details about the originating area. These summary LSAs from another area are injected directly into the routing table and without making the router rerun its SPF algorithm.

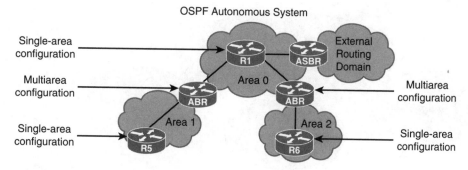

Figure 3-2 *OSPF Hierarchy*

OSPF uses a two-layer area hierarchy:

- **Backbone area, or area 0:** Two principal requirements for the backbone area are that it must connect to all other nonbackbone areas and this area must be always contiguous; it is not allowed to have split up the backbone area. Generally, end users are not found within a backbone area.

- **Nonbackbone area:** The primary function of this area is to connect end users and resources. Nonbackbone areas are usually set up according to functional or geographic groupings. Traffic between different nonbackbone areas must always pass through the backbone area.

In the multi-area topology there are some special commonly used OSPF terms:

- **ABR:** A router that has interfaces connected to at least two different OSPF areas, including the backbone area. ABRs contain LSDB information for each area, make route calculation for each area and advertise routing information between areas.

- **ASBR:** ASBR is a router that has at least one of its interfaces connected to an OSPF area and at least one of its interfaces connected to an external non-OSPF domain.

- **Internal router:** A router that has all its interfaces connected to only one OSPF area. This router is completely internal to this area.

- **Backbone router:** A router that has at least one interface connected to the backbone area.

The optimal number of routers per area varies based on factors such as network stability, but in general it is recommended to have no more than 50 routers per single area.

Design Restrictions of OSPF

OSPF has special restrictions when multiple areas are configured in an OSPF routing domain or AS, as shown in Figure 3-3. If more than one area is configured, known as *multi-area OSPF*, one of these areas must be area 0. This is called the *backbone area*. When designing networks or starting with a single area, it is good practice to start with the core layer, which becomes area 0, and then expand into other areas later.

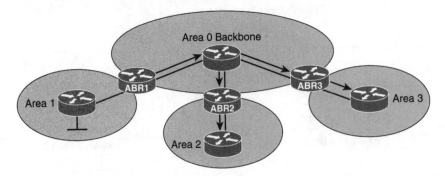

Figure 3-3   *Multi-Area OSPF*

The backbone has to be at the center of all other areas, and other areas have to be connected to the backbone. The main reason is that OSPF expects all areas to inject routing information into the backbone area, which distributes that information into other areas.

Another important requirement for the backbone area is that it must be contiguous. In other words, splitting up area 0 is not allowed.

However, in some cases, these two conditions cannot be met. Later in this chapter in the section, "OSPF Virtual Links," you will learn about the use of virtual links as a solution.

OSPF Message Types

OSPF uses five types of routing protocol packets, which share a common protocol header. Every OSPF packet is directly encapsulated in the IP header. The IP protocol number for OSPF is 89.

- **Type 1: Hello packet:** Hello packets are used to discover, build, and maintain OSPF neighbor adjacencies. To establish adjacency, OSPF peers at both sides of the link must agree on some parameters contained in the Hello packet to become OSPF neighbors.

- **Type 2: Database Description (DBD) packet:** When the OSPF neighbor adjacency is already established, a DBD packet is used to describe LSDB so that routers can compare whether databases are in sync.

- **Type 3: Link-State Request (LSR) packet:** The LSR packet is used within the database synchronization process. A router sends an LSR to request that its OSPF neighbors send the most recent version of LSAs that are missing in its database.

- **Type 4: Link-State Update (LSU) packet:** LSU packets contain several types of LSAs. LSU packets are used for the flooding of LSAs and sending LSA responses to LSR packets. Responses are sent only to the directly connected neighbors who have previously requested LSAs in LSR packets. In case of flooding, neighbor routers are responsible for re-encapsulation of received LSA information in new LSU packets.

- **Type 5: Link-State Acknowledgment (LSAck) packet:** LSAcks are used to make flooding of LSAs reliable. Each LSA received must be explicitly acknowledged. Multiple LSAs can be acknowledged in a single LSAck packet.

Basic OSPF Configuration

This section explores how to configure and establish OSPF neighbor relationship. You will observe the impact of the interface MTU and OSPF hello/dead timer parameters on the OSPF neighbor relationship formation. In addition, you will learn what the roles are of the DR/BDR routers and how to control the DR/BDR election process.

The topology in Figure 3-4 shows five routers, R1 to R5. R1, R4, and R5 are already pre-configured, while R2 and R3 will be configured in this section.

R1, R4, and R5 are connected to common multiaccess Ethernet segment. R1 and R2 are connected over serial Frame Relay interface, and R1 and R3 are also connected over Ethernet link.

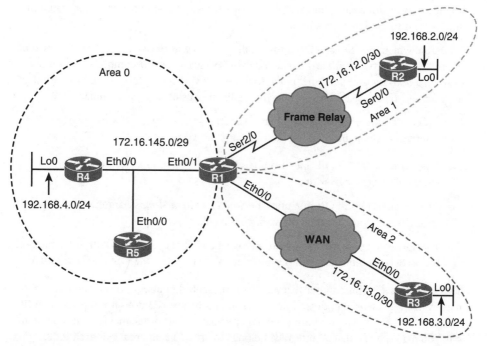

Figure 3-4 *Topology for Basic OSPF Configuration*

Example 3-1 begins the configuration of OSPF on WAN and LAN interfaces on R2 and R3. Use the process numbers 2 and 3 on R2 and R3, respectively.

Example 3-1   *Configuration OSPF on R2 and R3*

```
R2# configure terminal
Enter configuration commands, one per line.  End with CNTL/Z.
R2(config)# router ospf 2
R2(config-router)# network 172.16.12.0 0.0.0.3 area 1
R2(config-router)# network 192.168.2.0 0.0.0.255 area 1

R3# configure terminal
Enter configuration commands, one per line.  End with CNTL/Z.
R3(config)# router ospf 3
R3(config-router)# network 172.16.13.0 0.0.0.3 area 2
R3(config-router)# network 192.168.3.0 0.0.0.255 area 2
```

To enable the OSPF process on the router, use the **router ospf** *process-id* command. Process ID numbers between neighbors do not need to match for the routers to establish an OSPF adjacency. The OSPF process number ID is an internally used identification parameter for an OSPF routing process and only has local significance. However, it is good practice to make the process ID number the same on all routers. If necessary, you can specify multiple OSPF routing processes on a router, but you need to know the implications of doing so. Multiple OSPF processes on the same router is not common and beyond the scope of this book.

To define which interfaces will run the OSPF process and to define the area ID for those interfaces, use **network** *ip-address wildcard-mask* **area** *area-id* command. A combination of *ip-address* and *wildcard-mask* together allows you to define one or multiple interfaces to be associated with a specific OSPF area using a single command.

Cisco IOS Software sequentially evaluates the *ip-address wildcard-mask* pair specified in the **network** command for each interface as follows:

- It performs a logical OR operation between a *wildcard-mask* argument and the interface's primary IP address.

- It performs a logical OR operation between a *wildcard-mask* argument and the *ip-address* argument in the network command.

- The software compares the two resulting values. If they match, OSPF is enabled on the associated interface, and this interface is attached to the OSPF area specified.

This area ID is a 32-bit number that may be represented in integer or dotted-decimal format. When represented in dotted-decimal format, the area ID does not represent an IP address; it is only a way of writing an integer value in dotted-decimal format. For example, you may specify that an interface belongs to area 1 using **area 1** or **area 0.0.0.1** notation in the **network** command. To establish OSPF full adjacency, two neighbor routers must be in the same area. Any individual interface can only be attached to a single area. If the address ranges specified for different areas overlap, IOS will adopt the first area in the **network** command list and ignore subsequent overlapping portions. To avoid conflicts, you must pay special attention to ensure that address ranges do not overlap.

In Example 3-2, the OSPF router IDs of R2 and R3 are configured using the **router-id** command.

Example 3-2 *Configuration of OSPF Router IDs*

```
R2(config-router)# router-id 2.2.2.2
% OSPF: Reload or use "clear ip ospf process" command, for this to take effect
```

```
R3(config-router)# router-id 3.3.3.3
% OSPF: Reload or use "clear ip ospf process" command, for this to take effect
```

The OSPF router ID is a fundamental parameter for the OSPF process. For the OSPF process to start, Cisco IOS must be able to identify a unique OSPF router ID. Similar to EIGRP, the OSPF router ID is a 32-bit value expressed as an IPv4 address. At least one primary IPv4 address on an interface in the up/up state must be configured for a router to be able to choose router ID; otherwise, an error message is logged, and the OSPF process does not start.

To choose the OSPF router ID at the time of OSPF process initialization, the router uses the following criteria:

1. Use the router ID specified in the **router-id** *ip-address* command. You can configure an arbitrary value in the IPv4 address format, but this value must be unique. If the IPv4 address specified with the **router-id** command overlaps with the router ID of another already-active OSPF process, the **router-id** command fails.

2. Use the highest IPv4 address of all active loopback interfaces on the router.

3. Use the highest IPv4 address among all active nonloopback interfaces.

After the three-step OSPF router ID selection process has finished, and if the router is still unable to select an OSPF router ID, an error message will be logged. An OSPF process that failed to select a router ID retries the selection process every time an IPv4 address becomes available. (An applicable interface changes its state to up/up or an IPv4 address is configured on an applicable interface.)

In Example 3-3, the OSPF routing process is cleared on R2 and R3 for the manually configured router ID to take effect.

Example 3-3 *Clearing the OSPF Processes on R2 and R3*

```
R2# clear ip ospf process
Reset ALL OSPF processes? [no]: yes
R2#
*Nov 24 08:37:24.679: %OSPF-5-ADJCHG: Process 2, Nbr 1.1.1.1 on Serial0/0 from
```

```
FULL to DOWN, Neighbor Down: Interface down or detached
R2#
*Nov 24 08:39:24.734: %OSPF-5-ADJCHG: Process 2, Nbr 1.1.1.1 on Serial0/0 from
LOADING to FULL, Loading Done
```

```
R3# clear ip ospf 3 process
Reset OSPF process 3? [no]: yes
R3#
*Nov 24 09:06:00.275: %OSPF-5-ADJCHG: Process 3, Nbr 1.1.1.1 on Ethernet0/0 from
FULL to DOWN, Neighbor Down: Interface down or detached
R3#
*Nov 24 09:06:40.284: %OSPF-5-ADJCHG: Process 3, Nbr 1.1.1.1 on Ethernet0/0 from
LOADING to FULL, Loading Done
```

Once an OSPF router ID is selected, it is not changed even if the interface that is used to select it changed its operational state or its IP address. To change the OSPF router ID, you must reset the OSPF process with the **clear ip ospf process** command or reload the router.

In production networks, the OSPF router ID cannot be changed easily. Changing the OSPF router ID requires reset of all OSPF adjacencies, resulting in a temporary routing outage. The router also has to originate new copies of all originating LSAs with the new router ID.

You can either clear the specific OSPF process by specifying the process ID, or you can reset all OSPF processes by using the **clear ip ospf process** command.

The newly configured OSPF router ID is verified on R2 and R3 using **show ip protocols** commands in Example 3-4. Large output of this command can optionally be filtered using the pipe function, also shown in Example 3-4.

Example 3-4   *Verifying the Router IDs on R2 and R3*

```
R2# show ip protocols
*** IP Routing is NSF aware ***

Routing Protocol is "ospf 2"
  Outgoing update filter list for all interfaces is not set
  Incoming update filter list for all interfaces is not set
  Router ID 2.2.2.2
  Number of areas in this router is 1. 1 normal 0 stub 0 nssa
  Maximum path: 4
  Routing for Networks:
    172.16.12.0 0.0.0.3 area 1
    192.168.2.0 0.0.0.255 area 1
  Routing Information Sources:
    Gateway         Distance      Last Update
    1.1.1.1              110      00:02:55
  Distance: (default is 110)
```

```
R3# show ip protocols | include ID
  Router ID 3.3.3.3
```

The OSPF neighborship on R2 and R3 is verified in Example 3-5 using the **show ip ospf neighbor** command.

Example 3-5 *Verifying OSPF Neighborships on R2 and R3*

```
R2# show ip ospf neighbor

Neighbor ID      Pri    State         Dead Time    Address        Interface
1.1.1.1            1    FULL/DR        00:01:57     172.16.12.1    Serial0/0
```

```
R3# show ip ospf neighbor

Neighbor ID      Pri    State         Dead Time    Address        Interface
1.1.1.1            1    FULL/DR        00:00:39     172.16.13.1    Ethernet0/0
```

The command **show ip ospf neighbor** displays OSPF neighbor information on a per-interface basis. The significant fields of the outputs are as follows:

- **Neighbor ID:** Represents neighbor router ID.

- **Priority:** Priority on the neighbor interface used for the DR/BDR election.

- **State:** A Full state represents the final stage of OSPF neighbor establishment process and denotes that the local router has established full neighbor adjacency with the remote OSPF neighbor. DR means that DR/BDR election process has been completed and that the remote router with the router ID 1.1.1.1 has been elected as the designated router (DR).

- **Dead Time:** Represents value of the dead timer. When this timer expires, the router terminates the neighbor relationship. Each time a router receives an OSPF Hello packet from a specific neighbor, it resets the dead timer back to its full value.

- **Address:** Primary IPv4 address of the neighbor router.

- **Interface:** Local interface over which an OSPF neighbor relationship is established.

Example 3-6 verifies the OSPF-enabled interfaces on R2 and R3 using the **show ip ospf interface** command.

Example 3-6 *Verifying the OSPF-Enabled Interfaces on R2 and R3*

```
R2# show ip ospf interface
Loopback0 is up, line protocol is up
   Internet Address 192.168.2.1/24, Area 1, Attached via Network Statement
   Process ID 2, Router ID 2.2.2.2, Network Type LOOPBACK, Cost: 1
<Output omitted>
Serial0/0 is up, line protocol is up
```

```
    Internet Address 172.16.12.2/30, Area 1, Attached via Network Statement
    Process ID 2, Router ID 2.2.2.2, Network Type NON_BROADCAST, Cost: 64
<Output omitted>
```

```
R3# show ip ospf interface
Loopback0 is up, line protocol is up
    Internet Address 192.168.3.1/24, Area 2, Attached via Network Statement
    Process ID 3, Router ID 3.3.3.3, Network Type LOOPBACK, Cost: 1
<Output omitted>
Ethernet0/0 is up, line protocol is up
    Internet Address 172.16.13.2/30, Area 2, Attached via Network Statement
    Process ID 3, Router ID 3.3.3.3, Network Type BROADCAST, Cost: 10
<Output omitted>
```

Output of the **show ip ospf interface** command shows you all interfaces enabled in the OSPF process. For each enabled interface, you can see detailed information such as OSPF area ID, OSPF process ID, and how the interface was included into the OSPF process. In the output, you can see that both interfaces on both routers were included via the **network** statement, configured with the **network** command.

In Example 3-7, the OSPF routes are verified in the routing table on R5 using the **show ip route ospf** command.

Example 3-7 *Verifying the OSPF Routes on R5*

```
R5# show ip route ospf
Codes: L - local, C - connected, S - static, R - RIP, M - mobile, B - BGP
       D - EIGRP, EX - EIGRP external, O - OSPF, IA - OSPF inter area
       N1 - OSPF NSSA external type 1, N2 - OSPF NSSA external type 2
       E1 - OSPF external type 1, E2 - OSPF external type 2
       i - IS-IS, su - IS-IS summary, L1 - IS-IS level-1, L2 - IS-IS level-2
       ia - IS-IS inter area, * - candidate default, U - per-user static route
       o - ODR, P - periodic downloaded static route, H - NHRP, l - LISP
       + - replicated route, % - next hop override


Gateway of last resort is not set


      172.16.0.0/16 is variably subnetted, 4 subnets, 3 masks
O IA     172.16.12.0/30 [110/74] via 172.16.145.1, 00:39:00, Ethernet0/0
O IA     172.16.13.0/30 [110/20] via 172.16.145.1, 00:19:29, Ethernet0/0
      192.168.2.0/32 is subnetted, 1 subnets
O IA     192.168.2.1 [110/75] via 172.16.145.1, 00:07:27, Ethernet0/0
      192.168.3.0/32 is subnetted, 1 subnets
O IA     192.168.3.1 [110/21] via 172.16.145.1, 00:08:30, Ethernet0/0
O     192.168.4.0/24 [110/11] via 172.16.145.4, 00:39:10, Ethernet0/0
```

Among the routes originated within the OSPF autonomous system, OSPF clearly distinguishes two types of routes: intra-area routes and interarea routes. Intra-area routes are routes that are originated and learned in the same local area. Code for the intra-area routes in the routing table is O. The second type is interarea routes, which originate in other areas and are inserted into the local area to which your router belongs. Code for the interarea routes in the routing table is O IA. Interarea routes are inserted into other areas on the ABR.

The prefix 192.168.4.0/24 is an example of intra-area route from the R5 perspective. It originated from router R4, which is part of the area 0, the same area as R5.

Prefixes from R2 and R3, which are part of area 1 and area 2, are shown in the routing table on R5 as interarea routes. Prefixes were inserted into area 0 as interarea routes by R1, which plays the role of ABR.

Prefixes 192.168.2.0/24 and 192.168.3.0/24 configured on the loopback interfaces of R2 and R3 are displayed in the R5 routing table as host routes 192.168.2.1/32 and 192.168.3.1/32. By default, OSPF will advertise any subnet configured on the loopback interface as /32 host route. To change this default behavior, you can optionally change OSPF network type on the loopback interface from the default loopback to point-to-point using the **ip ospf network point-to-point** interface command.

OSPF database routes on R5 are observed in Example 3-8 using the **show ip ospf route** command.

Example 3-8   *OSPF Routes on R5*

```
R5# show ip ospf route

               OSPF Router with ID (5.5.5.5) (Process ID 1)


             Base Topology (MTID 0)


   Area BACKBONE(0)


   Intra-area Route List
*    172.16.145.0/29, Intra, cost 10, area 0, Connected
       via 172.16.145.5, Ethernet0/0
*>   192.168.4.0/24, Intra, cost 11, area 0
       via 172.16.145.4, Ethernet0/0


     Intra-area Router Path List
i 1.1.1.1 [10] via 172.16.145.1, Ethernet0/0, ABR, Area 0, SPF 2


     Inter-area Route List
*>   192.168.2.1/32, Inter, cost 75, area 0
       via 172.16.145.1, Ethernet0/0
*>   192.168.3.1/32, Inter, cost 21, area 0
```

```
          via 172.16.145.1, Ethernet0/0
*>  172.16.12.0/30, Inter, cost 74, area 0
          via 172.16.145.1, Ethernet0/0
*>  172.16.13.0/30, Inter, cost 20, area 0
          via 172.16.145.1, Ethernet0/0
```

The **show ip ospf route** command clearly separates the lists of intra-area and interarea
routes. In addition, output of the command displays essential information about ABRs,
including the router ID, IPv4 address in the current area, interface that advertises routes
into the area, and the area ID.

For interarea routes, the metric for the route (cost), the area into which the route is distributed, and the interface over which the route is inserted are displayed.

In Example 3-9, the OSPF neighbor adjacency and the associated OSPF packet types
on R3 are observed using the **debug ip ospf adj** and **clear ip ospf process** commands.
Disable **debug** when the OSPF session is reestablished.

Example 3-9 *Observing Formation of OSPF Neighbor Adjacencies*

```
R3# debug ip ospf adj
OSPF adjacency debugging is on
R3# clear ip ospf process
Reset ALL OSPF processes? [no]: yes
*Jan 17 13:02:37.394: OSPF-3 ADJ   Lo0: Interface going Down
*Jan 17 13:02:37.394: OSPF-3 ADJ   Lo0: 3.3.3.3 address 192.168.3.1 is dead, state
  DOWN
*Jan 17 13:02:37.394: OSPF-3 ADJ   Et0/0: Interface going Down
*Jan 17 13:02:37.394: OSPF-3 ADJ   Et0/0: 1.1.1.1 address 172.16.13.1 is dead, state
  DOWN
*Jan 17 13:02:37.394: %OSPF-5-ADJCHG: Process 3, Nbr 1.1.1.1 on Ethernet0/0 from
  FULL to DOWN, Neighbor Down: Interface down or detached
<Output omitted>
*Jan 17 13:02:37.394: OSPF-3 ADJ   Lo0: Interface going Up
*Jan 17 13:02:37.394: OSPF-3 ADJ   Et0/0: Interface going Up
*Jan 17 13:02:37.395: OSPF-3 ADJ   Et0/0: 2 Way Communication to 1.1.1.1, state 2WAY
*Jan 17 13:02:37.396: OSPF-3 ADJ   Et0/0: Backup seen event before WAIT timer
*Jan 17 13:02:37.396: OSPF-3 ADJ   Et0/0: DR/BDR election
*Jan 17 13:02:37.396: OSPF-3 ADJ   Et0/0: Elect BDR 3.3.3.3
*Jan 17 13:02:37.396: OSPF-3 ADJ   Et0/0: Elect DR 1.1.1.1
*Jan 17 13:02:37.396: OSPF-3 ADJ   Et0/0: Elect BDR 3.3.3.3
*Jan 17 13:02:37.396: OSPF-3 ADJ   Et0/0: Elect DR 1.1.1.1
*Jan 17 13:02:37.396: OSPF-3 ADJ   Et0/0: DR: 1.1.1.1 (Id)    BDR: 3.3.3.3 (Id)
*Jan 17 13:02:37.396: OSPF-3 ADJ   Et0/0: Nbr 1.1.1.1: Prepare dbase exchange
*Jan 17 13:02:37.396: OSPF-3 ADJ   Et0/0: Send DBD to 1.1.1.1 seq 0x95D opt 0x52
  flag 0x7 len 32
*Jan 17 13:02:37.397: OSPF-3 ADJ   Et0/0: Rcv DBD from 1.1.1.1 seq 0x691 opt 0x52
  flag 0x7 len 32  mtu 1500 state EXSTART
```

```
*Jan 17 13:02:37.397: OSPF-3 ADJ    Et0/0: First DBD and we are not SLAVE
*Jan 17 13:02:37.397: OSPF-3 ADJ    Et0/0: Rcv DBD from 1.1.1.1 seq 0x95D opt 0x52
   flag 0x2 len 152  mtu 1500 state EXSTART
*Jan 17 13:02:37.397: OSPF-3 ADJ    Et0/0: NBR Negotiation Done. We are the MASTER
*Jan 17 13:02:37.397: OSPF-3 ADJ    Et0/0: Nbr 1.1.1.1: Summary list built, size 0
*Jan 17 13:02:37.397: OSPF-3 ADJ    Et0/0: Send DBD to 1.1.1.1 seq 0x95E opt 0x52
   flag 0x1 len 32
*Jan 17 13:02:37.398: OSPF-3 ADJ    Et0/0: Rcv DBD from 1.1.1.1 seq 0x95E opt 0x52
   flag 0x0 len 32  mtu 1500 state EXCHANGE
*Jan 17 13:02:37.398: OSPF-3 ADJ    Et0/0: Exchange Done with 1.1.1.1
*Jan 17 13:02:37.398: OSPF-3 ADJ    Et0/0: Send LS REQ to 1.1.1.1 length 96 LSA count
   6
*Jan 17 13:02:37.399: OSPF-3 ADJ    Et0/0: Rcv LS UPD from 1.1.1.1 length 208 LSA
   count 6
*Jan 17 13:02:37.399: OSPF-3 ADJ    Et0/0: Synchronized with 1.1.1.1, state FULL
*Jan 17 13:02:37.399: %OSPF-5-ADJCHG: Process 3, Nbr 1.1.1.1 on Ethernet0/0 from
   LOADING to FULL, Loading Done
R3# undebug all
```

An OSPF adjacency is established in several steps. In the first step, routers that intend to establish full OSPF neighbor adjacency exchange OSPF Hello packets. Both OSPF neighbors are in the Down state, the initial state of a neighbor conversation that indicates that no Hello's have been heard from the neighbor. When a router receives a Hello from the neighbor but has not yet seen its own router ID in the neighbor Hello packet, it will transit to the Init state. In this state, the router will record all neighbor router IDs and start including them in Hellos sent to the neighbors. When the router sees its own router ID in the Hello packet received from the neighbor, it will transit to the 2-Way state. This means that bidirectional communication with the neighbor has been established.

On multi-access links, OSPF neighbors first determine the designated router (DR) and backup designated router (BDR) roles, which optimize the exchange of information in broadcast segments.

In the next step, routers start to exchange content of OSPF databases. The first phase of this process is to determine master/slave relationship and choose the initial sequence number for adjacency formation. To accomplish this, routers exchange DBD packets. When the router receives the initial DBD packet it transitions the state of the neighbor from which this packet is received to ExStart state, populates its Database Summary list with the LSAs that describe content of the neighbor's database, and sends its own empty DBD packet. In the DBD exchange process, the router with the higher router ID will become master, and it will be the only router that can increment sequence numbers.

With master/slave selection complete, database exchange can start. R3 will transit R1's neighbor state to Exchange. In this state, R3 describes its database to the R1 by sending DBD packets that contain the headers of all LSAs in the Database Summary list. The Database Summary list describes all LSAs in the router's database, but not the full content of the OSPF database. To describe the content of the database, one or multiple DBD packets may be exchanged. A router compares the content of its own Database

Summary list with the list received from the neighbor, and if there are differences, it adds missing LSAs to the Link State Request list. At this point, routers enter the Loading state. R3 sends an LSR packet to the neighbor requesting full content of the missing LSAs from the LS Request list. R1 replies with the LSU packets, which contain full versions of the missing LSAs.

Finally, when neighbors have a complete version of the LSDB, both neighbors transit to the Full state, which means that databases on the routers are synchronized and that neighbors are fully adjacent.

Optimizing OSPF Adjacency Behavior

Multiaccess networks, either broadcast (such as Ethernet) or nonbroadcast (such as Frame Relay), represent interesting issues for OSPF. All routers sharing the common segment will be part of the same IP subnet. When forming adjacency on multiaccess network, if every router tried to establish full OSPF adjacency with all other routers on the segment, this may not represent an issue for the smaller multiaccess broadcast networks, but it could be an issue for the nonbroadcast multiaccess (NBMA) networks, where in most cases you do not have full-mesh private virtual circuit (PVC) topology. In these NBMA networks neighbors would not be able to synchronize their OSPF databases directly among themselves. A logical solution in this case is to have a central point of OSPF adjacency responsible for the database synchronization and advertisement of the segment to the other routers, as shown in Figure 3-5.

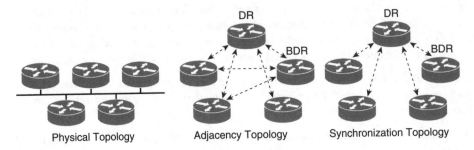

Figure 3-5   *OSPF Adjacencies on Multiaccess Networks*

As the number of routers on the segment grows, the number of OSPF adjacencies increases exponentially. If every router had to synchronize its OSPF database with every other router, this would be inefficient. For example, if every router on the segment advertised all its routing information to all other routers on the segment, in a full-mesh of OSPF adjacencies the OSPF routers would receive a large amount of redundant link-state information. Again, the solution for this problem is to establish a central point with which every other router forms adjacency and which advertises segment as a whole to the rest of the network.

Thus, the routers on the multiaccess segment elect a designated router (DR) and backup designated router (BDR), which centralizes communications for all routers connected to the segment. The DR and BDR improve network functioning in the following ways:

- **Reducing routing update traffic:** The DR and BDR act as a central point of contact for link-state information exchange on a multiaccess network; therefore, each router must establish a full adjacency with the DR and the BDR only. Each router, rather than exchanging link-state information with every other router on the segment, sends the link-state information to the DR and BDR only, by using a dedicated IPv4 multicast address 224.0.0.6 or FF02::6 for IPv6. The DR represents the multiaccess network in the sense that it sends link-state information from each router to all other routers in the network. This flooding process significantly reduces the router-related traffic on the segment.

- **Managing link-state synchronization:** The DR and BDR ensure that the other routers on the network have the same link-state information about the common segment. In this way, the DR and BDR reduce the number of routing errors.

Only LSAs are sent to the DR/BDR. The normal routing of packets on the segment will go to the best next-hop router.

When the DR is operating, the BDR does not perform any DR functions. Instead, the BDR receives all the information, but the DR performs the LSA forwarding and LSDB synchronization tasks. The BDR performs the DR tasks only if the DR fails. When the DR fails, the BDR automatically becomes the new DR, and a new BDR election occurs.

In Example 3-10, the DR/BDR status on R1, R4, and R5 are observed using the **show ip ospf neighbor** command. Routers R1, R4, and R5 are all connected to the same shared network segment, where OSPF will automatically attempts to optimize adjacencies.

Example 3-10 *Neighbor Status of R1, R4, and R5*

```
R1# show ip ospf neighbor

Neighbor ID     Pri   State           Dead Time   Address         Interface
4.4.4.4           1   FULL/BDR        00:00:37    172.16.145.4    Ethernet0/1
5.5.5.5           1   FULL/DR         00:00:39    172.16.145.5    Ethernet0/1
2.2.2.2           1   FULL/DR         00:01:53    172.16.12.2     Serial2/0
3.3.3.3           1   FULL/DR         00:00:35    172.16.13.2     Ethernet0/0


R4# show ip ospf neighbor

Neighbor ID     Pri   State           Dead Time   Address         Interface
1.1.1.1           1   FULL/DROTHER    00:00:39    172.16.145.1    Ethernet0/0
5.5.5.5           1   FULL/DR         00:00:39    172.16.145.5    Ethernet0/0


R5# show ip ospf neighbor

Neighbor ID     Pri   State           Dead Time   Address         Interface
1.1.1.1           1   FULL/DROTHER    00:00:39    172.16.145.1    Ethernet0/0
4.4.4.4           1   FULL/BDR        00:00:35    172.16.145.4    Ethernet0/0
```

When R1, R4, and R5 start establishing OSPF neighbor adjacency, they first send OSPF Hello packets to discover which OSPF neighbors are active on the common Ethernet segment. After the bidirectional communication between routers is established and they are all in the OSPF neighbor 2-Way state, the DR/BDR election process begins. The OSPF Hello packet contains three specific fields used for the DR/BDR election: Designated Router, Backup Designated Router, and Router Priority.

The Designated Router and Backup Designate Router fields are populated with a list of routers claiming to be DR and BDR. From all routers listed, the router with the highest priority becomes the DR, and the one with the next highest priority becomes the BDR. If the priority values are equal, the router with the highest OSPF router ID becomes the DR, and the one with the next highest OSPF router ID becomes the BDR.

The DR/BDR election process takes place on broadcast and NBMA networks. The main difference between the two is the type of IP address used in the Hello packet. On the multiaccess broadcast networks, routers use multicast destination IPv4 address 224.0.0.6 to communicate with the DR (called AllDRRouters), and the DR uses multicast destination IPv4 address 224.0.0.5 to communicate with all other non-DR routers (called AllSPFRouters). On NBMA networks, the DR and adjacent routers communicate using unicast addresses.

The DR/BDR election process not only occurs when the network first becomes active but also when the DR becomes unavailable. In this case, the BDR will immediately become the DR, and the election of the new BDR starts.

In the topology, R5 has been elected as the DR and R4 as the BDR due to having the highest router ID values on the segment. R1 became a DROTHER. On the multiaccess segment, it is normal behavior that the router in DROTHER status is fully adjacent with DR/BDR and in 2-WAY state with all other DROTHER routers present on the segment.

In Example 3-11, the interface on R5 is shut down toward R1 and R4. Now, reexamine the DR/BDR status on R1 and R4. After the shutdown on the interface, wait until neighbor adjacencies expire before reexamining the DR/BDR state.

Example 3-11   *R5's Ethernet 0/0 Interface Shutdown*

```
R5(config)# interface ethernet 0/0
R5(config-if)# shutdown
*Dec  8 16:20:25.080: %OSPF-5-ADJCHG: Process 1, Nbr 1.1.1.1 on Ethernet0/0 from
FULL to DOWN, Neighbor Down: Interface down or detached
*Dec  8 16:20:25.080: %OSPF-5-ADJCHG: Process 1, Nbr 4.4.4.4 on Ethernet0/0 from
FULL to DOWN, Neighbor Down: Interface down or detached


R1# show ip ospf neighbor

Neighbor ID     Pri   State        Dead Time    Address        Interface
4.4.4.4          1    FULL/DR      00:00:32     172.16.145.4   Ethernet0/1
2.2.2.2          1    FULL/DR      00:01:36     172.16.12.2    Serial2/0
```

```
3.3.3.3              1    FULL/DR        00:00:39    172.16.13.2    Ethernet0/0
```

```
R4# show ip ospf neighbor

Neighbor ID        Pri   State          Dead Time   Address        Interface
1.1.1.1             1    FULL/BDR       00:00:33    172.16.145.1   Ethernet0/0
```

When R5's Ethernet 0/0 interface is shut down, the DR router on the segment becomes immediately unavailable. As a result, a new DR/BDR election takes place. The output of the **show ip ospf neighbor** command shows that R4 has become the DR and R1 the BDR.

Next, in Example 3-12, R5's interface toward R1 and R4 is enabled. Examine the DR/BDR status on R1, R4, and R5.

Example 3-12 *R1's Ethernet 0/0 Interface Reenabled*

```
R5(config)# interface ethernet 0/0
R5(config-if)# no shutdown
*Dec 10 08:49:26.491: %OSPF-5-ADJCHG: Process 1, Nbr 1.1.1.1 on Ethernet0/0 from
LOADING to FULL, Loading Done
*Dec 10 08:49:30.987: %OSPF-5-ADJCHG: Process 1, Nbr 4.4.4.4 on Ethernet0/0 from
LOADING to FULL, Loading Done
```

```
R1# show ip ospf neighbor

Neighbor ID        Pri   State          Dead Time   Address        Interface
4.4.4.4             1    FULL/DR        00:00:36    172.16.145.4   Ethernet0/1
5.5.5.5             1    FULL/DROTHER   00:00:38    172.16.145.5   Ethernet0/1
2.2.2.2             1    FULL/DR        00:01:52    172.16.12.2    Serial2/0
3.3.3.3             1    FULL/DR        00:00:33    172.16.13.2    Ethernet0/0
```

```
R4# show ip ospf neighbor

Neighbor ID        Pri   State          Dead Time   Address        Interface
1.1.1.1             1    FULL/BDR       00:00:30    172.16.145.1   Ethernet0/0
5.5.5.5             1    FULL/DROTHER   00:00:34    172.16.145.5   Ethernet0/0
```

```
R5# show ip ospf neighbor

Neighbor ID        Pri   State          Dead Time   Address        Interface
1.1.1.1             1    FULL/BDR       00:00:33    172.16.145.1   Ethernet0/0
4.4.4.4             1    FULL/DR        00:00:37    172.16.145.4   Ethernet0/0
```

When R5's Ethernet 0/0 interface is reenabled, a new DR/BDR election process will not take place even though R5 has the highest OSPF router ID on the segment. Once a DR and BDR are elected, they are not preempted. This rule makes the multiaccess segment more stable by preventing the election process from occurring whenever a new router becomes active. It means that the first two DR-eligible routers on the link will be elected as DR and BDR. A new election will occur only when one of them fails.

Using OSPF Priority in the DR/BDR Election

One of the fields in the OSPF Hello packet used in the DR/BDR election process is the Router Priority field. Every broadcast and NBMA OSPF-enabled interface is assigned a priority value between 0 and 255. By default, in Cisco IOS, the OSPF interface priority value is 1 and can be manually changed by using the **ip ospf priority** interface command. When electing a DR and BDR, the routers view the OSPF priority value of other routers during the Hello packet exchange process, and then use the following conditions to determine which router to select:

■ The router with the highest priority value is elected as the DR.

■ The router with the second-highest priority value is the BDR.

■ In case of a tie where two routers have the same priority value, router ID is used as the tiebreaker. The router with the highest router ID becomes the DR. The router with the second-highest router ID becomes the BDR.

■ A router with a priority that is set to 0 cannot become the DR or BDR. A router that is not the DR or BDR is called a DROTHER.

The OSPF priority is configured on R1 using the **ip ospf priority** interface command, shown in Example 3-13. The OSPF process is cleared on R4 to reinitiate the DR/BDR election process. Setting the OSPF interface priority to a value higher than 1 will influence the DB/BDR election in favor of R1.

Example 3-13 *Configuring the OSPF Priority on an Interface*

```
R1(config)# interface ethernet 0/1
R1(config-if)# ip ospf priority 100

R4# clear ip ospf process
Reset ALL OSPF processes? [no]: yes
*Dec 10 13:08:48.610: %OSPF-5-ADJCHG: Process 1, Nbr 1.1.1.1 on Ethernet0/0 from
FULL to DOWN, Neighbor Down: Interface down or detached
*Dec 10 13:08:48.610: %OSPF-5-ADJCHG: Process 1, Nbr 5.5.5.5 on Ethernet0/0 from
FULL to DOWN, Neighbor Down: Interface down or detached
*Dec 10 13:09:01.294: %OSPF-5-ADJCHG: Process 1, Nbr 1.1.1.1 on Ethernet0/0 from
LOADING to FULL, Loading Done
*Dec 10 13:09:04.159: %OSPF-5-ADJCHG: Process 1, Nbr 5.5.5.5 on Ethernet0/0 from
LOADING to FULL, Loading Done
```

In this example, the OSPF interface priority value is configured to 100. This influences the DR/BDR election, so that the R1 router will become DR after the OSPF process is cleared on the current DR, R4.

In Example 3-14, the **show ip ospf interface Ethernet 0/1** command on R1 verifies that it has been elected as a new DR.

Example 3-14 *R1 Is the New DR*

```
R1# show ip ospf interface ethernet 0/1
Ethernet0/1 is up, line protocol is up
  Internet Address 172.16.145.1/29, Area 0, Attached via Network Statement
  Process ID 1, Router ID 1.1.1.1, Network Type BROADCAST, Cost: 10
  Topology-MTID    Cost    Disabled    Shutdown    Topology Name
       0            10       no          no          Base
  Transmit Delay is 1 sec, State DR, Priority 100
  Designated Router (ID) 1.1.1.1, Interface address 172.16.145.1
  Backup Designated router (ID) 5.5.5.5, Interface address 172.16.145.5
  Timer intervals configured, Hello 10, Dead 40, Wait 40, Retransmit 5
    oob-resync timeout 40
    Hello due in 00:00:06
  Supports Link-local Signaling (LLS)
  Cisco NSF helper support enabled
  IETF NSF helper support enabled
  Index 1/3, flood queue length 0
  Next 0x0(0)/0x0(0)
  Last flood scan length is 1, maximum is 5
  Last flood scan time is 0 msec, maximum is 1 msec
  Neighbor Count is 2, Adjacent neighbor count is 2
    Adjacent with neighbor 4.4.4.4
    Adjacent with neighbor 5.5.5.5  (Backup Designated Router)
  Suppress hello for 0 neighbor(s)
```

The Ethernet 0/1 interface on R1 has been assigned the OSPF priority value of 100, too, and when the new DR/BDR election process took place, the state of the R1 has become DR. The **show ip ospf interface** command on R1 shows that R1 is elected as the DR and that R5 is elected as the BDR. R1 is fully adjacent with two neighbors: R4 and R5.

OSPF Behavior in NBMA Hub-and-Spoke Topology

Special issues may arise when trying to interconnect multiple OSPF sites over an NBMA network. For example, if the NBMA topology is not fully meshed, a broadcast or multicast that is sent by one router will not reach all the other routers. Frame Relay and ATM are two examples of NBMA networks. By default, OSPF treats NBMA environments like any other broadcast media environment, such as Ethernet; however, NBMA clouds are usually built as hub-and-spoke topologies using private virtual circuits (PVCs) or switched virtual circuits (SVCs). The hub-and-spoke topology shown in Figure 3-6 means that the NBMA network is only a partial mesh. In these cases, the physical topology does not provide multiaccess capability, on which OSPF relies. In a hub-and-spoke NBMA environment, you will need to have the hub router acting as the DR and spoke routers acting as the DROTHER routers. On the spoke router interfaces, you want to configure an OSPF priority value of 0 so that the spoke routers never participate in the DR election.

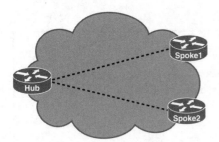

Figure 3-6 *Hub-and-Spoke Topology*

In addition, OSPF is not able to automatically discover OSPF neighbors over an NBMA network like Frame Relay. Neighbors must be statically configured on at least one router by using the **neighbor** *ip_address* configuration command in the router configuration mode.

In our example network the effect of a priority changed is tested using Ethernet interfaces. Example 3-15 shows setting the OSPF priority on R4's and R5's Ethernet 0/0 interfaces to 0 using the **ip ospf priority** interface command. Setting the OSPF interface priority to 0 prevents the router from being a candidate for the DR/BDR role.

Example 3-15 *Setting the OSPF Priority to 0 on R4 and R5*

```
R4(config)# interface ethernet 0/0
R4(config-if)# ip ospf priority 0
```

```
R5(config)# interface ethernet 0/0
R5(config-if)# ip ospf priority 0
```

Setting the OSPF priority value to 0 on the Ethernet 0/0 interfaces for R4 and R5 means that these two routers will not participate in the DR/BDR election and will not be eligible to become the DR/BDR. These routers will be DROTHER routers.

The state of the DR/BDR status on R1, R4, and R5 is shown in Example 3-16.

Example 3-16 *DR/BDR States on R1, R4, and R5*

```
R1# show ip ospf neighbor

Neighbor ID     Pri   State           Dead Time   Address         Interface
4.4.4.4           0   FULL/DROTHER    00:00:36    172.16.145.4    Ethernet0/1
5.5.5.5           0   FULL/DROTHER    00:00:34    172.16.145.5    Ethernet0/1
```

```
2.2.2.2              1    FULL/DR        00:01:33    172.16.12.2    Serial2/0
3.3.3.3              1    FULL/DR        00:00:30    172.16.13.2    Ethernet0/0

R4# show ip ospf neighbor

Neighbor ID    Pri    State          Dead Time   Address        Interface
1.1.1.1        100    FULL/DR        00:00:37    172.16.145.1   Ethernet0/0
5.5.5.5          0    2WAY/DROTHER   00:00:37    172.16.145.5   Ethernet0/0

R5# show ip ospf neighbor

Neighbor ID    Pri    State          Dead Time   Address        Interface
1.1.1.1        100    FULL/DR        00:00:32    172.16.145.1   Ethernet0/0
4.4.4.4          0    2WAY/DROTHER   00:00:37    172.16.145.4   Ethernet0/0
```

The output of the **show ip ospf neighbor** commands on R1 shows that R1 is fully adjacent with R4 and R5 and that R4 and R5 have DROTHER functions. R4 is fully adjacent with the DR router R1, but it maintains a 2-Way state with its peer DROTHER router R5. Similarly, R5 is fully adjacent with DR R1 and maintains a 2-Way state with the DROTHER router R4. A 2-Way state between non-DR/BDR routers on the segment is normal behavior; they do not synchronize LSDBs directly, but over DR/BDR. By maintaining 2-Way state, DROTHER routers keep other DROTHER peers informed about their presence on the network.

The Importance of MTU

The IP MTU parameter determines the maximum size of an IPv4 packet that can be forwarded out the interface without fragmentation. If a packet with an IPv4 MTU larger than the maximum arrives at the router interface, it will be either discarded, if the DF bit in the packet header is set, or it will be fragmented. OSPF for IPv4 packets completely relies on IPv4 for the possible fragmentation. Although RFC 2328 does not recommend OSPF packet fragmentation, in some situations the size of the OSPF packet has greater value than the interface IPv4 MTU. If MTUs are mismatched between two neighbors, this could introduce issues with exchange of link-state packets, resulting in continuous retransmissions.

Note   The interface command for setting the IPv6 MTU parameter is **ipv6 mtu**. An IPv6 router does not fragment an IPv6 packet unless it is the source of the packet.

To prevent such issues, OSPF requires that the same IPv4 MTU be configured on both sides of the link. If neighbors have a mismatched IPv4 MTU configured, they will not be able to form full OSPF adjacency. They will be stuck in the ExStart adjacency state.

In Example 3-17, the IPv4 MTU size on the R3 Ethernet 0/0 interface is changed to 1400.

Example 3-17   *Configuration of the IPv4 MTU on R3's Ethernet 0/0 Interface*

```
R3(config)# interface ethernet 0/0
R3(config-if)# ip mtu 1400
```

After the IPv4 MTU size is changed on R3's Ethernet 0/0 interface, this creates a mismatch between IPv4 MTU sizes on the link between R3 and R1. This mismatch will result in R3 and R1 not being able to synchronize their OSPF databases, and a new full adjacency between them will not be established. This is observed in Example 3-18 using the **debug ip ospf adj** command on R3. The OSPF process is cleared to reset adjacency, and debug is disabled when the OSPF session is reestablished.

Example 3-18   *Observing a Mismatched MTU*

```
R3# debug ip ospf adj
R3# clear ip ospf process
Reset ALL OSPF processes? [no]: yes
*Jan 19 17:37:05.969: OSPF-3 ADJ    Et0/0: Interface going Up
*Jan 19 17:37:05.969: OSPF-3 ADJ    Et0/0: 2 Way Communication to 1.1.1.1, state 2WAY
*Jan 19 17:37:05.969: OSPF-3 ADJ    Et0/0: Backup seen event before WAIT timer
*Jan 19 17:37:05.969: OSPF-3 ADJ    Et0/0: DR/BDR election
*Jan 19 17:37:05.969: OSPF-3 ADJ    Et0/0: Elect BDR 3.3.3.3
*Jan 19 17:37:05.969: OSPF-3 ADJ    Et0/0: Elect DR 1.1.1.1
*Jan 19 17:37:05.969: OSPF-3 ADJ    Et0/0: Elect BDR 3.3.3.3
*Jan 19 17:37:05.969: OSPF-3 ADJ    Et0/0: Elect DR 1.1.1.1
*Jan 19 17:37:05.969: OSPF-3 ADJ    Et0/0: DR: 1.1.1.1 (Id)    BDR: 3.3.3.3 (Id)
*Jan 19 17:37:05.970: OSPF-3 ADJ    Et0/0: Nbr 1.1.1.1: Prepare dbase exchange
*Jan 19 17:37:05.970: OSPF-3 ADJ    Et0/0: Send DBD to 1.1.1.1 seq 0x21D6 opt 0x52
flag 0x7 len 32
*Jan 19 17:37:05.970: OSPF-3 ADJ    Et0/0: Rcv DBD from 1.1.1.1 seq 0x968 opt 0x52
flag 0x7 len 32  mtu 1500 state EXSTART
*Jan 19 17:37:05.970: OSPF-3 ADJ    Et0/0: Nbr 1.1.1.1 has larger interface MTU
*Jan 19 17:37:05.970: OSPF-3 ADJ    Et0/0: Rcv DBD from 1.1.1.1 seq 0x21D6 opt 0x52
flag 0x2 len 112  mtu 1500 state EXSTART
*Jan 19 17:37:05.970: OSPF-3 ADJ    Et0/0: Nbr 1.1.1.1 has larger interface MTU
R3# no debug ip ospf adj
```

The DBD packet carries information about largest nonfragmented packet that can be sent from the neighbor. In this situation, the IPv4 MTU values on different sides of the link are not equal. R3 will receive the DBD packet with an IPv4 MTU size of 1500, which is greater than its own MTU size of 1400. This will result in the inability of both R3 and R1 to establish full neighbor adjacency, and the output of the **debug** command will display that Nbr has a larger interface MTU message. Mismatched neighbors will stay in ExStart state. To form full OSPF adjacency, the IPv4 MTU needs to match on both sides of the link.

Note By default, the IPv6 MTU must also match between OSPFv3 neighbors. However, you can override this by using the **ospfv3 mtu-ignore** interface command.

In Example 3-19, the OSPF neighbor state is verified on R3 and R1.

Example 3-19 *Verifying the OSPF Neighbor States*

```
R3# show ip ospf neighbor

Neighbor ID     Pri    State           Dead Time    Address          Interface
1.1.1.1          1     EXSTART/BDR     00:00:38     172.16.13.1      Ethernet0/0


R1# show ip ospf neighbor

Neighbor ID     Pri    State           Dead Time    Address          Interface
4.4.4.4          0     FULL/DROTHER    00:00:39     172.16.145.4     Ethernet0/1
5.5.5.5          0     FULL/DROTHER    00:00:38     172.16.145.5     Ethernet0/1
2.2.2.2          1     FULL/DR         00:01:55     172.16.12.2      Serial2/0
3.3.3.3          1     EXCHANGE/DR     00:00:36     172.16.13.2      Ethernet0/0


R1# show ip ospf neighbor

Neighbor ID     Pri    State           Dead Time    Address          Interface
4.4.4.4          0     FULL/DROTHER    00:00:38     172.16.145.4     Ethernet0/1
5.5.5.5          0     FULL/DROTHER    00:00:31     172.16.145.5     Ethernet0/1
2.2.2.2          1     FULL/DR         00:01:31     172.16.12.2      Serial2/0
3.3.3.3          1     INIT/DROTHER    00:00:33     172.16.13.2      Ethernet0/0
```

Mismatching interface IPv4 MTU sizes on opposite sides of the OSPF link results in the inability to form full adjacency. R3, which detected that R1 has higher MTU, keeps the neighbor adjacency in ExStart state. R1 continues to retransmit initial BDB packet to R3, but R3 cannot acknowledge them because of the unequal IPv4 MTU. On R1, you can observe how the OSPF neighbor relationship state with R3 is unstable. Adjacency gets to the Exchange state, but is then terminated, starting again from the Init state up to the Exchange state.

The recommended way to solve such issues is to make sure that the IPv4 MTU matches between OSPF neighbors.

Manipulating OSPF Timers

Similar to EIGRP, OSPF uses two timers to check neighbor reachability: the hello and dead intervals. The values of hello and dead intervals are carried in OSPF Hello packets and serve as a keepalive message, with the purpose of acknowledging the presence of the router on the segment. The hello interval specifies the frequency of sending OSPF Hello packets in seconds. The OSPF dead timer specifies how long a router waits to receive a Hello packet before it declares a neighbor router as down.

OSPF requires that both hello and dead timers be identical for all routers on the segment to become OSPF neighbors. The default value of the OSPF hello timer on multiaccess broadcast and point-to-point links is 10 seconds, and is 30 seconds on all other network types, including NBMA. When you configure the hello interval, the default value of the dead interval is automatically adjusted to four times the hello interval. For broadcast and point-to-point links, it is 40 seconds, and for all other OSPF network types, it is 120 seconds.

To detect faster topological changes, you can lower the value of OSPF hello interval, with the downside of having more routing traffic on the link. The **debug ip ospf hello** command enables you to investigate hello timer mismatch.

In Example 3-20, R1, the different hello/dead timer values on Ethernet 0/1, and Frame Relay Serial 2/0 interfaces are observed using the **show ip ospf interface** command.

Example 3-20   *Examining the Hello/Dead Timers on R1 Interfaces*

```
R1# show ip ospf interface ethernet 0/1
Ethernet0/1 is up, line protocol is up
  Internet Address 172.16.145.1/29, Area 0, Attached via Network Statement
  Process ID 1, Router ID 1.1.1.1, Network Type BROADCAST, Cost: 10
  Topology-MTID    Cost    Disabled    Shutdown       Topology Name
       0            10        no          no             Base
  Transmit Delay is 1 sec, State DROTHER, Priority 1
  Designated Router (ID) 5.5.5.5, Interface address 172.16.145.5
  Backup Designated router (ID) 4.4.4.4, Interface address 172.16.145.4
  Timer intervals configured, Hello 10, Dead 40, Wait 40, Retransmit 5
<Output omitted>


R1# show ip ospf interface serial 2/0
Serial2/0 is up, line protocol is up
  Internet Address 172.16.12.1/30, Area 1, Attached via Network Statement
  Process ID 1, Router ID 1.1.1.1, Network Type NON_BROADCAST, Cost: 64
  Topology-MTID    Cost    Disabled    Shutdown       Topology Name
       0            64        no          no             Base
  Transmit Delay is 1 sec, State BDR, Priority 1
  Designated Router (ID) 2.2.2.2, Interface address 172.16.12.2
  Backup Designated router (ID) 1.1.1.1, Interface address 172.16.12.1
  Timer intervals configured, Hello 30, Dead 120, Wait 120, Retransmit 5
<Output omitted>
```

The default value of the OSPF hello interval on broadcast multiaccess (Ethernet) and point-to-point links is 10 seconds, and the default value of the dead interval is four times hello (40 seconds). Default values of the OSPF hello and dead timers on all other OSPF network types, including nonbroadcast (NBMA) like Frame Relay on the Serial 2/0 interface, are 30 seconds and 120 seconds, respectively.

On low-speed links, you might want to alter default OSPF timer values to achieve faster convergence. The negative aspect of lowering the OSPF hello interval is the overhead of more frequent routing updates causing higher router utilization and more traffic on the link.

In Example 3-21, the default OSPF hello and dead intervals on R1's Frame Relay Serial 2/0 interface are modified. You can change the OSPF by using the **ip ospf hello-interval** and **ip ospf dead-interval** interface commands.

Example 3-21   *Modifying the Hello and Dead Intervals on R1's Serial Interface*

```
R1(config)# interface serial 2/0
R1(config-if)# ip ospf hello-interval 8
R1(config-if)# ip ospf dead-interval 30
*Jan 20 13:17:34.441: %OSPF-5-ADJCHG: Process 1, Nbr 2.2.2.2 on Serial2/0 from
FULL to DOWN, Neighbor Down: Dead timer expired
```

Once the default OSPF hello and dead interval values on the Frame Relay link are changed, both routers will detect hello timer mismatch. As a result, the dead timer will not be refreshed, so it will expire, declaring the OSPF neighbor relationship as down.

Note   When you are changing only the OSPF hello interval, OSPF automatically changes the dead interval to four times the hello interval.

In Example 3-22, R2's default OSPF hello and dead timers on the Frame Relay Serial 0/0 interface are changed so that they match respective values configured on R1.

Example 3-22   *Modifying the Hello and Dead Intervals on R2's Serial Interface*

```
R2(config)# interface serial 0/0
R2(config-if)# ip ospf hello-interval 8
R2(config-if)# ip ospf dead-interval 30
*Jan 20 13:38:58.976: %OSPF-5-ADJCHG: Process 2, Nbr 1.1.1.1 on Serial0/0 from
LOADING to FULL, Loading Done
```

When you are changing OSPF hello and dead timers on R2 so that they match the timers on R1, both routers on the link will be able to establish adjacency and elect the DR/BDR on the NBMA segment. Routers will then exchange and synchronize LSDBs and form full neighbor adjacency.

On R2, the OSPF neighbor state is verified by using the **show ip ospf neighbor detail** command, as demonstrated in Example 3-23.

Example 3-23   *Verifying the OSPF Neighbor States on R2*

```
R2# show ip ospf neighbor detail
Neighbor 1.1.1.1, interface address 172.16.12.1
   In the area 1 via interface Serial0/0
   Neighbor priority is 1, State is FULL, 6 state changes
   DR is 172.16.12.2 BDR is 172.16.12.1
   Poll interval 120
   Options is 0x12 in Hello (E-bit, L-bit)
   Options is 0x52 in DBD (E-bit, L-bit, O-bit)
   LLS Options is 0x1 (LR)
   Dead timer due in 00:00:26
   Neighbor is up for 00:14:57
   Index 1/1, retransmission queue length 0, number of retransmission 0
   First 0x0(0)/0x0(0) Next 0x0(0)/0x0(0)
   Last retransmission scan length is 0, maximum is 0
   Last retransmission scan time is 0 msec, maximum is 0 msec
```

The output of the **show ip ospf neighbor detail** command confirms that full OSPF adjacency with R1 is established. The output also shows additional information about neighbor router ID, DR/BDR roles, and how long the neighbor session has been established.

OSPF Neighbor Relationship over Point-to-Point Links

Figure 3-7 shows a point-to-point network joining a single pair of routers. A T1 serial line that is configured with a data link layer protocol such as PPP or High-Level Data Link Control (HDLC) is an example of a point-to-point network.

Figure 3-7   *Point-to-Point link*

On these types of networks, the router dynamically detects its neighboring routers by multicasting its Hello packets to all OSPF routers, using the 224.0.0.5 address. On point-to-point networks, neighboring routers become adjacent whenever they can communicate directly. No DR or BDR election is performed; there can be only two routers on a point-to-point link, so there is no need for a DR or BDR.

The default OSPF hello and dead timers on point-to-point links are 10 seconds and 40 seconds, respectively.

OSPF Neighbor Relationship over Layer 3 MPLS VPN

Figure 3-8 shows a Layer 3 MPLS VPN architecture, where the ISP provides a peer-to-peer VPN architecture. In this architecture, provider edge (PE) routers participate in customer routing, guaranteeing optimum routing between customer sites. Therefore, the PE routers carry a separate set of routes for each customer, resulting in perfect isolation between customers.

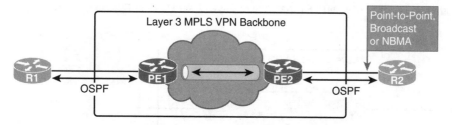

Figure 3-8 *Layer 3 MPLS VPN*

The following applies to Layer 3 MPLS VPN technology, even when running OSPF as a provider edge - customer edge (PE-CE) routing protocol:

■ The customer routers should not be aware of MPLS VPN; they should run standard IP routing software.

■ The core routers in the provider network between the two PE routers are known as the P routers (not shown in the diagram). The P routers do not carry customer VPN routes for the MPLS VPN solution to be scalable.

■ The PE routers must support MPLS VPN services and traditional Internet services.

To OSPF, the Layer 3 MPLS VPN backbone looks like a standard corporate backbone that runs standard IP routing software. Routing updates are exchanged between the customer routers and the PE routers that appear as normal routers in the customer network. OSPF is enabled on proper interfaces by using the **network** command. The standard design rules that are used for enterprise Layer 3 MPLS VPN backbones can be applied to the design of the customer network. The service provider routers are hidden from the customer view, and CE routers are unaware of MPLS VPN. Therefore, the internal topology of the Layer 3 MPLS backbone is totally transparent to the customer. The PE routers receive IPv4 routing updates from the CE routers and install them in the appropriate virtual routing and forwarding (VRF) table. This part of the configuration, and operation, is the responsibility of a service provider.

The PE-CE can have any OSPF network type: point-to-point, broadcast, or even non-broadcast multiaccess.

The only difference between a PE-CE design and a regular OSPF design is that the customer has to agree with the service provider about the OSPF parameters (area ID, authentication password, and so on); usually, these parameters are governed by the service provider.

OSPF Neighbor Relationship over Layer 2 MPLS VPN

Figure 3-9 shows a Layer 2 MPLS VPN. The MPLS backbone of the service provider is used to enable Layer 2 Ethernet connectivity between the customer routers R1 and R2, whether an Ethernet over MPLS (EoMPLS) or Layer 2 MPLS VPN Ethernet service is used.

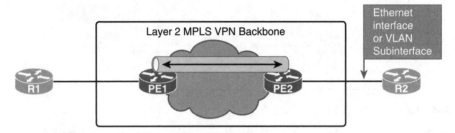

Figure 3-9   *Layer 2 MPLS VPN*

R1 and R2 thus exchange Ethernet frames. PE router PE1 takes the Ethernet frames that are received from R1 on the link to PE1, encapsulates them into MPLS packets, and forwards them across the backbone to router PE2. PE2 decapsulates the MPLS packets and reproduces the Ethernet frames on the link toward R2. EoMPLS and Layer 2 MPLS VPN typically do not participate in Spanning Tree Protocol (STP) and bridge protocol data unit (BPDU) exchanges, so EoMPLS and Layer 2 MPLS VPNs are transparent to the customer routers.

The Ethernet frames are transparently exchanged across the MPLS backbone. Keep in mind that customer routers can be connected either in a port-to-port fashion, in which PE routers take whatever Ethernet frame is received and forward the frames across the Layer 2 MPLS VPN backbone, or in a VLAN subinterface fashion in which frames for a particular VLAN—identified with subinterface in configuration—are encapsulated and sent across the Layer 2 MPLS VPN backbone.

When deploying OSPF over EoMPLS, there are no changes to the existing OSPF configuration from the customer perspective.

OSPF needs to be enabled, and network commands must include the interfaces that are required by the relevant OSPF area to start the OSPF properly.

R1 and R2 form a neighbor relationship with each other over the Layer 2 MPLS VPN backbone. From an OSPF perspective, the Layer 2 MPLS VPN backbone, PE1, and PE2 are all invisible.

A neighbor relationship is established between R1 and R2 directly, and it behaves in the same way as on a regular Ethernet broadcast network.

OSPF Neighbor States

OSPF neighbors go through multiple neighbor states before forming full OSPF adjacency, as illustrated in Figure 3-10.

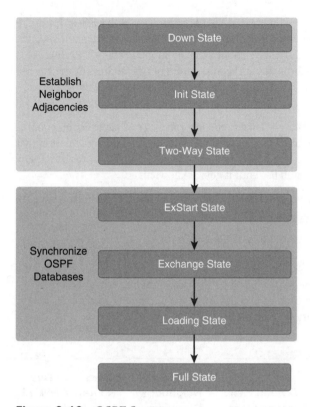

Figure 3-10 *OSPF States*

The following is a brief summary of the states that an interface passes through before becoming adjacent to another router:

■ **Down:** No information has been received on the segment.

■ **Init:** The interface has detected a Hello packet coming from a neighbor, but bidirectional communication has not yet been established.

■ **2-Way:** There is bidirectional communication with a neighbor. The router has seen itself in the Hello packets coming from a neighbor. At the end of this stage, the DR and BDR election would have been done if necessary. When routers are in the 2-Way state, they must decide whether to proceed in building an adjacency. The decision is based on whether one of the routers is a DR or BDR or the link is a point-to-point or a virtual link.

■ **ExStart:** Routers are trying to establish the initial sequence number that is going to be used in the information exchange packets. The sequence number ensures that routers always get the most recent information. One router will become the master and the other will become the slave. The master (primary) router will poll the slave (secondary) for information.

■ **Exchange:** Routers will describe their entire LSDB by sending database description (DBD) packets. A DBD includes information about the LSA entry header that appears in the router's LSDB. The entries can be about a link or about a network. Each LSA entry header includes information about the link-state type, the address of the advertising router, the link's cost, and the sequence number. The router uses the sequence number to determine the "newness" of the received link-state information.

■ **Loading:** In this state, routers are finalizing the information exchange. Routers have built a link-state request list and a link-state retransmission list. Any information that looks incomplete or outdated will be put on the request list. Any update that is sent will be put on the retransmission list until it gets acknowledged.

■ **Full:** In this state, adjacency is complete. The neighboring routers are fully adjacent. Adjacent routers will have similar LSDBs.

OSPF Network Types

OSPF defines distinct types of networks based on their physical link types, as shown in Table 3-1. OSPF operation on each type is different, including how adjacencies are established and which configuration is required.

Table 3-1   *OSPF Network Types*

OSPF Network Type	Uses DR/BDR	Default Hello Interval (sec)	Dynamic Neighbor Discovery	More than Two Routers Allowed in Subnet
Point-to-point	No	10	Yes	No
Broadcast	Yes	10	Yes	Yes
Nonbroadcast	Yes	30	No	Yes
Point-to-multipoint	No	30	Yes	Yes
Point-to-multipoint nonbroadcast	No	30	No	Yes
Loopback	No	—	—	No

These are the most common network types that are defined by OSPF:

■ **Point-to-point:** Routers use multicast to dynamically discover neighbors. There is no DR/BDR election because only two routers can be connected on a single point-to-point segment. It is a default OSPF network type for serial links and point-to-point Frame Relay subinterfaces.

■ **Broadcast:** Multicast is used to dynamically discover neighbors. The DR and BDR are elected to optimize the exchange of information. It is a default OSPF network type for Ethernet links.

- **Nonbroadcast:** Used on networks that interconnect more than two routers but without broadcast capability. Frame Relay and ATM are examples of NBMA networks. Neighbors must be statically configured, followed by DR/BDR election. This network type is the default for all physical interfaces and multipoint subinterfaces using Frame Relay encapsulation.

- **Point-to-multipoint:** OSPF treats this network type as a logical collection of point-to-point links even though all interfaces belong to the common IP subnet. Every interface IP address will appear in the routing table of the neighbors as a host /32 route. Neighbors are discovered dynamically using multicast. No DR/BDR election occurs.

- **Point-to-multipoint nonbroadcast:** Cisco extension that has the same characteristics as point-to-multipoint type except for the fact that neighbors are not discovered dynamically. Neighbors must be statically defined, and unicast is used for communication. Can be useful in point-to-multipoint scenarios where multicast and broadcast are not supported.

- **Loopback:** Default network type on loopback interfaces.

You can change OSPF network type by using the interface configuration mode command **ip ospf network** *network_type*.

Configuring Passive Interfaces

Passive interface configuration is a common method for hardening routing protocols and reducing the use of resources. The passive interface is supported by OSPF, and a sample configuration is shown in Example 3-24.

Example 3-24 *Passive Interface Configuration for OSPF*

```
Router(config)# router ospf 1
Router(config-router)# passive-interface default
Router(config-router)# no passive-interface serial 1/0
```

When you configure a passive interface under the OSPF process, the router stops sending and receiving OSPF Hello packets on the selected interface. The passive interface should be used only on interfaces where the router is not expected to form any OSPF neighbor adjacency. A specific interface can be configured as passive, or passive interface can be configured as the default. If the default option is used, any interfaces that need to form a neighbor adjacency must be exempted with the **no passive-interface** configuration command.

Building the Link-State Database

OSPF, as a link-state protocol, uses several different packets to exchange the information about network topology between routers. These packets are called *link-state advertisements* (LSAs), and they describe the network topology in great detail. Each router stores the received LSA packets in the link-state database (LSDB). After LSDBs are synced between the routers, OSPF uses the shortest path first (SPF) algorithm to calculate the best routes. The best intra-area routes are calculated individually by each OSPF router. For the best interarea route calculation, the internal router must rely also on the best path information received from the ABRs.

Upon completing this section, you will be able to do the following:

- List and describe different LSA types

- Describe how OSPF LSAs are also reflooded at periodic intervals

- Describe the exchange of information in a network without a designated router

- Describe the exchange of information in a network with a designated router

- Explain when SPF algorithms occur

- Describe how the cost of intra-area routes is calculated

- Describe how the cost of interarea routes is calculated

- Describe rules selecting between intra-area and interarea routes

OSPF LSA Types

Knowing the detailed topology of the OSPF area is required for a router to calculate the best paths. Topology details are described by LSAs, which are the building blocks of the OSPF LSDB. Individually, LSAs act as database records. In combination, they describe the entire topology of an OSPF network area. Figure 3-11 shows a sample topology, highlighting the most common types of OSPF LSAs, which are described in further detail in the list that follows.

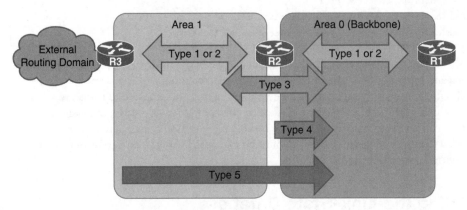

Figure 3-11 *OSPF LSA Types*

- **Type 1, Router LSA:** Every router generates router link advertisements for each area to which it belongs. Router link advertisements describe the state of the router links to the area and are flooded only within that particular area. For all types of LSAs, there are 20-byte LSA headers. One of the fields of the LSA header is the link-state ID. The link-state ID of the type 1 LSA is the originating router ID.

- **Type 2, Network LSA:** DRs generate network link advertisements for multiaccess networks. Network link advertisements describe the set of routers that are attached to a particular multiaccess network. Network link advertisements are flooded in the area that contains the network. The link-state ID of the type 2 LSA is the IP interface address of the DR.

- **Type 3, Summary LSA:** An ABR takes the information that it learned in one area and describes and summarizes it for another area in the summary link advertisement. This summarization is not on by default. The link-state ID of the type 3 LSA is the destination network number.

- **Type 4, ASBR Summary LSA:** The ASBR summary link advertisement informs the rest of the OSPF domain how to get to the ASBR. The link-state ID includes the router ID of the described ASBR.

- **Type 5, Autonomous System LSA:** Autonomous system external link advertisements, which are generated by ASBRs, describe routes to destinations that are external to the autonomous system. They get flooded everywhere, except into special areas. The link-state ID of the type 5 LSA is the external network number.

Other LSA types include the following:

- **Type 6:** Specialized LSAs that are used in multicast OSPF applications

- **Type 7:** Used in special area type NSSA for external routes

- **Type 8, 9:** Used in OSPFv3 for link-local addresses and intra-area prefix

- **Type 10, 11:** Generic LSAs, also called *opaque*, which allow future extensions of OSPF

Examining the OSPF Link-State Database

This section analyzes the OSPF LSDB and the different types of LSAs using the topology in Figure 3-12. All routers have already been preconfigured with OSPF. In the figure, R1 is an ABR between areas 0, 1, and 2. R3 acts as the ASBR between the OSPF routing domain and an external domain. LSA types 1 and 2 are flooded between routers within an area. Type 3 and type 5 LSAs are flooded when exchanging information about backbone and standard areas. Type 4 LSAs are injected into the backbone by the ABR because all routers in the OSPF domain need to reach the ASBR (R3).

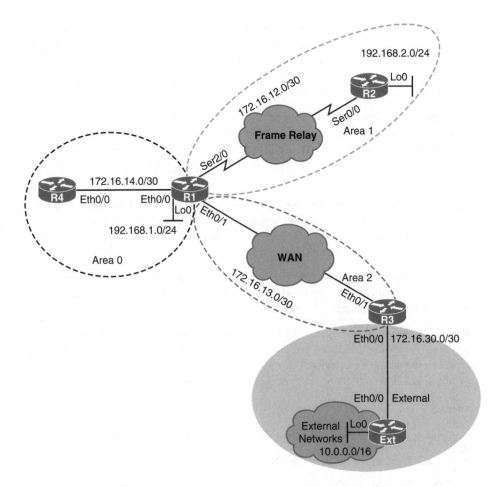

Figure 3-12   *OSPF Topology*

OSPF Link-State Database

Example 3-25 shows R4's routing table, which includes several OSPF routes because all the routers have already been configured.

Example 3-25   *R4's Routing Table*

```
R4# show ip route
Codes: L - local, C - connected, S - static, R - RIP, M - mobile, B - BGP
       D - EIGRP, EX - EIGRP external, O - OSPF, IA - OSPF inter area
       N1 - OSPF NSSA external type 1, N2 - OSPF NSSA external type 2
       E1 - OSPF external type 1, E2 - OSPF external type 2
       i - IS-IS, su - IS-IS summary, L1 - IS-IS level-1, L2 - IS-IS level-2
       ia - IS-IS inter area, * - candidate default, U - per-user static route
       o - ODR, P - periodic downloaded static route, H - NHRP, l - LISP
```

```
            + - replicated route, % - next hop override

Gateway of last resort is not set


      10.0.0.0/16 is subnetted, 1 subnets
O E2      10.0.0.0 [110/20] via 172.16.14.1, 00:46:48, Ethernet0/0
      172.16.0.0/16 is variably subnetted, 4 subnets, 2 masks
O IA     172.16.12.0/30 [110/74] via 172.16.14.1, 03:19:12, Ethernet0/0
O IA     172.16.13.0/30 [110/20] via 172.16.14.1, 03:19:12, Ethernet0/0
C        172.16.14.0/30 is directly connected, Ethernet0/0
L        172.16.14.2/32 is directly connected, Ethernet0/0
O      192.168.1.0/24 [110/11] via 172.16.14.1, 00:36:19, Ethernet0/0
O IA   192.168.2.0/24 [110/75] via 172.16.14.1, 00:47:59, Ethernet0/0
```

Notice the intra-area route 192.168.1.0/24 and interarea routes describing WAN links 172.16.12.0/30, 172.16.13.0/30, and the remote subnet 192.168.2.0/24 on R2. There is also routing information about an OSPF external route that is describing network 10.0.0.0/16. This route is injected into OSPF on R3, which has connectivity to external networks.

Example 3-26 displays the OSPF database on R4.

Example 3-26 *R4's OSPF LSDB*

```
R4# show ip ospf database

            OSPF Router with ID (4.4.4.4) (Process ID 1)


            Router Link States (Area 0)


Link ID          ADV Router       Age        Seq#        Checksum Link count
1.1.1.1          1.1.1.1          291        0x8000000B 0x00966C 2
4.4.4.4          4.4.4.4          1993       0x80000007 0x001C4E 1


            Net Link States (Area 0)


Link ID          ADV Router       Age        Seq#        Checksum
172.16.14.2      4.4.4.4          1993       0x80000006 0x0091B5


            Summary Net Link States (Area 0)


Link ID          ADV Router       Age        Seq#        Checksum
172.16.12.0      1.1.1.1          291        0x80000007 0x00C567
172.16.13.0      1.1.1.1          291        0x80000007 0x009CC5
192.168.2.0      1.1.1.1          1031       0x80000002 0x002E5D
```

```
                    Summary ASB Link States (Area 0)

Link ID          ADV Router       Age         Seq#          Checksum
3.3.3.3          1.1.1.1          1031        0x80000002 0x0035EB


                    Type-5 AS External Link States

Link ID          ADV Router       Age         Seq#          Checksum   Tag
10.0.0.0          3.3.3.3         977         0x80000002  0x000980     0
```

The OSPF database contains all LSAs that describe the network topology. The **show ip ospf database** command displays the content of the LSDB and verifies information about specific LSAs.

The output reveals the presence of different LSA types. For each LSA type, you can see which router advertised it, the age of the LSA, and the value of the link ID.

In Example 3-26, notice two different type 1 LSAs, or router link advertisements, generated by routers with router ID 1.1.1.1 and 4.4.4.4.

Example 3-27 displays the details of R4's type 1 LSAs

Example 3-27   *R4 Type 1 LSA Details*

```
R4# show ip ospf database router

            OSPF Router with ID (4.4.4.4) (Process ID 1)


               Router Link States (Area 0)


Routing Bit Set on this LSA in topology Base with MTID 0
LS age: 321
Options: (No TOS-capability, DC)
LS Type: Router Links
Link State ID: 1.1.1.1
Advertising Router: 1.1.1.1
LS Seq Number: 8000000B
Checksum: 0x966C
Length: 48
Area Border Router
Number of Links: 2


  Link connected to: a Stub Network
   (Link ID) Network/subnet number: 192.168.1.0
   (Link Data) Network Mask: 255.255.255.0
   Number of MTID metrics: 0
    TOS 0 Metrics: 1
```

```
Link connected to: a Transit Network
 (Link ID) Designated Router address: 172.16.14.2
 (Link Data) Router Interface address: 172.16.14.1
  Number of MTID metrics: 0
   TOS 0 Metrics: 10


LS age: 2023
Options: (No TOS-capability, DC)
LS Type: Router Links
Link State ID: 4.4.4.4
Advertising Router: 4.4.4.4
LS Seq Number: 80000007
Checksum: 0x1C4E
Length: 36
Number of Links: 1

  Link connected to: a Transit Network
   (Link ID) Designated Router address: 172.16.14.2
   (Link Data) Router Interface address: 172.16.14.2
    Number of MTID metrics: 0
     TOS 0 Metrics: 10
```

Type 1 LSAs are generated by every router and flooded within the area. They describe the state of the router links in that area. R4 has two type 1 LSAs in the database: one received from R1 with router ID 1.1.1.1, and one that was generated by R4.

The content of the displayed LSA reveals that R1 is an ABR with two links. The output shows details for both links, to what kind of network the links are connected, and their settings, such as the IP configuration. Link can be connected to a stub, to another router (point-to-point), or to a transit network. The transit network describes Ethernet or NMBA segment, which can include two or more routers. If the link is connected to a transit network, the LSA also includes the info about the DR address.

The LSDB keeps copies of all LSAs, including those that were generated locally on the router. An example of a local LSA is the second advertisement that is displayed in the output. It includes the same topology parameters as the first LSA, but this time from a perspective of router R4.

OSPF identifies all LSAs using a 32-bit LSID. When generating a type 1 LSA, the router uses its own router ID as the value of LSID.

Using the **self-originate** command argument, Example 3-28 displays locally generated type 1 LSAs on R4.

Example 3-28 *Locally Generated Type 1 LSAs on R4*

```
R4# show ip ospf database router self-originate

                OSPF Router with ID (4.4.4.4) (Process ID 1)


                Router Link States (Area 0)


  LS age: 23
  Options: (No TOS-capability, DC)
  LS Type: Router Links
  Link State ID: 4.4.4.4
  Advertising Router: 4.4.4.4
  LS Seq Number: 80000008
  Checksum: 0x1A4F
  Length: 36
  Number of Links: 1


    Link connected to: a Transit Network
     (Link ID) Designated Router address: 172.16.14.2
     (Link Data) Router Interface address: 172.16.14.2
     Number of MTID metrics: 0
       TOS 0 Metrics: 10
```

The output shows the type 1 LSA, which describes the interface that is enabled in OSPF area 0 on router R4.

R4 has an interface that is connected to a transit network; therefore, the DR information is also included. You can see that R4 is the DR on the segment.

Example 3-29 shows the OSPF database on router R2.

Example 3-29 *R2's OSPF LSDB*

```
R2# show ip ospf database

            OSPF Router with ID (2.2.2.2) (Process ID 1)


                Router Link States (Area 1)


Link ID         ADV Router      Age         Seq#        Checksum Link count
1.1.1.1         1.1.1.1         403         0x80000008 0x0097B7 1
2.2.2.2         2.2.2.2         1088        0x80000008 0x006E5C 2


                Net Link States (Area 1)


Link ID         ADV Router      Age         Seq#        Checksum
```

```
172.16.12.2     2.2.2.2         587         0x80000003 0x00A5B6


                Summary Net Link States (Area 1)


Link ID         ADV Router      Age         Seq#       Checksum
172.16.13.0     1.1.1.1         403         0x80000007 0x009CC5
172.16.14.0     1.1.1.1         403         0x80000007 0x0091CF
192.168.1.0     1.1.1.1         403         0x80000002 0x00B616


                Summary ASB Link States (Area 1)


Link ID         ADV Router      Age         Seq#       Checksum
3.3.3.3         1.1.1.1         1143        0x80000002 0x0035EB


                Type-5 AS External Link States


Link ID         ADV Router      Age         Seq#       Checksum Tag
10.0.0.0        3.3.3.3         1089        0x80000002 0x000980 0
```

OSPF type 1 LSAs are exchanged only within OSPF areas. Router R2, which has interfaces that are configured in OSPF area 1, should not see any type 1 LSAs that were originated on R4. The output of the OSPF database from R2 confirms this. No type 1 LSA with the advertising router parameter set to 4.4.4.4 can be found in the LSDB.

Example 3-30 displays the LSAs on R1.

Example 3-30 *R1's OSPF LSDB*

```
R1# show ip ospf database


                OSPF Router with ID (1.1.1.1) (Process ID 1)


                Router Link States (Area 0)
Link ID         ADV Router      Age         Seq#       Checksum Link count
1.1.1.1         1.1.1.1         445         0x8000000B 0x00966C 2
4.4.4.4         4.4.4.4         103         0x80000008 0x001A4F 1
<Output omitted>
                Router Link States (Area 1)
Link ID         ADV Router      Age         Seq#       Checksum Link count
1.1.1.1         1.1.1.1         445         0x80000008 0x0097B7 1
2.2.2.2         2.2.2.2         1133        0x80000008 0x006E5C 2
 <Output omitted>
                Router Link States (Area 2)
Link ID         ADV Router      Age         Seq#       Checksum Link count
1.1.1.1         1.1.1.1         445         0x80000008 0x00DDA5 1
3.3.3.3         3.3.3.3         1131        0x8000000A 0x00521D 1
 <Output omitted>
```

Notice that router R1 is the only router that is in multiple areas. As an ABR, its OSPF database includes type 1 LSAs from all three areas.

OSPF Type 2 Network LSA

Figure 3-13 shows a type 2 LSA, which is generated for every transit broadcast or NBMA network within an area.

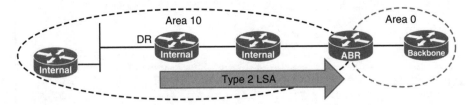

Figure 3-13   *OSPF Type 2 LSA*

The DR of the network is responsible for advertising the network LSA. A type 2 network LSA lists each of the attached routers that make up the transit network, including the DR itself, and the subnet mask that is used on the link. The type 2 LSA then floods to all routers within the transit network area. Type 2 LSAs never cross an area boundary. The link-state ID for a network LSA is the IP interface address of the DR that advertises it.

Example 3-31 shows R4's OSPF LSDB with a focus on the type 2 LSAs.

Example 3-31   *R4's Type 2 LSAs*

```
R4# show ip ospf database


            OSPF Router with ID (4.4.4.4) (Process ID 1)


            Router Link States (Area 0)


Link ID         ADV Router      Age        Seq#       Checksum Link count
1.1.1.1         1.1.1.1         486        0x8000000B 0x00966C 2
4.4.4.4         4.4.4.4         142        0x80000008 0x001A4F 1


            Net Link States (Area 0)


Link ID         ADV Router      Age        Seq#       Checksum
172.16.14.2     4.4.4.4         142        0x80000007 0x008FB6
<Output omitted>
```

Notice that R4 has only one type 2 LSA in its LSDB. This is expected because there is only one multiaccess network in area 0.

Example 3-32 shows the details of a type 2 LSA on router R4.

Example 3-32 *R4's Type 2 LSA Details*

```
R4# show ip ospf database network


            OSPF Router with ID (4.4.4.4) (Process ID 1)


                 Net Link States (Area 0)


Routing Bit Set on this LSA in topology Base with MTID 0
LS age: 170
Options: (No TOS-capability, DC)
LS Type: Network Links
Link State ID: 172.16.14.2 (address of Designated Router)
Advertising Router: 4.4.4.4
LS Seq Number: 80000007
Checksum: 0x8FB6
Length: 32
Network Mask: /30
        Attached Router: 4.4.4.4
        Attached Router: 1.1.1.1
```

The content of the displayed type 2 LSA describes the network segment listing the DR
address, the attached routers, and the used subnet mask. This information is used by
each router participating in OSPF to build the exact picture of the described multiaccess
segment, which cannot be fully described with just type 1 LSAs.

OSPF Type 3 Summary LSA

ABRs do not forward type 1 and 2 LSAs between areas to improve OSPF scalability.
However, other routers still need to learn how to reach interarea subnets in other areas.
OSPF advertises these subnets on ABRs by using type 3 summary LSAs, as shown in
Figure 3-14.

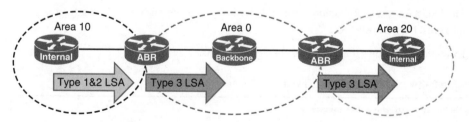

Figure 3-14 *OSPF Type 3 LSA*

The ABRs generate type 3 summary LSAs to describe any networks that are owned by an
area to the rest of the areas in the OSPF autonomous system, as shown in the figure.

Summary LSAs are flooded throughout a single area only, but are regenerated by ABRs
to flood into other areas.

Notice that the figure only illustrates how information is propagated from area 10 to the other areas. Type 3 LSAs are also advertised by ABRs in other direction, from area 20 to area 0, and from area 0 into area 10.

By default, OSPF does not automatically summarize groups of contiguous subnets. OSPF does not summarize a network to its classful boundary. A type 3 LSA is advertised into the backbone area for every subnet that is defined in the originating area, which can cause flooding problems in larger networks.

As a best practice, you can use manual route summarization on ABRs to limit the amount of information that is exchanged between the areas.

Example 3-33 displays R4's OSPF LSDB, with the focus on type 3 LSAs.

Example 3-33 *R4's Type 3 LSAs*

```
R4# show ip ospf database


            OSPF Router with ID (4.4.4.4) (Process ID 1)


            Router Link States (Area 0)
Link ID         ADV Router      Age        Seq#       Checksum Link count
1.1.1.1         1.1.1.1         583        0x8000000B 0x00966C 2
4.4.4.4         4.4.4.4         238        0x80000008 0x001A4F 1
            Net Link States (Area 0)
Link ID         ADV Router      Age        Seq#       Checksum
172.16.14.2     4.4.4.4         238        0x80000007 0x008FB6
            Summary Net Link States (Area 0)
Link ID         ADV Router      Age        Seq#       Checksum
172.16.12.0     1.1.1.1         583        0x80000007 0x00C567
172.16.13.0     1.1.1.1         583        0x80000007 0x009CC5
192.168.2.0     1.1.1.1         1322       0x80000002 0x002E5D
<Output omitted>
```

The LSDB on router R4 includes three different type 3 summary LSAs, all advertised into area 1 by the ABR R1.

Example 3-34 shows the details of R4's type 3 LSAs.

Example 3-34 *R4's Type 3 LSA Details*

```
R4# show ip ospf database summary


            OSPF Router with ID (4.4.4.4) (Process ID 1)


            Summary Net Link States (Area 0)


Routing Bit Set on this LSA in topology Base with MTID 0
```

```
LS age: 608
Options: (No TOS-capability, DC, Upward)
LS Type: Summary Links(Network)
Link State ID: 172.16.12.0 (summary Network Number)
Advertising Router: 1.1.1.1
LS Seq Number: 80000007
Checksum: 0xC567
Length: 28
Network Mask: /30
     MTID: 0          Metric: 64


Routing Bit Set on this LSA in topology Base with MTID 0
LS age: 608
Options: (No TOS-capability, DC, Upward)
LS Type: Summary Links(Network)
Link State ID: 172.16.13.0 (summary Network Number)
Advertising Router: 1.1.1.1
LS Seq Number: 80000007
Checksum: 0x9CC5
Length: 28
Network Mask: /30
     MTID: 0          Metric: 10


Routing Bit Set on this LSA in topology Base with MTID 0
LS age: 1348
Options: (No TOS-capability, DC, Upward)
LS Type: Summary Links(Network)
Link State ID: 192.168.2.0 (summary Network Number)
Advertising Router: 1.1.1.1
LS Seq Number: 80000002
Checksum: 0x2E5D
Length: 28
Network Mask: /24
     MTID: 0        Metric: 65
```

The output in the examples shows detailed information about three type 3 LSAs in the LSDB. Each type 3 LSA has a link-state ID field, which carries the network address, and together with the attached subnet mask describes the interarea network. Notice that all three LSAs were advertised by the router having router ID set to 1.1.1.1, which is the ABR router R1.

OSPF Type 4 ASBR Summary LSA

Figure 3-15 shows a type 4 summary LSA generated by an ABR only when an ASBR exists within an area. A type 4 LSA identifies the ASBR and provides a route to the

ASBR. The link-state ID is set to the ASBR router ID. All traffic that is destined to an external autonomous system requires routing table knowledge of the ASBR that originated the external routes.

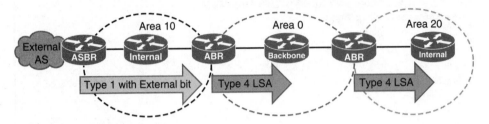

Figure 3-15   *OSPF Type 4 LSA*

In the figure, the ASBR sends a type 1 router LSA with a bit (known as the *external bit*) that is set to identify itself as an ASBR. When the ABR (identified with the border bit in the router LSA) receives this type 1 LSA, it builds a type 4 LSA and floods it to the backbone, area 0. Subsequent ABRs regenerate a type 4 LSA to flood it into their areas.

Example 3-35 shows R4's OSPF LSDB with a focus on type 4 LSAs.

Example 3-35   *R4's Type 4 LSAs*

```
R4# show ip ospf database

            OSPF Router with ID (4.4.4.4) (Process ID 1)

            Router Link States (Area 0)

Link ID         ADV Router      Age         Seq#        Checksum Link count
1.1.1.1         1.1.1.1         666         0x8000000B 0x00966C 2
4.4.4.4         4.4.4.4         321         0x80000008 0x001A4F 1

            Net Link States (Area 0)

Link ID         ADV Router      Age         Seq#        Checksum
172.16.14.2     4.4.4.4         321         0x80000007 0x008FB6

            Summary Net Link States (Area 0)

Link ID         ADV Router      Age         Seq#        Checksum
172.16.12.0     1.1.1.1         666         0x80000007 0x00C567
172.16.13.0     1.1.1.1         666         0x80000007 0x009CC5
192.168.2.0     1.1.1.1         1405        0x80000002 0x002E5D


            Summary ASB Link States (Area 0)

```

```
Link ID          ADV Router         Age        Seq#       Checksum
3.3.3.3          1.1.1.1            1405       0x80000002 0x0035EB


                 Type-5 AS External Link States


Link ID          ADV Router         Age        Seq#       Checksum Tag
10.0.0.0         3.3.3.3            1351       0x80000002 0x000980 0
```

There is only one type 4 LSA present in the R4 OSPF database. The type 4 LSA was generated by ABR R1 and describing the ASBR with the router ID 3.3.3.3.

Example 3-36 shows the details of the type 4 LSA on R4.

Example 3-36 *R4's Type 4 LSA Details*

```
R4# show ip ospf database asbr-summary


               OSPF Router with ID (4.4.4.4) (Process ID 1)


                  Summary ASB Link States (Area 0)


Routing Bit Set on this LSA in topology Base with MTID 0
LS age: 1420
Options: (No TOS-capability, DC, Upward)
LS Type: Summary Links(AS Boundary Router)
Link State ID: 3.3.3.3 (AS Boundary Router address)
Advertising Router: 1.1.1.1
LS Seq Number: 80000002
Checksum: 0x35EB
Length: 28
Network Mask: /0
      MTID: 0          Metric: 10
```

A type 4 LSA contains information about the existence of the ASBR in the OSPF autonomous system. The information is advertised to R4 from R1, which recognizes the ASBR capability of R3 with a router ID of 3.3.3.3.

OSPF Type 5 External LSA

Figure 3-16 shows type 5 external LSAs used to describe routes to networks outside the OSPF autonomous system. Type 5 LSAs are originated by the ASBR and are flooded to the entire autonomous system.

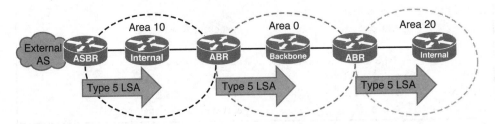

Figure 3-16 *OSPF Type 5 LSA*

The link-state ID is the external network number. Because of the flooding scope and depending on the number of external networks, the default lack of route summarization can also be a major issue with external LSAs. Therefore, you should consider summarization of external network numbers at the ASBR to reduce flooding problems.

Example 3-37 shows R4's OSPF LSDB, with a focus on type 5 LSAs.

Example 3-37 *R4's OSPF LSDB*

```
R4# show ip ospf database

            OSPF Router with ID (4.4.4.4) (Process ID 1)


                Router Link States (Area 0)

Link ID         ADV Router      Age         Seq#        Checksum Link count
1.1.1.1         1.1.1.1         724         0x8000000B 0x00966C 2
4.4.4.4         4.4.4.4         380         0x80000008 0x001A4F 1


                Net Link States (Area 0)

Link ID         ADV Router      Age         Seq#        Checksum
172.16.14.2     4.4.4.4         380         0x80000007 0x008FB6


                Summary Net Link States (Area 0)

Link ID         ADV Router      Age         Seq#        Checksum
172.16.12.0     1.1.1.1         724         0x80000007 0x00C567
172.16.13.0     1.1.1.1         724         0x80000007 0x009CC5
192.168.2.0     1.1.1.1         1463        0x80000002 0x002E5D


                Summary ASB Link States (Area 0)

Link ID         ADV Router      Age         Seq#        Checksum
3.3.3.3         1.1.1.1         1463        0x80000002 0x0035EB


            Type-5 AS External Link States
```

```
Link ID          ADV Router       Age        Seq#        Checksum Tag
10.0.0.0         3.3.3.3          1410       0x80000002 0x000980 0
```

The LSDB on R4 contains one external LSA describing external network 10.0.0.0, which was advertised into OSPF by router R3 with a router ID 3.3.3.3.

Example 3-38 shows the details of a type 5 LSA on R4.

Example 3-38 *R4's Type 5 LSA Details*

```
R4# show ip ospf database external


                OSPF Router with ID (4.4.4.4) (Process ID 1)


                Type-5 AS External Link States


Routing Bit Set on this LSA in topology Base with MTID 0
LS age: 1434
Options: (No TOS-capability, DC, Upward)
LS Type: AS External Link
Link State ID: 10.0.0.0 (External Network Number )
Advertising Router: 3.3.3.3
LS Seq Number: 80000002
Checksum: 0x980
Length: 36
Network Mask: /16
      Metric Type: 2 (Larger than any link state path)
      MTID: 0
      Metric: 20
      Forward Address: 0.0.0.0
      External Route Tag: 0
```

An external LSA on R4 describes the external network 10.0.0.0 with the subnet mask /16. The LSA is advertised by the R3 with a router ID 3.3.3.3. The zero forwarding address tells the rest of the routers in the OSPF domain that ASBR itself is the gateway to get to the external routes. Router R4 gathers information described in the type 5 LSA combined with the information received in the type 4 LSA, which describes the ASBR capability of router R3. This way, R4 learns how to reach the external networks.

Periodic OSPF Database Changes

Although OSPF does not refresh routing updates periodically, it does reflood LSAs every 30 minutes. Each LSA includes the link-state age variable, which counts the age of the LSA packet. When a network change occurs, the LSA's advertising router generates an updated LSA to reflect the change in the network topology. Each updated LSA includes incremented sequence number so that other routers can distinguish an updated LSA from the old one.

If the LS age variable reaches 30 minutes, meaning that there was no updated LSA created in the last half an hour, it gets automatically regenerated with an increased sequence number and flooded through the OSPF autonomous system. Only the router that originally generated the LSA, the one with the directly connected link, will resend the LSA every 30 minutes.

The output of the OSPF LSDB reveals the value of the current link-state age timer for all LSAs. In a normally operating network, you will not see the age variable with values higher than 1800 seconds.

When an LSA reaches a max age of 60 minutes in the LSDB, it is removed from the LSDB, and the router will perform a new SPF calculation. The router floods the LSA to other routers, informing them to remove the LSA as well.

Because this update is only used to refresh the LSDB, it is sometimes called a *paranoid update*.

Exchanging and Synchronizing LSDBs

Once a bidirectional adjacency is formed, OSPF neighbors follow an exact procedure to synchronize the LSDBs between them.

When routers that are running OSPF are initialized, an exchange process using the hello protocol is the first procedure. The exchange process that happens when routers appear on the network is illustrated in the Figure 3-17 and detailed in the list that follows.

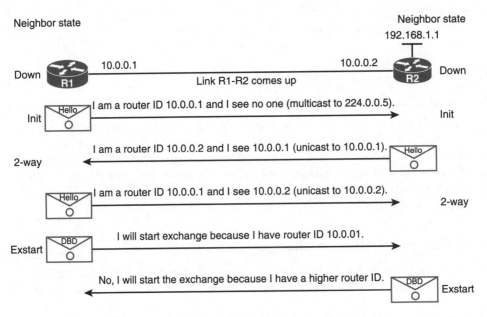

Figure 3-17 *Establishing Neighbor Adjacencies*

- Router R1 is enabled on the LAN and is in a down state because it has not exchanged information with any other router. It begins by sending a Hello packet through each of its interfaces that are participating in OSPF, even though it does not know the identity of the DR or of any other routers. The Hello packet is sent out using the multicast address 224.0.0.5.

- All directly connected routers that are running OSPF receive the Hello packet from router R1 and add R1 to their lists of neighbors. After adding R1 to the list, other routers are in the Init state.

- Each router that received the Hello packet sends a unicast reply Hello packet to R1 with its corresponding information. The neighbor field in the Hello packet includes all neighboring routers and R1.

- When R1 receives these Hello packets, it adds all the routers that had its router ID in their Hello packets to its own neighbor relationship database. After this process, R1 is in the 2-way state with R2. At this point, all routers that have each other in their lists of neighbors have established bidirectional communication.

If the link type is a broadcast network, like Ethernet, a DR and BDR election occurs before the neighboring state proceeds to the next phase.

In the ExStart state, a master-slave relationship is determined between the adjacent neighbors. The router with the higher router ID acts as the master during the exchange process. In Figure 3-17, R2 becomes the master.

Routers R1 and R2 exchange one or more DBD packets while they are in the Exchange state. A DBD includes information about the LSA entry header that appears in the LSDB of the router. The entries can be about a link or a network. Each LSA entry header includes information about the link-state type, the address of the advertising router, the cost of the link, and the sequence number. The router uses the sequence number to determine the "newness" of the received link-state information. A router will ignore a received LSA if it has the same sequence number as the router already has for that LSA.

When the router receives the DBD, it performs these actions, as shown in Figure 3-18:

- It acknowledges the receipt of the DBD using the LSAck packet.

- It compares the information that it received with the information that it has. If the DBD has a more up-to-date link-state entry, the router sends an LSR to the other router. When routers start sending LSRs, they are in the loading state.

- The other router responds with the complete information about the requested entry in an LSU packet. Again, when the router receives an LSU, it returns an LSAck.

The router adds the new link-state entries to its LSDB.

When all LSRs have been satisfied for a given router, the adjacent routers are considered synchronized. They are in a Full state, and their LSDBs should be identical. The routers must be in a Full state before they can route traffic.

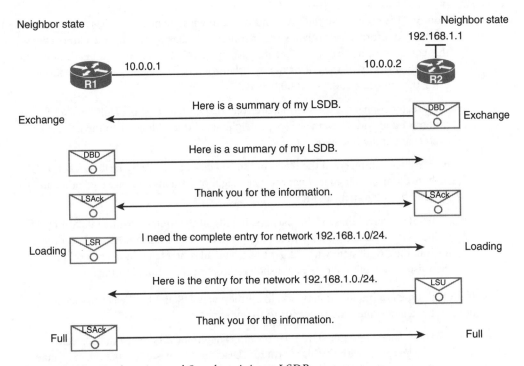

Figure 3-18   *Exchanging and Synchronizing a LSDB*

Synchronizing the LSDB on Multiaccess Networks

On multiaccess segments like Ethernet, OSPF optimizes the LSDB synchronization and the exchange of LSAs. When routers form a neighbor relationship on a multiaccess segment, the DR and BDR election takes place when routers are in the 2-Way state. The router with a highest OSPF priority, or highest router ID in case of a tie, is elected as a DR. Similarly, the router with the second highest priority or router ID becomes the BDR.

While the DR and BDR proceed in establishing the neighborship with all routers on the segment, other routers establish full adjacency only with the DR and BDR. The neighbor state of other neighbors stays in the 2-Way state.

Non-DR router exchange their databases only with the DR. The DR takes care to synchronize any new or changed LSAs with the rest of the routers on the segment.

In the flooding process that is illustrated in Figure 3-19, routers perform the following steps:

Step 1.   A router notices a change in a link state and multicasts an LSU packet (which includes the updated LSA entry) to all OSPF DRs and BDRs at multicast address 224.0.0.6. An LSU packet may contain several distinct LSAs.

Step 2.   The DR acknowledges receipt of the change and floods the LSU to others on the network using the OSPF multicast address 224.0.0.5.

Step 3.   After receiving the LSU, each router responds to the DR with an LSAck. To make the flooding procedure reliable, each LSA must be acknowledged separately.

Step 4.   The router updates its LSDB using the LSU that includes the changed LSA.

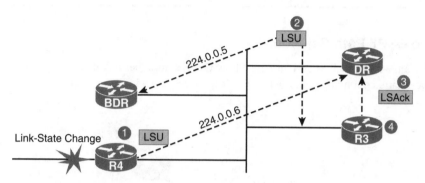

Figure 3-19 *Synchronizing the LSDB on an Multiaccess Network*

Running the SPF Algorithm

Every time there is a change in the network topology, OSPF needs to reevaluate its shortest path calculations. OSPF uses SPF to determine best paths toward destinations. The network topology that is described in the LSDB is used as an input for calculation. Network topology change can influence best path selection; therefore, routers must rerun SPF each time there is an intra-area topology change.

Interarea changes, which are described in type 3 LSAs, do not trigger the SPF recalculation because the input information for the best path calculation remains unchanged. The router determines the best paths for interarea routes based on the calculation of the best path toward the ABR. The changes that are described in type 3 LSAs do not influence how the router reaches the ABR; therefore, SPF recalculation is not needed.

You can verify how often the SPF algorithm was executed by using the **show ip ospf** command, as shown in Example 3-39. The output will also show you when the algorithm was last executed.

Example 3-39 *Verifying OSPF Frequency of the SPF Algorithm*

```
R1# show ip ospf | begin Area
    Area BACKBONE(0) (Inactive)
        Number of interfaces in this area is 1
        Area has no authentication
        SPF algorithm last executed 00:35:04:959 ago
        SPF algorithm executed 5 times
        Area ranges are
        Number of opaque link LSA 0. Checksum Sum 0x000000
```

```
        Number of DCbitless LSA 0
        Number of indication LSA 0
        Number of DoNotAge LSA 0
        Flood list length 0
    Area 1
```

Configuring OSPF Path Selection

In this section, we will analyze and influence how OSPF determines link costs to calculate the best path, continuing with the previous topology shown in Figure 3-20.

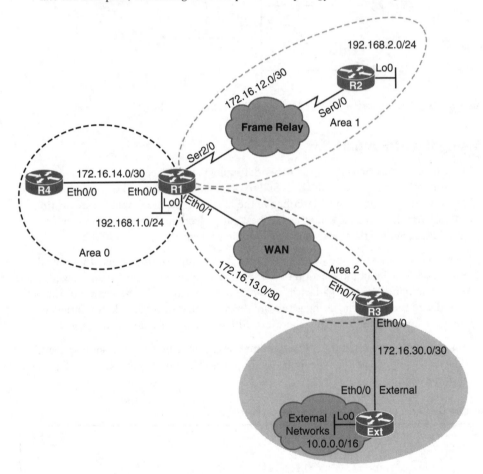

Figure 3-20 *Topology for OSPF Path Selection*

OSPF Path Selection

In Example 3-40, the output of the **show ip ospf** command verifies how many times the SFP algorithm was executed.

Example 3-40   *Verifying the SPF Calculations on R1*

```
R1# show ip ospf | begin Area
    Area BACKBONE(0)
        Number of interfaces in this area is 2
        Area has no authentication
        SPF algorithm last executed 00:02:17.777 ago
        SPF algorithm executed 3 times
        Area ranges are
        Number of LSA 7. Checksum Sum 0x0348C4
        Number of opaque link LSA 0. Checksum Sum 0x000000
        Number of DCbitless LSA 0
        Number of indication LSA 0
        Number of DoNotAge LSA 0
        Flood list length 0
<Output omitted>
```

The command output shows you how many times SPF has already run, together with the information about the last execution.

On R1, the link toward R4 is disabled and reenabled in Example 3-41. The number of SPF executions is verified afterward.

Example 3-41   *SPF Calculated on R1*

```
R1(config)# interface ethernet 0/0
R1(config-if)# shutdown
*Jan 31 12:33:20.617: %OSPF-5-ADJCHG: Process 1, Nbr 4.4.4.4 on Ethernet0/0 from
FULL to DOWN, Neighbor Down: Interface down or detached
*Jan 31 12:33:22.613: %LINK-5-CHANGED: Interface Ethernet0/0, changed state to
administratively down
*Jan 31 12:33:23.617: %LINEPROTO-5-UPDOWN: Line protocol on Interface Ethernet0/0,
changed state to down
R1(config-if)# no shutdown
*Jan 31 12:33:29.125: %LINK-3-UPDOWN: Interface Ethernet0/0, changed state to up
*Jan 31 12:33:30.129: %LINEPROTO-5-UPDOWN: Line protocol on Interface Ethernet0/0,
changed state to up
*Jan 31 12:33:35.040: %OSPF-5-ADJCHG: Process 1, Nbr 4.4.4.4 on Ethernet0/0 from
LOADING to FULL, Loading Done
R1(config-if)# do show ip ospf | begin Area
    Area BACKBONE(0)
        Number of interfaces in this area is 2
        Area has no authentication
        SPF algorithm last executed 00:00:07.752 ago
        SPF algorithm executed 5 times
        Area ranges are
        Number of LSA 7. Checksum Sum 0x033ACB
        Number of opaque link LSA 0. Checksum Sum 0x000000
```

```
        Number of DCbitless LSA 0
        Number of indication LSA 0
        Number of DoNotAge LSA 0
        Flood list length 0
<Output omitted>
```

Disabling the interface on R1 in area 0 triggers SPF calculation. Enabling the interface back into the OSPF triggers another SPF calculation. As a result, the counter displayed in the output has increased.

Link flap caused two recalculations of SPF algorithm. Frequent changes of link status can lead to frequent SPF calculation, which can utilize router resources.

OSPF Best Path Calculation

Once LSDBs are synchronized among OSPF neighbors, each router needs to determine on its own the best paths over the network topology.

When SPF is trying to determine the best path toward a known destination, it compares total costs of specific paths against each other. The paths with the lowest costs are selected as the best paths. The OSPF cost is an indication of the overhead to send packets over an interface. OSPF cost is computed automatically for each interface that is assigned into an OSPF process, using the following formula:

Cost = Reference bandwidth / Interface bandwidth

The cost value is a 16-bit positive number between 1 and 65,535, where a lower value is a more desirable metric. Reference bandwidth is set to 100 Mbps by default.

On high-bandwidth links (100 Mbps and more), automatic cost assignment no longer works. (It would result in all costs being equal to 1.) On these links, OSPF costs must be set manually on each interface.

For example, a 64-Kbps link gets a metric of 1562, and a T1 link gets a metric of 64. Cost is applied on all router link paths, and route decisions are made on the total cost of a path. The metric is only relevant on an outbound path; route decisions are not made for inbound traffic. The OSPF cost is recomputed after every bandwidth change, and the Dijkstra's algorithm determines the best path by adding all link costs along a path.

Example 3-42 reveals the interface bandwidth and the OSPF cost of the Frame Relay interface on R1.

Example 3-42 *Examining the Interface Bandwidth and OSPF Cost on R1*

```
R1# show interface serial 2/0
Serial2/0 is up, line protocol is up
  Hardware is M4T
  Internet address is 172.16.12.1/30
  MTU 1500 bytes, BW 1544 Kbit/sec, DLY 20000 usec,
     reliability 255/255, txload 1/255, rxload 1/255
```

```
    Encapsulation FRAME-RELAY, crc 16, loopback not set
<Output omitted>


R1# show ip ospf interface serial 2/0
Serial2/0 is up, line protocol is up
  Internet Address 172.16.12.1/30, Area 1, Attached via Network Statement
  Process ID 1, Router ID 1.1.1.1, Network Type NON_BROADCAST, Cost: 64
  Topology-MTID    Cost    Disabled    Shutdown    Topology Name
        0           64         no          no          Base
  Transmit Delay is 1 sec, State BDR, Priority 1
  Designated Router (ID) 2.2.2.2, Interface address 172.16.12.2
  Backup Designated router (ID) 1.1.1.1, Interface address 172.16.12.1
  Timer intervals configured, Hello 30, Dead 120, Wait 120, Retransmit 5
 <Output omitted>
```

The first command in the output displays bandwidth of the serial interface, which connects R1 with R2. The second output shows that OSPF calculated the cost of 64 for this interface. The cost was calculated by dividing the reference bandwidth of 100 Mbps with the actual interface bandwidth.

Default OSPF Costs

OSPF calculates the default interface costs, based on the interface type and the default reference bandwidth, shown in Table 3-2.

Table 3-2 *Default OSPF Costs*

Link Type	Default Cost
T1 (1.544-Mbps serial link)	64
Ethernet	10
Fast Ethernet	1
Gigabit Ethernet	1
10-Gigabit Ethernet	1

The default reference bandwidth of 100 Mbps is not suitable to calculate OSPF costs for links faster than Fast Ethernet. All such links gets assigned cost of 1, and OSPF cannot optimally choose the shortest path as it treats all the high-speed links as equal.

To improve OSPF behavior, you can adjust reference bandwidth to a higher value by using the **auto-cost reference-bandwidth** OSPF configuration command.

In Example 3-43, the reference bandwidth on R1 is changed to 10 Gbps.

Example 3-43   *Modifying the Reference Bandwidth on R1*

```
R1(config)# router ospf 1
R1(config-router)# auto-cost reference-bandwidth 10000
% OSPF: Reference bandwidth is changed.
        Please ensure reference bandwidth is consistent across all routers.
```

You can change the OSPF reference bandwidth under OSPF configuration mode by using the **auto-cost reference-bandwidth** command. The reference bandwidth value is inserted in megabits per second.

Notice also the warning that is displayed by the prompt. Only consistent reference bandwidth across OSPF domain ensures that all routers calculate the best paths correctly.

Example 3-44 highlights the OSPF link cost of R1's serial interface.

Example 3-44   *R1's OSPF Cost on Serial 2/0*

```
R1# show ip ospf interface serial 2/0
Serial2/0 is up, line protocol is up
  Internet Address 172.16.12.1/30, Area 1, Attached via Network Statement
  Process ID 1, Router ID 1.1.1.1, Network Type NON_BROADCAST, Cost: 6476
  Topology-MTID    Cost    Disabled    Shutdown     Topology Name
       0           6476      no          no            Base
<Output omitted>
```

The changed OSPF reference bandwidth results in updated OSPF costs for all interfaces. The cost for Serial 2/0 interface has increased from 64 to 6476. The new cost was calculated based on reference bandwidth of 10 Gbps divided by the interface speed of 1.544 Mbps.

In Example 3-45, the interface bandwidth is changed on R1's Serial 2/0 interface.

Example 3-45   *Changing the Interface Bandwidth on R1's Serial 2/0 Interface*

```
R1(config)# interface serial 2/0
R1(config-if)# bandwidth 10000
```

Changing the OSPF reference bandwidth influences the cost of all local interfaces included in the OSPF. Commonly, you will need to influence the cost just for a specific interface on the router. Using the **bandwidth** command, you can change how IOS treats a specific interface by default. Bandwidth setting changes the artificial value of the interface bandwidth that is derived by IOS based on the interface type. A manually set bandwidth value on the interface overrides the default value and is used by OSPF as input to the interface cost calculation.

Modifying the bandwidth not only influences OSPF but also other routing protocols like EIGRP, which takes the bandwidth into account when calculating the EIGRP metric.

The interface bandwidth and the OSPF cost of the serial interface on R1 are verified in Example 3-46.

Example 3-46 *Verifying the Interface Bandwidth and OSPF Cost on R1's Serial 2/0 Interface*

```
R1# show interfaces serial 2/0
Serial2/0 is up, line protocol is up
  Hardware is M4T
  Internet address is 172.16.12.1/30
  MTU 1500 bytes, BW 10000 Kbit/sec, DLY 20000 usec,
<Output omitted>
R1# show ip ospf interface serial 2/0
Serial2/0 is up, line protocol is up
  Internet Address 172.16.12.1/30, Area 1, Attached via Network Statement
  Process ID 1, Router ID 1.1.1.1, Network Type NON_BROADCAST, Cost: 1000
  Topology-MTID   Cost   Disabled   Shutdown     Topology Name
       0          1000     no         no              Base
<Output omitted>
```

The interface verification command displays the updated interface bandwidth, which was manually set to 10 Mbps. The change of the interface bandwidth is also reflected in the newly calculated OSPF cost, which is shown in the second output. The cost was calculated by dividing the reference bandwidth of 10000 Mbps with the configured bandwidth of 10 Mbps.

In Example 3-47, the OSPF cost of the serial interface link on R1 is changed using the **ip ospf cost** interface command.

Example 3-47 *Changing the OSPF Cost on an Interface*

```
R1(config)# interface serial 2/0
R1(config-if)# ip ospf cost 500
```

Using the OSPF interface configuration command, you can directly change the OSPF cost of specific interface. Cost of the interface can be set to a value between 1 and 65,535. This command overrides whatever value is calculated based on the reference bandwidth and the interface bandwidth.

The OSPF cost of the serial interface on R1 is verified in Example 3-48.

Example 3-48 *Verifying the OSPF Interface Costs on R1*

```
R1# show ip ospf interface brief
Interface   PID   Area      IP Address/Mask      Cost  State Nbrs F/C
Lo0         1     0         192.168.1.1/24       1     P2P   0/0
Et0/0       1     0         172.16.14.1/30       1000  DR    1/1
Se2/0       1     1         172.16.12.1/30       500   BDR   1/1
Et0/1       1     2         172.16.13.1/30       1000  BDR   1/1
```

To verify the OSPF cost, you can also use the **brief** keyword in the **show ip ospf interface** command. The verification command displays the summarized information on all OSPF-enabled interfaces, including the cost of the interface. You can notice the updated cost of the serial interface, which was manually configured in the previous step. In the output, you can observe the manually configured cost setting of the serial interface.

Calculating the Cost of Intra-Area Routes

To calculate the cost of intra-area routes, the router first analyzes OSPF database and identifies all subnets within its area. For each possible route, OSPF calculates the cost to reach the destination by summing up the individual interface costs. For each subnet, the route with the lowest total cost is selected as the best route.

Analyzing the topology in the Figure 3-21 from R1's perspective, notice that it can reach intra-area network A either via ABR1 or ABR2. The autonomous system path through ABR1 is associated with the lower cost, so it will be selected as the best path.

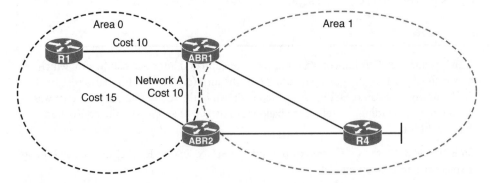

Figure 3-21   *Calculating the Cost of Intra-Area Routes*

In a scenario where two paths would have the same lowest total cost, both routes would be selected as the best paths and inserted in the routing table. As a result, a router would perform equal-cost load balancing.

Calculating the Cost of Interarea Routes

The internal OSPF router within an area receives only summarized info about interarea routes. As a result, the cost of an interarea route cannot be calculated the same way as for the intra-area routes.

When ABRs propagate information about the interarea routes with type 3 LSAs, they include their lowest cost to reach a specific subnet in the advertisement. The internal router adds its cost to reach a specific ABR to the cost announced in a type 3 LSA. Then it selects the route with the lowest total cost as the best route.

Router R1, in Figure 3-22, learns about network B from both ABRs. ABR2 in type 3 LSA reports the lowest cost to reach network B as 6, while ABR1 reports the cost of 21.

Router R1 determines the lowest cost to reach both ABRs and adds this cost to the one received in LSA. Router R1 selects the route via ABR2 as the total lowest cost route and tries to install it into the routing table.

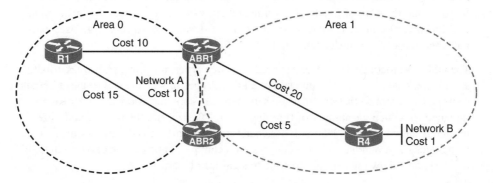

Figure 3-22 *Calculating the Cost of Interarea Routes*

Selecting Between Intra-Area and Interarea Routes

To eliminate the single point of failure on area borders, at least two ABRs are used in most networks. As a result, ABR can learn about a specific subnet from internal routers and also from the other ABR. ABR can learn an intra-area route and also an interarea route for the same destination. Even though the interarea route could have lower cost to the specific subnet, the intra-area path is always the preferred choice.

In the example topology in Figure 3-23, ABR1 learns about network B directly from a router R4 and also from the ABR2. Even though the interarea path has a cost of 16, the intra-area path with a total cost of 21 is selected as the best path.

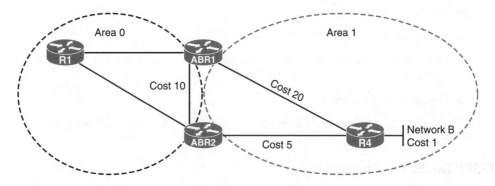

Figure 3-23 *Selecting Between Intra-Area and Interarea Routes*

Optimizing OSPF Behavior

Scalability, improved CPU and memory utilization, and the ability to mix small routers with large routers are all the benefits of using proper route summarization techniques. A key feature of the OSPF protocol is the ability to summarize routes at area and autonomous system boundaries.

Route summarization is important because it reduces the amount of the OSPF LSA flooding and the sizes of LSDBs and routing tables, which also reduces the memory and the CPU utilization on the routers. An OSPF network can scale to very large sizes, partially because of the route summarization.

The OSPF protocol defines several special-case area types, including stub areas, totally stubby areas, and NSSAs. The purpose of all three types of stub areas is to inject default routes into an area so that external and summary LSAs are not flooded. Stub areas are designed to reduce the amount of flooding, the LSDB size, and the routing table size in routers within the area. Network designers should always consider using stub area techniques when building networks. Stub area techniques improve performance in OSPF networks and allow the network to scale to significantly larger sizes.

Default routes reduce the routing table size, and also reduce the memory and the CPU utilization. OSPF injects a default route unconditionally or based on the presence of a default route inside the routing table.

This section defines different types of route summarization and describes the configuration commands for each type. It also describes the OSPF area types and the benefits of default routes.

Upon completing this section, you will be able to do the following:

- Describe the properties of OSPF route summarization
- Describe benefits of route summarization in OSPF
- Configure summarization on ABR
- Configure summarization on ASBR
- Configure the cost of OSPF default route
- Describe how you can use default routes and stub routing to direct traffic toward the Internet
- Describe the NSSA areas
- Configure the default route using the **default-information originate** command

OSPF Route Summarization

Route summarization is a key to scalability in OSPF. Route summarization helps solve two major problems:

- Large routing tables
- Frequent LSA flooding throughout the autonomous system

Every time that a route disappears in one area, routers in other areas also get involved in shortest-path calculation. To reduce the size of the area database, you can configure summarization on an area boundary or autonomous system boundary.

Normally, type 1 and type 2 LSAs are generated inside each area and translated into type 3 LSAs in other areas. With route summarization, the ABRs or ASBRs consolidate multiple routes into a single advertisement. ABRs summarize type 3 LSAs, and ASBRs summarize type 5 LSAs. Instead of advertising many specific prefixes, advertise only one summary prefix.

If the OSPF design includes many ABRs or ASBRs, suboptimal routing is possible. This is one of the drawbacks of summarization.

Route summarization requires a good addressing plan—an assignment of subnets and addresses that is based on the OSPF area structure and lends itself to aggregation at the OSPF area borders.

Benefits of Route Summarization

Route summarization directly affects the amount of bandwidth, CPU power, and memory resources that the OSPF routing process consumes. Without route summarization, every specific-link LSA is propagated into the OSPF backbone and beyond, causing unnecessary network traffic and router overhead.

With route summarization, only the summarized routes are propagated into the backbone (area 0), as illustrated in Figure 3-24. Summarization prevents every router from having to rerun the SPF algorithm, increases the stability of the network, and reduces unnecessary LSA flooding. Also, if a network link fails, the topology change is not propagated into the backbone (and other areas by way of the backbone). Specific-link LSA flooding outside the area does not occur.

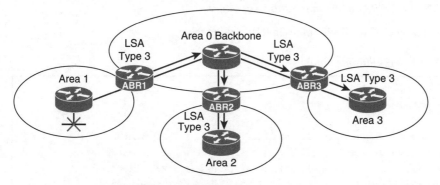

Figure 3-24 *OSPF Route Summarization*

Receiving a type 3 LSA into its area does not cause a router to run the SPF algorithm. The routes being advertised in the type 3 LSAs are appropriately added to or deleted from the router's routing table, but an SPF calculation is not done.

Configuring OSPF Route Summarization

In this section, we will implement route summarization on the area borders in an OSPF environment, shown in Figure 3-25. We will summarize the OSPF network using different subnet sizes and examine the impact of summarization on the OSPF database and routing.

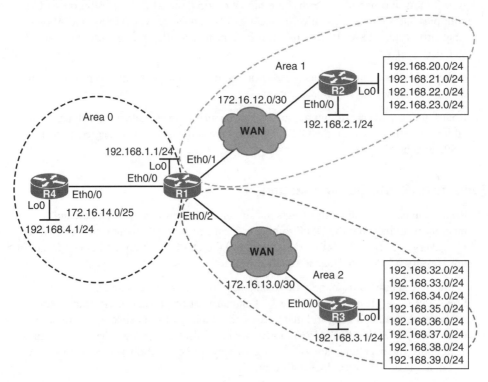

Figure 3-25 *OSPF Route Summarization Topology*

Example 3-49 displays OSPF routes in R1's routing table.

Example 3-49 *OSPF Routes in R1's Routing Table*

```
R1# show ip route ospf
<Output omitted>

O     192.168.2.0/24 [110/11] via 172.16.12.2, 00:41:47, Ethernet0/1
O     192.168.3.0/24 [110/11] via 172.16.13.2, 00:40:01, Ethernet0/2
O     192.168.4.0/24 [110/11] via 172.16.14.2, 00:38:09, Ethernet0/0
O     192.168.20.0/24 [110/11] via 172.16.12.2, 00:41:37, Ethernet0/1
O     192.168.21.0/24 [110/11] via 172.16.12.2, 01:03:46, Ethernet0/1
O     192.168.22.0/24 [110/11] via 172.16.12.2, 01:03:36, Ethernet0/1
O     192.168.23.0/24 [110/11] via 172.16.12.2, 01:03:26, Ethernet0/1
O     192.168.32.0/24 [110/11] via 172.16.13.2, 00:40:14, Ethernet0/2
O     192.168.33.0/24 [110/11] via 172.16.13.2, 00:57:01, Ethernet0/2
```

```
O      192.168.34.0/24 [110/11] via 172.16.13.2, 00:01:16, Ethernet0/2
O      192.168.35.0/24 [110/11] via 172.16.13.2, 00:01:06, Ethernet0/2
O      192.168.36.0/24 [110/11] via 172.16.13.2, 00:00:56, Ethernet0/2
O      192.168.37.0/24 [110/11] via 172.16.13.2, 00:00:46, Ethernet0/2
O      192.168.38.0/24 [110/11] via 172.16.13.2, 00:00:32, Ethernet0/2
O      192.168.39.0/24 [110/11] via 172.16.13.2, 00:00:18, Ethernet0/2
```

Apart from the loopback networks (192.168.x.0/24 where x is the router ID), notice the four Class C networks advertised by R2 (192.168.20.0/24 to 192.168.23.0/24) and eight Class C networks advertised by R3 (192.168.32.0/24 to 192.168.39.0/24).

Example 3-50 displays OSPF routes in R4's routing table.

Example 3-50 *OSPF Routes in R4's Routing Table*

```
R4# show ip route ospf
<Output omitted>


     172.16.0.0/16 is variably subnetted, 4 subnets, 3 masks
O IA     172.16.12.0/30 [110/20] via 172.16.14.1, 01:17:30, Ethernet0/0
O IA     172.16.13.0/30 [110/20] via 172.16.14.1, 01:17:30, Ethernet0/0
O        192.168.1.0/24 [110/11] via 172.16.14.1, 01:17:30, Ethernet0/0
O IA  192.168.2.0/24 [110/21] via 172.16.14.1, 00:49:23, Ethernet0/0
O IA  192.168.3.0/24 [110/21] via 172.16.14.1, 00:47:37, Ethernet0/0
O IA  192.168.20.0/24 [110/21] via 172.16.14.1, 00:49:08, Ethernet0/0
O IA  192.168.21.0/24 [110/21] via 172.16.14.1, 01:11:23, Ethernet0/0
O IA  192.168.22.0/24 [110/21] via 172.16.14.1, 01:11:13, Ethernet0/0
O IA  192.168.23.0/24 [110/21] via 172.16.14.1, 01:11:03, Ethernet0/0
O IA  192.168.32.0/24 [110/21] via 172.16.14.1, 00:47:50, Ethernet0/0
O IA  192.168.33.0/24 [110/21] via 172.16.14.1, 01:04:37, Ethernet0/0
O IA  192.168.34.0/24 [110/21] via 172.16.14.1, 00:02:26, Ethernet0/0
O IA  192.168.35.0/24 [110/21] via 172.16.14.1, 00:02:16, Ethernet0/0
O IA  192.168.36.0/24 [110/21] via 172.16.14.1, 00:02:06, Ethernet0/0
O IA  192.168.37.0/24 [110/21] via 172.16.14.1, 00:01:56, Ethernet0/0
O IA  192.168.38.0/24 [110/21] via 172.16.14.1, 00:01:43, Ethernet0/0
O IA  192.168.39.0/24 [110/21] via 172.16.14.1, 00:01:28, Ethernet0/0
```

Notice that the same networks are listed as interarea summary routes. They are being flooded into each area without any summarization on the area borders. You can see the respective routes that are received from the other areas on R2 and R3 as well.

Example 3-51 shows the OSPF database on R4.

Example 3-51 *R4's OSPF LSDB*

```
R4# show ip ospf database

          OSPF Router with ID (4.4.4.4) (Process ID 1)
```

```
                    Router Link States (Area 0)

Link ID          ADV Router      Age        Seq#        Checksum Link count
1.1.1.1          1.1.1.1         1110       0x80000006 0x008A7E 2
4.4.4.4          4.4.4.4         1406       0x80000005 0x00D915 2


                    Net Link States (Area 0)

Link ID          ADV Router      Age        Seq#        Checksum
172.16.14.1      1.1.1.1         1373       0x80000003 0x004192


                    Summary Net Link States (Area 0)

Link ID          ADV Router      Age        Seq#        Checksum
172.16.12.0      1.1.1.1         553        0x80000008 0x00A5BC
172.16.13.0      1.1.1.1         553        0x80000008 0x009AC6
192.168.2.0      1.1.1.1         1541       0x80000006 0x0008B5
192.168.3.0      1.1.1.1         3607       0x80000007 0x008C3A
192.168.20.0     1.1.1.1         1541       0x8000000B 0x00376F
192.168.21.0     1.1.1.1         1800       0x80000004 0x003A72
192.168.22.0     1.1.1.1         1800       0x80000004 0x002F7C
192.168.23.0     1.1.1.1         1800       0x80000004 0x002486
192.168.32.0     1.1.1.1         3607       0x80000007 0x004C5D
192.168.33.0     1.1.1.1         3607       0x80000008 0x003F68
192.168.34.0     1.1.1.1         3607       0x80000002 0x00406C
192.168.35.0     1.1.1.1         3607       0x80000002 0x003576
192.168.36.0     1.1.1.1         3607       0x80000002 0x002A80
192.168.37.0     1.1.1.1         3607       0x80000002 0x001F8A
192.168.38.0     1.1.1.1         3607       0x80000002 0x001494
192.168.39.0     1.1.1.1         3607       0x80000002 0x00099E
```

Notice the corresponding LSA 3 updates for each interarea summary route received from R1.

In Example 3-52, R1 summarizes four networks (192.168.20.0/24 to 192.168.23.0/24) in area 1 and the eight networks (192.168.32.0/24 to 192.168.39.0/24) in area 2 using the appropriate address blocks.

Example 3-52 *Configuring Summarization on the ABR*

```
R1(config)# router ospf 1
R1(config-router)# area 1 range 192.168.20.0 255.255.252.0
R1(config-router)# area 2 range 192.168.32.0 255.255.248.0
```

OSPF is a classless routing protocol, which carries subnet mask information along with route information. Therefore, OSPF supports multiple subnet masks for the same major network, which is known as *variable-length subnet masking* (VLSM). OSPF supports discontiguous subnets because the subnet masks are part of the LSDB. Network numbers in areas should be assigned contiguously to ensure that these addresses can be summarized into a minimal number of summary addresses.

In this scenario, the list of four networks advertised by R2 (192.168.20.0/24 to 192.168.23.0/24) in the routing table of the ABR can be summarized into one address block. The list of networks advertised by R3 (192.168.32.0/24 to 192.168.39.0/24) can also be aggregated by one summary address. All these networks will be summarized on the ABR R1. The block of addresses from 192.168.20.0 through 192.168.23.0/24 can be summarized using 192.168.20.0/22, and the block from 192.168.32.0 through 192.168.39.0/24 can be summarized using 192.168.32.0/21.

To consolidate and summarize routes at an area boundary, use the **area range** command in the router configuration mode. The ABR will summarize routes for a specific area before injecting them into a different area via the backbone as type 3 summary LSAs.

Example 3-53 examines the OSPF routing tables on R2, R3, and R4 with the route summarization on R1. Apart from the loopback networks, you will see the summary block of the other area, respectively.

Example 3-53   *OSPF Summarized Routes in the Routing Table*

```
R2# show ip route ospf
<Output omitted>


      172.16.0.0/16 is variably subnetted, 4 subnets, 3 masks
O IA     172.16.13.0/30 [110/20] via 172.16.12.1, 05:27:05, Ethernet0/0
O IA     172.16.14.0/25 [110/20] via 172.16.12.1, 05:07:35, Ethernet0/0
O IA  192.168.1.0/24 [110/11] via 172.16.12.1, 05:27:09, Ethernet0/0
O IA  192.168.3.0/24 [110/21] via 172.16.12.1, 01:24:16, Ethernet0/0
O IA  192.168.4.0/24 [110/21] via 172.16.12.1, 04:32:02, Ethernet0/0
O IA  192.168.32.0/21 [110/21] via 172.16.12.1, 00:57:42, Ethernet0/0

R3# show ip route ospf
<Output omitted>


      172.16.0.0/16 is variably subnetted, 4 subnets, 3 masks
O IA     172.16.12.0/30 [110/20] via 172.16.13.1, 05:25:50, Ethernet0/0
O IA     172.16.14.0/25 [110/20] via 172.16.13.1, 05:10:02, Ethernet0/0
O IA  192.168.1.0/24 [110/11] via 172.16.13.1, 05:25:50, Ethernet0/0
O IA  192.168.2.0/24 [110/21] via 172.16.13.1, 04:38:07, Ethernet0/0
O IA  192.168.4.0/24 [110/21] via 172.16.13.1, 04:34:29, Ethernet0/0
O IA  192.168.20.0/22 [110/21] via 172.16.13.1, 01:00:19, Ethernet0/0

R4# show ip route ospf
<Output omitted>
```

```
        172.16.0.0/16 is variably subnetted, 4 subnets, 3 masks
O IA      172.16.12.0/30 [110/20] via 172.16.14.1, 05:16:24, Ethernet0/0
O IA      172.16.13.0/30 [110/20] via 172.16.14.1, 05:16:24, Ethernet0/0
O     192.168.1.0/24 [110/11] via 172.16.14.1, 05:16:24, Ethernet0/0
O IA  192.168.2.0/24 [110/21] via 172.16.14.1, 04:48:17, Ethernet0/0
O IA  192.168.3.0/24 [110/21] via 172.16.14.1, 01:36:53, Ethernet0/0
O IA  192.168.20.0/22 [110/21] via 172.16.14.1, 01:10:29, Ethernet0/0
O IA  192.168.32.0/21 [110/21] via 172.16.14.1, 01:10:19, Ethernet0/0
```

In the routing table of R4, you will see the two summarized address blocks from areas 1 and 2.

Example 3-54 shows the OSPF database on the backbone router R4.

Example 3-54 *R4's OSPF LSDB*

```
R4# show ip ospf database
<Output omitted>


            Summary Net Link States (Area 0)


Link ID         ADV Router      Age      Seq#        Checksum
172.16.12.0     1.1.1.1         599      0x8000000B 0x009FBF
172.16.13.0     1.1.1.1         599      0x8000000B 0x0094C9
192.168.2.0     1.1.1.1         1610     0x80000009 0x0002B8
192.168.3.0     1.1.1.1         98       0x80000004 0x0001BD
192.168.20.0    1.1.1.1         599      0x8000000F 0x002085
192.168.32.0    1.1.1.1         98       0x80000005 0x009B0C
```

Notice the type 3 LSAs for the two summarized address blocks from areas 1 and 2. The type 3 LSAs for the specific networks are no longer in the database.

Example 3-55 displays the OSPF routing table on R1. Notice the two routes to the Null 0 interface. What is the purpose of these routes?

Example 3-55 *OSPF Routes in R1's Routing Table*

```
R1# show ip route ospf
<Output omitted>

O     192.168.2.0/24 [110/11] via 172.16.12.2, 01:18:25, Ethernet0/1
O     192.168.3.0/24 [110/11] via 172.16.13.2, 01:18:25, Ethernet0/2
O     192.168.4.0/24 [110/11] via 172.16.14.2, 01:18:25, Ethernet0/0
O     192.168.20.0/22 is a summary, 01:18:25, Null0
O     192.168.20.0/24 [110/11] via 172.16.12.2, 01:18:25, Ethernet0/1
O     192.168.21.0/24 [110/11] via 172.16.12.2, 01:18:25, Ethernet0/1
O     192.168.22.0/24 [110/11] via 172.16.12.2, 01:18:25, Ethernet0/1
```

```
O      192.168.23.0/24 [110/11] via 172.16.12.2, 01:18:25, Ethernet0/1
O      192.168.32.0/21 is a summary, 01:18:25, Null0
O      192.168.32.0/24 [110/11] via 172.16.13.2, 01:18:25, Ethernet0/2
O      192.168.33.0/24 [110/11] via 172.16.13.2, 01:18:25, Ethernet0/2
O      192.168.34.0/24 [110/11] via 172.16.13.2, 01:18:25, Ethernet0/2
O      192.168.35.0/24 [110/11] via 172.16.13.2, 01:18:25, Ethernet0/2
O      192.168.36.0/24 [110/11] via 172.16.13.2, 01:18:25, Ethernet0/2
O      192.168.37.0/24 [110/11] via 172.16.13.2, 01:18:25, Ethernet0/2
O      192.168.38.0/24 [110/11] via 172.16.13.2, 01:18:25, Ethernet0/2
O      192.168.39.0/24 [110/11] via 172.16.13.2, 01:18:25, Ethernet0/2
```

Cisco IOS Software creates a summary route to the Null0 interface when manual summarization is configured, to prevent routing loops. For example, if the summarizing router receives a packet to an unknown subnet that is part of the summarized range, the packet matches the summary route based on the longest match. The packet is forwarded to the Null0 interface (in other words, it is dropped), which prevents the router from forwarding the packet to a default route and possibly creating a routing loop.

Summarization on ABRs

OSPF offers two methods of route summarization:

- Summarization of internal routes performed on the ABRs
- Summarization of external routes performed on the ASBRs

Without summarization of internal routes, all the prefixes from an area are passed into the backbone as type 3 interarea routes. When summarization is enabled, the ABR intercepts this process and instead injects a single type 3 LSA, which describes the summary route into the backbone, shown in Figure 3-26. Multiple routes inside the area are summarized.

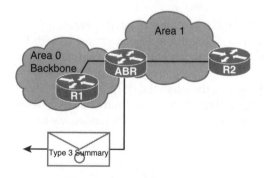

Figure 3-26 *Type 3 Summary LSA*

To consolidate and summarize routes at an area boundary, use the following command in router configuration mode:

area *area-id* **range** *ip-address mask* [**advertise** | **not-advertise**] [**cost** *cost*]

Table 3-3 shows the parameters used with this command. To remove the summarization, use the **no** form of this command.

Table 3-3   area range *Command Parameters*

Parameter	Description
area-id	Identifier of the area about which routes are to be summarized. It can be specified as either a decimal value or as an IP address.
ip-address	IP address.
mask	IP address mask.
advertise	(Optional) Sets the address range status to advertise and generates a type 3 summary LSA.
not-advertise	(Optional) Sets the address range status to DoNotAdvertise. The Type 3 summary LSA is suppressed, and the component networks remain hidden from other networks.
cost *cost*	(Optional) Metric or cost for this summary route, which is used during OSPF SPF calculation to determine the shortest paths to the destination. The value can be 0 to 16,777,215.

An internal summary route is generated if at least one subnet within the area falls in the summary address range and the summarized route metric is equal to the lowest cost of all the subnets within the summary address range. Interarea summarization can only be done for the intra-area routes of connected areas, and the ABR creates a route to Null0 to avoid loops in the absence of more specific routes.

Summarization on ASBRs

Summarization can also be performed for external routes, as illustrated in Figure 3-27. Each route that is redistributed into OSPF from other protocols is advertised individually with an external LSA. To reduce the size of the OSPF LSDB, you can configure a summary for external routes. Summarization of external routes can be done on the ASBR for type 5 LSAs (redistributed routes) before injecting them into the OSPF domain. Without summarization, all the redistributed external prefixes from external autonomous systems are passed into the OSPF area. A summary route to Null0 is created automatically for each summary range.

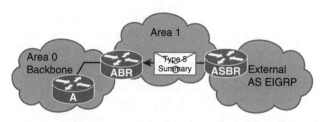

Figure 3-27   *Type 5 Summary LSA*

To create aggregate addresses for OSPF at an autonomous system boundary, use the following command in router configuration mode:

```
summary-address {{ip-address mask} | {prefix mask}} [not-advertise] [tag tag]
```

The ASBR will summarize external routes before injecting them into the OSPF domain as type 5 external LSAs. Table 3-4 shows the parameters used with the **summary-address** command. To remove a the summarization, use the **no** form of this command.

Table 3-4   **summary-address** *Command Parameters*

Parameter	Description
ip-address	Summary address designated for a range of addresses.
mask	IP subnet mask used for the summary route.
prefix	IP route prefix for the destination.
mask	IP subnet mask used for the summary route.
not-advertise	(Optional) Suppress routes that match the specified prefix/mask pair. This keyword applies to OSPF only.
tag *tag*	(Optional) Tag value that can be used as a "match" value for controlling redistribution via route maps. This keyword applies to OSPF only.

It is recommended practice dictates implementing contiguous IP addressing to achieve optimal summarization results.

OSPF Virtual Links

OSPF's two-tiered area hierarchy requires that if more than one area is configured, one of the areas must be area 0, the backbone area. All other areas must be directly connected to area 0, and area 0 must be contiguous. OSPF expects all nonbackbone areas to inject routes into the backbone, so that the routes can be distributed to other areas.

A virtual link is a link that allows discontiguous area 0s to be connected, or a disconnected area to be connected to area 0, via a transit area. The OSPF virtual link feature should be used only in very specific cases, for temporary connections or for backup after a failure. Virtual links should not be used as a primary backbone design feature.

The virtual link relies on the stability of the underlying intra-area routing. Virtual links cannot go through more than one area, nor through stub areas. Virtual links can only run through standard nonbackbone areas. If a virtual link needs to be attached to the backbone across two nonbackbone areas, two virtual links are required, one per area.

In Figure 3-28, two companies running OSPF have merged and a direct link does not yet exist between their backbone areas. The resulting area 0 is discontiguous. A logical link (virtual link) is built between the two ABRs, routers A and B, across area 1, a nonbackbone area. The routers at each end of the virtual link become part of the backbone and act as ABRs. This virtual link is similar to a standard OSPF adjacency, except that in a virtual link, neighboring routers do not have to be directly attached.

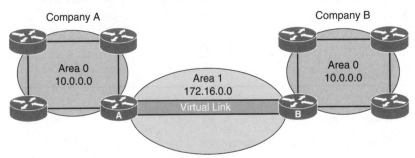

Figure 3-28   *Virtual Links Are Used to Connect a Discontiguous Area 0*

Figure 3-29 illustrates another example where a nonbackbone area is added to an OSPF network, and a direct physical connection to the existing OSPF area 0 does not yet exist. In this case, area 20 is added, and a virtual link across area 10 is created to provide a logical path between area 20 and the backbone area 0. The OSPF database treats the virtual link between ABR1 and ABR2 as a direct link. For greater stability, loopback interfaces are used as router IDs, and virtual links are created using these loopback addresses.

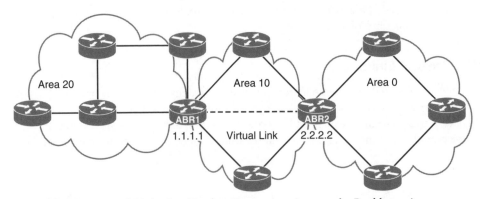

Figure 3-29   *Virtual Links Are Used to Connect an Area to the Backbone Area*

The hello protocol works over virtual links as it does over standard links, in 10-second intervals. However, LSA updates work differently on virtual links. An LSA usually refreshes every 30 minutes. However, LSAs learned through a virtual link have the DoNotAge (DNA) option set so that the LSA does not age out. This DNA technique is required to prevent excessive flooding over the virtual link.

Configuring OSPF Virtual Links

Use the following router configuration command to define an OSPF virtual link:

```
area area-id virtual-link router-id [authentication [message-digest| null]]
[hello-interval seconds] [retransmit-interval seconds] [transmit-
delay seconds] [dead-interval seconds] [[authentication-key
key] | [message-digest-key key-id md5 key]]
```

To remove a virtual link, use the **no** form of this command.

Table 3-5 describes the options available with the **area** *area-id* **virtual-link** command. Make sure that you understand the effect of these options before changing them. For instance, the smaller the hello interval, the faster the detection of topological changes, but the more routing traffic. You should be conservative with the setting of the retransmit interval, or the result is needless retransmissions. The value should be larger for serial lines and virtual links. The transmit delay value should take into account the interface's transmission and propagation delays.

Table 3-5   **area** *area-id* **virtual-link** *Command Parameters*

Parameter	Description
area-id	Specifies the area ID of the transit area for the virtual link. This ID can be either a decimal value or in dotted-decimal format, like a valid IP address. There is no default.
	The transit area cannot be a stub area.
router-id	Specifies the router ID of the virtual link neighbor. The router ID appears in the **show ip ospf** display. This value is in an IP address format. There is no default.
authentication	(Optional) Specifies an authentication type.
message-digest	(Optional) Specifies the use of MD5 authentication.
null	(Optional) Overrides simple password or MD5 authentication if configured for the area. No authentication is used.
hello-interval *seconds*	(Optional) Specifies the time (in seconds) between the hello packets that the Cisco IOS Software sends on an interface. The unsigned integer value is advertised in the Hello packets. The value must be the same for all routers and access servers attached to a common network. The default is 10 seconds.

Parameter	Description
retransmit-interval *seconds*	(Optional) Specifies the time (in seconds) between LSA retransmissions for adjacencies belonging to the interface. The value must be greater than the expected round-trip delay between any two routers on the attached network. The default is 5 seconds.
transmit-delay *seconds*	(Optional) Specifies the estimated time (in seconds) to send an LSU packet on the interface. This integer value must be greater than 0. LSAs in the update packet have their age incremented by this amount before transmission. The default value is 1 second.
dead-interval *seconds*	(Optional) Specifies the time (in seconds) that must pass without hello packets being seen before a neighboring router declares the router down. This is an unsigned integer value. The default is 4 times the default hello interval, or 40 seconds. As with the hello interval, this value must be the same for all routers and access servers attached to a common network.
authentication-key *key*	(Optional) Specifies the password used by neighboring routers for simple password authentication. It is any continuous string of up to eight characters. There is no default value.
message-digest-key *key-id* **md5** *key*	(Optional) Identifies the key ID and key (password) used between this router and neighboring routers for MD5 authentication. There is no default value.

In the example in Figure 3-30, area 0 is discontiguous. A virtual link is used as a backup strategy to temporarily connect area 0. Area 1 is used as the transit area. Router A builds a virtual link to Router B, and Router B builds a virtual link to the Router A. Each router points at the other router's router ID.

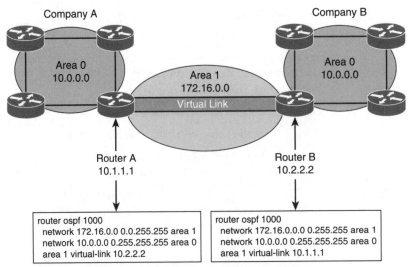

Figure 3-30   *OSPF Virtual Link Configuration: Split Area 0*

Figure 3-31 presents another example network. The configurations for routers R1 and R3 are provided in Example 3-56.

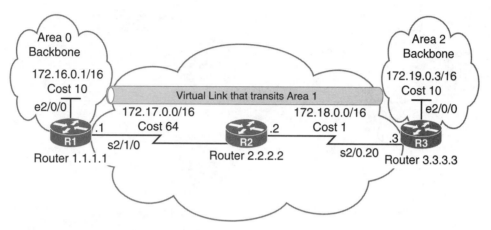

Figure 3-31   *OSPF Virtual Link Across Area 1*

Example 3-56   *Configuring a Virtual Link Between R1 and R3*

```
R1(config)# router ospf 2
R1(config-router)# area 1 virtual-link 3.3.3.3


R3(config)# router ospf 2
R3(config-router)# area 1 virtual-link 1.1.1.1
```

Configuring OSPF Stub Areas

In this section, you will learn how to implement special area types in an OSPF environment, using the topology in Figure 3-32. The stub and totally stubby areas are deployed to reduce the size of the OSPF database and routing table:

- **Stub area:** This area type does not accept information about routes external to the autonomous system, such as routes from non-OSPF sources. If routers need to route to networks outside the autonomous system, they use a default route, indicated as 0.0.0.0. Stub areas cannot contain ASBRs (except that the ABRs may also be ASBRs). The stub area does not accept external routes.

- **Totally stubby area:** This Cisco proprietary area type does not accept external autonomous system routes or summary routes from other areas internal to the autonomous system. If a router needs to send a packet to a network external to the area, it sends the packet using a default route. Totally stubby areas cannot contain ASBRs (except that the ABRs may also be ASBRs). A totally stubby area does not accept external or interarea routes.

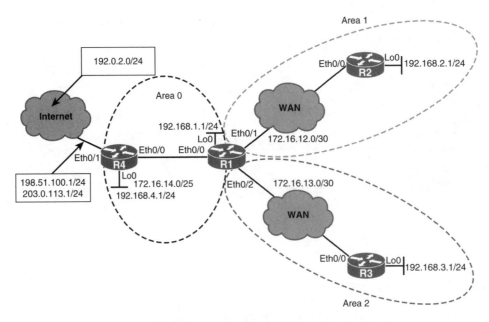

Figure 3-32   *Topology for Stub and Totally Stubby Areas*

OSPF Stub Areas

Example 3-57 displays the OSPF routes in the routing tables of R2 and R3, including external OSPF routes.

Example 3-57   *OSPF Routes in R2's and R3's Routing Tables*

```
R2# show ip route ospf
<Output omitted>


      172.16.0.0/16 is variably subnetted, 4 subnets, 3 masks
O IA    172.16.13.0/30 [110/20] via 172.16.12.1, 00:56:16, Ethernet0/0
O IA    172.16.14.0/25 [110/20] via 172.16.12.1, 00:56:16, Ethernet0/0
O IA  192.168.1.0/24 [110/11] via 172.16.12.1, 00:56:16, Ethernet0/0
O IA  192.168.3.0/24 [110/21] via 172.16.12.1, 00:54:50, Ethernet0/0
O IA  192.168.4.0/24 [110/21] via 172.16.12.1, 00:46:00, Ethernet0/0
O E2  198.51.100.0/24 [110/20] via 172.16.12.1, 00:01:47, Ethernet0/0
O E2  203.0.113.0/24 [110/20] via 172.16.12.1, 00:01:47, Ethernet0/0


R3# show ip route ospf
<Output omitted>


      172.16.0.0/16 is variably subnetted, 4 subnets, 3 masks
O IA    172.16.12.0/30 [110/20] via 172.16.13.1, 00:53:58, Ethernet0/0
O IA    172.16.14.0/25 [110/20] via 172.16.13.1, 00:53:58, Ethernet0/0
```

```
O IA   192.168.1.0/24  [110/11]  via 172.16.13.1, 00:53:58, Ethernet0/0
O IA   192.168.2.0/24  [110/21]  via 172.16.13.1, 00:53:58, Ethernet0/0
O IA   192.168.4.0/24  [110/21]  via 172.16.13.1, 00:45:10, Ethernet0/0
O E2   198.51.100.0/24 [110/20]  via 172.16.13.1, 00:00:57, Ethernet0/0
O E2   203.0.113.0/24  [110/20]  via 172.16.13.1, 00:00:57, Ethernet0/0
```

The two external routes, 198.51.100.0/24 and 203.0.113.0/24, are being redistributed into the OSPF domain by R4, which acts as the ASBR and provides Internet connectivity.

Area 0 is the backbone area. The backbone area is the central entity to which all other areas connect. All other areas connect to this area to exchange and route information. The OSPF backbone includes all the properties of a standard OSPF area.

Area 1 is a standard nonbackbone area, in which the type 5 LSAs are flooded from R1. This default area accepts link updates, route summaries, and external routes.

Area 2 is also a standard nonbackbone area. The type 5 LSAs are exchanged through the backbone area (R4 and R1) and the standard nonbackbone areas.

A critical design aspect arises in environments with thousands of external routes. The multitude of type 5 LSAs and the corresponding external routes consumes substantial resources. It also makes the network more difficult to monitor and manage.

Example 3-58 shows ABR R1's area 1 configured as a stub area. The stub area offers you a powerful method of reducing the size of the OSPF database and routing tables. This area does not accept information about routes that are external to the AS, such as routes from non-OSPF sources. Stub areas cannot contain ASBRs, except when ABRs are also ASBRs.

Example 3-58   *Configuring R1's Area 1 as a Stub Area*

```
R1(config)# router ospf 1
R1(config-router)# area 1 stub
%OSPF-5-ADJCHG: Process 1, Nbr 2.2.2.2 on Ethernet0/1 from FULL to DOWN, Neighbor
Down: Adjacency forced to reset
```

Configuring a stub area reduces the size of the LSDB inside the area, resulting in reduced memory requirements for routers in that area. External network LSAs (type 5), such as those that are redistributed from other routing protocols into OSPF, are not permitted to flood into a stub area.

The **area stub** router configuration mode command is used to define an area as a stub area. Each router in the stub area must be configured with the **area stub** command. The Hello packets that are exchanged between OSPF routers contain a stub area flag that must match on neighboring routers. Until the **area 1 stub** command is enabled on R2 in this scenario, the adjacency between R1 and R2 will be down.

Example 3-59 shows R2's area 1 configured as a stub area. R2 is an internal router or leaf router in R2. Once you configure the area 1 as a stub on R2, the stub area flag in the OSPF Hello packets will start matching between R1 and R2. The routers establish an adjacency and exchange routing information.

Example 3-59 *Configuring R2's Area 1 as a Stub Area*

```
R2(config)# router ospf 1
R2(config-router)# area 1 stub
%OSPF-5-ADJCHG: Process 1, Nbr 1.1.1.1 on Ethernet0/0 from LOADING to FULL, Loading
Done
```

Example 3-60 examines the OSPF routing table on R2 and verifies its connectivity to the Internet destinations 203.0.113.2 and 192.0.2.1. Why can you reach 203.0.113.2 and not 192.0.2.1, although both IP addresses exist on the upstream Internet router? _____

_____

Example 3-60 *Verifying R2's Connectivity to the Internet*

```
R2# show ip route ospf
<Output omitted>


O*IA  0.0.0.0/0 [110/11] via 172.16.12.1, 00:19:27, Ethernet0/0
        172.16.0.0/16 is variably subnetted, 4 subnets, 3 masks
O IA    172.16.13.0/30 [110/20] via 172.16.12.1, 00:19:27, Ethernet0/0
O IA    172.16.14.0/25 [110/20] via 172.16.12.1, 00:19:27, Ethernet0/0
O IA  192.168.1.0/24 [110/11] via 172.16.12.1, 00:19:27, Ethernet0/0
O IA  192.168.3.0/24 [110/21] via 172.16.12.1, 00:19:27, Ethernet0/0
O IA  192.168.4.0/24 [110/21] via 172.16.12.1, 00:19:27, Ethernet0/0


R2# ping 192.0.2.1
Type escape sequence to abort.
Sending 5, 100-byte ICMP Echos to 192.0.2.1, timeout is 2 seconds:
U.U.U
Success rate is 0 percent (0/5)


R2# ping 203.0.113.2
Type escape sequence to abort.
Sending 5, 100-byte ICMP Echos to 203.0.113.1, timeout is 2 seconds:
!!!!!
Success rate is 100 percent (5/5), round-trip min/avg/max = 1/1/1 ms
```

Routing from a stub area to the outside is based on a default route (0.0.0.0). If a packet is addressed to a network that is not in the routing table of an internal router, the router automatically forwards the packet to the ABR (R1), which sends a 0.0.0.0 LSA. Forwarding the packet to the ABR allows routers within the stub to reduce the size of their routing tables, because a single default route replaces many external routes.

The routes that appear in the routing table of R2 include the default route and interarea routes, all designated with an IA in the routing table.

You can reach 203.0.113.2 because the 203.0.113.0/24 is being flooded as a type 5 LSA into the backbone area. The first leg of reachability is provided by the default route injected into the stub area by the ABR. The second leg, through the backbone area, is ensured by the existing external route.

You cannot reach 192.0.2.1 because its network is not advertised into the OSPF domain as an external route. Despite the default route out of the stub area to the ABR, the ABR drops traffic to that destination because it does not have a path to the destination. This problem could be solved by advertising a default external route from the ASBR (R4) into the OSPF domain.

In Example 3-61, the ASBR (R4) is confirmed to have a default static route configured. The default route is then advertised into the OSPF domain.

Example 3-61 *Propagating a Default Route Using OSPF on R4*

```
R4# show ip route static
<Output omitted>
Gateway of last resort is 198.51.100.2 to network 0.0.0.0
S*    0.0.0.0/0 [1/0] via 198.51.100.2
R4(config)# router ospf 1
R4(config-router)# default-information originate
```

To be able to perform routing from an OSPF autonomous system toward external networks or toward the Internet, you must either know all the destination networks or create a default route. The most scalable and optimized way is through the use of a default route.

To generate a default external route into an OSPF routing domain, use the **default-information originate** router configuration command, as shown in Example 3-61. This command will generate a type 5 LSA for 0.0.0.0/0 when the advertising router already has a default route.

The ABR (R1), shown in Example 3-62, examines the injected default route in the OSPF routing table and database. Connectivity to the external destination 192.0.2.1 is verified with the **show ip ospf database** command.

Example 3-62 *Verifying R1's Default Route*

```
R1# show ip route ospf
<Output omitted>

Gateway of last resort is 172.16.14.2 to network 0.0.0.0

O*E2  0.0.0.0/0 [110/1] via 172.16.14.2, 00:00:15, Ethernet0/0
O       192.168.2.0/24 [110/11] via 172.16.12.2, 19:08:02, Ethernet0/1
O       192.168.3.0/24 [110/11] via 172.16.13.2, 19:46:45, Ethernet0/2
O       192.168.4.0/24 [110/11] via 172.16.14.2, 19:46:45, Ethernet0/0
O E2  198.51.100.0/24 [110/20] via 172.16.14.2, 19:46:45, Ethernet0/0
O E2  203.0.113.0/24 [110/20] via 172.16.14.2, 19:46:45, Ethernet0/0
```

```
R1# show ip ospf database
<Output omitted>
              Type-5 AS External Link States

Link ID         ADV Router      Age       Seq#        Checksum Tag
0.0.0.0         4.4.4.4         121       0x80000001 0x00C2DF 1
198.51.100.0    4.4.4.4         1131      0x80000027 0x0054B7 0
203.0.113.0     4.4.4.4         1131      0x80000027 0x00E943 0


R1# ping 192.0.2.1
Type escape sequence to abort.
Sending 5, 100-byte ICMP Echos to 192.0.2.1, timeout is 2 seconds:
!!!!!
Success rate is 100 percent (5/5), round-trip min/avg/max = 1/1/1 ms
```

On the ABR, you can see the default route, injected into the backbone area as a type 5 LSA. It appears in the routing table with the symbols O (OSPF), * (default route), E2 (external type 2). You can also see the appropriate LSA 5 in the OSPF database.

Notice the external IP address 192.0.2.1 because the default route directs the traffic via the ASBR. The ASBR has a default static toward the upstream router.

In Example 3-63, connectivity from R2 in the stub area is verified to the external destination 192.0.2.1.

Example 3-63 *Verifying R2's Connectivity to an External Destination*

```
R2# ping 192.0.2.1
Type escape sequence to abort.
Sending 5, 100-byte ICMP Echos to 192.0.2.1, timeout is 2 seconds:
!!!!!
Success rate is 100 percent (5/5), round-trip min/avg/max = 1/1/1 ms
```

Having flooded the default route as a type 5 LSA into the backbone area, you can now verify that R2 can reach the external IP address 192.0.2.1. The traffic to that destination first follows the default route injected into the stub area by the ABR, and then the default route injected into the backbone by the ASBR.

OSPF Totally Stubby Areas

Next, the ABR's (R1's) area 2 is configured as a totally stubby area, shown in Example 3-64.

Example 3-64 *Configuring Area 2 as a Totally Stubby Area on the ABR*

```
R1(config)# router ospf 1
R1(config-router)# area 2 stub no-summary
%OSPF-5-ADJCHG: Process 1, Nbr 3.3.3.3 on Ethernet0/2 from FULL to
DOWN, Neighbor Down: Adjacency forced to reset
```

The totally stubby area is a Cisco proprietary enhancement that further reduces the number of routes in the routing table. A totally stubby area is a stub area that blocks external type 5 LSAs and summary type 3 and type 4 LSAs (interarea routes) from entering the area. Because it blocks these routes, a totally stubby area recognizes only intra-area routes and the default route of 0.0.0.0. ABRs inject the default summary link 0.0.0.0 into the totally stubby area. Each router picks the closest ABR as a gateway to everything outside the area.

Totally stubby areas minimize routing information further than stub areas and increase the stability and scalability of OSPF internetworks. Using totally stubby areas is typically a better solution than using stub areas, as long as the ABR is a Cisco router.

To configure an area as totally stubby, you must configure all the routers inside the area as stub routers. Use the **area stub** command with the **no-summary** keyword on the ABR to configure it as totally stubby. In this example, configuring the total stub on the ABR (R1) breaks the adjacency within area 2 until R3 is configured as a member of a stub area. The adjacency fails because the stub flag in the Hello packets does not match between R1 and R3.

Example 3-65 shows the configuration of an internal router or leaf router (R3) as a stub router in a totally stubby area.

Example 3-65   *OSPF Routes in R1's Routing Table*

```
R3(config)# router ospf 1
R3(config-router)# area 2 stub
%OSPF-5-ADJCHG: Process 1, Nbr 1.1.1.1 on Ethernet0/0 from LOADING to FULL, Loading
Done
```

Once R3 in area 2 is configured as a stub, the stub area flag in the OSPF Hello packets will start matching between R1 and R3. The routers establish an adjacency and exchange routing information. R3 may or may not be configured with the **no-summary** keyword. The **no-summary** keyword has no effect when the router is not an ABR and thus does not advertise any interarea summaries.

Example 3-66 verifies R3's routing table and LSDB information in the totally stubby area.

Example 3-66   *OSPF Routes in R1's Routing Table*

```
R3# show ip route ospf
<Output omitted>
Gateway of last resort is 172.16.13.1 to network 0.0.0.0
O*IA  0.0.0.0/0 [110/11] via 172.16.13.1, 00:18:08, Ethernet0/0

R3# show ip ospf data
<Output omitted>
```

```
                    Summary Net Link States (Area 2)

Link ID          ADV Router       Age        Seq#        Checksum
0.0.0.0          1.1.1.1          1285       0x80000001  0x0093A6
```

```
R3# ping 192.0.2.1
Type escape sequence to abort.
Sending 5, 100-byte ICMP Echos to 192.0.2.1, timeout is 2 seconds:
!!!!!
Success rate is 100 percent (5/5), round-trip min/avg/max = 1/1/1 ms
```

The leaf router (R3) in the totally stubby area has the smallest possible routing table.
Only the intra-area routes are maintained. Interarea and external routes are not visible in
the routing tables for each stub area, but are accessible via the intra-area default routes
for that stub area. The ABR (R1) blocks interarea and external LSAs and inserts the
default route instead.

Despite the minimal routing information about external reachability the leaf router
can ping the outside address 192.0.2.1. The traffic to that destination first follows the
default route injected into the totally stubby area by the ABR, and then the default
route injected into the backbone by the ASBR (R4).

Cost of the Default Route in a Stub Area

By default, the ABR of a stub area will advertise a default route with a cost of 1. You
can change the cost of the default route by using the **area default-cost** command. The
default-cost option provides the metric for the summary default route that is generated
by the ABR into the stub area.

To specify a cost for the default summary route sent into a stub or not so stubby area
(NSSA), use the following command in router configuration mode:

```
area area-id default-cost cost
```

To remove the assigned default route cost, use the **no** form of this command. Table 3-6
shows the parameters available for this command.

Table 3-6 *Parameters for the* area default-cost *Command*

Parameter	Description
area-id	Identifier for the stub or NSSA. The identifier can be specified as either a decimal value or as an IP address.
cost	Cost for the default summary route used for a stub or NSSA. The acceptable value is a 24-bit number.

The **area default-cost** command is used only on an ABR attached to a stub or not-so-stubby area (NSSA). Use the **default-cost** option only on an ABR attached to the stub area. The **default-cost** option provides the metric for the summary default route generated by the ABR into the stub area.

The option of tuning the cost of the default route in the stub area is useful in stub areas with redundant exit points to the backbone area, as shown in Figure 3-33. The primary exit point can be configured using a lower cost. The secondary exit point would advertise a higher cost and thus attract external traffic only when the primary ABR fails. This distribution pattern applies only to external traffic. The traffic to interarea networks will follow the shortest path.

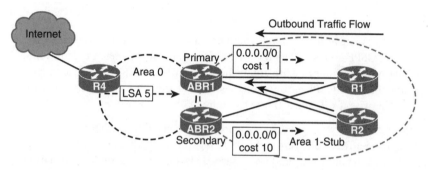

Figure 3-33   *Cost of the Default Route in a Stub Area*

The default-information originate Command

To generate a default external route into an OSPF routing domain, use the following command in router configuration mode:

```
default-information originate [always] [metric metric-value] [metric-type type-
value] [route-map map-name]
```

To disable this feature, use the **no** form of this command. Table 3-7 shows the parameters available for this command.

Table 3-7   *Parameters for the* **default-information originate** *Command*

Parameter	Description
always	(Optional) Always advertises the default route regardless of whether the software has a default route.
metric *metric-value*	(Optional) Metric used for generating the default route. If you omit a value and do not specify a value using the default-metric router configuration command, the default metric value is 1. The value used is specific to the protocol.

Parameter	Description
metric-type *type-value*	(Optional) External link type associated with the default route advertised into the OSPF routing domain. It can be one of the following values: 1: Type 1 external route 2: Type 2 external route The default is type 2 external route.
route-map *map-name*	(Optional) Routing process will generate the default route if the route map is satisfied.

There are two ways to advertise a default route into a standard area. You can advertise 0.0.0.0/0 into the OSPF domain when the advertising router already has a default route. Use the **default-information originate** command to allow the ASBR to originate a type 5 default route inside the OSPF autonomous system. The default route must be in the routing table otherwise it will not be propagated by OSPF.

You can use different keywords in the configuration command to configure dependency on IP routing table entries. To advertise 0.0.0.0/0 regardless of whether the advertising router already has a default route, add the keyword **always** to the **default-information originate** command. The default route will be propagated by OSPF whether or not there is a default route.

Whenever you use the **redistribute** or the **default-information** command to redistribute routes into an OSPF routing domain, the router automatically becomes an ASBR. You can also use a route map to define dependency on any condition inside the route map. The **metric** and *metric-type* options allow you to specify the OSPF cost and metric type of the injected external route.

Other Stubby Area Types

The NSSA is a nonproprietary extension of the existing stub area feature that allows the injection of external routes in a limited fashion into the stub area.

Redistribution into an NSSA creates a special type of LSA known as a type 7 LSA, which can exist only in an NSSA. An NSSA ASBR (router ASBR1 in the Figure 3-34) generates this LSA, and an NSSA ABR translates it into a type 5 LSA, which gets propagated into the OSPF domain. Type 7 LSAs have a propagate (P) bit in the LSA header to prevent propagation loops between the NSSA and the backbone area. The NSSA retains the majority of other stub area features. An important difference is the default behavior regarding the default route. ABR must be configured with additional commands before it starts announcing it into the NSSA area.

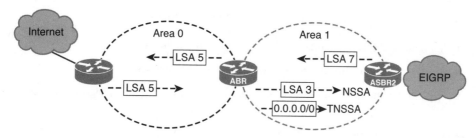

Figure 3-34 *NSSA Area*

The type 7 LSA is described in the routing table as an O N2 or O N1 (N means NSSA). N1 means that the metric is calculated like external type 1 (E1); N2 means that the metric is calculated like external type 2 (E2). The default is O N2.

> **Note** The E1 metric adds external and internal costs together to reflect the whole cost to the destination. The E2 metric takes only the external cost, which is reflected in the OSPF cost.

The totally NSSA feature is an extension to the NSSA feature like the totally stubby feature is an extension to the stub area feature. It is a Cisco proprietary feature that blocks type 3, 4, and 5 LSAs. A single default route replaces both inbound-external (type 5) LSAs and summary (type 3 and 4) LSAs in the totally NSSA area. The ABRs for the totally NSSA area must be configured to prevent the flooding of summary routes for other areas into the NSSA area. Only ABRs control the propagation of type 3 LSAs from the backbone. If an ABR is configured on any other routers in the area, it will have no effect at all.

To configure an area as an NSSA, you must configure all routers inside the area for NSSA functionality. The **area nssa** router configuration mode command is used to define each router in the NSSA area as not-so-stubby. Totally NSSA functionality requires one more step; you must configure each ABR for totally NSSA functionality. The **area nssa** command with the **no-summary** keyword is used to define the ABR as totally not-so-stubby.

OSPFv3

OSPF is a widely used IGP in IPv4, IPv6, and dual-stack (IPv4/IPv6) environments. The OSPF upgrade to support IPv6 generated a number of significant changes to how the protocol behaves. Understanding the differences between OSPFv2 and OSPFv3 is required for the successful deployment and operation of an IPv6 network using OSPF for routing. This section describes OSPFv3, the IPv6-capable version of the OSPF routing protocol, including its operations, configuration, and commands.

Upon completing this section, you will be able to do the following:

■ Implement OSPFv3 in a dual-stack (IPv4/IPv6) environment

■ Configure external route summarization and load balancing in OSPFv3

■ Explain the limitations and where you need to be careful when configuring OSPFv3

Configuring OSPFv3

In this section, you will learn how to implement OSPFv3 in a dual-stack (IPv4/IPv6) environment. Using the IPv6 topology in Figure 3-35 for IPv6 and Figure 3-36 for IPv4, routers R2, R3, and R4 have been completely preconfigured. R1 has been preconfigured with the necessary IPv4/IPv6 addresses, but does not have any routing protocol configuration. On R1, we will first configure OSPFv3 for IPv6 in the traditional way, in which a dedicated OSPF process serves the IPv6 protocol. Then we will migrate the configuration to the newest configuration approach, in which a single OSPFv3 process serves both address families, IPv4 and IPv6.

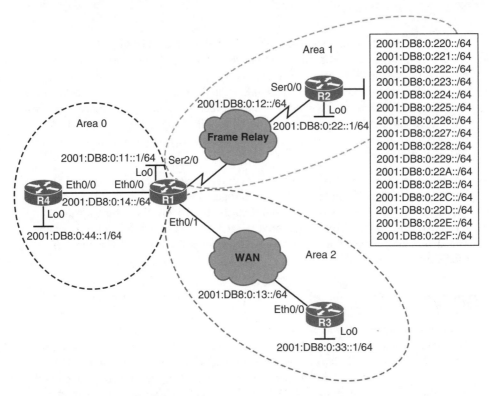

Figure 3-35 *IPv6 Topology OSPFv3*

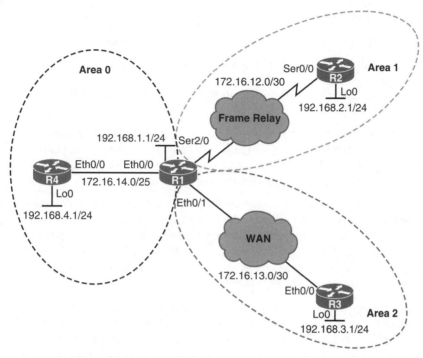

Figure 3-36 *IPv4 Topology OSPFv3*

Implementing OSPFv3

Example 3-67 shows R1 enabled for IPv6 unicast routing and starting an IPv6 OSPF router process with ID 1. R1 is configured with a router ID 1.1.1.1 and loopback 0 is as a passive interface.

Example 3-67 *Enabling OSPFv3 on R1*

```
R1(config)# ipv6 unicast-routing
R1(config)# ipv6 router ospf 1
R1(config-rtr)# router-id 1.1.1.1
R1(config-rtr)# passive-interface Loopback0
```

OSPFv3 is the IPv6-capable version of the OSPF routing protocol. It is a rewrite of the OSPF protocol to support IPv6, although the foundation remains the same as in IPv4 and OSPFv2. The OSPFv3 metric is still based on interface cost. The packet types and neighbor discovery mechanisms are the same in OSPFv3 as they are for OSPFv2. OSPFv3 also supports the same interface types, including broadcast, point-to-point, point-to-multipoint, NBMA, and virtual links. LSAs are still flooded throughout an OSPF domain, and many of the LSA types are the same, though a few have been renamed or newly created.

Cisco IOS routers offer two OSPF configuration methods for IPv6:

- Using the traditional **ipv6 router ospf** global configuration command

- Using the new-style **router ospfv3** global configuration command

We will first examine the traditional configuration approach, and then migrate the configuration to the new style.

To start any IPv6 routing protocols, you need to enable IPv6 unicast routing using the **ipv6 unicast-routing** command. In the traditional configuration approach, the OSPFv3 and OSPFv2 processes run independently on a router. In the traditional way, the OSPF process for IPv6 is started using the **ipv6 router ospf** command.

The OSPF process for IPv6 does not require an IPv4 address to be configured on the router, but it does require a 32-bit value for the router ID, which uses IPv4 address notation. The router ID is defined using the **router-id** command. If the router ID is not specifically configured, the system will try to dynamically choose an ID from the currently active IPv4 addresses, using the same process as OSPFv2 does for IPv4. If there is no active IPv4 address, the process will fail to start.

In the **ipv6 router ospf** configuration mode, you can specify the passive interfaces (using the **passive-interface** command), enable summarization, and fine-tune the operation, but you do not enable the process on specific interfaces. There is no **network** command. To activate the OSPF process on required interfaces, you will need the **ipv6 ospf** command in the interface configuration mode.

In Example 3-68, R1 is enabled for the OSPF-for-IPv6 process on its active interfaces. Interface Loopback 0 and Ethernet 0/0 are assigned to area 0, Serial 2/0 to area 1, and Ethernet 0/1 to area 2. The **exit** interface command does not need to be used between interfaces. It is only used in this example to better illustrate that OSPF-for-IPv6 is enabled on each specific interface.

Example 3-68   *Enabling OSPFv3 on the Interface*

```
R1(config)# interface Loopback0
R1(config-if)# ipv6 ospf 1 area 0
R1(config-if)# exit
R1(config)# interface Ethernet0/0
R1(config-if)# ipv6 ospf 1 area 0
R1(config-if)# exit
R1(config)# interface Serial2/0
R1(config-if)# ipv6 ospf 1 area 1
R1(config-if)# exit
R1(config)# interface Ethernet0/1
R1(config-if)# ipv6 ospf 1 area 2
 %OSPFv3-5-ADJCHG: Process 1, Nbr 4.4.4.4 on Ethernet0/0 from LOADING to FULL,
Loading Done
 %OSPFv3-5-ADJCHG: Process 1, Nbr 3.3.3.3 on Ethernet0/1 from LOADING to FULL,
Loading Done
```

To enable the OSPF-for-IPv6 process on an interface and assign that interface to an area, use the **ipv6 ospf** *ospf-process* **area** *area-id* command in the interface configuration mode. To be able to enable OSPFv3 on an interface, the interface must be enabled for IPv6. This occurs when the interface is configured with a global unicast IPv6 address.

Example 3-69 examines R1's OSPF adjacencies and routing table.

Example 3-69 *R1's Adjacencies and Routing Table*

```
R1# show ipv6 ospf neighbor

            OSPFv3 Router with ID (1.1.1.1) (Process ID 1)


Neighbor ID     Pri   State          Dead Time    Interface ID    Interface
4.4.4.4           1   FULL/DR        00:00:37     3               Ethernet0/0
3.3.3.3           1   FULL/DR        00:00:35     4               Ethernet0/1
R1# show ipv6 route ospf
<Output omitted>
O   2001:DB8:0:33::/64 [110/11]
      via FE80::A8BB:CCFF:FE00:AD10, Ethernet0/1
O   2001:DB8:0:44::/64 [110/11]
      via FE80::A8BB:CCFF:FE00:AE00, Ethernet0/0
```

After enabling the OSPF process on IPv6 interfaces you can verify the adjacencies and the IPv6 routing table. You can selectively display the OSPF-populated part of the routing table if you use the **show ipv6 route** command with the **ospf** keyword.

Why is the OSPF adjacency with R2, via Serial2/0, not working? On NBMA interfaces, the NBMA network type is by default used in OSPF routing. On such links, at least one side needs to define the OSPF neighbor, similarly as in OSPFv2. The **neighbor** command in the IPv6 environment requires that the IPv6 link-local address is specified for the peer, instead of using an IPv6 global unicast address. The IPv6 link-local addresses start with the FE80 prefix. In this scenario, the link-local address of R2 is FE80::2.

Example 3-70 specifies the IPv6 neighbor, FE80::2, for OSPFv3 on the NBMA interface Serial 2/0.

Example 3-70 *Specifying the Neighbor on an NBMA Interface*

```
R1(config)# interface serial 2/0
R1(config-if)# ipv6 ospf neighbor FE80::2
 %OSPFv3-5-ADJCHG: Process 1, Nbr 2.2.2.2 on Serial2/0 from LOADING to FULL, Loading
Done
```

OSPF adjacencies over NBMA links require that IPv6 connectivity for both the link-local and the global addresses is established. Depending on the transport network, this may require mapping of IPv6 addresses to Layer 2 circuit identifiers. In this scenario, R1 and R2 have been pre-configured with the necessary mappings. The relevant configuration on R1, including the neighbor address, is shown in Example 3-71:

Example 3-71   *R1's Partial Running-Config*

```
R1# show running-config interface serial 2/0
Building configuration...

Current configuration : 404 bytes
!
interface Serial2/0
 ip address 172.16.12.1 255.255.255.252
 encapsulation frame-relay
 ipv6 address FE80::1 link-local
 ipv6 address 2001:DB8:0:12::1/64
 ipv6 ospf 1 area 1
 ipv6 ospf neighbor FE80::2
 serial restart-delay 0
 frame-relay map ip 172.16.12.2 102 broadcast
 frame-relay map ipv6 2001:DB8:0:12::2 102 broadcast
 frame-relay map ipv6 FE80::2 102 broadcast
 no frame-relay inverse-arp
end
```

Example 3-72 examines the IPv6 OSPF database on R1.

Example 3-72   *R1's OSPF LSDB*

```
R1# show ipv6 ospf database

            OSPFv3 Router with ID (1.1.1.1) (Process ID 1)

            Router Link States (Area 0)

ADV Router      Age         Seq#        Fragment ID  Link count  Bits
  1.1.1.1       854         0x80000003  0               1        B
  4.4.4.4       871         0x80000002  0               1        None

            Net Link States (Area 0)

ADV Router      Age         Seq#        Link ID    Rtr count
  4.4.4.4       871         0x80000001  3              2

            Inter Area Prefix Link States (Area 0)

ADV Router      Age         Seq#        Prefix
  1.1.1.1       845         0x80000001  2001:DB8:0:12::/64
  1.1.1.1       845         0x80000001  2001:DB8:0:13::/64
  1.1.1.1       845         0x80000001  2001:DB8:0:33::/64
```

```
<Output omitted>


                    Link (Type-8) Link States (Area 0)


ADV Router          Age         Seq#        Link ID     Interface
  1.1.1.1           870         0x80000001  3           Et0/0
  4.4.4.4           1056        0x80000002  3           Et0/0


                    Intra Area Prefix Link States (Area 0)


ADV Router          Age         Seq#        Link ID     Ref-lstype  Ref-LSID
  1.1.1.1           865         0x80000003  0           0x2001      0
  4.4.4.4           871         0x80000003  0           0x2001      0
  4.4.4.4           871         0x80000001  3072        0x2002      3
```

OSPFv3 (for IPv6) renames two LSA types and defines two additional LSA types that do not exist in OSPFv2 (for IPv4).

The two renamed LSA types are as follows:

- **Interarea prefix LSAs for ABRs (Type 3):** Type 3 LSAs advertise internal networks to routers in other areas (interarea routes). Type 3 LSAs may represent a single network or a set of networks summarized into one advertisement. Only ABRs generate summary LSAs. In OSPF for IPv6, addresses for these LSAs are expressed as prefix/prefix length instead of address and mask. The default route is expressed as a prefix with length 0.

- **Interarea router LSAs for ASBRs (Type 4):** Type 4 LSAs advertise the location of an ASBR. Routers that are trying to reach an external network use these advertisements to determine the best path to the next hop. ASBRs generate Type 4 LSAs.

The two new LSA types are as follows:

- **Link LSAs (Type 8):** Type 8 LSAs have local-link flooding scope and are never flooded beyond the link with which they are associated. Link LSAs provide the link-local address of the router to all other routers attached to the link. They inform other routers attached to the link of a list of IPv6 prefixes to associate with the link. In addition, they allow the router to assert a collection of option bits to associate with the network LSA that will be originated for the link.

- **Intra-area prefix LSAs (Type 9):** A router can originate multiple intra-area prefix LSAs for each router or transit network, each with a unique link-state ID. The link-state ID for each intra-area prefix LSA describes its association to either the router LSA or the network LSA. The link-state ID also contains prefixes for stub and transit networks.

Example 3-73 reexamines the OSPFv3 adjacencies and routing table on R1.

Example 3-73 *R1's OSPFv3 Adjacencies and Routing Table*

```
R1# show ipv6 ospf neighbor

          OSPFv3 Router with ID (1.1.1.1) (Process ID 1)


Neighbor ID     Pri   State          Dead Time   Interface ID   Interface
4.4.4.4           1   FULL/DR        00:00:39    3              Ethernet0/0
2.2.2.2           1   FULL/DR        00:01:43    3              Serial2/0
3.3.3.3           1   FULL/DR        00:00:39    4              Ethernet0/1
R1# show ipv6 route ospf
<Output omitted>
O    2001:DB8:0:22::/64 [110/65]
      via FE80::2, Serial2/0
O    2001:DB8:0:33::/64 [110/11]
      via FE80::A8BB:CCFF:FE00:AD10, Ethernet0/1
O    2001:DB8:0:44::/64 [110/11]
      via FE80::A8BB:CCFF:FE00:AE00, Ethernet0/0
O    2001:DB8:0:220::/64 [110/65]
      via FE80::2, Serial2/0
O    2001:DB8:0:221::/64 [110/65]
      via FE80::2, Serial2/0
<Output omitted>
```

After enabling the OSPF on the NBMA interface, notice an additional adjacency across Serial 2/0 and multiple OSPF intra-area routes received via this interface.

OSPFv3 for IPv4 and IPv6

OSPFv3 does not only support exchange of IPv6 routes, but it also supports exchange of IPv4 routes.

The newest OSPFv3 configuration approach utilizes a single OSPFv3 process. It is capable of supporting IPv4 and IPv6 within a single OSPFv3 process. OSPFv3 builds a single database with LSAs that carry IPv4 and IPv6 information. The OSPF adjacencies are established separately for each address family. Settings that are specific to an address family (IPv4/IPv6) are configured inside that address family router configuration mode.

Running single OSPFv3 for both IPv4 and IPv6 is supported since Cisco IOS Software Release 15.1(3)S.

Example 3-74 shows R1's configuration of an OSPFv3 process using the new configuration style (**router ospfv3**), using process number 1, OSPF router ID 1.1.1.1, and making the Loopback 0 interface passive.

Example 3-74 *Configuring OSPFv3 Using the* **router ospfv3** *Command*

```
R1(config)# router ospfv3 1
R1(config-router)# router-id 1.1.1.1
R1(config-router)# passive-interface Loopback0
```

The new-style OSPFv3 process is enabled using the **router ospfv3** *process-number* command. Within the OSPF process configuration mode, the OSPF router ID is defined (using the **router-id** *ospf-process-ID* command), the passive interfaces are set, and per-process OSPF behavior can be tuned.

Example 3-75 displays the OSPFv3 router configuration on R1 using the **show running-config | section router** command. The old-style OSPF router configuration (**ipv6 router ospf**) has disappeared and has been replaced by the new-style router ospfv3 with an address family sub-mode.

Example 3-75 *R1's OSPFv3 Configuration*

```
R1# show running-config | section router
router ospfv3 1
 router-id 1.1.1.1
 !
 address-family ipv6 unicast
  passive-interface Loopback0
  router-id 1.1.1.1
 exit-address-family
```

The router ID is displayed in the router configuration mode that is valid globally for all address families.

The **address-family ipv6 unicast** has been automatically created on R1. Cisco IOS Software has parsed the previous old-style OSPFv3 configuration and found that the OSPF process was enabled only for IPv6. Consequently, when you chose the new-style configuration, the IPv6 address family has been instantiated and the IPv4 address family does not show in the configuration.

The passive-interface configuration is actually a setting that is valid per address family. You can have dissimilar settings for IPv4 and IPv4. Therefore this command has been placed in the address family submode.

Example 3-76 verifies R1's OSPFv3 operation by verifying its adjacencies, routing table, and database. The OSPFv3 operation can be verified using the old-style commands (**show ipv6 ospf neighbor**, **show ipv6 ospf database**) or the new-style commands, such as **show ospfv3 neighbor** and **show ospfv3 database**.

Example 3-76 *R1's OSPFv3 Adjacencies, Routing Table, and LSDB*

```
R1# show ospfv3 neighbor


          OSPFv3 1 address-family ipv6 (router-id 1.1.1.1)


Neighbor ID     Pri   State          Dead Time   Interface ID   Interface
4.4.4.4           1   FULL/DR        00:00:37    3              Ethernet0/0
2.2.2.2           1   FULL/DR        00:01:44    3              Serial2/0
3.3.3.3           1   FULL/DR        00:00:35    4              Ethernet0/1
R1# show ipv6 route ospf
IPv6 Routing Table - default - 28 entries
Codes: C - Connected, L - Local, S - Static, U - Per-user Static route
       B - BGP, HA - Home Agent, MR - Mobile Router, R - RIP
       H - NHRP, I1 - ISIS L1, I2 - ISIS L2, IA - ISIS interarea
       IS - ISIS summary, D - EIGRP, EX - EIGRP external, NM - NEMO
       ND - ND Default, NDp - ND Prefix, DCE - Destination, NDr - Redirect
       O - OSPF Intra, OI - OSPF Inter, OE1 - OSPF ext 1, OE2 - OSPF ext 2
       ON1 - OSPF NSSA ext 1, ON2 - OSPF NSSA ext 2, l - LISP
O   2001:DB8:0:22::/64 [110/65]
     via FE80::2, Serial2/0
O   2001:DB8:0:33::/64 [110/11]
     via FE80::A8BB:CCFF:FE00:AD10, Ethernet0/1
O   2001:DB8:0:44::/64 [110/11]
     via FE80::A8BB:CCFF:FE00:AE00, Ethernet0/0
O   2001:DB8:0:220::/64 [110/65]
     via FE80::2, Serial2/0
O   2001:DB8:0:221::/64 [110/65]
     via FE80::2, Serial2/0
O   2001:DB8:0:222::/64 [110/65]
     via FE80::2, Serial2/0
O   2001:DB8:0:223::/64 [110/65]
     via FE80::2, Serial2/0
O   2001:DB8:0:224::/64 [110/65]
     via FE80::2, Serial2/0
O   2001:DB8:0:225::/64 [110/65]
     via FE80::2, Serial2/0
O   2001:DB8:0:226::/64 [110/65]
     via FE80::2, Serial2/0
O   2001:DB8:0:227::/64 [110/65]
     via FE80::2, Serial2/0
O   2001:DB8:0:228::/64 [110/65]
     via FE80::2, Serial2/0
O   2001:DB8:0:229::/64 [110/65]
     via FE80::2, Serial2/0
```

```
O   2001:DB8:0:22A::/64 [110/65]
       via FE80::2, Serial2/0
O   2001:DB8:0:22B::/64 [110/65]
       via FE80::2, Serial2/0
O   2001:DB8:0:22C::/64 [110/65]
       via FE80::2, Serial2/0
O   2001:DB8:0:22D::/64 [110/65]
       via FE80::2, Serial2/0
O   2001:DB8:0:22E::/64 [110/65]
       via FE80::2, Serial2/0
O   2001:DB8:0:22F::/64 [110/65]
       via FE80::2, Serial2/0
R1# show ospfv3 database


           OSPFv3 1 address-family ipv6 (router-id 1.1.1.1)


              Router Link States (Area 0)


ADV Router        Age        Seq#       Fragment ID  Link count  Bits
   1.1.1.1        793        0x80000006 0            1           B
   4.4.4.4        135        0x8000000D 0            1           None


              Net Link States (Area 0)


ADV Router        Age        Seq#       Link ID    Rtr count
   4.4.4.4        379        0x80000006 3          2


              Inter Area Prefix Link States (Area 0)


ADV Router        Age        Seq#       Prefix
   1.1.1.1        301        0x80000006 2001:DB8:0:12::/64
   1.1.1.1        301        0x80000006 2001:DB8:0:33::/64
   1.1.1.1        301        0x80000006 2001:DB8:0:13::/64
   1.1.1.1        1301       0x80000004 2001:DB8:0:22::/64
   1.1.1.1        1301       0x80000004 2001:DB8:0:220::/64
   1.1.1.1        1301       0x80000004 2001:DB8:0:221::/64
   1.1.1.1        1301       0x80000004 2001:DB8:0:222::/64
   1.1.1.1        1301       0x80000004 2001:DB8:0:223::/64
   1.1.1.1        1301       0x80000004 2001:DB8:0:224::/64
   1.1.1.1        1301       0x80000004 2001:DB8:0:225::/64
   1.1.1.1        1301       0x80000004 2001:DB8:0:226::/64
   1.1.1.1        1301       0x80000004 2001:DB8:0:227::/64
   1.1.1.1        1301       0x80000004 2001:DB8:0:228::/64
   1.1.1.1        1301       0x80000004 2001:DB8:0:229::/64
   1.1.1.1        1301       0x80000004 2001:DB8:0:22A::/64
```

```
1.1.1.1         1301        0x80000004   2001:DB8:0:22B::/64
1.1.1.1         1301        0x80000004   2001:DB8:0:22C::/64
1.1.1.1         1301        0x80000004   2001:DB8:0:22D::/64
1.1.1.1         1301        0x80000004   2001:DB8:0:22E::/64
1.1.1.1         1301        0x80000004   2001:DB8:0:22F::/64


                Link (Type-8) Link States (Area 0)


ADV Router      Age         Seq#         Link ID     Interface
1.1.1.1         793         0x80000006   3           Et0/0
4.4.4.4         135         0x8000000B   3           Et0/0


                Intra Area Prefix Link States (Area 0)


ADV Router      Age         Seq#         Link ID     Ref-lstype   Ref-LSID
1.1.1.1         793         0x80000006   0           0x2001       0
4.4.4.4         379         0x8000000F   0           0x2001       0
4.4.4.4         379         0x80000006   3072        0x2002       3


                Router Link States (Area 1)


ADV Router      Age         Seq#         Fragment ID  Link count  Bits
1.1.1.1         793         0x80000007   0            1           B
2.2.2.2         1464        0x80000029   0            1           None


                Net Link States (Area 1)


ADV Router      Age         Seq#         Link ID     Rtr count
2.2.2.2         1464        0x80000004   3           2


                Inter Area Prefix Link States (Area 1)


ADV Router      Age         Seq#         Prefix
1.1.1.1         301         0x80000006   2001:DB8:0:33::/64
1.1.1.1         301         0x80000006   2001:DB8:0:13::/64
1.1.1.1         301         0x80000006   2001:DB8:0:11::1/128
1.1.1.1         301         0x80000006   2001:DB8:0:44::/64
1.1.1.1         301         0x80000006   2001:DB8:0:14::/64


                Link (Type-8) Link States (Area 1)


ADV Router      Age         Seq#         Link ID     Interface
1.1.1.1         793         0x80000006   11          Se2/0
2.2.2.2         1962        0x80000029   3           Se2/0
```

```
                Intra Area Prefix Link States (Area 1)

ADV Router       Age        Seq#        Link ID    Ref-lstype  Ref-LSID
  2.2.2.2        1464       0x80000040  0          0x2001      0
  2.2.2.2        1464       0x80000004  3072       0x2002      3


                Router Link States (Area 2)

ADV Router       Age        Seq#        Fragment ID  Link count  Bits
  1.1.1.1        793        0x80000006      0            1        B
  3.3.3.3        1901       0x8000002B      0            1        None


                Net Link States (Area 2)

ADV Router       Age        Seq#        Link ID    Rtr count
  3.3.3.3        376        0x80000006  4          2


                Inter Area Prefix Link States (Area 2)

ADV Router       Age        Seq#        Prefix
  1.1.1.1        301        0x80000006  2001:DB8:0:12::/64
  1.1.1.1        301        0x80000006  2001:DB8:0:11::1/128
  1.1.1.1        301        0x80000006  2001:DB8:0:44::/64
  1.1.1.1        301        0x80000006  2001:DB8:0:14::/64
  1.1.1.1        1301       0x80000004  2001:DB8:0:22::/64
  1.1.1.1        1301       0x80000004  2001:DB8:0:220::/64
  1.1.1.1        1301       0x80000004  2001:DB8:0:221::/64
  1.1.1.1        1301       0x80000004  2001:DB8:0:222::/64
  1.1.1.1        1301       0x80000004  2001:DB8:0:223::/64
  1.1.1.1        1301       0x80000004  2001:DB8:0:224::/64
  1.1.1.1        1301       0x80000004  2001:DB8:0:225::/64
  1.1.1.1        1301       0x80000004  2001:DB8:0:226::/64
  1.1.1.1        1301       0x80000004  2001:DB8:0:227::/64
  1.1.1.1        1301       0x80000004  2001:DB8:0:228::/64
  1.1.1.1        1301       0x80000004  2001:DB8:0:229::/64
  1.1.1.1        1301       0x80000004  2001:DB8:0:22A::/64
  1.1.1.1        1301       0x80000004  2001:DB8:0:22B::/64
  1.1.1.1        1301       0x80000004  2001:DB8:0:22C::/64
  1.1.1.1        1301       0x80000004  2001:DB8:0:22D::/64
  1.1.1.1        1301       0x80000004  2001:DB8:0:22E::/64
  1.1.1.1        1301       0x80000004  2001:DB8:0:22F::/64


                Link (Type-8) Link States (Area 2)

ADV Router       Age        Seq#        Link ID    Interface
```

```
1.1.1.1          793        0x80000006  4          Et0/1
3.3.3.3          1901       0x80000028  4          Et0/1


                 Intra Area Prefix Link States (Area 2)

ADV Router       Age        Seq#        Link ID   Ref-lstype  Ref-LSID
3.3.3.3          376        0x8000002B     0        0x2001         0
3.3.3.3          376        0x80000006   4096       0x2002         4
```

Despite the change of the OSPFv3 configuration to the new-style approach, the OSPF connectivity has been retained. In fact, R1 now uses a mixed configuration: new-style process configuration, and old-style interface commands. Example 3-77 shows the old-style interface commands.

Example 3-77 *OSPFv3 Old-Style OSPF Configuration Commands*

```
interface Loopback0
 ipv6 ospf 1 area 0
!
interface Ethernet0/0
 ipv6 ospf 1 area 0
!
interface Ethernet0/1
 ipv6 ospf 1 area 2
!
interface Serial2/0
 ipv6 ospf 1 area 1
 ipv6 ospf neighbor FE80::2
```

In Example 3-78, R1 is enabled using the OSPFv3 IPv6 address family on the active interfaces using the new-style configuration approach. Once again, the **exit** interface command is not needed but used make the configuration clearer.

Example 3-78 *OSPFv3 New-Style OSPF Configuration Commands*

```
R1(config)# interface Loopback 0
R1(config-if)# ospfv3 1 ipv6 area 0
R1(config-if)# exit
R1(config)# interface Ethernet 0/0
R1(config-if)# ospfv3 1 ipv6 area 0
R1(config-if)# exit
R1(config)# interface Serial 2/0
R1(config-if)# ospfv3 1 ipv6 area 1
R1(config-if)# exit
R1(config)# interface Ethernet 0/1
R1(config-if)# ospfv3 1 ipv6 area 2
```

The preferred interface mode command for the new style OSPFv3 configuration is the **ospfv3** *process-id* **{ipv4|ipv6} area** *area-id* command. It allows you to selectively activate the OSPFv3 process for an address family (IPv4 or IPv6) on a given interface.

With the OSPFv3 address families feature, you may have two device processes per interface, but only one process per AF. If the IPv4 AF is used, an IPv4 address must first be configured on the interface. For IPv6 AF it is enough, if only IPv6 is enabled on the interface, as OSPFv3 uses link-local addresses. A single IPv4 or IPv6 OSPFv3 process running multiple instances on the same interface is not supported.

Example 3-79 verifies the resulting configuration and operation on R1. The interface configuration can be viewed using the **show running-config interface** command. The **include** keyword can be used to display only the interface commands that include a certain information.

Example 3-79 *Verifying OSPFv3 Configuration and Operation on R1*

```
R1# show running-config interface Loopback 0 | include ospf
 ospfv3 1 ipv6 area 0
R1# show running-config interface Ethernet 0/0 | include ospf
 ospfv3 1 ipv6 area 0
R1# show running-config interface Serial 2/0 | include ospf
 ospfv3 1 ipv6 area 1
 ospfv3 1 ipv6 neighbor FE80::2
R1# show running-config interface Ethernet 0/1 | include ospf
 ospfv3 1 ipv6 area 2
R1# show ospfv3 neighbor

          OSPFv3 1 address-family ipv6 (router-id 1.1.1.1)

Neighbor ID     Pri   State        Dead Time   Interface ID    Interface
4.4.4.4           1   FULL/DR      00:00:32    3               Ethernet0/0
2.2.2.2           1   FULL/DR      00:01:48    3               Serial2/0
3.3.3.3           1   FULL/DR      00:00:31    4               Ethernet0/1
```

The configuration on R1 shows that the new-style interface-mode commands have replaced the old-style (**ipv6 ospf**) commands. The configuration of the NBMA interface (Serial 2/0) shows that the neighbor commands has been automatically updated with the **ospfv3** *process-id* **ipv6 neighbor** command.

The OSPF operation has not been affected. The OSPFv3 adjacencies, database, and routing table are functional.

Example 3-80 shows R1 enabled the OSPFv3 process enabled for IPv4 and the Loopback 0 interface is configured as passive. To activate OSPFv3 for IPv4, you need to configure the **ospfv3** *process-number* **ipv4 area** *area-id* command in the configuration mode of the desired interface.

Example 3-80   *Enabling OSPFv3 for IPv4*

```
R1(config)# interface Loopback0
R1(config-if)# ospfv3 1 ipv4 area 0
R1(config-if)# exit
R1(config)# interface Ethernet0/0
R1(config-if)# ospfv3 1 ipv4 area 0
R1(config-if)# exit
R1(config)# interface Ethernet0/1
R1(config-if)# ospfv3 1 ipv4 area 2
R1(config)# exit
R1(config-if)# interface Serial2/0
R1(config-if)# ospfv3 1 ipv4 area 1
R1(config-if)# ospfv3 1 ipv4 neighbor FE80::2
R1(config-if)# exit
R1(config)# router ospfv3 1
R1(config-router)# address-family ipv4 unicast
R1(config-router-af)# passive-interface Loopback0
%OSPFv3-5-ADJCHG: Process 1, IPv4, Nbr 0.0.0.0 on Serial2/0 from ATTEMPT to DOWN,
Neighbor Down: Interface down or detached
%OSPFv3-5-ADJCHG: Process 1, IPv4, Nbr 3.3.3.3 on Ethernet0/1 from LOADING to FULL,
Loading Done
%OSPFv3-5-ADJCHG: Process 1, IPv4, Nbr 4.4.4.4 on Ethernet0/0 from LOADING to FULL,
Loading Done
```

This way some (or all) of the links can be enabled for IPv4 forwarding and be configured with IPv4 addresses. For example, pockets of IPv4-only devices may exist around the edges running an IPv4 static or dynamic routing protocol. In that scenario, you could forward IPv4 or IPv6 traffic between these pockets. The transit device needs both IPv4 and IPv6 forwarding stacks (that is, a dual stack).

This feature allows a separate (possibly incongruent) topology to be constructed for the IPv4 address family. It installs IPv4 routes in the IPv4 RIB, and then the forwarding occurs natively. The OSPFv3 process fully supports an IPv4 AF topology and can redistribute routes from and into any other IPv4 routing protocol.

An OSPFv3 process can be configured to be IPv4 or IPv6. The **address-family** command is used to determine which AF will run in the OSPFv3 process. Once the address family is selected, you can enable multiple instances on a link and enable address–family-specific commands.

On the NBMA links, such as the interface Serial 2/0 in this scenario, you need to define the OSPF neighbor. In the new-style OSPFv3 you must configure the IPv6 link-local address of the peer as the OSPF neighbor. Both address families use IPv6 as the underlying transport.

Example 3-81 examines R1's OSPFv3 adjacencies. The OSPF adjacencies can be displayed using the **show ospfv3 neighbor** command for both address families.

Example 3-81 *R1's OSPFv3 Adjacencies for Both IPv4 and IPv6 Address Families*

```
R1# show ospfv3 neighbor


            OSPFv3 1 address-family ipv4 (router-id 1.1.1.1)


Neighbor ID     Pri   State         Dead Time   Interface ID   Interface
4.4.4.4          1    FULL/DR       00:00:34    3              Ethernet0/0
2.2.2.2          1    FULL/DR       00:01:38    3              Serial2/0
3.3.3.3          1    FULL/DR       00:00:36    4              Ethernet0/1


            OSPFv3 1 address-family ipv6 (router-id 1.1.1.1)


Neighbor ID     Pri   State         Dead Time   Interface ID   Interface
4.4.4.4          1    FULL/DR       00:00:35    3              Ethernet0/0
2.2.2.2          1    FULL/DR       00:01:58    3              Serial2/0
3.3.3.3          1    FULL/DR       00:00:34    4              Ethernet0/1
```

In Example 3-82, R1's IPv4 routing table is displayed computed from the OSPFv3 database. The IPv4 routing table, computed from the OSPFv3 database, can be displayed using the **show ip route ospfv3** command. The **ospfv3** keyword filters the content of the routing table and displays only the OSPFv3 routes.

Note that command **show ip route ospf** will not show any routes.

Example 3-82 *R1's IPv4 Routing Table with OSPFv3 Routes*

```
R1# show ip route ospfv3
<Output omitted>


      192.168.2.0/32 is subnetted, 1 subnets
O        192.168.2.2 [110/64] via 172.16.12.2, 00:27:49, Serial2/0
      192.168.3.0/32 is subnetted, 1 subnets
O        192.168.3.3 [110/10] via 172.16.13.2, 00:30:08, Ethernet0/1
      192.168.4.0/32 is subnetted, 1 subnets
O        192.168.4.4 [110/10] via 172.16.14.4, 00:30:08, Ethernet0/0
```

The OSPFv3 database for R1 is examined in Example 3-83. A router maintains a single OSPFv3 database, which contains various LSAs. Some LSAs carry IPv4-related information, others carry IPv6-related information, and others carry mixed information. You have to examine specific LSA types to see which address family is described by a given LSA.

Note that old-style verification commands like **show ip ospf database** will not show any information.

Example 3-83   *R1's OSPFv3 LSDB*

```
R1# show ospfv3 database inter-area prefix
            OSPFv3 1 address-family ipv4 (router-id 1.1.1.1)
                    Inter Area Prefix Link States (Area 0)
  LS Type: Inter Area Prefix Links
  Advertising Router: 1.1.1.1
<Output omitted>
  Prefix Address: 172.16.12.0
  Prefix Length: 30, Options: None
<Output omitted>


            OSPFv3 1 address-family ipv6 (router-id 1.1.1.1)
                    Inter Area Prefix Link States (Area 0)
  LS Type: Inter Area Prefix Links
  Advertising Router: 1.1.1.1
<Output omitted>
  Prefix Address: 2001:DB8:0:12::
  Prefix Length: 64, Options: None
<Output omitted>
```

Example 3-84 shows the IPv6 routing tables for R3 and R4. Configuring the areas using one of the stub options can help reduce the size of the routing tables.

Example 3-84   *OSPFv3 Routes in the Routing Tables of R3 and R4*

```
R3# show ipv6 route ospf
<Output omitted>
OI  2001:DB8:0:11::1/128 [110/10]
     via FE80::A8BB:CCFF:FE00:AB10, Ethernet0/1
OI  2001:DB8:0:12::/64 [110/74]
     via FE80::A8BB:CCFF:FE00:AB10, Ethernet0/1
OI  2001:DB8:0:14::/64 [110/20]
     via FE80::A8BB:CCFF:FE00:AB10, Ethernet0/1
OI  2001:DB8:0:22::/64 [110/75]
     via FE80::A8BB:CCFF:FE00:AB10, Ethernet0/1
OI  2001:DB8:0:44::/64 [110/21]
     via FE80::A8BB:CCFF:FE00:AB10, Ethernet0/1
OI  2001:DB8:0:220::/64 [110/75]
     via FE80::A8BB:CCFF:FE00:AB10, Ethernet0/1
OI  2001:DB8:0:221::/64 [110/75]
     via FE80::A8BB:CCFF:FE00:AB10, Ethernet0/1
OI  2001:DB8:0:222::/64 [110/75]
     via FE80::A8BB:CCFF:FE00:AB10, Ethernet0/1
OI  2001:DB8:0:223::/64 [110/75]
     via FE80::A8BB:CCFF:FE00:AB10, Ethernet0/1
```

```
OI   2001:DB8:0:224::/64 [110/75]
         via FE80::A8BB:CCFF:FE00:AB10, Ethernet0/1
OI   2001:DB8:0:225::/64 [110/75]
         via FE80::A8BB:CCFF:FE00:AB10, Ethernet0/1
OI   2001:DB8:0:226::/64 [110/75]
         via FE80::A8BB:CCFF:FE00:AB10, Ethernet0/1
OI   2001:DB8:0:227::/64 [110/75]
         via FE80::A8BB:CCFF:FE00:AB10, Ethernet0/1
OI   2001:DB8:0:228::/64 [110/75]
         via FE80::A8BB:CCFF:FE00:AB10, Ethernet0/1
OI   2001:DB8:0:229::/64 [110/75]
         via FE80::A8BB:CCFF:FE00:AB10, Ethernet0/1
OI   2001:DB8:0:22A::/64 [110/75]
         via FE80::A8BB:CCFF:FE00:AB10, Ethernet0/1
OI   2001:DB8:0:22B::/64 [110/75]
         via FE80::A8BB:CCFF:FE00:AB10, Ethernet0/1
OI   2001:DB8:0:22C::/64 [110/75]
         via FE80::A8BB:CCFF:FE00:AB10, Ethernet0/1
OI   2001:DB8:0:22D::/64 [110/75]
         via FE80::A8BB:CCFF:FE00:AB10, Ethernet0/1
OI   2001:DB8:0:22E::/64 [110/75]
         via FE80::A8BB:CCFF:FE00:AB10, Ethernet0/1
OI   2001:DB8:0:22F::/64 [110/75]
         via FE80::A8BB:CCFF:FE00:AB10, Ethernet0/1


R4# show ipv6 route ospf
<Output omitted>
O    2001:DB8:0:11::1/128 [110/10]
         via FE80::A8BB:CCFF:FE00:AB00, Ethernet0/0
OI   2001:DB8:0:12::/64 [110/74]
         via FE80::A8BB:CCFF:FE00:AB00, Ethernet0/0
OI   2001:DB8:0:13::/64 [110/20]
         via FE80::A8BB:CCFF:FE00:AB00, Ethernet0/0
OI   2001:DB8:0:22::/64 [110/75]
         via FE80::A8BB:CCFF:FE00:AB00, Ethernet0/0
OI   2001:DB8:0:33::/64 [110/21]
         via FE80::A8BB:CCFF:FE00:AB00, Ethernet0/0
OI   2001:DB8:0:220::/64 [110/75]
         via FE80::A8BB:CCFF:FE00:AB00, Ethernet0/0
OI   2001:DB8:0:221::/64 [110/75]
         via FE80::A8BB:CCFF:FE00:AB00, Ethernet0/0
OI   2001:DB8:0:222::/64 [110/75]
         via FE80::A8BB:CCFF:FE00:AB00, Ethernet0/0
OI   2001:DB8:0:223::/64 [110/75]
         via FE80::A8BB:CCFF:FE00:AB00, Ethernet0/0
```

```
OI  2001:DB8:0:224::/64 [110/75]
      via FE80::A8BB:CCFF:FE00:AB00, Ethernet0/0
OI  2001:DB8:0:225::/64 [110/75]
      via FE80::A8BB:CCFF:FE00:AB00, Ethernet0/0
OI  2001:DB8:0:226::/64 [110/75]
      via FE80::A8BB:CCFF:FE00:AB00, Ethernet0/0
OI  2001:DB8:0:227::/64 [110/75]
      via FE80::A8BB:CCFF:FE00:AB00, Ethernet0/0
OI  2001:DB8:0:228::/64 [110/75]
      via FE80::A8BB:CCFF:FE00:AB00, Ethernet0/0
OI  2001:DB8:0:229::/64 [110/75]
      via FE80::A8BB:CCFF:FE00:AB00, Ethernet0/0
OI  2001:DB8:0:22A::/64 [110/75]
      via FE80::A8BB:CCFF:FE00:AB00, Ethernet0/0
OI  2001:DB8:0:22B::/64 [110/75]
      via FE80::A8BB:CCFF:FE00:AB00, Ethernet0/0
OI  2001:DB8:0:22C::/64 [110/75]
      via FE80::A8BB:CCFF:FE00:AB00, Ethernet0/0
OI  2001:DB8:0:22D::/64 [110/75]
      via FE80::A8BB:CCFF:FE00:AB00, Ethernet0/0
OI  2001:DB8:0:22E::/64 [110/75]
      via FE80::A8BB:CCFF:FE00:AB00, Ethernet0/0
OI  2001:DB8:0:22F::/64 [110/75]
      via FE80::A8BB:CCFF:FE00:AB00, Ethernet0/0
```

When you display the IPv6 routing tables on R3 and R4, you will see numerous OSPF interarea routes. Making the nonbackbone area 2 a stub area can reduce the size of the R3 routing table. Summarizing the interarea routes on the area border router can reduce R4's routing table in area 0.

In Example 3-85, ABR R1 and area 2 router R3 are configured to act as a totally stubby area for IPv6.

Example 3-85 *Area 2 Routers Configured as a Totally Stubby Area*

```
R1(config)# router ospfv3 1
R1(config-router)# address-family ipv6 unicast
R1(config-router-af)# area 2 stub no-summary
%OSPFv3-5-ADJCHG: Process 1, IPv6, Nbr 3.3.3.3 on Ethernet0/1 from FULL to DOWN,
Neighbor Down: Adjacency forced to reset

R3(config)# router ospfv3 1
R3(config-router)# address-family ipv6 unicast
R3(config-router-af)# area 2 stub
%OSPFv3-5-ADJCHG: Process 1, IPv6, Nbr 1.1.1.1 on Ethernet0/1 from LOADING to FULL,
Loading Done
```

Features specific to an address family are configured for the given address family. The stubbiness or total stubbiness of an area, for example, could be enabled individually for IPv4, IPv6, or both. In this scenario, area 2 is configured as a stub area for the IPv6 address family.

OSPF uses a stub feature flag in the Hello packets. This flag must match between the neighbors for the adjacency to be established. The flag is exchanged individually for each address family. This example illustrates how the adjacency fails if only one side has the area configured as stub, and then succeeds when both R1 and R3 have matching configuration.

The IPv6 and IPv4 routing in area 2 is verified by examining the routing table of R3 in Example 3-86.

Example 3-86 *Examining the Differences Between R3's IPv4 and IPv6 Routing Tables*

```
R3# show ipv6 route ospf
<Output omitted>
OI   ::/0 [110/11]
     via FE80::A8BB:CCFF:FE00:AB10, Ethernet0/1
R3# show ip route ospfv3
<Output omitted>
O IA     172.16.12.0/30 [110/74] via 172.16.13.1, 00:09:55, Ethernet0/1
O IA     172.16.14.0/25 [110/20] via 172.16.13.1, 00:09:55, Ethernet0/1
       192.168.1.0/32 is subnetted, 1 subnets
O IA     192.168.1.1 [110/10] via 172.16.13.1, 00:09:55, Ethernet0/1
       192.168.2.0/32 is subnetted, 1 subnets
O IA     192.168.2.2 [110/74] via 172.16.13.1, 00:09:55, Ethernet0/1
       192.168.4.0/32 is subnetted, 1 subnets
O IA     192.168.4.4 [110/20] via 172.16.13.1, 00:09:55, Ethernet0/1
```

When viewing the OSPF routing table for IPv4 and IPv6, notice the difference in the area 2 operations between the two address families. Area 2 acts as a standard area for IPv4 and therefore you see all external and interarea routes received via the backbone area. Area 2 acts as a totally stubby area for IPv6. Therefore you see a default route toward the ABR.

Example 3-87 summarizes the IPv6 networks advertised by R2 (2001:DB8:0:220::/64 to 2001:DB8:0:22F::/64) using the smallest possible address block.

Example 3-87 *Summarizing an IPv6 Address Block on R1*

```
R1(config)# router ospfv3 1
R1(config-router)# address-family ipv6 unicast
R1(config-router-af)# area 1 range 2001:DB8:0:220::/60
```

Like in IPv4, OSPFv3 supports IPv6 address summarization. Interarea routes can be summarized on area border routers using the **area** *area-id* **range** command in the desired address family mode. In this scenario, a set of IPv6 network addresses are summarized using the address block 2001:DB8:0:220::/60.

Although not demonstrated in these examples, you can summarize external routes on the ASBRs. To perform such summarization for IPv6, you would use the **summary-prefix** command in the IPv6 address family router configuration mode.

Example 3-88 verifies the IPv6 summarization effects in the backbone area by viewing the IPv6 routing table on the backbone router R4. R4 contains the summary address 2001:DB8:0:220::/60 instead of the individual smaller networks.

Example 3-88   *OSPF Routes in R1's Routing Table*

```
R4# show ipv6 route ospf
<Output omitted>
O    2001:DB8:0:11::1/128 [110/10]
       via FE80::A8BB:CCFF:FE00:AB00, Ethernet0/0
OI   2001:DB8:0:12::/64 [110/74]
       via FE80::A8BB:CCFF:FE00:AB00, Ethernet0/0
OI   2001:DB8:0:13::/64 [110/20]
       via FE80::A8BB:CCFF:FE00:AB00, Ethernet0/0
OI   2001:DB8:0:22::/64 [110/75]
       via FE80::A8BB:CCFF:FE00:AB00, Ethernet0/0
OI   2001:DB8:0:33::/64 [110/21]
       via FE80::A8BB:CCFF:FE00:AB00, Ethernet0/0
OI   2001:DB8:0:220::/60 [110/75]
       via FE80::A8BB:CCFF:FE00:AB00, Ethernet0/0
```

Configuring Advanced OSPFv3

OSPFv3 offers you a set of tools that is very similar to that of OSPFv2 to fine-tune the OSPFv3 functionality.

Networks on the ASBR can be summarized during redistribution into OSPFv3. To configure an IPv6 summary prefix in Open Shortest Path First Version 3 (OSPFv3), use the following command in OSPFv3 router configuration mode, IPv6 address family configuration mode, or IPv4 address family configuration mode:

```
summary-prefix prefix [ not-advertise | tag tag-value ] [ nssa-only]
```

To restore the default, use the **no** form of this command. Table 3-8 describes the command parameters.

Table 3-8 *Parameters for* **summary-prefix** *Command*

Parameter	Description
prefix	IPv6 route prefix for the destination.
not-advertise	(Optional) Suppresses routes that match the specified prefix and mask pair. This keyword applies to OSPFv3 only.
tag *tag-value*	(Optional) Specifies the tag value that can be used as a match value for controlling redistribution via route maps. This keyword applies to OSPFv3 only.
nssa-only	(Optional) Limits the scope of the prefix to the area. Sets the NSSA-only attribute for the summary route (if any) generated for the specified prefix.

Example 3-89 shows a sample configuration. Redistribution is discussed in Chapter 4.

Example 3-89 *Configuring the* **summary-prefix** *Command on an ASBR*

```
Router(config)# router ospfv3 1
Router(config-router)# address-family ipv6 unicast
Router(config-router-af)# summary-prefix 2001:db8:1::/56
```

Load-balancing behavior can also be controlled on OSPFv3 routers. To control the maximum number of equal-cost routes that a process for OSPFv3 routing can support, use the **maximum-paths** command in IPv6 or IPv4 address family configuration mode, shown in Example 3-90. The range in OSPFv3 is from 1 through 64.

Example 3-90 **maximum-paths** *Command Configured in Address Family Mode*

```
Router(config)# router ospfv3 1
Router(config-router)# address-family ipv6 unicast
Router(config-router-af)# maximum-paths 8
```

OSPFv3 Caveats

The OSPF processes: traditional OSPFv2, traditional OSPFv3, and new OSPFv3 that uses the address families to supports both IP stacks, differ in the transport protocols.

The traditional OSPFv2 method, configured with the **router ospf** command, uses IPv4 as the transport mechanism. The traditional OSPFv3 method, configured with the **ipv6 router ospf** command, uses IPv6 as the transport protocol. The new OSPFv3 framework, configured with the **router ospfv3** command, uses IPv6 as the transport mechanism for both address families. Therefore, it will not peer with routers running the traditional OSPFv2 protocol.

The OSPFv3 address families feature is supported as of Cisco IOS Release 15.1(3)S and Cisco IOS Release 15.2(1)T. Cisco devices that run software older than these releases and third-party devices will not form neighbor relationships with devices running the address family feature for the IPv4 address family because they do not set the address family bit. Therefore, those devices will not participate in the IPv4 address family SPF calculations and will not install the IPv4 OSPFv3 routes in the IPv4 Routing Information Base (RIB).

Summary

In this chapter, you learned about establishing OSPF neighbor relationships, building the OSPF link-state database, optimizing OSPF behavior, configuring OSPFv2 and OSPFv3. Some key points in this chapter are:

- OSPF uses a two-layer hierarchical approach dividing networks into a backbone area (area 0) and nonbackbone areas.

- For its operation, OSPF uses five packet types: Hello, DBD, LSR, LSU, and LSAck.

- OSPF neighbors go through several different neighbor states before adjacency results in Full state.

- OSPF elects DR/BDR routers on a multiaccess segment to optimize exchange of information.

- The most common OSPF network types are point-to-point, broadcast, nonbroadcast, and loopback.

- OSPF uses several different LSA types to describe the network topology.

- LSAs are stored in an LSDB, which is synchronized with every network change.

- OSPF calculates interface costs based on default reference bandwidth and interface bandwidth.

- Using SPF, OSPF determines the total lowest cost paths and selects them as the best routes.

- Intra-area routes are always preferred over interarea routes.

- Route summarization improves CPU utilization, reduces LSA flooding, and reduces routing table sizes.

- The **area range** command is used summarize at the ABR. The **summary-address** command is sued to summarize at the ASBR.

- Default routes can be used in OSPF to prevent the need for specific route to each destination network.

- OSPF uses the **default-information originate** command to inject a default route.

- There are several OSPF area types: normal, backbone, stub, totally stubby, NSSA, and totally stubby NSSA.

- Use the **area** *area-id* stub router configuration command to define an OSPF as stubby.

- Use the **area** *area-id* **stub** command with the **no-summary** keyword only on the ABR to define an area as totally stubby.

- For stub areas, external routes are not visible in the routing table, but are accessible via the intra-area default route.

- For totally stubby areas, interarea and external routes are not visible in the routing table, but are accessible via the intra-area default route.

- OSPFv3 for IPv6 supports the same basic mechanisms that OSPFv2 for IPv4, including the use of areas to provide network segmentation and LSAs to exchange routing updates.

- OSPFv3 features two new LSA types and has renamed two traditional LSA types.

- OSPFv3 uses link-local addresses to source LSAs.

- OSPFv3 is enabled per-interface on Cisco routers.

- New-style OSPFv3 and traditional OSPFv3 for IPv6, configured with **ipv6 router ospf**, can coexist in the network to provide IPv6 routing.

Review Questions

Answer the following questions, and then see Appendix A, "Answers to Review Questions," for the answers.

1. What is the OSPF transport?

   a. IP/88
   b. TCP/179
   c. IP/89
   d. IP/86
   e. UDP/520

2. An Area Border Router maintains _____.

   a. A single database for all areas
   b. A separate database for each area with which it is connected
   c. Two databases: one for the backbone and one for all other areas
   d. A separate routing table for each area

3. Which two methods does OSPF employ to conserve the computing resources?

   a. Area-based segregation including stub areas
   b. LSDB
   c. Summarization
   d. Redistribution
   e. Network types

4. What is the difference between an LSA 3 and an LSA 4?

   a. LSA 3 is a summary LSA, and LSA 4 is E1.

   b. LSA 3 is E1, and LSA 4 is a summary.

   c. LSA 3 is a summary for networks, and LSA 4 is a summary for ASBRs.

   d. LSA 3 is a summary for ASBRs, and LSA 4 is a summary for networks.

5. Which two LSAs describe intra-area routing information?

   a. Summary

   b. External 1

   c. External 2

   d. Router

   e. Network

6. An OSPF router receives an LSA and checks the sequence number of the LSA. This number matches the sequence number of an LSA that the receiving router already has. What does the receiving router do with the received LSA?

   a. Ignores the LSA

   b. Adds the LSA to the database

   c. Sends the newer LSU to the source router

   d. Floods the LSA to the other routers

7. What are the two reasons why route summarization is important?

   a. Reduces LSA type 1 flooding

   b. Reduces LSA type 3 flooding

   c. Reduces the size of the routing table

   d. Reduces the size of the neighbor table

8. Route summarization reduces the flooding of which two of the following LSA types?

   a. Router

   b. Network

   c. Summary

   d. External

   e. NSSA

9. Stub area design can improve _____.

   a. CPU utilization on routers in the stub

   b. The number of adjacencies in the stub

   c. Ability to reach outside networks

   d. LSDB size on routers in the backbone

10. Which feature characterizes both OSPFv2 and OSPFv3?

   a. Router ID in IPv4 format

   b. Router ID in IPv6 format

   c. Process activation using the **network** command

   d. The same LSA types

11. Which address would you configure in the neighbor command to set up an OSPFv3 adjacency over an NBMA link?

   a. Local IPv4 address

   b. Neighbor's IPv4 address

   c. Interface link local IPv6 address

   d. Local global IPv6 address

   e. Neighbor's link-local IPv6 address

   f. Neighbor's global IPv6 address

12. You can run a single OSPFv3 process using the **ipv6 router ospf** command to support a support a dual-stack environment. (True or false?)

   a. True

   b. False

13. Which of the following is not a characteristic of link-state routing protocols?

   a. They respond quickly to network changes.

   b. They broadcast every 30 minutes.

   c. They send triggered updates when a network change occurs.

   d. They may send periodic updates, known as link-state refresh, at long time intervals, such as every 30 minutes.

14. Link-state routing protocols use a two-layer area hierarchy composed of which two areas?

   a. Backbone area

   b. Transmit area

   c. Regular area

   d. Linking area

15. Which IPv4 address is used to send an updated LSA entry to OSPF DRs and BDRs?

   a. Unicast 224.0.0.5

   b. Unicast 224.0.0.6

   c. Multicast 224.0.0.5

   d. Multicast 224.0.0.6

16. To ensure an accurate database, how often does OSPF flood (refresh) each LSA record?

   a. Every 60 minutes.

   b. Every 30 minutes.

   c. Every 60 seconds.

   d. Every 30 seconds.

   e. Flooding each LSA record would defeat the purpose of a link-state routing protocol, which strives to reduce the amount of routing traffic it generates.

17. What kind of router generates LSA type 5 in a standard area?

   a. DR

   b. ABR

   c. ASBR

   d. ADR

18. Where does a type 1 LSA flood to?

   a. To immediate peers

   b. To all other routers in the area where it originated

   c. To routers located in other areas

   d. To all areas

19. How does a routing table reflect the link-state information of an intra-area route?

   a. The route is marked with O.

   b. The route is marked with I.

   c. The route is marked with IO.

   d. The route is marked with EA.

   e. The route is marked with O IA.

20. Which type of external route is the default?

   a. E1.

   b. E2.

   c. E5.

   d. There is no default external route. OSPF adapts and chooses the most accurate one.

21. How is the cost of an E1 external route calculated?

   a. The sum of the internal cost of each link the packet crosses

   b. The sum of the external cost and the internal cost of each link the packet crosses

   c. The external cost only

   d. The sum of all area costs, even those that are not used

Chapter 4

Manipulating Routing Updates

This chapter covers the following topics:

- Using Multiple IP Routing Protocols on a Network

- Implementing Route Redistribution

- Controlling Routing Update Traffic

This chapter starts with a discussion of network performance issues related to routing and using multiple IP routing protocols on a network. Implementing route redistribution between different routing protocols is described, and methods of controlling the routing information sent between these routing protocols are explored, including using distribute lists, prefix lists, and route maps.

Note This chapter on manipulating routing updates is placed before the chapter on Border Gateway Protocol (BGP) because knowledge of route redistribution and route maps is required for the BGP discussion.

Using Multiple IP Routing Protocols on a Network

Simple routing protocols work well for simple networks, but as networks grow and become more complex, it may be necessary to change the routing protocols. Often, the transition between routing protocols takes place gradually, so there are multiple routing protocols that are operating in the network for variable lengths of time.

A router can connect networks that use different routing protocols (referred to as routing domains or autonomous systems). For example, router R1 in Figure 4-1 interconnects the Enhanced Interior Gateway Routing Protocol (EIGRP) routing domain and the Open Shortest Path First (OSPF) Protocol routing domain in AS1. R1 also connects to an Internet service provider (ISP) using Border Gateway Protocol (BGP). R1 is called a boundary router (also called an *edge router*) because it interconnects the different autonomous systems.

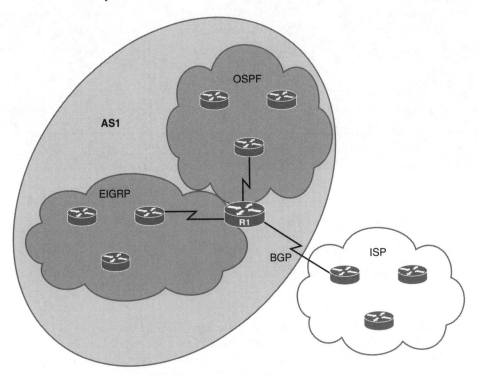

Figure 4-1   *Routers Can Run Multiple Routing Protocols*

The problem is that each routing protocol collects different types of information and reacts to topology changes in its own way. For example, the OSPF metric is based on link cost, and the EIGRP metric is based on a composite metric.

Another problem is that running multiple routing protocols increases the CPU and memory load on the router. For example, R1 in Figure 4-1 would now have to maintain separate routing, topology, and database tables and exchange and process routing information at different intervals.

Finally, routing protocols were also not designed to interoperate with one another. For instance, the different OSPF and EIGRP metrics are incompatible and exchanging routing information between these two metrics adds an additional CPU and memory load on the router.

Upon completing this section, you will be able to do the following:

■ Describe the need for using more than one protocol in a network

■ Describe how routing protocols interact

■ Describe solutions for operating in a multiple routing protocol environment

Why Run Multiple Routing Protocols?

Although it is desirable to run a single routing protocol throughout an entire IP internetwork, multiprotocol routing may be required for various reasons, including the following:

- When migrating from an older Interior Gateway Protocol (IGP) to a new IGP. Multiple redistribution boundaries may exist until the new protocol has completely displaced the old protocol. The same applies to company mergers between companies that are each using a different routing protocol.

- In mixed-router vendor environments. In these environments, you can use a routing protocol that is specific to Cisco, such as EIGRP, in the Cisco portion of the network and a common standards-based routing protocol, like OSPF, to communicate with devices from other vendors.

- When the use of a new protocol is desired, but the old routing protocol is needed for host systems (for example, for UNIX host-based routers that are running RIP).

- When some departments do not want to upgrade their routers to support a new routing protocol.

Running Multiple Routing Protocols

When running multiple routing protocols, a router may learn of a route from different routing sources. If a router learns of a specific destination from two different routing domains, the route with the lowest administrative distance would get installed in routing table.

Administrative Distance

The administrative distance is used to rate a routing protocol's believability (also called its trustworthiness). Each routing protocol is prioritized in order from most to least believable using an assigned value called the *administrative distance*. This criterion is the first thing a router uses to determine which routing protocol to believe if more than one protocol provides route information for the same destination.

The path with the lowest administrative distance to a destination when compared to the other routes in the table, is installed in the routing table. Routes with a higher administrative distance are rejected.

Table 4-1 lists the common default administrative metrics of routing protocols. Lower administrative distances are considered more believable (better).

Table 4-1 *Default Administrative Distances of Common Routing Protocols*

Route Source	Default Administrative Distance
EIGRP and EIGRP for IPv6 summary route	5
External BGP	20

Route Source	Default Administrative Distance
Internal EIGRP, EIGRP for IPv6	90
OSPFv2, OSPFv3	110
RIPv1, RIPv2, RIPng	120
Internal BGP	200
Unreachable	255

For instance, in Figure 4-1, R1 in AS1 is running two routing processes (that is, EIGRP and OSPF) within the autonomous system. Assume that EIGRP and OSPF have learned of routes to a 192.168.24.0/24 network using their internal metrics and processes. Each routing process would attempt to install their route toward 192.168.24.0/24 into the routing table. R1 would install the path provided by EIGRP because EIGRP has a lower administrative distance of 90 compared to OSPF with an administrative distance of 110.

Multiple Routing Protocols Solutions

Careful routing protocol design and traffic optimization solutions should be implemented when supporting complex multiprotocol networks. These solutions include the following:

- Summarization

- Redistribution between routing protocols

- Route filtering

Summarization was discussed in Chapter 2, "EIGRP Implementation," and Chapter 3, "OSPF Implementation." This chapter discusses redistribution and route filtering.

Implementing Route Redistribution

Upon completing this section, you will be able to do the following:

- Describe the need for route redistribution

- Identify some considerations for route redistribution

- Describe how to configure and verify route redistribution

- Identify the different types of route redistribution

Defining Route Redistribution

Cisco routers allow internetworks using multiple routing protocols to exchange routing information using the *route redistribution* feature.

Route redistribution is defined as the capability of boundary routers connecting different routing domains to exchange and advertise routing information between those routing domains (autonomous systems). Redistribution shares routing information about routes that the router has learned with other routing protocols.

Planning to Redistribute Routes

Network administrators must manage the migration from one routing protocol to another, or to multiple protocols, carefully and thoughtfully; otherwise, redistribution can lead to routing loops, which negatively affect an internetwork.

When redistributing between routing protocols, the two routing protocols will most likely have different requirements and capabilities, so it is important for network administrators to create a detailed plan before making any routing protocol changes. An accurate topology map of the network and an inventory of all network devices are critical for success.

Within each autonomous system, internal routers typically have complete knowledge of their network. Boundary routers running multiple protocols are usually configured to redistribute routes between routing domains. To have a scalable solution and limit the amount of routing update traffic, the redistribution process must selectively insert the routes that are learned.

When a router redistributes routes, it only propagates routes that are in the routing table. Therefore, a router can redistribute dynamically learned routes, static routes, and direct connected routes.

Redistributing Routes

Redistribution is always performed *outbound*. This means that the router doing redistribution does not change its own routing table. Only downstream routers receiving the redistributed routes could add them to their respective routing tables.

For instance, Figure 4-2 illustrates two routing domains interconnected by the boundary router R1. The routing table of R2 contains directly connected and OSPF networks, and the R3 routing table contains directly connected and EIGRP routes. R1 has active OSPF and EIGRP processes and its routing table contains directly connected routes, OSPF domain routes, and EIGRP domain routes. Without redistribution, routers in the OSPF domain are not aware of EIGRP routes, and routers in the EIGRP domain are not aware of OSPF routes.

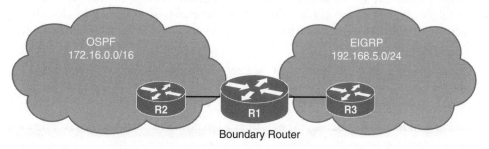

Figure 4-2 *Routing Domains Interconnected by a Boundary Router*

As shown in Figure 4-3, to advertise the EIGRP routes to the OSPF domain, the OSPF process on R1 is configured to redistribute the EIGRP routes in its routing table to its OSPF neighbors. Likewise, to advertise the OSPF routes to the EIGRP domain, the EIGRP process on R1 is configured to redistribute the OSPF routes in its routing table to its EIGRP neighbors.

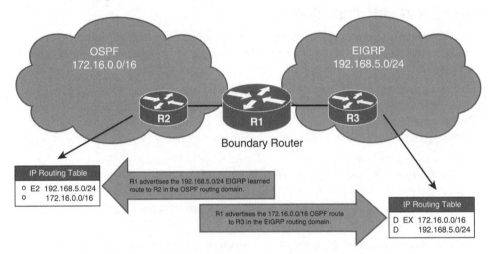

Figure 4-3   *Routing Domains Interconnected by a Boundary Router*

Notice how the OSPF domain now contains the EIGRP route as indicated in the routing table of R2 with an O E2 designation. The EIGRP domain now contains the OSPF route as indicated in the routing table of R3 with a D EX designation. Routers in each autonomous system can now make informed routing decisions for these networks.

Note   To improve routing table stability and decrease the size of routing tables, boundary routers should be configured to redistribute summarized routes.

Seed Metrics

When a router advertises a link that is directly connected to one of its interfaces, the initial, or *seed* metric (also called the default metric) used is derived from the characteristics of that interface, and the metric increments as the routing information is passed to other routers.

For OSPF, the seed metric is based on the interface's bandwidth. For EIGRP, the seed metric is based on the interface bandwidth and delay. For RIP, the seed metric starts with a hop count of 0 and increases in increments from router to router.

When a router is redistributing, the redistributed route must have a metric appropriate for the receiving protocol.

Because redistributed routes are learned from other sources (such as other routing protocols), a boundary router must be capable of translating the metric of the received route from the source routing protocol into the receiving routing protocol. For example, if a boundary router receives a RIP route, the route has hop count as a metric. To redistribute the route into OSPF, the router must translate the hop count into a cost metric that the other OSPF routers will understand.

The seed or default metric is defined during redistribution configuration. After the seed metric for a redistributed route is established, the metric increments normally within the autonomous system.

Note   An exception to the normal metric increment behavior is an OSPF E2 route. An OSPF external type 2 route maintains the initial metric regardless of how far they are propagated across an autonomous system.

The seed metric can be configured using either of the following:

- The **default-metric** router configuration command, which establishes the seed metric for all redistributed routes. The default metric specified applies to all protocols being redistributed into this protocol.

- The **redistribute** router configuration command using either the **metric** option or a route map. Using the **metric** parameter in the **redistribute** command, set a specific metric for the protocol being redistributed. A metric configured in a **redistribute** command overrides the value in the **default-metric** command for that one protocol.

To help prevent suboptimal routing and routing loops, always set the initial seed metric to a value that is larger than the largest metric within the receiving autonomous system. For example, when RIP routes are redistributed into OSPF and the highest OSPF metric is 50, the redistributed RIP routes should be assigned an OSPF metric higher than 50.

Default Seed Metrics

Default seed metric value for redistributed routes for each IP routing protocol is as follows:

- Routes redistributed into EIGRP and RIP are assigned a metric of 0, which is interpreted as infinity or unreachable. This informs the router that the route is unreachable and should not be advertised. Therefore, a seed metric *must* be specified when redistributing routes into RIP and EIGRP; otherwise, the routes will not be redistributed. Exceptions to this rule are redistributed connected or static routes and routes that are being redistributed between two EIGRP autonomous systems.

- Routes redistributed into OSPF are assigned a default type 2 (E2) metric of 20. However, redistributed BGP routes are assigned a default type 2 metric of 1. (Note that when redistributing OSPF into OSPF, metrics associated with both intra-area and interarea routes are preserved.)

- Routes redistributed into for BGP maintain their IGP routing metrics.

Note   Routes redistributed into Intermediate System-to-Intermediate System (IS-IS) Protocol are assigned a default metric of 0. But unlike RIP or EIGRP, a seed metric of 0 is not treated as unreachable by IS-IS. Configuring a seed metric for redistribution into IS-IS is recommended.

Table 4-2 lists the default seed metric value for routes that are redistributed into each IP routing protocol.

Table 4-2   *Default Seed Metrics*

Protocol That Route Is Redistributed Into	Default Seed Metric
RIP	0, which is interpreted as infinity and unreachable.
EIGRP	0, which is interpreted as infinity and unreachable.
OSPF	20. The exception is for BGP routes, which have a default seed metric of 1. (All default to type E2.)
BGP	BGP metric is set to IGP metric value.

The example in Figure 4-4 displays the configuration of boundary router R1 to redistribute RIP routes from the RIP domain into OSPF with a seed metric of 30.

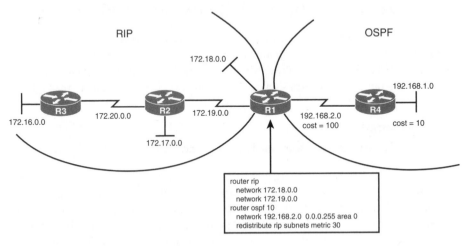

Figure 4-4   *Redistributing RIP Routes into OSPF*

Figure 4-5 displays the resulting routing tables.

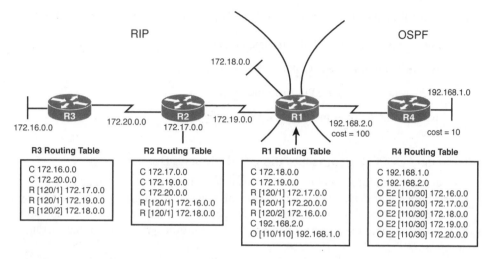

Figure 4-5 *Resulting Routing Tables*

Remember that redistribution is performed outbound; therefore, the routing tables of R1, R2, and R3 remain unchanged. The R4 routing table has changed and now includes the RIP routes as O E2 routes with a metric of 30. Notice how the cost of the serial link from R1 to R4 was not added to the metric of these routes. This is because they are redistributed as E2 type routes automatically by OSPF. The metrics of the three networks in the RIP cloud are irrelevant in the OSPF cloud because R4 would forward any traffic for these three networks to R1, which in turn would forward the traffic within the RIP network appropriately.

Configuring and Verifying Basic Redistribution in IPv4 and IPv6

This section discusses how to perform basic redistribution configuration using the topology in Figure 4-6. For OSPFv2 and OSPFv3, R1 and R3 are in area 0 and R3 and R4 are in area 2. R3 is the ABR.

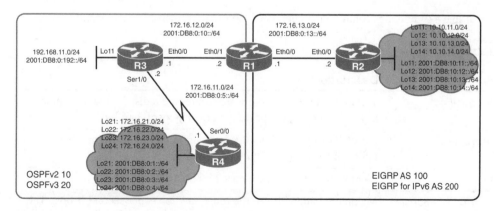

Figure 4-6 *Basic Redistribution Topology*

In the example, redistribution will be configured on the boundary router R1 to redistribute

- OSPFv2 routes into the EIGRP routing domain

- OSPFv3 routes into the EIGRP for IPv6 routing domain

- EIGRP routes into the OSPFv2 routing domain

- EIGRP for IPv6 routes into the OSPFv3 routing domain

Redistributing OSPFv2 Routes into the EIGRP Routing Domain

To redistribute routes from one routing domain into another routing domain, use the **redistribute** router configuration command. This command identifies the source routing protocol (the protocol from which updates are accepted) and how those routes should be redistributed into the target routing protocol (the protocol that is accepting routing updates).

It is important to note that **routes** are redistributed *into* a routing protocol, so the **redistribute** command is configured under the routing process that is to *receive* the redistributed routes.

Because different routing protocols use different metrics, the **redistribute** command parameters vary between routing protocols.

To configure redistribution into EIGRP, the following command syntax is used:

```
Router(config-router)# redistribute protocol process-id [metric bandwidth-metric
delay-metric reliability-metric effective-bandwidth-metric mtu-bytes] [route-map
map-tag]
```

Note   The preceding simplified command syntax lists commonly used parameters of the EIGRP **redistribute** command. Refer to Cisco.com for the complete syntax.

Table 4-3 describes common parameters of the EIGRP **redistribute** command.

Table 4-3   *EIGRP* redistribute *Command Parameters*

Parameter	Description
protocol	The source protocol from which routes are redistributed. Common keywords include **connected**, **static**, **rip**, **ospf**, and **bgp**.
process-id	For BGP or EIGRP, this value is an autonomous system number. For OSPF, this value is an OSPF process ID.
metric	(Optional) Specifies the metric for redistributed routes.
bandwidth-metric	Maximum bandwidth of the route, in kilobits per second (Kbps). The range is from 1 to 4,294,967,295.

Parameter	Description
delay-metric	EIGRP route delay metric, in 10s of microseconds. The range is from 1 to 4,294,967,295.
reliability-metric	EIGRP reliability metric. The range is from 0 to 255. An EIGRP metric of 255 signifies 100 percent reliability.
effective-bandwidth-metric	Effective bandwidth of the route. The range is from 1 to 255. Effective bandwidth of 255 denotes 100 percent load.
mtu	Smallest allowed MTU in bytes.
route-map	(Optional) Route map that should be interrogated to filter the importation of routes from this source routing protocol to the current routing protocol. If not specified, all routes are redistributed. If this keyword is specified, but no route map tags are listed, no routes will be imported.
map-tag	Route map name.

Note The command parameters of the **redistribute** command vary depending on the target protocol. For example, some parameters of the EIGRP **redistribute** command will be different than the OSPF **redistribute** command.

Example 4-1 configures the EIGRP 100 process to redistribute all known OSPFv2 routes on R1. The **redistribute** command also configures specific metrics for those redistributed routes. Recall that EIGRP must have metrics provided; otherwise, the source routes would be assigned a metric of infinity and not get propagated.

Example 4-1 *Redistributing OSPF Routes into EIGRP*

```
R1(config)# router eigrp 100
R1(config-router)# redistribute ospf 10 metric 1500 100 255 1 1500
```

Alternatively, the metric could have been applied using the **default-metric** command as shown in Example 4-2.

Example 4-2 *Redistributing OSPF Routes into EIGRP with Default Metric*

```
R1(config)# router eigrp 100
R1(config-router)# default-metric 1500 100 255 1 1500
R1(config-router)# redistribute ospf 10
```

The difference in implementation is as follows:

- Example 4-1 assigns the metric specifically to the redistributed OSPF routes.

- Example 4-2 assigns a default metric for all redistributed routes. For instance, if static routes were also redistributed along with the OSPF routes, then they would also be assigned the metric specified by the **default-metric** command.

The EIGRP metric configured in this example is interpreted as follows:

■ Bandwidth in Kbps = 1,500,000 bps. The route's minimum bandwidth in kilobits per second (Kbps). It can be 1 or any positive integer.

■ Delay in tens of microseconds = 100. Route delay in tens of microseconds. It can be 0 or any positive integer.

■ Reliability = 255 (maximum). The likelihood of successful packet transmission, expressed as a number from 0 to 255, where 255 indicates that the route is 100 percent reliable, and 0 means unreliable.

■ Load = 1 (minimum). The route's effective loading, expressed as a number from 1 to 255, where 255 indicates that the route is 100 percent loaded.

■ Maximum transmission unit (MTU) = 1500 bytes. Maximum transmission unit. The maximum packet size in bytes along the route; an integer greater than or equal to 1.

Note   Recall from Chapter 2 that MTU is included in the EIGRP update but is actually not used in the metric calculation.

Next, verify that OSPF routes are now redistributed into EIGRP autonomous system 100. To do so, use the **show ip route** command on R2, as shown in Example 4-3.

Example 4-3   *Verifying Redistributed OSPF Routes on R2*

```
R2# show ip route
Codes: L - local, C - connected, S - static, R - RIP, M - mobile, B - BGP
       D - EIGRP, EX - EIGRP external, O - OSPF, IA - OSPF inter area
       N1 - OSPF NSSA external type 1, N2 - OSPF NSSA external type 2
       E1 - OSPF external type 1, E2 - OSPF external type 2
       i - IS-IS, su - IS-IS summary, L1 - IS-IS level-1, L2 - IS-IS level-2
       ia - IS-IS inter area, * - candidate default, U - per-user static route
       o - ODR, P - periodic downloaded static route, H - NHRP, l - LISP
       + - replicated route, % - next hop override

Gateway of last resort is not set

      10.0.0.0/8 is variably subnetted, 8 subnets, 2 masks
C        10.10.11.0/24 is directly connected, Loopback11
L        10.10.11.1/32 is directly connected, Loopback11
C        10.10.12.0/24 is directly connected, Loopback12
L        10.10.12.1/32 is directly connected, Loopback12
C        10.10.13.0/24 is directly connected, Loopback13
L        10.10.13.1/32 is directly connected, Loopback13
C        10.10.14.0/24 is directly connected, Loopback14
```

```
L           10.10.14.1/32 is directly connected, Loopback14
         172.16.0.0/16 is variably subnetted, 8 subnets, 3 masks
D EX        172.16.11.0/30 [170/1757696] via 172.16.13.1, 00:00:05, Ethernet0/0
D EX        172.16.12.0/24 [170/1757696] via 172.16.13.1, 00:00:05, Ethernet0/0
C           172.16.13.0/24 is directly connected, Ethernet0/0
L           172.16.13.2/32 is directly connected, Ethernet0/0
D EX        172.16.21.1/32 [170/1757696] via 172.16.13.1, 00:00:05, Ethernet0/0
D EX        172.16.22.1/32 [170/1757696] via 172.16.13.1, 00:00:05, Ethernet0/0
D EX        172.16.23.1/32 [170/1757696] via 172.16.13.1, 00:00:05, Ethernet0/0
D EX        172.16.24.1/32 [170/1757696] via 172.16.13.1, 00:00:05, Ethernet0/0
         192.168.11.0/32 is subnetted, 1 subnets
D EX        192.168.11.1 [170/1757696] via 172.16.13.1, 00:00:05, Ethernet0/0

R2#
```

Notice that all of the OSPF routes are now present in the routing table of R2. They are imported into the routing table as D EX (EIGRP external) routes because they have been redistributed from the OSPF domain.

By default, EIGRP routes learned within an autonomous system have an administrative distance of 90. However, external routes have an administrative distance of 170. Therefore, internal EIGRP (D) routes are preferred over external EIGRP (D EX) routes.

Redistributing OSPFv3 Routes into the EIGRP for IPv6 Routing Domain

Example 4-4 configures the EIGRP 200 process to redistribute all known OSPFv3 routes on R1 with specific metrics.

Example 4-4 *Redistributing OSPFv3 Routes into EIGRP for IPv6*

```
R1(config)# ipv6 router eigrp 200
R1(config-rtr)# redistribute ospf 20 metric 1500 100 255 1 1500
```

Next, verify that OSPFv3 routes are now redistributed into EIGRP autonomous system 200. Only list EIGRP routes. To do so, use the **show ipv6 route eigrp** command on R2, as shown in Example 4-5.

Example 4-5 *Verifying Redistributed OSPFv3 Routes on R2*

```
R2# show ipv6 route eigrp
IPv6 Routing Table - default - 17 entries
Codes: C - Connected, L - Local, S - Static, U - Per-user Static route
       B - BGP, HA - Home Agent, MR - Mobile Router, R - RIP
       H - NHRP, I1 - ISIS L1, I2 - ISIS L2, IA - ISIS interarea
       IS - ISIS summary, D - EIGRP, EX - EIGRP external, NM - NEMO
       ND - ND Default, NDp - ND Prefix, DCE - Destination, NDr - Redirect
       O - OSPF Intra, OI - OSPF Inter, OE1 - OSPF ext 1, OE2 - OSPF ext 2
```

```
        ON1 - OSPF NSSA ext 1, ON2 - OSPF NSSA ext 2, 1 - LISP
EX  2001:DB8:0:1::1/128 [170/1757696]
     via FE80::A8BB:CCFF:FE01:6C00, Ethernet0/0
EX  2001:DB8:0:2::1/128 [170/1757696]
     via FE80::A8BB:CCFF:FE01:6C00, Ethernet0/0
EX  2001:DB8:0:3::1/128 [170/1757696]
     via FE80::A8BB:CCFF:FE01:6C00, Ethernet0/0
EX  2001:DB8:0:4::1/128 [170/1757696]
     via FE80::A8BB:CCFF:FE01:6C00, Ethernet0/0
EX  2001:DB8:0:5::/64 [170/1757696]
     via FE80::A8BB:CCFF:FE01:6C00, Ethernet0/0
EX  2001:DB8:0:192::1/128 [170/1757696]
     via FE80::A8BB:CCFF:FE01:6C00, Ethernet0/0


R2#
```

The OSPFv3 routes are imported with an external route tag (EX). Notice that the directly connected route between R1 and R2 (that is, 2001:DB8:0:10::/64) is not displayed. The reason is because EIGRP for IPv6 does not automatically include connected routes.

With IPv4, connected interfaces are automatically advertised into routing protocol for interfaces on which the source protocol is running. Therefore, in IPv4 there is no need to explicitly define that connected subnets must be advertised to the target routing protocol.

However, in IPv6, it is up to the administrator to decide whether the connected subnets are included into redistribution. For connected interfaces to be advertised to in a target routing protocol, the **include-connected** keyword must be used with the **redistribute** command. With this keyword, the target routing protocol is instructed to redistribute the routes that are learned by the source protocol and also the connected interfaces if the source routing protocol is running on them.

Example 4-6 configures the EIGRP 200 process to redistribute all known OSPFv3 routes and connected routes on R1 with specific metrics.

Example 4-6   *Redistributing Connected Routes into EIGRP for IPv6*

```
R1(config)# ipv6 router eigrp 200
R1(config-rtr)# redistribute ospf 20 metric 1500 100 255 1 1500 include-connected
```

Again, verify that OSPFv3 routes and directly connected routes are now redistributed into EIGRP autonomous system 200 using the **show ipv6 route eigrp** command on R2, as shown in Example 4-7.

Example 4-7 *Verifying Redistributed OSPFv3 Routes on R2*

```
R2# show ipv6 route eigrp
IPv6 Routing Table - default - 18 entries
Codes: C - Connected, L - Local, S - Static, U - Per-user Static route
       B - BGP, HA - Home Agent, MR - Mobile Router, R - RIP
       H - NHRP, I1 - ISIS L1, I2 - ISIS L2, IA - ISIS interarea
       IS - ISIS summary, D - EIGRP, EX - EIGRP external, NM - NEMO
       ND - ND Default, NDp - ND Prefix, DCE - Destination, NDr - Redirect
       O - OSPF Intra, OI - OSPF Inter, OE1 - OSPF ext 1, OE2 - OSPF ext 2
       ON1 - OSPF NSSA ext 1, ON2 - OSPF NSSA ext 2, l - LISP
EX  2001:DB8:0:1::1/128 [170/1757696]
     via FE80::A8BB:CCFF:FE01:6C00, Ethernet0/0
EX  2001:DB8:0:2::1/128 [170/1757696]
     via FE80::A8BB:CCFF:FE01:6C00, Ethernet0/0
EX  2001:DB8:0:3::1/128 [170/1757696]
     via FE80::A8BB:CCFF:FE01:6C00, Ethernet0/0
EX  2001:DB8:0:4::1/128 [170/1757696]
     via FE80::A8BB:CCFF:FE01:6C00, Ethernet0/0
EX  2001:DB8:0:5::/64 [170/1757696]
     via FE80::A8BB:CCFF:FE01:6C00, Ethernet0/0
EX  2001:DB8:0:10::/64 [170/1757696]
     via FE80::A8BB:CCFF:FE01:6C00, Ethernet0/0
EX  2001:DB8:0:192::1/128 [170/1757696]
     via FE80::A8BB:CCFF:FE01:6C00, Ethernet0/0
R1(config-router)# redistribute ospf 20 metric 1500 100 255 1 1500 include-connected
```

Notice that now the connected route is also redistributed into the EIGRP for IPv6 routing domain.

Redistributing EIGRP Routes into the OSPFv2 Routing Domain

When redistributing into OSPF, the default metric is usually 20, the default metric type is 2, and subnets are not redistributed by default.

To configure redistribution into OSPF, use the following command syntax:

```
Router(config-router)# redistribute protocol process-id [metric metric-value]
[metric-type type-value] [route-map map-tag] [subnets]
```

Note The preceding simplified command syntax lists commonly used parameters of the OSPF **redistribute** command. Refer to Cisco.com for the complete syntax.

Table 4-4 describes common parameters of the OSPF **redistribute** command.

Table 4-4 *OSPF* redistribute *Command Parameters*

Parameter	Description
protocol	The source protocol from which routes are redistributed. Common keywords include **connected**, **static**, **rip**, **eigrp**, and **bgp.**
process-id	For BGP or EIGRP, this value is an autonomous system number. For OSPF, this value is an OSPF process ID.
metric *metric-value*	(Optional) This parameter is used to specify the metric for the redistributed route. If it is not explicitly specified, then the redistributed routes are assigned a metric of 20 by default.
metric-type *type-value*	(Optional) This OSPF parameter specifies the external link type. This can be **1** for type 1 external routes, or **2** for type 2 external routes. The default is 2.
route-map	(Optional) Route map that should be interrogated to filter the importation of routes from this source routing protocol to the current routing protocol. If not specified, all routes are redistributed. If this keyword is specified, but no route map tags are listed, no routes will be imported.
map-tag	Route map name.
subnets	(Optional) For redistributing routes into OSPF, the scope of redistribution for the specified protocol. By default, no subnets are defined.

Note The command parameters of the **redistribute** command vary depending on the target protocol. For example, the parameters of the EIGRP **redistribute** command will be different than the OSPF **redistribute** command.

The **subnets** keyword is necessary for classless networks to be advertised. Without this keyword, only routes that are in the routing table with the default classful mask will be redistributed.

For instance, the R2 router only has subnets configured on its interfaces; therefore, if the **subnets** keyword is omitted, no networks from R2 will be redistributed to R3 and R4 routers.

Example 4-8 configures the OSPF 10 process to redistribute all known EIGRP routes, including subnets. Recall that OSPF assigns a default metric of 20 when no other metric is specifically defined.

Example 4-8 *Redistributing EIGRP Routes into OSPF*

```
R1(config)# router ospf  10
R1(config-router)# redistribute eigrp 100 subnets
```

Next, verify that EIGRP routes are now redistributed into the OSPF routing domain. Filter the output to display only OSPF-learned routes. To do so, use the **show ip route ospf** command on R3, as shown in Example 4-9.

Example 4-9   *Verifying Redistributed EIGRP Routes on R3*

```
R3# show ip route ospf
Codes: L - local, C - connected, S - static, R - RIP, M - mobile, B - BGP
       D - EIGRP, EX - EIGRP external, O - OSPF, IA - OSPF inter area
       N1 - OSPF NSSA external type 1, N2 - OSPF NSSA external type 2
       E1 - OSPF external type 1, E2 - OSPF external type 2
       i - IS-IS, su - IS-IS summary, L1 - IS-IS level-1, L2 - IS-IS level-2
       ia - IS-IS inter area, * - candidate default, U - per-user static route
       o - ODR, P - periodic downloaded static route, H - NHRP, l - LISP
       + - replicated route, % - next hop override

Gateway of last resort is not set

      10.0.0.0/24 is subnetted, 4 subnets
O E2     10.10.11.0 [110/20] via 172.16.12.2, 00:02:29, Ethernet0/0
O E2     10.10.12.0 [110/20] via 172.16.12.2, 00:02:29, Ethernet0/0
O E2     10.10.13.0 [110/20] via 172.16.12.2, 00:02:29, Ethernet0/0
O E2     10.10.14.0 [110/20] via 172.16.12.2, 00:02:29, Ethernet0/0
      172.16.0.0/16 is variably subnetted, 9 subnets, 3 masks
O E2     172.16.13.0/24 [110/20] via 172.16.12.2, 00:02:29, Ethernet0/0
O        172.16.21.1/32 [110/65] via 172.16.11.1, 2d20h, Serial1/0
O        172.16.22.1/32 [110/65] via 172.16.11.1, 2d20h, Serial1/0
O        172.16.23.1/32 [110/65] via 172.16.11.1, 2d20h, Serial1/0
O        172.16.24.1/32 [110/65] via 172.16.11.1, 2d20h, Serial1/0
R3#
```

External link-state advertisements (LSAs) appear in the routing table and are marked as external type 1 (E1) or external type 2 (E2) routes. The cost of an external route varies depending on the external type that is configured on the Area System Border Router (ASBR). The following external packet types can be configured:

- **E1:** Type O E1 external routes calculate the cost by adding the external cost to the internal cost of each link that the packet crosses. Use this type when there are multiple ASBRs advertising an external route to the same autonomous system to avoid suboptimal routing.

- **E2 (default):** The external cost of O E2 routes is fixed and does not change across OSPF domain. Use this type if only one ASBR is advertising an external route to the autonomous system.

If external routes are received as E2 routes (default setting), the cost is the same regardless of the topology in the OSPF domain. If external routes are received as E1 routes, the internal OSPF cost is added to the external cost. If an OSPF router receives both type E1 and type E2 routes for the same destination, the type E1 route is always preferred over type E2 regardless of the actual calculated cost.

In this topology, R1 is the only ASBR and therefore the default type 2 routes would be suitable. Although, not required in this topology, Example 4-10 displays how to redistribute the EIGRP routes into OSPF as type 1 (E1) routes.

Example 4-10 *Redistributing EIGRP Routes into OSPF as External Type 1 Routes*

```
R1(config)# router ospf  10
R1(config-router)# redistribute eigrp 100 metric-type 1 subnets
```

Next, verify that EIGRP routes are now redistributed into the OSPF routing domain as external type 1 routes using the **show ip route ospf** command on R3, as shown in Example 4-11.

Example 4-11 *Verifying Redistributed EIGRP External Type 1 Routes on R3*

```
R3# show ip route ospf
Codes: L - local, C - connected, S - static, R - RIP, M - mobile, B - BGP
       D - EIGRP, EX - EIGRP external, O - OSPF, IA - OSPF inter area
       N1 - OSPF NSSA external type 1, N2 - OSPF NSSA external type 2
       E1 - OSPF external type 1, E2 - OSPF external type 2
       i - IS-IS, su - IS-IS summary, L1 - IS-IS level-1, L2 - IS-IS level-2
       ia - IS-IS inter area, * - candidate default, U - per-user static route
       o - ODR, P - periodic downloaded static route, H - NHRP, l - LISP
       + - replicated route, % - next hop override

Gateway of last resort is not set

      10.0.0.0/24 is subnetted, 4 subnets
O E1    10.10.11.0 [110/30] via 172.16.12.2, 00:00:02, Ethernet0/0
O E1    10.10.12.0 [110/30] via 172.16.12.2, 00:00:02, Ethernet0/0
O E1    10.10.13.0 [110/30] via 172.16.12.2, 00:00:02, Ethernet0/0
O E1    10.10.14.0 [110/30] via 172.16.12.2, 00:00:02, Ethernet0/0
      172.16.0.0/16 is variably subnetted, 9 subnets, 3 masks
O E1    172.16.13.0/24 [110/30] via 172.16.12.2, 00:00:02, Ethernet0/0
O       172.16.21.1/32 [110/65] via 172.16.11.1, 2d21h, Serial1/0
O       172.16.22.1/32 [110/65] via 172.16.11.1, 2d21h, Serial1/0
O       172.16.23.1/32 [110/65] via 172.16.11.1, 2d21h, Serial1/0
O       172.16.24.1/32 [110/65] via 172.16.11.1, 2d21h, Serial1/0

R3#
```

Notice now that the redistributed EIGRP routes are now identified as type 1 routes and that their metric increased normally.

Redistributing EIGRP for IPv6 Routes into the OSPFv3 Routing Domain

Example 4-12 configures the OSPF 20 process to redistribute all known EIGRP routes on R1.

Example 4-12 *Redistributing EIGRP for IPv6 Routes into OSPFv3*

```
R1(config)# ipv6 router ospf 20
R1(config-rtr)# redistribute eigrp 200 include-connected
```

Next, verify that EIGRP for IPv6 routes are now redistributed into the OSPFv3 routing domain. Only list OSPFv3 routes. To do so, use the **show ipv6 route ospf** command on R3, as shown in Example 4-13.

Example 4-13 *Verifying Redistributed EIGRP for IPv6 Routes on R3*

```
R3# show ipv6 route ospf
IPv6 Routing Table - default - 16 entries
Codes: C - Connected, L - Local, S - Static, U - Per-user Static route
       B - BGP, HA - Home Agent, MR - Mobile Router, R - RIP
       H - NHRP, I1 - ISIS L1, I2 - ISIS L2, IA - ISIS interarea
       IS - ISIS summary, D - EIGRP, EX - EIGRP external, NM - NEMO
       ND - ND Default, NDp - ND Prefix, DCE - Destination, NDr - Redirect
       O - OSPF Intra, OI - OSPF Inter, OE1 - OSPF ext 1, OE2 - OSPF ext 2
       ON1 - OSPF NSSA ext 1, ON2 - OSPF NSSA ext 2, l - LISP
O    2001:DB8:0:1::1/128 [110/64]
     via FE80::FF:FE0F:C16F, Serial1/0
O    2001:DB8:0:2::1/128 [110/64]
     via FE80::FF:FE0F:C16F, Serial1/0
O    2001:DB8:0:3::1/128 [110/64]
     via FE80::FF:FE0F:C16F, Serial1/0
O    2001:DB8:0:4::1/128 [110/64]
     via FE80::FF:FE0F:C16F, Serial1/0
OE2 2001:DB8:0:13::/64 [110/20]
     via FE80::A8BB:CCFF:FE01:6C10, Ethernet0/0
OE2 2001:DB8:10:11::/64 [110/20]
     via FE80::A8BB:CCFF:FE01:6C10, Ethernet0/0
OE2 2001:DB8:10:12::/64 [110/20]
     via FE80::A8BB:CCFF:FE01:6C10, Ethernet0/0
OE2 2001:DB8:10:13::/64 [110/20]
     via FE80::A8BB:CCFF:FE01:6C10, Ethernet0/0
OE2 2001:DB8:10:14::/64 [110/20]
     via FE80::A8BB:CCFF:FE01:6C10, Ethernet0/0

R3#
```

Again, notice how the EIGRP for IPv6 routes are automatically identified as external type 2 routes with the default cost of 20. To help understand this behavior, use the **show ipv6 route ospf** command on R4, as shown in Example 4-14.

Example 4-14 *Verifying Redistributed EIGRP for IPv6 Routes on R4*

```
R4# show ipv6 route ospf
IPv6 Routing Table - default - 18 entries
Codes: C - Connected, L - Local, S - Static, U - Per-user Static route
       B - BGP, HA - Home Agent, MR - Mobile Router, R - RIP
       H - NHRP, I1 - ISIS L1, I2 - ISIS L2, IA - ISIS interarea
       IS - ISIS summary, D - EIGRP, EX - EIGRP external, NM - NEMO
       ND - ND Default, NDp - ND Prefix, DCE - Destination, NDr - Redirect
       O - OSPF Intra, OI - OSPF Inter, OE1 - OSPF ext 1, OE2 - OSPF ext 2
       ON1 - OSPF NSSA ext 1, ON2 - OSPF NSSA ext 2, l - LISP
O   2001:DB8:0:10::/64 [110/74]
     via FE80::A8BB:CCFF:FE01:6E00, Serial0/0
OE2 2001:DB8:0:13::/64 [110/20]
     via FE80::A8BB:CCFF:FE01:6E00, Serial0/0
OI  2001:DB8:0:192::1/128 [110/64]
      via FE80::A8BB:CCFF:FE01:6E00, Serial0/0
OE2 2001:DB8:10:11::/64 [110/20]
      via FE80::A8BB:CCFF:FE01:6E00, Serial0/0
OE2 2001:DB8:10:12::/64 [110/20]
      via FE80::A8BB:CCFF:FE01:6E00, Serial0/0
OE2 2001:DB8:10:13::/64 [110/20]
      via FE80::A8BB:CCFF:FE01:6E00, Serial0/0
OE2 2001:DB8:10:14::/64 [110/20]
      via FE80::A8BB:CCFF:FE01:6E00, Serial0/0

R4#
```

Again, the redistributed EIGRP for IPv6 routes are identified by the default external type 2, and the metric has remained unchanged.

Example 4-15 displays how **redistribute** routes as external type 1 routes.

Example 4-15 *Redistributing EIGRP for IPv6 Routes as External Type 2 into OSPFv3*

```
R1(config)# ipv6 router ospf 20
R1(config-rtr)# redistribute eigrp 200 metric-type 1 include-connected
```

Next, verify that EIGRP for IPv6 routes are now redistributed as external type 1 routes into the OSPFv3 routing domain using the **show ipv6 route ospf** command on R4, as shown in Example 4-16.

Example 4-16 *Verifying Redistributed External Type 1 EIGRP for IPv6 Routes on R4*

```
R4# show ipv6 route ospf
IPv6 Routing Table - default - 18 entries
Codes: C - Connected, L - Local, S - Static, U - Per-user Static route
       B - BGP, HA - Home Agent, MR - Mobile Router, R - RIP
       H - NHRP, I1 - ISIS L1, I2 - ISIS L2, IA - ISIS interarea
       IS - ISIS summary, D - EIGRP, EX - EIGRP external, NM - NEMO
       ND - ND Default, NDp - ND Prefix, DCE - Destination, NDr - Redirect
       O - OSPF Intra, OI - OSPF Inter, OE1 - OSPF ext 1, OE2 - OSPF ext 2
       ON1 - OSPF NSSA ext 1, ON2 - OSPF NSSA ext 2, l - LISP
O    2001:DB8:0:10::/64 [110/74]
     via FE80::A8BB:CCFF:FE01:6E00, Serial0/0
OE1  2001:DB8:0:13::/64 [110/94]
     via FE80::A8BB:CCFF:FE01:6E00, Serial0/0
OI   2001:DB8:0:192::1/128 [110/64]
     via FE80::A8BB:CCFF:FE01:6E00, Serial0/0
OE1  2001:DB8:10:11::/64 [110/94]
     via FE80::A8BB:CCFF:FE01:6E00, Serial0/0
OE1  2001:DB8:10:12::/64 [110/94]
     via FE80::A8BB:CCFF:FE01:6E00, Serial0/0
OE1  2001:DB8:10:13::/64 [110/94]
     via FE80::A8BB:CCFF:FE01:6E00, Serial0/0
OE1  2001:DB8:10:14::/64 [110/94]
     via FE80::A8BB:CCFF:FE01:6E00, Serial0/0

R4#
```

Notice how EIGRP routes are now redistributed into OSPF with type 1 metric. The total cost for external routes that are shown in the routing table includes the costs of intra-area OSPF links. The total cost of 94 includes the default cost for redistributed routes (20), the cost of Ethernet link R1-R3 (10), and the cost of serial link R3-R4 (64).

Types of Redistribution Techniques

This section describes one-point and multipoint redistribution techniques and how to prevent loops in a redistribution environment.

One-Point Redistribution

One-point redistribution has only one boundary router redistributing between two routing domains.

Two one-point redistribution methods are available:

- **One-way redistribution:** This method only redistributes the networks learned from one routing protocol into the other routing protocol. In the example in Figure 4-7, R1 is the one-point of redistribution between autonomous system 1 (AS1) and autonomous system 2 (AS2). With this method, R1 performs one-way redistribution because it only redistributes AS1 routes into the AS2 routing domain. AS2 routes are not being redistributed in AS1. Typically, AS1 routers would require the use of a default route or one or more static routes to reach AS2 routes.

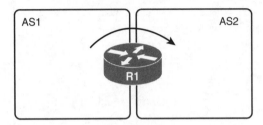

Figure 4-7   *One-Point One-Way Redistribution*

- **Two-way redistribution:** This method redistributes routes between the two routing processes in both directions. In the example in Figure 4-8, R1 is the one-point of redistribution between AS1 and AS2. R1 provides two-way redistribution because it redistributes AS1 routes into AS2 and AS2 routes into AS1.

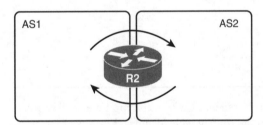

Figure 4-8   *One-Point Two-Way Redistribution*

One-way or two-way redistribution at one point is always safe, because one-point redistribution represents the only exit and entrance from one routing protocol to another. Routing loops cannot be inadvertently created.

Multipoint Redistribution

One-point redistribution has only one boundary router redistributing between two routing domains.

Two multipoint redistribution methods are available:

- **Multipoint one-way redistribution:** This method consists of two or more boundary routers only redistributing networks learned from one routing protocol into the other routing protocol. In the example in Figure 4-9, the boundary routers R3 and R4 are both redistributing AS1 routes into the AS2 routing domain. Again, AS1 routers would require the use of a default route or one or more static routes to reach AS2 routes.

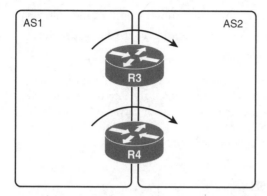

Figure 4-9 *Multipoint One-Way Redistribution*

■ **Multipoint two-way redistribution:** Also referred to as *mutual redistribution*, this
method consists of two or more boundary routers redistributing routes in both
directions. In the example in Figure 4-10, the boundary routers R3 and R4 provide
two-way redistribution because they redistribute AS1 routes into AS2 and AS2
routes into AS1.

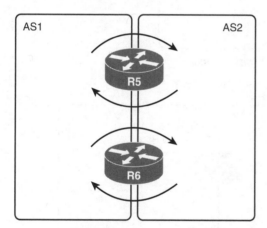

Figure 4-10 *Multipoint Two-Way Redistribution*

Multipoint redistribution is likely to introduce potential routing loops. Multipoint
one-way redistribution is problematic, and multipoint two-way redistribution is highly
dangerous. Typical problems with multipoint redistribution involve the difference in the
administrative distances of the protocols and their incompatible metrics, especially when
statically assigned seed metrics are used in redistribution points.

Redistribution Problems

Generic multipoint two-way redistribution requires careful design and configuration.
Routing protocols have incompatible metrics, and during redistribution, the metric information can be lost.

Problems that can occur during multipoint two-way redistribution include the following:

- Suboptimal routing. (Only part of the total cost is considered in routing decisions.)
- Self-sustained routing loops upon route loss.

Figure 4-11 illustrates a two-way multipoint redistribution issue where the cost of the internal links in AS1 (that is, 10 Mbps) differs from the cost of the internal links in AS2 (that is, 100 Mbps). In the figure, it is obvious that the best path between R1 and R4 is via R3, but during redistribution from AS2 to AS1, the metric is lost, and R1 is sending the packets toward R4 via R2, resulting in suboptimal routing.

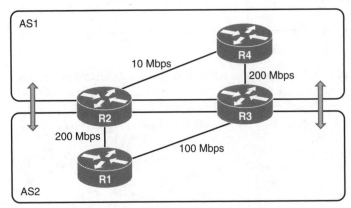

Figure 4-11   *Two-Way Multipoint Redistribution Issue*

Figure 4-12 shows another more detailed example.

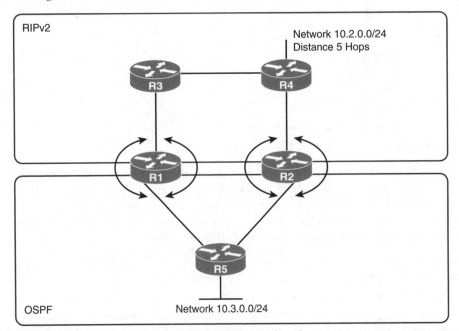

Figure 4-12   *Detailed Two-Way Multipoint Redistribution Issue*

With this type of multipoint two-way redistribution, routing loops or suboptimal routing may occur.

As an example, look at the 10.2.0.0/24 network. As this network is learned natively within the RIP part of the network, R4 first sees it with a hop count of 5. R4 then propagates this route to R3 and R2 with a hop count of 6. R3 propagates the route to R1 with a hop count of 7, and R2 redistributes it into OSPF. Now R1 has a choice to make. It has a route to the 10.2.0.0/24 network from RIP with an AD of 120 (RIP) and the same network with an AD of 110 (OSPF). Because OSPF has a better (lower) AD, R1 redistributes the network back to RIP with the metric that is set in the **redistribute** command.

However, if the **redistribute** command is configured to assign a static metric of 3 hops (or lower), then R3 starts preferring the path R1-R5-R2-R4 to reach 10.2.0.0/24, because the hop count advertised by R1 is 3, and the hop count advertised by R4 is 6.

This results in suboptimal routing. Worse, because R3 now prefers the path to R1, it will advertise this to R4 with a hop count of 4. R4 now has the choice of the route from R3 with a hop count of 4 or the true path to the 10.2.0.0/24 network with a hop count of 5. R4 will select the path to R3 and advertise this to R2. There is now a routing loop (R4, R2, R5, R1, R3, and R4). Packets destined for the 10.2.0.0/24 network that enter this loop will bounce around the loop and never reach the destination, 10.2.0.0/24.

Preventing Routing Loops in a Redistribution Environment

The safest way to perform redistribution is to redistribute routes in only one direction, on only one boundary router within the network. (Note, however, that this results in a single point of failure in the network.)

If redistribution must be done in both directions or on multiple boundary routers, the redistribution should be tuned to avoid problems such as suboptimal routing and routing loops.

The following recommendations should be considered to prevent routing loops in a multipoint redistribution scenario:

■ Only redistribute internal routes from one autonomous system to another (and vice versa).

■ Tag routes in redistribution points and filter based on these tags when configuring redistribution in the other direction.

■ Propagate metrics from one autonomous system to another autonomous system properly. (Even though this is not sufficient to prevent loops.)

■ Use default routes to avoid having to do two-way redistribution.

Verifying Redistribution Operation

The best way to verify redistribution operation is as follows:

- Know your network topology, particularly where redundant routes exist.

- Study the routing tables on a variety of routers in the internetwork using the **show ip route** [*ip-address*] EXEC command. For example, check the routing table on the boundary router and on some of the internal routers in each autonomous system.

- Examine the topology table of each configured routing protocol to ensure that all appropriate prefixes are being learned.

- Perform a trace using the **traceroute** [*ip-address*] EXEC command on some of the routes that go across the autonomous systems to verify that the shortest path is being used for routing. Be sure to run traces to networks for which redundant routes exist.

- If you encounter routing problems, use the **traceroute** and **debug** commands to observe the routing update traffic on the boundary routers and on the internal routers.

Controlling Routing Update Traffic

Many IP routing challenges can be solved using route redistribution. Having a method to manipulate the redistribution process increases options and flexibility.

In some scenarios, the redistribution of route information is designed to have the same metric and external route type for all redistributed routes. In other scenarios, metric or external route type must be changed during redistribution. In other cases, only a subset of routes need to be redistributed.

Upon completing this section, you will be able to do the following:

- Describe the general mechanics and need for route filtering

- Identify how to use and configure distribute lists

- Identify how to use and configure prefix lists

- Identify how to use and configure route maps

- Describe how to modify administrative distance

Why Filter Routes?

To understand the need for router filtering, consider the topology in Figure 4-13.

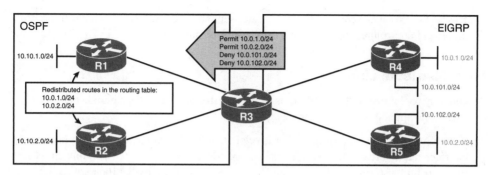

Figure 4-13   *Route Filtering Scenario*

In the example in Figure 4-13, only a portion of routes from the EIGRP domain is distributed into OSPF on the boundary router R3. Specifically, the 10.0.1.0/24 and 10.0.2.0/24 should be permitted, and the 10.0.101.0/24 and 10.0.102.0/24 should be denied.

Cisco IOS allows manipulation of redistributed route information by using route filtering features. For example, a route filter option such as a route map could be used to accomplish to support the requirement of the network in Figure 4-13.

Route Filtering Methods

Routing updates compete with user data for bandwidth and router resources, yet routing updates are critical because they carry the information that routers need to make sound routing decisions. To ensure that the network operates efficiently, routing updates must be controlled and tuned.

Information about networks must be sent where it is needed and filtered from where it is not needed. This can involve controlling routing update traffic using static and default routes, and passive interfaces. However, more advanced route filtering mechanisms are available to help control or prevent routing updates.

Advanced route filtering methods include the following:

- **Distribute lists:** A distribute list allows an access control lists (ACLs) to be applied to routing updates.

- **Prefix lists:** A prefix list is an alternative to ACLs designed to filter routes. It can be used with distribute lists, route maps, and other commands.

- **Route maps:** Route maps are complex access lists that allow conditions to be tested against a packet or route, and then actions taken to modify attributes of the packet or route.

No one type of route filter is appropriate for every situation. Therefore, it is important to understand the various techniques available to help make better route filtering decisions.

This section discusses controlling the updates sent and received by dynamic routing protocols and controlling the routes redistributed into routing protocols.

Using Distribute Lists

One way to control routing updates is to use a distribute list. A distribute list allows an ACL to be applied to routing updates.

Classic ACLs do not affect traffic that is originated by the router, so applying one to an interface has no effect on the outgoing routing advertisements. When you link an ACL to a distribute list, routing updates can be controlled no matter what their source is.

ACLs are configured in the global configuration mode and are then associated with a distribute list under the routing protocol. The ACL should permit the networks that should be advertised or redistributed and deny the networks that should be filtered.

The router then applies the ACL to the routing updates for that protocol. Options in the **distribute-list** command allow updates to be filtered based on three factors:

■ Incoming interface

■ Outgoing interface

■ Redistribution from another routing protocol

Using a distribute list gives the administrator great flexibility in determining just which routes will be permitted and which will be denied.

Configuring Distribute Lists

To filter routing update traffic for any protocol, define an ACL and apply it to a specific routing protocol using the **distribute-list** command. A distribute list enables the filtering of routing updates coming into or out of a specific interface from neighboring routers using the same routing protocol. A distribute list also allows the filtering of routes redistributed from other routing protocols or sources.

A distribute list filter can be applied for received, sent or redistributed routes. Table 4-5 describes common parameters for the **distribute-list** router configuration command, the syntax for which is as follows:

```
distribute-list [access-list-number | name] out [interface-type interface-number |
routing process | autonomous-system-number] command.
```

Table 4-5   distribute-list out *Command Parameters*

Parameter	Description
*access-list-number	name*	Specifies the standard access list number or name
out	Applies the access list to outgoing routing updates
interface-type interface-number	(Optional) Specifies the name of the interface out of which updates are filtered
*routing process	autonomous-system-number]*	(Optional) Used when redistribution from another routing process or autonomous system number has been specified.

Table 4-6 describes common parameters of the following command:

```
distribute-list [access-list-number | name] in [interface-type interface-number]
```

Table 4-6   distribute-list in *Command Parameters*

Parameter	Description
*access-list-number	name*	Specifies the standard access list number or name
in	Applies the access list to incoming routing updates
interface-type interface-number	(Optional) Specifies the interface type and number from which updates are filtered

It is important to understand the differences between these commands:

- The **distribute-list out** command filters updates going *out* of the interface or routing protocol specified in the command, *into* the routing process under which it is configured.

- The **distribute-list in** command filters updates going *into* the interface specified in the command, *into* the routing process under which it is configured.

Use the **distribute-list out** command to assign the access list to filter outgoing routing updates or to assign it to routes that are being redistributed into the protocol.

Distribute List and ACL Example

To understand how to use a distribute list with an ACL, refer to the topology in Figure 4-14.

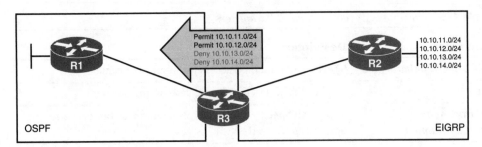

Figure 4-14   *Route Filtering Using Distribute List and ACL Scenario*

In this example, R3 must redistribute EIGRP routes into the OSPF domain with a metric of 40. However, the administrator only wants to allow the 10.10.11.0/24 and 10.10.12.0/24 routes to be propagated. All other routes should not be permitted.

As shown in Example 4-17, the configuration satisfies this route filtering redistribution requirement using ACLs with a distribute list.

Example 4-17   *Route Filtering Using Outgoing Distribute List and ACL*

```
R3(config)# ip access-list standard ROUTE-FILTER
R3(config-std-nacl)# remark Outgoing Route Filter used with Distribute List
R3(config-std-nacl)# permit 10.10.11.0 0.0.0.255
R3(config-std-nacl)# permit 10.10.12.0 0.0.0.255
R3(config-std-nacl)# exit
R3(config)# router ospf 10
R3(config-router)# redistribute eigrp 100 metric 40 subnets
R3(config-router)# distribute-list ROUTE-FILTER out eigrp 100
R3(config-router)#
```

The **distribute-list out** command defines that prefixes matched by the ROUTE-FILTER ACL will be redistributed from EIGRP 100 to the OSPF routing process. Recall that an implicit **deny any** statement at the end of the access list prevents routing updates about any other networks from being advertised. As a result, networks 10.10.13.0 and 10.10.14.0 are hidden from the rest of the network.

Use the **distribute-list in** command to filter incoming routing updates that are coming in through an interface. This command prevents most routing protocols from placing the filtered routes in their databases. When this command is used with OSPF, the routes are placed in the database but not in the routing table.

For example, as an alternative to using the **distribute-list out** command in Example 4-17, a **distribute-list in** could be used on the R1 routers. Example 4-18 displays the required configuration on R1.

Example 4-18 *Route Filtering Using Incoming Distribute List and ACL*

```
R1(config)# ip access-list standard ROUTE-FILTER
R1(config-std-nacl)# remark Incoming Route Filter used with Distribute List
R1(config-std-nacl)# permit 10.10.11.0 0.0.0.255
R1(config-std-nacl)# permit 10.10.12.0 0.0.0.255
R1(config-std-nacl)# exit
R1(config)# router ospf 10
R1(config-router)# distribute-list ROUTE-FILTER in Ethernet 0/0
R1(config-router)#
```

The **distribute-list in** command in the example filters the networks that are received in updates from interface Ethernet 0/0 according to the ROUTE-FILTER ACL.

Although Example 4-18 satisfies the requirements, Example 4-17 is more efficient because it is configured on the redistributing router.

A distribute list hides network information, which could be considered a drawback in some circumstances. For example, to avoid routing loops in a network with redundant paths, a distribute list might permit routing updates for only specific paths. In this case, other routers in the network might not know about the other ways to reach the filtered networks, so if the primary path goes down, the backup paths are not used because the rest of the network does not know they exist. When redundant paths exist, you should use other techniques.

Using Prefix Lists

Traditionally, route filtering was accomplished using ACLs with the **distribute-list** command; however, using ACLs as route filters for distribute lists has several drawbacks, including the following:

- A subnet mask cannot be easily matched.

- Access lists are evaluated sequentially for every IP prefix in the routing update.

- Extended access lists can be cumbersome to configure.

The following sections detail the characteristics of prefix lists and how they can be used with distribute lists or route maps to filter instead of ACLs. The configuration and verification of prefix lists is also covered.

Prefix List Characteristics

Using the **ip prefix-list** command has several benefits in comparison with using the **access-list** command. The intended use of prefix lists is limited to route filtering, where access lists were originally intended to be used for packet filtering and were then extended to route filtering.

Prefix lists are similar to access lists in many ways. A prefix list can consist of any number of lines, each of which indicates a test and a result. The router can interpret the lines in the specified order, although Cisco IOS Software optimizes prefix lists for processing in a tree structure. When a router evaluates a route against the prefix list, the first line that matches will result in either a "permit" or "deny." If none of the lines in the list match, the result is "implicitly deny."

The advantages of using prefix lists include the following:

- **Friendlier command-line interface:** The CLI is easier to understand and use compared to using extended access lists to filter updates.

- **Faster processing:** A significant performance improvement over access lists in loading and route lookup of large lists. A router transforms a prefix list into a tree structure, with each branch of the tree serving as a test. Cisco IOS Software determines a verdict of either permit or deny much faster this way than when sequentially interpreting access lists.

- **Support for incremental modifications:** Sequence numbers are assigned to **ip prefix-list** statements, making it easier to edit. Statements can be added in between sequence numbers or specific statements can be deleted. If no sequence number is specified, a default one is applied.

- **Greater flexibility:** Routers match networks in a routing update against the prefix list using as many bits as indicated. A prefix list can specify the exact size of the subnet mask, or it can indicate that the subnet mask must be in a specified range. For example, a prefix list created to match 10.0.0.0/16 would match 10.0.0.0/16 routes but not 10.1.0.0/16 routes or 10.0.x.x/17 (or greater).

Testing is done using prefixes. The router compares the indicated number of bits in the prefix with the same number of bits in the network number in the update. If they match, testing continues with an examination of the number of bits set in the subnet mask. The prefix list line can indicate a range in which the number must be in order to pass the test. If you do not indicate a range in the prefix line, the subnet mask must match the prefix size.

Configuring Prefix Lists

To create a prefix list, you use the following global configuration command, the options for which are described in Table 4-7:

```
ip prefix-list {list-name | list-number} [seq seq-value] {deny | permit} network/
length [ge ge-value] [le le-value]
```

Table 4-7 ip prefix-list *Command Description*

Parameter	Description
list-name	The name of the prefix list that will be created (case sensitive).
list-number	The number of the prefix list that will be created.
seq *seq-value*	A 32-bit sequence number of the prefix-list statement, used to determine the order in which the statements are processed when filtering. Default sequence numbers are in increments of 5 (5, 10, 15, and so on). If no sequence value is configured, a new entry is assigned a sequence number equal to the current maximum sequence number plus 5.
deny | **permit**	The action taken when a match is found.
network/length	The prefix to be matched and the length of the prefix. The network is a 32-bit address. The length is a decimal number.
ge *ge-value*	The range of the prefix length to be matched for prefixes that are more specific than network/length. The range is assumed to be from *ge value* to 32 if only the **ge** attribute is specified.
le *le-value*	The range of the prefix length to be matched for prefixes that are more specific than network/length. The range is assumed to be from length to *le value* if only the **le** attribute is specified.

The **ge** and **le** keywords are optional. They can be used to specify the range of the prefix length to be matched for prefixes that are more specific than network/length.

Distribute List and Prefix List Example

To understand how to use a distribute list with a prefix list, refer to the topology in Figure 4-15.

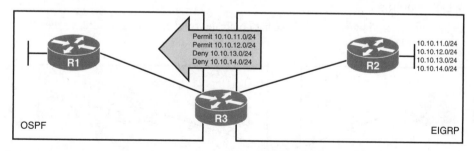

Figure 4-15 *Route Filtering Using Distribute List and Prefix List Scenario*

In this example, R3 must redistribute EIGRP routes into the OSPF domain with a metric of 40. However, the administrator only wants to allow the 10.10.11.0/24 and 10.10.12.0/24 routes to be propagated. All other routes should not be permitted.

As shown in Example 4-19, the configuration satisfies this route filtering redistribution requirement using prefix lists with a distribute list.

Example 4-19   *Route Filtering Using Distribute List and Prefix List*

```
R3(config)# ip prefix-list FILTER-ROUTES description Outgoing Route Filter
R3(config)# ip prefix-list FILTER-ROUTES seq 5 permit 10.10.11.0/24
R3(config)# ip prefix-list FILTER-ROUTES seq 10 permit 10.10.12.0/24
R3(config)# router ospf 10
R3(config-router)# redistribute eigrp 100 metric 40 subnets
R3(config-router)# distribute-list prefix FILTER-ROUTES out eigrp 100
```

A quick look at the R1 routing table is displayed in Example 4-20.

Example 4-20   *Route Filtering Using Distribute List and Prefix List*

```
R1# show ip route ospf
<Output omitted>


     10.0.0.0/8 is variably subnetted, 6 subnets, 2 masks
O E2    10.10.11.0/24 [110/40] via 172.16.12.2, 01:09:26, Ethernet0/0
O E2    10.10.12.0/24 [110/40] via 172.16.12.2, 01:09:26, Ethernet0/0
O       10.10.21.1/32 [110/65] via 172.16.11.1, 01:48:04, Serial1/0
O       10.10.22.1/32 [110/65] via 172.16.11.1, 01:48:04, Serial1/0
O       10.10.23.1/32 [110/65] via 172.16.11.1, 01:48:04, Serial1/0
O       10.10.24.1/32 [110/65] via 172.16.11.1, 01:48:04, Serial1/0


<Output omitted>
```

The output confirms that R1 is only receiving the routes filtered by the prefix list.

Prefix List Examples

To help understand how the **ip prefix-list** command can be used filter, refer to the topology in Figure 4-16.

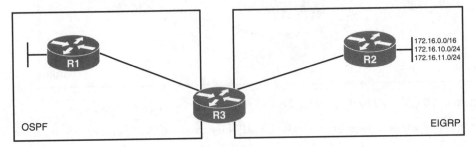

Figure 4-16   *Network Used in Prefix List Option Testing*

In this scenario, R3 is redistributing the EIGRP routes into the OSPF routing domain and is using the TEST prefix list. Table 4-8 contains variations of the **ip prefix-list** command and the resulting filter.

Table 4-8 ip prefix-list *Examples*

Examples	Resulting Filter
ip prefix-list TEST permit 172.0.0.0/8 le 24	R1 learns about 172.16.0.0/16, 172.16.10.0/24, and 172.16.11.0/24. These are the routes that match the first 8 bits of 172.0.0.0 and have a prefix length between 8 and 24.
ip prefix-list TEST permit 172.0.0.0/8 le 16	R1 learns only about 172.16.0.0/16. This is the only route that matches the first 8 bits of 172.0.0.0 and has a prefix length between 8 and 16.
ip prefix-list TEST permit 172.0.0.0/8 ge 17	R1 learns only about 172.16.10.0/24 and 172.16.11.0/24. (In other words, Router A ignores the /8 parameter and treats the command as if it has the parameters **ge 17 le 32**.)
ip prefix-list TEST permit 172.0.0.0/8 ge 16 le 24	R1 learns about 172.16.0.0/16, 172.16.10.0/24, and 172.16.11.0/24. (In other words, Router A ignores the /8 parameter and treats the command as if it has the parameters **ge 16 le 24**.)
ip prefix-list TEST permit 172.0.0.0/8 ge 17 le 23	R1 does not learn about any networks.
ip prefix-list TEST permit 0.0.0.0/0 le 32	R1 learns about all EIGRP routes.
ip prefix-list TEST permit 0.0.0.0/0	R1 learns only about a default route (if one exists).

Verifying Prefix Lists

The EXEC commands related to prefix lists are described in Table 4-9. Use the **show ip prefix-list ?** command to see all the **show** commands available for prefix lists.

Table 4-9 *Commands Used to Verify Prefix Lists*

Command	Description
show ip prefix-list [detail | summary]	Displays information on all prefix lists. Specifying the detail keyword includes the description and the hit count (the number of times the entry matches a route) in the display.
show ip prefix-list [detail | summary] *prefix-list-name*	Displays a table showing the entries in a specific prefix list.
show ip prefix-list *prefix-list-name* [*network/length*]	Displays the policy associated with a specific network/length in a prefix list.
show ip prefix-list *prefix-list-name* [seq *sequence-number*]	Displays the prefix list entry with a given sequence number.
show ip prefix-list *prefix-list-name* [*network/length*] **longer**	Displays all entries of a prefix list that are more specific than the given network and length.
show ip prefix-list *prefix-list-name* [*network/length*] **first-match**	Displays the entry of a prefix list that matches the network and length of the given prefix.
clear ip prefix-list *prefix-list-name* [*network/length*]	Resets the hit count shown on prefix list entries.

A sample output is displayed in Example 4-21.

Example 4-21 show ip prefix-list detail *Command Output*

```
R3# show ip prefix-list detail
Prefix-list with the last deletion/insertion: SUPER-NET ip prefix-list SUPER-NET:
   Description: Only permit the supernet route
   count: 1, range entries: 0, sequences: 5 - 5, refcount: 1
seq 5 permit 172.0.0.0/8 (hit count: 0, refcount: 1)
```

In the output, R1 has a prefix list called SUPER-NET that has only one entry (sequence number 5). The hit count of 0 means that no routes match this entry.

Manipulating Redistribution Using ACLs, Prefix Lists, and Distribute Lists

This example provides an overview of configure route manipulation using ACLs with a distribute list, and using prefix lists with a distribute list using the topology in Figure 4-17.

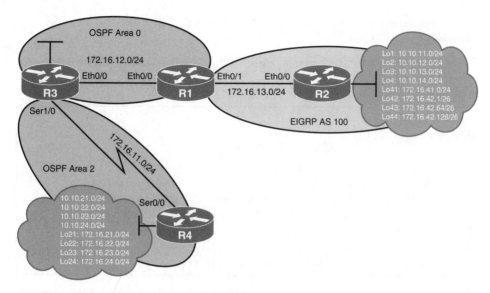

Figure 4-17 *Manipulating Redistribution Topology*

In the example, R1 will be configured to support mutual redistribution. Specifically, R1 will

- Redistribute OSPF routes into the EIGRP routing domain using ACLs and a distribute list

- Redistribute OSPF routes into the EIGRP routing domain using prefix lists and a distribute list

Redistributing OSPFv2 Routes into the EIGRP Routing Domain Using an ACL and Distribute List

Example 4-22 configures redistribution from OSPF into EIGRP using an ACL and a distribute list on R1. R1 will be configured to specifically filter and not redistribute the 10.10.21.0/24, 10.10.22.0/24, 10.10.23.0/24, and 10.10.24.0/24 routes into the EIGRP routing domain.

Example 4-22 *Redistributing OSPF Routes into EIGRP*

```
R1(config)# access-list 5 deny 10.10.21.0 0.0.0.255
R1(config)# access-list 5 deny 10.10.22.0 0.0.0.255
R1(config)# access-list 5 deny 10.10.23.0 0.0.0.255
R1(config)# access-list 5 deny 10.10.24.0 0.0.0.255
R1(config)# access-list 5 permit any
R1(config)# router eigrp 100
R1(config-router)# redistribute ospf 10 metric 1500 100 255 1 1500
R1(config-router)# distribute-list 5 out ospf 10
```

In the configuration, access list 5 and the distribute list deny the specified networks from being redistributed.

Next, Example 4-23 displays a partial output of the resulting routing table on R2.

Example 4-23   *Verifying Redistributed Routes on R2*

```
R2# show ip route eigrp
<Output omitted>


        172.16.0.0/16 is variably subnetted, 16 subnets, 4 masks
D EX      172.16.11.0/30 [170/1757696] via 172.16.13.1, 1w0d, Ethernet0/0
D EX      172.16.12.0/24 [170/1757696] via 172.16.13.1, 1w0d, Ethernet0/0
D EX      172.16.21.1/32 [170/1757696] via 172.16.13.1, 1w0d, Ethernet0/0
D EX      172.16.22.1/32 [170/1757696] via 172.16.13.1, 1w0d, Ethernet0/0
D EX      172.16.23.1/32 [170/1757696] via 172.16.13.1, 1w0d, Ethernet0/0
D EX      172.16.24.1/32 [170/1757696] via 172.16.13.1, 1w0d, Ethernet0/0
```

Notice how all the OSPF routes except those identified by the ACL are displayed in the routing table.

Redistributing EIGRP Routes into the OSPF Routing Domain Using a Prefix List and Distribute List

Example 4-24 configures redistribution from EIGRP to OSPF using a prefix list and a distribute list on R1. R1 will be configured to specifically filter and only redistribute all matching prefixes in the range of 172.16.0.0/16 to /24 into the OSPF routing domain.

Example 4-24   *Redistributing EIGRP into OSPF*

```
R1(config)# ip prefix-list EIGRP-TO-OSPF seq 5 permit 172.16.0.0/16 le 24
R1(config)# router ospf 10
R1(config-router)# redistribute eigrp 100 metric 40 subnets
R1(config-router)# distribute-list prefix EIGRP-TO-OSPF out eigrp 100
```

Next, Example 4-25 verifies the hits by using the **show ip prefix-list** detail command on R1.

Example 4-25   *Verifying Prefix List on R1*

```
R1# show ip prefix-list detail
Prefix-list with the last deletion/insertion: EIGRP_TO_OSPF
ip prefix-list EIGRP_TO_OSPF:
   count: 1, range entries: 1, sequences: 5 - 5, refcount: 3
   seq 5 permit 172.16.0.0/16 le 24 (hit count: 2, refcount: 1)
```

Because there are only two networks on R2 router that matches the prefix list (172.16.41.1/24 and 172.16.13.2/24), the hit count counter is increased by two.

Finally, the partial output of the **show ip route ospf** command in Example 4-26 verifies the routing table on R4.

Example 4-26 *Verifying Routing Table on R4*

```
R4# show ip route ospf
<Output omitted>


Gateway of last resort is not set


      172.16.0.0/16 is variably subnetted, 13 subnets, 3 masks
O IA     172.16.12.0/24 [110/74] via 172.16.11.2, 1w1d, Serial0/0
O E2     172.16.13.0/24 [110/20] via 172.16.11.2, 00:17:38, Serial0/0
O E2     172.16.41.0/24 [110/20] via 172.16.11.2, 00:17:38, Serial0/0
```

Using Route Maps

Route maps provide another technique to manipulate and control routing protocol updates. Route maps may be used for a variety of purposes. After describing route map applications and operation, this section explores the use of route maps as a tool to filter and manipulate routing updates. All the IP routing protocols can use route maps for redistribution filtering.

Understanding Route Maps

Route maps are complex access lists that allow some conditions to be tested against the packet or route in question using **match** commands. If the conditions match, some actions can be taken to modify attributes of the packet or route. These actions are specified by **set** commands.

A collection of **route-map** statements that have the same route map name is considered one route map. Within a route map, each **route-map** statement is numbered and therefore can be edited individually.

The statements in a route map correspond to the lines of an access list. Specifying the match conditions in a route map is similar in concept to specifying the source and destination addresses and masks in an access list.

One major difference between route maps and access lists is that route maps can use the **set** commands to modify the packet or route.

Route Map Applications

Network administrators use route maps for a variety of purposes. Several of the more common applications for route maps are as follows:

■ **Route filtering during redistribution:** Redistribution nearly always requires some amount of route filtering. Although distribute lists can be used for this purpose, route maps offer the added benefit of manipulating routing metrics through the use of **set** commands. The route map is applied using the **redistribute** command.

■ **Policy-based routing (PBR):** Route maps can be used to match source and destination addresses, protocol types, and end-user applications. When a match occurs, a **set** command can be used to define the interface or next-hop address to which the packet should be sent. PBR allows an administrator to define routing policy other than basic destination-based routing using the routing table. The route map is applied to an interface using the **ip policy route-map** interface configuration command.

■ **BGP:** Route maps are the primary tools for implementing BGP policy. Network administrators assign route maps to specific BGP sessions (neighbors) to control which routes are allowed to flow in and out of the BGP process. In addition to filtering, route maps provide sophisticated manipulation of BGP path attributes. The route map is applied using the BGP **neighbor** router configuration command. Route maps for BGP are discussed in Chapter 6, "Enterprise Internet Connectivity."

Configuring Route Maps

There are three steps when creating a route map:

Step 1.   Define the route map using the **route-map** global configuration command.

Step 2.   Define the matching conditions using the **match** command and optionally the action to be taken when each condition is matched using the **set** command.

Step 3.   Apply the route map.

To define a route map, use the **route-map** *map-tag* [**permit** | **deny**] [*sequence-number*] global configuration command. Table 4-10 explains the parameters of this command in detail.

Table 4-10   route-map *Command Parameters*

Parameter	Description
map-tag	Name of the route map.
permit | **deny**	(Optional) A parameter that specifies the action to be taken if the route map match conditions are met. The meaning of **permit** or **deny** is dependent on how the route map is used. The default for the **route-map** command is **permit**, with a sequence number of 10.
sequence-number	(Optional) A sequence number that indicates the position that a new **route-map** statement will have in the list of **route-map** statements already configured with the same name.

A route map may be made up of multiple **route-map** statements (with different sequence numbers). The statements are processed top-down, similar to an access list. The first match found for a route is applied. The sequence number is also used for inserting or deleting specific **route-map** statements in a specific place in the route map.

The sequence number specifies the order in which conditions are checked. For example, if two statements in a route map are named MYMAP, one with sequence 10 and the other with sequence 20, sequence 10 is checked first. If the match conditions in sequence 10 are not met, sequence 20 is checked.

Route map sequence numbers do not automatically increment. When the *sequence-number* parameter of the **route-map** command is not used, the following occurs:

- If no other entry is already defined with the supplied **route-map** *map-tag*, an entry is created, with the *sequence-number* set to 10.

- If only one entry is already defined with the supplied **route-map** tag, that entry is the default entry for the **route-map** command, and the *sequence-number* of the entry is unchanged. (The router assumes you are editing the one entry that is already defined.)

- If more than one entry is already defined with the supplied **route-map** tag, an error message is displayed, indicating that the *sequence-number* is required.

- If the **no route-map map-tag** command is specified (without the *sequence-number* parameter), the whole route map is deleted.

Like an access list, an implicit **deny any** appears at the end of a route map. The consequences of this **deny** depend on how the route map is being used.

The **match** *condition* route map configuration commands are used to define the conditions to be checked. The **set** *condition* route map configuration commands are used to define the actions to be followed if there is a match and the action to be taken is **permit**. (The consequences of a **deny** action depend on how the route map is being used.)

A **route-map** statement without any **match** statements will be considered matched.

A single **match** statement may contain multiple conditions. Only one condition in the same **match** statement must be true for that **match** statement to be considered a match. (This is a logical OR operation.)

A **route-map** statement may contain multiple **match** statements. All **match** statements within a **route-map** statement must be considered true for the **route-map** statement to be considered matched. (This is a logical AND operation.)

For example, IP standard, extended access lists, or prefix lists can be used to establish match criteria using the **match ip address** {*access-list-number* | *name*} [...*access-list-number* | *name*] | **prefix-list** *prefix-list-name* [..*prefix-list-name*] route map configuration command. If multiple access lists or prefix lists are specified, matching any one results in a match. A standard IP access list can be used to specify match criteria for a packet's source address. Extended access lists can be used to specify match criteria based on source and destination addresses, application, protocol type, type of service (ToS), and precedence.

Another way to explain how a route map works is to use a simple example and see how it would be interpreted. Example 4-27 shows a sample route map-like configuration. (Note that on a router all the conditions and actions shown would be replaced with specific conditions and actions, depending on the exact **match** and **set** commands used.)

Example 4-27   *Demonstration of the* **route-map** *Command*

```
route-map DEMO permit 10
  match X Y Z
  match A
  set B
  set C
route-map DEMO permit 20
  match Q
  set R
route-map DEMO permit 30
```

The route map named DEMO in Example 4-27 is interpreted as follows:

If {(X or Y or Z) and (A) match} then {set B and C}

Else

If Q matches then set R

Else

Set nothing

Route Map Match and Set Statements

The **match** *condition* route map configuration commands are used to define the conditions to be checked. Table 4-11 lists some of the variety of **match** commands that can be configured. Not all the **match** commands listed here are used for redistribution purposes; the table includes commands for BGP and PBR.

Table 4-11   **match** *Commands*

Command	Description
match ip address {*access-list-number*	*name*} [...*access-list-number*	*name*]	**prefix-list** *prefix-list-name* [..*prefix-list-name*]	Matches any routes that have a network number that is permitted by a standard or extended access list or prefix list. Multiple access lists or prefix lists can be specified; matching any one results in a match.
match length *min max*	Matches based on a packet's Layer 3 length.
match interface *type number*	Matches any routes that have the next hop out of one of the interfaces specified.

Command	Description
match ip next-hop {*access-list-number* | *access-list-name*} [*...access-list-number* | *... access-list-name*]	Matches any routes that have a next-hop router address permitted by one of the access lists specified.
match ip route-source {*access-list-number* | *access-list-name*} [*...access-list-number* | *... access-list-name*]	Matches routes that have been advertised by routers and access servers that have an address permitted by one of the access lists specified.
match metric *metric-value*	Matches routes that have the metric specified.
match route-type [external | internal | level-1 | level-2 | local]	Matches routes of the specified type.
match community {*list-number* | *list-name*}	Matches a BGP community.
match tag *tag-value*	Matches based on the tag of a route.

The **set** *condition* route map configuration commands change or add characteristics, such as metrics, to any routes that have met a match criterion and the action to be taken is **permit**. (The consequences of a **deny** action depend on how the route map is being used.) Table 4-12 lists some of the variety of **set** commands that are available. Not all the **set** commands listed here are used for redistribution purposes; the table includes commands for BGP and PBR.

Table 4-12   set *Commands*

Command	Description
set metric *metric-value*	Sets the metric value for a routing protocol.
set metric-type [type-1 | type-2 | internal | external]	Sets the metric type for the destination routing protocol.
set default interface *type number* [*...type number*]	Indicates where to send output packets that pass a match clause of a route map for policy routing and for which the Cisco IOS Software has no explicit route to the destination.
set interface *type number* [*...type number*]	Indicates where to send output packets that pass a match clause of a route map for policy routing.
set ip default next-hop *ip-address* [*...ip-address*]	Indicates where to send output packets that pass a match clause of a route map for policy routing and for which the Cisco IOS Software has no explicit route to the destination.
set ip default next-hop verify-availability	Forces the router to check the CDP database to determine if an entry is available for the next hop that is specified by the **set ip default next-hop** command. This command is used to prevent traffic from being "black holed" if the configured next hop becomes unavailable.
set ip next-hop *ip-address* [*...ip-address*]	Indicates where to send output packets that pass a match clause of a route map for policy routing.

Command	Description
set ip next-hop verify-availability	Forces the router to check the Cisco Discovery Protocol (CDP) database or use object tracking to determine if the next hop that is specified for policy-based routing is available.
set ip vrf	Indicates where to forward packets that pass a match clause of a route map for policy routing when the next hop must be under a specified Virtual Routing and Forwarding (VRF) name.
set next-hop	Specifies the address of the next hop.
**set level [level-1	level-2	stub-area	backbone]**	Indicates at what level or type of area to import routes into (for IS-IS and OSPF routes).
**set as-path {tag	prepend** *as-path-string*}	Modifies an autonomous system path for BGP routes.
set automatic-tag	Automatically computes the BGP tag value.
set community {*community-number* [**additive**] [*well-known-community*]	**none**}	Sets the BGP community attribute.
set local-preference *bgp-path-attributes*	Specifies a local preference value for the BGP autonomous system path.
set weight *bgp-weight*	Specifies the BGP weight value.
set origin *bgp-origin-code*	Specifies the BGP origin code.
set tag	Specifies the tag value for destination routing protocol.

Configuring Route Redistribution Using Route Maps

Use route maps when you want detailed control over how routes are redistributed between routing protocols. The **redistribute** command has a **route-map** keyword with a *map-tag* parameter. This parameter refers to a route map configured with the **route-map** command.

It is important to understand what the **permit** and **deny** mean when redistributing. When used with a **redistribute** command, a **route-map** statement with **permit** indicates that the matched route is to be redistributed, and a **route-map** statement with **deny** indicates that the matched route is not to be redistributed.

Using Route Maps with Redistribution

For an example of using a route map for redistribution, see Figure 4-18.

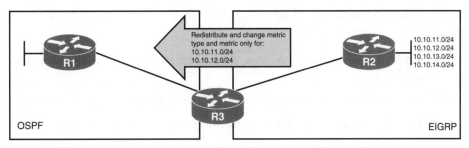

Figure 4-18 *Redistribution using Route Maps Topology*

Example 4-28 redistributes networks 10.10.11.0/24 and 10.10.12.0/24 from EIGRP into OSPF. Traffic that is matched by the route map RM-INTO-OSPF is defined by the prefix list FILTER-ROUTES. The **set** command specifies the routing actions to perform such as change of metric and change of metric type for the matched prefixes defined by prefix list. In this case we are setting metric to 25 and metric type to external type 1 for matched routes.

Example 4-28 *Redistributing OSPF Routes into EIGRP*

```
R3(config)# ip prefix-list FILTER-ROUTES permit 10.10.11.0/24
R3(config)# ip prefix-list FILTER-ROUTES permit 10.10.12.0/24
R3(config)# route-map RM-INTO-OSPF permit 10
R3(config-route-map)# match ip address prefix-list FILTER-ROUTES
R3(config-route-map)# set metric 25
R3(config-route-map)# set metric-type type-1
R3(config-route-map)# exit
R3(config)# router ospf 10
R3(config-router)# redistribute eigrp 100 subnets route-map RM-INTO-OSPF
```

Manipulating Redistribution Using Route Maps

This example provides an overview of configure route redistribution using route maps using the topology in Figure 4-19.

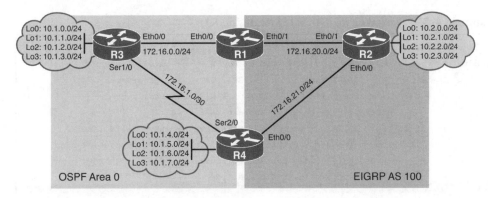

Figure 4-19 *Manipulating Redistribution using Route Maps Topology*

In this example, R1 and R4 will be performing multipoint two-way redistribution. Specifically

- R1 and R4 will be configured to support mutual redistribution without any filtering mechanism.

- R1 and R4 will be configured to support mutual redistribution using route maps.

- Change administrative distance for certain routes to enable optimal routing.

Mutual Redistribution without Route Filtering

Example 4-29 configures mutual redistribution on R1.

Example 4-29 *Mutual Redistribution Without Filters on R1*

```
R1(config)# router eigrp 100
R1(config-router)# redistribute ospf 10 metric 10000 10 200 5 1500
R1(config-router)# exit
R1(config)# router ospf 10
R1(config-router)# redistribute eigrp 100 subnets
```

Example 4-30 configures mutual redistribution on R4.

Example 4-30 *Mutual Redistribution Without Filters on R4*

```
R4(config)# router eigrp 100
R4(config-router)# redistribute ospf 10 metric 10000 10 200 5 1500
R4(config-router)# exit
R4(config)# router ospf 10
R4(config-router)# redistribute eigrp 100 subnets
```

Next, verify the routing table on R3 using the **show ip route ospf** command, as shown in Example 4-31.

Example 4-31 *Verifying Redistributed Routes on R3*

```
R3# show ip route ospf
Codes: L - local, C - connected, S - static, R - RIP, M - mobile, B - BGP
       D - EIGRP, EX - EIGRP external, O - OSPF, IA - OSPF inter area
       N1 - OSPF NSSA external type 1, N2 - OSPF NSSA external type 2
       E1 - OSPF external type 1, E2 - OSPF external type 2
       i - IS-IS, su - IS-IS summary, L1 - IS-IS level-1, L2 - IS-IS level-2
       ia - IS-IS inter area, * - candidate default, U - per-user static route
       o - ODR, P - periodic downloaded static route, H - NHRP, l - LISP
       + - replicated route, % - next hop override

Gateway of last resort is not set
```

```
        10.0.0.0/8 is variably subnetted, 16 subnets, 2 masks
O          10.1.4.0/24 [110/65] via 172.16.1.2, 00:20:02, Serial1/0
O          10.1.5.0/24 [110/65] via 172.16.1.2, 00:20:02, Serial1/0
O          10.1.6.0/24 [110/65] via 172.16.1.2, 00:20:02, Serial1/0
O          10.1.7.0/24 [110/65] via 172.16.1.2, 00:20:02, Serial1/0
O E2       10.2.0.0/24 [110/20] via 172.16.0.2, 00:58:31, Ethernet0/0
O E2       10.2.1.0/24 [110/20] via 172.16.0.2, 00:58:31, Ethernet0/0
O E2       10.2.2.0/24 [110/20] via 172.16.0.2, 00:58:31, Ethernet0/0
O E2       10.2.3.0/24 [110/20] via 172.16.0.2, 00:58:31, Ethernet0/0
        172.16.0.0/16 is variably subnetted, 6 subnets, 3 masks
O E2       172.16.20.0/24 [110/20] via 172.16.0.2, 00:58:31, Ethernet0/0
O E2       172.16.21.0/24 [110/20] via 172.16.0.2, 00:58:31, Ethernet0/0
```

Notice the redistributed EIGRP network as OSPF routes in the routing table. An example of two redistributed loopback routes is highlighted. Also notice how the link networks like 172.16.20.0/24 and 172.16.21.0/24 were redistributed.

Mutual Redistribution with Route Maps

Next, ACLs and route maps will be used to manipulate the redistributed routes. Example 4-32 creates two ACLs on R1 and two route maps.

Example 4-32 *Mutual Redistribution with Route Maps on R1*

```
R1(config)# access-list 10 permit 10.2.0.0 0.0.3.255
R1(config)# access-list 20 permit 10.1.0.0 0.0.7.255
R1(config)# route-map INTO-OSPF permit 10
R1(config-route-map)# match ip address 10
R1(config-route-map)# exit
R1(config)# route-map INTO-EIGRP permit 10
R1(config-route-map)# match ip address 20
R1(config-route-map)# set metric 10000 10 200 5 1500
```

Example 4-33 creates two ACLs on R2 and two route maps.

Example 4-33 *Mutual Redistribution with Route Maps on R4*

```
R4(config)# access-list 10 permit 10.2.0.0 0.0.3.255
R4(config)# access-list 20 permit 10.1.0.0 0.0.7.255
R4(config)# route-map INTO-OSPF permit 10
R4(config-route-map)# match ip address 10
R4(config-route-map)# exit
R4(config)# route-map INTO-EIGRP permit 10
R4(config-route-map)# match ip address 20
R4(config-route-map)# set metric 10000 10 200 5 1500
```

Example 4-34 applies the configured route map to the **redistribute** command under the OSPF and EIGRP processes on R1.

Example 4-34 *Applying Route Maps to the* **Redistribute** *Command on R1*

```
R1(config)# router eigrp 100
R1(config-router)# redistribute ospf 10 route-map INTO-EIGRP
R1(config-router)# exit
R1(config)# router ospf 10
R1(config-router)# redistribute eigrp 100 subnets route-map INTO-OSPF
```

Example 4-35 applies the configured route map to the **redistribute** command under the OSPF and EIGRP processes on R4.

Example 4-35 *Applying Route Maps to the* **Redistribute** *Command on R1*

```
R4(config)# router eigrp 100
R4(config-router)# redistribute ospf 10 route-map INTO-EIGRP
R4(config-router)# exit
R4(config)# router ospf 10
R4(config-router)# redistribute eigrp 100 subnets route-map INTO-OSPF
```

Next, verify the routing table on R3 using the **show ip route ospf** command, as shown in Example 4-36.

Example 4-36 *Verifying Redistributed Routes on R3*

```
R3# show ip route ospf
<Output omitted>


Gateway of last resort is not set


      10.0.0.0/8 is variably subnetted, 16 subnets, 2 masks
O        10.1.4.0/24 [110/65] via 172.16.1.2, 00:30:02, Serial1/0
O        10.1.5.0/24 [110/65] via 172.16.1.2, 00:33:48, Serial1/0
O        10.1.6.0/24 [110/65] via 172.16.1.2, 00:33:48, Serial1/0
O        10.1.7.0/24 [110/65] via 172.16.1.2, 00:33:38, Serial1/0
O E2     10.2.0.0/24 [110/20] via 172.16.0.2, 01:40:23, Ethernet0/0
O E2     10.2.1.0/24 [110/20] via 172.16.0.2, 01:40:23, Ethernet0/0
O E2     10.2.2.0/24 [110/20] via 172.16.0.2, 01:40:23, Ethernet0/0
O E2     10.2.3.0/24 [110/20] via 172.16.0.2, 01:40:23, Ethernet0/0
```

Notice that now the link networks 172.16.20.0/24 are not present any more as OSPF routes in the routing table.

Change Administrative Distance to Enable Optimal Routing

A route redistributed into a routing protocol by default inherits the default administrative distance of that routing protocol. Occasionally, such as when using route redistribution, you might need to modify a protocol's default administrative distance to manipulate the routing process.

Example 4-37 examines the routing table of R1.

Example 4-37 *Examine the Routing Table of R1*

```
R1# show ip route
Codes: L - local, C - connected, S - static, R - RIP, M - mobile, B - BGP
       D - EIGRP, EX - EIGRP external, O - OSPF, IA - OSPF inter area
       N1 - OSPF NSSA external type 1, N2 - OSPF NSSA external type 2
       E1 - OSPF external type 1, E2 - OSPF external type 2
       i - IS-IS, su - IS-IS summary, L1 - IS-IS level-1, L2 - IS-IS level-2
       ia - IS-IS inter area, * - candidate default, U - per-user static route
       o - ODR, P - periodic downloaded static route, H - NHRP, l - LISP
       + - replicated route, % - next hop override

Gateway of last resort is not set

      10.0.0.0/24 is subnetted, 12 subnets
O        10.1.0.0 [110/11] via 172.16.0.1, 03:47:09, Ethernet0/0
O        10.1.1.0 [110/11] via 172.16.0.1, 03:47:09, Ethernet0/0
O        10.1.2.0 [110/11] via 172.16.0.1, 03:47:09, Ethernet0/0
O        10.1.3.0 [110/11] via 172.16.0.1, 03:47:09, Ethernet0/0
O        10.1.4.0 [110/75] via 172.16.0.1, 00:32:22, Ethernet0/0
O        10.1.5.0 [110/75] via 172.16.0.1, 00:36:08, Ethernet0/0
O        10.1.6.0 [110/75] via 172.16.0.1, 00:36:08, Ethernet0/0
O        10.1.7.0 [110/75] via 172.16.0.1, 00:35:58, Ethernet0/0
D        10.2.0.0 [90/409600] via 172.16.20.2, 03:41:39, Ethernet0/1
D        10.2.1.0 [90/409600] via 172.16.20.2, 03:41:39, Ethernet0/1
D        10.2.2.0 [90/409600] via 172.16.20.2, 03:41:39, Ethernet0/1
D        10.2.3.0 [90/409600] via 172.16.20.2, 03:41:39, Ethernet0/1
      172.16.0.0/16 is variably subnetted, 6 subnets, 3 masks
C        172.16.0.0/24 is directly connected, Ethernet0/0
L        172.16.0.2/32 is directly connected, Ethernet0/0
O        172.16.1.0/30 [110/74] via 172.16.0.1, 01:04:30, Ethernet0/0
C        172.16.20.0/24 is directly connected, Ethernet0/1
L        172.16.20.1/32 is directly connected, Ethernet0/1
D        172.16.21.0/24 [90/281856] via 172.16.20.2, 03:41:39, Ethernet0/1
```

The highlighted route 10.1.4.0/24 describes one of the loopback interfaces on R4. Notice how R1 prefers the path learned via OSPF to reach this network, even though it crosses a slow serial link. The alternative EIGRP path has faster links, but it also has a higher administrative distance. The reason is because it is an external EIGRP route and is therefore assigned an administrative value of 170, which is higher than the OSPF administrative distance of 110.

One way you can improve routing is to manipulate administrative distance of routes. If the EIGRP external route administrative distance is lowered below the OSPF value, the 10.1.4.0/24 route should be directed over the EIGRP domain.

Example 4-38 changes the administrative distance for external EIGRP routes from 170 to 100 on R1.

Example 4-38   *Changing External Route Administrative Distance on R1*

```
R1(config)# router eigrp 100
R1(config-router)# distance eigrp 90 100
R1(config-router)# ^Z
R1#
R1#
*Jul 21 16:08:00.454: %DUAL-5-NBRCHANGE: EIGRP-IPv4 100: Neighbor 172.16.20.2
(Ethernet0/1) is down: route configuration changed
R1#
*Jul 21 16:08:03.705: %DUAL-5-NBRCHANGE: EIGRP-IPv4 100: Neighbor 172.16.20.2
(Ethernet0/1) is up: new adjacency
```

The **distance eigrp** command changes local default values for internal and external routes in the EIGRP domain. In this example, the default EIGRP administrative distance of 90 is configured for internal EIGRP routes, and external routes are assigned an administrative distance of 100. This value is less than the OSPF administrative value of 110 and should make R1 prefer the path through the EIGRP domain to reach the 10.1.4.0/24 network. Also notice how R1 has its renegotiated adjacency with R2.

Example 4-39 verifies the routing table of R1 to see whether it now prefers the EIGRP path to 10.1.4.0/24.

Example 4-39   *Examine the Routing Table of R1*

```
R1# show ip route
<Output omitted>

Gateway of last resort is not set

      10.0.0.0/24 is subnetted, 12 subnets
D EX    10.1.0.0 [100/284416] via 172.16.20.2, 00:00:26, Ethernet0/1
D EX    10.1.1.0 [100/284416] via 172.16.20.2, 00:00:26, Ethernet0/1
D EX    10.1.2.0 [100/284416] via 172.16.20.2, 00:00:26, Ethernet0/1
D EX    10.1.3.0 [100/284416] via 172.16.20.2, 00:00:26, Ethernet0/1
D EX    10.1.4.0 [100/284416] via 172.16.20.2, 00:00:26, Ethernet0/1
D EX    10.1.5.0 [100/284416] via 172.16.20.2, 00:00:26, Ethernet0/1
D EX    10.1.6.0 [100/284416] via 172.16.20.2, 00:00:26, Ethernet0/1
```

```
D EX      10.1.7.0 [100/284416] via 172.16.20.2, 00:00:26, Ethernet0/1
D         10.2.0.0 [90/409600] via 172.16.20.2, 00:00:26, Ethernet0/1
D         10.2.1.0 [90/409600] via 172.16.20.2, 00:00:26, Ethernet0/1
D         10.2.2.0 [90/409600] via 172.16.20.2, 00:00:26, Ethernet0/1
D         10.2.3.0 [90/409600] via 172.16.20.2, 00:00:26, Ethernet0/1
          172.16.0.0/16 is variably subnetted, 6 subnets, 3 masks
C         172.16.0.0/24 is directly connected, Ethernet0/0
L         172.16.0.2/32 is directly connected, Ethernet0/0
O         172.16.1.0/30 [110/74] via 172.16.0.1, 01:10:33, Ethernet0/0
C         172.16.20.0/24 is directly connected, Ethernet0/1
L         172.16.20.1/32 is directly connected, Ethernet0/1
D         172.16.21.0/24 [90/281856] via 172.16.20.2, 00:00:26, Ethernet0/1
```

Now notice how the path for network 10.1.4.0/24 is learned via EIGRP with an administrative value of 100. This way R1 can reach network 10.1.4.0/24 without crossing a slow serial link.

However, another problem was accidentally created by altering the default external EIGRP metric to 100. It now has introduced a nonoptimal path from R1 towards all networks announced by R3. For example, when R1 wants to reach an R3 networks (10.1.0.0/24, 10.1.1.0/24, 10.1.2.0/24, 10.1.3.0/24), it will now be routed to R2, R4, and then R3 instead of going directly to R3 from R1.

Various solutions could be implemented, but the decision has been made to make the four R3 routes more attractive by lowering the administrative distance of those specific routes.

Example 4-40 identifies the four R3 routes and lowers their administrative distance to 95.

Example 4-40 *Altering Administrative Distance of R3 Routes*

```
R1(config)# access-list 30 permit 10.1.0.0 0.0.3.255
R1(config)# router ospf 10
R1(config-router)# distance 95 10.1.3.1 0.0.0.0 30
```

Note The **distance** *admin-distance source-address source-wildcard-mask* [*access-list*] router configuration command can be used to change the administrative distance for RIP, OSPF, EIGRP, and BGP. For EIGRP, however, this command only works for EIGRP internal routes; it does not work for EIGRP external routes. For OSPF the *source-address* parameter is the source router ID.

In the example, ACL 30 identifies the four R3 routes, and this time the **distance** command assigns an administrative distance of 95 to updates from R3's router ID that match the routes listed in ACL 30.

Example 4-41 verifies the routing table of R1 to see which path is the preferred path to 10.1.0.0/24.

Example 4-41 *Verifying the Routing Table of R1*

```
R1# show ip route
<Output omitted>


Gateway of last resort is not set


      10.0.0.0/24 is subnetted, 12 subnets
O       10.1.0.0 [95/11] via 172.16.0.1, 02:43:27, Ethernet0/0
O       10.1.1.0 [95/11] via 172.16.0.1, 02:43:27, Ethernet0/0
O       10.1.2.0 [95/11] via 172.16.0.1, 02:43:27, Ethernet0/0
O       10.1.3.0 [95/11] via 172.16.0.1, 02:43:27, Ethernet0/0
D EX    10.1.4.0 [100/284416] via 172.16.20.2, 02:43:27, Ethernet0/1
D EX    10.1.5.0 [100/284416] via 172.16.20.2, 02:43:27, Ethernet0/1
D EX    10.1.6.0 [100/284416] via 172.16.20.2, 02:43:27, Ethernet0/1
D EX    10.1.7.0 [100/284416] via 172.16.20.2, 02:43:27, Ethernet0/1
D       10.2.0.0 [90/409600] via 172.16.20.2, 02:43:27, Ethernet0/1
D       10.2.1.0 [90/409600] via 172.16.20.2, 02:43:27, Ethernet0/1
D       10.2.2.0 [90/409600] via 172.16.20.2, 02:43:27, Ethernet0/1
D       10.2.3.0 [90/409600] via 172.16.20.2, 02:43:27, Ethernet0/1
      172.16.0.0/16 is variably subnetted, 6 subnets, 3 masks
C       172.16.0.0/24 is directly connected, Ethernet0/0
L       172.16.0.2/32 is directly connected, Ethernet0/0
O       172.16.1.0/30 [110/74] via 172.16.0.1, 02:43:27, Ethernet0/0
C       172.16.20.0/24 is directly connected, Ethernet0/1
L       172.16.20.1/32 is directly connected, Ethernet0/1
D       172.16.21.0/24 [90/281856] via 172.16.20.2, 02:43:27, Ethernet0/1
R1#
```

Notice that now the preferred path to the R3 routes (10.1.0.0/24, 10.1.1.0/24, 10.1.2.0/24, 10.1.3.0/24) is from R1 to R3.

Manipulating Redistribution Using Route Tagging

Another option to manipulate two-way multipoint redistribution is to use route tagging. Two-way multipoint redistribution can introduce routing loops in the network. One option to prevent redistribution of already redistributed routes is to use route tagging.

See the topology in Figure 4-20.

In this example, R4 tags all routes that are redistributed from EIGRP into OSPF with route tag 50. Router R1 can then be configured to redistribute all OSPF routes into EIGRP except those that are tagged with route tag 50.

Example 4-42 configures a route map that will set route tag to 50, using the **set tag** *tag* route map configuration command, and attaches the route map to the **redistribution** command to manipulate the redistribution process and mark all redistributed routes with the configured tag.

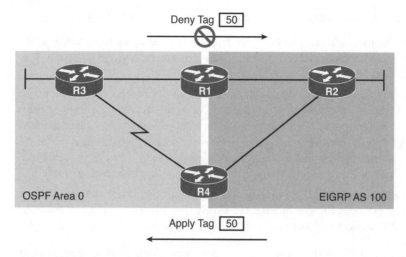

Figure 4-20 *Route Tagging Topology*

Example 4-42 *Tagging External Routes on R4*

```
R4(config)# route-map EIGRP-TO-OSPF permit 10
R4(config-route-map)# set tag 50
R4(config-route-map)# exit
R4(config)# router ospf 10
R4(config-router)# redistribute eigrp 100 subnets route-map EIGRP-TO-OSPF
```

Example 4-43 configures the route map on R1 with **deny** redistribution of routes based on the matched tag 50 and **permit** redistribution of all other routes. To match routes with tags, use the **match tag** *tag* route map configuration command and attach the route map to the **redistribute** command.

Example 4-43 *Matching External Routes on R1*

```
R1(config)# route-map OSPF-TO-EIGRP deny 10
R1(config-route-map)# match tag 50
R1(config-route-map)# exit
R1(config)# route-map OSPF-TO-EIGRP permit 20
R1(config-route-map)# exit
R1(config)# router eigrp 100
R1(config-router)# redistribute ospf 10 metric 1000 1 255 1 1500 route-map OSPF-
TO-EIGRP
```

Caveats of Redistribution

Redistribution of routing information adds to the complexity of a network and increases the potential for routing confusion, so you should use it only when necessary.

The key issues that arise when you are using redistribution are as follows:

■ **Routing loops:** Depending on how redistribution is employed, routers may send routing information that is received from one autonomous system back into that same autonomous system.

■ **Incompatible routing information:** Because each routing protocol uses different metrics to determine the best path, path selection using the redistributed route information may be suboptimal. The metric information about a route cannot be translated exactly into a different protocol, so the path that a router chooses might not be the best. To prevent suboptimal routing, as a rule, assign a seed metric to redistributed routes that is higher than any routes that are native to the redistributing protocol.

■ **Inconsistent convergence time:** Different routing protocols converge at different rates. For example, RIP converges more slowly than EIGRP. So, if a link goes down, the EIGRP network will learn about it before the RIP network.

Good planning will ensure that these issues do not cause problems in your network. It can eliminate the majority of issues, but additional configuration might be required. You might resolve some issues by changing the administrative distance, manipulating the metrics, and filtering using distribute lists and route maps.

Summary

This chapter covered how to support multiple routing protocols by using redistribution and route filtering techniques, through discussion of the following topics:

■ Reasons for using more than one routing protocol (migration, host system needs, mixed-vendor environment, political and geographic borders, Multiprotocol Label Switching [MPLS] virtual private networks [VPNs]).

■ Routing information can be exchanged between them (referred to as redistribution), and how Cisco routers operate in a multiple routing protocol environment.

■ Route redistribution is always performed *outbound*. The router doing redistribution does not change its routing table.

■ A router assigns a seed metric to redistributed routes using the **default-metric** router configuration command or the **redistribute** command with the **metric** parameter.

■ The redistribution techniques, one-point and multipoint:

■ The two methods of one-point route redistribution are one-way and two-way. Suboptimal routing is a possible issue with these techniques.

■ The two methods of multipoint route redistribution are one-way and two-way. Multipoint redistribution is likely to introduce potential routing loops.

■ To prevent routing issues, use one of the following options:

■ Redistribute a default route from the core autonomous system into the edge autonomous system, and redistribute routes from the edge routing protocols into the core routing protocol.

- Redistribute multiple static routes about the core autonomous system networks into the edge autonomous system, and redistribute routes from the edge routing protocols into the core routing protocol.

- Redistribute routes from the core autonomous system into the edge autonomous system with filtering to block out inappropriate routes.

- Redistribute all routes from the core autonomous system into the edge autonomous system, and from the edge autonomous system into the core autonomous system, and then modify the administrative distance associated with redistributed routes so that they are not the selected routes when multiple routes exist for the same destination.

- Configuration of redistribution between various IP routing protocols:

  - To redistribute into EIGRP, use the **redistribute** *protocol* [*process-id*] [**match** *route-type*] [**metric** *metric-value*] [**route-map** *map-tag*] router configuration command.

  - To redistribute into OSPF, use the **redistribute** *protocol* [*process-id*] [**metric** *metric-value*] [**metric-type** *type-value*] [**route-map** *map-tag*] [**subnets**] [**tag** *tag-value*] router configuration command.

- Using the **show ip route** [*ip-address*] and **traceroute** [*ip-address*] commands to verify route redistribution.

- Distribute lists, allowing an access list to be applied to routing updates:

  - The **distribute-list** {*access-list-number* | *name*} **out** [*interface-name*] router configuration command assigns the access list to filter outgoing routing updates. This command filters updates going out of the interface or routing protocol specified in the command, into the routing process under which it is configured.

  - The **distribute-list** {*access-list-number* | *name*} [**route-map** *map-tag*] **in** [*interface-type interface-number*] router configuration command assigns the access list to filter routing updates coming in through an interface. This command filters updates going into the interface specified in the command, into the routing process under which it is configured.

- Prefix lists can be used with distribute lists as an alternative to ACLs, with improvements in performance, support for incremental modifications, a more user-friendly command-line interface, and greater flexibility. Prefix lists are configured with the **ip prefix-list** {*list-name* | *list-number*} [**seq** *seq-value*] {**deny** | **permit**} *network/length* [**ge** *ge-value*] [**le** *le-value*] global configuration command.

- Whether a prefix in a prefix list is permitted or denied is based on the following rules:

  - An empty prefix list permits all prefixes.

  - If a prefix is permitted, the route is used. If a prefix is denied, the route is not used.

  - Prefix lists consist of statements with sequence numbers. The router begins the search for a match at the top of the prefix list, which is the statement with the lowest sequence number.

- When a match occurs, the router does not need to go through the rest of the prefix list. For efficiency, you might want to put the most common matches (permits or denies) near the top of the list by specifying a lower sequence number.

- An implicit **deny** is assumed if a given prefix does not match any entries in a prefix list.

- Prefix list sequence numbers:

  - Sequence numbers are generated automatically, unless you disable this automatic generation.

  - A prefix list is an ordered list. The sequence number is significant when a given prefix is matched by multiple entries of a prefix list, in which case the one with the smallest sequence number is considered the real match.

  - The evaluation of a prefix list starts with the lowest sequence number and continues down the list until a match is found, in which case the **permit** or **deny** statement is applied to that network and the remainder of the list is not evaluated.

- Using route maps for route filtering during redistribution, PBR, and BGP.

- The characteristics of route maps, configured using the **route-map** *map-tag* [**permit** | **deny**] [*sequence-number*] global configuration command:

  - Route maps allow some conditions to be tested against the packet or route in question using **match** commands. If the conditions match, some actions can be taken to modify attributes of the packet or route; these actions are specified by **set** commands.

  - A collection of **route-map** statements that have the same route map name is considered one route map.

  - Within a route map, each **route-map** statement is numbered and therefore can be edited individually.

  - The default for the **route-map** command is **permit**, with a *sequence-number* of 10.

  - Only one condition listed on the same **match** statement must match for the entire statement to be considered a match. However, all **match** statements within a **route-map** statement must match for the route map to be considered matched.

  - When used with a **redistribute** command, a **route-map** statement with **permit** indicates that the matched route is to be redistributed, and a **route-map** statement with **deny** indicates that the matched route is not to be redistributed.

References

For additional information, see these resources:

- Cisco IOS Software Releases support page: http://www.cisco.com/cisco/web/psa/default.html?mode=prod&level0=268438303

- Cisco IOS Master Command List, All Releases: http://www.cisco.com/c/en/us/td/docs/ios/mcl/allreleasemcl/all_book.html

Review Questions

Answer the following questions, and then see Appendix A, "Answers to Review Questions," for the answers.

1. What two methods can be used to filter routes?

   a. Cisco NetFlow

   b. Default routes

   c. Distribute lists with prefix lists

   d. IP SLA

   e. Route maps

2. Which are two reasons to use multiple routing protocols in a network?

   a. When migrating from an older IGP to a new IGP, multiple redistribution boundaries might exist until the new protocol has displaced the old protocol completely.

   b. When adding new Layer 2 switches that affect the STP domain.

   c. When different departments do not want to upgrade their routers to support a new routing protocol.

   d. When connecting to a new service provider.

3. Which two statements about redistribution are true?

   a. Redistribution is always performed inbound.

   b. Redistribution is always performed outbound.

   c. Redistribution is performed inbound and outbound.

   d. The routing table on the router doing the redistribution changes.

   e. The routing table on the router doing the redistribution does not change.

4. What are two issues that arise with redistribution?

   a. Compatible routing information

   b. Inconsistent convergence times

   c. Routing loops

   d. Large routing tables

   e. Cannot summarize routes

5. When configuring a seed metric for redistributed routes, what is the recommended metric setting?

  a. Do not set a seed metric.

  b. Set the seed metric to a value less than the largest metric within the autonomous system.

  c. Set the seed metric to a value matching the largest metric within the autonomous system.

  d. Set the seed metric to a value greater than the largest metric within the autonomous system.

6. Which two of the following accurately match the default seed metric for the respective routing protocol?

  a. EIGRP default seed metric is 0.

  b. EIGRP default seed metric is infinite.

  c. EIGRP default seed metric is 10000 100 1 255 1500.

  d. OSPF default seed metric is 0.

  e. OSPF default seed metric is infinite.

  f. OSPF default seed metric is 20.

7. What is the safest way to perform redistribution between two routing protocols?

  a. Multipoint one-way redistribution

  b. Multipoint two-way redistribution

  c. No point no-way redistribution

  d. One-point one-way redistribution

  e. One-point two-way redistribution

8. Which two statements about route maps are true?

  a. A **route-map** statement without any **match** statements will be considered matched.

  b. A sequence number must be assigned when using the **route-map** command.

  c. Route maps can be used to manipulate redistribution, manipulate paths using policy-based routing, and assign attributes in BGP.

  d. When a **match** statement contains multiple conditions, all the conditions in the statement must be true for that match statement to be considered a match.

9. What option correctly identifies the prompt and configuration command to redistribute EIGRP 10 traffic into OSPF 1 based on a route map called TESTING?

  a. R1(config)# **router ospf 1**
     R1(config-router)# **redistribute eigrp 10 route-map TESTING**

  b. R1(config)# **router ospf 1**
     R1(config-router)# **redistribute ospf 1 route-map TESTING**

  c. R1(config)# **router eigrp 10**
     R1(config-router)# **redistribute eigrp 10 route-map TESTING**

  d. R1(config)# **router eigrp 10**
     R1(config-router)# **redistribute ospf 1 route-map TESTING**

10. What does the router configuration command **distance 95 10.1.3.1 0.0.0.0 30** do in OSPF?

  a. Sets the administrative distance to 30 for updates as identified in ACL 95 from any neighbor

  b. Sets the administrative distance to 30 for updates as identified in ACL 95 from the neighbor with a router ID of 10.1.3.1

  c. Sets the administrative distance to 30 for updates as identified in ACL 95 from the neighbor with the next-hop address of 10.1.3.1

  d. Sets the administrative distance to 95 for updates as identified in ACL 30 from any neighbor

  e. Sets the administrative distance to 95 for updates as identified in ACL 30 from the neighbor with a router ID of 10.1.3.1

  f. Sets the administrative distance to 95 for updates as identified in ACL 30 from the neighbor with the next-hop address of 10.1.3.1

11. Correctly identify what the following router configuration commands do.

```
R1(config)# route-map TEST deny 10
R1(config-route-map)#  match tag 80
R1(config-route-map)# route-map TEST permit 20
R1(config-route-map)# router ospf 1
R1(config-router)#  redistribute eigrp 10 route-map TEST
```

  a. Routes with a tag of 80 will be redistributed from EIGRP into OSPF.

  b. Routes with a tag of 80 will be redistributed from OSPF into EIGRP.

  c. Routes with a tag of 80 are denied from being redistributed from EIGRP into OSPF.

  d. Routes with a tag of 80 are denied from being redistributed from OSPF into EIGRP.

  e. Routes with an administrative distance of 80 are denied from being redistributed from EIGRP into OSPF.

  f. Routes with an administrative distance of 80 are denied from being redistributed from OSPF into EIGRP.

12. Which parameter does a router use to select the best path when it learns two or more routes to the same destination (with the same prefix length) from different routing protocols?

  a. Administrative distance

  b. ACL filters

  c. Highest metric

  d. Lowest metric

  e. Prefix list filters

  f. Route map

13. In IPv6, what keyword must be used with the **redistribute** command for connected interfaces to be advertised to a target routing protocol?

    a. connected

    b. include-connected

    c. route-map

    d. static

    e. No keyword is required because IPv6 automatically includes connected routes when redistribution is configured.

14. Refer to the topology in Figure 4-21. Which prefix list configured on R3 would allow R1 to only learn about networks 172.16.10.0/24 and 172.16.11.0/24? (R3 would not learn about network 172.16.0.0/16.)

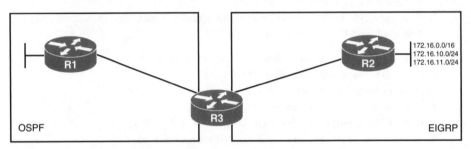

Figure 4-21 *Network Used in Prefix List Option Testing*

    a. ip prefix-list TEST permit 172.0.0.0/8 ge 16 le 24

    b. ip prefix-list TEST permit 172.0.0.0/8 ge 17

    c. ip prefix-list TEST permit 172.0.0.0/8 ge 17 le 23

    d. ip prefix-list TEST permit 172.0.0.0/8 le 16

    e. ip prefix-list TEST permit 172.0.0.0/8 le 24

15. What does the router configuration command **distance eigrp 80 100** do in EIGRP?

    a. It changes local default administrative distance of EIGRP 80 value for redistributed external routes to 100.

    b. It changes local default administrative distance of EIGRP 80 value for redistributed internal routes to 100.

    c. It changes local default administrative distance of EIGRP 100 value for redistributed external routes to 100.

    d. It changes local default administrative distance of EIGRP 100 value for redistributed internal routes to 100.

    e. It changes local default administrative distance EIGRP values for redistributed external routes to 80 and redistributed internal routes to 100.

    f. It changes local default administrative distance EIGRP values for internal routes to 80 and external routes to 100.

Chapter 5

Path Control Implementation

This chapter covers the following topics:

- Using Cisco Express Forwarding Switching

- Understanding Path Control

- Implementing Path Control Using Policy-Based Routing

- Implementing Path Control Using Cisco IOS IP SLAs

Given that bandwidth of modern networks is continually increasing at a steady rate, packet switching efficiency is important. As a network administrator, it is important to understand packet switching methods and their evolution.

Packets are usually routed by destination address but sometimes this approach is not flexible enough. For example, traffic path may have to be optimized for a specific application, or the traffic path may be controlled based on the network performance.

This chapter starts by discussing the Cisco Express Forwarding (CEF) switching method. Next we discuss path control fundamentals and explore two path control tools; policy-based routing (PBR) and Cisco IOS IP service-level agreements (SLAs).

Using Cisco Express Forwarding Switching

Packet forwarding is a core router function, therefore high-speed packet forwarding is very important. Throughout the years, various methods of packet switching have been developed. Cisco IOS platform-switching mechanisms evolved from process switching to fast switching, and eventually to CEF switching.

Upon completing this section, you will be able to do the following:

- Describe the different switching mechanisms that a Cisco router uses

- Describe how Cisco Express Forwarding (CEF) works

- Describe how to verify that CEF is working

- Describe how to verify the content of the CEF tables

- Describe how to enable and disable CEF by interface and globally

Control and Data Plane

A Layer 3 device employs a distributed architecture in which the control plane and data plane are relatively independent. For example, the exchange of routing protocol information is performed in the control plane by the route processor, whereas data packets are forwarded in the data plane by an interface microcoded processor.

The main functions of the control layer between the routing protocol and the firmware data plane microcode include the following:

- Managing the internal data and control circuits for the packet-forwarding and control functions.

- Extracting the other routing and packet-forwarding-related control information from Layer 2 and Layer 3 bridging and routing protocols and the configuration data, and then conveying the information to the interface module for control of the data plane.

- Collecting the data plane information, such as traffic statistics, from the interface module to the route processor.

- Handling certain data packets that are sent from the Ethernet interface modules to the route processor.

Cisco Switching Mechanisms

A Cisco router can use one of three methods to forward packets:

- **Process switching:** This switching method is the slowest of the three methods. Every packet is examined by the CPU in the control plane and all forwarding decisions are made in software. As illustrated in Figure 5-1, each packet must be processed by the CPU individually. When a packet arrives on the ingress interface, it is forwarded to the control plane where the CPU matches the destination address with an entry in its routing table. It then determines the exit interface and forwards the packet. The router does this for every packet, even if the destination is the same for a stream of packets. Process switching is the most CPU-intensive method that is available in Cisco routers. It greatly degrades performance and is generally used only as a last resort or during troubleshooting.

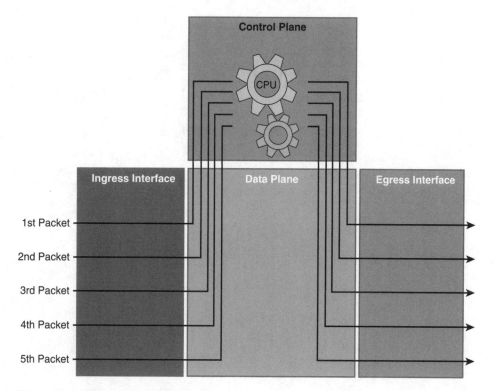

Figure 5-1 *Process-Switched Packets*

■ **Fast switching:** This switching method is faster than process switching. With fast switching, the initial packet of a traffic flow is process switched. This means that it is examined by the CPU and the forwarding decision is made in software. However, the forwarding decision is also stored in the data plane hardware fast-switching cache. When subsequent frames in the flow arrive, the destination is found in the hardware fast-switching cache and the frames are then forwarded without interrupting the CPU. As illustrated in Figure 5-2, notice how only the first packet of a flow is process switched and added to the fast-switching cache. The next four packets are quickly processed based on the information in the fast-switching cache; the initial packet of a traffic flow is process switched.

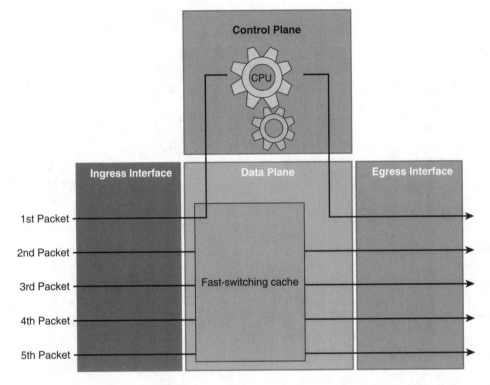

Figure 5-2 *Fast-Switched Packets*

■ **Cisco Express Forwarding:** This switching method is the fastest switching mode and is less CPU-intensive than fast switching and process switching. The control plane CPU of a CEF-enabled router creates two hardware-based tables called the Forwarding Information Base (FIB) table and an adjacency table using Layer 3 and 2 tables including the routing and Address Resolution Protocol (ARP) tables. When a network has converged, the FIB and adjacency tables contain all the information a router would have to consider when forwarding a packet. As illustrated in Figure 5-3, these two tables are then used to make hardware-based forwarding decisions for all frames in a data flow, even the first frame. The FIB contains precomputed reverse lookups and next-hop information for routes, including the interface and Layer 2 information.

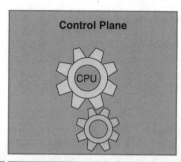

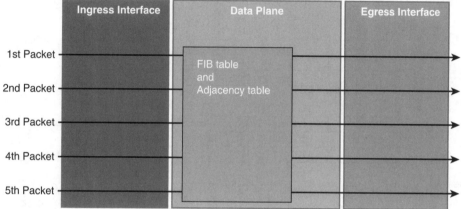

Figure 5-3 *CEF-Switched Packets*

A common analogy used to describe the three packet-forwarding mechanisms is as follows:

- Process switching solves a problem by doing math long hand, even if it is the identical problem.

- Fast switching solves a problem by doing math long hand one time and remembering the answer for subsequent identical problems.

- CEF solves every possible problem ahead of time in a spreadsheet.

While CEF is the fastest switching mode, some limitations apply. Some features are not compatible with CEF. In some rare instances, too, the functions of CEF can actually degrade performance.

Note Packets that cannot be CEF switched, such as packets destined to the router itself, are "punted." This means that the packet will be fast switched or process switched.

Process and Fast Switching

To help further understand the differences between these switching methods, consider the following sequence of process-switching and fast-switching events that occur when a packet arrives for a destination that was just learned through Enhanced Interior Gateway Routing Protocol (EIGRP).

As shown in Figure 5-4, an EIGRP update containing a new route to 10.0.0.0/8 is added to the EIGRP topology table. The EIGRP diffusing update algorithm (DUAL) deems this a successor route and offers the new entry to the routing table. The routing table deems that this is the best path to network 10.0.0.0/8 and adds a new routing table entry. Note that the fast-switching cache does not automatically get updated.

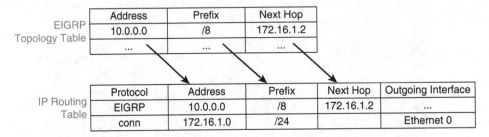

EIGRP Topology Table

Address	Prefix	Next Hop
10.0.0.0	/8	172.16.1.2
...	...	...

IP Routing Table

Protocol	Address	Prefix	Next Hop	Outgoing Interface
EIGRP	10.0.0.0	/8	172.16.1.2	...
conn	172.16.1.0	/24		Ethernet 0

Figure 5-4   *EIGRP Entry Added to the Routing Table*

When the first packet of a packet flow arrives for destination 10.0.0.0/8, the router initially looks for the destination in its fast-switching cache. Because the destination is not in the fast-switching cache, the router must perform process switching.

Therefore, a full routing table lookup is performed. The process performs a recursive lookup to find the outgoing interface. As shown in Figure 5-5, the routing table locates the entry for network 10.0.0.0/8 and identifies the next hop as 172.16.1.2. The router then performs a recursive lookup and discovers that this is out of interface Ethernet 0.

IP Routing Table

Protocol	Address	Prefix	Next Hop	Outgoing Interface
EIGRP	10.0.0.0	/8	172.16.1.2	...
conn	172.16.1.0	/24	...	Ethernet 0

Figure 5-5   *Routing Table Lookup*

Process switching might trigger an ARP request or find the Layer 2 address in the ARP cache. For example, the MAC address of 172.16.1.2 was found in the ARP cache, as shown in Figure 5-6.

ARP Cache

IP Address	MAC Address
172.16.1.2	0c.00.11.22.33.44
...	...

Figure 5-6   *Content of ARP Cache*

The router then forwards the packet out of its Ethernet 0 interface to the next hop IP address 172.16.1.2 with MAC address 0c.00.11.22.33.44.

This information is also added to the fast-switching cache in the data plane, as shown in Figure 5-7.

	Address	Prefix	Layer 2 Header	Interface
Fast-Switching Cache	10.0.0.0	/8	0c.00.11.22.33.44	Ethernet 0
	...	...	...	...

Figure 5-7 *Content of the Data Plane Fast-Switching Cache*

Specifically, an entry is created in the fast-switching cache to ensure that the subsequent packets for the same destination prefix will be fast switched. All subsequent packets for the same destination are fast switched:

- The switching occurs in the interrupt code. (The packet is processed immediately.)

- Fast destination lookup is performed (no recursion).

- The encapsulation uses a pregenerated Layer 2 header that contains the destination IP Address and Layer 2 source MAC address. (No ARP request or ARP cache lookup is necessary.)

Cisco Express Forwarding

CEF uses special strategies to switch data packets to their destinations. It caches the information that is generated by the Layer 3 routing engine even before the router encounters any data flows.

CEF separates the control plane software from the data plane hardware, thereby achieving higher data throughput. The control plane is responsible for building the FIB table and adjacency tables in software. The data plane is responsible for forwarding IP unicast traffic using hardware.

As shown in Figure 5-8, CEF caches routing information in the FIB table.

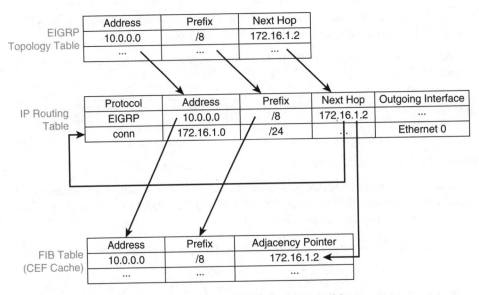

Figure 5-8   *CEF Caches Routing Information in the FIB Table*

The FIB is derived from the IP routing table and is arranged for maximum lookup throughput. CEF IP destination prefixes are stored from the most-specific to the least-specific entry. The FIB lookup is based on the Layer 3 destination address prefix (longest match), so it matches the structure of CEF entries. When the CEF FIB table is full, a wildcard entry redirects frames to the Layer 3 engine. The FIB table is updated after each network change, but only once, and contains all known routes; there is no need to build a route cache by central-processing initial packets from each data flow. Each change in the IP routing table triggers a similar change in the FIB table because it contains all next-hop addresses that are associated with all destination networks.

CEF also caches Layer 2 next-hop addresses and frame header rewrite information for all FIB entries in the adjacency table, as shown in Figure 5-9.

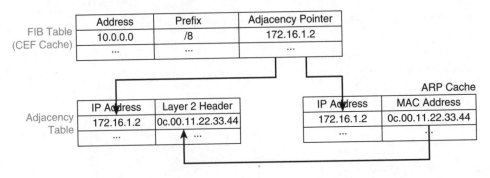

Figure 5-9   *CEF Caches Layer 2 Information in the Adjacency Table*

The adjacency table is derived from the ARP table, and it contains Layer 2 header rewrite (MAC) information for each next hop that is contained in the FIB. Nodes in the network are said to be adjacent if they are within a single hop from each other. The adjacency table maintains Layer 2 next-hop addresses and link-layer header information for all FIB entries. The adjacency table is populated as adjacencies are discovered. Each time that an adjacency entry is created (such as through ARP), a link-layer header for that adjacent node is precomputed and is stored in the adjacency table.

CEF uses a specific process to build forwarding tables in the hardware and then uses the information from those tables to forward packets at line speed.

Not all packets can be CEF switched and processed in the hardware. When traffic cannot be processed in the hardware, it must be received by software processing of the Layer 3 engine. This traffic does not receive the benefit of expedited hardware-based forwarding. A number of different packet types may force the Layer 3 engine to process them. Some examples of IP exception packets are packets that have the following characteristics:

- They use IP header options.

- They have an expiring IP Time To Live (TTL) counter.

- They are forwarded to a tunnel interface.

- They arrive with unsupported encapsulation types.

- They are routed to an interface with unsupported encapsulation types.

- They exceed the maximum transmission unit (MTU) of an output interface and must be fragmented.

Analyzing Cisco Express Forwarding

This section discusses how to verify CEF operations using the topology in Figure 5-10.

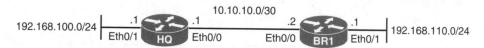

Figure 5-10 *CEF Reference Topology*

In the example, you will

- Verify the content of the CEF tables

- Enable and disable CEF by interface and globally

Verify the Content of the CEF Tables

To inspect the content of the FIB table on the HQ router, use the **show ip cef** privileged EXEC command, as shown in Example 5-1.

Example 5-1   *Verifying the FIB Table on HQ*

```
HQ# show ip cef
Prefix                  Next Hop            Interface
0.0.0.0/0               no route
0.0.0.0/8               drop
0.0.0.0/32              receive
10.10.10.0/30           attached            Ethernet0/0
10.10.10.0/32           receive             Ethernet0/0
10.10.10.1/32           receive             Ethernet0/0
10.10.10.3/32           receive             Ethernet0/0
127.0.0.0/8             drop
192.168.100.0/24        attached            Ethernet0/1
192.168.100.0/32        receive             Ethernet0/1
192.168.100.1/32        receive             Ethernet0/1
192.168.100.255/32      receive             Ethernet0/1
224.0.0.0/4             drop
224.0.0.0/24            receive
240.0.0.0/4             drop
255.255.255.255/32      receive
HQ#
```

There are entries in the FIB table for every local network connected to HQ. Every entry in the routing table has a preconfigured entry in the FIB table. Only local networks are listed because HQ is currently not configured with any routing protocol. For instance, notice that HQ has no information about remote network 192.168.110.0/24.

To inspect the content of the adjacency table on the HQ router, use the **show adjacency** privileged EXEC command, as shown in Example 5-2

Example 5-2   *Verifying the Adjacency Table on HQ*

```
HQ# show adjacency
Protocol Interface              Address
HQ#
```

While the FIB table had entries, notice that the adjacency table has none. The reason is because the adjacency table is built from the ARP table. However, no traffic has yet been generated and therefore the ARP table and consequently the adjacency table are also empty.

To add entries to the ARP table, Example 5-3 initiates traffic toward the neighboring router BR1 using ping.

Example 5-3 *Initiate Traffic from HQ*

```
HQ# ping 10.10.10.2

Type escape sequence to abort.
Sending 5, 100-byte ICMP Echos to 10.10.10.2, timeout is 2 seconds:
.!!!!
Success rate is 80 percent (4/5), round-trip min/avg/max = 1/1/1 ms
HQ#
```

Notice that the first packet was lost. This is because the HQ router was waiting for an ARP reply from BR1, which is needed to complete a new ARP entry on HQ.

Example 5-4 verifies the content of the adjacency and FIB tables.

Example 5-4 *Verify the CEF Tables*

```
HQ# show adjacency

Protocol Interface              Address
IP        Ethernet0/0            10.10.10.2(7)

HQ# show ip cef

Prefix              Next Hop          Interface
0.0.0.0/0           no route
0.0.0.0/8           drop
0.0.0.0/32          receive
10.10.10.0/30       attached          Ethernet0/0
10.10.10.0/32       receive           Ethernet0/0
10.10.10.1/32       receive           Ethernet0/0
10.10.10.2/32       attached          Ethernet0/0
10.10.10.3/32       receive           Ethernet0/0
127.0.0.0/8         drop
192.168.100.0/24    attached          Ethernet0/1
192.168.100.0/32    receive           Ethernet0/1
192.168.100.1/32    receive           Ethernet0/1
192.168.100.255/32  receive           Ethernet0/1
224.0.0.0/4         drop
224.0.0.0/24        receive
240.0.0.0/4         drop
255.255.255.255/32  receive

HQ#
```

Notice now that there is an entry in the adjacency table. The HQ router learned about the new end host via the ARP protocol. Subsequently, the new entry is also inserted into the FIB table.

Next we will enable a routing protocol to learn about remote networks. BR1 has been preconfigured for EIGRP, and Example 5-5 enables EIGRP on HQ.

Example 5-5 *Enable EIGRP on HQ*

```
HQ(config)# router eigrp 1
HQ(config-router)# network 192.168.100.0 0.0.0.255
HQ(config-router)# network 10.10.10.0 0.0.0.3
HQ(config-router)#
*Jul 29 16:35:15.745: %DUAL-5-NBRCHANGE: EIGRP-IPv4 1: Neighbor 10.10.10.2
(Ethernet0/0) is up: new adjacency
HQ(config-router)#
HQ#
```

Notice the information message indicating that an EIGRP adjacency has been established with BR1. Example 5-6 verifies that the BR1 LAN has been added to the routing table.

Example 5-6 *Verify the Routing Table on HQ*

```
HQ# show ip route eigrp
Codes: L - local, C - connected, S - static, R - RIP, M - mobile, B - BGP
       D - EIGRP, EX - EIGRP external, O - OSPF, IA - OSPF inter area
       N1 - OSPF NSSA external type 1, N2 - OSPF NSSA external type 2
       E1 - OSPF external type 1, E2 - OSPF external type 2
       i - IS-IS, su - IS-IS summary, L1 - IS-IS level-1, L2 - IS-IS level-2
       ia - IS-IS inter area, * - candidate default, U - per-user static route
       o - ODR, P - periodic downloaded static route, H - NHRP, l - LISP
       + - replicated route, % - next hop override


Gateway of last resort is not set

D    192.168.110.0/24 [90/307200] via 10.10.10.2, 00:03:17, Ethernet0/0
HQ#
```

As highlighted in the output, the HQ has learned a new EIGRP route to 192.168.110.0/24 network. Next, Example 5-7 verifies the adjacency and FIB tables on HQ.

Example 5-7 *Verify the CEF Tables on HQ*

```
HQ# show adjacency
Protocol Interface            Address
IP       Ethernet0/0          10.10.10.2(11)
HQ# show ip cef
```

```
Prefix                  Next Hop          Interface
0.0.0.0/0               no route
0.0.0.0/8               drop
0.0.0.0/32              receive
10.10.10.0/30           attached          Ethernet0/0
10.10.10.0/32           receive           Ethernet0/0
10.10.10.1/32           receive           Ethernet0/0
10.10.10.2/32           attached          Ethernet0/0
10.10.10.3/32           receive           Ethernet0/0
127.0.0.0/8             drop
192.168.100.0/24        attached          Ethernet0/1
192.168.100.0/32        receive           Ethernet0/1
192.168.100.1/32        receive           Ethernet0/1
192.168.100.255/32      receive           Ethernet0/1
192.168.110.0/24        10.10.10.2        Ethernet0/0
224.0.0.0/4             drop
224.0.0.0/24            receive
240.0.0.0/4             drop
255.255.255.255/32      receive
HQ#
```

The adjacency table has remained the same because the ARP table did not change. However, the FIB table has a new entry for the 192.168.110.0/24 network. This is because the routing table changed when a new route was learned via EIGRP.

Another useful CEF command is the **show ip interface** *interface* command. The command output can be used to verify the CEF status of the particular interface.

Example 5-8 verifies that CEF is enabled for interface Ethernet 0/0 on the HQ router.

Example 5-8 *Verify the CEF-Enabled Interface HQ*

```
HQ# show ip interface ethernet 0/0
Ethernet0/0 is up, line protocol is up
  Internet address is 10.10.10.1/30
  Broadcast address is 255.255.255.255
  Address determined by non-volatile memory
  MTU is 1500 bytes
  Helper address is not set
  Directed broadcast forwarding is disabled
  Multicast reserved groups joined: 224.0.0.10
  Outgoing access list is not set
  Inbound  access list is not set
  Proxy ARP is enabled
  Local Proxy ARP is disabled
  Security level is default
  Split horizon is enabled
```

```
    ICMP redirects are always sent
    ICMP unreachables are always sent
    ICMP mask replies are never sent
    IP fast switching is enabled
    IP fast switching on the same interface is disabled
    IP Flow switching is disabled
    IP CEF switching is enabled
    IP CEF switching turbo vector
    IP multicast fast switching is enabled
    IP multicast distributed fast switching is disabled
    IP route-cache flags are Fast, CEF
    Router Discovery is disabled
    IP output packet accounting is disabled
    IP access violation accounting is disabled
    TCP/IP header compression is disabled
    RTP/IP header compression is disabled
    Policy routing is disabled
    Network address translation is disabled
    BGP Policy Mapping is disabled
    Input features: MCI Check
    IPv4 WCCP Redirect outbound is disabled
    IPv4 WCCP Redirect inbound is disabled
    IPv4 WCCP Redirect exclude is disabled
HQ#
```

Notice the highlighted line confirms that CEF is enabled on this interface.

CEF for IPv4 is enabled by default on all interfaces while CEF for IPv6 is disabled by default. However, CEF for IPv6 is enabled automatically when IPv6 unicast routing is configured by using the **ipv6 unicast** command on your devices.

> **Note**   As a prerequisite to use CEF for IPv6, CEF for IPv4 must be enabled.

Although CEF for IPv6 is not required, the next two examples confirm the previous statements for CEF for IPv6. Example 5-9 verifies the status of CEF for IPv6 on HQ.

Example 5-9   *Verify the Status of CEF for IPv6 on HQ*

```
HQ# show ipv6 cef
%IPv6 CEF not running
HQ#
```

Example 5-10 enables IPv6 unicast routing and verifies the status of CEF for IPv6 on HQ.

Example 5-10   *Enable and Verify CEF for IPv6 on HQ*

```
HQ(config)# ipv6 unicast-routing
HQ(config)# exit
*Jul 29 16:53:16.000: %SYS-5-CONFIG_I: Configured from console by console
HQ# show ipv6 cef
::/0
  no route
::/127
  discard
FE80::/10
  receive for Null0
FF00::/8
  multicast
HQ#
```

Notice how enabling IPv6 unicast routing automatically enabled CEF for IPv6.

Enable and Disable CEF by Interface and Globally

CEF should be used whenever possible. However, CEF may have to be disabled for troubleshooting purposes.

CEF for IPv4 can be disabled by specific interface using the **no ip route-cache cef** interface configuration command or globally using the **no ip cef** global configuration command.

Example 5-11 disables CEF for IPv4 on Ethernet 0/0 and verifies the interface status.

Example 5-11   *Disable CEF for IPv4 on Ethernet 0/0 on HQ*

```
HQ(config)# interface ethernet 0/0
HQ(config-if)# no ip route-cache cef
HQ(config-if)# ^Z
HQ#
*Jul 29 17:10:14.737: %SYS-5-CONFIG_I: Configured from console by console
HQ# show ip interface ethernet 0/0 | include switching
  IP fast switching is enabled
  IP fast switching on the same interface is disabled
  IP Flow switching is disabled
  IP CEF switching is disabled
  IP multicast fast switching is enabled
  IP multicast distributed fast switching is disabled
HQ#
```

Notice that the interface now has CEF disabled but fast-switching has been automatically enabled.

Note   CEF for IPv4 can be re-enabled on an interface using the **ip route-cache cef** interface configuration command.

Example 5-12 verifies if CEF is still enabled globally.

Example 5-12   *Verify the Global Status of CEF on HQ*

```
HQ# show ip cef
Prefix              Next Hop           Interface
0.0.0.0/0           no route
0.0.0.0/8           drop
0.0.0.0/32          receive
10.10.10.0/30       attached           Ethernet0/0
10.10.10.0/32       receive            Ethernet0/0
10.10.10.1/32       receive            Ethernet0/0
10.10.10.2/32       attached           Ethernet0/0
10.10.10.3/32       receive            Ethernet0/0
127.0.0.0/8         drop
192.168.100.0/24    attached           Ethernet0/1
192.168.100.0/32    receive            Ethernet0/1
192.168.100.1/32    receive            Ethernet0/1
192.168.100.255/32  receive            Ethernet0/1
192.168.110.0/24    10.10.10.2         Ethernet0/0
224.0.0.0/4         drop
224.0.0.0/24        receive
240.0.0.0/4         drop
255.255.255.255/32  receive
HQ#
```

HQ still maintains a CEF table even though CEF for IPv4 has been disabled on Ethernet 0/0.

Example 5-13 disables CEF for IPv4 globally on HQ.

Example 5-13   *Disabled and verify CEF for IPv4 on HQ*

```
HQ(config)# no ip cef
HQ(config)# end
HQ#
*Jul 29 17:14:36.676: %SYS-5-CONFIG_I: Configured from console by console
HQ# show ip cef
%IPv4 CEF not running
HQ#
```

Notice how CEF for IPv4 is now completely disabled on HQ.

Note   CEF for IPv4 can be re-enabled globally using the **ip cef** global configuration command.

Understanding Path Control

Upon completing this section, you will be able to do the following:

- Identify the need for path control

- Describe how to use policy-based routing (PBR) to control path selection

- Describe how to use IP service-level agreement (IP SLA) to control path selection

The Need for Path Control

Networks are designed to use redundancy to provide high availability. However, having redundancy does not guarantee resistance to failure. The use of multiple routing protocols and redundant connectivity options can result in inefficient paths for forwarding packets to their destinations. Each routing protocol has a different administrative distance, metric, and convergence time. Suboptimal routing often occurs after redistribution because redistribution resets the administrative distance and metric.

Convergence time is also important. First, protocols converge in different ways from each other and for different network designs. Second, slow convergence can result in an application sending traffic timeouts before a backup path is found to a destination. Path control is required to avoid performance issues and to optimize paths.

Note   To establish a global strategy for path control, the physical connectivity and the services that are running over the network infrastructure must be taken into account.

Path control tools can be used to change the default destination forwarding and optimize the path of the packets for some specific application.

Other examples of path control include switching traffic to the backup link if there is a primary link failure, or forwarding some traffic to the backup link if the primary link is congested. Path control mechanisms can improve performance in such a situation. Similarly, load balancing can divide traffic among parallel paths.

It is important to provide predictable and deterministic control over traffic patterns. Unfortunately, there is not a "one-command" solution to implement path control. Instead, as shown in Figure 5-11, many tools are available.

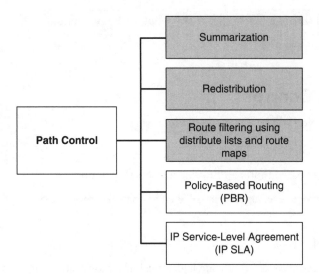

Figure 5-11   *Path Control Tools*

You can use all of these tools as part of an integrated strategy to implement path control. The shaded path control tools in Figure 5-11 were discussed in previous chapters. The focus of this section is on PBR and IP SLA.

Implementing Path Control Using Policy-Based Routing

This section describes another use for route maps, with PBR. PBR enables the administrator to define a routing policy other than basic destination-based routing using the routing table. With PBR, route maps can be used to match source and destination addresses, protocol types, and end-user applications. When a match occurs, a **set** command can be used to define items, such as the interface or next-hop address to which the packet should be sent.

PBR Features

PBR is a powerful and flexible tool that offers significant benefits in terms of implementing user-defined policies to control traffic in the internetwork.

PBR adds flexibility in a difficult-to-manage environment by providing the ability to route traffic that is based on network needs. It also provides solutions in cases where legal, contractual, or political constraints dictate that traffic be routed through specific paths.

Benefits of implementing PBR in a network include the following:

- **Source-based transit-provider selection:** PBR policies can be implemented by ISPs and other organizations to route traffic that originates from different sets of users through different Internet connections across the policy routers.

■ **QoS:** PBR policies can be implemented to provide quality of service (QoS) to differentiated traffic by setting the type of service (ToS) values in the IP packet headers in routers at the periphery of the network and then leveraging queuing mechanisms to prioritize traffic in the network's core or backbone. This setup improves network performance by eliminating the need to classify the traffic explicitly at each WAN interface in the network's core or backbone.

■ **Cost savings:** PBR policies can be implemented to direct the bulk traffic associated with a specific activity to use a higher-bandwidth, high-cost link for a short time and to continue basic connectivity over a lower-bandwidth, low-cost link for interactive traffic.

■ **Load sharing:** PBR policies can be implemented based on the traffic characteristics to distribute traffic among multiple paths. This is in addition to the default dynamic load-sharing capabilities that are provided by destination-based routing that is supported by Cisco IOS Software.

Steps for Configuring PBR

PBR is applied to incoming or locally generated packets sent by the router to bypass and overrule the routing table. It enables an administrator to configure different routing rules beyond the original IP routing table. For example, it can be used is to route packets that are based on the source IP address instead of the destination IP address.

Consider, for example, the topology in Figure 5-12. In the example, the network policy dictates that ISP #1 should be used as the default gateway for all user traffic; however, traffic from the web server should to go through ISP 2. This can easily be achieved with path control.

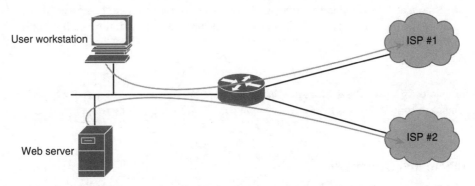

Figure 5-12 *PBR Routing Packets Based on Source Address*

The implementation plan for this configuration would include the following steps:

1. Enable PBR by configuring a route map using the **route-map** global configuration command.

2. Implement the traffic-matching configuration, specifying which traffic will be manipulated. This is done using the **match** commands within the route map.

3. Define the action for the matched traffic. This is done using the **set** commands within the route map.

4. Optionally, fast-switched PBR or CEF-switched PBR can be enabled. Fast-switched PBR must be enabled manually. CEF-switched PBR is automatically enabled when CEF switching is enabled (which it is by default in recent IOS versions) and PBR is enabled.

5. Apply the route map to incoming traffic or to traffic locally generated on the router. In this example, the route map would be applied to the incoming interface using the **ip policy route-map** interface configuration command.

6. Verify PBR configuration with basic connectivity and path verification commands, as well as policy routing **show** commands.

Configuring PBR

The **route-map** *map-tag* [**permit | deny**] [*sequence-number*] global configuration command is used to create a route map. The command can be configured as **permit** or **deny**. The following defines how these options work:

- If the statement is marked as **permit**, such as in **route-map MY-MAP permit 10**, packets that meet all the match criteria are policy-based routed.

- If the statement is marked as **deny**, such as in **route-map MY-MAP deny 10**, a packet meeting the match criteria is not policy-based routed. Instead, it is sent through the normal forwarding channels and destination-based routing is performed.

- If no match is found in the route map, the packet is *not* dropped. It is forwarded through the normal routing channel, which means that destination-based routing is performed.

Note   To drop a packet that does not match the specified criteria, configure a **set** statement to route the packets to interface null 0 as the last entry in the route map.

PBR **match** Commands

The **match** *condition* route map configuration commands are used to define the conditions to be checked. The **match ip address** and **match length** listed in Table 5-1 can be used for PBR.

Table 5-1   *PBR* match *Commands*

Command	Description
match ip address *{access-list-number	name}* *[...access-list-number	name]*	Matches any packets that have a source address that is permitted by a standard or extended access control list (ACL). Multiple ACLs can be specified. Matching any one results in a match.
match length *min max*	Matches based on a packet's Layer 3 length.

A standard IP ACL can be used to specify match criteria for a packet's source address, and an extended ACL can be used to specify match criteria based on source and destination addresses, application, protocol type, and ToS.

You can use the **match length** command to establish criteria based on the packet length between specified minimum and maximum values. For example, a network administrator could use the match length as the criterion that distinguishes between interactive and file transfer traffic because file transfer traffic usually has larger packet sizes.

PBR **set** Commands

If the **match** statements are satisfied, you can use the **set ip next-hop** or **set interface** commands listed in Table 5-2 to specify the criteria for forwarding packets through the router.

Table 5-2   *PBR* set *Commands*

Command	Description
set ip next-hop *ip-address* *[...ip-address]*	Command identifies the IP address of an adjacent next-hop router to forward packets to. If more than one IP address is specified, the first IP address associated with a currently up and connected interface is used to route the packets.
set interface *type number* *[...type number]*	Command identifies the exit interface to forward packets out of. If more than one interface is specified, the first interface that is found to be up is used to forward the packets.

Configuring PBR on an Interface

To identify a route map to use for policy routing on an interface, use the **ip policy route-map** *map-tag* interface configuration command. The *map-tag* parameter is the name of the route map to use for policy routing. It must match a map tag specified by a **route-map** command.

Remember that policy-based routing is configured on the interface that *receives* the packets, not on the interface from which the packets are forwarded.

Packets originating on the router are not normally policy routed. *Local policy routing* enables packets originating on the router to take a route other than the obvious shortest path. To identify a route map to use for local policy routing, use the **ip local policy route-map** *map-tag* global configuration command. This command applies the specified route map to packets originating on the router.

Verifying PBR

To display the route maps used for policy routing on the router's interfaces, use the **show ip policy** EXEC command.

To display configured route maps, use the **show route-map** [*map-name*] EXEC command, where *map-name* is an optional name of a specific route map.

Use the **debug ip policy** EXEC command to display IP policy routing packet activity. This command shows in detail what policy routing is doing. It displays information about whether a packet matches the criteria and, if so, the resulting routing information for the packet.

Note   Because the **debug ip policy** command generates a significant amount of output, use it only when traffic on the IP network is low so that other activity on the system is not adversely affected.

To discover the routes that the packets follow when traveling to their destination from the router, use the **traceroute** EXEC command. To change the default parameters and invoke an extended **traceroute**, enter the command without a destination argument. You are then stepped through a dialog to select the desired parameters.

To check host reachability and network connectivity, use the **ping** EXEC command. You can use the **ping** command's extended command mode to specify the supported header options by entering the command without any arguments.

Configuring PBR Example

This section discusses how to use PBR to influence path selection using the topology in Figure 5-13.

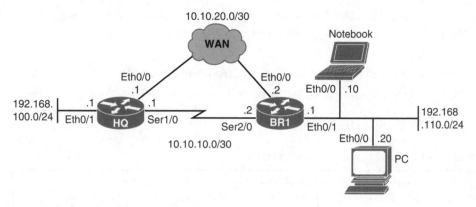

Figure 5-13 *PBR Reference Topology*

In the example, you will

- Verify normal traffic paths as selected by the traditional destination-based routing

- Configure PBR to alter the traffic flow for one client station

- Verify both the PBR configuration and the new traffic path

Verify Normal Traffic Paths

Example 5-14 verifies the traffic path from the PC to HQ LAN using the **traceroute** command.

Example 5-14 *Verifying Connectivity Between PC and HQ LAN*

```
PC> traceroute 192.168.100.1
Type escape sequence to abort.
Tracing the route to 192.168.100.1
VRF info: (vrf in name/id, vrf out name/id)
  1 192.168.110.1 1 msec 0 msec 0 msec
  2 10.10.20.1 1 msec * 1 msec
PC>
```

Example 5-15 verifies the traffic path from the Notebook to the HQ LAN.

Example 5-15 *Verifying Connectivity Between Notebook and HQ LAN*

```
Notebook> traceroute 192.168.100.1
Type escape sequence to abort.
Tracing the route to 192.168.100.1
VRF info: (vrf in name/id, vrf out name/id)
  1 192.168.110.1 0 msec 0 msec
  2 10.10.20.1 1 msec * 1 msec
Notebook>
```

Notice from the highlighted output that traffic from both clients is going through the faster WAN link (network 10.10.20.0/30) to the HQ router.

Configure PBR to Alter the Traffic Flow from the Notebook

A route map will be created to identify traffic from the Notebook and make it use the serial link. To do so, an ACL is configured as shown in Example 5-16 to match traffic coming from the Notebook client.

Example 5-16 *Identify Traffic from Notebook*

```
BR1(config)# ip access-list extended PBR-ACL
BR1(config-ext-nacl)# permit ip host 192.168.110.10 any
BR1(config-ext-nacl)# exit
```

Next a route map named PBR-Notebook is configured, as shown in Example 5-17.

Example 5-17 *Configure Route Map on BR1*

```
BR1(config)# route-map PBR-Notebook
BR1(config-route-map)# match ip address PBR-ACL
BR1(config-route-map)# set ip next-hop 10.10.10.1
BR1(config-route-map)# exit
```

The route map matches the configured ACL and sets the next hop IP address to the serial interface of HQ.

The route map should then be applied to the inbound interface of the router. As shown in Example 5-18, the route map is applied to the inbound Ethernet 0/1 interface.

Example 5-18 *Apply Route Map to Inbound Interface*

```
BR1(config)# interface ethernet 0/1
BR1(config-if)# ip policy route-map PBR-Notebook
BR1(config-if)# exit
BR1(config)# exit
```

Note To alter the traffic generated by the local router, the route map must be applied using the **ip local policy route-map** *map-tap* global configuration command.

Verify the PBR Configuration and Traffic Path

Example 5-19 verifies the configured route map.

Example 5-19 *Verify Configured Route Maps*

```
BR1# show route-map
route-map PBR-Notebook, permit, sequence 10
  Match clauses:
    ip address (access-lists): PBR-ACL
  Set clauses:
    ip next-hop 10.10.10.1
  Policy routing matches: 0 packets, 0 bytes
BR1#
```

The route map output states that incoming traffic defined with the access list PBR-ACL is forwarded to 10.10.10.1, which corresponds to the IP address of HQ configured on the serial link.

Example 5-20 verifies the configured policy.

Example 5-20 *Verify Configured Policy*

```
BR1# show ip policy
Interface       Route map
Ethernet0/1     PBR-Notebook
BR1#
```

Example 5-21 verifies the traffic path from the PC to HQ LAN.

Example 5-21 *Verifying Connectivity Between PC and HQ LAN*

```
PC> traceroute 192.168.100.1
Type escape sequence to abort.
Tracing the route to 192.168.100.1
VRF info: (vrf in name/id, vrf out name/id)
  1 192.168.110.1 1 msec 1 msec 0 msec
  2 10.10.20.1 1 msec *  1 msec
PC>
```

As expected, the traffic path for the PC client remained the same and its traffic is going through the WAN link (network 10.10.20.0/30).

Example 5-22 verifies the traffic path from the Notebook to the HQ LAN to see if the path is altered.

Example 5-22 *Verify Connectivity Between Notebook and HQ LAN*

```
Notebook> traceroute 192.168.100.1
Type escape sequence to abort.
Tracing the route to 192.168.100.1
VRF info: (vrf in name/id, vrf out name/id)
  1 192.168.110.1 1 msec 0 msec 1 msec
  2 10.10.10.1 5 msec *  5 msec
Notebook>
```

Notice how the Notebook client is now going through the serial link (network 10.10.10.0/30).

You can configure the privileged EXEC **debug ip policy** command to analyze the detailed policy-based routing operation and verify the actual traffic path. Example 5-23 enables PBR debugging on BR1.

Example 5-23   *Enable PBR Debugging*

```
BR1# debug ip policy
Policy routing debugging is on
BR1#
```

For the command to display the output, traffic must be present on the network. Therefore, Example 5-24 initiates traffic from the PC to the HQ router using the **ping** command.

Example 5-24   *Initiate Traffic from the PC*

```
PC> ping 192.168.100.1
Type escape sequence to abort.
Sending 5, 100-byte ICMP Echos to 192.168.100.1, timeout is 2 seconds:
!!!!!
Success rate is 100 percent (5/5), round-trip min/avg/max = 1/1/1 ms
PC>
```

The ping automatically generates the debug output displayed in Example 5-25.

Example 5-25   *Debug Output Generated by PC Ping*

```
BR1#
*Aug  4 17:36:42.981: IP: s=192.168.110.20 (Ethernet0/1), d=192.168.100.1, len 100,
FIB policy rejected(no match) - normal forwarding
*Aug  4 17:36:42.982: IP: s=192.168.110.20 (Ethernet0/1), d=192.168.100.1, len 100,
FIB policy rejected(no match) - normal forwarding
*Aug  4 17:36:42.983: IP: s=192.168.110.20 (Ethernet0/1), d=192.168.100.1, len 100,
FIB policy rejected(no match) - normal forwarding
*Aug  4 17:36:42.984: IP: s=192.168.110.20 (Ethernet0/1), d=192.168.100.1, len 100,
FIB policy rejected(no match) - normal forwarding
*Aug  4 17:36:42.984: IP: s=192.168.110.20 (Ethernet0/1), d=192.168.100.1, len 100,
FIB policy rejected(no match) - normal forwarding
BR1#
```

Notice that the traffic flow information is displayed in the output block, beginning with "IP: ..," which includes source, incoming interface, and destination. The output clearly states that there is no policy match and that traffic is treated with normal (destination-based) forwarding.

Example 5-26 initiates traffic from the Notebook to the HQ router using the **ping** command.

Example 5-26   *Initiate Traffic from the Notebook*

```
Notebook> ping 192.168.100.1
Type escape sequence to abort.
Sending 5, 100-byte ICMP Echos to 192.168.100.1, timeout is 2 seconds:
!!!!!
Success rate is 100 percent (5/5), round-trip min/avg/max = 1/1/1 ms
Notebook>
```

The ping automatically generates the debug output displayed in Example 5-27.

Example 5-27   *Debug Output Generated by Notebook Ping*

```
BR1#
*Aug  4 17:39:53.147: IP: s=192.168.110.10 (Ethernet0/1), d=192.168.100.1, len 100,
FIB policy match
*Aug  4 17:39:53.147: IP: s=192.168.110.10 (Ethernet0/1), d=192.168.100.1, len 100,
PBR Counted
*Aug  4 17:39:53.147: IP: s=192.168.110.10 (Ethernet0/1), d=192.168.100.1,
g=10.10.10.1, len 100, FIB policy routed
*Aug  4 17:39:53.152: IP: s=192.168.110.10 (Ethernet0/1), d=192.168.100.1, len 100,
FIB policy match
*Aug  4 17:39:53.152: IP: s=192.168.110.10 (Ethernet0/1), d=192.168.100.1, len 100,
PBR Counted
*Aug  4 17:39:53.152: IP: s=192.168.110.10 (Ethernet0/1), d=192.168.100.1,
g=10.10.10.1, len 100, FIB policy routed
*Aug  4 17:39:53.158: IP: s=192.168.110.10 (Ethernet0/1), d=192.168.100.1, len 100,
FIB policy match
*Aug  4 17:39:53.158: IP: s=192.168.110.10 (Ethernet0/1), d=192.168.100.1, len 100,
PBR Counted
*Aug  4 17:39:53.158: IP: s=192.168.110.10 (Ethernet0/1), d=192.168.100.1,
g=10.10.10.1, len 100, FIB policy routed
*Aug  4 17:39:53.163: IP: s=192.168.110.10 (Ethernet0/1), d=192.168.100.1, len 100,
FIB policy match
*Aug  4 17:39:53.163: IP: s=192.168.110.10 (Ethernet0/1), d=192.168.100.1, len 100,
PBR Counted
*Aug  4 17:39:53.163: IP: s=192.168.110.10 (Ethernet0/1), d=192.168.100.1,
g=10.10.10.1, len 100, FIB policy routed
BR1#
*Aug  4 17:39:53.168: IP: s=192.168.110.10 (Ethernet0/1), d=192.168.100.1, len 100,
FIB policy match
*Aug  4 17:39:53.168: IP: s=192.168.110.10 (Ethernet0/1), d=192.168.100.1, len 100,
PBR Counted
*Aug  4 17:39:53.168: IP: s=192.168.110.10 (Ethernet0/1), d=192.168.100.1,
g=10.10.10.1, len 100, FIB policy routed
BR1#
```

The output clearly states that there is a policy match and that traffic is forwarded to
10.10.10.1.

Implementing Path Control Using Cisco IOS IP SLAs

This section describes how to enable path control using the Cisco IP SLA feature.

PBR and IP SLA

PBR is a static path control mechanism. It cannot respond dynamically to changes in network health. For example, refer to the topology displayed in Figure 5-14.

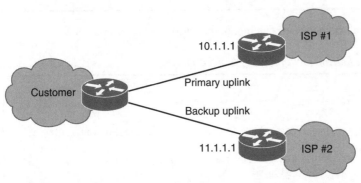

Figure 5-14   *IP SLA Reference Topology*

In the example, the customer router has static default routes to ISPs configured. The route to ISP 2 has a higher administrative distance, so only the primary uplink is used.

Assume, however, that the network policy states that when packet loss on the primary link exceeds 5 percent the backup link should be used instead. This cannot be accomplished with PBR alone.

In this scenario, a dynamic response is exactly what is needed. Cisco IP SLA can be coupled with PBR or with static routes to achieve dynamic path control.

IP SLA Features

Cisco IOS IP SLAs perform network performance measurement within Cisco devices. The IP SLAs use active traffic monitoring (generation of traffic in a continuous, reliable, and predictable manner) for measuring network performance.

Cisco IOS IP SLAs actively send simulated data across the network to measure performance between multiple network locations or across multiple network paths. The information collected includes data about response time, one-way latency, jitter, packet loss, voice-quality scoring, network resource availability, application performance, and server response time. In its simplest form, Cisco IOS IP SLAs verify whether a network element, such as an IP address on a router interface or an open TCP port on an IP host, is active and responsive.

Cisco IOS IP SLA Sources and Targets

The Cisco IOS IP SLA feature allows performance measurements to be taken within and between Cisco devices, or between a Cisco device and a host, providing data about service levels for IP applications and services.

All the IP SLA measurement probe operations are configured on the IP SLAs *source*, such as a Cisco IOS router. The source sends probe packets to the *target* device, which can be a server or an IP host, such as shown in Figure 5-15.

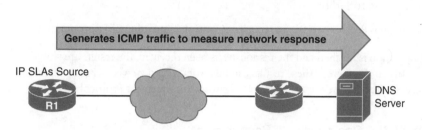

Figure 5-15   *R1 with IP SLA Enabled*

In this example, R1 is the IP SLA source and the target is an IP server.

If the target is another Cisco IOS device, the target can be configured as an IP SLA responder. A responder can provide accurate measurements without the need for dedicated probes or any complex or per-operation configuration. The example in Figure 5-16 displays R1 as an IP SLA source and R2 enabled as an IP SLA responder.

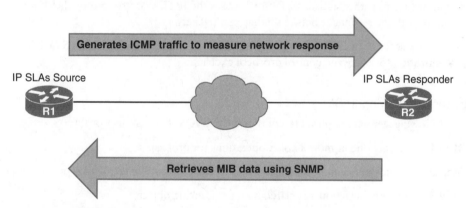

Figure 5-16   *R1 and R2 with IP SLA Enabled*

Notice how the IP SLA source can still probe the target like in the previous example. However, the IP SLA responder can be configured to capture specific data that can be retrieved by the source using the CLI or through an SNMP tool that supports the operation of IP SLAs. The IP SLA measurement accuracy is improved when the target is an IP SLA responder.

Cisco IOS IP SLA Operations

An *IP SLA operation* is a measurement that includes protocol, frequency, traps, and thresholds. This operation can be used with both types of target devices.

For example, the network manager can configure the IP SLA source with the

- Target device IP address
- Protocol to use for probe
- User Datagram Protocol (UDP) or Transfer Control Protocol (TCP) port number

When the operation is finished and the response has been received, the results are stored in the IP SLA MIB on the source. These results can be retrieved and viewed using command-line interface (CLI) commands or using Simple Network Management Protocol (SNMP).

Cisco IOS IP SLA Operation with Responders

Using an IP SLA responder provides enhanced measurement accuracy—without the need for dedicated third-party external probe devices—and additional statistics that are not otherwise available via standard Internet Control Message Protocol (ICMP)-based measurements.

When a network manager configures an IP SLA operation on the IP SLA source, reaction conditions can also be defined, and the operation can be scheduled to be run for a period of time to gather statistics. The source uses the IP SLA control protocol to communicate with the responder before sending test packets.

To increase security of IP SLAs control messages, you can use message digest 5 (MD5) authentication to secure the control protocol exchange.

Steps for Configuring IP SLAs

The following steps are required to configure Cisco IOS IP SLAs functionality:

Step 1.   Define one or more IP SLA operations (or probes).

Step 2.   Define one or more tracking objects to track the state of IOS IP SLA operations.

Step 3.   Define the action associated with the tracking object.

Step 1: Configuring Cisco IOS IP SLA Operations

This section describes some of the configuration commands used to define IP SLAs operations.

Use the **ip sla** *operation-number* global configuration command to begin configuring a Cisco IOS IP SLA operation and to enter IP SLA configuration mode. The *operation-number* is the identification number of the IP SLA operation to be configured.

IP SLA Configuration Mode Commands

Once in IP SLA configuration mode, a variety of commands are available, as shown in Example 5-28.

Example 5-28 *IP SLA Options*

```
BR1(config-ip-sla)# ?
IP SLAs entry configuration commands:
  dhcp          DHCP Operation
  dns           DNS Query Operation
  ethernet      Ethernet Operations
  exit          Exit Operation Configuration
  ftp           FTP Operation
  http          HTTP Operation
  icmp-echo     ICMP Echo Operation
  icmp-jitter   ICMP Jitter Operation
  mpls          MPLS Operation
  path-echo     Path Discovered ICMP Echo Operation
  path-jitter   Path Discovered ICMP Jitter Operation
  tcp-connect   TCP Connect Operation
  udp-echo      UDP Echo Operation
  udp-jitter    UDP Jitter Operation
  voip          Voice Over IP Operation

BR1(config-ip-sla)#
```

Note There are many configurable IP SLA command options available. Refer to Cisco. com for more information.

The focus of this section is on the **icmp-echo** command. The command is used to verify connectivity by sending ICMP echo requests to a destination.

The complete command syntax is **icmp-echo** {*destination-ip-address* | *destination-hostname*} [**source-ip** {*ip-address* | *hostname*} | **source-interface** *interface-name*]. The parameters of these commands are defined in Table 5-3.

Table 5-3 **icmp-echo** *Command Parameters*

Parameter	Description
destination-ip-address | *destination-hostname*	Destination IPv4 or IPv6 address or hostname.
source-ip {*ip-address* | *hostname*}	(Optional) Specifies the source IPv4 or IPv6 address or hostname. When a source IP address or hostname is not specified, the IP SLA chooses the IP address nearest to the destination.
source-interface *interface-name*	(Optional) Specifies the source interface for the operation.

IP SLA ICMP Echo Configuration Mode Commands

Configuring the **icmp-echo** command enters the IP SLA echo configuration mode. A variety of IP SLA ICMP echo configuration commands are available, as shown in Example 5-29.

Example 5-29   *IP SLA Options*

```
BR1(config-ip-sla-echo)# ?
IP SLAs Icmp Echo Configuration Commands:
  default           Set a command to its defaults
  exit              Exit operation configuration
  frequency         Frequency of an operation
  history           History and Distribution Data
  no                Negate a command or set its defaults
  owner             Owner of Entry
  request-data-size Request data size
  tag               User defined tag
  threshold         Operation threshold in milliseconds
  timeout           Timeout of an operation
  tos               Type Of Service
  verify-data       Verify data
  vrf               Configure IP SLAs for a VPN Routing/Forwarding instance

BR1(config-ip-sla-echo)#
```

Note   There are many configurable IP SLA ICMP echo command options available. Refer to Cisco.com for more information.

Use the **frequency** *seconds* IP SLA configuration submode command to set the rate at which a specified IP SLA operation repeats. The *seconds* parameter is the number of seconds between the IP SLA operations; the default is 60.

Use the **timeout** *milliseconds* IP SLA configuration submode command to set the amount of time a Cisco IOS IP SLA operation waits for a response from its request packet. The *milliseconds* parameter is the number of milliseconds (ms) the operation waits to receive a response from its request packet. It is recommended that the value of the milliseconds parameter be based on the sum of both the maximum round-trip time (RTT) value for the packets and the processing time of the IP SLA operation.

Note   When deploying the Cisco IOS IP SLAs solution, consider the impact of the additional probe traffic being generated, including how that traffic affects bandwidth utilization and congestion levels. Tuning the configuration (for example, with the **frequency** and **delay** commands) becomes critical to mitigate possible issues related to excessive transitions and route changes in the presence of flapping tracked objects.

Schedule the IP SLA Operation

Once a Cisco IP SLA operation is configured, it needs to be scheduled using the **ip sla schedule** global configuration command. The complete command syntax is **ip sla schedule** *operation-number* [**life** {**forever** | *seconds*}] [**start-time** {*hh:mm* [*:ss*] [*month day* | *day month*] | **pending** | **now** | **after** *hh:mm:ss*}] [**ageout** *seconds*] [**recurring**]. Table 5-4 describes the parameters of these commands.

Table 5-4 ip sla schedule *Command Parameters*

Parameter	Description
operation-number	Number of the IP SLA operation to schedule.
life *forever*	(Optional) Schedules the operation to run indefinitely.
life *seconds*	(Optional) Number of seconds the operation actively collects information. The default is 3600 seconds (1 hour).
start-time	(Optional) Time when the operation starts.
hh:mm[*:ss*]	Specifies an absolute start time using hour, minute, and (optionally) second. Use the 24-hour clock notation. For example, start time 01:02 means "start at 1:02 a.m.," and start time 13:01:30 means "start at 1:01 p.m. and 30 seconds." The current day is implied unless you specify a *month* and *day*.
month	(Optional) Name of the month to start the operation in. If month is not specified, the current month is used. Use of this argument requires that a day be specified. You can specify the month by using either the full English name or the first three letters of the month.
day	(Optional) Number of the day (in the range 1 to 31) to start the operation on. If a day is not specified, the current day is used. Use of this argument requires that a month be specified.
pending	(Optional) No information is collected. This is the default value.
now	(Optional) Indicates that the operation should start immediately.
after *hh:mm:ss*	(Optional) Indicates that the operation should start *hh* hours, *mm* minutes, and *ss* seconds after this command was entered.
ageout *seconds*	(Optional) Number of seconds to keep the operation in memory when it is not actively collecting information. The default is 0 seconds (never ages out).
recurring	(Optional) Indicates that the operation will start automatically at the specified time and for the specified duration every day.

Step 2: Configuring Cisco IOS IP SLA Tracking Objects

This section examines some of the configuration commands used to define tracking objects, to track the state of IOS IP SLA operations.

Use the **track** *object-number* **ip sla** *operation-number* {**state** | **reachability**} global configuration command to track the state of an IOS IP SLA operation, and enter track configuration mode. Table 5-5 describes the parameters of these commands.

Table 5-5   **track ip sla** *Command Parameters*

Parameter	Description
object-number	Object number representing the object to be tracked. The range is from 1 to 500.
operation-number	Number used for the identification of the IP SLA's operation you are tracking.
state	Tracks the operation return code.
reachability	Tracks whether the route is reachable.

Once in IP SLA track configuration mode, use the optional **delay** {**up** *seconds* [**down** *seconds*] | [**up** *seconds*] **down** *seconds*} track configuration command to specify a period of time to delay communicating state changes of a tracked object. Table 5-6 describes the parameters of this command.

Table 5-6   **delay** *Command Parameters*

Parameter	Description
up	Time to delay the notification of an up event.
down	Time to delay the notification of a down event.
seconds	Delay value, in seconds. The range is from 0 to 180. The default is 0.

Step 3: Defining an Action Associated with a Tracking Object

Many types of actions can be associated with a tracked object. A simple path control action is to use the **ip route** *prefix mask* {*ip-address* | *interface-type interface-number* [*ip-address*]} [**track** *number*] global configuration command. The command can be used with the **track** keyword to establish a static route that tracks an object.

Verifying Path Control Using IOS IP SLAs

This section describes some of the commands used to verify path control using IOS IP SLAs.

To display configuration values including all defaults for all Cisco IOS IP SLA operations, or for a specified operation, use the **show ip sla configuration** [*operation*] command. The *operation* parameter is the number of the IP SLA operation for which the details will be displayed.

Configuring IP SLA Example

This section discusses how to use IP SLA to influence path selection using the topology in Figure 5-17.

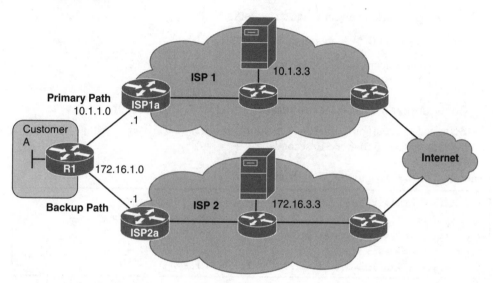

Figure 5-17 *IP SLA Reference Topology*

In this scenario, Customer A is multihoming to two Internet service providers (ISPs). The link from R1 to ISP1a should be the primary path, and the link from R1 to ISP2a should be the backup path. To accomplish this, R1 is configured with the following two default floating static routes:

- The static route to ISP1a (ISP-1), which has been assigned an administrative distance of 2

- The static route to ISP2a (ISP-2), which has been assigned an administrative distance of 3

Because the link to ISP1a has a lower administrative distance, it becomes the default gateway and therefore the primary path.

What would happen if a link within the ISP 1 infrastructure were to fail? A problem would arise because the link from R1 to ISP1a would still remain up. Therefore, R1 would continue to use primary path because the current default static route is still valid.

The solution is to promote the backup path as the preferred default static route until the problem is resolved. This will be accomplished using the Cisco IOS IP SLA feature.

Configure IP SLAs to continuously check the reachability of a specific destination (such as the ISP's DNS server or any other specific destination) and conditionally announce the default route only if the connectivity is verified.

In the example, you will

- Configure an IP SLA operation with the ISP 1 DNS server

- Define a tracking object assign an action

- Configure an IP SLA operation with the ISP 2 DNS server

- Define a tracking object assign an action

Configuring an IP SLA Operation with the ISP 1 DNS Server

Example 5-30 configures IP SLA 11 to continuously send ICMP echo requests to the DNS server (10.1.3.3) every 10 seconds.

Example 5-30 *Configure IP SLA for ISP 1*

```
R1(config)# ip sla 11
R1(config-ip-sla)# icmp-echo 10.1.3.3 source-interface ethernet 0/0
R1(config-ip-sla-echo)# frequency 10
R1(config-ip-sla-echo)# exit
R1(config)# ip sla schedule 11 start-time now life forever
```

The first part defines probe number 11 using the **ip sla monitor 11** command. Next the SLA test operation using the **icmp-echo 10.1.3.3 source-interface Ethernet 0/0** command. This configures the router to send the ICMP echoes to destination 10.1.3.3 using the Ethernet 0/0 interface as a source. The **frequency 10** command schedules the connectivity test to repeat every 10 seconds.

The **ip sla schedule 11 start-time now life forever** command defines the start and end times of the connectivity test for probe 11. The start time is now, and the end time is forever.

Defining a Tracking Object and Assigning an Action

Example 5-31 configures the tracking object, which is linked to the probe 11.

Example 5-31 *Configure the IP SLA Tracking Object*

```
R1(config)# track 1 ip sla 11 reachability
R1(config-track)# delay down 10 up 1
R1(config-track)# exit
R1(config)# ip route 0.0.0.0 0.0.0.0 10.1.1.1 2 track 1
```

Tracking object 1 is linked to the previously defined probe 11 so that the reachability of the 10.1.3.3 is tracked. Generate a notification after the link is down for 10 seconds, and notify 1 second after it comes back up.

The last step defines an action based on the status of the tracking object. In this case, the default static route via 10.1.1.1 is assigned an administrative distance of 2.

When IP SLA is used with static routes, the administrator controls whether the route in question will be active, based on the status of the tracked object. In this example, the IP SLA is tracking that object, and as long as the DNS server is reachable, the default route to ISP1a will be in the routing table. Therefore, if 10.1.3.3 is reachable, a static default route via 10.1.1.1 with an administrative distance of 2 will be in the routing table.

Configuring an IP SLA Operation with the ISP 2 DNS Server

Next, the IP SLA operation has to be configured to track the DNS server of ISP 2. Example 5-32 configures IP SLA 22 to continuously send ICMP echo requests to the DNS server (172.16.3.3) every 10 seconds.

Example 5-32 *Configure IP SLA for ISP 2*

```
R1(config)# ip sla 22
R1(config-ip-sla)# icmp-echo 172.16.3.3 source-interface ethernet 0/0
R1(config-ip-sla-echo)# frequency 10
R1(config-ip-sla-echo)# exit
R1(config)# ip sla schedule 22 start-time now life forever
```

Defining a Tracking Object and Assigning an Action

Example 5-33 configures the tracking object, which is linked to the probe 22.

Example 5-33 *Configure the IP SLA Tracking Object*

```
R1(config)# track 2 ip sla 22 reachability
R1(config-track)# delay down 10 up 1
R1(config-track)# exit
R1(config)# ip route 0.0.0.0 0.0.0.0 172.16.1.1 3 track 2
```

Tracking object 2 is linked to the previously defined probe 22 so that as long as the ISP 2 DNS server is reachable, the default route to ISP2a will be floating. If the link to the ISP 1 DNS server ever fails, this second route would become active.

With the **show ip sla configuration** command, you can verify the configured probes and their attributes, such as operation type, target address, source interface, and scheduling information.

To verify configured tracking objects, use the **show track** command. Here, you can verify that the mapping between the tracking object and the probe is correct. Also, the status of the tracking object is displayed.

Configuring PBR and IP SLA Example

To achieve dynamic path control, IP SLA must be used in combination with either static routes or PBR. For example, consider the reference topology in Figure 5-18.

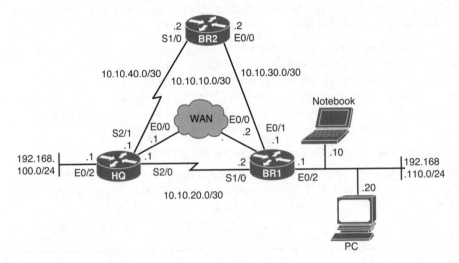

Figure 5-18 *PBR and IP SLA Reference Topology*

In this scenario, traffic paths for the clients at first branch office (router BR1) will be optimized using PBR and IP SLA. EIGRP is already configured between HQ and BR1, and all traffic flows over the Ethernet WAN link because it has the lowest EIGRP metric route.

The new network policy for BR1 dictates that

- Web traffic to the HQ site should be redirected over the serial link.

- All other traffic from Notebook should go via BR2 but only if BR2 is reachable.

In the example, you will

- Redirect web traffic from clients on the BR1 router going to the HQ router over the serial link using PBR

- Ensure that BR2 is reachable by using an IP SLA ICMP echo test to its WAN interface

- Redirect all other traffic from Notebook to router BR2 if BR2 is reachable

Redirecting Web Traffic from BR1 to HQ Using PBR

In this example, PBR is implemented to match interesting web traffic and setting the next-hop IP address for the matched traffic.

Example 5-34 creates a named ACL on BR1 called PBR-WWW-TRAFFIC. The ACL matches all HTTP and HTTPS traffic from any client to any server.

Example 5-34 *Match Web Traffic*

```
BR1(config)# ip access-list extended PBR-WWW-TRAFFIC
BR1(config-ext-nacl)# remark Permit only Web traffic
BR1(config-ext-nacl)# permit tcp any any eq 80
BR1(config-ext-nacl)# permit tcp any any eq 443
BR1(config-ext-nacl)# exit
```

Next, Example 5-35 creates a route map called PBR-2-HQ that matches the ACL and sets the next hop for the traffic to IP address of serial interface on HQ router.

Example 5-35 *Create the PBR*

```
BR1(config)# route-map PBR-2-HQ
BR1(config-route-map)# match ip address PBR-WWW-TRAFFIC
BR1(config-route-map)# set ip next-hop 10.10.20.1
BR1(config-route-map)# exit
```

Finally, Example 5-36 applies the inbound route map as a policy to the Ethernet 0/2 LAN interface.

Example 5-36 *Apply Route Map to the Interface*

```
BR1(config)# interface ethernet 0/2
BR1(config-if)# ip policy route-map PBR-2-HQ
BR1(config-if)# exit
```

Ensuring That BR2 Is Reachable Using IP SLA

The second part of the new network policy was that all other traffic from Notebook should go via BR2 but only if BR2 is reachable. To do so, an IP SLA will be configured to track the WAN interface of BR2, as shown in Example 5-37.

Example 5-37 *Create IP SLA Probing the BR2 WAN Interface*

```
BR1(config)# ip sla 1
BR1(config-ip-sla)# icmp-echo 10.10.30.2 source-interface Ethernet 0/1
BR1(config-ip-sla-echo)# frequency 10
BR1(config-ip-sla-echo)# exit
BR1(config)# ip sla schedule 1 start-time now life forever
```

Specifically, probe number 1 is created and is configured to send ICMP echoes to the BR2 WAN interface (10.10.30.2) every 10 seconds. The start and end times are configured to start now and never end.

Example 5-38 defines a new tracking object which is linked to IP SLA probe 1.

Example 5-38 *Create Tracking Object*

```
BR1(config)# track 1 ip sla 1
BR1(config-track)# delay down 5 up 1
BR1(config-track)# exit
```

Tracking object 1 is now linked to IP SLA probe 1. It essentially tracks the reachability of BR2 WAN interface and generates a notification after the link is down for 5 seconds and 1 second after it comes back up.

Redirect Traffic from Notebook to BR2 If Reachable

This next task redirects all non-web traffic from Notebook to be forwarded to BR2 but only if the previously configured IP SLA operation verifies reachability to the BR2 WAN interface.

Example 5-39 creates a new ACL to match all interesting traffic from the Notebook host.

Example 5-39 *Create ACL to Track Notebook Traffic*

```
BR1(config)# ip access-list extended PBR-FROM-B
BR1(config-ext-nacl)# Remark Match all traffic from the Notebook host
BR1(config-ext-nacl)# permit ip host 192.168.110.10 any
BR1(config-ext-nacl)# exit
```

Now you have to add a new entry to an existing route-map as shown in Example 5-40. Reference the newly created access list, and finally set the next appropriate hop. When doing so, make sure to include the **verify-availability** keyword and reference the created IP SLA tracking object with **track** keyword.

Example 5-40 *Add New Entry to PBR-2-HQ Route MAP*

```
BR1(config)# route-map PBR-2-HQ permit 20
BR1(config-route-map)# match ip address PBR-FROM-B
BR1(config-route-map)# set ip next-hop verify-availability 10.10.30.2 1 track 1
BR1(config-route-map)# end
```

If you want to use IP SLA with PBR, you have to use the **verify-availability** keywords when you set the next hop within a route map. If the status of the tracked object is up, the **set ip next-hop** command is used and the traffic is redirected. If the status of the tracked object is down, however, the command is bypassed, and destination-based routing is used to forward a packet.

Example 5-41 verifies that the PBR-2-HQ is defined and applied.

Example 5-41 *Verify Route Maps on BR1*

```
BR1# show route-map
route-map PBR-2-HQ, permit, sequence 10
  Match clauses:
    ip address (access-lists): PBR-WWW-TRAFFIC
  Set clauses:
    ip next-hop 10.10.20.1
  Policy routing matches: 0 packets, 0 bytes
route-map PBR-2-HQ, permit, sequence 20
  Match clauses:
    ip address (access-lists): PBR-FROM-B
  Set clauses:
    ip next-hop verify-availability 10.10.30.2 1 track 1   [up]
  Policy routing matches: 0 packets, 0 bytes
BR1#
```

The output confirms that the route map PBR-2-HQ is defined. Sequence 10 addresses the first part of the new network policy that web traffic from the BR1 LAN should be redirected over the serial link. Sequence 20 addresses the second part of the new network policy that all other traffic from Notebook should go via BR2 but only if BR2 is reachable.

Example 5-42 verifies that the route map is applied to the inbound Ethernet 0/0 interface.

Example 5-42 *Verify That the Route Map Is Applied*

```
BR1# show running-config interface ethernet 0/2
Building configuration...

Current configuration : 99 bytes
!
interface Ethernet0/2
 ip address 192.168.110.1 255.255.255.0
 ip policy route-map PBR-2-HQ
end

BR1#
```

Example 5-43 verifies the IP SLA operation.

Example 5-43 *Verify IP SLA Operations on BR1*

```
BR1# show ip sla summary
IPSLAs Latest Operation Summary
Codes: * active, ^ inactive, ~ pending
```

```
ID            Type         Destination      Stats      Return      Last
                                           (ms)       Code        Run
--------------------------------------------------------------------------
*1            icmp-echo    10.10.30.2       RTT=1      OK          1 second ago


BR1#
```

Notice that it is the correct type of operation (that is, icmp-echo) to the right destination (10.10.30.2) and that its return code is OK, which indicates that the BR2 WAN interface is reachable.

Example 5-44 verifies the tracking objects.

Example 5-44   *Verify Tracking Objects on BR1*

```
BR1# show track
Track 1
  IP SLA 1 state
  State is Up
    1 change, last change 00:29:37
  Delay up 1 sec, down 5 secs
  Latest operation return code: OK
  Latest RTT (millisecs) 1
  Tracked by:
    ROUTE-MAP 0
BR1#
```

Notice that tracking object 1 is linked to IP SLA probe 1. Its state is up and operational.

Finally, Example 5-45 verifies the path taken from the Notebook computer to the HQ LAN interface.

Example 5-45   *Verify the Path from Notebook to the HQ LAN*

```
Notebook> traceroute 192.168.100.1
Type escape sequence to abort.
Tracing the route to 192.168.100.1
VRF info: (vrf in name/id, vrf out name/id)
  1 192.168.110.1 1 msec 0 msec
  2 10.10.30.2 5 msec 3 msec 5 msec
  3 10.10.40.1 5 msec 6 msec *
Notebook>
```

Notice that the IP address of BR2 router is listed in the output of the **traceroute** command.

Summary

In this chapter, you learned about CEF and implementing path control. The chapter focused on the following topics:

- Packet-switching mechanisms on a Cisco IOS platform, including process switching, fast switching, and CEF switching.

- Overview of path control tools, including PBR and Cisco IOS IP SLAs.

- Using PBR to control path selection, providing benefits including source-based transit provider selection, QoS, cost savings, and load sharing. PBR is applied to *incoming* packets; enabling PBR causes the router to evaluate all packets incoming on the interface using a route map configured for that purpose.

- Configuring and verifying PBR, including the following steps:

  - Choose the path control tool to use; for PBR, **route-map** commands are used

  - Implement the traffic-matching configuration, specifying which traffic will be manipulated; **match** commands are used within route maps

  - Define the action for the matched traffic, using **set** commands within route maps

  - Apply the route map to incoming traffic or to traffic locally generated on the router

  - Verify path control results, using **show** commands

- Cisco IOS IP SLAs, which use active traffic monitoring, generating traffic in a continuous, reliable, and predictable manner, to measure network performance. IOS IP SLAs can be used in conjunction with other tools, including the following:

  - Object tracking, to track the reachability of specified objects

  - Cisco IOS IP SLAs probes, to send different types of probes toward the desired objects

  - Static routes with tracking options, as a simpler alternative to PBR

  - Route maps with PBR, to associate the results of the tracking to the routing process

- Cisco IOS IP SLA terminology, including the following:

  - All the Cisco IOS IP SLA measurement probe operations are configured on the IP SLA source, either by the CLI or through an SNMP tool that supports IP SLA operation. The source sends probe packets to the target.

  - There are two types of IP SLA operations: those in which the target device is running the IP SLA responder component, and those in which the target device is not running the IP SLA responder component (such as a web server or IP host).

  - An IP SLA operation is a measurement that includes protocol, frequency, traps, and thresholds.

- Configuring and verifying IOS IP SLAs.

References

For additional information, see these resources:

- Cisco IOS Software Releases support page: http://www.cisco.com/cisco/web/psa/default.html?mode=prod&level0=268438303

- Cisco IOS Master Command List, All Releases: http://www.cisco.com/c/en/us/td/docs/ios/mcl/allreleasemcl/all_book.html

- The Cisco IOS IP SLAs Command Reference: http://www.cisco.com/en/US/docs/ios/ipsla/command/reference/sla_book.html

Review Questions

Answer the following questions, and then see Appendix A, "Answers to Review Questions," for the answers.

1. Which packet switching method examines the first packet in each flow and the forwarding decision is cached in hardware for subsequent packets in the flows?

   a. Cisco Express Forwarding (CEF) switching
   b. Cut-through switching
   c. Fast switching
   d. Process switching
   e. Store-and-forward switching

2. Which packet switching method is the fastest and creates forwarding tables?

   a. Cisco Express Forwarding (CEF) switching
   b. Cut-through switching
   c. Fast switching
   d. Process switching
   e. Store-and-forward switching

3. Which packet switching method examines every packet and all forwarding decisions are made in software?

   a. Cisco Express Forwarding (CEF) switching
   b. Cut-through switching
   c. Fast switching
   d. Process switching
   e. Store-and-forward switching

4. Which three of the following packets cannot be CEF switched and must be processed in software?

   a. Packets that exceed the MTU of an output interface and must be fragmented

   b. Packets that need to be translated by NAT

   c. Packets that are forwarded to a tunnel interface

   d. Packets whose destination IP address is in the FIB table

   e. Packets with an expiring TTL counter

5. To which packets on an interface is PBR applied?

6. When a route map is used for PBR, which of the following are true statements? (Choose three.)

   a. If no match is found in the route map, the packet is dropped.

   b. If no match is found in the route map, the packet is not dropped.

   c. If the statement is marked as **deny**, a packet meeting the match criteria is dropped.

   d. If the statement is marked as **deny**, a packet meeting the match criteria is sent through the normal forwarding channels.

   e. If the statement is marked as **permit** and the packet meets all the match criteria, the **set** commands are applied.

   f. If the statement is marked as **permit** and the packet meets all the match criteria, the packet is sent through the normal forwarding channels.

7. Which three statements are true about IP SLAs?

   a. A Cisco IOS device can be an IP SLAs responder.

   b. A Cisco IOS device can be an IP SLAs source.

   c. A web server can be an IP SLA responder.

   d. A web server can be an IP SLA source.

   e. Operations are configured on the IP SLAs source.

   f. Operations are configured on the IP SLAs responder

8. Fill in the blank: _____ use active traffic monitoring, generating traffic in a continuous, reliable, and predictable manner to measure network performance.

9. Write the command to track the reachability of IOS IP SLA operation number 100 with object number 2.

10. Write the command to start IP SLA operation number 100 immediately and have it never end.

Chapter 6

Enterprise Internet Connectivity

This chapter covers the following topics:

- Planning Enterprise Internet Connectivity

- Establishing Single-Homed IPv4 Internet Connectivity

- Establishing Single-Homed IPv6 IPv6 Internet Connectivity

- Improving Internet Connectivity Resilience

The Internet has become a vital resource for most organizations, requiring a single connection to an Internet service provider (ISP) or redundant connections to multiple ISPs. Planning for such connectivity is an important task and is covered first in this chapter. The details of single connections for IPv4 and IPv6 are then described. The chapter concludes with a discussion of using multiple ISP connections to improve Internet connectivity resilience.

Note The term *IP* is used for generic IP and applies to both IPv4 and IPv6. Otherwise, the terms *IPv4* and *IPv6* are used for the specific protocols.

Note Appendix B, "IPv4 Supplement," contains job aids and supplementary information related to IPv4, including a review of IPv4 addressing and IPv4 access control lists (ACLs). Before reading the rest of this chapter, you are encouraged to review any of the material you find unfamiliar in Appendix B.

Planning Enterprise Internet Connectivity

One of the most important tasks when designing the network topology is planning for enterprise Internet connectivity. There are multiple ways of connecting to ISPs; the choice depends on the needs of the organization. For example, some enterprises only need web and e-mail access, whereas others require constant access to mission-critical servers. Understanding the process of how IP addresses are assigned and how public IP addresses are distributed are key elements of Internet connectivity planning.

Upon completion of this section, you will be able to do the following:

■ Identify the Internet connectivity needs of organizations

■ Identify the different types of ISP connectivity

■ Describe public IP address assignments and the need for provider-independent IP addressing

■ Describe autonomous system numbers

Connecting Enterprise Networks to an ISP

Modern corporate IP networks connect to the global Internet, use the Internet for some of their data transport needs, and provide services via the Internet to customers and business partners. To meet these needs, many systems—from web servers to mainframes to workstations—must be accessible from anywhere in the world.

Enterprise Connectivity Requirements

Enterprise connectivity requirements can be categorized as one of the following:

■ **Outbound:** In the rare case that only one-way connectivity outbound from clients to the Internet is required, private IPv4 addresses with Network Address Translation (NAT) are used for IPv4 connections, allowing clients on a private network to communicate with servers on the public Internet. This situation would be similar to that found in most homes, where no connections are needed from the Internet into the home network.

■ **Inbound:** Typically, though, two-way connectivity is needed, so that clients external to the enterprise network can access resources in the enterprise network. In this case, both public and private IPv4 address space is needed, as are routing and security considerations. E-mail and remote-access virtual private networks (VPNs) are examples of services used by enterprise clients residing external to the organization, and site-to-site VPNs and public web servers are examples of services that may be used by other organizations, such as business partners.

The type of redundancy required for enterprise network to ISP connectivity must be evaluated. Options include the following:

- **Edge device redundancy:** Deploying redundant edge devices, such as routers, protects your network against device failure. If one router fails, Internet connectivity can still be established through the redundant router.

- **Link redundancy:** Using redundant links protects your network against link failure between your router and the ISP router.

- **ISP redundancy:** If you are hosting important servers in your network or accessing mission-critical servers in the Internet, it is best to have two redundant ISPs. If a failure occurs in one ISP network, traffic can be automatically rerouted through the second ISP.

ISP Redundancy

When using redundant ISP connections, an organization (the ISP's customer) can be connected to a single ISP or to multiple ISPs. There are various names for these different types of connections, as illustrated in Figure 6-1:

- **Single-homed:** With a connection to a single ISP when no link redundancy is used, the customer is *single-homed*. If the ISP network fails, connectivity to the Internet is interrupted. Single-homed ISP connectivity is used in cases when a loss in Internet connectivity is not problematic to a customer. (These days however, the Internet is usually a vital resource.)

- **Dual-homed:** With a connection to a single ISP, redundancy can be achieved if two links toward the same ISP are used effectively. This is called being *dual-homed*. There are two options for dual homing: Both links can be connected to one customer router, or to enhance the resiliency further, the two links can terminate at separate routers in the customer's network. In either case, routing must be properly configured to allow both links to be used.

- **Multihomed:** With connections to multiple ISPs, redundancy is built in to the design. A customer connected to multiple ISPs is said to be *multihomed*, and is thus resistant to a single ISP failure. Connections from different ISPs can terminate on the same router, or on different routers to further enhance the resiliency. The customer is responsible for announcing its own IP address space to upstream ISPs, but should avoid forwarding any routing information between ISPs (otherwise the customer becomes a transit provider between the two ISPs). The routing used must be capable of reacting to dynamic changes. Multihoming also allows load balancing of traffic between ISPs.

- **Dual multihomed:** To enhance the resiliency further with connections to multiple ISPs, a customer can have two links toward each ISP. This solution is called being *dual multihomed* and typically has multiple edge routers, one per ISP.

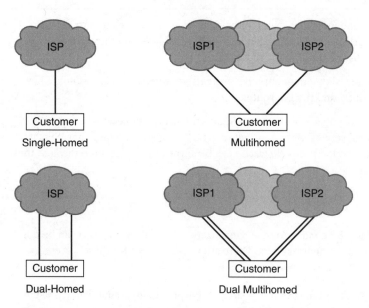

Figure 6-1   *Types of ISP Connectivity*

Public IP Address Assignment

The Internet Assigned Numbers Authority (IANA) and the regional Internet registries (RIRs) are involved with public IP address assignment.

The Internet Assigned Numbers Authority

The IANA is the umbrella organization responsible for allocating the numbering systems that are used in the technical standards (also known as the protocols) that comprise the Internet. The IANA describes its role as follows:

> "The IANA team is responsible for the operational aspects of coordinating the Internet's unique identifiers and maintaining the trust of the community to provide these services in an unbiased, responsible and effective manner."

IANA responsibilities include the following:

- Coordinate the global pool of IPv4 and IPv6 addresses, and provide them to RIRs

- Coordinate the global pool of autonomous system numbers and provide them to RIRs

- Manage the Domain Name Service (DNS) root zone

- Manage the IP numbering systems (in conjunction with standards bodies)

The IANA is operated by the Internet Corporation for Assigned Names and Numbers (ICANN), formed in 1998 as a not-for-profit public-benefit corporation with participants from all over the world dedicated to keeping the Internet secure, stable, and interoperable.

Both IPv4 and IPv6 addresses are generally assigned in a hierarchical structure. IP addresses and IP address space ranges are typically assigned to subscribers by their ISP. ISPs obtain allocations of IP addresses from RIR.

As illustrated in Figure 6-2, the IANA's role is to allocate IP addresses from the pools of unallocated addresses to the RIRs. The IANA does not make allocations directly to ISPs or end users except in specific circumstances, such as allocations of multicast addresses or other protocol-specific needs.

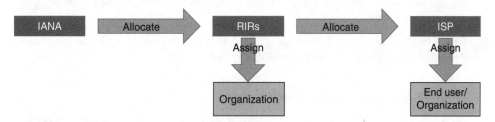

Figure 6-2   *The IANA Allocates Public Addresses*

Regional Internet Registries

RIRs are nonprofit corporations established for the purpose of administration and registration of IP address space and autonomous system numbers. There are five RIRs, as follows:

- **African Network Information Centre (AfriNIC):** Responsible for the continent of Africa

- **Asia Pacific Network Information Centre (APNIC):** Administers the numbers for the Asia Pacific region

- **American Registry for Internet Numbers (ARIN):** Has jurisdiction over assigning numbers for Canada, the United States, and several islands in the Caribbean Sea and North Atlantic Ocean

- **Latin American and Caribbean Internet Addresses Registry (LACNIC):** Responsible for allocation in Latin America and portions of the Caribbean

- **Réseaux IP Européens Network Coordination Centre (RIPE NCC):** Administers the numbers for Europe, the Middle East, and Central Asia

Public IP Address Space

ISPs distribute addresses from their assigned address space.

End users typically request a public address space from their ISP. (Provider-independent address space is an exception and is described later in this section.) ISPs may assign one public IPv4 address or a range of IPv4 addresses. For clients that need access to resources on the Internet, client private addresses are translated to public addresses.

Public addresses are also used for enterprise servers that need to be accessible from the Internet; these servers are configured either with public addresses or with private addresses that are statically translated to public addresses.

In the IPv6 world, ISPs may assign /64 blocks of addresses to home users; this is the smallest range of addresses that ISPs can assign. ISPs usually assign /48 blocks to enterprise users. Some RIRs have a policy that all customers, including home users, be assigned a /48 address space; the actual allocation is up to the ISPs. Other ranges, such as /52 and /56 (which has been suggested for home sites), may also be assigned, depending on customer needs.

Blocks of IP addresses can be provider independent (PI) or provider aggregatable (PA), as described in more detail in the sections that follow.

Provider Aggregatable Address Space

A PA block of IP addresses is used in simple topologies, where no redundancy is needed. PA address space is assigned by the ISP to its customer, from its address space. If the customer changes its ISP, the new ISP will give the customer a new PA address space, and all devices with public IP addresses will have to be renumbered; the old address space cannot be transferred to the new ISP.

Provider-Independent Address Space

For a multihomed connection, a PI address space is required because the enterprise network needs to be independent of the ISP's address space. The PI address space must be acquired from an RIR; it is assigned directly to an organization by the RIR, and is not related to any ISP.

This address space can be routed through other service providers, resulting in more flexibility when planning connections to ISPs and when migrating between service providers.

After successfully processing an address space request, the RIR assigns the PI address space and a public autonomous system number (ASN) (described in the next section) that uniquely defines the enterprise's network and its address spaces. This ASN is not related to any ISP.

The enterprise then configures their Internet gateway routers to advertise the newly assigned IP address space to neighboring ISPs; the Border Gateway Protocol (BGP) is typically used for this task. (BGP is described further in Chapter 7, "BGP Implementation.")

Autonomous System Numbers

To understand ASNs and BGP, it is first necessary to understand one of the ways that routing protocols are categorized, whether they are interior or exterior, as follows:

- **Interior Gateway Protocol (IGP):** An IGP is a routing protocol that exchanges routing information within an autonomous system. Routing Information Protocol (RIP), Open Shortest Path First (OSPF) Protocol, Intermediate System-to-Intermediate System (IS-IS) Protocol, and Enhanced Interior Gateway Routing Protocol (EIGRP) are examples of IGPs for IPv4.

- **Exterior Gateway Protocol (EGP):** An EGP is a routing protocol that exchanges routing information between different autonomous systems. BGP is an example of an EGP.

BGP is an interdomain routing protocol (IDRP), which is also known as an EGP. All the routing protocols you have seen so far in this book are IGPs.

Figure 6-3 illustrates the concept of IGPs and EGPs.

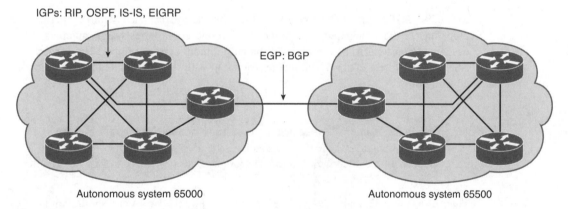

Figure 6-3 *IGPs Operate Within an Autonomous System, and EGPs Operate Between Autonomous Systems*

BGP Version 4 (BGP-4) is the latest version of BGP for IPv4. It is defined in RFC 4271, *A Border Gateway Protocol (BGP-4)*. As noted in this RFC, the classic definition of an autonomous system is "a set of routers under a single technical administration, using an IGP and common metrics to determine how to route packets within the autonomous system, and using an inter-autonomous system routing protocol to determine how to route packets to other autonomous systems."

> **Note** Extensions to BGP-4, known as MP-BGP (or BGP4+), have been defined to support multiple protocols, including IPv6. These multiprotocol extensions to BGP are defined in RFC 4760, *Multiprotocol Extensions for BGP-4.*

Autonomous systems might use more than one IGP, with potentially several sets of metrics. The important characteristic of an autonomous system from the BGP point of view is that the autonomous system appears to other autonomous systems to have a single coherent interior routing plan, and it presents a consistent picture of which destinations can be reached through it. All parts of the autonomous system must be connected to each other.

Another way to look at an autonomous system is as a collection of routing prefixes (sets of address spaces) under the same administrative control. An ASN is used to uniquely identify each autonomous system. Similar to IP addresses, ASNs are managed by the IANA and assigned to RIRs. RIRs in turn assign ASNs to ISPs and to organizations with PI address space.

The ASN is a very important parameter required when configuring BGP.

The ASN is a 16-bit number, with a range of 0 to 65,535. RFC 1930, *Guidelines for Creation, Selection, and Registration of an Autonomous System (AS)*, provides guidelines for the use of ASNs.

RFC 6793, *BGP Support for Four-Octet Autonomous System (AS) Number Space*, preparing for the anticipated depletion of BGP 16-bit autonomous system numbers, describes extensions to BGP to use a 32-bit autonomous system number. This longer ASN can be expressed in a 32-bit integer format or with two 16-bit integers concatenated with dot (.).

Note   The Cisco document "Explaining 4-Octet Autonomous System (AS) Numbers for Cisco IOS," explains how the new numbering scheme can be implemented in Cisco routers. The link to this document is in the "References" section at the end of this chapter.

The ASNs 0, 65,535, and 4,294,967,295 are reserved by the IANA and should not be used in any routing environment. The IANA defines the following two ASN ranges to be used for private purposes, much like the private IPv4 addresses:

- 64,512 through 65,534

- 4,200,000,000 through 4,294,967,294 (64,086.59904 through 65,535.65534)

The IANA also defines the following two ranges for use in documentation and in sample code:

- 64,496 through 64,511

- 65,536 through 65,551 (1.0 – 1.15)

You need to use an IANA-assigned autonomous system number, rather than a private autonomous system number, only if your organization plans to use BGP to connect to the Internet.

Establishing Single-Homed IPv4 Internet Connectivity

When single-homed organizations connect to the Internet using IPv4, the address used comes from the ISP. This can be a static IPv4 addresses or can be allocated dynamically, using the Dynamic Host Configuration Protocol (DHCP).

Because there are not enough public IPv4 addresses available to enable Internet connectivity for all of an organization's devices, mechanisms such as NAT need to be implemented to conserve public IPv4 addresses. With NAT, private address ranges are used for internal client devices; these are translated to public addresses to provide Internet connectivity. NAT simplifies addressing tasks and also reduces problems that could occur when the same address ranges are used within intranets.

Upon completion of this section, you will be able to do the following:

- Describe how to configure your router with both a provider-assigned static IPv4 address and a provider-assigned DHCP address

- Understand DHCP operation and describe how to use a router as a DHCP server and relay agent

- Identify the various types of NAT

- Describe the NAT virtual interface (NVI) feature, configuration, and verification

Configuring a Provider-Assigned IPv4 Address

Statically assigned IPv4 addresses are useful in cases where a company or organization wants to have its servers or services publicly accessible. These static addresses can be linked to a domain name, such as www.cisco.com, which allows clients to find and access these servers and services.

The ISP provides you with a static IPv4 address, which you configure on your router. This is a straightforward two-step process:

Step 1. Assign the static IPv4 address on the router's Internet-facing interface.

Step 2. Configure a default route that will forward all traffic intended for the Internet to the ISP.

Example 6-1 illustrates this configuration on the R1 router shown in Figure 6-4.

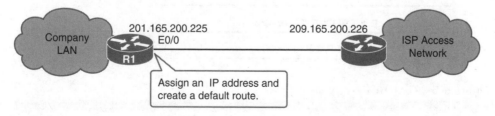

Figure 6-4 *Configuring a Static Provider-Assigned IPv4 Address*

Example 6-1   *Static Provider-Assigned IPv4 Address Configuration*

```
R1(config)# interface Ethernet 0/0
R1(config-if)# ip address 209.165.200.225 255.255.255.224
R1(config-if)# no shutdown
R1(config-if)# exit
R1(config)# ip route 0.0.0.0 0.0.0.0 209.165.200.226
```

In this example, the ISP provides a static IPv4 address of 209.165.200.225/27. The address is assigned on the interface pointing to the ISP, and a default route is created with a next-hop IPv4 address 209.165.200.226, which is the IPv4 address of the ISP's router.

Note   Of course, these same commands can be used to assign any address to a router's interface and configure an appropriate default route, including when using a PI address or a private address on an internal network.

DHCP Operation

DHCP is built on the client/server model, where designated DHCP servers allocate IPv4 addresses and deliver configuration parameters to dynamically configured hosts. DHCP is defined in RFC 2131, *Dynamic Host Configuration Protocol*.

In the DHCP negotiation process, illustrated in Figure 6-5, the client sends a DHCPDISCOVER broadcast message to locate a DHCP server. A DHCP server offers configuration parameters to the client in a DHCPOFFER unicast message. Typical configuration parameters are an IPv4 address, a domain name, and a lease period for the IPv4 address.

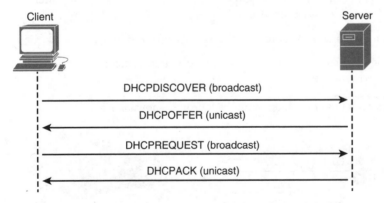

Figure 6-5   *The DHCP Negotiation Process*

A DHCP client may receive offers from multiple DHCP servers and can accept any one of the offers; however, the client usually accepts the first offer that it receives. In addition, the offer from the DHCP server is not a guarantee that the address will be allocated to the client, but the server usually reserves the address until the client has had a chance to formally request the address, which is done in a DHCPREQUEST broadcast message.

The DHCP server confirms that the IPv4 address has been allocated to the client by returning a DHCPACK unicast message to the client.

Four other DHCP messages are possible:

- **DHCPDECLINE:** A message sent from a client to a server indicating that the address is already in use

- **DHCPNAK:** A message sent from a server indicating that it is refusing a client's request for configuration

- **DHCPRELEASE:** A message sent from a client indicating to a server that it is giving up a lease

- **DHCPINFORM:** A message sent from a client indicating that it already has an IPv4 address, but is requesting other configuration parameters from the DHCP server, such as a DNS address

Obtaining a Provider-Assigned IPv4 Address with DHCP

When dynamic assignment is used by the ISP, no manual address assignment is needed; instead, DHCP client functionality needs to be enabled on the router interface. Other configuration information can also be obtained through DHCP, such as the default gateway address.

To enable the DHCP client functionality, use the **ip address dhcp** interface configuration command. The client will send out DHCP discover and request messages, and configure the interface with the information received from the DHCP server.

If the optional default gateway information is contained within the reply from the DHCP server, the router will install a static default route in its routing table, with the default gateway's IPv4 address as the next hop. The default route is installed with an administrative distance (AD) of 254, making it a floating static route; the high AD prevents the injected route from being used if other manually configured or dynamically learned default routes exist. You can disable this functionality by issuing the **no ip dhcp client request router** interface configuration command.

Example 6-2 illustrates this configuration on the R1 router shown in Figure 6-6. The routing table entry for the injected default static route is also displayed.

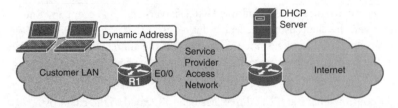

Figure 6-6   *Configuring a Provider-Assigned IPv4 Address with DHCP*

Example 6-2   *Configuration and Verification of a Provider-Assigned IPv4 Address with DHCP*

```
R1(config)# interface Ethernet 0/0
R1(config-if)# ip address dhcp
R1(config-if)# end


R1# show ip route 0.0.0.0
Routing entry for 0.0.0.0/0, supernet
Known via "static", distance 254, metric 0, candidate default path
  Routing Descriptor Blocks:
  * 209.165.200.226
      Route metric is 0. traffic share count is 1
```

Note   Again, these same commands can be used to configure any router's interface to obtain an address via DHCP, including when using a PI address or a private address on an internal network.

Configuring a Router as a DHCP Server and DHCP Relay Agent

A Cisco router can be configured to be a DHCP server and a DHCP relay agent. When configuring a router as a DHCP server, you create a pool to define all of the DHCP parameters, with the **ip dhcp pool** *name* global configuration command. The *name* parameter is locally significant to the router only. Within DHCP configuration mode, you define the parameters. Figure 6-7 shows a network, and Example 6-3 displays the DHCP server configuration on the R2 router.

Figure 6-7   *Network for Configuring a DHCP Server and DHCP Relay Agent Examples*

Example 6-3 *Configuring a Router as a DHCP Server*

```
R2(config)# ip dhcp pool MYLAN
R2(dhcp-config)# network 10.0.20.0 255.255.255.0
R2(dhcp-config)# default-router 10.0.20.1
R2(dhcp-config)# lease 2
R2(dhcp-config)# exit
R2(config)# ip dhcp excluded-address 10.0.20.1 10.0.20.49
```

In this example, R2 defines a DHCP pool called MYLAN. A client will be given an address in the 10.0.20.0/24 network, defined with the **network** *network-number mask* DHCP configuration command. This address will be leased for 2 days, defined by the **lease** *days* DHCP configuration command. The client will also be given a default gateway (router) address of 10.0.20.1, defined with the **default-router** *address* DHCP configuration command; this is R1's address. Addresses in the range 10.0.20.1 through 10.0.20.49 will not be given to clients, as defined by the **ip dhcp excluded-address** *first-ip-address last-ip-address* global configuration command.

In this network example, the client and the DHCP server reside on different subnets. A DHCP client uses a broadcast to find a DHCP server. Because routers do not forward broadcasts by default, the client would not be able to communicate with the DHCP server, by default. To allow this communication, router R1 must be configured as a DHCP relay agent, using the **ip helper-address** *address* interface configuration command. The address parameter is the address of the DHCP server. The command must be configured on the interface on which the router receives the broadcasts; this would be R1's Gi0/0 interface in this example. Example 6-4 displays the DHCP relay agent configuration on the R1 router.

Example 6-4 *Configuring a Router as a DHCP Relay Agent*

```
R1(config)# interface gi0/0
R1(config-if)# ip helper-address 172.16.1.1
```

NAT

The NAT protocol is used when connecting multiple devices on internal private networks to a public network such as the Internet using a limited number of public IPv4 addresses. It was originally designed for conserving IPv4 address space because the IPv4 address space is not big enough to uniquely identify all devices that need Internet connectivity.

RFC 1918, *Address Allocation for Private Internets*, has set aside the following IPv4 address space for private use:

- **Class A network:** 10.0.0.0 to 10.255.255.255

- **Class B network:** 172.16.0.0 to 172.31.255.255

- **Class C network:** 192.168.0.0 to 192.168.255.255

Private addresses are reserved IPv4 addresses to be used only internally within a company's network. These private addresses are not to be used on the Internet, so they must be translated to a public address when anything is sent on the Internet. NAT is the mechanism used to perform this translation.

NAT is usually implemented on border devices such as firewalls or routers, which allows devices within an organization to have private addresses. In this case, NAT only translates traffic when it needs to be sent to the Internet, and the border device translates private addresses to public addresses and vice versa, keeping a mapping between the two for return traffic. NAT can be configured to translate all private addresses to only one public address or to pick from a pool of public addresses.

NAT can also be used when there is an addressing overlap between intranets. An example of this would be when two companies merge and both were using the same private address range. In this case, NAT can be used to translate one intranet's private addresses into another private range, thus avoiding the addressing conflict and enabling devices from one intranet to communicate with devices on the other.

It is important to understand the different types of NAT and how and when to use them, in addition to understanding the NAT terminology.

NAT uses the terms *inside* and *outside*. Inside means internal to your network, and outside means external to your network. NAT includes the following four types of addresses:

- **Inside local address:** The IPv4 address assigned to a device on the internal network.

- **Inside global address:** The IPv4 address of an internal device as it appears to the external network. This is the address to which the inside local address is translated.

- **Outside local address:** The IPv4 address of an external device as it appears to the internal network. If outside addresses are being translated, this is the address to which the outside global address is translated.

- **Outside global address:** The IPv4 address assigned to a device on the external network.

A good way to remember what is local and what is global is to add the word *visible*. An address that is locally visible normally implies a private IPv4 address, and an address that is globally visible normally implies a public IPv4 address. The rest is simple. Inside means internal to your network, and outside means external to your network. So, for example, an inside global address means that the device is physically inside your network and has an address that is visible from the Internet. This could be a web server, for instance.

The inside and outside definition is important for NAT operation. When a packet travels from an inside domain to an outside domain, it is routed first and then translated and forwarded out the exit interface. When a packet travels from an outside domain to an inside domain, the process is reversed.

The three types of NAT are as follows:

- **Static NAT:** Static NAT is one-to-one translation. Static NAT is particularly useful when a device must be accessible from outside the network. (For example, when a server with a static IPv4 address needs to be accessible from the Internet, that server's private address can be translated to a public address.)

- **Dynamic NAT:** Dynamic NAT is many-to-many translation, using a pool of addresses. When an inside device accesses an outside network, it is assigned an available IPv4 address from the pool on a first-come, first-serve basis. When using dynamic NAT, you need to ensure that there are enough addresses available in the pool to satisfy the total number of user sessions. An example of when this type of NAT could be used is when two companies that are using the same private address space merge; dynamic NAT readdressing could be used as a temporary measure until the entire network is readdressed.

- **Port Address Translation (PAT):** PAT is many-to-one translation; for example, it maps multiple inside local IPv4 addresses to a single inside global IPv4 address by tracking port numbers. PAT is also known as *NAT overloading*. It is a form of dynamic NAT and is the most common type of NAT. PAT is used in business and home routers, allowing multiple devices to access the Internet, even though only one public IPv4 address is available.

The **show ip nat translations** command is used to verify which addresses are currently being translated. Figure 6-8 illustrates the types of NAT addresses. Example 6-5 illustrates the **show ip nat translations** command output from the R1 router.

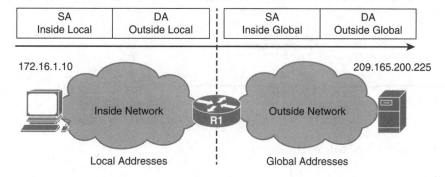

Figure 6-8 *Network for NAT Example*

Example 6-5 *NAT Verification*

```
R1# show ip nat translations
Pro    Inside global    Inside local    Outside local      Outside global
icmp   209.165.201.5:4  172.16.1.10:4   209.165.200.255:4  209.165.200.255:4
---    209.165.201.5:4  172.16.1.10     ---                ---
```

Usually, as is the case in this example, only inside addresses are translated, so the outside local and outside global addresses are identical.

Configuring Static NAT

Configuring static NAT is a simple process. You first define *inside* and *outside* interfaces, using the **ip nat inside** and **ip nat outside** interface configuration commands. You next specify which inside local address should be translated to which inside global address, using the **ip nat inside source static** *local-ip global-ip* global configuration command. Table 6-1 describes the parameters for this command.

Table 6-1   **ip nat inside source static** *Global Configuration Command*

Parameter	Description
local-ip	The inside local IPv4 address assigned to a host on the inside network.
global-ip	The inside global IPv4 address of an inside host as it appears to the outside world

Packets arriving on the inside interface and having a source address that matches the defined *local-ip* address will have the source address translated to the *global-ip* address. Return packets that have a destination address that matches the *global-ip* address will have the destination address translated to the *local-ip* address. You configure one **ip nat inside source static** command for each address that you need to translate.

Example 6-6 illustrates the configuration on the R1 router in Figure 6-9. The PC's address, 172.16.1.10, will be translated to 209.165.201.5 when the PC sends packets to the Internet.

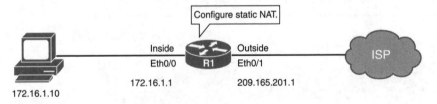

Figure 6-9   *Network for Static NAT Example*

Example 6-6   *Static NAT Configuration*

```
Router(config)# interface Ethernet 0/1
Router(config-if)# ip address 209.165.201.1 255.255.255.240
Router(config-if)# ip nat outside
Router(config-if)# exit
Router(config)# interface Ethernet 0/0
Router(config-if)# ip address 172.16.1.1 255.255.255.0
Router(config-if)# ip nat inside
Router(config-if)# exit
Router(config)# ip nat inside source static 172.16.1.10 209.165.201.5
```

Configuring Dynamic NAT

Whereas static NAT provides a permanent mapping between a single inside local and a single inside global address, dynamic NAT maps many inside local to many inside global addresses (a many-to-many mapping).

Dynamic NAT takes these inside global addresses from a NAT pool on a first-come, first-served basis. This is why you have to be careful to provide enough addresses for the NAT pool to satisfy all initiated connections.

Like static NAT, you first identify each interface as an *inside* or *outside* interface. You then define the set of inside local addresses to be translated, using an ACL. The next step is to define the set of inside global addresses to which the inside local addresses will be translated, using the **ip nat pool** *name start-ip end-ip* {**netmask** *netmask* | **prefix-length** *prefix-length*} global configuration command; the parameters of this command are shown in Table 6-2.

Table 6-2   **ip nat pool** *Global Configuration Command*

Parameter	Description
name	Name of the pool
start-ip	Starting IPv4 address that defines the range of addresses in the address pool
end-ip	Ending IPv4 address that defines the range of addresses in the address pool
netmask	Specifies the subnet mask of the network to which the pool addresses belong
prefix-length	Alternative way of specifying the subnet mask of the network to which the pool addresses belong

Finally, the ACL-to-NAT pool mapping is defined by the following global configuration command:

```
ip nat inside source list {access-list-number | access-list-name} pool name
```

Table 6-3 describes the parameters for this command.

Table 6-3   **ip nat inside source list** *Global Configuration Command*

Parameter	Description
access-list-number	Identifies a standard IPv4 access list. The source address of packets that are permitted by the access list is dynamically translated to an inside global addresses from the named pool.

Parameter	Description
access-list-name	Identifies a standard IPv4 access list. The source address of packets that are permitted by the access list is dynamically translated to an inside global addresses from the named pool.
name	Name of the pool from which the inside global IPv4 addresses are dynamically allocated.

Example 6-7 illustrates the configuration on the R1 router in Figure 6-10. In this example, the addresses of both PCs are permitted by the ACL. The pool, called NAT-POOL, defines the range 209.165.201.5/28 to 209.165.201.10/28. When a PC sends packets to the Internet, its source address will be translated to an address from the pool.

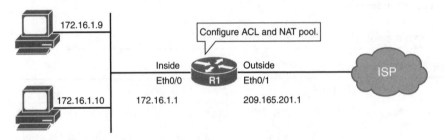

Figure 6-10   *Network for Dynamic NAT Example*

Example 6-7   *Dynamic NAT Configuration*

```
Router(config)# access-list 1 permit 172.16.1.0 0.0.0.255
Router(config)# ip nat pool NAT-POOL 209.165.201.5 209.165.201.10
  netmask 255.255.255.240
Router(config)# interface Ethernet 0/1
Router(config-if)# ip address 209.165.201.1 255.255.255.240
Router(config-if)# ip nat outside
Router(config-if)# exit
Router(config)# interface Ethernet 0/0
Router(config-if)# ip address 172.16.1.1 255.255.255.0
Router(config-if)# ip nat inside
Router(config-if)#exit
Router(config)# ip nat inside source list 1 pool NAT-POOL
```

Configuring PAT

Port Address Translation (PAT), also known as NAT overloading, is the most widely used form of NAT. It maps multiple inside local addresses to a one or few inside global addresses by keeping track of both IPv4 address and port numbers mappings.

PAT allows multiple devices to share a single or few inside global addresses. Most home routers operate in this manner; your ISP assigns one public address to your router, yet several members of your family can simultaneously surf the Internet.

PAT ensures that each session is unique by possibly modifying port numbers as well as IPv4 addresses when performing translations. If a mapping can be made without modifying source port numbers, it is done; however, if a previous mapping exists in the translations table that would match the newly translated IPv4 header (because the source port number is already in use), PAT will search for a new unique mapping. If more than one inside global address is available, it will try to keep the source port number the same and use an available address. If this is not possible (for example if there is only one inside global address), PAT will modify the source port number when translating, creating unique mapping.

Incoming packets from the outside network are delivered to the destination device on the inside network by looking for a match in the NAT translations table and translating IPv4 headers, both address and port number, accordingly. This mechanism is called connection tracking.

To configure PAT, you again first identify each interface as an *inside* or *outside* interface, and define the set of inside local addresses to be translated, using an ACL. To configure PAT, you use the following global configuration command:

```
ip nat inside source list {access-list-number | access-list-name} {interface type
number} [overload]
```

This command translates all addresses permitted by the ACL to the address of the specified outside interface; the **overload** parameter does the PAT. Table 6-4 describes the parameters for this command.

Table 6-4 ip nat inside source list overload *Global Configuration Command*

Parameter	Description
access-list-number	Identifies a standard IP access list. The source address of packets that are permitted by the access list is translated to the address of the specified interface.
access-list-name	Identifies a standard IP access list. The source address of packets that are permitted by the access list is translated to the address of the specified interface.
type number	Specifies the interface type and number from which the inside global address will be taken.
overload	(Optional) Enables the router to use one inside global address for many inside local addresses. When overloading is configured, the Transmission Control Protocol (TCP) or User Datagram Protocol (UDP) port number of each inside host distinguishes between the multiple conversations using the same local IP address.

Note   There are many other options for these commands. For example, you can add the **overload** keyword to the **ip nat inside source list** {*access-list-number* | *access-list-name*} **pool** *name* command to do PAT using a pool of addresses.

Example 6-8 illustrates the configuration on the R1 router in Figure 6-10, from the previous example. In this configuration, the addresses of both PCs are permitted by the ACL. When a PC sends packets to the Internet, its address will be translated to the address of the Ethernet 0/1 interface, and the source port number of the packet will also be translated as necessary.

Example 6-8   *PAT Configuration*

```
Router(config)# access-list 1 permit 172.16.1.0 0.0.0.255
Router(config)# interface Ethernet 0/0
Router(config-if)# ip address 172.16.1.1 255.255.255.0
Router(config-if)# ip nat inside
Router(config-if)# interface Ethernet 0/1
Router(config-if)# ip address 209.165.201.1 255.255.255.240
Router(config-if)# ip nat outside
Router(config-if)# exit
Router(config)# ip nat inside source list 1 interface Ethernet 0/1 overload
```

Limitations of NAT

NAT provides benefits to a network, but it also has some limitations that you need to consider, including the following:

- **End-to-end visibility issues:** Many applications depend on end-to-end functionality, with unmodified packets being forwarded from source to destination. By changing end-to-end addresses, NAT effectively blocks such applications. For example, some security applications, such as digital signatures, fail because the source IP addresses change. Applications that use physical addresses rather than a qualified domain name do not reach destinations that are translated across the NAT router. Also, because of address changes along the way, the traceability of endpoints is lost, which can make troubleshooting challenging.

  Another visibility problem is session initiation from the outside network; services that require the initiation of TCP connections from the outside network, or stateless protocols such as those using UDP, can be disrupted. Unless the NAT router makes a specific effort to support such protocols, incoming packets cannot reach their destination.

- **Tunneling becomes more complex:** Using NAT can complicate tunneling protocols, such as IPsec, because NAT modifies the values in the headers and thus interferes with the integrity checks done by IPsec and other tunneling protocols.

- **In certain topologies, standard NAT may not work correctly:** In Figure 6-11, the R1 router is configured to perform PAT for the LAN clients and static NAT for the web server. When a client on the Internet wants to access the web server, it gets the server's public IP address from DNS and attempts to access the server. The router statically translates the server's public IP address (its inside global address) to its inside local address, and forwards packets to the server.

When a client on the LAN tries to access the server, it similarly gets the same public IP address for the server from DNS, and tries to access the server. However, attempts to connect to the server will fail because of how NAT operates. When packets go from inside to outside, they are first routed and then translated; the packets from the LAN client are routed to the outside interface and the LAN client's address is translated by PAT. When packets travel from outside to inside, they are translated and routed. In this case however, the packets from the LAN client do not come into the router's outside interface; therefore, they are never translated so they are never routed back to the interface where the server is located. The result is that the LAN client cannot connect to the web server.

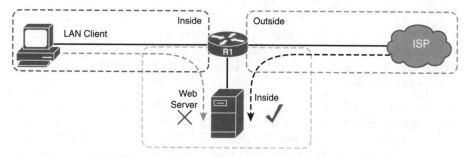

Figure 6-11   *Network for Limitations of NAT Example*

NAT Virtual Interface

As of Cisco IOS Software Release 12.3(14)T Cisco introduced a new feature, NAT virtual interface (NVI), which removes the requirement to configure an interface as inside or outside. The NVI order of operations is also slightly different than NAT. Recall that classic NAT first performs routing and then translation when going from an inside interface to an outside interface, and vice versa when the traffic flow is reversed. NVI, however, performs routing, translation, and routing again; NVI performs the routing operation twice, before and after translation, before forwarding the packet to an exit interface. The whole process is symmetrical, no matter which way the traffic is flowing. Because of the added routing step, packets can flow, in classic NAT terms, from an inside to an inside interface; as described in the previous section, this scenario fails if classic NAT is used.

Configuring NAT Virtual Interface

This section uses an example to illustrate how to configure NVI. This section includes both static and dynamic NVI translations and the verification of these translations.

Figure 6-12 displays the network diagram for this example. In this network, the server's address will be translated statically, and the PC's address will be translated dynamically.

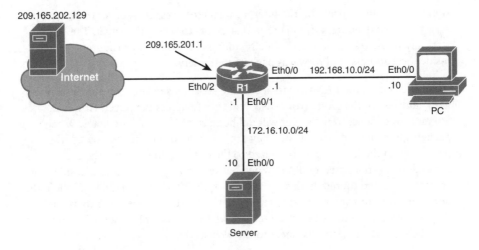

Figure 6-12 *Network for NVI Example*

The first step is to identify the addresses to be translated dynamically using an access list. Because only the 192.168.10.0/24 segment should be translated dynamically, a standard access list using the **access-list 10 permit 192.168.10.0 0.0.0.255** global configuration command is created.

Next, you create the NAT pool to be used for dynamic NAT translations. For this example, we use the address range 209.165.201.5/27 through 209.165.201.10/27 in the pool. The required command is **ip nat pool TEST1 209.165.201.5 209.165.201.10 prefix-length 27**. Recall that the IP addresses in the pool are used on a first-come, first-served basis, so ensure that the pool is big enough to satisfy all client connections.

You then configure the dynamic and static NAT translations.

Clients from the 192.168.10.0/24 segment should be translated dynamically, getting their inside global addresses from the TEST1 pool. To create a dynamic mapping, use the **ip nat source list 10 pool TEST1** global configuration command. This command maps all inside local addresses permitted by the access list to the addresses defined in the pool.

> **Note**   NVI can also use PAT by using the **overload** keyword in the translation commands, similar to what is shown in the earlier "Configuring PAT" section. For example, you could use the **ip nat source list 10 interface Ethernet0/2 overload** command.

The server's inside local address 172.16.10.10 should be statically mapped to its inside global address of 209.165.201.2. The **ip nat source static 172.16.10.10 209.165.201.2** global configuration command creates this mapping.

Example 6-9 illustrates the configuration on the R1 router.

Example 6-9 *NVI Configuration Example*

```
R1(config)# access-list 10 permit 192.168.10.0 0.0.0.255
R1(config)# ip nat pool TEST1 209.165.201.5 209.165.201.10 prefix-length 27
R1(config)# ip nat source list 10 pool TEST1
R1(config)# ip nat source static 172.16.10.10 209.165.201.2
```

Note Notice that there are no **inside** or **outside** keywords used in these commands. Because NVI does not require that you define inside or outside interfaces, those keywords are also not used in the translation commands.

When NAT is configured, an NVI0 interface is created; it is used when translating IPv4 addresses. To verify this, issue the **show ip interface brief** command. Example 6-10 provides this command output on R1; you can see that the NVI0 interface was created

Example 6-10 **show ip interface brief** *Command Output*

```
R1# show ip interface brief
Interface        IP-Address      OK?  Method  Status                    Protocol
Ethernet0/0      192.168.10.1    YES  manual  up                        up
Ethernet0/1      172.16.10.1     YES  manual  up                        up
Ethernet0/2      209.165.201.1   YES  manual  up                        up
Ethernet0/3      unassigned      YES  NVRAM   administratively down     down
NVI0             192.168.10.1    YES  unset   up                        up
```

Recall that NVI performs two routing operations instead of one. When a packet enters the NAT router on any NAT-enabled interface, it is matched against the NAT translation table. If there is a match, the packet is routed to the NVI0 interface, where translation takes place. After the translation process, the packet is routed again and forwarded to the appropriate interface.

The NVI0 interface is assigned an IPv4 address, which is needed for Cisco IOS internal operation. The assigned IPv4 address has no influence on NAT behavior; it is copied from the first physical interface or from the first interface on which NAT is enabled.

To configure interfaces to use NVI and to participate in the translation process, use the **ip nat enable** interface configuration command. Example 6-11 shows the configuration of this command on the R1 router.

Example 6-11 *Configuring NAT NVI*

```
R1(config)# interface ethernet 0/0
R1(config-if)# ip nat enable
R1(config-if)# interface ethernet 0/1
R1(config-if)# ip nat enable
R1(config-if)# interface ethernet 0/2
R1(config-if)# ip nat enable
```

Verifying NAT Virtual Interface

Now that NVI is configured, you check connectivity using the **ping** command. Example 6-12 provides sample output of checking connectivity to the Internet server from the PC and the internal server, and from the PC to the internal server's private and public addresses.

Example 6-12   *Testing Connectivity to the Server*

```
PC# ping 209.165.202.129
Type escape sequence to abort.
Sending 5, 100-byte ICMP Echos to 209.165.202.129, timeout is 2 seconds:
!!!!!
Success rate is 100 percent (5/5), round-trip min/avg/max = 1/1/1 ms

Server# ping 209.165.202.129
Type escape sequence to abort.
Sending 5, 100-byte ICMP Echos to 209.165.202.129, timeout is 2 seconds:
!!!!!
Success rate is 100 percent (5/5), round-trip min/avg/max = 1/1/1 ms

PC# ping 172.16.10.10
Type escape sequence to abort.
Sending 5, 100-byte ICMP Echos to 172.16.10.10, timeout is 2 seconds:
!!!!!
Success rate is 100 percent (5/5), round-trip min/avg/max = 1/1/1 ms

PC# ping 209.165.201.2
Type escape sequence to abort.
Sending 5, 100-byte ICMP Echos to 209.165.201.2, timeout is 2 seconds:
!!!!!
Success rate is 100 percent (5/5), round-trip min/avg/max = 1/1/1 ms
```

All pings are successful. With NAT NVI, there is no problem of going from inside to inside using translated addresses.

To observe NVI translations, you can issue the **show ip nat nvi translations** command; note the use of the **nvi** keyword. Example 6-13 provides this command output on R1.

Example 6-13   show ip nat nvi translations *Command Output*

```
R1# show ip nat nvi translations
Pro Source global      Source local       Destin  local        Destin  global
icmp 209.165.201.2:0   172.16.10.10:0     209.165.202.129:0    209.165.202.129:0
--- 209.165.201.2      172.16.10.10       ---                  ---
icmp 209.165.201.5:0   192.168.10.10:0    209.165.202.129:0    209.165.202.129:0
icmp 209.165.201.5:1   192.168.10.10:1    172.16.10.10:1       172.16.10.10:1
icmp 209.165.201.5:2   192.168.10.10:2    209.165.201.2:2      172.16.10.10:2
--- 209.165.201.5      192.168.10.10      ---                  ---
```

Notice that the output of the command differs slightly from legacy NAT command output. Because NVI no longer uses inside and outside, the terms *inside global*, *inside local*, *outside local*, and *outside global* are no longer used in the translations table. Instead, the terms *source global*, *source local*, *destin local*, and *destin global* are used, respectively. The definition of the terms, however, remains the same.

As you can see from the output example, the server's private address, source local, is correctly translated to its public address, source global, as defined in the static mapping. Also, the PC's private address, source local, was translated to the first available address from the NAT pool, source global.

If you use the **show ip nat translations** command to see the status of traditional NAT, you will see that it is empty, because traditional NAT is not being performed. Example 6-14 provides this command output on R1.

Example 6-14   show ip nat translations *Command Output*

```
R1# show ip nat translations
Pro Inside global    Inside local    Outside local    Outside global
```

The **show ip nat nvi statistics** command can be used to display NVI statistics and to indicate which interfaces are participating in NAT. Example 6-15 provides this command output on R1.

Example 6-15   show ip nat nvi statistics *Command Output*

```
R1# show ip nat nvi statistics
Total active translations: 4 (1 static, 3 dynamic; 2 extended)
NAT Enabled interfaces:
  Ethernet0/0, Ethernet0/1, Ethernet0/2
Hits: 34  Misses: 4
CEF Translated packets: 10, CEF Punted packets: 0
Expired translations: 0
Dynamic mappings:
-- Source [Id: 3] access-list 10 pool TEST1 refcount 2
 pool TEST1: netmask 255.255.255.224
       start 209.165.201.5 end 209.165.201.10
       type generic, total addresses 6, allocated 1 (16%), misses 0
```

The Hits and Misses count in this command output provide you with valuable information. The Hits counter increases every time a translation is found in the translations table. If no translation is found, a new translation is inserted in the table, and the Misses counter is increased. If NAT is operating normally, these counters should increase over time.

Establishing Single-Homed IPv6 Internet Connectivity

IPv6 is similar to IPv4, but it is a different protocol, so some of the concepts that you are familiar with in IPv4 have changed in IPv6. With IPv6 gaining in popularity, it is becoming increasingly necessary to understand how to connect your organization to the IPv6 Internet. Because with IPv6 every IPv6-enabled node has global reachability, it is important to understand that implementing IPv6 in your network also comes with some security risks. You should be both aware of them and know how to protect your network against them.

Upon completion of this section, you will be able to do the following:

- Describe the various ways that your router can obtain an IPv6 address

- Understand DHCP for IPv6 (DHCPv6) operation and describe the use of a router as a DHCPv6 server and relay agent

- Describe the use of NAT for IPv6

- Identify how to configure IPv6 ACLs

- Describe the need to secure IPv6 Internet connectivity

Obtaining a Provider-Assigned IPv6 Address

Multiple IPv6 addressing methods have been developed to facilitate address assignment with little or no human intervention, similar to those for IPv4. These methods automate the assignment of addresses and other configuration parameters, because manual assignment is especially inconvenient and error prone with the 128-bit IPv6 address.

The IPv6 address assignment methods are as follows:

- Manual assignment

- Stateless address autoconfiguration (SLAAC)

- Stateless DHCPv6

- Stateful DHCPv6

- DHCPv6 prefix delegation (DHCPv6-PD)

The sections that follow explore these methods in more detail.

Note   The first four of these methods can be used to assign any IPv6 address, whether it is a PA address, a PI address, or an address on an internal network.

Note   IPv6 address guidelines are explored in RFC 7381, *Enterprise IPv6 Deployment Guidelines*.

Manual Assignment

As with IPv4, an IPv6 address can be statically assigned by a network administrator. This assignment method can be error-prone and introduces significant administrative overhead, especially because of the 128-bit length of IPv6 addresses. However, it is necessary in some cases (for example, if an enterprise receives a manual address allocation from their ISP).

Within an enterprise, there are a variety of thoughts on designing an IPv6 addressing plan. For security, some recommendations include choosing addresses that are not easily guessed and avoiding any embedded existing IPv4 addresses. However, embedding IPv4 information can help ease troubleshooting and operation of the network, which may be desirable. (For more on this topic, see the *How to Write an IPv6 Address Plan* Cisco Live presentation; the link to the presentation is in the "References" section at the end of this chapter.)

Configuring Basic IPv6 Internet Connectivity

This section uses an example to illustrate how to configure basic IPv6 Internet connectivity.

Figure 6-13 displays the network diagram for this example. In this network, the ISP has allocated the 2001:DB8:10:10::10/64 IPv6 address for you to use on your Internet connection. The Internet-facing interface on R1, Ethernet 0/2, needs to be configured with this IPv6 address. A default route pointing to the ISP (2001:DB8:10:10::1/64) needs to be created; it will be used to forward all nonlocal traffic to the Internet.

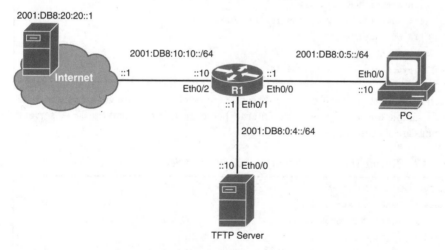

Figure 6-13 *Network for Basic IPv6 Internet Connectivity Example*

Recall that you need to use the **ipv6 unicast-routing** global configuration command to enable the forwarding of IPv6 unicast datagrams; this command is also required before you configure IPv6 static or dynamic routing. The **ipv6 unicast-routing** command also causes the router to send ICMPv6 router advertisement (RA) messages.

Use the **ipv6 address** *address/prefix-length* interface configuration command to configure an IPv6 address and prefix (specified in the *address/prefix-length* parameters) for an interface and enable IPv6 processing on the interface.

IPv6 static routes can be configured with the **ipv6 route** *ipv6-prefix/prefix-length next-hop-address* global configuration command. Table 6-5 describes the parameters of this command.

Table 6-5 ipv6 route *Command Parameters*

Parameter	Description
ipv6-prefix/prefix-length	Specifies the IPv6 network that is the destination of the static route and its prefix length
next-hop-address	Specifies the address of the next hop that can be used to reach the specified network

The default static route uses ::/0 in the *ipv6-prefix/prefix-length* parameter.

Example 6-16 shows the configuration on the R1 router.

Example 6-16 *Example Basic IPv6 Configuration*

```
R1(config)# ipv6 unicast-routing
R1(config)# interface Ethernet 0/2
R1(config-if)# ipv6 address 2001:DB8:10:10::10/64
R1(config-if)# no shutdown
R1(config-if)# exit
R1(config)# ipv6 route ::/0 2001:DB8:10:10::1
```

You can accomplish the verification of basic IPv6 connectivity by pinging. Example 6-17 provides sample output of pinging the Internet server from the PC and the TFTP server. Both pings are successful.

Example 6-17 *Testing IPv6 Connectivity to the Internet Server*

```
PC# ping 2001:db8:20:20::1
Type escape sequence to abort.
Sending 5, 100-byte ICMP Echos to 2001:DB8:20:20::1, timeout is 2 seconds:
!!!!!
Success rate is 100 percent (5/5), round-trip min/avg/max = 1/1/1 ms


Server# ping 2001:db8:20:20::1
Type escape sequence to abort.
Sending 5, 100-byte ICMP Echos to 2001:DB8:20:20::1, timeout is 2 seconds:
!!!!!
Success rate is 100 percent (5/5), round-trip min/avg/max = 1/1/4 ms
```

Stateless Address Autoconfiguration

SLAAC provides the capability for a device to obtain IPv6 addressing information without any intervention from the network administrator. This is achieved with the help of RAs, which are sent by routers on the local link. RA messages include one or more prefixes, prefix lifetime information, flag information, and default router lifetime information. The source IPv6 link-local address of the RA message is used by the host as its IPv6 default router address. IPv6 hosts listen for these RAs and use the advertised prefix, which must be 64 bits long. The host generates the remaining 64 host bits either by using the IEEE EUI-64 format or by creating a random sequence of bits. If the generated IPv6 address is unique, it can be applied to the interface. This process introduces plug-and-play functionality to the network, which significantly reduces administrative overhead; however, it provides no way of tracking address assignment.

IEEE EUI-64

IEEE EUI-64 format interface IDs are derived from an interface's 48-bit IEEE 802 MAC address using the following process:

1. The MAC address is split into two 24-bit parts.

2. 0xFFFE is inserted between the two parts, resulting in a 64-bit value.

3. The seventh bit of the first octet is inverted. (In a MAC address, this bit indicates the scope and has a value of 0 for global scope and 1 for local scope; it will be 0 for globally unique MAC addresses. In the EUI-64 format used for IPv6 interface IDs, the meaning of this bit is opposite, so the bit is inverted.)

For example, a MAC address of 00AA.BBBB.CCCC would result in an IPv6 EUI-64 format interface ID of 02AA:BBFF:FEBB:CCCC.

Enabling SLAAC

Use the **ipv6 address autoconfig [default]** interface configuration command to enable automatic configuration of IPv6 addresses using SLAAC on a router interface and to enable IPv6 processing on the interface. The optional **default** keyword causes a default route to be installed using that default router sending the RAs as the default router. You can specify the **default** keyword on only one interface.

Note that the commands configured on a router determine when it generates router solicitation (RS) and RA messages:

- Routers configured with the **ipv6 unicast-routing** command generate RA messages; these routers by default have the **no ipv6 nd suppress-ra** interface configuration command. They do not generate RS messages.

- Routers configured with the **ipv6 address autoconfig** command, and not configured with the **ipv6 unicast-routing** command, generate RS messages only. They do not generate RA messages.

DHCPv6 Operation

In the IPv6 world, there are two types of DHCPv6:

- **Stateless:** Used to supply additional parameters to clients that already have an IPv6 address

- **Stateful:** Similar to DHCP for IPv4 (DHCPv4)

Stateless and stateful DHCPv6 are described in the next two sections; this section provides an overview of DHCPv6 operation and how it differs from its IPv4 counterpart. DHCPv6 is defined in RFC 3315, *Dynamic Host Configuration Protocol for IPv6 (DHCPv6)*.

Acquiring data for a client in DHCPv6 is similar to the process in DHCPv4, with a few exceptions. One difference is that in IPv6 a client may detect the presence of routers on the link using Neighbor Discovery (ND) protocol messages. If at least one router is found, the client examines the RA messages to determine if DHCPv6 should be used. If the RA messages allow the use of DHCPv6 on the link, or if no router is found, the client starts a DHCPv6 solicit phase to find a DHCP server. Another difference is that servers may be configured with policies for global addresses (for example, "do not give an address to a printer").

In the DHCPv6 negotiation process, the client sends a SOLICIT message to find a DHCPv6 server and request assignment of addresses and other configuration information. This message is sent to the *all-DHCP-agents* multicast address (FF02::1:2) with link-local scope; agents include both servers and relays.

Any DHCPv6 servers that can meet the client's requirement respond to the client with an ADVERTISE message.

A DHCPv6 client builds a list of potential servers by sending a SOLICIT message and collecting ADVERTISE message replies from servers. These messages are ranked based on preference value; servers may add an explicit preference option to their ADVERTISE messages. If the client needs to acquire prefixes from a server, only servers that have advertised prefixes are considered.

The client chooses one of the servers and sends a REQUEST message to it, asking it to confirm the addresses and other information that were advertised.

The server responds with a REPLY message that contains the confirmed addresses and configuration information.

Like with DHCPv4, a DHCPv6 client renews its lease after a period of time by sending a RENEW message.

In addition to the four-way exchange, DHCPv6 can also use a shortened two-way exchange, with only SOLICIT and REPLY messages. By default, the four-message exchange is used; when the **rapid-commit** option is enabled by both the client and server, the two-message exchange is used.

Stateless DCHPv6

Stateless DHCPv6 works in combination with SLAAC. An IPv6 host gets its addressing and default router information using SLAAC, from information contained within an RA. However, the IPv6 host also queries a DHCPv6 server for other information it needs, such as the DNS or NTP server addresses. The query for other configurations is triggered by the *other configuration* flag bit set in the RA. In this case, the DHCPv6 server does not assign IPv6 addresses, and therefore does not need to maintain any dynamic state information for the clients; therefore, it is called *stateless*. Note that because of the use of SLAAC, however, the issue of address tracking is still not resolved. The RA link-local address is still used as the default router address.

Configuring a router to be a stateless DHCPv6 client is the same as configuring it to use SLAAC.

Just as for IPv4, a Cisco router can be configured as a DHCPv6 server and relay agent. The network in Figure 6-14 is used to illustrate the configuration of a stateless (and stateful in the next section) DHCPv6 relay agent and server.

Figure 6-14 *Network for Stateless and Stateful DHCPv6 Server and Relay Agent Examples*

Example 6-18 displays the configuration of router R1 as the DHCPv6 relay agent and of router R2 as the DHCPv6 server, both for stateless DHCPv6.

Example 6-18 *Configuring Stateless DHCPv6 Relay Agent (R1) and Server (R2)*

```
R1(config)# ipv6 unicast-routing
R1(config)# interface gigabitEthernet 0/0
R1(config-if)# ipv6 nd other-config-flag
R1(config-if)# ipv6 dhcp relay destination 2001:DB8:CAFE:1::1

R2(config)# ipv6 dhcp pool IPV6-STATELESS
R2(config-dhcpv6)# dns-server 2001:DB8:CAFE:1::99
R2(config-dhcpv6)# domain-name www.example.com
R2(config)# interface gigabitEthernet 0/0
R2(config-if)# ipv6 dhcp server IPV6-STATELESS
```

On R1, the **ipv6 nd other-config-flag** command sets the *other configuration flag* bit in the RAs sent on the Gigabit Ethernet 0/0 interface toward the client. The **ipv6 dhcp relay destination 2001:DB8:CAFE:1::1** command configures R1 as a relay agent; the address specified is the address of the DHCPv6 server, R2.

On R2, the **ipv6 dhcp pool IPV6-STATELESS** command creates the DHCPv6 pool. The DNS server and domain name are specified with the **dns-server 2001:DB8:CAFE:1::99** and **domain-name www.example.com** commands, respectively. Finally the **ipv6 dhcp server IPV6-STATELESS** command enables the Gigabit Ethernet 0/0 interface as a DHCPv6 server, using the specified pool.

Stateful DHCPv6

When stateful DHCPv6 is implemented, RAs use the *managed address configuration* flag bit to tell IPv6 hosts to get their addressing and additional information only from the DHCPv6 server. This flag tells the hosts to disregard the prefixes in the RA and instead query the DHCPv6 server for addressing and other information. The DHCPv6 server then allocates addresses to the host and tracks the allocated address. Note that the default router address is still received from the RA link-local address.

To allow a router to acquire an IPv6 address on an interface from a DHCPv6 server, use the **ipv6 address dhcp** interface configuration command.

Example 6-19 displays the configuration of router R1 as the DHCPv6 relay agent and of router R2 as the DHCPv6 server, both for stateful DHCPv6.

Example 6-19 *Configuring Stateful DHCPv6 Relay Agent (R1) and Server (R2)*

```
R1(config)# ipv6 unicast-routing
R1(config)# interface gigabitEthernet 0/0
R1(config-if)# ipv6 nd managed-config-flag
R1(config-if)# ipv6 dhcp relay destination 2001:DB8:CAFE:1::1


R2(config)# ipv6 dhcp pool IPV6-STATEFUL
R2(config-dhcpv6)# address prefix 2001:DB8:CAFE:2::/64
R2(config-dhcpv6)# dns-server 2001:DB8:CAFE:1::99
R2(config-dhcpv6)# domain-name www.example.com
R2(config)# interface gigabitEthernet 0/0
R2(config-if)# ipv6 dhcp server IPV6-STATEFUL
```

On R1, the **ipv6 nd managed-config-flag** command sets the *managed address configuration* bit in the RAs sent on the Gigabit Ethernet 0/0 interface toward the client. The **ipv6 dhcp relay destination 2001:DB8:CAFE:1::1** command configures R1 as a relay agent; the address specified is the address of the DHCPv6 server, R2.

On R2, the **ipv6 dhcp pool IPV6-STATEFUL** command creates the DHCPv6 pool. The pool's prefix, containing addresses for clients, is defined in the **address prefix 2001:DB8:CAFE:2::/64** command. The DNS server and domain name are specified with the **dns-server 2001:DB8:CAFE:1::99** and **domain-name www.example.com** commands, respectively. Finally, the **ipv6 dhcp server IPV6-STATEFUL** command enables the Gigabit Ethernet 0/0 interface as a DHCPv6 server, using the specified pool.

DHCPv6 Prefix Delegation

DHCPv6-PD is an extension to DHCPv6. It is used by an ISP to automate the process of assigning prefixes to a customer for use within the customer's network. The prefix delegation occurs between a provider-edge (PE) device and customer premise equipment (CPE) using the DHCPv6-PD option. Once the ISP has delegated prefixes to a customer, the customer may further subnet and assign prefixes to the links in their network.

NAT for IPv6

In IPv4, NAT is typically used to translate private addresses to public addresses when communicating on the Internet. In IPv6, we do not have to worry about private-to-public address translation, but some forms of NAT are still used. This section introduces NAT IPv6-to-IPv4 (NAT64) and IPv6-to-IPv6 Network Prefix Translation (NPTv6).

NAT64

NAT Protocol Translation (NAT-PT) was the initial translation scheme for facilitating communication between IPv6 and IPv4. NAT-PT has been deprecated and replaced by NAT64.

NAT64 is described in RFC 6146, *Stateful NAT64: Network Address and Protocol Translation from IPv6 Clients to IPv4 Servers*. With NAT64, one or multiple public IPv4 addresses are shared by many IPv6-only devices, using overloading. IPv6 address assignment can be any of those discussed earlier in this chapter.

NAT64 performs both address and IP header translation. An example use of NAT64 is to provide IPv4 Internet connectivity to IPv6 devices, during the transition to a full IPv6 Internet.

NPTv6

NPTv6 is described in RFC 6296, *IPv6-to-IPv6 Network Prefix Translation*. (Note that at the time of this writing this RFC has an "experimental," not "standard," status.) NPTv6 is a one-to-one stateless translation; one IPv6 address in an inside network, such as an organization's LAN, is translated to one IPv6 address in an outside network, the IPv6 Internet. The idea for NPTv6 is that an organization's internal IPv6 addressing can be independent of its ISP's address space, making it easier to change ISPs. NPTv6 provides only network layer translation; port numbers are not translated.

One use of NPTv6 is when an organization has connections to two ISPs. In this multi-homed case, NPTv6 translates to either of the ISP's address space. RFC 6296 has been updated (as documented in *draft-bonica-v6-multihome-0*; see the "References" section for the link to this document) to also maintain transport layer sessions if a connection to one ISP fails, which would be useful in this case.

IPv6 ACLs

ACLs are often used for security purposes; for example, they can be used to permit or deny the flow of packets through an interface. For IPv6 ACLs, some configuration commands and details differ somewhat from IPv4 ACLs, but the concepts remain the same.

IPv6 ACL Characteristics

One change from IPv4 is that IPv6 ACLs are always named and extended.

The other important difference from IPv4 is the change to, or rather the addition to, the implicit **deny** statement at the end of every ACL. IPv6 relies on various protocols to function correctly; one of those is the ND protocol. ND is to IPv6 what ARP is to IPv4, so it is important that ND not be disrupted. For this reason, two additional implicit statements are added before the *implicit* **deny any** statement at the end of each IPv6 ACL. For IPv6, there are three implicit rules at the end of each ACL, as follows:

- **permit icmp any any nd-na**
- **permit icmp any any nd-ns**
- **deny ipv6 any any**

The first of these rules permits all ND neighbor advertisement (NA) messages. The second permits all ND neighbor solicitation (NS) messages. The last denies all other IPv6 packets. If you want to log all packets that are denied, you may be tempted to do as you would in IPv4 and simply add a **deny ipv6 any any log** command to your ACL. However, this explicit **deny** command would override all three implicit rules, not just the last one, and would result in the neighbor discovery traffic being blocked. You would need to instead explicitly configure the two **permit nd** statements, followed by the explicit **deny** statement.

Configuring IPv6 ACLs

This section uses an example to illustrate how to configure an IPv6 ACL, which will be configured on router R1 in Figure 6-15.

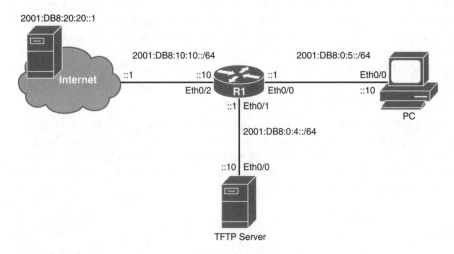

Figure 6-15   *Network for IPv6 ACL Example*

The ACL should block all ICMP echo requests and Telnet requests to the TFTP server. TFTP traffic from the Internet should only be allowed to the TFTP server, not to other internal hosts.

Example 6-20 illustrates the configuration on the R1 router. Notice that the commands for configuring IPv6 ACLs are very similar to commands for configuring IPv4 named extended ACLs; the structure of ACL statements has not changed.

Example 6-20   *IPv6 ACL Configuration Example*

```
R1(config)# ipv6 access-list SECURE_HOSTS
R1(config-ipv6-acl)# remark DENY PING TO TFTP SERVER
R1(config-ipv6-acl)# deny icmp any host 2001:DB8:0:4::10 echo-request
R1(config-ipv6-acl)# remark DENY TELNET TO TFTP SERVER
R1(config-ipv6-acl)# deny tcp any host 2001:DB8:0:4::10 eq telnet
R1(config-ipv6-acl)# remark ALLOW TFTP ONLY TO TFTP SERVER
R1(config-ipv6-acl)# permit udp any host 2001:DB8:0:4::10 eq tftp
R1(config-ipv6-acl)# deny udp any any eq tftp
R1(config-ipv6-acl)# remark ALLOW ALL OTHER TRAFFIC
R1(config-ipv6-acl)# permit ipv6 any any
```

This ACL blocks all inbound echo request and telnets to the TFTP server, and permits inbound TFTP traffic only to the TFTP server but not to other internal hosts. All other IPv6 traffic is allowed. ACL concepts have not changed in IPv6, so more-specific statements should go before less-specific statements because the ACL is processed top-down.

If your ACL does not allow all other IPv6 traffic, a recommendation specific to IPv6 ACLs is to allow ICMPv6 Packet Too Big messages, by using the **permit icmp any any packet-too-big** command. The reason for this is that IPv6 fragmentation occurs at the source of the packet and not on the routers along the path; the maximum transmission unit (MTU) discovery process has moved from the routers to IPv6 hosts, reducing the routers' processing resources and allowing IPv6 networks to work more efficiently. However, if a router receives a packet that it cannot forward because the packet is too big (bigger than the MTU), it sends an ICMPv6 Packet Too Big message. The information in this message is used as part of the path MTU discovery process.

To apply an ACL to an interface, use the **ipv6 traffic-filter** *ACL-name* {**in|out**} interface configuration command; notice that the **traffic-filter** keyword is used rather than the **access-group** keyword that is used in IPv4 ACLs. The additional configuration on the R1 router is illustrated in Example 6-21. The ACL is applied inbound on the Internet-facing interface so that it filters all inbound traffic.

Example 6-21   *Applying IPv6 ACL Configuration*

```
R1(config)# interface Ethernet 0/2
R1(config-if)# ipv6 traffic-filter SECURE_HOSTS in
```

Of course, you could configure a separate ACL to restrict Telnet access and apply it to the vty lines. To apply an ACL to a vty line, use the **ipv6 access-class** *ACL-name* line configuration command. This would save you the administrative burden of placing an ACL on multiple physical interfaces.

Now that the IPv6 ACL is configured, you verify it by sending a variety of traffic. Example 6-22 provides sample output of the first set of tests from the Internet server:

- The first test is a ping to the TFTP server. The ping attempt does not work because of the configured ACL. The output AAAAA tells you that the host is *Administratively Unreachable*. This usually means that an ACL is blocking traffic.

- The second test is a Telnet to the TFTP server. Because the ACL was configured to deny Telnet access to the TFTP server, the attempt should fail, which it does.

- The final of these tests attempts to TFTP from the PC to the Internet server. Again, this test should fail, and it does.

Example 6-22 *First Tests of IPv6 ACL*

```
Inet# ping 2001:DB8:0:4::10
Type escape sequence to abort.
Sending 5, 100-byte ICMP Echos to 2001:DB8:0:4::10, timeout is 2 seconds:
AAAAA
Success rate is 0 percent (0/5)


Inet# telnet 2001:DB8:0:4::10
Trying 2001:DB8:0:4::10 ...
% Destination unreachable; gateway or host down


Inet# copy tftp://2001:DB8:0:5::10/startup-config null:
Accessing tftp://2001:DB8:0:5::10/startup-config...
%Error opening tftp://2001:DB8:0:5::10/startup-config (Timed out)
```

Example 6-23 provides sample output of some more tests from the Internet server; these tests should all be successful:

- The first test is a ping to the internal PC; it is successful.

- The second test is a Telnet to the PC; it is successful.

- The final test attempts to TFTP from the TFTP server to the Internet Server. Again, this test should be successful, and it is.

Example 6-23 *Final Tests of IPv6 ACL*

```
Inet# ping 2001:DB8:0:5::10
Type escape sequence to abort.
Sending 5, 100-byte ICMP Echos to 2001:DB8:0:5::10, timeout is 2 seconds:
```

```
!!!!!
Success rate is 100 percent (5/5), round-trip min/avg/max = 1/1/1 ms


Inet# telnet 2001:DB8:0:5::10
Trying 2001:DB8:0:5::10 ... Open


PC>exit


[Connection to 2001:DB8:0:5::10 closed by foreign host]
Inet# copy tftp://2001:DB8:0:4::10/startup-config null:
Accessing tftp://2001:DB8:0:4::10/startup-config...
Loading startup-config from 2001:DB8:0:4::10: !
[OK - 963 bytes]
```

Example 6-24 provides sample output from the **show ipv6 access-list** command, including the configured statements in the ACL, the number of matches, and the sequence number on each statement. You can examine the number of matches to confirm that your ACL is catching the correct packets.

Example 6-24   show ipv6 access-list *Command Output*

```
R1# show ipv6 access-list
IPv6 access list SECURE_HOSTS
    deny icmp any host 2001:DB8:0:4::10 echo-request (5 matches) sequence 20
    deny tcp any host 2001:DB8:0:4::10 eq telnet (1 match) sequence 40
    permit udp any host 2001:DB8:0:4::10 eq tftp (4 matches) sequence 60
    deny udp any any eq tftp (6 matches) sequence 70
    permit ipv6 any any (44 matches) sequence 90
```

Securing IPv6 Internet Connectivity

When connecting your organization to the Internet via IPv6, you need to ensure that you properly secure your infrastructure and end hosts.

Enabling IPv6 Internet connectivity results in several new attack vulnerabilities in your infrastructure. Protocols such as neighbor discovery can easily be exploited, similar to attacks on IPv4's ARP.

In addition, end hosts connected to the Internet are usually no longer hidden behind the NAT as they typically are with IPv4. This enables an attacker to try to connect to any TCP or UDP port to which end hosts are listening.

To secure end hosts that are connected to the IPv6 Internet, the use of a stateful firewall is recommended. Either each individual host can be secured using a software solution, or a hardware appliance can be installed within the network infrastructure.

You should also harden the IPv6 protocols being used by disabling unnecessary functions and optimizing default settings.

Improving Internet Connectivity Resilience

A single-homed Internet connectivity design has many disadvantages because of the single points of failure. If Internet access is crucial, improving the resilience of Internet connectivity is important.

Upon completion of this section, you will be able to do the following:

- Describe the disadvantages of single-homed Internet connectivity

- Describe dual-homed Internet connectivity

- Describe multihomed Internet connectivity

Drawbacks of a Single-Homed Internet Connectivity

Single-homed Internet connectivity is a simple way to connect your enterprise environment to the Internet, but the design has many drawbacks because of the single points of failure, as illustrated in Figure 6-16. In this design there is no redundancy toward the ISP. This approach would typically only be used in smaller networks where Internet access is not crucial to the enterprise.

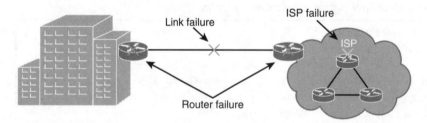

Figure 6-16 *Single-Homed Internet Connectivity Has Many Disadvantages*

Link failure between the enterprise Internet gateway and the ISP's PE router can result from many possible causes, but the most common are when a cable is cut (for example, by construction workers) and a bad connector on a patch panel.

The enterprise's Internet gateway is another single point of failure; if it fails, you lose Internet connectivity. Power outage, module failure, power supply failure, or a bug in the router's software are the most common causes for router failure.

There is also a possibility that the ISP has problems in their own network. In this situation, Internet access can be degraded or totally disabled, or some portion of Internet resources may become unavailable.

Based on the importance of Internet access for corporate processes, some improvements to redundancy can be made.

Dual-Homed Internet Connectivity

In a dual-homed design, there are two (or more) connections, using one or more Internet routers, to the same ISP. The ISP may also have multiple routers to connect to specific customers.

Dual-Homed Connectivity Options

Figure 6-17 illustrates the dual-homed options.

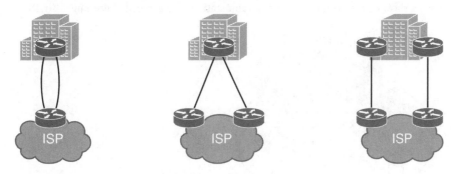

Figure 6-17 *Dual-Homed Internet Connectivity Options*

The additional link in a dual-homed design provides redundancy. If the primary link fails, the redundant link can be used for traffic forwarding. Common practice in a dual-homed design is to deploy two CE routers on the enterprise side and two PE devices on the ISP side.

Even in a dual-homed design, there are still some single points of failure, though. For example, if the ISP network fails, you still lose Internet connectivity. Another single point of failure is if a single CE router is used; if it fails, connectivity is lost. This is why you should use two devices for Internet connectivity.

A dual-homed design with dual CE and ISP devices is the preferred design option when connecting to a single ISP provider. The devices must be properly configured to ensure correct packet routing in case of failure.

Configuring Best Path for Dual-Homed Internet Connectivity

When a second Internet link is added to a network, new possibilities for traffic routing become available.

In dual-homed networks, one link is usually used as a primary link. In case of primary link failure, the second (backup) link is used for traffic forwarding. Either static routing toward the ISP or BGP with the ISP are commonly used to route outbound traffic.

Traffic can also be load balanced over both links. In this case, BGP should be used to route outbound traffic.

Internet routing information must also be available to the organization's internal routing protocol. In simple networks, static routes with different ADs (called floating static routes) can be used. Alternatively, you can redistribute a default route or a subset of Internet routes into your internal routing protocol. When using redistribution between BGP and IGP, you have to be careful because BGP can process many more routes than IGP protocols.

First-hop redundancy protocols (FHRPs) can also be used to properly route packets to the appropriate Internet gateway. Supported FHRPs are Cisco's Hot Standby Router

Protocol (HSRP) and Gateway Load Balancing Protocol (GLBP), in addition to the standard Virtual Router Redundancy Protocol (VRRP).

Figure 6-18 shows a network in which a default static route is redistributed into EIGRP.

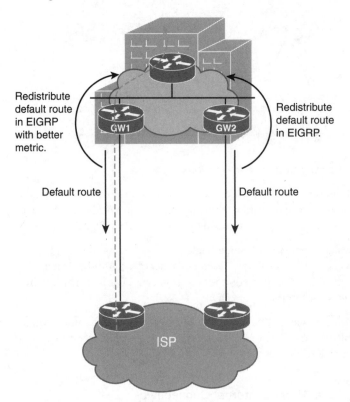

Figure 6-18   *Redistributing Default Routes with Dual-Homed Internet Connectivity*

Example 6-25 provides the configuration of the GW1 and GW2 routers.

Example 6-25   *Configuration of GW1 and GW2 Routers*

```
!GW1 has default route to one ISP router
ip route 0.0.0.0 0.0.0.0 209.165.201.129
router eigrp 1
 redistribute static metric 20000 1 255 1 1500

!GW2 has default route to the other ISP router
ip route 0.0.0.0 0.0.0.0 209.165.202.129
router eigrp 1
 redistribute static metric 10000 1 255 1 1500
```

Both Internet border routers (GW1 and GW2) advertise the default route, but notice that the first number in the **redistribute** command is different; this is the **bandwidth** parameter used in EIGRP metric calculations. The primary router, GW1, has a higher bandwidth and therefore advertises the better route so that traffic goes through it. If this router fails, traffic is redirected to the secondary router, GW2.

Multihomed Internet Connectivity

The multihomed Internet design offers the highest level of redundancy. It resolves all single points of failure issues and provides a reliable link to the Internet. As illustrated in Figure 6-19, two routers are commonly used as Internet gateways, and each router is connected to a different ISP using one or more physical links.

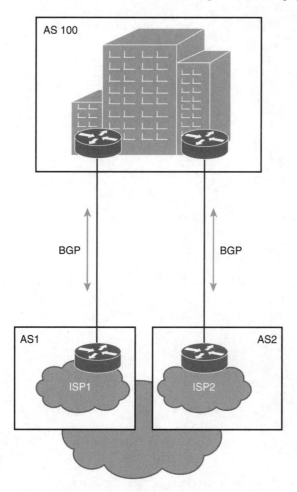

Figure 6-19 *A Multihomed Internet Connectivity Design Connects to Two ISPs*

Establishing a multihomed environment involves meeting some requirements:

- You must have PI address space and your own autonomous system number.

- You must establish connectivity with two independent ISPs.

The Internet gateways use BGP to advertise your PI address space to both ISPs and to learn routes from both ISPs. Figure 6-20 illustrates some of the options for the routes which the ISPs can send. The ISPs advertise your PI address space to all other devices.

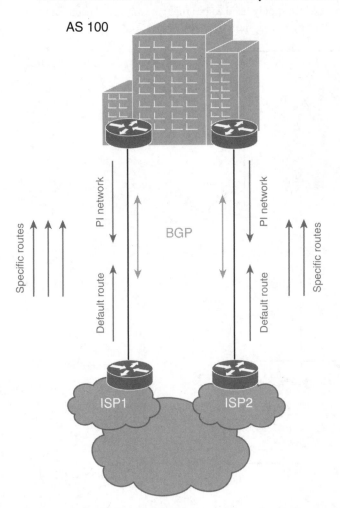

Figure 6-20   *Options for Routes That ISPs in a Multihomed Design Can Send*

The ISPs can send the following to your network:

- The ISPs can send only a default route. Your border Internet routers then typically select one default route as the best, and send all traffic to that ISP.

- The ISPs can send a partial routing table (of a subset of routes originated near the ISP) and a default route. This option allows you to use all the links to the ISPs. In this case, the border Internet routers calculate the best paths to each destination and use this for optimal routing. In Figure 6-19, for example, traffic to customers connected to ISP1 will usually be routed to ISP1, and traffic to customers connected to ISP2 will be redirected to ISP2.

- The ISPs could also send you a full routing table. In this case, your border Internet gateways calculate optimal paths for all Internet traffic.

When configuring your border Internet gateways, be careful. Route filtering is usually required both inbound and outbound. For example, if you do not filter your outbound routing information, your routes will be advertised to all ISPs, and your network may became a transit network. In other words, traffic from one ISP to another ISP may flow through your network, which is not a desirable result!

Receiving partial or full BGP routing updates from ISPs has important implications for your network. The more routing information the BGP process on your router receives, the more accurate and optimal routing paths it can calculate. Better routing information provides better link utilization, as well.

However, there are also disadvantages. BGP configuration can be complex, and full routing tables consume a lot of router resources. In 2009, there were about 300,000 IPv4 prefixes in a full routing table; by 2014, this number had grown to approximately 500,000! When IPv6 prefixes are also added, there will be even larger numbers of routes. All of this data has to be stored in RAM and processed by the CPU when calculating best routes. Therefore, it is important to plan for enough resources on your border Internet gateways. For example, to store the full IPv4 routing table, at least 2 GB of RAM is suggested on Cisco IOS devices; IOS XE routers need even more RAM.

Summary

This chapter covered how enterprises can connect to the Internet through discussion of the following topics:

- Internet connectivity requirements: outbound only, or also inbound.

- Internet connectivity redundancy options: edge device, link, and ISP.

- The four connection redundancy types:

  - **Single-homed:** One connection to one ISP

  - **Dual-homed:** Two connections to one ISP

  - **Multihomed:** One connection to each of multiple (usually two) ISPs

  - **Dual multihomed:** Two connections to each of two ISPs

- Public IP address assignment: The IANA assigns to RIRs; RIRs assign to ISPs and organizations.

- IP addresses, which can be PI or PA.

- Routing protocols that are either IGPs (and operate within an autonomous system) or EGPs (and operate between autonomous systems). BGP is the protocol used between autonomous systems on the Internet.

- The range of private autonomous system numbers: 64,512 to 65,534 and 4,200,000,000 through 4,294,967,294 (64,086.59904 through 65,535.65534).

- Provider-assigned IPv4 addresses, which can be configured statically or via DHCP.

- DHCPv4 operation, including the DHCPDISCOVER, DHCPOFFER, DHCPREQUEST, and DHCPACK messages.

- The use of NAT for IPv4, typically to translate private addresses to public addresses.

- The four types of NAT addresses:

  - **Inside local address:** The IPv4 address assigned to a device on the internal network.

  - **Inside global address:** The IPv4 address of an internal device as it appears to the external network. This is the address to which the inside local address is translated.

  - **Outside local address:** The IPv4 address of an external device as it appears to the internal network. If outside addresses are being translated, this is the address to which the outside global address is translated.

  - **Outside global address:** The IPv4 address assigned to a device on the external network.

- The three types of NAT: static (one-to-one), dynamic (many-to-many), and PAT (many-to-one).

- The order of operations for NAT: It first performs routing and then translation when going from an inside interface to an outside interface, and vice versa when the traffic flow is reversed.

- NAT issues, including when an inside device tries to communicate with a device on another inside interface.

- NVI, which removes the requirement to configure an interface as inside or outside. NVI also operates differently; it performs routing, translation, and routing again. The whole process is symmetrical, no matter which way the traffic is flowing.

- Configuring a Cisco router to be a DHCP server and a DHCP relay agent, for both IPv4 and IPv6.

- IPv6 addresses, which can be configured with the following methods:

  - Manual Assignment

  - SLAAC

- Stateless DHCPv6

- Stateful DHCPv6

- DHCPv6-PD

- DHCPv6 operation, including the SOLICIT, ADVERTISE, REQUEST, and REPLY messages.

- Two types of NAT for IPv6: NAT64 and NPTv6.

- IPv6 ACLs, which include three implicit rules at the end of each ACL, as follows:

  - **permit icmp any any nd-na**

  - **permit icmp any any nd-ns**

  - **deny ipv6 any any**

- Applying an IPv6 ACL to an interface, using the **ipv6 traffic-filter** *ACL-name* {**in|out**} interface configuration command. Notice the **traffic-filter** keyword is used rather than the **access-group** keyword that is used in IPv4 ACLs.

- The need to secure devices connected to the IPv6 Internet.

- The drawbacks of single-homed Internet connectivity because of the single points of failure: link failure, ISP failure, or router failure.

- Using a dual-homed design to improve redundancy: two (or more) connections, using one or more Internet routers, to the same ISP. The ISP may also have multiple routers to connect to specific customers. Static routes or BGP are used. One link can be primary, or traffic can be load balanced over both links.

- Using a multihomed design to further improve redundancy; two routers are used as Internet gateways, and each router is connected to a different ISP using one or more physical links.

- The options for what ISPs can send to your network in a multihomed design:

  - Only a default route

  - A partial routing table (of a subset of routes originated near the ISP) and a default route

  - A full routing table

- How receiving full routing tables consume a lot of router resources.

References

For additional information, see these resources:

- Cisco IOS Software Releases support page: http://www.cisco.com/cisco/web/psa/default.html?mode=prod&level0=268438303

- Cisco IOS Master Command List, All Releases: http://www.cisco.com/c/en/us/td/docs/ios/mcl/allreleasemcl/all_book.html

- "Explaining 4-Octet Autonomous System (AS) Numbers for Cisco IOS," at http://www.cisco.com/en/US/prod/collateral/iosswrel/ps6537/ps6554/ps6599/white_paper_C11_516823.html

- "NAT64 Technology: Connecting IPv6 and IPv4 Networks" at http://www.cisco.com/c/en/us/products/collateral/ios-nx-os-software/enterprise-ipv6-solution/white_paper_c11-676278.html

- "Why Would Anyone Need an IPv6-to-IPv6 Network Prefix Translator?" at http://blogs.cisco.com/enterprise/why-would-anyone-need-an-ipv6-to-ipv6-network-prefix-translator/

- "Cisco Live On-Demand Library" at https://www.ciscolive.com/online/connect/search.ww?cid=000052088

- "BRKRST-2667 - How to write an IPv6 Addressing Plan (2014 San Francisco)" Presentation at https://www.ciscolive.com/online/connect/sessionDetail.ww?SESSION_ID=78667&backBtn=true

- "NAT64 Technology: Connecting IPv6 and IPv4 Networks" at http://www.cisco.com/c/en/us/products/collateral/ios-nx-os-software/enterprise-ipv6-solution/white_paper_c11-676278.html

- Multihoming with IPv6-to-IPv6 Network Prefix Translation (NPTv6), draft-bonica-v6-multihome-03: http://tools.ietf.org/html/draft-bonica-v6-multihome-03

- RFCs are available at http://tools.ietf.org/html/

- "Autonomous System (AS) Numbers" at: http://www.iana.org/assignments/as-numbers/as-numbers.xhtml

Review Questions

Answer the following questions, and then see Appendix A, "Answers to Review Questions," for the answers.

1. What type of addresses are needed for inbound Internet connectivity so that clients external to an enterprise network can access resources in the enterprise network?

    a. Private only

    b. Public only

    c. Both private and public

    d. Either private or public, but not both

2. Which type of Internet connectivity provides the most redundancy?

    a. Single-homed
    b. Dual-homed
    c. Multihomed
    d. Dual multihomed

3. In which order are public IP addresses allocated?

    a. The IANA allocates to ISPs, which allocate to RIRs.
    b. The IANA allocates to RIRs, which allocate to ISPs.
    c. The RIRs allocates to the IANA, which allocates to ISPs.
    d. The RIRs allocates to ISPs, which allocate to the IANA.

4. What type of protocol is BGP?

    a. IGP
    b. EGP
    c. PI
    d. PA

5. Which command configures a router to be a DHCP client?

    a. (config)# **ip address client**
    b. (config-if)# **ip address client**
    c. (config-if)# **ip dhcp address**
    d. (config-if)# **ip address dhcp**
    e. (config)# **ip address dhcp**

6. You are configuring your router to be a DHCP relay agent. Which command should you use?

    a. Use the following command on the interface connected to the client: (config-if)# **ip helper-address** *server-address*
    b. Use the following command on the interface connected to the server: (config-if)# **ip helper-address** *server-address*
    c. Use the following command: (config)# **ip helper-address** *server-address*
    d. Use the following command on the interface connected to the client: (config-if)# **ip helper-address** *client-address*
    e. Use the following command on the interface connected to the server: (config-if)# **ip helper-address** *client-address*

7. Your router is configured to do NAT and is translating the address of a PC, 10.1.1.1, to the address 209.165.200.225. Which is the correct name for the 209.165.200.225 address?

    a. Inside local address
    b. Inside global address
    c. Outside local address
    d. Outside global address

8. Which of the following does many-to-many translation?

   a. Static NAT

   b. Dynamic NAT

   c. NAT overloading

   d. PAT

9. What does PAT use to distinguish between sessions that use the same address?

   a. Source port number

   b. Destination port number

   c. Protocol number

   d. Type code

10. You are configuring your router to do NVI so that a PC can connect to the Internet. Which command do you configure on the interface connected to the PC?

   a. ip nat inside

   b. ip nat outside

   c. ip nat enable

   d. ip nat nvi

11. Which is the corresponding NAT term for the NVI term *source local*?

   a. Inside local address

   b. Inside global address

   c. Outside local address

   d. Outside global address

12. Which command configures a router to obtain its address via SLAAC?

   a. (config-if)# **ipv6 address slaac**

   b. (config-if)# **ipv6 address autoconfig**

   c. (config-if)# **ipv6 address dhcp**

   d. (config-if)# **ipv6 address dhcpv6**

13. Which command configures a router to obtain its address via stateless DHCPv6?

   a. (config-if)# **ipv6 address slaac**

   b. (config-if)# **ipv6 address autoconfig**

   c. (config-if)# **ipv6 address dhcp**

   d. (config-if)# **ipv6 address dhcpv6**

14. Which command configures a router to obtain its address via stateful DHCPv6?

   a. (config-if)# **ipv6 address slaac**

   b. (config-if)# **ipv6 address autoconfig**

   c. (config-if)# **ipv6 address dhcp**

   d. (config-if)# **ipv6 address dhcpv6**

15. Which protocol would you use to provide IPv4 Internet connectivity to IPv6 devices?

a. NAT-PT

b. NAT64

c. NPTv6

d. PAT

16. You have created an IPv6 ACL called mylist. Which command would you configure to use this ACL to check inbound packets on an interface?

a. ipv6 traffic-filter mylist in

b. ipv6 access-class mylist in

c. ipv6 access-group mylist in

d. ipv6 access-list mylist in

17. Which rules are implicit at the end of every IPv6 ACL?

a. permit icmp any any nd-na; permit icmp any any nd-ns; permit ipv6 any any

b. deny icmp any any nd-na; deny icmp any any nd-ns; permit ipv6 any any

c. permit icmp any any nd-na; permit icmp any any nd-ns; deny ipv6 any any

d. deny icmp any any nd-na; deny icmp any any nd-ns; deny ipv6 any any

18. Which is a characteristic of dual-homed connectivity?

a. Single point of failure due to link failure

b. Single point of failure due to ISP failure

c. No single points of failure

d. Use of two ISPs

19. Approximately how many IPv4 routes are in the full Internet routing table (in 2014)?

a. 10,000

b. 100,000

c. 300,000

d. 500,000

Chapter 7

BGP Implementation

This chapter covers the following topics:

- BGP Terminology, Concepts, and Operation
- Implementing Basic BGP
- BGP Attributes and the Path-Selection Process
- Controlling BGP Routing Updates
- Implementing BGP for IPv6 Internet Connectivity

As described in Chapter 6, "Enterprise Internet Connectivity," enterprises may use the Border Gateway Protocol (BGP) when connecting to their Internet service providers (ISPs).

Configuring and troubleshooting BGP can be complex. A BGP administrator must understand the various options involved in properly configuring BGP for scalable internetworking. This chapter focuses on how enterprises can use BGP when connecting to the Internet. BGP terminology and concepts are introduced, and BGP configuration, verification, and troubleshooting techniques are provided. The chapter also describes BGP attributes and how they can be configured to control the BGP path-selection process. Various tools for manipulating BGP updates are introduced. The chapter concludes by exploring BGP for IPv6 Internet connectivity.

Note The term *IP* is used for generic IP and applies to both IP Version 4 (IPv4) and IPv6. Otherwise, the terms *IPv4* and *IPv6* are used for the specific protocols.

BGP Terminology, Concepts, and Operation

This section provides an introduction to BGP and an explanation of various BGP terminology and concepts, including the following:

- Using BGP between autonomous systems

- Comparing BGP with other scalable routing protocols

- BGP path vector characteristics

- BGP characteristics

- BGP tables

- BGP message types

- When to use BGP

- When not to use BGP

BGP Use Between Autonomous Systems

Recall from Chapter 6 that an Exterior Gateway Protocol (EGP) is a routing protocol that exchanges routing information between different autonomous systems. BGP is an example of an EGP and is a very robust and scalable routing protocol; BGP is the routing protocol used on the Internet. Figure 7-1 illustrates the use of BGP between autonomous systems.

The main goal of BGP is to provide an interdomain routing system that guarantees the loop-free exchange of routing information between autonomous systems. BGP routers exchange information about paths to destination networks.

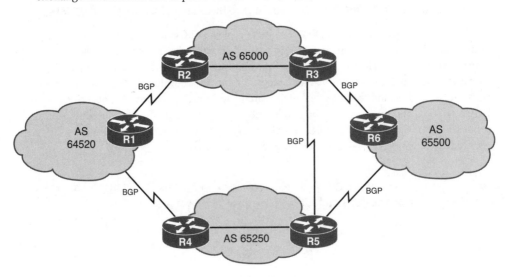

Figure 7-1   *BGP Is Used Between Autonomous Systems*

Note   BGP is a successor to an earlier protocol that was called simply Exterior Gateway Protocol (EGP). (Note the dual use of EGP.) This original EGP was developed to isolate networks from each other at the early stages of the Internet.

ISPs and their customers, such as universities, corporations, and other enterprises, usually use an Interior Gateway Protocol (IGP) such as Open Shortest Path First (OSPF) Protocol or Enhanced Interior Gateway Routing Protocol (EIGRP) for the exchange of routing information within their networks. Any communication between these enterprises and the Internet or between the ISPs is accomplished by BGP.

Note   A distinction exists between an ordinary autonomous system and one that has been configured with BGP to implement a transit policy. The latter is called an ISP or a service provider (SP).

BGP's interdomain routing enables connectivity between autonomous systems and is usually based on a set of policies, not just the technical characteristics of the underlying infrastructure. This capability differentiates BGP from the IGPs, which focus only on finding the optimum (usually fastest) route between two points, without respect to routing policies.

Comparison with Other Scalable Routing Protocols

BGP works differently than IGPs. Table 7-1 compares some of BGP's key characteristics to the other scalable IP routing protocols discussed in this book.

Table 7-1   *Comparison of Scalable Routing Protocols*

Protocol	Interior or Exterior	Type	Hierarchy Required?	Metric
OSPF	Interior	Link state	Yes	Cost
EIGRP	Interior	Advanced distance vector	No	Composite
BGP	Exterior	Path vector	No	Path vectors (attributes)

As shown in Table 7-1, OSPF and EIGRP are interior protocols, whereas BGP is an exterior protocol.

OSPF is a link-state protocol, whereas EIGRP is an advanced distance vector protocol. BGP is also a distance vector protocol, with many enhancements; it is usually called a path vector protocol.

Link-state routing protocols, including OSPF, require a hierarchical design as the network expands, especially to support proper address summarization. For OSPF, this hierarchical design is implemented by separating a large internetwork into smaller internetworks called areas. EIGRP and BGP do not require a hierarchical topology.

Internal routing protocols look at the path metric to get somewhere and choose the best path from one point in a corporate network to another based on certain metrics. OSPF uses cost, which on Cisco routers is based on bandwidth, as its metric. EIGRP uses a composite metric, with bandwidth and accumulated delay considered by default.

In contrast, BGP does not look at bandwidth for the best path. Rather, BGP is a policy-based routing protocol that allows an autonomous system to control traffic flow using multiple BGP attributes. Routers running BGP exchange network reachability information, called path vectors or attributes, including a list of the full path of BGP autonomous system numbers that a router should take to reach a destination network. BGP allows an organization to fully use all of its bandwidth by manipulating these path attributes.

BGP Path Vector Characteristics

Internal routing protocols announce a list of networks along with the metric to get to each network. In contrast, BGP routers exchange network reachability information, called path vectors, made up of path attributes, as illustrated in Figure 7-2. The path vector information includes a list of the full path of BGP autonomous system numbers (hop by hop) necessary to reach a destination network; this is the *AS-path* attribute. Other attributes include the IP address to get to the next autonomous system (the *next-hop* attribute) and how the networks at the end of the path were introduced into BGP (the *origin code* attribute). The "BGP Attributes" section, later in this chapter, describes all the BGP attributes in detail.

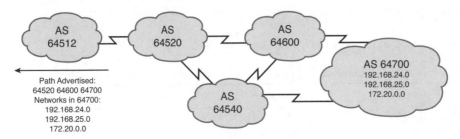

Figure 7-2 *BGP Uses Path Vector Routing*

The autonomous system path information is used to construct a graph of loop-free autonomous systems and to identify routing policies so that restrictions on routing behavior can be enforced based on the autonomous system path.

The BGP autonomous system path is guaranteed to always be loop free: A router running BGP does not accept a routing update that already includes its autonomous system number in the path list because the update has already passed through its autonomous system, and accepting it again would result in a routing loop.

BGP is designed to scale to huge internetworks, such as the Internet.

BGP allows routing-policy decisions to be applied to the path of BGP autonomous system numbers so that routing behavior can be enforced at the autonomous system level and to determine how data will flow through the autonomous system. These policies can be implemented for all networks owned by an autonomous system, for a certain classless interdomain routing (CIDR) block of network numbers (prefixes), or for individual networks or subnetworks. The policies are based on the attributes carried in the routing information and configured on the routers.

BGP specifies that a BGP router can advertise to its peers (neighbors) in neighboring autonomous systems only those routes that it uses. This rule reflects the hop-by-hop routing paradigm generally used throughout the current Internet. Some policies cannot be supported by the hop-by-hop routing paradigm. For example, BGP does not allow one autonomous system to send traffic to a neighboring autonomous system, intending that the traffic take a different route from that taken by traffic originating in that neighboring autonomous system. In other words, you cannot influence how a neighboring autonomous system will route your traffic, but you can influence how your traffic gets to a neighboring autonomous system. However, BGP can support any policy conforming to the hop-by-hop routing paradigm.

Because the current Internet uses only the hop-by-hop routing paradigm, and because BGP can support any policy that conforms to that paradigm, BGP is highly applicable as an inter-autonomous system routing protocol for the current Internet.

For example, in Figure 7-3, the following are some of the paths possible for autonomous system 64512 to reach networks in autonomous system 64700 through autonomous system 64520:

- 64520 64600 64700

- 64520 64600 64540 64550 64700

- 64520 64540 64600 64700

- 64520 64540 64550 64700

Autonomous system 64512 does not see all these possibilities. Autonomous system 64520 advertises to autonomous system 64512 only its best path (in this case, 64520 64600 64700), the same way that IGPs announce only their best least-metric routes. This path is the only path through autonomous system 64520 that autonomous system 64512 sees. All packets that are destined for 64700 via 64520 take this path because it is the autonomous system-by-autonomous system (hop-by-hop) path that autonomous system 64520 uses to reach the networks in autonomous system 64700. Autonomous system 64520 does not announce the other paths, such as 64520 64540 64600 64700, because it does not choose any of those paths as the best path, based on the BGP routing policy in autonomous system 64520.

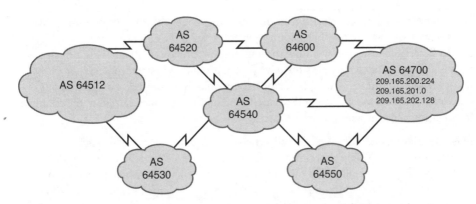

Figure 7-3   *BGP Supports the Internet's Hop-by-Hop Routing Paradigm*

Autonomous system 64512 does not learn of the second-best path, or any other paths from 64520, unless the best path through autonomous system 64520 becomes unavailable.

Even if autonomous system 64512 were aware of another path through autonomous system 64520 and wanted to use it, autonomous system 64520 would not route packets along that other path because autonomous system 64520 selected 64520 64600 64700 as its best path, and all autonomous system 64520 routers will use that path as a matter of BGP policy. BGP does not let one autonomous system send traffic to a neighboring autonomous system, intending that the traffic take a different route from that taken by traffic originating in the neighboring autonomous system.

To reach the networks in autonomous system 64700, autonomous system 64512 can choose to use the path through autonomous system 64520 or it can choose to go through the path that autonomous system 64530 is advertising. Autonomous system 64512 selects the best path to take based on its own BGP routing policies.

BGP Characteristics

What type of protocol is BGP? BGP is sometimes categorized as an advanced distance vector protocol, but it is actually a path vector protocol. BGP has many differences from standard distance vector protocols, such as the Routing Information Protocol (RIP).

BGP uses the Transmission Control Protocol (TCP) as its transport protocol, which provides connection-oriented reliable delivery. In this way, BGP assumes that its communication is reliable and, therefore, BGP does not have to implement any retransmission or error-recovery mechanisms, like EIGRP does. BGP information is carried inside TCP segments using port 179; these segments are carried inside IP packets. Figure 7-4 illustrates this concept.

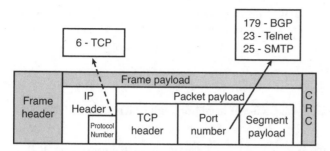

Figure 7-4 *BGP Is Carried Inside TCP Segments, Which Are Inside IP Packets*

Two routers speaking BGP (called *BGP speakers*) establish a TCP connection with one another and exchange messages to open and confirm the connection parameters. These two routers are called BGP *peer* routers or BGP *neighbors*.

After the TCP connection is made, the routers exchange their full BGP tables (described in the upcoming "BGP Tables" section). However, because the connection is reliable, BGP routers need to send only changes (incremental updates) after that. Periodic routing updates are not required on a reliable link, so triggered updates are used. BGP sends keepalive messages, similar to the hello messages sent by OSPF and EIGRP.

BGP is the only IP routing protocol to use TCP as its transport layer. OSPF and EIGRP reside directly above the IP layer, and RIP uses the User Datagram Protocol (UDP) for its transport layer. OSPF and EIGRP have their own internal functions to ensure that update packets are explicitly acknowledged. These protocols use a one-for-one window so that if either OSPF or EIGRP has multiple packets to send, the next packet cannot be sent until an acknowledgment from the first update packet is received. This process can be very inefficient and cause latency issues if thousands of update packets must be exchanged over relatively slow serial links. However, OSPF and EIGRP rarely have thousands of update packets to send. For example, EIGRP can hold more than 100 networks in one EIGRP update packet, so 100 EIGRP update packets can hold up to 10,000 networks. Most organizations do not have 10,000 subnets.

BGP, however, has many more networks on the Internet to advertise (as of 2014 there were 500,000, and growing); it uses TCP to handle the acknowledgment function. TCP uses a dynamic window, which allows for up to 65,576 bytes to be outstanding before it stops and waits for an acknowledgment. For example, if 1000-byte packets are being sent and the maximum window size is being used, BGP would have to stop and wait for an acknowledgment only if 65 packets had not been acknowledged.

Note The CIDR report, at http://www.cidr-report.org/, is a good reference site to see the current size of the Internet routing tables and other related information.

TCP is designed to use a sliding window, where the receiver sends an acknowledgment before the number of octets specified by the window have been received (such as the halfway point of the sending window). This method allows any TCP application, such as BGP, to continue streaming packets without having to stop and wait, as OSPF or EIGRP would require.

BGP Tables

BGP keeps a neighbor table containing a list of neighbors with which it has a BGP connection.

As shown in Figure 7-5, a router running BGP also keeps its own table for storing BGP information received from and sent to other routers.

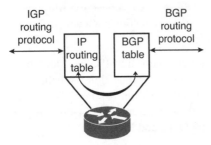

Figure 7-5   *A Router Running BGP Keeps a BGP Table, Separate from the IP Routing Table*

This table of BGP information is known by many names in various documents, including the following:

- BGP table
- BGP topology table
- BGP topology database
- BGP routing table
- BGP forwarding database

It is important to remember that this BGP table is separate from the IP routing table in the router.

The router offers the best routes from the BGP table to the IP routing table and can be configured to share information between the two tables (by redistribution).

For BGP to establish an adjacency, you must configure it explicitly for each neighbor. BGP forms a TCP relationship with each of the configured neighbors and keeps track of the state of these relationships by periodically sending a BGP/TCP keepalive message.

Note   BGP sends BGP/TCP keepalives by default every 60 seconds.

After establishing an adjacency, the neighbors exchange their best BGP routes. Each router collects these routes from each neighbor with which it successfully established an adjacency and places them in its BGP table; all routes that have been learned from each neighbor are placed in the BGP table. Each path learned is associated with BGP attributes. The single best route for each network is selected from the BGP table using these attributes in the BGP route-selection process (discussed in the section "BGP Path Selection," later in this chapter) and then offered to the IP routing table. (As described in the referenced section, one of the criteria for being selected as the best BGP route is that the next-hop IP address is reachable. Therefore, BGP routes with an unreachable next hop will not be propagated to other routers.)

Each router compares the offered BGP routes to any other possible paths to those networks in its IP routing table, and the best route, based on administrative distance, is installed in the IP routing table. External BGP (eBGP) routes (BGP routes learned from an external autonomous system) have a default administrative distance of 20. Internal BGP (iBGP) routes (BGP routes learned from within the autonomous system) have a default administrative distance of 200.

A router may have a best BGP route to a destination, but that route might not be installed in the IP routing table because it has a higher administrative distance than another route. That best BGP route will still be propagated to other BGP routers, though.

Note   A route does not have to be in the IP routing table for BGP to advertise it. BGP advertises the best route from the BGP table.

BGP Message Types

BGP defines the following message types, as described in this section:

- Open
- Keepalive
- Update
- Notification

Note   Keepalive messages have a length of 19 bytes. Other messages may be between 19 and 4096 bytes long.

Open and Keepalive Messages

After a TCP connection is established, the first message sent by each side is an open message. If the open message is acceptable, a keepalive message confirming the open message is sent back by the side that received the open message.

When the open is confirmed, the BGP connection is established, and update, keepalive, and notification messages can be exchanged.

BGP peers initially exchange their full BGP routing tables. From then on, incremental updates are sent as the table changes. Keepalive packets are sent to ensure that the connection is alive between the BGP peers, and notification packets are sent in response to errors or special conditions.

An open message includes the following information:

- **Version:** This 8-bit field indicates the message's BGP version number. The highest common version that both routers support is used. BGP implementations today use the current version, BGP-4.

- **My autonomous system:** This 16-bit field indicates the sender's autonomous system number. The peer router verifies this information; if it is not the autonomous system number expected, then the BGP session is torn down.

- **Hold time:** This 16-bit field indicates the maximum number of seconds that can elapse between the successive keepalive or update messages from the sender. Upon receipt of an open message, the router calculates the value of the hold timer to use with this neighbor by using the smaller of its configured hold time (which has a default of 180 seconds) and the hold time received in the open message.

Note   A minimum hold time can be configured. If the received hold time is lower than the minimum hold time, a neighbor relationship will not be formed.

- **BGP router identifier (router ID):** This 32-bit field indicates the sender's BGP identifier. The BGP router ID is an IP address assigned to that router and is determined at startup. The BGP router ID is chosen the same way the OSPF router ID is chosen: It is the highest active IP address on the router, unless a loopback interface with an IP address exists, in which case it is the highest such loopback IP address. Alternatively, the router ID can be statically configured, overriding the automatic selection.

- **Optional parameters:** A length field indicates the total length of the optional parameters field in octets. These parameters are Type, Length, and Value (TLV) encoded. An example of an optional parameter is session authentication.

BGP does not use any transport protocol-based keepalive mechanism to determine whether peers can be reached. Instead, BGP keepalive messages are exchanged between peers often enough to keep the hold timer from expiring. If the negotiated hold time interval is 0, periodic keepalive messages are not sent. Keepalive messages consist of only a message header and have a length of 19 bytes; they are sent every 60 seconds by default.

Update Messages

An update message has information on one path only; multiple paths require multiple messages. All the attributes in the update message refer to that path, and the networks are those that can be reached through that path. An update message might include the following fields:

- **Withdrawn routes:** A list of IP address prefixes for routes that are being withdrawn from service, if any.

- **Path attributes:** The AS-path, origin, local preference, and so forth, as discussed in the "BGP Attributes" section later in this chapter. Each path attribute includes the attribute type, attribute length, and attribute value (TLV). The attribute type consists of the attribute flags, followed by the attribute type code.

- **Network layer reachability information (NLRI):** A list of networks (IP address prefixes and their prefix lengths) that can be reached by this path.

Notification Messages

A BGP router sends a notification message when it detects an error condition. The BGP router closes the BGP connection immediately after sending the notification message. Notification messages include an error code, an error subcode, and data related to the error.

BGP Neighbor States

BGP is a state machine that takes a router through the following states with its neighbors:

- Idle
- Connect
- Active
- Open sent
- Open confirm
- Established

Only when the connection is in the established state are update, keepalive, and notification messages exchanged.

Neighbor states are discussed in more detail in the "Understanding and Troubleshooting BGP Neighbor States" section, later in this chapter.

When to Use BGP

BGP use in an autonomous system is most appropriate when the effects of BGP are well understood and at least one of the following conditions exists:

- The autonomous system allows packets to transit through it to reach other autonomous systems (for example, it is a service provider).

- The autonomous system has multiple connections to other autonomous systems.

- Routing policy and route selection for traffic entering and leaving the autonomous system must be manipulated.

If an enterprise wants its traffic to be differentiated from its ISP's traffic on the Internet, the enterprise must connect to its ISP using BGP. If, instead, an enterprise is connected to its ISP with a static route, traffic from that enterprise on the Internet is indistinguishable from traffic from the ISP.

BGP was designed to allow ISPs to communicate and exchange packets. These ISPs have multiple connections to one another and have agreements to exchange updates. BGP is the protocol that is used to implement these agreements between two or more autonomous systems. If BGP is not properly controlled and filtered, it has the potential to allow an outside autonomous system to affect the traffic flow to your autonomous system. For example, if you are a customer connected to ISP A and ISP B (for redundancy), you want to implement a routing policy to ensure that ISP A does not send traffic to ISP B via your autonomous system. You want to be able to receive traffic destined for your autonomous system through each ISP, but you do not want to waste valuable resources and bandwidth within your autonomous system to route traffic for your ISPs.

When Not to Use BGP

BGP is not always the appropriate solution to interconnect autonomous systems. For example, if there is only one exit path from the autonomous system, a default or static route is appropriate. Using BGP will not accomplish anything except to use router CPU resources and memory. If the routing policy that will be implemented in an autonomous system is consistent with the policy implemented in the ISP autonomous system, it is not necessary or even desirable to configure BGP in that autonomous system. The only time BGP will be required is when the local policy differs from the ISP policy.

Do not use BGP if one or more of the following conditions exist:

- A single connection to the Internet or another autonomous system.

- Lack of memory or processor power on edge routers to handle constant BGP updates.

- You have a limited understanding of route filtering and the BGP path-selection process.

- If the routing policy that will be implemented in an autonomous system is consistent with the policy implemented in the ISP autonomous system.

In these cases, use static or default routes instead, as discussed in Chapter 1, "Basic Network and Routing Concepts."

Implementing Basic BGP

This section introduces BGP neighbor relationships and how they are established. Basic BGP configuration and verification is explored, and this section also covers some BGP attributes and monitoring of BGP operation. This section also describes the neighbor states through which BGP progresses to establish a BGP session and how to use knowledge of these states when troubleshooting BGP. The commands used to clear BGP sessions, needed after a policy change is implemented, are also explained. Specifically, the sections that follow address all of these topics:

- BGP neighbor relationships

- Basic BGP configuration requirements

- Entering BGP configuration mode

- Defining BGP neighbors and activating BGP sessions

- Basic BGP configuration and verification

BGP Neighbor Relationships

No single router can handle communications with the tens of thousands of the routers that run BGP and are connected to the Internet, representing more than 48,000 autonomous systems (at the time of this writing). A BGP router forms a direct neighbor relationship with a limited number of other BGP routers. Through these BGP neighbors, a BGP router learns of the paths through the Internet to reach any advertised network.

Recall that any router that runs BGP is called a BGP speaker. A BGP peer, also known as a BGP neighbor, is a BGP speaker that is configured to form a neighbor relationship with another BGP speaker for the purpose of directly exchanging BGP routing information with one another.

A BGP speaker has a limited number of BGP neighbors with which it peers and forms a TCP-based relationship, as illustrated in Figure 7-6. BGP peers can be either internal or external to the autonomous system. Both types of neighbors require a TCP connection to be established.

Note   A BGP peer must be configured under the BGP process with a **neighbor remote-as** command. This command instructs the BGP process to establish a relationship with the neighbor at the address listed in the command and to exchange BGP routing updates with that neighbor. This command is described in the upcoming "Defining BGP Neighbors and Activating BGP Sessions" section.

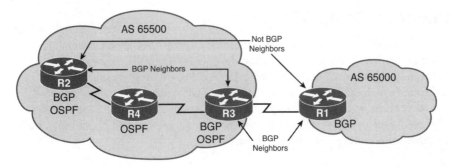

Figure 7-6 *Routers That Have Formed a BGP Connection Are BGP Neighbors or Peers*

External BGP Neighbors

When BGP is running between routers in different autonomous systems, it is called external BGP. Routers running eBGP are usually directly connected to each other, as shown in Figure 7-7.

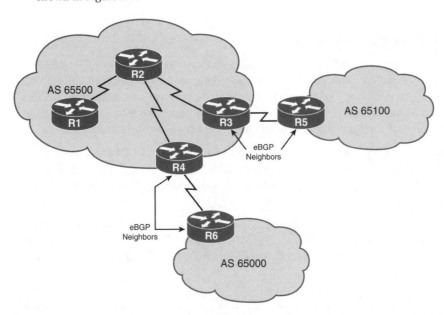

Figure 7-7 *eBGP Neighbors Belong to Different Autonomous Systems*

An eBGP neighbor is a router running in a different autonomous system. An IGP is not run between the eBGP neighbors. For two routers to exchange BGP routing updates, the TCP transport layer on each side must successfully pass the TCP three-way handshake before the BGP session can be established. Therefore, the IP address used in the **neighbor** command must be reachable without using an IGP. This can be accomplished by pointing at an address that can be reached through a directly connected network or by configuring a static route to that IP address. Generally, the neighbor address used is the address of the directly connected network.

An enterprise network can have a connection to one or several ISPs, and the ISPs themselves might be connected to several other ISPs. For each such connection between different autonomous systems, an eBGP is session required between eBGP neighboring routers. In Figure 7-7, an eBGP relationship is established between routers R4 and R6, and another eBGP relationship is established between routers R3 and R5. The neighbors will then exchange BGP routing updates with one another. In Figure 7-7, the autonomous system 65500 routers learn the paths to the external autonomous systems from their respective eBGP neighbors.

There are several requirements for an eBGP neighbor relationship (also called an eBGP neighborship):

- **Different autonomous system number:** eBGP neighbors must reside in different autonomous systems to be able to form an eBGP relationship.

- **Define neighbors:** A TCP session must be established before starting BGP routing update exchanges.

- **Reachability:** The IP addresses used in the **neighbor** command must be reachable; eBGP neighbors are usually directly connected.

Note   If a BGP neighbor is not directly connected, a router must have a route to the neighbor's address installed in its routing table; a default route does not suffice for this use.

Internal BGP Neighbors

When BGP is running between routers within the same autonomous system, it is called internal BGP. iBGP is run within an autonomous system to exchange BGP information so that all internal BGP speakers have the same BGP routing information about outside autonomous systems and so this information can be passed to other autonomous systems.

There are several requirements for an iBGP neighbor relationship (also known as an iBGP neighborship):

- **Same autonomous system number:** iBGP neighbors must reside in the same autonomous system to be able to form an iBGP relationship.

- **Define neighbors:** A TCP session must be established between neighbors before they start exchanging BGP routing updates.

- **Reachability:** iBGP neighbors must be reachable. An IGP typically runs inside the autonomous system, and provides this reachability.

Routers running iBGP do not have to be directly connected to each other, as long as they can reach each other so that TCP handshaking can be performed to set up the BGP neighbor relationships. The iBGP neighbor can be reached by a directly connected network, static routes, or an internal routing protocol. Because multiple paths generally exist within an autonomous system to reach other routers, a loopback address is usually used in the BGP **neighbor** command to establish the iBGP sessions.

For example, in Figure 7-8, routers R1, R4, and R3 learn the paths to the external autonomous systems from their respective eBGP neighbors (routers R7, R6, and R5). If the link between routers R4 and R6 goes down, router R4 must learn new routes to the external autonomous systems. Other BGP routers within autonomous system 65500 that were using router R4 to get to external networks must also be informed that the path through router R4 is unavailable. Those BGP routers within autonomous system 65500 need to have the alternative paths through routers R1 and R3 in their BGP topology database.

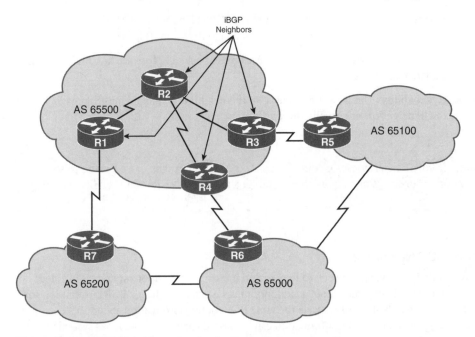

Figure 7-8   *iBGP Neighbors Are in the Same Autonomous System*

As described in the next section, you must set up a full mesh of iBGP sessions between all routers in the transit path in autonomous system 65500 so that each router in the transit path within the autonomous system learns about paths to the external networks via iBGP.

iBGP on All Routers in a Transit Path

This section explains why iBGP route propagation requires all routers in the transit path in an autonomous system to run full-meshed iBGP.

iBGP in a Transit Autonomous System

BGP was originally intended to run along the borders of an autonomous system, with the routers in the middle of the autonomous system ignorant of the details of BGP—hence the name *Border Gateway* Protocol. A transit autonomous system, such as autonomous system 65102 in Figure 7-9, is an autonomous system that routes traffic from one external autonomous system to another external autonomous system. As mentioned earlier, transit autonomous systems are typically ISPs. All routers in a transit autonomous system must have complete knowledge of external routes. Theoretically, one way to achieve this goal is to redistribute BGP routes into an IGP at the edge routers; however, this approach has problems.

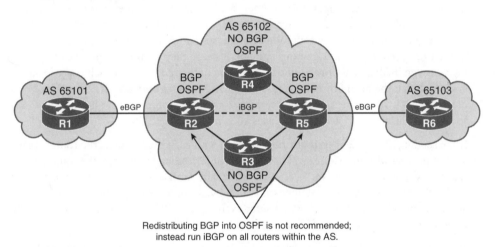

Redistributing BGP into OSPF is not recommended;
instead run iBGP on all routers within the AS.

Figure 7-9 *BGP in a Transit Autonomous System*

Because the current Internet routing table is very large, redistributing all the BGP routes into an IGP is not a scalable way for the interior routers within an autonomous system to learn about the external networks. Another method that you can use is to run iBGP on all routers within the autonomous system.

iBGP in a Nontransit Autonomous System

A nontransit autonomous system, such as an organization that is multihoming with two ISPs, does not pass routes between the ISPs. To make proper routing decisions, however, the BGP routers within the autonomous system still require knowledge of all BGP routes passed to the autonomous system.

As discussed, BGP does not work in the same manner as IGPs. Because the designers of BGP could not guarantee that an autonomous system would run BGP on all routers, a method had to be developed to ensure that iBGP speakers could pass updates to one another while ensuring that no routing loops would exist.

TCP and Full Mesh

As mentioned earlier, TCP was selected as the transport layer for BGP because TCP can move a large volume of data reliably. With the very large full Internet routing table changing constantly, using TCP for windowing and reliability was determined to be the best solution, as opposed to developing a BGP one-for-one windowing capability like OSPF or EIGRP.

TCP sessions cannot be multicast or broadcast because TCP has to ensure the delivery of packets to each recipient. Because TCP cannot use broadcasting or multicasting, BGP cannot use it either.

To avoid routing loops within an autonomous system, BGP specifies that routes learned through iBGP are never propagated to other iBGP peers; this is sometimes referred to as the BGP split-horizon rule. Thus, each iBGP router needs to send routes to all the other iBGP neighbors in the same autonomous system (so that they all have a complete picture of the routes sent to the autonomous system). Because they cannot use broadcast or multicast, an iBGP neighbor relationship must be configured between each pair of routers. Recall that the **neighbor** command enables BGP updates between BGP speakers. By default, each BGP speaker is assumed to have a **neighbor** statement for all other iBGP speakers in the autonomous system; this is known as *full-mesh iBGP*.

If the sending iBGP neighbor is not fully meshed with each iBGP router, the routers that are not peering with this router will have different IP routing tables than the routers that are peering with it. The inconsistent routing tables can cause routing loops or routing black holes, because the default assumption by all routers running BGP within an autonomous system is that each BGP router exchanges iBGP information directly with all other BGP routers in the autonomous system.

When all iBGP neighbors are fully meshed and a change is received from an external autonomous system, the receiving BGP router in the local autonomous system is responsible for informing all of its iBGP neighbors of the change. iBGP neighbors that receive this update do not send it to any other iBGP neighbor because they assume that the sending iBGP neighbor is fully meshed with all other iBGP speakers and has sent each iBGP neighbor the update.

BGP Partial-Mesh and Full-Mesh Examples

The top network in Figure 7-10 illustrates iBGP update behavior in a partially meshed neighbor environment. Router R2 receives an eBGP update from router R1. Router R2 has two iBGP neighbors, routers R3 and R4, but does not have an iBGP neighbor relationship with router R5. Therefore, routers R3 and R4 learn about any networks that were added or withdrawn behind router R2. Even if routers R3 and R4 have iBGP neighbor sessions with router R5, they assume that the autonomous system is fully meshed for iBGP and do not replicate the update and send it to router R5. Sending the iBGP update to router R5 is router R2's responsibility because it is the router with firsthand knowledge of the networks in and beyond autonomous system 65101. So, router R5 does not learn of any networks through router R2 and does not use router R2 to reach any networks in autonomous system 65101 or other autonomous systems behind autonomous system 65101.

In the lower portion of Figure 7-10, iBGP is fully meshed. When router R2 receives an eBGP update from router R1, it updates all three of its iBGP peers, router R3, router R4, and router R5. OSPF, the IGP, is used to route the TCP segment containing the BGP update from router R2 to router R5, because these two routers are not directly connected. The update is sent once to each neighbor and not duplicated by any other iBGP neighbor (which also reduces unnecessary traffic). In fully meshed iBGP, each router assumes that every other internal router has a **neighbor** statement that points to each iBGP neighbor.

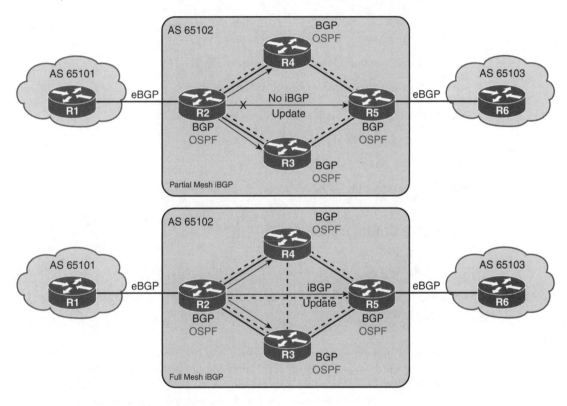

Figure 7-10 *Partial-Mesh Versus Full-Mesh iBGP*

> **Note**   BGP route reflectors are an alternative to running full-mesh iBGP and are discussed in Appendix C, "BGP Supplement."

When all routers running BGP in an autonomous system are fully meshed and have the same database as a result of a consistent routing policy, they can apply the same path-selection formula. The path-selection results will therefore be uniform across the autonomous system. Uniform path selection across the autonomous system means no routing loops and a consistent policy for exiting and entering the autonomous system.

Basic BGP Configuration Requirements

Before configuring BGP, a network administrator must define the network requirements, including the internal connectivity (for iBGP) and the external connectivity to the ISP (for eBGP).

The next step is to gather the parameters needed to provide the BGP configuration details. For basic BGP, these details include the following:

- The autonomous system numbers (of your own network and of all remote autonomous systems)

- The IP addresses of all the neighbors (peers) involved

- The networks that are to be advertised into BGP

Basic BGP configuration requires the following main steps:

Step 1.   Define the BGP process.

Step 2.   Establish the neighbor relationships.

Step 3.   Advertise the networks into BGP.

Entering BGP Configuration Mode

Note   The syntax of some BGP configuration commands is similar to the syntax of commands used to configure internal routing protocols. However, there are significant differences in how BGP functions.

Use the **router bgp** *autonomous-system* global configuration command to enter BGP configuration mode and identify the local autonomous system in which this router belongs. In the command, *autonomous-system* identifies the local autonomous system. The BGP process needs to be informed of its autonomous system so that when BGP neighbors are configured it can determine whether they are iBGP or eBGP neighbors.

The **router bgp** command alone does not activate BGP on a router. You must enter at least one subcommand under the **router bgp** command to activate the BGP process on the router.

Only one instance of BGP can be configured on a router at a time. For example, if you configure your router in autonomous system 65000 and then try to configure the **router bgp 65100** command, the router informs you that you are currently configured for autonomous system 65000.

Defining BGP Neighbors and Activating BGP Sessions

Use the **neighbor** *ip-address* **remote-as** *autonomous-system* router configuration command to activate a BGP session for external and internal neighbors and to identify a peer router with which the local router will establish a session, as described in Table 7-2.

Table 7-2   neighbor remote-as *Command Description*

Parameter	Description
ip-address	Identifies the peer router
autonomous-system	Identifies the peer router's autonomous system

The IP address used in the **neighbor remote-as** command is the destination address for all BGP packets going to this neighboring router. For a BGP relationship to be established, this address must be reachable, because BGP attempts to establish a TCP session and exchange BGP updates with the device at this IP address.

The value placed in the *autonomous-system* field of the **neighbor remote**-as command determines whether the communication with the neighbor is an eBGP or iBGP session. If the *autonomous-system* field configured in the **router bgp** command is identical to the field in the **neighbor remote-as** command, BGP initiates an internal session, and the IP address specified does not have to be directly connected. If the field values differ, BGP initiates an external session, and the IP address specified must be directly connected, by default.

The network shown in Figure 7-11 uses the BGP **neighbor** commands. Examples 7-1 through 7-3 show the configurations of routers R1, R2, and R3. Router R1 in autonomous system 65101 has two neighbor statements. In the first statement, **neighbor 10.2.2.2** (R2) is in the same autonomous system as router R1 (65101); this neighbor statement defines R2 as an iBGP neighbor. Autonomous system 65101 runs EIGRP between all internal routers. Router R1 has an EIGRP path to reach address 10.2.2.2. As an iBGP neighbor, R2 can be multiple routers away from R1.

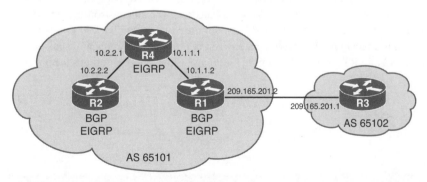

Figure 7-11   *BGP Network with iBGP and eBGP Neighbor Relationships*

Example 7-1 *Configuration of Router R1*

```
router bgp 65101
  neighbor 10.2.2.2 remote-as 65101
  neighbor 209.165.201.1 remote-as 65102
```

Example 7-2 *Configuration of Router R2*

```
router bgp 65101
  neighbor 10.1.1.2 remote-as 65101
```

Example 7-3 *Configuration of Router R3*

```
router bgp 65102
  neighbor 209.165.201.2 remote-as 65101
```

Router R1 in Figure 7-11 knows that router R3 is an external neighbor because the **neighbor** statement for R3 uses autonomous system 65102, which differs from the autonomous system number of R1, autonomous system 65101. Router R1 can reach autonomous system 65102 via 209.165.201.2, which is directly connected to R1.

Note   The network in Figure 7-11 is used just to illustrate the difference between configuring iBGP and eBGP sessions. As mentioned earlier, if router R2 connects to another autonomous system all routers in the transit path (R1, R4, and R2 in this figure) should be running fully meshed BGP.

Basic BGP Configuration and Verification

This section presents an example to illustrate how to configure and verify basic BGP.

Figure 7-12 displays the network diagram for this example. Internal and external BGP sessions will first be established, and network prefixes will be advertised via BGP. **Show** commands will be used to observe how BGP propagates and maintains routing information. BGP sessions will then be established between the router's loopback interface IP addresses; this is a technique for making an environment more resilient against link failures. Routers R2 and R3 are already running OSPF and can reach each other's loopback 0 address.

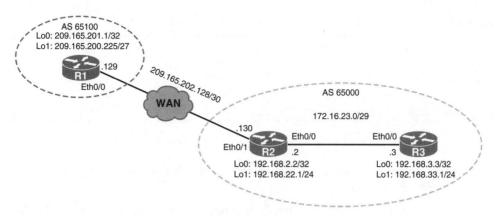

Figure 7-12 *Network for Basic BGP Configuration Example*

Configuring and Verifying an eBGP Session

Let's start with the R1 router and configure it for BGP and with an eBGP session with R2.

Recall that the **router bgp** *autonomous-system* global configuration command identifies the local router's autonomous system; for R1, this is 65100. The **neighbor** *ip-address* **remote-as** *autonomous-system* router configuration command identifies the IP address and autonomous system of the neighbor. R1's neighbor is R2 in autonomous system 65000. An eBGP relationship must span a maximum of one hop by default, so the IP addresses for an eBGP session must be that of a directly connected neighbor. Example 7-4 shows the configuration for the R1 router.

Example 7-4 *Starting Up BGP and Establishing an eBGP Session on R1*

```
R1(config)# router bgp 65100
R1(config-router)# neighbor 209.165.202.130 remote-as 65000
```

Similarly, Example 7-5 shows the configuration on router R2, specifying R1 as its eBGP neighbor.

Example 7-5 *Starting Up BGP and Establishing an eBGP Session on R2*

```
R2(config)# router bgp 65000
R2(config-router)# neighbor 209.165.202.129 remote-as 65100
```

You can examine the BGP sessions by looking at an overall BGP summary or detailed information about all or individual BGP peers. The **show ip bgp summary** command displays the overall status of all BGP connections. Example 7-6 provides sample output on R1.

Example 7-6   show ip bgp summary *Command Output on R1*

```
R1# show ip bgp summary
BGP router identifier 209.165.201.1, local AS number 65100
BGP table version is 1, main routing table version 1
Neighbor          V    AS MsgRcvd MsgSent   TblVer  InQ  OutQ  Up/Down  State/PfxRcd
209.165.202.130   4  65000      91      93        1    0     0  01:20:28           0
```

The first part of this command output describes the local router:

- **BGP router identifier:** The IP address that all other BGP speakers recognize as representing this router

- **Local AS number:** The local router's autonomous system number

The next part of this command output describes the BGP table:

- **BGP table version:** This is the version number of the local BGP table; it increases when the BGP table changes.

- **Main routing table version:** This is the last version of BGP database that was injected into the main routing table.

The rest of this command output describes the current neighbor status, one for each configured neighbor:

- **Neighbor:** The IP address, used in the **neighbor** statement, with which this router is setting up a relationship.

- **Version (V):** The version of BGP this router is running with the listed neighbor.

- **AS:** The listed neighbor's autonomous system number.

- **Messages received (MsgRcvd):** The number of BGP messages received from this neighbor.

- **Messages sent (MsgSent):** The number of BGP messages sent to this neighbor.

- **TblVer:** The last version of the BGP table that was sent to this neighbor.

- **In queue (InQ):** The number of messages from this neighbor that are waiting to be processed.

- **Out queue (OutQ):** The number of messages queued and waiting to be sent to this neighbor. TCP flow control prevents this router from overwhelming a neighbor with a large update.

- **Up/down:** The length of time this neighbor has been in the current BGP state (established, active, or idle).

- **State:** The current state of the BGP session: active, idle, open sent, open confirm, or idle (admin). The admin state indicates that the neighbor is administratively shut down; this state is created by using the **neighbor** *ip-address* **shutdown** router configuration command. The active state means that the router is attempting to create a TCP connection to this neighbor. (Neighbor states are discussed in more detail in the "Understanding and Troubleshooting BGP Neighbor States" section, later in this chapter.) Note that if the session is in the established state, a state is not displayed. Instead, a number representing the PfxRcd is displayed, as described next.

■ **Prefix received (PfxRcd):** When the session is in the established state, this value represents the number of BGP network entries received from this neighbor.

In Example 7-6, there is a zero in the PfxRcd column; this indicates that the state is established but no network prefixes have been received yet.

You can use the information in the **show ip bgp summary** command to verify that BGP sessions are up and established. If they are not, you will have to further investigate the BGP configuration to locate the problem. You can also verify the IP address and autonomous system number of the configured BGP neighbors with this command. If the session is established, the number of messages that have been sent and received, as displayed in the output of this command, can indicate BGP stability. For example, you could issue the command a few times, and calculate how many messages have been exchanged during that period.

The **show ip bgp neighbors** command supplies additional information, such as the negotiated capabilities, supported address families, and others. Example 7-7 provides sample output on R1.

Example 7-7   show ip bgp neighbors *Command Output on R1*

```
R1# show ip bgp neighbors
BGP neighbor is 209.165.202.130,  remote AS 65000, external link
  BGP version 4, remote router ID 192.168.22.1
  BGP state = Established, up for 01:21:17
  Last read 00:00:25, last write 00:00:00, hold time is 180, keepalive interval is
60 seconds
  Neighbor sessions:
    1 active, is not multisession capable (disabled)
  Neighbor capabilities:
    Route refresh: advertised and received(new)
    Four-octets ASN Capability: advertised and received
    Address family IPv4 Unicast: advertised and received
    Enhanced Refresh Capability: advertised and received
    Multisession Capability:
    Stateful switchover support enabled: NO for session 1
  Message statistics:
    InQ depth is 0
    OutQ depth is 0

                        Sent       Rcvd
  Opens:                   1          1
```

```
       Notifications:        0          0
       Updates:              1          1
       Keepalives:          92         90
       Route Refresh:        0          0
       Total:               94         92
   Default minimum time between advertisement runs is 30 seconds


 For address family: IPv4 Unicast
   Session: 209.165.202.130
<Output omitted>
```

The **show ip bgp neighbors** command is useful to get information about the TCP sessions and the BGP parameters of the sessions including TCP timers and counters. You can also examine the details of a specific session if you add the neighbor IP address to the command. This command also has optional parameters that can be included for a specific neighbor, as shown in Example 7-8. You can use these parameters to examine specific BGP routing information that was sent to or received from the neighbor, which can be useful when you are troubleshooting path selection.

Example 7-8   show ip bgp neighbors *Command Options*

```
R1# show ip bgp neighbors 209.165.202.130 ?
   advertised-routes   Display the routes advertised to a BGP neighbor
   dampened-routes     Display the dampened routes received from neighbor (eBGP
                       peers only)
   flap-statistics     Display flap statistics of the routes learned from
                       neighbor (eBGP peers only)
   paths               Display AS paths learned from neighbor
   policy              Display neighbor polices per address-family
   received            Display information received from a BGP neighbor
   received-routes     Display the received routes from neighbor
   routes              Display routes learned from neighbor
   |                   Output modifiers
   <cr>
```

Example 7-9 provides sample output from the same commands used on R1 on R2.

Example 7-9   show ip bgp summary *and* show ip bgp neighbors *Command Output on R2*

```
R2# show ip bgp summary
BGP router identifier 192.168.22.1, local AS number 65000
BGP table version is 1, main routing table version 1


Neighbor        V     AS MsgRcvd MsgSent   TblVer  InQ  OutQ Up/Down State/PfxRcd
209.165.202.129 4  65100     116     114        1    0     0 01:41:20        0
```

```
R2# show ip bgp neighbor
BGP neighbor is 209.165.202.129,  remote AS 65100, external link
  BGP version 4, remote router ID 209.165.201.1
  BGP state = Established, up for 01:41:32
  Last read 00:00:41, last write 00:00:47, hold time is 180, keepalive interval is
60 seconds
  Neighbor sessions:
    1 active, is not multisession capable (disabled)
  Neighbor capabilities:
    Route refresh: advertised and received(new)
<Output omitted>
```

Notice that the R2 output is a mirrored image of the information on R1.

Configuring and Verifying an iBGP Session

Now that the eBGP sessions are established, let's next configure the iBGP session between R2 and R3, using the addresses on the connection between the routers. An iBGP session is configured using the **neighbor** *ip-address* **remote-as** *autonomous-system* router configuration command, in the same way as the external sessions are established. Recall that the router automatically identifies an internal session by examining the autonomous system number and comparing it with the local autonomous system number. For an iBGP session, the neighbor IP addresses do not have to be directly connected (although in this example they are). Example 7-10 shows the configuration on both routers.

Example 7-10 *Establishing iBGP Relationships on R2 and R3*

```
R2(config)# router bgp 65000
R2(config-router)# neighbor 172.16.23.3 remote-as 65000

R3(config)# router bgp 65000
R3(config-router)# neighbor 172.16.23.2 remote-as 65000
```

You can verify iBGP sessions in the same ways as you monitor external BGP sessions. Example 7-11 and Example 7-12 provide command output on the R2 and R3 routers. Notice that the iBGP connection is identified as an *internal link* in the **show ip bgp neighbors** command output. Again, the command output on the R3 router is a mirrored perspective of the iBGP connection information on R2.

Example 7-11 *Examining BGP Sessions on R2*

```
R2# show ip bgp summary
BGP router identifier 192.168.22.1, local AS number 65000
BGP table version is 1, main routing table version 1
```

```
Neighbor          V    AS  MsgRcvd  MsgSent  TblVer  InQ  OutQ  Up/Down   State/PfxRcd
172.16.23.3       4  65000   13       13        1     0     0   00:08:23        0
209.165.202.129   4  65100  287      284        1     0     0   04:16:06        0


R2# show ip bgp neighbors
BGP neighbor is 172.16.23.3,  remote AS 65000, internal link
  BGP version 4, remote router ID 192.168.33.1
  BGP state = Established, up for 00:08:38
<Output omitted>
```

Example 7-12 *Examining iBGP Session on R3*

```
R3# show ip bgp summary
BGP router identifier 192.168.33.1, local AS number 65000
BGP table version is 1, main routing table version 1
Neighbor          V     AS MsgRcvd MsgSent  TblVer  InQ OutQ Up/Down State/PfxRcd
172.16.23.2       4   65000   109     110       1     0    0 01:36:17        0


R3# show ip bgp neighbors
BGP neighbor is 172.16.23.2,  remote AS 65000, internal link
  BGP version 4, remote router ID 192.168.22.1
  BGP state = Established, up for 01:37:20
  Last read 00:00:06, last write 00:00:03, hold time is 180, keepalive interval is
60 seconds
  Neighbor sessions:
    1 active, is not multisession capable (disabled)
  Neighbor capabilities:
    Route refresh: advertised and received(new)
<Output omitted>
```

Advertising Networks in BGP and Verifying That They Are Propagated

Now that the sessions are established, we need to configure the routers to advertise networks. Use the **network** *network-number* [**mask** *network-mask*] router configuration command to inject routes that are present in the IPv4 routing table into the BGP table so that they can be advertised in BGP. Table 7-3 describes this command.

Table 7-3 network *Command Description*

Parameter	Description
network-number	Identifies an IPv4 network to be advertised by BGP.
mask *network-mask*	(Optional) Identifies the subnet mask to be advertised by BGP. If the network mask is not specified, the default mask is the classful mask.

It is important to note that the BGP **network** command determines which networks this router advertises. This is a different concept from what you are used to when configuring IGPs. Unlike for IGPs, the **network** command does not start BGP on specific interfaces. Rather, it indicates to BGP which networks it should originate from this router. The list of **network** commands must include all networks in your autonomous system that you want to advertise, not just those locally connected to your router.

The **mask** parameter indicates that BGP-4 allows classless prefixes; it can advertise subnets and supernets.

Note Before Cisco IOS Software Release 12.0, there was a limit of 200 **network** commands per BGP router. This limit has now been removed. The router's resources, such as the configured NVRAM or RAM, determine the maximum number of network commands that you can now use.

Notice the difference between the **neighbor** command and the **network** command: The **neighbor** command tells BGP where to advertise; the **network** command tells BGP what to advertise.

The sole purpose of the **network** command is to notify BGP which networks to advertise. If the **mask** parameter is not specified, this command announces only the classful network number; at least one subnet of the specified major network must be present in the IP routing table to allow BGP to start announcing the classful network as a BGP route.

However, if you specify the **mask** *network-mask*, an exact match to the network (both address and mask) must exist in the routing table for the network to be advertised. Before BGP announces a route, it checks to see whether it can reach it. For example, if you want to advertise the 192.168.0.0/24 route, and by mistake you configure network **192.168.0.0 mask 255.255.0.0** instead of **network 192.168.0.0 mask 255.255.255.0**, BGP looks for 192.168.0.0/16 in the routing table. In this case, it would find 192.168.0.0/24 but will not find 192.168.0.0/16. Because the routing table does not contain a specific match to the network, BGP does not announce the 192.168.0.0/24 network to any neighbors.

If you want to advertise the CIDR block 192.168.0.0/16, you might try configuring network 192.168.0.0 mask 255.255.0.0. Again, BGP looks for 192.168.0.0/16 in the routing table, and if it never finds 192.168.0.0/16, BGP does not announce the 192.168.0.0/16 network to any neighbors. In this case, you can configure a static route to the CIDR block toward the null interface, with the **ip route 192.168.0.0 255.255.0.0 null0** command, so that BGP can find an exact match in the routing table. After finding an exact match in the routing table, BGP announces the 192.168.0.0/16 network to its neighbors.

The BGP Table, the IP Routing Table, and the network Command

To summarize the relationship between the BGP table, the IP routing table and the **network** command: The **network** command allows a BGP router to inject a network that is in its IP routing table into its BGP table and advertise that network to its BGP neighbors. BGP neighbors exchange their best BGP routes. The neighbor router that receives that network information puts the information in its BGP table and selects its best BGP route for that network. The best route is offered to its IP routing table.

On R3, let's advertise the network prefix that is configured on the loopback 1 interface (192.168.33.0/24) in BGP. Example 7-13 provides the configuration.

Example 7-13 *Advertising the Loopback 1 Network on R3*

```
R3(config)#router bgp 65000
R3(config-router)#network 192.168.33.0 mask 255.255.255.0
```

On R3, examine the BGP table, using the **show ip bgp** command, to see the announced prefix. Example 7-14 provides sample output.

Example 7-14 *Examining the BGP Table on R3*

```
R3# show ip bgp
BGP table version is 2, local router ID is 192.168.33.1
Status codes: s suppressed, d damped, h history, * valid, > best, i - internal,
              r RIB-failure, S Stale, m multipath, b backup-path, f RT-Filter,
              x best-external, a additional-path, c RIB-compressed,
Origin codes: i - IGP, e - EGP, ? - incomplete
RPKI validation codes: V valid, I invalid, N Not found

     Network          Next Hop            Metric LocPrf Weight Path
 *>  192.168.33.0     0.0.0.0                  0          32768 i
```

When the **show ip bgp** command is used without optional qualifiers, the entire BGP table is displayed. An abbreviated list of information about each route is displayed, one line per prefix. The output is sorted in network number order; if the BGP table contains more than one entry for the same network, the alternative routes are displayed on successive lines. The network number is printed on the first of these lines only.

The *status codes* are shown at the beginning of each line of output, and the *origin codes* are shown at the end of each line. A row with an asterisk (*) in the first column means that the table entry is valid. Some of the other options for the first column are as follows:

- An *s* indicates that the specified routes are suppressed (usually because routes have been summarized and only the summarized route is being sent).

- A *d*, for dampening, indicates that the route is being dampened (penalized) for going up and down too often. Although the route might be up right now, it is not advertised until the penalty has expired.

- An *h*, for history, indicates that the route is unavailable and is probably down. Historic information about the route exists, but a best route does not exist.

- An *r*, for Routing Information Base (RIB) failure, indicates that the route was not installed in the RIB; the RIB is another name for the IP routing table. The reason that the route is not installed can be displayed using the **show ip bgp rib-failure** command, as described in the next section.

- An *S*, for stale, indicates that the route is stale. (This is used in a nonstop forwarding-aware router.)

A greater-than sign (>) in the second column indicates the best path for a route selected by BGP. This route is offered to the IP routing table.

The third column is either blank or has an *i* in it. If it is blank, BGP learned that route from an external peer. If it has an *i*, an iBGP neighbor advertised this route to this router.

The fourth column lists the networks that the router learned.

Some, but not all, of the BGP attributes that are associated with the route are displayed. The fifth column lists all the next-hop addresses for each route. If this column contains 0.0.0.0, this router originated the route. (For BGP the next-hop address is not always on a router that is directly connected to this router, as explored later in this example.)

The next three columns list three BGP path attributes associated with the path: metric, which is also called the multi-exit discriminator (MED); local preference; and weight.

The column with the Path header may contain a sequence of autonomous systems in the path. From left to right, the first autonomous system listed is the adjacent autonomous system from which this network was learned. The last number (the rightmost autonomous system number) is this network's originating autonomous system. The autonomous system numbers between these two represent the exact path that a packet takes back to the originating autonomous system. If the path column is blank, the route is from the current autonomous system.

The last column signifies how this route was entered into BGP on the original router (the origin attribute). If the last column has an *i* in it, the original router probably used a **network** command to introduce this network into BGP. The character *e* signifies that the original router learned this network from EGP, which is the historic predecessor to BGP. A question mark (?) signifies that the original BGP process cannot absolutely verify this network's availability because it is redistributed from an IGP into the BGP process.

On R2, examine the BGP table and BGP portion of the routing table. Example 7-15 provides sample output.

Example 7-15 *Examining the BGP Table and Routing Table on R2*

```
R2# show ip bgp
BGP table version is 4, local router ID is 192.168.22.1
Status codes: s suppressed, d damped, h history, * valid, > best, i - internal,
<Output omitted>


     Network          Next Hop          Metric LocPrf Weight Path
*>i 192.168.33.0     172.16.23.3            0     100      0 i


R2# show ip route bgp
<Output omitted>
B     192.168.33.0/24 [200/0] via 172.16.23.3, 01:20:57
```

R2's BGP table indicates that the 192.168.33.0/24 prefix is an internal route (it has *i* in the third column) and its next-hop attribute is the originating neighbor's IP address. The next-hop attribute is also visible in the routing table. The next hop identifies the path toward the destination network. Within an autonomous system, the next hop does not change; it points to the router that advertised the route.

Examine R1's BGP and routing tables next. Example 7-16 provides sample output.

Example 7-16 *Examining the BGP Table and Routing Table on R2*

```
R1# show ip bgp
BGP table version is 4, local router ID is 209.165.201.1
Status codes: s suppressed, d damped, h history, * valid, > best, i - internal,
<Output omitted>
     Network          Next Hop          Metric LocPrf Weight Path
*>  192.168.33.0     209.165.202.130                    0 65000 i


R1# show ip route bgp
<Output omitted>
B     192.168.33.0/24 [20/0] via 209.165.202.130, 01:16:42
```

R1's BGP table shows the 192.168.33.0/24 prefix; however, this time it is not marked as an internal route. (There is no *i* in the third column.) Therefore, this is an external route. Notice that the next-hop attribute is the IP address of the neighbor in the adjacent autonomous system. The next-hop attribute informs the router where to send the traffic towards the given network. BGP, like IGPs, is a hop-by-hop routing protocol. However, unlike IGPs, BGP routes autonomous system by autonomous system, not router by router, and the default next hop is the next autonomous system. The next-hop address for a network from another autonomous system is an IP address of the entry point of the next autonomous system along the path to that destination network. Therefore, for eBGP, the next-hop address is the IP address of the neighbor that sent the update.

For R1, notice that the AS-path attribute lists autonomous system 65000 as the only autonomous system in the path to the announced destination.

Now let's configure R2 to advertise in BGP the network prefix that is configured on its loopback 1 interface (192.168.22.0/24) and verify that it is propagated to R1. Example 7-17 provides R2's configuration, and Example 7-18 provides the resulting output on R1.

Example 7-17   *Advertising R2's Loopback Subnet*

```
R2(config)# router bgp 65000
R2(config-router)#network 192.168.22.0 mask 255.255.255.0
```

Example 7-18   *Confirming That R1 Sees R2's Loopback Subnet*

```
R1# show ip bgp
BGP table version is 5, local router ID is 209.165.201.1
Status codes: s suppressed, d damped, h history, * valid, > best, i - internal,
<Output omitted>


     Network          Next Hop          Metric LocPrf  Weight Path
*>   192.168.22.0     209.165.202.130        0            0 65000 i
*>   192.168.33.0     209.165.202.130                     0 65000 i


R1# show ip route bgp
<Output omitted>


B     192.168.22.0/24 [20/0] via 209.165.202.130, 00:01:15
B     192.168.33.0/24 [20/0] via 209.165.202.130, 13:48:43
```

Notice that the next-hop attribute on R1 is R2's address and the administrative distance of the learned eBGP routes defaults to 20. Because this value is lower than the value of all IGPs, an eBGP route is preferred by default. Therefore, routers forward traffic to external domains rather than deliver it locally within an IGP domain; this behavior helps prevent loops.

Now let's verify that R3 can see R2's loopback network. Example 7-19 provides the resulting output on R3.

Example 7-19   *Confirming That R3 Sees R1's Loopback Subnet*

```
R3# show ip bgp
BGP table version is 3, local router ID is 192.168.33.1
Status codes: s suppressed, d damped, h history, * valid, > best, i - internal,
<Output omitted>
     Network          Next Hop          Metric LocPrf  Weight Path
*>i 192.168.22.0      172.16.23.2            0    100      0 i
*>   192.168.33.0     0.0.0.0                0          32768 i


R3# show ip route bgp
<Output omitted>


B     192.168.22.0/24 [200/0] via 172.16.23.2, 05:56:53
```

The next-hop attribute on R3 is R2's address, and the route is installed in R3's routing table. Because the default administrative distance of iBGP routes is 200, which is higher than the value of all IGPs, if a router receives advertisements about the same network prefix via iBGP and an IGP, the IGP route will be preferred. Routers will therefore forward traffic through an internal domain according to the IGP information rather than via iBGP. This behavior helps prevent traffic from black-holing on routers that do not run BGP within a local domain.

Now let's advertise R1's loopback interface prefix (209.165.200.224/27) and verify that it is propagated to R2 and R3. Example 7-20 provides the configuration on R1, and Example 7-21 displays the resulting output on R2 and R3.

Example 7-20 *Advertising R1's Loopback Subnet*

```
R1(config)# router bgp 65100
R1(config-router)# network 209.165.200.224 mask 255.255.255.224
```

Example 7-21 *Confirming That R2 and R3 See R1's Loopback Subnet*

```
R2# show ip bgp
BGP table version is 6, local router ID is 192.168.22.1
Status codes: s suppressed, d damped, h history, * valid, > best, i - internal,
<Output omitted>
     Network          Next Hop          Metric  LocPrf  Weight  Path
 *>  192.168.22.0     0.0.0.0                0           32768  i
 *>i 192.168.33.0     172.16.23.3            0     100       0  i
 *>  209.165.200.224/27
                      209.165.202.129        0               0  65100 i


R2# show ip route bgp
<Output omitted>

B     192.168.33.0/24 [200/0] via 172.16.23.3, 20:15:50
      209.165.200.0/27 is subnetted, 1 subnets
B        209.165.200.224 [20/0] via 209.165.202.129, 00:00:56


R3# show ip bgp
BGP table version is 3, local router ID is 192.168.33.1
Status codes: s suppressed, d damped, h history, * valid, > best, i - internal,
              r RIB-failure, S Stale, m multipath, b backup-path, f RT-Filter,
              x best-external, a additional-path, c RIB-compressed,
Origin codes: i - IGP, e - EGP, ? - incomplete
RPKI validation codes: V valid, I invalid, N Not found

     Network          Next Hop          Metric LocPrf Weight Path
 *>i 192.168.22.0     172.16.23.2            0    100      0 i
```

```
*>   192.168.33.0     0.0.0.0                    0         32768 i
*  i 209.165.200.224/27
                        209.165.202.129          0    100    0 65100 i

R3# show ip route bgp
<Output omitted>
B     192.168.22.0/24 [200/0] via 172.16.23.2, 05:56:53


R3# show ip route 209.165.202.129
% Network not in table
```

R2 receives the 209.165.200.224/27 information via BGP, with a next-hop attribute of R1; the route is installed in the routing table.

R3 receives the external prefix 209.165.200.224/27 in BGP and stores it in its BGP table. Notice, though, that the entry is not designated as a best route; the > character is missing. This is because R3 does not have a route to the next-hop address (209.165.202.129), and therefore the route is not installed in the routing table.

Using the Next-Hop-Self Feature

How BGP establishes an iBGP relationship differs significantly from the way that IGPs behave. An internal protocol, such as RIP, EIGRP, or OSPF, always uses the source IP address of a routing update as the next-hop address for each network from that update that is placed in the routing table. Recall that BGP routes autonomous system by autonomous system, not router by router, and the default next hop is the next autonomous system. As such, for BGP the next hop is the IP address that is used to reach the next autonomous system.

As a result, for eBGP, the next-hop address is the IP address of the neighbor that sent the update. For iBGP, however, the next hop advertised by eBGP is carried into iBGP, by default.

It is sometimes necessary to override a router's default behavior and force it to advertise itself as the next-hop address for routes sent to a neighbor. The **neighbor** *ip-address* **next-hop-self** router configuration command enables you to force BGP to use the source IP address of the update as the next hop for each network it advertises to the neighbor, rather than letting the protocol choose the next-hop address to use.

In our example network, let's configure R2 to set the next-hop address to itself when advertising prefixes to R3 and verify R3's routing table. Example 7-22 provides the configuration on R2, and Example 7-23 displays the resulting output on R3.

Example 7-22 *Configuring R2 to Advertise Itself as the Next-Hop*

```
R2(config)# router bgp 65000
R2(config-router)# neighbor 172.16.23.3 next-hop-self
```

Example 7-23 *Confirming That R3 Sees R1's Loopback Subnet*

```
R3# show ip bgp
<Output omitted>


     Network              Next Hop          Metric  LocPrf  Weight  Path
 *>i 192.168.22.0        172.16.23.2            0     100        0  i
 *>  192.168.33.0        0.0.0.0                0             32768  i
 *>i 209.165.200.224/27
                 172.16.23.2                    0     100        0  65100 i
R3#show ip route bgp
<Output omitted>


B    192.168.22.0/24 [200/0] via 172.16.23.2, 06:57:03
     209.165.200.0/27 is subnetted, 1 subnets
B       209.165.200.224 [200/0] via 172.16.23.2, 00:02:51
```

R3 now has a route to R1's loopback subnet via R2's next-hop address (172.16.23.2).
This address is directly connected to R3, so it is reachable.

Understanding and Troubleshooting BGP Neighbor States

After the TCP handshake is complete, the BGP application tries to set up a session with
the neighbor. BGP is a state machine that takes a router through the following states with
its neighbors:

- **Idle:** The router is searching the routing table to see whether a route exists to reach
  the neighbor.

- **Connect:** The router found a route to the neighbor and has completed the three-
  way TCP handshake.

- **Open sent:** An open message was sent, with the parameters for the BGP session.

- **Open confirm:** The router received agreement on the parameters for establishing a
  session.

  Alternatively, the router goes into the active state if there is no response to the open
  message.

- **Established:** Peering is established and routing begins.

After you enter the **neighbor remote-as** command, BGP starts in the *idle* state, and the
BGP process checks that it has a route to the IP address listed. BGP should be in the idle
state for only a few seconds. However, if BGP does not find a route to the neighboring
IP address, it stays in the idle state. If it finds a route, it goes to the *connect* state when
the TCP handshaking synchronize acknowledge (SYN ACK) packet returns (when the
TCP three-way handshake is complete). After the TCP connection is set up, the BGP
process creates a BGP open message and sends it to the neighbor. After BGP dispatches

this open message, the BGP peering session changes to the *open sent* state. If there is no response for 5 seconds, the state changes to the *active* state. If a response does come back in a timely manner, BGP goes to the *open confirm* state and starts scanning (evaluating) the routing table for the paths to send to the neighbor. When these paths have been found, BGP then goes to the *established* state and begins routing between the neighbors.

The BGP state is shown in the last column of the **show ip bgp summary** command output.

> **Note**   You can observe the states that two BGP routers are going through to establish a session by using **debug** commands. In Cisco IOS Software Release 12.4 and newer, you can use the **debug ip bgp ipv4 unicast** command (or the **debug bgp ipv4 unicast events** command) to see this process.

Idle State Troubleshooting

The idle state indicates that the router does not know how to reach the IP address listed in the **neighbor** statement. The most common reason for the idle state is that the neighbor is not announcing the IP address or network that the neighbor statement of the router is pointing to. Check the following two conditions to troubleshoot this problem:

- Ensure that the neighbor announces the route in its local routing protocol (IGP) (for iBGP neighbors).

- Verify that you have not entered an incorrect IP address in the **neighbor** statement.

Active State Troubleshooting

If the router is in the active state, this means that it has found the IP address in the **neighbor** statement and has created and sent out a BGP open packet but has not received a response (an open confirm packet) back from the neighbor.

One common cause of this is when the neighbor does not have a return route to the source IP address. Ensure that the source IP address or network of the packets is advertised into the local routing protocol (IGP) on the neighboring router.

Another common problem associated with the active state is when a BGP router attempts to peer with another BGP router that does not have a **neighbor** statement peering back at the first router, or the other router is peering with the wrong IP address on the first router. Check to ensure that the other router has a **neighbor** statement peering at the correct address of the router that is in the active state.

If the state toggles between idle and active, the autonomous system numbers might be misconfigured. You see a message similar to the following console message at the router with the wrong autonomous system number configured in the neighbor statement:

```
%BGP-3-NOTIFICATION: sent to neighbor 172.31.1.3 2/2 (peer in wrong AS) 2 bytes FDE6
FFFF FFFF FFFF FFFF FFFF FFFF FFFF FFFF 002D 0104 FDE6 00B4 AC1F 0203 1002 0601 0400
0100 0102 0280 0002 0202 00
```

At the remote router, you see a message similar to the following message:

```
%BGP-3-NOTIFICATION: received from neighbor 172.31.1.1 2/2 (peer in wrong AS) 2
bytes FDE6
```

BGP Session Resilience

In the example network we are configuring, R2 and R3 have only one connection between them. If the interface to which the IP address used in the **neighbor** command goes down, the BGP neighbor relationship would be lost.

In cases where multiple paths exist to reach an iBGP neighboring routers, the routers could peer with each other's loopback interface address and the BGP session would not be lost because loopback interfaces are always available as long as the router itself does not fail. This peering arrangement adds resiliency to the iBGP sessions because they are not tied into a physical interface, which might go down for any number of reasons.

To peer with the loopback interface of an iBGP neighbor, configure each router with a **neighbor** command using the neighbor's loopback address. Both routers must have a route to the loopback address of the other neighbor in their routing table; check to ensure that both routers are announcing their loopback addresses into the IGP. In our example network, the routers are running OSPF and do have a route to each other's loopback 0 address.

On R2 and R3, change the iBGP peer addresses to the respective loopback 0 addresses (192.168.2.2 and 192.168.3.3). Example 7-24 provides the configuration on R2 and R3. As this example illustrates, you can change the neighbor address by deleting the previous IP address of that neighbor and reapplying the configuration for it using the peer's new address. Each router will now send BGP packets to the other router's loopback 0 address.

Example 7-24   *Configuring R2 and R3 to Establish a Neighbor Relationship over Their Loopback Interfaces*

```
R2(config)# router bgp 65000
R2(config-router)# no neighbor 172.16.23.3
R2(config-router)# neighbor 192.168.3.3 remote-as 65000
R2(config-router)# neighbor 192.168.3.3 next-hop-self

R3(config)# router bgp 65000
R3(config-router)# no neighbor 172.16.23.2
R3(config-router)# neighbor 192.168.2.2 remote-as 65000
```

Verify the session status between R2 and R3. Example 7-25 displays the output on the two routers.

Example 7-25 *Verifying That R2 and R3 Are Neighbors*

```
R2# show ip bgp summary
<Output omitted>


Neighbor          V    AS MsgRcvd MsgSent   TblVer  InQ OutQ Up/Down  State/PfxRcd
192.168.3.3       4 65000       0       0        1    0    0 00:14:59 Idle
209.165.202.129 4 65100    2980    2981        9    0    0 1d21h            1

R3# show ip bgp summary
<Output omitted>


Neighbor          V    AS MsgRcvd MsgSent   TblVer  InQ OutQ Up/Down  State/PfxRcd
192.168.2.2       4 65000       0       0        1    0    0 never    Idle
```

Notice in Example 7-25 that the state is *idle*. The BGP **neighbor** statement tells the BGP process the destination IP address of each update packet. The router must decide which IP address to use as the source IP address in the BGP routing update. When a router creates a packet, whether it is a routing update, a ping, or any other type of IP packet, the router does a lookup in the routing table for the destination address. The routing table lists the appropriate interface to get to the destination address. The address of this outbound interface is used as that packet's source address by default.

For BGP packets, this source IP address must match the address in the corresponding **neighbor** statement on the other router. (In other words, the other router must have a BGP relationship with the packet's source IP address.) Otherwise, the routers will not be able to establish the BGP session, and the packet will be ignored. BGP does not accept unsolicited updates; it must be aware of every neighboring router and have a **neighbor** statement for it.

Sourcing BGP from Loopback Address

In this case, R2 and R3 do not establish the BGP session because, despite correct neighbor IP addresses, each router expects the BGP packets to be originated from the loopback 0 address of the other peer. You must tell BGP to use a loopback interface address rather than a physical interface address as the source address for all BGP packets, including those that initiate the BGP neighbor TCP connection. Use the **neighbor** *ip-address* **update-source loopback** *interface-number* router configuration command to cause the router to use the address of the specified loopback interface as the source address for BGP connections to this neighbor. The **neighbor update-source** command is necessary for both routers.

Note If the **neighbor** *ip-address* **next-hop-self** command is also used with this neighbor, then the address of the specified loopback interface will also be the next-hop address for routes sent to this neighbor.

On R2 and R3, let's source the iBGP packets from the loopback 0 addresses and verify the peering. Example 7-26 displays the configuration and output on the two routers.

Example 7-26 *Configuring and Verifying R2 and R3 Have Established a Neighbor Relationship over Their Loopback Interfaces*

```
R2(config)# router bgp 65000
R2(config-router)# neighbor 192.168.3.3 update-source Loopback 0

R3(config)# router bgp 65000
R3(config-router)# neighbor 192.168.2.2 update-source Loopback 0

R3# show ip bgp summary
<Output omitted>


Neighbor        V     AS    MsgRcvd  MsgSent  TblVer  InQ  OutQ   Up/Down   State/PfxRcd
192.168.2.2     4   65000        8        8      12    0     0   00:02:38             2
```

The **show ip bgp summary** command output in Example 7-26 has a 2 in the State/PfxRcd column; this indicates that the BGP session between the two routers is in the established state and R3 has received two prefixes from its neighbor, R3.

Establishing the BGP session between the loopback IP addresses can also help increase the resilience of an eBGP connection. If multiple paths between two eBGP neighbors exist, the session will survive no matter which path remains available. The loopback addresses must be reachable from both sides, respectively. In contrast to internal enterprise networks, where an IGP provides reachability for the loopback addresses used for iBGP peering, you typically need to configure static routes to the respective remote loopback IP address.

On R1 and R2, let's configure a static route to reach the other router's loopback 0 address, because these routers are not running an IGP, and then configure eBGP peering between the loopback 0 addresses and verify the peering. Example 7-27 displays the configuration and output on the two routers.

Example 7-27 *Configuring and Verifying R1 and R2 Have Established a Neighbor Relationship over Their Loopback Interfaces*

```
R1(config)# ip route 192.168.2.2 255.255.255.255 209.165.202.130
R1(config)# router bgp 65100
R1(config-router)# no neighbor 209.165.202.130
R1(config-router)# neighbor 192.168.2.2 remote-as 65000
R1(config-router)# neighbor 192.168.2.2 update-source Loopback 0

R2(config)# ip route 209.165.201.1 255.255.255.255 209.165.202.129
R2(config)# router bgp 65000
R2(config-router)# no neighbor 209.165.202.129
R2(config-router)# neighbor 209.165.201.1 remote-as 65100
R2(config-router)# neighbor 209.165.201.1 update-source Loopback 0
```

```
R1# show ip bgp summary
<Output omitted>
Neighbor        V     AS MsgRcvd MsgSent   TblVer  InQ OutQ Up/Down  State/PfxRcd
192.168.2.2     4  65000       0       0        1    0    0 never        Idle
```

Example 7-27 illustrates that the eBGP connection between the loopback addresses remains idle, despite the routing setup and BGP neighbor configuration that would suffice for similar iBGP peering. The session does not become established because eBGP neighbor addresses must be by default directly adjacent.

eBGP Multihop

To fix this issue, you must also enable multihop eBGP, with the **neighbor** *ip-address* **ebgp-multihop** [*ttl*] router configuration command.

This command allows the router to accept and attempt BGP connections to external peers residing on networks that are not directly connected. This command increases the default of one hop for eBGP peers by changing the default Time To Live (TTL) value of 1 (with the *ttl* parameter) and therefore allowing routes to the eBGP loopback address. By default, the TTL is set to 255 with this command. This command is useful when redundant paths exist between eBGP neighbors. Other scenarios where the directly adjacent IP addresses cannot be used include peering with third-party routers, connections over a Layer 3 hop, and advanced Multiprotocol Label Switching (MPLS) virtual private network (VPN) solutions.

Let's configure eBGP multihop between routers R1 and R2 and verify that the peering works this time. Example 7-28 displays the configuration and output on the two routers.

Example 7-28   *Configuring and Verifying R1 and R2 with eBGP Multihop*

```
R1(config)# router bgp 65100
R1(config-router)# neighbor 192.168.2.2 ebgp-multihop

R2(config)# router bgp 65000
R2(config-router)# neighbor 209.165.201.1 ebgp-multihop

R1# show ip bgp summary
<Output omitted>

Neighbor        V     AS  MsgRcvd MsgSent TblVer  InQ OutQ  Up/Down   State/PfxRcd
192.168.2.2     4  65000        6       5     12    0    0  00:00:30          2
```

This time the eBGP connection is successfully established, as indicated by the 2 in the State/PfxRcd column on the R1 router in Example 7-28; R1 has received two prefixes from its neighbor R2.

> **Note**   Recall that BGP is not designed to perform load balancing. Paths are chosen because of policy, not based on bandwidth. BGP will choose only a single best path. Using the loopback addresses and the **neighbor ebgp-multihop** command as shown in this example allows load balancing, and redundancy, across the two paths between the autonomous systems.

Resetting BGP Sessions

BGP can potentially handle huge volumes of routing information. When a BGP policy configuration change occurs (such as when access lists, timers, or attributes are changed), the router cannot go through the huge table of BGP information and recalculate which entry is no longer valid in the local table. Nor can the router determine which route or routes, already advertised, should be withdrawn from a neighbor. There is an obvious risk that the first configuration change will immediately be followed by a second, which would cause the whole process to start all over again. To avoid such a problem, the Cisco IOS Software applies changes on only those updates received or sent *after* the BGP policy configuration change has been performed. The new policy, enforced by the new filters, is applied only on routes received or sent after the change.

If the network administrator wants the policy change to be applied on all routes, he or she must trigger an update to force the router to let all routes pass through the new filter. If the filter is applied to outgoing information, the router has to resend the BGP table through the new filter. If the filter is applied to incoming information, the router needs its neighbor to resend its BGP table so that it passes through the new filter.

There are two ways to trigger an update: a hard reset, and a soft reset, which is also called a route refresh. The following sections detail these methods of triggering an update.

Hard Reset of BGP Sessions

Resetting a session is a method of informing the neighbor or neighbors of a policy change. If BGP sessions are reset, all information received on those sessions is invalidated and removed from the BGP table. The remote neighbor detects a BGP session down state and, likewise, invalidates the received routes. After a period of 30 to 60 seconds, the BGP sessions are reestablished automatically, and the BGP table is exchanged again, but through the new filters. However, resetting the BGP session disrupts packet forwarding.

Use the **clear ip bgp** * or **clear ip bgp** {*neighbor-address*} privileged EXEC command to cause a hard reset of the BGP neighbors involved, where * indicates all sessions and the *neighbor-address* identifies the address of a specific neighbor for which the BGP sessions will be reset. A "hard reset" means that the router issuing either of these commands will close the appropriate TCP connections, reestablish those TCP sessions as appropriate, and resend all information to each of the neighbors affected by the particular command that is used.

Caution   Clearing the BGP table and resetting BGP sessions will disrupt routing, so do not use these commands unless you have to.

The **clear ip bgp** * command causes the BGP forwarding table on the router on which this command is issued to be completely deleted; all networks must be relearned from every neighbor. If a router has multiple neighbors, this action is a very dramatic event. This command forces all neighbors to resend their entire tables simultaneously.

If, instead, the **clear ip bgp** *neighbor-address* command is used, one neighbor is reset at a time. The impact is less severe on the router issuing this command. However, it takes longer to change policy to all the neighbors because each must be done individually rather than all at once as it is with the **clear ip bgp** * command. The **clear ip bgp** *neighbor-address* command still performs a hard reset and must reestablish the TCP session with the specified address used in the command, but this command affects only a single neighbor at a time, not all neighbors simultaneously.

Soft Reset or Route Refresh

Use the **clear ip bgp** {* | *neighbor-address*} **out** privileged EXEC command to cause BGP to do a soft reset for outbound updates. The router on which this command is issued does not reset the BGP session. Instead, the router creates a new update and sends the whole table to the specified neighbors. This update includes withdrawal commands for networks that the neighbor will not see anymore, based on the new outbound policy.

Outbound BGP soft configuration does not have any memory overhead. This command is highly recommended when you are changing an outbound policy, but does not help if you are changing an inbound policy.

Cisco IOS Software Releases 12.0(2)S and 12.0(6)T introduced a BGP soft reset enhancement feature, also known as *route refresh*, that provides automatic support for dynamic soft reset of inbound BGP routing table updates that is not dependent on locally stored routing table update information. In the past, routers consumed additional memory to store copies of received BGP tables that could be used for generating new inbound updates. Issuing the **clear ip bgp** {* | *neighbor-address*} **in** privileged EXEC command will trigger the specified BGP neighbor to resend its BGP table.

Note   To determine whether a BGP router supports this route refresh capability, use the **show ip bgp neighbors** command. The following message is displayed in the output when the router supports the route refresh capability:

```
Received route refresh capability from peer.
```

Note   The **clear ip bgp soft** command performs a soft reconfiguration of both inbound and outbound updates.

On R2 let's enable BGP update debugging with the **debug ip bgp updates** command, and then on R1 perform a soft reset outbound for its neighbor relationship with R2. Example 7-29 displays the commands and output on the two routers.

Example 7-29   *Soft Reset of Outbound BGP Updates*

```
R2# debug ip bgp updates
BGP updates debugging is on for address family: IPv4 Unicast


R1# clear ip bgp 192.168.2.2 out

R2#
BGP: nbr_topo global 209.165.201.1 IPv4 Unicast:base (0xEC245CF8:1) rcvd Refresh
Start-of-RIB
BGP: nbr_topo global 209.165.201.1 IPv4 Unicast:base (0xEC245CF8:1) refresh_epoch is
3
BGP(0): 209.165.201.1 rcvd UPDATE w/ attr: nexthop 209.165.201.1, origin i, metric
0, merged path 65100, AS_PATH
BGP(0): 209.165.201.1 rcvd 209.165.200.224/27...duplicate ignored
BGP: nbr_topo global 209.165.201.1 IPv4 Unicast:base (0xEC245CF8:1) rcvd Refresh
End-of-RIB
R2# no debug all
All possible debugging has been turned off
```

In Example 7-29, notice that when you trigger a soft reset outbound on R1 toward R2, all prefixes existing in the BGP table that have not been received from R2 are re-sent to R2. In this case, the received information is a duplicate of a previous entry and R2 ignores it.

Do not forget to disable the debug with the **no debug all** command, as is done at the end of Example 7-29.

When a BGP session is reset using soft reconfiguration, the following commands can be useful for monitoring the BGP routes received, sent, or filtered, as illustrated in Figure 7-13:

- **show ip bgp neighbors** {*address*} **received-routes:** Displays all received routes (both accepted and rejected) from the specified neighbor.

- **show ip bgp neighbors** {*address*} **routes:** Displays all routes that are received and accepted from the specified neighbor. This output is a subset of the output displayed by the **received-routes** keyword.

- **show ip bgp:** Displays entries in the BGP table.

- **show ip bgp neighbors** {*address*} **advertised-routes:** Displays all BGP routes that have been advertised to neighbors.

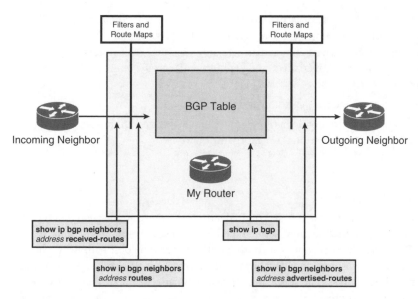

Figure 7-13 *Monitoring Soft Reconfiguration*

BGP Attributes and the Path-Selection Process

BGP can be used to perform policy-based routing. To manipulate the best paths that are chosen by BGP, you need to understand the different attributes that BGP uses and how BGP selects the best path that is based on these attributes. This section describes how BGP selects one best path, and introduces the attributes used in this decision process and how to configure them.

BGP Path Selection

A router running BGP may receive updates about destinations from multiple neighbors, some in different autonomous systems, and therefore multiple paths might exist to reach a given network. These are kept in the BGP table. As paths for the network are evaluated, those determined not to be the best path are eliminated from the selection criteria but kept in the BGP table in case the best path becomes inaccessible.

BGP chooses only a single best path to reach a specific destination.

BGP is not designed to perform load balancing; paths are chosen because of policy, not based on bandwidth. The BGP selection process eliminates any multiple paths until a single best path is left.

The best BGP path is submitted to the IP routing table manager process and is evaluated against any other routing protocols that can also reach that network. The route from the routing protocol with the lowest administrative distance is installed in the routing table.

Note   You can use the **maximum-paths** *paths* router configuration command for BGP if your router has multiple paths, with the same attributes, to different routers in the same remote autonomous system. This command affects only the number of routes kept in the IP routing table; it allows multiple paths to be kept in the IP routing table. However, BGP *still selects one best path for the BGP table.*

For BGP, the *paths* parameter in this command defaults to one.

See the Cisco.com document "Load Sharing with BGP in Single and Multihomed Environments: Sample Configurations" for more information.

BGP Path-Selection Process

The BGP path decision process is based on BGP attributes; these are discussed in the upcoming "BGP Attributes" section. When faced with multiple routes to the same destination, BGP chooses the best route for routing traffic toward the destination. To choose the best route, BGP considers only routes with no autonomous system loops and a valid, reachable next-hop address. The following process summarizes how BGP chooses the best route on a Cisco router:

Step 1.   Prefer the route with the highest weight. (The weight is Cisco proprietary and is local to the router only.)

Step 2.   If multiple routes have the same weight, prefer the route with the highest local preference. (The local preference is used within an autonomous system.)

Step 3.   If multiple routes have the same local preference, prefer the route that was originated by the local router. (A locally originated route has a next hop of 0.0.0.0 in the BGP table.)

Step 4.   If none of the routes were originated by the local router, prefer the route with the shortest AS-path.

Step 5.   If the AS-path length is the same, prefer the lowest-origin code (IGP < EGP < incomplete).

Step 6.   If all origin codes are the same, prefer the path with the lowest MED. (The MED is exchanged between autonomous systems.)

The MED comparison is done only if the neighboring autonomous system is the same for all routes considered, unless the **bgp always-compare-med** router configuration command is enabled.

Note   The most recent Internet Engineering Task Force (IETF) decision about BGP MED assigns a value of infinity to a missing MED, making a route lacking the MED variable the least preferred. The default behavior of BGP routers running Cisco IOS Software is to treat routes without the MED attribute as having a MED of 0, making a route lacking the MED variable the most preferred. To configure the router to conform to the IETF standard, use the **bgp bestpath med missing-as-worst** router configuration command.

Step 7.   If the routes have the same MED, prefer external paths (eBGP) over internal paths (iBGP).

Step 8.   If only internal paths remain, prefer the path through the closest IGP neighbor. This means that the router prefers the shortest internal path within the autonomous system to reach the destination (the shortest path to the BGP next hop).

Step 9.   For eBGP paths, select the oldest route, to minimize the effect of routes going up and down (flapping).

Step 10. Prefer the route with the lowest neighbor BGP router ID value.

Step 11. If the BGP router IDs are the same, prefer the route with the lowest neighbor IP address.

Only the best path is offered to the IP routing table and propagated to the router's BGP neighbors.

Note   The route-selection decision process summarized here does not cover all cases, but it is sufficient for a basic understanding of how BGP selects routes.

Suppose, for example, that there are seven paths to reach network 192.0.2.0. All paths have no autonomous system loops and valid next-hop addresses, so all seven paths proceed to Step 1, which examines the weight of the paths. All seven paths have a weight of 0, so they all proceed to Step 2, which examines the paths' local preference. Four of the paths have a local preference of 200, and the other three have a local preference of 100, 100, and 150. The four with a local preference of 200 continue the evaluation process to the next step. The other three remain in the BGP forwarding table but are currently disqualified as the best path.

BGP continues the evaluation process until only a single best path remains. The single best path that remains is offered to the IP routing table as the best BGP path.

The Path-Selection Decision Process with a Multihomed Connection

An autonomous system rarely implements BGP with only one eBGP connection, so generally multiple paths exist for each network in the BGP forwarding database.

Note   If you are running BGP in a network with only one eBGP connection, it is loop free. If the next hop can be reached, the path is submitted to the IP routing table. Because there is only one path, there is no benefit to manipulating its attributes.

Using the 11-step route-selection process, only the best path is put in the routing table and propagated to the router's BGP neighbors. Without route manipulation, the most common reason for path selection is Step 4, the preference for the shortest AS-path.

Step 1 looks at weight, which by default is set to 0 for routes that were not originated by this router.

Step 2 compares local preference, which by default is set to 100 for all networks. Both Step 1 and Step 2 have an effect only if the network administrator configures the weight or local preference to a nondefault value.

Step 3 looks at networks that are owned by this autonomous system. If one of the routes is injected into the BGP table by the local router, the local router prefers it to any routes received from other BGP routers.

Step 4 selects the path that has the fewest autonomous systems to cross. This is the most common reason a path is selected in BGP. If a network administrator does not like the path with the fewest autonomous systems, he or she needs to manipulate weight or local preference to change which outbound path BGP chooses.

Step 5 looks at how a network was introduced into BGP. This introduction is usually either with **network** commands (*i* for an origin code) or through redistribution (*?* for an origin code).

Step 6 looks at MED to judge where the neighbor autonomous system wants this autonomous system to send packets for a given network. The Cisco IOS Software sets the MED to 0 by default. Therefore, MED does not participate in path selection unless the network administrator of the neighbor autonomous system manipulates the paths using MED.

If multiple paths have the same number of autonomous systems to traverse, the second most common decision point is Step 7, which states that an externally learned path from an eBGP neighbor is preferred over a path learned from an iBGP neighbor. A router in an autonomous system prefers to use the ISP's bandwidth to reach a network rather than using internal bandwidth to reach an iBGP neighbor on the other side of its own autonomous system.

If the autonomous system path length is equal and the router in an autonomous system has no eBGP neighbors for that network (only iBGP neighbors), it makes sense to take the quickest path to the nearest exit point. Step 8 looks for the closest iBGP neighbor; the IGP metric determines what closest means. (For example, RIP uses hop count, and OSPF uses the least cost, which by default is based on bandwidth in the Cisco IOS.)

If the autonomous system path length is equal and the costs via all iBGP neighbors are equal, or if all neighbors for this network are eBGP, the oldest path (Step 9) is the next common reason for selecting one path over another. eBGP neighbors rarely establish sessions at the exact same time. One session is likely older than another, so the paths through that older neighbor are considered more stable because they have been up longer.

If all these criteria are equal, the next most common decision is to take the neighbor with the lowest BGP router ID, which is Step 10.

If the BGP router IDs are the same (for example, if the paths are to the same BGP router), Step 11 states that the route with the lowest neighbor IP address is used.

BGP Attributes

BGP routers send BGP update messages about destination networks to other BGP routers. Update messages can contain NLRI, which is a list of one or more networks (IP address prefixes and their prefix lengths), and path attributes, which are a set of BGP metrics describing the path to these networks (routes). BGP uses the path attributes to determine the best path to the networks. The following are some terms defining how these attributes are implemented:

- An attribute is either well-known or optional, mandatory or discretionary, and transitive or nontransitive. An attribute might also be partial.

- Not all combinations of these characteristics are valid; path attributes fall into four separate categories:

  - Well-known mandatory

  - Well-known discretionary

  - Optional transitive

  - Optional nontransitive

- Only optional transitive attributes might be marked as partial.

These characteristics are described in the following sections.

BGP Path Attribute Format

A BGP update message includes a variable-length sequence of path attributes describing the route. A path attribute is of variable length and consists of three fields:

- Attribute type, which consists of a 1-byte attribute flags field and a 1-byte attribute-type code field
- Attribute length
- Attribute value

The first bit of the attribute flags field indicates whether the attribute is optional or well known. The second bit indicates whether an optional attribute is transitive or nontransitive. The third bit indicates whether a transitive attribute is partial or complete. The fourth bit indicates whether the attribute length field is 1 or 2 bytes. The rest of the flag bits are unused and are set to 0.

Well-Known Attributes

A well-known attribute is one that all BGP implementations must recognize and propagate to BGP neighbors.

There are two types of well-known attributes:

- **Well-known mandatory attribute:** A well-known mandatory attribute *must* appear in all BGP update messages.

> **Note**   If a well-known attribute is missing from an update message, a notification error is generated. This ensures that all BGP implementations agree on a standard set of attributes.

- **Well-known discretionary attribute:** A well-known discretionary attribute does not have to be present in all BGP update messages. (In other words, it is recognized by all BGP implementations but does not have to be in every update message.)

Optional Attributes

Attributes that are not well known are called optional. BGP routers that implement an optional attribute might propagate it to other BGP neighbors, depending on its meaning. Optional attributes are either transitive or nontransitive, as follows:

- **Optional transitive:** BGP routers that do not implement an optional transitive attribute should pass it to other BGP routers untouched and mark the attribute as partial.

- **Optional nontransitive:** BGP routers that do not implement an optional nontransitive attribute must delete the attribute and must not pass it to other BGP routers.

Defined BGP Attributes

The attributes defined by BGP include the following:

- **Well-known mandatory attributes**
  - AS-path
  - Next-hop
  - Origin
- **Well-known discretionary attributes**
  - Local preference
  - Atomic aggregate
- **Optional transitive attributes**
  - Aggregator
  - Community
- **Optional nontransitive attribute**
  - MED

In addition, Cisco has defined a weight attribute for BGP. The weight is configured locally on a router and is not propagated to any other BGP routers.

The AS-path, next-hop, origin, local preference, community, MED, and weight attributes are discussed more fully in the following sections. The atomic aggregate attribute informs the neighbor autonomous system that the originating router has aggregated (summarized) the routes. The aggregator attribute specifies the BGP router ID and autonomous system number of the router that performed the route aggregation. Both of these attributes are discussed in Appendix C, as is BGP community configuration.

> **Note**   Appendix C describes how BGP route summarization is configured, using both the **network** and the **aggregate-address** *ip-address mask* [**summary-only**] [**as-set**] router configuration commands.

BGP Attribute Type Codes

Cisco uses the following attribute type codes:

- **Origin:** Type code 1
- **AS-path:** Type code 2
- **Next-hop:** Type code 3
- **MED:** Type code 4
- **Local preference:** Type code 5
- **Atomic aggregate:** Type code 6
- **Aggregator:** Type code 7
- **Community:** Type code 8 (Cisco defined)
- **Originator ID:** Type code 9 (Cisco defined)
- **Cluster list:** Type code 10 (Cisco defined)

The originator ID and cluster list attributes are discussed in Appendix C.

The AS-Path Attribute

The AS-path attribute is the list of autonomous system numbers that a route has traversed to reach a destination, with the number of the autonomous system that originated the route at the end of the list.

The AS-path attribute is a well-known mandatory attribute. Whenever a route update passes through an autonomous system, the autonomous system number is *prepended* to that update. (In other words, it is put at the beginning of the list when the update is advertised to the next eBGP neighbor.)

In Figure 7-14, router R1 in autonomous system 64520 advertises network 209.165.200.224. When that route traverses autonomous system 65500, router R3 prepends its own autonomous system number to it. When the route reaches router R2, it has two autonomous system numbers attached to it. From router R2's perspective, the path to reach 209.165.200.224 is (65500, 64520).

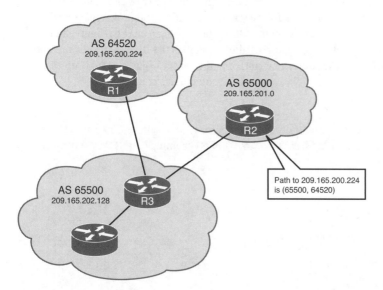

Figure 7-14 *Router R3 Prepends Its Own Autonomous System Number as It Passes Routes from Router R1 to Router R2*

The same applies for 209.165.201.0 and 209.165.202.128. Router R1's path to 209.165.201.0 is (65500 65000); it traverses autonomous system 65500 and then autonomous system 65000. Router R3 has to traverse path (65000) to reach 209.165.201.0 and path (64520) to reach 209.165.200.224.

BGP routers use the AS-path attribute to ensure a loop-free environment. If a BGP router receives a route in which its own autonomous system is part of the AS-path attribute, it does not accept the route.

Autonomous system numbers are prepended only by routers advertising routes to eBGP neighbors. Routers advertising routes to iBGP neighbors do not change the AS-path attribute.

The Next-Hop Attribute

The BGP next-hop attribute is a well-known mandatory attribute that indicates the next-hop IP address that is to be used to reach a destination.

As discussed earlier, for eBGP the next-hop address is the IP address of the neighbor that sent the update, but for iBGP the next hop advertised by eBGP is carried into iBGP by default. Recall that this behavior can be overridden by configuring a router to advertise itself as the next-hop address for routes sent to its neighbor.

The Origin Attribute

The origin is a well-known mandatory attribute that defines the origin of the path information. The origin attribute can be one of three values:

- **IGP:** The route is interior to the originating autonomous system. This normally happens when a **network** command is used to advertise the route via BGP. An origin of IGP is indicated with an *i* in the BGP table.

- **EGP:** The route is learned via EGP. This is indicated with an *e* in the BGP table. EGP is considered a historic routing protocol and is not supported on the Internet because it performs only classful routing and does not support CIDR.

- **Incomplete:** The route's origin is unknown or is learned via some other means. This usually occurs when a route is redistributed into BGP. (Redistribution is discussed in Chapter 4, "Manipulating Routing Updates," and in Appendix C.) An incomplete origin is indicated with a *?* in the BGP table.

The Local-Preference Attribute

Local preference is a well-known discretionary attribute that indicates to routers in the autonomous system which path is preferred to exit the autonomous system.

A path with a *higher* local preference is preferred.

The term *local* refers to inside the autonomous system. The local preference attribute is sent only to iBGP neighbors; it is not passed to eBGP peers. Thus, local preference is an attribute that is configured on a router and exchanged only among routers within the same autonomous system. The default value for local preference on a Cisco router is 100.

The Community Attribute

BGP communities are one way to filter incoming or outgoing routes. BGP communities allow routers to *tag* routes with an indicator (the *community*) and allow other routers to make decisions based on that tag. Any BGP router can tag routes in incoming and outgoing routing updates, or when doing redistribution. Any BGP router can filter routes in incoming or outgoing updates or can select preferred routes based on communities (the tag).

BGP communities are used for destinations (routes) that share some common properties and, therefore, share common policies; routers act on the community rather than on individual routes. Communities are not restricted to one network or one autonomous system, and they have no physical boundaries.

Communities are optional transitive attributes. If a router does not understand the concept of communities, it defers to the next router. However, if the router does understand the concept, it must be configured to propagate the community; otherwise, communities are dropped by default.

> **Note**   BGP community configuration is detailed in Appendix C.

The MED Attribute

The MED attribute, also called the *metric*, is an optional nontransitive attribute.

> **Note**   The MED attribute is called the metric in the Cisco IOS. In the output of the **show ip bgp** command for example, the MED is displayed in the *metric* column.

The MED indicates to *external* neighbors the preferred path *into* an autonomous system. This is a dynamic way for an autonomous system to try to influence another autonomous system as to which way it should choose to reach a certain route if there are multiple entry points into the autonomous system.

A *lower* metric value is preferred.

Unlike local preference, the MED is exchanged between autonomous systems. The MED is sent to eBGP peers; those routers propagate the MED within their autonomous system, and the routers within the autonomous system use the MED, but do not pass it on to the next autonomous system. When the same update is passed on to another autonomous system, the metric will be set back to the default of 0.

It is important to note the difference between MED and local preference: MED influences inbound traffic to an autonomous system, whereas local preference influences outbound traffic from an autonomous system.

By default, a router compares the MED attribute only for paths from neighbors in the same autonomous system.

By using the MED attribute, BGP is the only protocol that can try to affect the path used to send traffic into an autonomous system. However, keep in mind that there is no guarantee that neighboring autonomous system will take the MED attribute into account; it may have already decided on the path based on other attributes.

For example, in Figure 7-15, router R2 and R3 are configured as shown in Example 7-30. Prefix lists and route maps are used in this configuration. Chapter 4 describes prefix lists and how to configure them. Recall that the **ip prefix-list** {*list-name* | *list-number*} [**seq** *seq-value*] {**deny** | **permit**} *network/length* [**ge** *ge-value*] [**le** *le-value*] global configuration command is used to create a prefix list. To apply a route map for BGP routes, use the **neighbor** *ip address* **route-map** *name* {**in** | **out**} router configuration command.

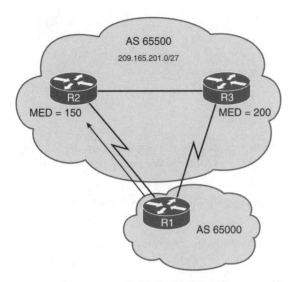

Figure 7-15 *MED Attribute: Router R2 Is the Best Next Hop to Get to Autonomous System 65500*

Example 7-30 *Configuration of Router R2 and R3 in Figure 7-15*

```
R2(config)# ip prefix-list PF1 permit 209.165.201.0/27
R2(config)# route-map SET-MED permit 10
R2(config-route-map)# match ip address prefix-list PF1
R2(config-route-map)# set metric 150
R2(config-route-map)# route-map SET-MED permit 20
R2(config-route-map)# exit
R2(config)# router bgp 65550
R2(config-router)# neighbor 209.165.202.129 route-map SET-MED out
```
```
R3(config)# ip prefix-list PF1 permit 209.165.201.0/27
R3(config)# route-map SET-MED permit 10
R3(config-route-map)# match ip address prefix-list PF1
R3(config-route-map)# set metric 200
R3(config-route-map)# route-map SET-MED permit 20
R3(config-route-map)# exit
R3(config)# router bgp 65550
R3(config-router)# neighbor 209.165.202.133 route-map SET-MED out
```

In Example 7-30, when sending the route 209.165.201.0/27 to R1 in autonomous system 65000, R2 sets the MED to 150 and R3 sets the MED attribute to 200. When router R1 receives update messages from routers R2 and R3 (which include the path attributes), it picks router R2 as the best next hop to get to the route 209.165.201.0/27 in autonomous system 65500 because the MED from router R2 of 150 is less than the MED from router R3 of 200.

Note By default, the MED comparison is done only if the neighboring autonomous system is the same for all routes considered. For the router to compare metrics from neighbors coming from different autonomous systems, the **bgp always-compare-med** router configuration command must be configured on the router.

The Weight Attribute (Cisco Only)

The weight attribute is a Cisco-defined attribute used for the path-selection process. The weight attribute is configured locally and provides local routing policy only; it is *not* propagated to *any* BGP neighbors.

Routes with a *higher* weight are preferred when multiple routes to the same destination exist.

The weight can have a value from 0 to 65535. Paths that the router originates have a weight of 32768 by default, and other paths have a weight of 0 by default.

The weight attribute applies when using one router with multiple exit points out of an autonomous system. Compare this to the local preference attribute, which is used when two or more routers provide multiple exit points.

In Figure 7-16, routers R2 and R3 learn about network 209.165.201.0 from autonomous system 65250 and propagate the update to router R1. Router R1 has two ways to reach 209.165.201.0 and must decide which way to go. In the example, router R1 is configured to set the weight of updates coming from router R2 to 200 and the weight of those coming from router R3 to 150. Because the weight for router R2's updates is higher than the weight for router R3's updates, router R1 uses router R2 as a next hop to reach 209.165.201.0.

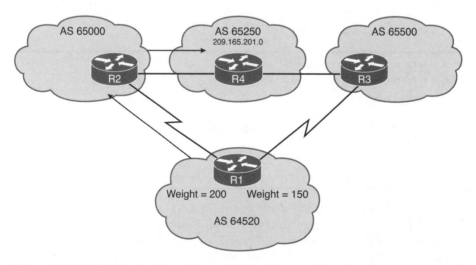

Figure 7-16 *Weight Attribute: Router R1 Uses Router R2 as the Next Hop to Reach 209.165.201.0*

Changing the Weight for All Updates from a Neighbor

The **neighbor** *ip-address* **weight** *weight* router configuration command is used to assign a weight to updates from a neighbor connection, as described in Table 7-4.

Table 7-4 **neighbor weight** *Command Description*

Parameter	Description
ip-address	The BGP neighbor's IP address.
weight	The weight to assign. Acceptable values are 0 to 65535. The default is 32768 for local routes (routes that the router originates). Other routes have a weight of 0 by default.

Changing the Weight Using Route Maps

The network shown in Figure 7-17 is used as an example to demonstrate how to change the weight attribute using route maps. Example 7-31 shows a partial configuration of router R1.

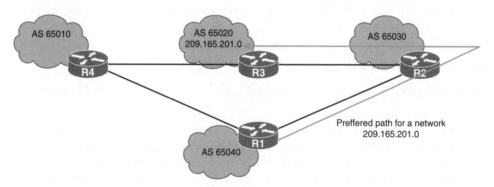

Figure 7-17 *Weight Attribute: Router R1 Uses Router R2 as the Next Hop to Reach 209.165.201.0*

Example 7-31 *Configuration of Router R1 in Figure 7-17*

```
R1(config)# ip prefix-list AS65020_ROUTES permit 209.165.201.0/24 le 28
R1(config)# route-map RM-SET-Weight permit 10
R1(config-route-map)# match ip address prefix-list AS65020_ROUTES
R1(config-route-map)# set weight 150
R1(config-route-map)# route-map RM-SET-Weight permit 20
R1(config-route-map)# set weight 100
R1(config-route-map)# exit
R1(config)# router bgp 65040
R1(config-router)# neighbor 209.165.202.129 route-map RM-SET-Weight in
```

In Example 7-31, the routing policy dictates the selection of autonomous system 65030 as the primary way out of autonomous system 65040 for the traffic destined to the 209.165.201.0 network. This is achieved by placing a higher weight (150) on all incoming announcements from autonomous system 65030 (from neighbor 209.165.202.129), which carry the information about this network.

The first step is to create a route map. The first line of the route map called RM-SET-Weight is a **permit** statement with a sequence number of 10; it defines the first **route-map** statement. Next, a rule for changing the BGP weight attribute is created. The **match** condition for this statement checks the AS65020_ROUTES prefix list, which matches the 209.165.201.0/24 route and any routes with the same first 24 bits and a mask of between /24 and /28 inclusive. The **set** command changes the weight attribute to 150 for all routes that are matched by the prefix list.

The second statement in the route map is a **permit** statement with a sequence number of 20; it does not have any **match** statements, so all remaining updates are permitted. It sets the weight to 100 for all routes that were not matched by the prefix list in the previous statement.

This route map is linked to neighbor 209.165.202.129 as an inbound route map. Therefore, as router R1 receives updates from 209.165.202.129 (R2), it processes them through the RM-SET-Weight route map and sets the weight accordingly as the routes are placed in router R1's BGP table.

Influencing BGP Path Selection

In this section, an example is used to illustrate how to configure and verify BGP attributes.

Figure 7-18 displays the network diagram for this example. All BGP sessions have already been established. GW1 and GW2 are advertising the networks configured on their loopback 1 interfaces into BGP, and ISP3 is advertising the two networks on its loopback 0 interface into BGP. GW1 and GW2 are running OSPF within autonomous system 65000.

After examining the current state, we will change some BGP attributes to alter the traffic path. First we will assign a higher weight for updates that are received by GW2 from GW1 to prefer GW1 as the exit point from the autonomous system 65000. Having verified that the weight has only local significance we will replace the weight-based configuration with a higher local preference setting on GW1 for updates that are received from ISP1. Finally, we will cause the inbound traffic to autonomous system 65000 to prefer the faster path by configuring AS-path prepending for updates advertised by GW2 to ISP2.

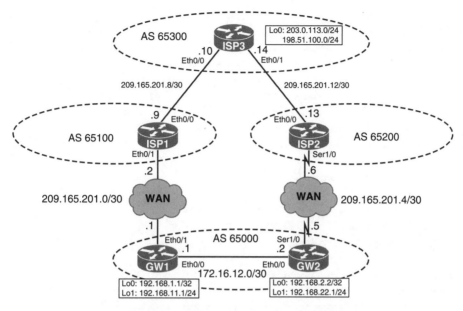

Figure 7-18   *Network for BGP Path Selection Example*

Lets' first verify the initial state of BGP on GW1 by examining the BGP table and routing table and then verifying connectivity to the external networks advertised by ISP3 (hosts 198.51.100.1 and 203.0.113.1). To verify connectivity between autonomous system 65000 and autonomous system 65300 on GW1, we need to source the traffic from an IP address that ISP3 can reach; because GW1 advertises its loopback 1 network (192.168.11.0/24) in BGP, ISP3 will be able to reach that network.

Example 7-32 provides GW1's output.

Example 7-32   *BGP Verification on GW1*

```
GW1# show ip bgp
BGP table version is 20, local router ID is 209.165.201.1
Status codes: s suppressed, d damped, h history, * valid, > best, i - internal,
              r RIB-failure, S Stale, m multipath, b backup-path, f RT-Filter,
              x best-external, a additional-path, c RIB-compressed,
Origin codes: i - IGP, e - EGP, ? - incomplete
RPKI validation codes: V valid, I invalid, N Not found

     Network          Next Hop          Metric LocPrf Weight Path
 *>  192.168.11.0     0.0.0.0                0          32768 i
 *>i 192.168.22.0     192.168.2.2            0    100      0 i
 *>  198.51.100.0     209.165.201.2                        0 65100 65300 i
 * i                  209.165.201.6          0    100      0 65200 65300 i
 *>  203.0.113.0      209.165.201.2                        0 65100 65300 i
 * i                  209.165.201.6          0    100      0 65200 65300 i
```

```
GW1# show ip route bgp
Codes: L - local, C - connected, S - static, R - RIP, M - mobile, B - BGP
       D - EIGRP, EX - EIGRP external, O - OSPF, IA - OSPF inter area
       N1 - OSPF NSSA external type 1, N2 - OSPF NSSA external type 2
       E1 - OSPF external type 1, E2 - OSPF external type 2
       i - IS-IS, su - IS-IS summary, L1 - IS-IS level-1, L2 - IS-IS level-2
       ia - IS-IS inter area, * - candidate default, U - per-user static route
       o - ODR, P - periodic downloaded static route, H - NHRP, l - LISP
       + - replicated route, % - next hop override

Gateway of last resort is not set

B     192.168.22.0/24 [200/0] via 192.168.2.2, 23:40:37
B     198.51.100.0/24 [20/0] via 209.165.201.2, 01:18:10
B     203.0.113.0/24 [20/0] via 209.165.201.2, 01:18:10

GW1# ping 198.51.100.1 source loopback 1
Type escape sequence to abort.
Sending 5, 100-byte ICMP Echos to 198.51.100.1, timeout is 2 seconds:
Packet sent with a source address of 192.168.11.1
!!!!!
Success rate is 100 percent (5/5), round-trip min/avg/max = 4/4/5 ms

GW1# traceroute 198.51.100.1 source loopback 1
Type escape sequence to abort.
Tracing the route to 198.51.100.1
VRF info: (vrf in name/id, vrf out name/id)
  1 209.165.201.2 0 msec 0 msec 1 msec
  2 209.165.201.10 4 msec *  4 msec
GW1# traceroute 203.0.113.1 source loopback 1
Type escape sequence to abort.
Tracing the route to 203.0.113.1
VRF info: (vrf in name/id, vrf out name/id)
  1 209.165.201.2 1 msec 0 msec 1 msec
  2 209.165.201.10 0 msec *  1 msec
GW1#
```

The BGP table and routing table on GW1 in Example 7-32 show that the ISP3 prefixes
198.51.100.0/24 and 203.0.113.0/24 have been received via both ISP paths (ISP1 and
ISP2). GW1 prefers the external routes via ISP1 because external BGP routes are preferred over internal BGP routes. ISP3's loopback networks are both reachable from
GW1.

Similarly, let's verify GW2's initial state and connectivity. Example 7-33 provides GW2's
output.

Example 7-33 *BGP Verification on GW2*

```
GW2# show ip bgp
BGP table version is 15, local router ID is 192.168.2.2
Status codes: s suppressed, d damped, h history, * valid, > best, i - internal,
              r RIB-failure, S Stale, m multipath, b backup-path, f RT-Filter,
              x best-external, a additional-path, c RIB-compressed,
Origin codes: i - IGP, e - EGP, ? - incomplete
RPKI validation codes: V valid, I invalid, N Not found

     Network          Next Hop         Metric LocPrf Weight Path
 *>i 192.168.11.0     192.168.1.1           0    100      0 i
 *>  192.168.22.0     0.0.0.0               0         32768 i
 *  i 198.51.100.0    209.165.201.2         0    100      0 65100 65300 i
 *>                   209.165.201.6                       0 65200 65300 i
 *  i 203.0.113.0     209.165.201.2         0    100      0 65100 65300 i
 *>                   209.165.201.6                       0 65200 65300 i
GW2# show ip route bgp
Codes: L - local, C - connected, S - static, R - RIP, M - mobile, B - BGP
       D - EIGRP, EX - EIGRP external, O - OSPF, IA - OSPF inter area
       N1 - OSPF NSSA external type 1, N2 - OSPF NSSA external type 2
       E1 - OSPF external type 1, E2 - OSPF external type 2
       i - IS-IS, su - IS-IS summary, L1 - IS-IS level-1, L2 - IS-IS level-2
       ia - IS-IS inter area, * - candidate default, U - per-user static route
       o - ODR, P - periodic downloaded static route, H - NHRP, l - LISP
       + - replicated route, % - next hop override


Gateway of last resort is not set

B     192.168.11.0/24 [200/0] via 192.168.1.1, 23:56:54
B     198.51.100.0/24 [20/0] via 209.165.201.6, 01:50:22
B     203.0.113.0/24 [20/0] via 209.165.201.6, 01:50:22


GW2# ping 198.51.100.1 source loopback 1
Type escape sequence to abort.
Sending 5, 100-byte ICMP Echos to 198.51.100.1, timeout is 2 seconds:
Packet sent with a source address of 192.168.22.1
!!!!!
Success rate is 100 percent (5/5), round-trip min/avg/max = 7/8/9 ms


GW2# traceroute 198.51.100.1 source loopback 1
Type escape sequence to abort.
Tracing the route to 198.51.100.1
VRF info: (vrf in name/id, vrf out name/id)
  1 209.165.201.6 8 msec 8 msec 8 msec
```

```
  2 209.165.201.14 8 msec *  6 msec

GW2# traceroute 203.0.113.1 source loopback 1
Type escape sequence to abort.
Tracing the route to 203.0.113.1
VRF info: (vrf in name/id, vrf out name/id)
  1 209.165.201.6 7 msec 9 msec 9 msec
  2 209.165.201.14 9 msec *  9 msec
GW2#
```

Similar to GW1, Example 7-33 verifies that GW2's BGP table contains ISP3's prefixes via both ISP paths (ISP1 and ISP2). Just like GW1, GW2 prefers the external routes via ISP2 because external BGP routes are preferred over internal BGP routes. In this case, however, this selection is really not the best path because the uplink to ISP2 is slower than the primary uplink to ISP1. ISP3's loopback networks are both reachable from GW2.

Now let's verify ISP3's initial state and connectivity. Example 7-34 provides this output, including checking connectivity to the networks advertised by GW1 and GW2 (hosts 192.168.11.1 and 192.168.22.1).

Example 7-34 *BGP Verification on ISP3*

```
ISP3# show ip bgp
<Output omitted>
     Network          Next Hop         Metric LocPrf Weight Path
  *   192.168.11.0     209.165.201.13                      0 65200 65000 i
  *>                   209.165.201.9                        0 65100 65000 i
  *   192.168.22.0     209.165.201.9                        0 65100 65000 i
  *>                   209.165.201.13                       0 65200 65000 i
  *>  198.51.100.0     0.0.0.0               0         32768 i
  *>  203.0.113.0      0.0.0.0               0         32768 i


ISP3# sh ip route bgp
<Output omitted>
Gateway of last resort is not set

B     192.168.11.0/24 [20/0] via 209.165.201.9, 00:10:53
B     192.168.22.0/24 [20/0] via 209.165.201.13, 00:10:56


ISP3# ping 192.168.11.1 source loopback 0
Type escape sequence to abort.
Sending 5, 100-byte ICMP Echos to 192.168.11.1, timeout is 2 seconds:
Packet sent with a source address of 198.51.100.1
!!!!!
Success rate is 100 percent (5/5), round-trip min/avg/max = 1/1/1 ms
```

```
ISP3# traceroute 192.168.22.1 source loopback 0
Type escape sequence to abort.
Tracing the route to 192.168.22.1
VRF info: (vrf in name/id, vrf out name/id)
  1 209.165.201.13 1 msec 0 msec 1 msec
  2 209.165.201.5 9 msec *  9 msec
ISP3#
```

The GW1 and GW2 loopback networks are both reachable from ISP3. The BGP and routing table on ISP3 show that the autonomous system 65000 prefixes 192.168.11.0/24 and 192.168.22.0/24 have been received via both ISP paths (ISP1 and ISP2). Both updates have the same attributes, so ISP3 selects the oldest path as the tie-break rule. Notice that because of this, in Example 7-34, ISP3 chose a different path for each of the two autonomous system 65000 prefixes! During testing we observed different results, depending on which routes came up first. Therefore, the path is not deterministic, and as shown in Example 7-34 for the 192.168.22.0 prefix, selecting the oldest path route can result in the lower-bandwidth serial WAN link between ISP2 and GW2 being used, which is an undesirable situation.

Changing the Weight

Let's explore ways to alter the path that traffic takes. We first change the default weight on GW2 for all updates received from GW1 to a nonzero value; this will cause the pre-fixes received via iBGP to be preferred. Example 7-35 shows the configuration and veri-fication on GW2.

Example 7-35 *Changing the Weight on GW2*

```
GW2(config)# router bgp 65000
GW2(config-router)# neighbor 192.168.1.1 weight 10

GW2# show ip bgp
<Output omitted>
     Network          Next Hop          Metric LocPrf Weight Path
 *>i 192.168.11.0     192.168.1.1            0    100      0 i
 *>  192.168.22.0     0.0.0.0                0         32768 i
 * i 198.51.100.0     209.165.201.2          0    100      0 65100 65300 i
 *>                   209.165.201.6                       0 65200 65300 i
 * i 203.0.113.0      209.165.201.2          0    100      0 65100 65300 i
 *>                   209.165.201.6                       0 65200 65300 i
GW2#
```

Notice in Example 7-35 that when the default weight for GW1 is configured on GW2, the BGP table on GW2 does *not* immediately reflect the policy change. BGP applies the new policy when new updates are exchanged, so we need to perform a hard or soft reset to resend the BGP updates from GW1 to GW2.

Example 7-36 shows a soft BGP inbound reset on GW2 for its GW1 neighbor, and the results.

Example 7-36   *Doing a Soft BGP Inbound Reset and Verifying Results*

```
GW2# clear ip bgp 192.168.1.1 in
GW2# sh ip bgp
<Output omitted>
      Network           Next Hop          Metric LocPrf Weight Path
 *>i 192.168.11.0      192.168.1.1             0    100     10 i
 *>  192.168.22.0      0.0.0.0                 0          32768 i
 *>i 198.51.100.0      209.165.201.2           0    100     10 65100 65300 i
 *                     209.165.201.6                        0 65200 65300 i
 *>i 203.0.113.0       209.165.201.2           0    100     10 65100 65300 i
 *                     209.165.201.6                        0 65200 65300 i
GW2#


GW2# traceroute 198.51.100.1 source loopback 1
Type escape sequence to abort.
Tracing the route to 198.51.100.1
VRF info: (vrf in name/id, vrf out name/id)
  1 172.16.12.1 1 msec 1 msec 0 msec
  2 209.165.201.2 1 msec 0 msec 1 msec
  3 209.165.201.10 3 msec *  5 msec
GW2#
```

As shown in Example 7-36, after a soft BGP inbound reset on GW2, GW1 resends the BGP updates to GW2 and GW2 applies the new policy with the non-zero weight value. GW2 now prefers updates received from GW1 over the external updates received from ISP2. The traffic path to external destinations (such as 198.51.100.1) now traverses GW1 and ISP1. Note that this new policy affects the routing decisions of GW2 but does not influence any other routers. GW1 will still prefer external routes and will send outbound traffic via ISP1.

Changing Local Preference

Local-preference settings *are* shared within an autonomous system, so this will affect both GW1 and GW2. One way to change the local preference is to change the default value of 100 with the **bgp default local-preference** *value* router configuration command; all BGP routes that are advertised would include this local preference value. Local preference can also be changed within a route map; let's do this and set a higher local preference on GW1 for updates that are received from ISP1. Example 7-37 shows the configuration; on GW2 we first remove the weight configuration, and then configure the local preference on GW1. The route map prefer_isp1 includes one statement that matches all updates and sets the local preference to 150. This route map is applied to updates from ISP1.

Example 7-37 *Changing Local Preference on GW1*

```
GW2(config)# router bgp 65000
GW2(config-router)# no neighbor 192.168.1.1 weight 10

GW1(config)# route-map prefer_isp1 permit 10
GW1(config-route-map)# set local-preference 150
GW1(config-route-map)# router bgp 65000
GW1(config-router)# neighbor 209.165.201.2 route-map prefer_isp1 in
```

We need to clear the BGP session on GW1 with ISP1 to make the local-preference setting effective, and then wait for BGP to converge (this takes a few minutes). Example 7-38 shows the resulting BGP table.

Example 7-38 *Clearing the BGP Session and Verifying Results*

```
GW1# clear ip bgp 209.165.201.2 in

GW1# show ip bgp
<Output omitted>
     Network          Next Hop          Metric LocPrf Weight Path
 *>  192.168.11.0     0.0.0.0                0          32768 i
 *>i 192.168.22.0     192.168.2.2            0    100      0 i
 *>  198.51.100.0     209.165.201.2               150      0 65100 65300 i
 *>  203.0.113.0      209.165.201.2               150      0 65100 65300 i
GW1#
```

The BGP table in Example 7-38 shows the local preference 150 for the external networks 198.51.100.0/24 and 203.0.113.0/24. Both external networks are still reached via ISP1. Notice that routes about these external networks received from GW2 have disappeared from GW1's BGP table. This is because GW2 now prefers the path over GW1 and only best paths are exchanged between BGP neighbors. Example 7-39 displays GW2's BGP table; the best path to the external networks has a local preference of 150 and is via GW1.

Example 7-39 *GW2 Traffic to ISP3's Networks Travels via GW1*

```
GW2# show ip bgp
<Output omitted>
     Network          Next Hop          Metric LocPrf Weight Path
 *>i 192.168.11.0     192.168.1.1            0    100     10 i
 *>  192.168.22.0     0.0.0.0                0          32768 i
 *>i 198.51.100.0     209.165.201.2          0    150      0 65100 65300 i
 *                    209.165.201.6                        0 65200 65300 i
 *>i 203.0.113.0      209.165.201.2          0    150      0 65100 65300 i
 *                    209.165.201.6                        0 65200 65300 i
GW2#
```

```
GW2# traceroute 198.51.100.1 source loopback 1
Type escape sequence to abort.
Tracing the route to 198.51.100.1
VRF info: (vrf in name/id, vrf out name/id)
  1 172.16.12.1 1 msec 0 msec 1 msec
  2 209.165.201.2 1 msec 0 msec 1 msec
  3 209.165.201.10 5 msec *  5 msec
GW2#
GW2# show ip route
<Output omitted>
      172.16.0.0/16 is variably subnetted, 2 subnets, 2 masks
C        172.16.12.0/30 is directly connected, Ethernet0/0
L        172.16.12.2/32 is directly connected, Ethernet0/0
      192.168.1.0/32 is subnetted, 1 subnets
O        192.168.1.1 [110/11] via 172.16.12.1, 00:03:20, Ethernet0/0
      192.168.2.0/32 is subnetted, 1 subnets
C        192.168.2.2 is directly connected, Loopback0
B     192.168.11.0/24 [200/0] via 192.168.1.1, 00:02:50
      192.168.22.0/24 is variably subnetted, 2 subnets, 2 masks
C        192.168.22.0/24 is directly connected, Loopback1
L        192.168.22.1/32 is directly connected, Loopback1
B     198.51.100.0/24 [200/0] via 209.165.201.2, 00:01:01
B     203.0.113.0/24 [200/0] via 209.165.201.2, 00:01:01
      209.165.201.0/24 is variably subnetted, 3 subnets, 2 masks
O        209.165.201.0/30 [110/20] via 172.16.12.1, 00:03:20, Ethernet0/0
C        209.165.201.4/30 is directly connected, Serial1/0
L        209.165.201.5/32 is directly connected, Serial1/0
```

Notice in Example 7-39 that the next-hop on GW2's routes to the external networks is ISP1's address (209.165.201.2); these routes are valid because GW2 learns about ISP1's IP address via OSPF, which runs between GW1 and GW2.

Setting the AS-Path

It is complicated to influence other autonomous systems to select a particular path for traffic that is returning to a specific autonomous system. Because it is unlikely that the operator of an autonomous system can request changes in router configurations in another autonomous system, it is nearly impossible to influence another autonomous system to select the desired path based on the weight and local-preference attributes because these require configuration changes in the neighboring autonomous system.

Note   Communities, described in Appendix C, can be used to set attributes, including weight and local preference, in other autonomous systems. For example, an ISP with multihomed customers could allow those customers to set the local preference using communities.

As you have seen, by default, if no BGP path-selection tools are configured to influence traffic flow, BGP uses the shortest autonomous system path, regardless of available bandwidth.

One way that an autonomous system can attempt to influence incoming traffic flow is by sending out eBGP updates with an extended AS-path attribute for undesired paths: The autonomous system path is extended with multiple copies of the autonomous system number of the sender. The receiver of this update is less likely to select the path as the best because its AS-path attribute appears to be longer. This feature is called *AS-path prepending*. There is no mechanism to calculate the optimal required prepended AS-path length because the administrator of an autonomous system has no control over whether other autonomous systems are also doing prepending.

To avoid clashes with BGP loop-prevention mechanisms, no other autonomous system number, except that of the sending autonomous system, should be prepended to the AS-path attribute. If another autonomous system number is prepended in the autonomous system path, the routers in the autonomous system that has been prepended will reject the update because of BGP loop-prevention mechanisms.

You can configure prepending on a router for all routing updates that you send to a neighbor or only on a subset of them.

When configuring path prepending, you need to decide how many occurrences of an autonomous system number to prepend. This decision will depend on the topology around your autonomous system. The more occurrences of the autonomous system number that you prepend, the larger the scope of the influence on the surrounding autonomous systems. In our example topology, GW2 needs to prepend a single instance of its autonomous system number to the AS-path advertised to ISP2 so that ISP3 will receive updates about the networks in autonomous system 65000 with a shorter path via ISP1 and a longer path via ISP2. On GW2 let's prepend one occurrence of the local autonomous system number to the AS-path advertised to ISP2 and resend the BGP updates to ISP2; this configuration is shown in Example 7-40. A hard or a soft reset can be done to trigger the updates.

Example 7-40 *GW2 Prepending an Autonomous System Number*

```
GW2(config)# route-map ASPath-Prepend permit 10
GW2(config-route-map)# set as-path prepend 65000
GW2(config-route-map)# router bgp 65000
GW2(config-router)# neighbor 209.165.201.6 route-map ASPath-Prepend out

GW2# clear ip bgp 209.165.201.6 out
```

The route map called ASPath-Prepend has only one statement, a **permit** statement with a sequence number of 10. There is no match condition for this statement, so it matches all updates. The **set as-path prepend** *as-path-string* route-map configuration command is used to modify the AS-path attribute. The *as-path-string* is prepended to the AS-path attribute of the route that is matched by the route map; the range of values is any valid autonomous system number from 1 to 65535. Multiple values can be entered. This route map is linked to neighbor ISP2 as an outbound route map. Therefore, as GW2 sends updates to ISP2, it processes them through the route map and all updates sent to ISP2 are prepended with the autonomous system number of the sender (65000), making that path less preferable for the returning traffic.

Example 7-41 displays the results on ISP3.

Example 7-41 *ISP3 Results after GW2 Prepends an Autonomous System Number*

```
ISP3# show ip bgp
<Output omitted>
     Network          Next Hop          Metric LocPrf Weight Path
 *   192.168.11.0     209.165.201.13                      0 65200 65000 65000 i
 *>                   209.165.201.9                        0 65100 65000 i
 *>  192.168.22.0     209.165.201.9                        0 65100 65000 i
 *                    209.165.201.13                       0 65200 65000 65000 i
 *>  198.51.100.0     0.0.0.0                0         32768 i
 *>  203.0.113.0      0.0.0.0                0         32768 i
ISP3#


ISP3# trace 192.168.22.1 source loopback0
Type escape sequence to abort.
Tracing the route to 192.168.22.1
VRF info: (vrf in name/id, vrf out name/id)
  1 209.165.201.9 1 msec 0 msec 1 msec
  2 209.165.201.1 0 msec 1 msec 0 msec
  3 172.16.12.2 0 msec *  1 msec
ISP3#
```

As shown in Example 7-41, ISP3's BGP table still includes two routes for each internal network 192.168.11.0/24 and 192.168.22.0/24. The preferred routes point to ISP1 and have a shorter AS-path consisting of only two autonomous system numbers (65100 65000). The other routes point to ISP2 and have a longer AS-path consisting of three autonomous system numbers (65200 65000 65000). The prepending of the autonomous system number on GW2 has caused ISP3 to prefer the path via the faster Ethernet link from ISP1 to GW1.

Let's verify that the other path will still work if the faster path is no longer available by shutting down the Ethernet link between ISP1 and GW1. After waiting for a few minutes, we verify outbound connectivity from GW1 to ISP3 and inbound connectivity from ISPF3 to GW1. Example 7-42 displays the configuration and results.

Example 7-42 *Verifying That a Redundant Path Is Available After Link Down*

```
GW1(config)# interface ethernet 0/1
GW1(config-if)# shutdown
GW1# show ip bgp
```

```
<Output omitted>
    Network          Next Hop        Metric LocPrf Weight Path
 *>   192.168.11.0    0.0.0.0              0         32768 i
 *>i 192.168.22.0     192.168.2.2          0    100      0 i
 *>i 198.51.100.0     209.165.201.6        0    100      0 65200 65300 i
 *>i 203.0.113.0      209.165.201.6        0    100      0 65200 65300 i
GW1#
GW1# trace 198.51.100.1 source loopback 1
Type escape sequence to abort.
Tracing the route to 198.51.100.1
VRF info: (vrf in name/id, vrf out name/id)
  1 172.16.12.2 0 msec 0 msec 0 msec
  2 209.165.201.6 9 msec 9 msec 9 msec
  3 209.165.201.14 9 msec *   9 msec
GW1#

ISP3# show ip bgp
<Output omitted>
    Network          Next Hop        Metric LocPrf Weight Path
 *>   192.168.11.0    209.165.201.13                    0 65200 65000 65000 i
 *>   192.168.22.0    209.165.201.13                    0 65200 65000 65000 i
 *>   198.51.100.0    0.0.0.0              0         32768 i
 *>   203.0.113.0     0.0.0.0              0         32768 i
ISP3#
ISP3# trace 192.168.11.1 source loopback 0
 Type escape sequence to abort.
 Tracing the route to 192.168.11.1
 VRF info: (vrf in name/id, vrf out name/id)
   1 209.165.201.13 1 msec 0 msec 1 msec
   2 209.165.201.5 9 msec 9 msec 9 msec
   3 172.16.12.1 9 msec *   6 msec
ISP3#
```

Notice in Example 7-42 that BGP will reconverge (after a few minutes) so that the secondary path via ISP2 is used. ISP2 is used to forward the traffic between autonomous system 65000 and autonomous system 65300, and on the return path, from autonomous system 65300 to autonomous system 65000.

Controlling BGP Routing Updates

If there are multiple paths between your network and ISP, you may need to filter certain information during the exchange of BGP updates to influence the route selection or to enforce an administrative policy. The "Filtering BGP Routing Updates" subsection that follows explores these filtering options.

BGP peer groups are used to group peers with similar policies together for a simpler, more efficient configuration. The "BGP Peer Groups," section that follows explores peer group operation and configuration.

Filtering BGP Routing Updates

BGP allows you to filter updates that are received from a neighbor or that are sent to a neighbor. The primary route filtering tools include route maps and prefix lists. We have seen these tools used for matching and setting attributes; they can also be used to permit or deny updates. If denied, the network advertisement is dropped from the BGP update.

> **Note**   Distribute lists can also be used for filtering BGP updates, either for the whole BGP process or within a **neighbor** command. Distribute lists for BGP filtering are not covered further in this book.

A common scenario where update filtering is used is in dual-homed enterprise environments. In this environment, an enterprise should advertise only its own address space to the ISPs. If the enterprise advertises address blocks received from an ISP, other ISPs may use the enterprise autonomous system to transit traffic and the enterprise becomes a transit autonomous system.

This section describes the steps needed to configure routing update filtering using prefix lists, AS-path access lists, and route maps.

BGP Filtering Using Prefix Lists

Chapter 4 describes prefix lists and how to configure them. This section introduces the use of prefix lists for BGP route filtering.

The **neighbor** *ip-address* **prefix-list** *prefix-list-name* {**in** | **out**} router configuration command is used to apply a prefix list to routes from or to a neighbor. Table 7-5 describes the parameters of this command.

Table 7-5   neighbor prefix-list *Command Description*

Parameter	Description
ip-address	IP address of the BGP neighbor.
prefix-list-name	Name of a prefix list.
in	Prefix list is applied to incoming advertisements.
out	Prefix list is applied to outgoing advertisements.

For example, consider Figure 7-19 and the configuration on router R2 in Example 7-43. The prefix list named ANY-8to24-NET is configured to match routes from any networks that have a mask length from 8 to 24 bits. The 0.0.0.0/0 network/length combination does not match a specific network; rather, it defines any network. The parameters **ge 8** and **le 24** specify that any network with the mask length between 8 and 24 matches the prefix list entry.

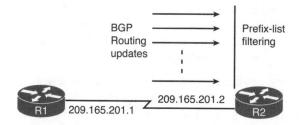

Figure 7-19 *Filtering BGP with Prefix Lists Examples*

Example 7-43 *Configuration for Router R2 in Figure 7-19*

```
router bgp 65001
  neighbor 209.165.201.1 remote-as 65002
  neighbor 209.165.201.1 prefix-list ANY-8to24-NET in
!
ip prefix-list ANY-8to24-NET permit 0.0.0.0/0 ge 8 le 24
```

The prefix list ANY-8to24-NET is applied to the incoming advertisements from the BGP neighbor 209.165.201.1. It permits routes from any network with a mask length from 8 to 24 bits.

Note Cisco IOS documentation for the **neighbor prefix-list** command says this command is used to "prevent distribution" of BGP neighbor information as specified in a prefix list. Other documentation interprets this statement incorrectly and assumes that routes permitted by the prefix list are denied (prevented) from being sent (with the **out** keyword) or received (with the **in** keyword).

Our testing confirmed that the **neighbor prefix-list** command actually behaves as we expected: Routes permitted by the prefix list are sent (with the **out** keyword) or received (with the **in** keyword).

You can use the **show ip prefix-list detail** command to display detailed information about configured prefix lists. Use the **clear ip prefix-list** *prefix-list-name* [*network/ length*] command to reset the hit count shown on prefix list entries in the **show ip prefix-list detail** command output.

BGP Filtering Using AS-Path Access Lists

Several scenarios may require filtering and selection of routing information based on the content of the AS-path attribute carried with each BGP route.

Recall that the AS-path attribute is the list of autonomous system numbers that a route has traversed to reach a destination, with the number of the autonomous system that originated the route at the end of the list. When a BGP route is sourced as a result of a **network** command in a BGP process or redistribution into a BGP process, the AS-path attribute is created and is empty. Each time the route is advertised by an egress router to another autonomous system, the AS-path attribute is modified by the egress router, which prepends its autonomous system number to the AS-path attribute.

Routers can filter incoming routes based on their AS-path attributes. For example, an autonomous system that wants to filter out all but the routes that are local to itself before sending them to a neighboring autonomous system can permit only routes with the empty AS-path to be sent, and deny sending all others. As another example, an autonomous system may not want routes from a specific autonomous system to be received from a certain neighbor; in this case, routes with that autonomous system in the AS-path can be filtered on the receiving router.

When routers filter BGP updates based on the content of the AS-path attribute, they use regular expressions. Regular expressions are commonly found in the UNIX environment and also in some Microsoft Windows-based applications. Regular expressions are a string-matching tool and consist of a string of characters. Some of these characters have special meanings, such as functioning as wildcards and operators. Table 7-6 provides some examples of special characters used in regular expressions. Some characters simply mean themselves (for example, A to Z, a to z, or 0 to 9). A regular expression is said to match a string if the ordinary characters and the applied meaning of the special operator characters can be translated into the matched string. When a regular expression matches, the selection test is said to be true. If it does not match, the test is false. For example, the combination ^$ means an empty string; this could be used when searching for all routes that are sourced in the local autonomous system.

Table 7-6   *Some Special Characters Used in Regular Expressions*

Parameter	Description
.	Matches any single character
*	Matchers 0 or more sequences of a pattern
^	Matches the beginning of a string
$	Matches the end of the string
_ (underscore)	Matches a comma, left brace, right brace, left parenthesis, right parenthesis, the beginning of a string, the end of a string, or a space

The autonomous system path access list is defined by the **ip as-path access-list** *access-list-number* {**permit** | **deny**} *regexp* global configuration command. The parameters of this command are described in Table 7-7.

Table 7-7   ip as-path access-list *Command Description*

Parameter	Description
access-list-number	Number from 1 to 500 that specifies the AS-path access list number.
permit	**deny**	Indicates whether this entry allows or blocks if the regular expression is true.
regexp	Regular expression that defines the AS-path filter. The autonomous system number is expressed in the range from 1 to 65535.

Note   See the Cisco.com document "Understanding Regular Expressions" for information about configuring regular expressions.

The **neighbor** *ip-address* **filter-list** *access-list-number* {**in** | **out**} router configuration command is used to apply an AS-path access list to routes from or to a neighbor. The parameters of this command are described in Table 7-8.

Table 7-8   neighbor filter-list *Command Description*

Parameter	Description
ip-address	IP address of the BGP neighbor.
access-list-number	Number of an AS-path access list.
in	Access list is applied to incoming routes.
out	Access list is applied to outgoing routes.

Routes that are permitted by the AS-path access list are permitted to be received from or sent to the neighbor, and those that are denied are not included. As in all access lists, the candidate to be permitted or denied is tested against the lines in the access list in the order in which the list is configured. The first match indicates "permit" or "deny," as specified in the line. If the end of the access list is reached without any explicit match, the candidate is implicitly denied.

Consider the multihomed ISP customer in Figure 7-20. Autonomous system 65000 does not want to act as a transit autonomous system between its service providers. This situation is avoided by ensuring that only locally sourced routes are sent to the ISP, and then the customer avoids receiving IP packets from the ISPs for destinations outside its own autonomous system. The configuration for the GW1 and GW2 routers is shown in Example 7-44. The AS-path access list permits only the empty string, matched by the regular expression ^$, which represents locally sourced routes. By applying this filter list on outgoing information to all neighbors, the customer announces only its local routes.

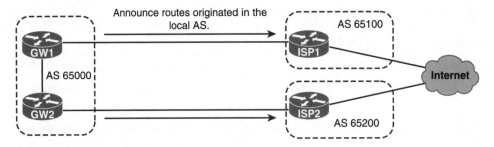

Figure 7-20 *Filtering BGP with AS-Path Access Lists Example*

Example 7-44 *Configuration for Routers GW1 and GW2 in Figure 7-20*

```
GW1(config)# ip as-path access-list 1 permit ^$
GW1(config)# router bgp 65000
GW1(config-router)# neighbor 209.165.201.1 filter-list 1 out
```

```
GW2(config)# ip as-path access-list 1 permit ^$
GW2(config)# router bgp 65000
GW2(config-router)# neighbor 209.165.201.5 filter-list 1 out
```

BGP Filtering Using Route Maps

Route maps offer great flexibility to manipulate BGP updates. A route map can match and set several different BGP attributes, including the following:

- Origin

- Next hop

- Community

- Local preference

- MED

Route maps can match based on other items, including the following:

- Network number and subnet mask (with an IP prefix list)

- Route originator

- Tag attached to an IGP route

- AS-path

- Route type (internal or external)

If all the match clauses within a route map statement are matched, the statement is considered to be a match, and the statement is executed (permitted or denied, as specified). When used for BGP filtering, a deny means that the route is ignored and a permit means that the route is processed further and the set clauses are applied. The set clauses allow one or more attributes to be changed or set to specific values before the route passes the route map.

To apply a route map to filter incoming or outgoing BGP routes, use the **neighbor route-map** router configuration command. The routes that are permitted may have their attributes set or changed, using **set** commands in the route map. This is useful when trying to influence route selection.

In the example network in Figure 7-21, the customer accepts only a default route from the two ISPs and uses the link to autonomous system 65100 as their primary link for outbound traffic. Example 7-45 shows the configuration of the customer GW router.

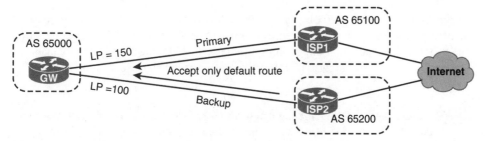

Figure 7-21 *Filtering BGP with Route Maps Example*

Example 7-45 *Configuration of GW in Figure 7-21*

```
router bgp 65000
  neighbor 209.165.201.1 remote-as 65100
  neighbor 209.165.201.1 route-map FILTER in
  neighbor 209.165.201.5 remote-as 65200
  neighbor 209.165.201.5 route-map FILTER in
!
route-map FILTER permit 10
 match ip address prefix-list default-only
 match as-path 10
 set local-preference 150
!
route-map FILTER permit 20
 match ip address prefix-list default-only
!
ip as-path access-list 10 permit ^65100$
ip prefix-list default-only permit 0.0.0.0/0
```

Router GW is configured for BGP with two neighbors using **neighbor remote-as** commands. Both neighbors are configured with the **neighbor route-map** command to filter the incoming routing update traffic according to the route map named FILTER. The route map FILTER allows only a default route into the customer's network, as defined by the prefix list *default-only*. The default route coming from ISP1 in autonomous system 65100, as defined in the AS-path access list 10, is assigned a local-preference value of 150, and all other default routes (in this case, the one coming from ISP2 in autonomous system 65200) will have the default local-preference value of 100. Because a higher local-preference value is preferred, the link to ISP1 autonomous system 65100 is preferred.

Filtering Order

Filter lists (for AS-path filtering), prefix lists, and route maps can be applied to either incoming or outgoing BGP information, or in any combination.

The incoming filter list, prefix list (or distribute list) and route map (in this order) must all permit the routes that are received from a neighbor before they will be accepted into the BGP table. Similarly, outgoing routes must pass the outgoing filter list, route map, and prefix list (or distribute list) (in this order) before they will be sent to the neighbor.

Note   The order in which BGP filtering mechanisms are processed may differ in different IOS versions. The order noted here was confirmed by Cisco during the development of the ROUTE course.

Clearing the BGP Session

Recall from the earlier "Resetting BGP Sessions" section that if you want a policy change, such as a BGP filter, to be applied, you must trigger an update to force the router to let the appropriate routes pass through the filter. You can do either a hard reset or a route refresh (soft reset).

BGP Peer Groups

In BGP, many neighbors are often configured with the same update policies (for example, they have the same filtering applied). On a Cisco IOS router, neighbors with the same update policies can be grouped into peer groups to simplify configuration and, more important, to make updating more efficient and improve performance. When a BGP router has many peers, this approach is highly recommended.

Peer Group Operation

A BGP peer group is a group of BGP neighbors of the router being configured that all have the same update policies.

Instead of separately defining the same policies for each neighbor, a peer group can be defined with these policies assigned to the peer group. Individual neighbors are then made members of the peer group. The policies of the peer group are similar to a template; the template is then applied to the individual members of the peer group.

Members of the peer group inherit all the peer group's configuration options. The router can also be configured to override these options for some members of the peer group if these options do not affect outbound updates. In other words, only options that affect the inbound updates can be overridden.

By default, Cisco IOS Software builds BGP updates for each neighbor individually. Building BGP updates involves a number of router-CPU-consuming tasks, including scanning the BGP table and applying various outgoing filtering mechanisms. When a router is configured with a large number of neighbors, the CPU load grows proportionally. Peer groups are more efficient than defining the same policies for each neighbor, because updates are generated only once per peer group (including all outgoing filter processing) rather than repetitiously for each neighboring router. The generated update is replicated for each neighbor that is part of the peer group. The actual TCP transmission still has to be done on a per-neighbor basis because of the connection-oriented characteristics of BGP sessions.

Thus, peer groups save processing time in generating the updates for all BGP neighbors and make the router configuration easier to read and manage.

BGP neighbors of a single router can be divided into several groups, each group having its own BGP parameters.

A peer group's configuration can have many BGP features, including the following:

- update-source
- next-hop-self
- ebgp-multihop
- Authentication of the BGP sessions (described in Chapter 8, "Routers and Routing Protocol Hardening")
- Change the weight of routes received
- Filter incoming or outgoing routes using a prefix list, a filter list, and a route map

When actual neighboring routers are assigned to the peer group on a router, all the attributes that are configured for the peer group are applied to all peer group members. The Cisco IOS Software optimizes the outgoing routes by running through the outgoing filters and route maps only once and then replicating the results to each of the peer group members. The Cisco IOS Software assigns a peer group leader, for which the software generates an update, and this update is replicated by the leader to all other members of the peer group.

Peer Group Configuration

The **neighbor** *peer-group-name* **peer-group** router configuration command is used to create a BGP peer group. The *peer-group-name* is the name of the BGP peer group to be created. The *peer-group-name* is local to the router on which it is configured; it is not passed to any other router.

Another syntax form of the **neighbor peer-group** command, the **neighbor** *ip-address* **peer-group** *peer-group-name* router configuration command, is used to assign neighbors as part of the group after the group has been created. Table 7-9 provides details of the parameters of this command. Using this command allows you to type the peer group name instead of typing the IP addresses of individual neighbors in other commands (for example, to link a policy to the group of neighboring routers). (Note that you must enter the **neighbor** *peer-group-name* **peer-group** command before the router will accept this second command.)

Table 7-9   neighbor peer-group *Command Description*

Parameter	Description
ip-address	The IP address of the neighbor that is to be assigned as a member of the peer group
peer-group-name	The name of the BGP peer group

A neighboring router can be part of only one peer group.

The **clear ip bgp peer-group** *peer-group-name* EXEC command is used to reset the BGP connections for all members of a BGP peer group. The *peer-group-name* is the name of the BGP peer group for which connections are to be cleared.

Caution   Resetting BGP sessions will disrupt routing.

Peer Group Configuration Example

There are several scenarios where the peer groups are applicable. For example, iBGP sessions are almost always identically configured. If a full mesh is deployed within an autonomous system, a large number of neighbor configurations might exist; configuring these separately results in a tremendous amount of redundant configuration.

Another use case is the configuration of an ISP router with multiple customer-owned BGP peers. The customer autonomous systems are all assumed to announce local networks only. All customer autonomous systems should receive BGP updates with the same set of Internet routes, and the customer autonomous systems are all assumed to generate only a few of prefixes. This situation makes the neighbor configuration almost identical for each of the customers, with only a few changes that are specific to each neighbor.

Figure 7-22 illustrates an enterprise border router that maintains multiple sessions with ISP-owned BGP neighbors. These external sessions share a number of common parameters that make them well suited for a peer group configuration. Example 7-46 provides the configuration of the GW1 router.

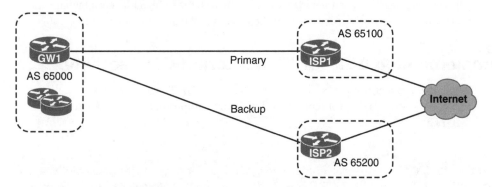

Figure 7-22 *BGP Peer Group Example*

Example 7-46 *Configuration of GW1 in Figure 7-22*

```
router bgp 65000
 neighbor ISP peer-group
 neighbor ISP filter-list 10 out
 neighbor ISP prefix-list desired-subnets in
 neighbor ISP route-map FILTER in
!
neighbor 209.165.201.1 remote-as 65100
neighbor 209.165.201.1 peer-group ISP
neighbor 209.165.201.5 remote-as 65200
neighbor 209.165.201.5 peer-group ISP
!
route-map FILTER permit 10
 match as-path 20
 set local-preference 150
!
route-map FILTER permit 20
!
ip as-path access-list 10 permit ^$
ip as-path access-list 20 permit ^65100_
!
ip prefix-list desired-subnets permit 0.0.0.0/0
ip prefix-list desired-subnets permit 0.0.0.0/0 ge 8 le 24
```

In Example 7-46, the peer group called ISP shares multiple common parameters: an outgoing filter list, an incoming prefix list, and an incoming route map. The individual neighbors, defined using their IP addresses and autonomous system numbers, have been assigned to the peer group. The filter list references the IP AS-path access list 10, which allows advertisements of only the networks originated in the local autonomous system. The incoming prefix list (desired-subnets) is used to accept the default route and subnets whose subnet masks are in the range 8 to 24. The route map FILTER sets a higher local preference for networks received from the primary ISP (autonomous system 65100).

Implementing BGP for IPv6 Internet Connectivity

The global Internet routing infrastructure is built using BGP. To make BGP-4 available for other network layer protocols, including IPv6, multiprotocol extensions for BGP-4 (MP-BGP) was introduced.

> **Note**   RFC 4760, *Multiprotocol Extensions for BGP-4*, defines multiprotocol extensions for BGP-4 (MP-BGP). RFC 2545, *Use of BGP-4 Multiprotocol Extensions for IPv6 Inter-Domain Routing*, defines how these extensions are used for IPv6.

MP-BGP is capable of carrying a rich set of routed protocols, including IPv4 and IPv6, over a transport protocol, such as IPv4 or IPv6.

This section covers the following topics:

- MP-BGP support for IPv6

- Exchanging IPv6 routes over an IPv4 session

- Exchanging IPv6 routes over an IPv6 session

- BGP for IPv6 configuration and verification

- Comparing IPv4 to Dual (IPv4/IPv6) BGP transport

- BGP filtering mechanisms for IPv6

MP-BGP Support for IPv6

Multiprotocol extensions are defined as new attributes. IPv6-specific extensions incorporated into MBGP include the following:

- A new identifier for the IPv6 address family.

- Scoped addresses. The next-hop attribute contains a global IPv6 address or a link-local address (only when there is link-local reachability with the peer). When link-local addresses are used for peering with a neighbor BGP router, these link-local IPv6 addresses are used as the next-hop addresses for the routes that are carried by BGP. In some cases, the next-hop IPv6 addresses need to be changed to a global IPv6 address, using a route map in the **neighbor** configuration statement.

■ The next-hop attribute and NLRI are expressed as IPv6 addresses and prefixes. (Recall that the NLRI field in a BGP update message lists the networks reachable on the BGP path described by the update message.)

MP-BGP can, of course, operate with multiple protocols. It operates by identifying two separate protocols: the carrier protocol and the passenger protocol.

In an all-IPv4 environment, BGP establishes sessions using IPv4 (using TCP port 179); IPv4 is the carrier protocol. The routes that BGP advertises, which is the passenger protocol, are also IPv4. Figure 7-23 illustrates this scenario.

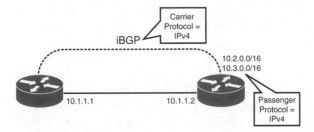

Figure 7-23   *BGP with IPv4 as Both the Carrier and Passenger Protocol*

Protocols other than IPv4, including IPv6, also need to advertise reachability information. MP-BGP extensions allow these other protocols to be carried using BGP. An analogy is that BGP is a truck that can transport multiple payloads. For example, the BGP "truck" could be IPv4, and it could be used to transport IPv6 (or other protocol) "payloads." In this case, the carrier protocol is IPv4 and the passenger protocol (the IPv6 prefixes being advertised) is IPv6. Figure 7-24 illustrates this scenario.

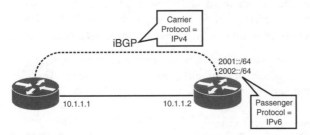

Figure 7-24   *BGP with IPv4 as the Carrier Protocol and IPv6 as the Passenger Protocol*

In an all-IPv6 environment, BGP can be used as both the carrier and passenger protocol, as illustrated in Figure 7-25. In this case, IPv6 is used to establish BGP sessions, and BGP advertises IPv6 prefixes; both the truck and the payload are IPv6.

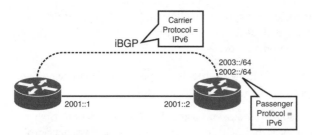

Figure 7-25   *BGP with IPv6 as Both the Carrier and Passenger Protocol*

IPv6 routes are carried with the use of the MP-BGP extension IPv6 NLRI, which defines a new *address family* that can be advertised using MP-BGP. Each protocol that uses MP-BGP has an address family defined.

Note   Either IPv4 or IPv6 can be used as the carrier protocol for other passenger protocols, such as multicast or MPLS VPNs. BGP uses the TCP protocol for peering; this has no relevance to the routes carried inside the BGP exchanges. IPv4 or IPv6 can be used at the network layer to transport a TCP connection.

Exchanging IPv6 Routes over an IPv4 Session

Existing IPv4 TCP sessions can carry IPv6 routing information when adding IPv6 support to a network. An existing neighbor can be activated for the IPv6 address family and IPv6 routing information will be sent over the same neighbor session.

MP-BGP allows the use of many address families to define the type of addresses being carried. The most common address families are IPv4, IPv6, and VPNv4 and VPNv6 (for MPLS VPN routes). This chapter discusses only the IPv4 and IPv6 address families.

The **address-family {ipv4 | ipv6} [unicast | multicast]** router configuration command enters address family configuration mode for configuring BGP routing sessions. The parameters in this command are described in Table 7-10.

Table 7-10   **address-family** *Command Description*

Parameter	Description
ipv4	Used for a routing session using IPv4 address prefixes.
ipv6	Used for a routing session using IPv6 address prefixes.
unicast	(Optional) Specifies unicast address prefixes. This is the default for both **ipv4** and **ipv6** keywords.
multicast	(Optional) Specifies multicast address prefixes.

In an IPv6 address family, a neighbor needs to be activated using the **neighbor** {*IPv4 address* | *IPv6 address*} **activate** address-family configuration command. The exchange of addresses with BGP neighbors is enabled for the IPv4 address family by default.

> **Note**   Address exchange for the IPv4 address family is enabled by default for each BGP routing session configured with the **neighbor remote-as** command unless you configure the **no bgp default ipv4-activate** command before configuring the **neighbor remote-as** command, or you disable address exchange for the IPv4 address family with a specific neighbor by using the **no neighbor activate** command.

The **network** *ipv6-address/prefix-length* command, this time in address family configuration mode, is used to specify the networks to be advertised. This command injects a prefix into the BGP database only for the specified address family. Table 7-11 describes the parameters in this command.

Table 7-11   network Command *for IPv6 Description*

Parameter	Description
ipv6-address	The IPv6 address to be used.
prefix-length	The length of the IPv6 prefix. A decimal value that indicates how many of the high-order contiguous bits of the address comprise the prefix (the network portion of the address). A slash mark must precede the decimal value.

Note that there is no **mask** keyword when defining the **network** command for IPv6 addresses.

Figure 7-26 illustrates a network used for an example. Partial configuration of the R1 router is provided in Example 7-47. R1 establishes a neighbor relationship with R2's IPv4 address. The IPv6 address family is activated, and both IPv4 and IPv6 routes are exchanged between neighbors.

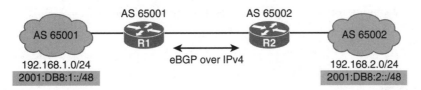

Figure 7-26   *Exchanging IPv6 Routes over an IPv4 BGP Session Example*

Example 7-47   *Partial Configuration of R1 in Figure 7-26*

```
router bgp 65001
 neighbor 192.168.2.2 remote-as 65002
!
 address-family ipv4 unicast
  network 192.168.1.0 mask 255.255.255.0
 address-family ipv6 unicast
  neighbor 192.168.2.2 activate
  network 2001:db8:1::/48
```

Exchanging IPv6 Routes over an IPv6 Session

Of course, MP-BGP also supports exchanging IPv6 routes over an IPv6 session.

By default, BGP sets its router ID to the IPv4 address of the highest address of the loopback interface, or if no loopback exists, to the highest IP address of the physical interface. If a router running BGP over IPv6 transport has no IPv4 addresses configured, you need to manually specify BGP router ID. The **bgp router-id** *ip-address* router configuration command configures a fixed router ID for the local BGP routing process; this command is required in an IPv6-only network. The *ip-address* parameter is an IPv4-address format 32-bit dotted-decimal number.

Figure 7-27 illustrates a network that is only running IPv6. Example 7-48 provides the partial configuration of the R1 router. In this example, an IPv6 BGP session is established between the routers; this session uses TCP over IPv6 and is used only for IPv6 routing. The IPv6 neighbor is activated in the IPv6 address family because it is not activated by default.

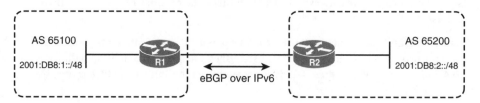

Figure 7-27   *Exchanging IPv6 Routes over an IPv6 BGP Session Example*

Example 7-48   *Partial Configuration of R1 in Figure 7-27*

```
router bgp 65100
 bgp router-id 1.1.1.1
 neighbor 2001:db8:2::2 remote-as 65200
!
address-family ipv6 unicast
  neighbor 2001:db8:2::2 activate
  network 2001:db8:1::/48
```

BGP for IPv6 Configuration and Verification

In this section, an example illustrates the configuration and verification of BGP for IPv6.

Figure 7-28 displays the network with the objectives for this example, and Figure 7-29 displays the network diagram and addressing.

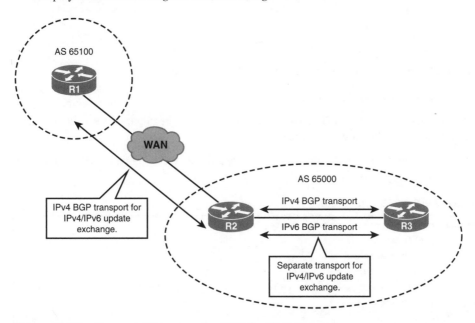

Figure 7-28   *Network Objectives for BGP for IPv6 Example*

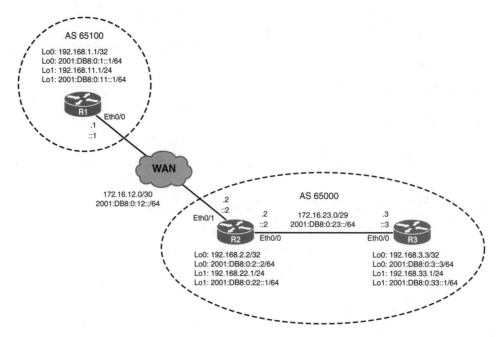

Figure 7-29   *Network and Addressing for BGP for IPv6 Example*

Initial State of Routers

The addressing and some BGP configuration have already been put on the routers. First, let's examine the initial state on the three routers.

Example 7-49 displays R1's initial state, including the BGP configuration, the BGP table, and connectivity to other routers.

Example 7-49   *R1's Initial State*

```
R1# show running-config | section router bgp
router bgp 65100
 bgp log-neighbor-changes
 neighbor 172.16.12.2 remote-as 65000
 !
 address-family ipv4
  network 192.168.11.0
  neighbor 172.16.12.2 activate
 exit-address-family
 !
 address-family ipv6
  network 2001:DB8:0:11::/64
  neighbor 172.16.12.2 activate
  neighbor 172.16.12.2 route-map nh out
 exit-address-family

R1# show bgp ipv4 unicast
```

```
<Output omitted>
    Network          Next Hop          Metric LocPrf Weight Path
 *>  192.168.11.0     0.0.0.0               0         32768 i
 *>  192.168.22.0     172.16.12.2           0             0 65000 i
 *>  192.168.33.0     172.16.12.2                         0 65000 i


R1# show bgp ipv6 unicast
BGP table version is 2, local router ID is 192.168.11.1
Status codes: s suppressed, d damped, h history, * valid, > best, i - internal,
              r RIB-failure, S Stale, m multipath, b backup-path, f RT-Filter,
              x best-external, a additional-path, c RIB-compressed,
Origin codes: i - IGP, e - EGP, ? - incomplete
RPKI validation codes: V valid, I invalid, N Not found


    Network          Next Hop          Metric LocPrf Weight Path
 *>  2001:DB8:0:11::/64
                      ::                    0         32768 i


R1# show bgp ipv4 unicast summary
BGP router identifier 192.168.11.1, local AS number 65100
BGP table version is 8, main routing table version 8
3 network entries using 444 bytes of memory
3 path entries using 192 bytes of memory
3/3 BGP path/bestpath attribute entries using 408 bytes of memory
1 BGP AS-PATH entries using 24 bytes of memory
0 BGP route-map cache entries using 0 bytes of memory
0 BGP filter-list cache entries using 0 bytes of memory
BGP using 1068 total bytes of memory
BGP activity 4/0 prefixes, 6/2 paths, scan interval 60 secs


Neighbor        V     AS MsgRcvd MsgSent    TblVer   InQ  OutQ Up/Down State/PfxRcd
172.16.12.2     4  65000      72      71         8     0     0 01:01:03          2


R1# show bgp ipv6 unicast summary
BGP router identifier 192.168.11.1, local AS number 65100
BGP table version is 2, main routing table version 2
1 network entries using 172 bytes of memory
1 path entries using 88 bytes of memory
1/1 BGP path/bestpath attribute entries using 136 bytes of memory
1 BGP AS-PATH entries using 24 bytes of memory
0 BGP route-map cache entries using 0 bytes of memory
0 BGP filter-list cache entries using 0 bytes of memory
BGP using 420 total bytes of memory
BGP activity 4/0 prefixes, 6/2 paths, scan interval 60 secs


Neighbor        V     AS MsgRcvd MsgSent    TblVer   InQ  OutQ Up/Down  State/PfxRcd
172.16.12.2     4  65000       0       0         1     0     0 never       (NoNeg)
```

From Example 7-49, we see that R1 has been preconfigured for IPv4 and IPv6 connectivity over an IPv4 BGP transport session with R2. The router has two address families. In the appropriate address family, it advertises the IPv4 or IPv6 network configured on its loopback 1 interface. R1 has an eBGP session with R2.

The **show bgp ipv4 unicast** command is equivalent to the **show ip bgp** command. You can use either to display the BGP IPv4 table. The IPv4 BGP table contains three networks, which indicates successful IPv4 route exchange.

The **show bgp ipv6 unicast** command is used to view the BGP IPv6 table. The IPv6 BGP table currently contains only the local network. (This is because the BGP processes on R2 and R3 have not been configured for IPv6 exchange, as you will see.)

The **show bgp ipv4 unicast summary** command is equivalent to the **show ip bgp summary** command and is used to display brief information about IPv4 peering. The **show bgp ipv6 unicast summary** command enables you to examine the overall information about peering for IPv6 addresses, whether over an IPv4 or IPv6 transport session. At this point, the peering for IPv6 prefixes is down as shown with the (NoNeg) state.

Example 7-50 displays R2's initial BGP configuration and BGP table.

Example 7-50 *R2's Initial State*

```
R2# show running-config | section router bgp
router bgp 65000
 bgp log-neighbor-changes
 network 192.168.22.0
 neighbor 172.16.12.1 remote-as 65100
 neighbor 192.168.3.3 remote-as 65000
 neighbor 192.168.3.3 update-source Loopback0
 neighbor 192.168.3.3 next-hop-self


R2# show ip bgp
<Output omitted>
     Network          Next Hop          Metric LocPrf Weight Path
 *>  192.168.11.0     172.16.12.1            0             0 65100 i
 *>  192.168.22.0     0.0.0.0                0         32768 i
 *>i 192.168.33.0     192.168.3.3            0    100      0 i
```

From Example 7-50, we see that R2 has been preconfigured for IPv4 connectivity using BGP. It does not use any address families at this point, and it only advertises the IPv4 network configured on the loopback 1 interface. The BGP table contains two remote networks, which indicates successful IPv4 route exchange with peers R1 and R3.

Example 7-51 displays R3's initial BGP configuration and BGP table, and connectivity test results with R1.

Example 7-51   *R3's Initial State*

```
R3# show running-config | section router bgp
router bgp 65000
 bgp log-neighbor-changes
 network 192.168.33.0
 neighbor 192.168.2.2 remote-as 65000
 neighbor 192.168.2.2 update-source Loopback0

R3# show ip bgp
<Output omitted>
     Network          Next Hop          Metric LocPrf Weight Path
 *>i 192.168.11.0     192.168.2.2            0    100      0 65100 i
 *>i 192.168.22.0     192.168.2.2            0    100      0 i
 *>  192.168.33.0     0.0.0.0                0          32768 i

R3# ping 192.168.11.1 source loopback 1
Type escape sequence to abort.
Sending 5, 100-byte ICMP Echos to 192.168.11.1, timeout is 2 seconds:
Packet sent with a source address of 192.168.33.1
!!!!!
Success rate is 100 percent (5/5), round-trip min/avg/max = 1/1/1 ms
```

From Example 7-51, we see that R3 has an iBGP session to R2. R3 receives and advertises IPv4 prefixes and can successfully communicate with other routers.

Enable eBGP IPv6 Route Exchange

On R2, let's enable IPv6 route exchange with its neighbor R1 over the existing IPv4 session. We will also announce the IPv6 network configured on the loopback 1 interface and verify the resulting configuration. Example 7-52 provides R2's configuration. We first enter the address-family IPv6 router configuration mode using the **address-family ipv6 unicast** command, and then activate a neighbor for IPv6 exchange and advertise the loopback 1 network.

Example 7-52   *R2 Exchanging IPv6 Routes*

```
R2(config)# router bgp 65000
R2(config-router)# address-family ipv6 unicast
R2(config-router-af)# neighbor 172.16.12.1 activate
R2(config-router-af)# network 2001:DB8:0:22::/64

R2# show running-config | section router bgp
router bgp 65000
 bgp log-neighbor-changes
 neighbor 172.16.12.1 remote-as 65100
```

```
 neighbor 192.168.3.3 remote-as 65000
 neighbor 192.168.3.3 update-source Loopback0
 !
 address-family ipv4
  network 192.168.22.0
  neighbor 172.16.12.1 activate
  neighbor 192.168.3.3 activate
  neighbor 192.168.3.3 next-hop-self
 exit-address-family
 !
 address-family ipv6
  network 2001:DB8:0:22::/64
  neighbor 172.16.12.1 activate
 exit-address-family
```

Notice in the configuration output in Example 7-52 that after any command is configured in an address family configuration mode, the BGP configuration syntax is converted automatically from the traditional IPv4 style to the address family approach.

Example 7-53 displays the eBGP session status on R1 so that we can verify if the received IPv6 route is installed in the routing table. We use the **show bgp ipv6 unicast summary** and the **show bgp ipv6 unicast neighbors** commands to verify that the eBGP session is up and running and that the IPv6 prefixes have been exchanged.

Example 7-53   *Verifying on R1 That IPv6 Routes Received*

```
R1# show bgp ipv6 unicast summary
BGP router identifier 192.168.11.1, local AS number 65100
BGP table version is 4, main routing table version 4
2 network entries using 344 bytes of memory
2 path entries using 176 bytes of memory
2/1 BGP path/bestpath attribute entries using 272 bytes of memory
1 BGP AS-PATH entries using 24 bytes of memory
0 BGP route-map cache entries using 0 bytes of memory
0 BGP filter-list cache entries using 0 bytes of memory
BGP using 816 total bytes of memory
BGP activity 23/18 prefixes, 46/41 paths, scan interval 60 secs


Neighbor        V    AS   MsgRcvd MsgSent  TblVer  InQ OutQ Up/Down   State/PfxRcd
172.16.12.2     4  65000      41      41       4    0    0 00:31:14              1


R1# show bgp ipv6 unicast neighbors
BGP neighbor is 172.16.12.2,  remote AS 65000, external link
  BGP version 4, remote router ID 192.168.22.1
  BGP state = Established, up for 00:31:45
  Last read 00:00:24, last write 00:00:11, hold time is 180, keepalive interval is
60 seconds
```

```
   Neighbor sessions:
     1 active, is not multisession capable (disabled)
   Neighbor capabilities:
<Output omitted>


R1# show bgp ipv6 unicast
BGP table version is 4, local router ID is 192.168.11.1
Status codes: s suppressed, d damped, h history, * valid, > best, i - internal,
              r RIB-failure, S Stale, m multipath, b backup-path, f RT-Filter,
              x best-external, a additional-path, c RIB-compressed,
Origin codes: i - IGP, e - EGP, ? - incomplete
RPKI validation codes: V valid, I invalid, N Not found


    Network          Next Hop          Metric LocPrf Weight Path
 *> 2001:DB8:0:11::/64

                     ::                      0         32768 i
 *  2001:DB8:0:22::/64
                     ::FFFF:172.16.12.2

                                            0           0 65000 i
R1# show ipv6 route bgp
IPv6 Routing Table - default - 8 entries
Codes: C - Connected, L - Local, S - Static, U - Per-user Static route
       B - BGP, HA - Home Agent, MR - Mobile Router, R - RIP
       H - NHRP, I1 - ISIS L1, I2 - ISIS L2, IA - ISIS interarea
       IS - ISIS summary, D - EIGRP, EX - EIGRP external, NM - NEMO
       ND - ND Default, NDp - ND Prefix, DCE - Destination, NDr - Redirect
       O - OSPF Intra, OI - OSPF Inter, OE1 - OSPF ext 1, OE2 - OSPF ext 2
       ON1 - OSPF NSSA ext 1, ON2 - OSPF NSSA ext 2, l - LISP
```

Notice in Example 7-53 that the eBGP IPv6 update received on R1 is not marked as best (using the > sign) in the BGP table, because the next-hop address is not reachable. Also notice that the next-hop address, ::FFFF:172.16.12.2, is an IPv6 address derived from the IPv4 next-hop address. Where did this strange address come from? Recall that this neighbor relationship is an IPv4 neighbor relationship, carrying IPv6 routes (under the IPv6 address family). Because an IPv6 route must have an IPv6 next hop, BGP dynamically created this IPv6 next-hop address from the actual IPv4 next-hop address. However, this is not a reachable IPv6 address; therefore, the route is not marked as best in the BGP table, and it does not appear in the IPv6 routing table.

Example 7-54 displays the eBGP session status on R2 and verifies that the received IPv6 route (from R1) is installed in the routing table.

Example 7-54   *Verifying on R2 That IPv6 Routes were Received*

```
R2# show bgp ipv6 unicast summary
BGP router identifier 192.168.22.1, local AS number 65000
BGP table version is 3, main routing table version 3
2 network entries using 344 bytes of memory
2 path entries using 176 bytes of memory
2/1 BGP path/bestpath attribute entries using 272 bytes of memory
1 BGP AS-PATH entries using 24 bytes of memory
0 BGP route-map cache entries using 0 bytes of memory
0 BGP filter-list cache entries using 0 bytes of memory
BGP using 816 total bytes of memory
BGP activity 5/0 prefixes, 8/3 paths, scan interval 60 secs


Neighbor        V   AS    MsgRcvd  MsgSent  TblVer  InQ  OutQ  Up/Down   State/PfxRcd
172.16.12.1     4   65100    47       47       3      0    0   00:36:18           1


R2# show bgp ipv6 unicast neighbors
BGP neighbor is 172.16.12.1,  remote AS 65100, external link
  BGP version 4, remote router ID 192.168.11.1
  BGP state = Established, up for 00:38:45
  Last read 00:00:52, last write 00:00:40, hold time is 180, keepalive interval is
60 seconds
  Neighbor sessions:
    1 active, is not multisession capable (disabled)
  Neighbor capabilities:
<Output omitted>


R2# show bgp ipv6 unicast
<Output omitted>
     Network          Next Hop          Metric LocPrf Weight Path
 *>  2001:DB8:0:11::/64
                      2001:DB8:0:12::1
                                          0              0 65100 i
 *>  2001:DB8:0:22::/64
                      ::                  0          32768 i


R2# show ipv6 route bgp
IPv6 Routing Table - default - 8 entries
Codes: C - Connected, L - Local, S - Static, U - Per-user Static route
       B - BGP, HA - Home Agent, MR - Mobile Router, R - RIP
       H - NHRP, I1 - ISIS L1, I2 - ISIS L2, IA - ISIS interarea
       IS - ISIS summary, D - EIGRP, EX - EIGRP external, NM - NEMO
       ND - ND Default, NDp - ND Prefix, DCE - Destination, NDr - Redirect
       O - OSPF Intra, OI - OSPF Inter, OE1 - OSPF ext 1, OE2 - OSPF ext 2
       ON1 - OSPF NSSA ext 1, ON2 - OSPF NSSA ext 2, l - LISP
B   2001:DB8:0:11::/64 [20/0]
     via FE80::A8BB:CCFF:FE00:C300, Ethernet0/1
```

Example 7-54 shows that the external route received from R1 is marked as best because it has a valid IPv6 next-hop address and is therefore reachable. The BGP router is installed in the IPv6 routing table. Where did this next-hop address come from? Recall in Example 7-49 that R1 has a command under the IPv6 address family: **neighbor 172.16.12.2 route-map nh out**. Example 7-55 displays this route map. It overwrites the next-hop parameter for all IPv6 routes with R1's IPv6 address on the link between R1 and R2; this address is reachable from R2. (Note that the address does not have to be directly connected to the neighbor, but it must be reachable from the neighbor's perspective.)

Example 7-55   *Route Map on R1*

```
R1# show route-map nh
route-map nh, permit, sequence 10
  Match clauses:
  Set clauses:
     ipv6 next-hop 2001:DB8:0:12::1
  Policy routing matches: 0 packets, 0 bytes
R1#
```

On R2, let's do something similar. Example 7-56 shows R2's configuration to set the next hop to the IPv6 address of the interface connecting to R1, using a route map.

Example 7-56   *Configuring a Route Map on R2*

```
R2(config)# route-map NH-R1
R2(config-route-map)# set ipv6 next-hop 2001:DB8:0:12::2
R2(config-route-map)# router bgp 65000
R2(config-router)# address-family ipv6 unicast
R2(config-router-af)# neighbor 172.16.12.1 route-map NH-R1 out
```

Now let's verify R1's reachability to R2 again. Example 7-57 shows the output and confirms that R1 now has IPv6 reachability to R2. The external route is valid on R1 and is installed in the IPv6 routing table. R1 and R2 have connectivity between their loopback 1 IPv6 addresses.

Example 7-57   *Verifying IPv6 Reachability on R1*

```
R1# show bgp ipv6 unicast
<Output omitted>


    Network          Next Hop          Metric LocPrf Weight Path
 *>  2001:DB8:0:11::/64
                     ::                      0          32768 i
 *>  2001:DB8:0:22::/64
                     2001:DB8:0:12::2
                                             0          0 65000 i
```

```
R1# show ipv6 route bgp
<Output omitted>
B   2001:DB8:0:22::/64 [20/0]
        via FE80::A8BB:CCFF:FE00:C410, Ethernet0/0

R1# ping 2001:DB8:0:22::1 source loopback 1
Type escape sequence to abort.
Sending 5, 100-byte ICMP Echos to 2001:DB8:0:22::1, timeout is 2 seconds:
Packet sent with a source address of 2001:DB8:0:11::1
!!!!!
Success rate is 100 percent (5/5), round-trip min/avg/max = 1/1/1 ms
```

Enable iBGP IPv6 Route Exchange

Now we will configure an iBGP session between the R2 and R3 loopback 0 IPv6 addresses and then use IPv6 transport to advertise the IPv6 networks configured on the loopback 1 interfaces in BGP.

Example 7-58 provides the configuration on R2 and R3. iBGP sessions for IPv6 route exchange are configured similarly to IPv4 sessions and typically are between the loopback interfaces and therefore also require the **neighbor update-source** command. Note that the **neighbor update-source** command affects both address families, and is therefore configured in the global BGP configuration mode.

Example 7-58 *Configuring iBGP over IPv6 on R2 and R3*

```
R2(config)# router bgp 65000
R2(config-router)# neighbor 2001:DB8:0:3::3 remote-as 65000
R2(config-router)# neighbor 2001:DB8:0:3::3 update-source Loopback 0
R2(config-router)# address-family ipv6 unicast
R2(config-router-af)# neighbor 2001:DB8:0:3::3 activate
R2(config-router-af)# neighbor 2001:DB8:0:3::3 next-hop-self

R3(config-router-af)# router bgp 65000
R3(config-router)# neighbor 2001:DB8:0:2::2 remote-as 65000
R3(config-router)# neighbor 2001:DB8:0:2::2 update-source Loopback 0
R3(config-router)# address-family ipv6 unicast
R3(config-router-af)# neighbor 2001:DB8:0:2::2 activate
R3(config-router-af)# neighbor 2001:DB8:0:2::2 next-hop-self
R3(config-router-af)# network 2001:DB8:0:33::/64
```

The next-hop address for external updates forwarded to internal peers is usually overwritten, and therefore requires the **neighbor next-hop-self** command. This command is address family specific and is configured in the address family IPv6 router configuration mode in Example 7-58.

The neighbor needs to be activated in the desired address family. In this scenario, we have separate BGP sessions for IPv4 and IPv6 exchange. The IPv6 neighbor is activated only in the IPv6 address family.

When IPv6 routes are exchanged over an IPv6 BGP session, the next-hop parameter is correctly configured automatically and there is no need for a route map to modify it.

Let's verify iBGP peering and connectivity for IPv6. We could do it on either peer; Example 7-59 shows the output on the R3 router. This output shows that the IPv6 iBGP neighbor is up and running and that the IPv6 networks are exchanged as expected. The BGP routes are being installed in the IPv6 routing table, and we have IPv6 connectivity between all routers in this topology.

Example 7-59   *Verifying iBGP Connectivity for IPv6 on R3*

```
R3# show bgp ipv6 unicast summary
BGP router identifier 192.168.3.3, local AS number 65000
BGP table version is 4, main routing table version 4
3 network entries using 516 bytes of memory
3 path entries using 264 bytes of memory
3/3 BGP path/bestpath attribute entries using 408 bytes of memory
1 BGP AS-PATH entries using 24 bytes of memory
0 BGP route-map cache entries using 0 bytes of memory
0 BGP filter-list cache entries using 0 bytes of memory
BGP using 1212 total bytes of memory
BGP activity 12/6 prefixes, 31/25 paths, scan interval 60 secs


Neighbor        V      AS MsgRcvd MsgSent   TblVer  InQ OutQ Up/Down  State/PfxRcd
2001:DB8:0:2::2 4   65000      24      23        4    0    0 00:16:38            2

R3# show bgp ipv6 unicast
<Output omitted>
    Network          Next Hop            Metric LocPrf Weight Path
 *>i 2001:DB8:0:11::/64
                     2001:DB8:0:2::2          0    100      0 65100 i
 *>i 2001:DB8:0:22::/64
                     2001:DB8:0:2::2          0    100      0 i
 *>  2001:DB8:0:33::/64
                     ::                       0           32768 i
R3# show ipv6 route bgp
<Output omitted>
B    2001:DB8:0:11::/64 [200/0]
     via 2001:DB8:0:2::2
B    2001:DB8:0:22::/64 [200/0]
     via 2001:DB8:0:2::2
```

```
R3# ping 2001:DB8:0:11::1 source loopback 1
Type escape sequence to abort.
Sending 5, 100-byte ICMP Echos to 2001:DB8:0:11::1, timeout is 2 seconds:
Packet sent with a source address of 2001:DB8:0:33::1
!!!!!
Success rate is 100 percent (5/5), round-trip min/avg/max = 1/1/1 ms
```

Comparing IPv4 to Dual (IPv4/IPv6) BGP Transport

As you have seen, both IPv4 and IPv6 address families can use a single IPv4 neighbor or two separate sessions can be established, one for each address family. There are advantages to both approaches.

Using a single IPv4 neighbor reduces the number of neighbor sessions. In an environment where a lot of neighbors are configured, this can significantly reduce the size and complexity of configuration. However, running IPv6 over an IPv4 session requires modification of the next-hop attribute.

In contrast, when using two separate sessions for IPv4 and IPv6, there is no need to implement route maps to overwrite the next-hop parameter. Exchange of IPv4 and IPv6 routes is completely independent; neighbor configuration and handling is duplicated. Note that IPv6 neighbors are not seen in the **show ip bgp summary** command output; use the **show bgp ipv6 unicast summary** command instead.

BGP Filtering Mechanisms for IPv6

MP-BGP offers the same set of IPv6 filtering and route manipulation capabilities that exist for IPv4. The mechanisms include incoming and outgoing prefix-lists, filter lists (for AS-path matching), and route maps, which provide a rich set of matching and manipulation tools. The order of incoming and outgoing filtering process is identical to IPv4.

The following sections provide two examples.

IPv6 Prefix List Filtering

You can filter BGP routing updates on the basis of prefix information from BGP update messages. Figure 7-30 illustrates an example network, and Example 7-60 provides the configuration on router R1. The configuration includes a prefix list named large_networks that allows only subnets with a subnet mask less or equal to 48 within the 2000::/3 address block. (This is the portion of the IPv6 address space currently allocated for global addresses.) The filter is applied to the inbound and outbound announcements received from and advertised to R1's BGP peer, R2.

Figure 7-30 *Network for IPv6 Prefix List Example*

Example 7-60 *Partial Configuration of R1 in Figure 7-30*

```
ipv6 prefix-list large_networks seq 5 permit 2000::/3 le 48
!
router bgp 65100
 bgp router-id 1.1.1.1
 neighbor 2001:DB8:2::2 remote-as 65200
 address-family ipv6
  neighbor 2001:DB8:2::2 activate
  neighbor 2001:DB8:2::2 prefix-list large_networks in
  neighbor 2001:DB8:2::2 prefix-list large_networks out
  network 2001:D00::/24
```

IPv6 Path Selection with BGP Local Preference

You can tune the BGP path selection by modifying the local preference on routes received from a peer. Figure 7-31 illustrates an example network, and Example 7-61 provides the configuration on router R1. In this example, routes received from autonomous system 65200 will have a local preference of 200 instead of the default of 100. Routes from autonomous system 65300 will have a local preference of 50. If the same route is received from both autonomous system 65200 and autonomous system 65300, the path via autonomous system 65200 will be preferred.

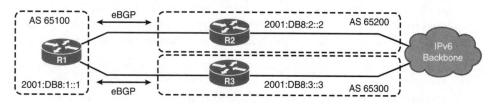

Figure 7-31 *Network for IPv6 Local Preference Example*

Example 7-61 *Partial Configuration of R1 in Figure 7-31*

```
router bgp 65100
 bgp router-id 1.1.1.1
 neighbor 2001:DB8:2::2 remote-as 65200
 neighbor 2001:DB8:3::3 remote-as 65300
 address-family ipv6
```

```
    neighbor 2001:DB8:2::2 activate
    neighbor 2001:DB8:3::3 activate
    neighbor 2001:DB8:2::2 route-map LP200 in
    neighbor 2001:DB8:3::3 route-map LP50 in
    network 2001:D00::/24
!
route-map LP50 permit 10
 set local-preference 50
!
route-map LP200 permit 10
 set local-preference 200
```

Summary

This chapter covered how enterprises can use BGP when connecting to the Internet through discussion of the following topics:

- BGP terminology and concepts, including the following:

    - BGP's use between autonomous systems and how it is different than other routing protocols described in this book

    - BGP's classification as a path vector protocol and its use of TCP port 179

    - BGP's loop-free guarantee, because it does not accept a routing update that already includes its autonomous system number in the AS-path list

    - The three tables used by BGP: the BGP table, IP routing table, and BGP neighbor table

    - The four BGP message types: open, keepalive, update, and notification

- When to use BGP: if the autonomous system allows packets to transit through it to reach other autonomous systems, if the autonomous system has multiple connections to other autonomous systems, or if the routing policy and route selection for traffic entering and leaving the autonomous system must be manipulated

- When not to use BGP: if there is only a single connection to the Internet or another autonomous system, if edge routers have a lack of memory or processing power, if you have a limited understanding of route filtering and the BGP path-selection process, or if the routing policy that will be implemented in an autonomous system is consistent with the policy implemented in the ISP autonomous system

- BGP neighbor (peer) relationships:

    - iBGP, when BGP runs between routers in the same autonomous system

    - eBGP, when BGP runs between routers that are in different autonomous systems. eBGP neighbors are typically directly connected.

■ The use of full-mesh iBGP on all routers in the transit path within the autonomous system

■ Basic BGP configuration, including the relationship between the BGP table, the IP routing table and the **network** command: The **network** command allows a BGP router to inject a network that is in its IP routing table into its BGP table and advertise that network to its BGP neighbors. BGP neighbors exchange their best BGP routes. The neighbor router that receives that network information puts the information in its BGP table and selects its best BGP route for that network. The best route is offered to its IP routing table.

■ Using BGP features, including next-hop-self, update source, and eBGP multihop.

■ Understanding and troubleshooting the BGP states: idle, connect, active, open sent, open confirm, and established.

■ Performing hard and soft resets of BGP sessions, required after a neighbor policy is changed.

■ The BGP attributes that can be either well-known or optional, mandatory or discretionary, and transitive or nontransitive. An attribute might also be partial. The BGP attributes are the following:

   ■ **AS-path:** Well-known mandatory. The list of autonomous system numbers that a route has traversed to reach a destination, with the number of the autonomous system that originated the route at the end of the list.

   ■ **Next hop:** Well-known mandatory. Indicates the next-hop IP address that is to be used to reach a destination. For eBGP, the next hop is the IP address of the neighbor that sent the update; for iBGP, the next hop advertised by eBGP is carried into iBGP by default.

   ■ **Origin:** Well-known mandatory. Defines the origin of the path information; can be IGP, EGP, or incomplete.

   ■ **Local preference:** Well-known discretionary. Indicates to routers in the autonomous system which path is preferred to exit the autonomous system. The path with a *higher* local preference is preferred. Sent only to iBGP neighbors.

   ■ **Atomic aggregate:** Well-known discretionary. Informs the neighbor autonomous system that the originating router has aggregated the routes.

   ■ **Aggregator:** Optional transitive. Specifies the BGP router ID and autonomous system number of the router that performed the route aggregation.

   ■ **Community:** Optional transitive. Allows routers to tag routes with an indicator (the community) and allows other routers to make decisions based on that tag.

   ■ **MED:** Optional nontransitive. Also called metric. Indicates to external neighbors the preferred path into an autonomous system. A *lower* value is preferred; exchanged between autonomous systems.

   ■ **Weight:** Cisco defined; provides local routing policy only and is not propagated to any BGP neighbors. Routes with a *higher* weight are preferred.

■ The 11-step BGP route-selection decision process is as follows:

1. Prefer the highest weight.

2. Prefer the highest local preference.

3. Prefer the route originated by the local router.

4. Prefer the shortest AS-path.

5. Prefer the lowest origin code.

6. Prefer the lowest MED.

7. Prefer the eBGP path over the iBGP path.

8. Prefer the path through the closest IGP neighbor.

9. Prefer the oldest route for eBGP paths.

10. Prefer the path with the lowest neighbor BGP router ID.

11. Prefer the route with the lowest neighbor IP address.

■ Verifying BGP configuration.

■ BGP path manipulation and filtering, including changing the weight, local preference, AS-path, and MED attributes. Prefix lists, distribute lists, filter lists, and route maps may be used.

■ Configuring BGP peer groups, a group of BGP neighbors of the router being configured that all have the same update policies.

■ Implementing MP-BGP for IPv6, including the following:

■ Exchanging IPv6 routes over an IPv4 session

■ Exchanging IPv6 routes over an IPv6 session

■ BGP filtering mechanisms used for IPv6.

References

For additional information, see these resources:

■ Cisco IOS Software Releases support page: http://www.cisco.com/cisco/web/psa/default.html?mode=prod&level0=268438303

■ Cisco IOS Master Command List, All Releases: http://www.cisco.com/c/en/us/td/docs/ios/mcl/allreleasemcl/all_book.html

■ RFCs, available at http://tools.ietf.org/html/

- "Load Sharing with BGP in Single and Multihomed Environments—Sample Configurations," at http://www.cisco.com/en/US/tech/tk365/technologies_configuration_example09186a00800945bf.shtml

- "The CIDR report," at http://www.cidr-report.org/

- "Understanding Regular Expressions," at http://www.cisco.com/c/en/us/td/docs/ios-xml/ios/fundamentals/configuration/15_sy/fundamentals-15-sy-book/cf-cli-search.html#GUID-A26947FE-801A-4597-8FD2-57FDCDD1AADB

Review Questions

Answer the following questions, and then see Appendix A, "Answers to Review Questions," for the answers.

1. On what does BGP base the selection of the best path?

   a. Speed

   b. Autonomous system routing policy

   c. Number of routers to reach a destination network

   d. Bandwidth and delay

2. Which two statements are true for BGP route advertisements and path selection?

   a. BGP selects the best path based on speed.

   b. BGP routers exchange attributes.

   c. BGP advertises paths.

   d. BGP paths can have loops.

3. Which two conditions are valid reasons to run BGP in an autonomous system?

   a. The autonomous system is an ISP.

   b. The autonomous system has only a single connection to another autonomous system.

   c. Path and packet flow manipulation is required in this autonomous system.

   d. There is a limited understanding of BGP routing and route filtering.

4. By default, which two are conditions for routers to be eBGP neighbors?

   a. Directly connected

   b. In the same autonomous system

   c. In different autonomous systems

   d. Running an IGP between them to establish an adjacency

5. Which command indicates to a BGP router whether an IP address belongs to an iBGP or an eBGP neighbor?

   a. neighbor *ip-address* **shutdown**

   b. neighbor *ip-address* **update-source** *interface-type interface-number*

   c. neighbor *ip-address* **remote-as** *autonomous-system*

   d. neighbor *ip-address* **next-hop-self**

6. Which BGP neighbor state is the proper state for normal BGP neighbor operations?

   a. Active

   b. Open confirm

   c. Idle

   d. Established

7. BGP, by default, will have how many paths for each destination?

   a. 1

   b. 2

   c. 4

   d. 6

8. Which of the following statements best illustrates the importance of BGP policies that influence route selection in a multihomed BGP network?

   a. The default BGP route selection does not always result in optimum routing.

   b. The default BGP route selection always results in optimum routing.

   c. After the route-selection behavior has been set, it cannot be changed.

   d. Since customers have redundant connections and receive all routes from both service providers, BGP policies are not necessary.

9. You can set the weight using a route map applied to a neighbor in the outgoing direction. True or false?

   a. True

   b. False

10. Why might a multihomed customer need prefix lists?

    a. To ensure that only valid IP prefixes are announced to the ISPs

    b. To set a limit on the number of prefixes that can be accepted from the ISPs

    c. To ensure that only private address space is advertised to the ISPs

    d. To verify that the customer has received full Internet route tables

11. Which three are appropriate reasons to apply AS-path filters?

    a. Ensure that only locally originated routes are announced

    b. Limit routes that are advertised from iBGP neighbors

    c. Select a subset of all received routes based on their originating autonomous system

    d. Limit route updates from a neighbor to specific routes originated in the autonomous system

    e. Change the weight or local preference attributes for all destination autonomous systems

12. Which statement about the BGP peer groups is accurate?

a. Peer groups can be used to hide the identity of BGP peers from external neighbors.

b. With BGP peer groups, the router CPU utilization that is imposed by BGP update generation is significantly reduced.

c. Network administrators should use peer groups to make smaller networks more productive.

d. With BGP peer groups, neighbor relationships are automatically created.

e. Peer groups should be used in all environments.

f. Peer groups are only used to configure eBGP peers with the same autonomous system number and parameters.

13. Which two are IPv6-specific extensions of MP-BGP?

a. IPv6-specific AS-path

b. IPv6 NLRI

c. IPv6 LSA

d. Next-hop attribute in IPv6 format

e. IPv6 Type Length Value (TLV)

f. BGP IPv6 prefix

14. Which two are advantages of exchanging IPv4 and IPv6 routes over a single IPv4 session?

a. Need to set the next hop

b. No need to set the next hop

c. Potentially simpler configuration

d. Fewer sessions

15. IPv4 BGP neighbors will exchange IPv6 routes by default. True or false?

a. True

b. False

16. Complete the following table to answer these questions about three BGP attributes:

- In which order are the attributes preferred (1, 2, or 3)?
- For the attribute, is the highest or lowest value preferred?
- Which other routers, if any, is the attribute sent to?

Attribute	Order Preferred In	Highest or Lowest Value Preferred?	Sent to Which Other Routers?
Local preference			
MED			
Weight			

17. Place the BGP route-selection criteria in order from the first step to the last step evaluated by placing a number in the blank provided.

___ Prefer the path with the lowest neighbor BGP router ID

___ Prefer the lowest MED

___ Prefer the shortest AS-path

___ Prefer the oldest route for eBGP paths

___ Prefer the lowest origin code

___ Prefer the highest weight

___ Prefer the path through the closest IGP neighbor

___ Prefer the highest local preference

___ Prefer the route originated by the local router

___ Prefer the route with the lowest neighbor IP address

___ Prefer the eBGP path over the iBGP path

Chapter 8

Routers and Routing Protocol Hardening

This chapter covers the following topics:

- Securing the Management Plane on Cisco Routers

- Describing Routing Protocol Authentication

- Configuring Authentication for EIGRP

- Configuring Authentication for OSPFv2 and OSPFv3

- Configuring Authentication for BGP peers

- Configuring VRF-lite

A router's security is critical to network security. Routers are typically the network-edge perimeter device and therefore exposed to a vast number of threats. Routers also exchange path information with other routers, and therefore it is imperative that routing updates are only accepted from authorized sources. A compromised router could be disastrous for an enterprise network.

A router's operational architecture can be categorized into three planes:

- **Management plane:** This plane is concerned with traffic that is sent to the Cisco IOS device and is used for device management. Securing this plane involves using strong passwords, user authentication, implementing role-based command-line interface (CLI), using Secure Shell (SSH), enable logging, using Network Time Protocol (NTP), securing Simple Network Management Protocol (SNMP), and securing system files.

- **Control plane:** This plane is concerned with packet forwarding decisions such as routing protocol operations. Securing this plane involves using routing protocol authentication.

- **Data plane:** This plane is also known as the forwarding plane because it is concerned with the forwarding of data through a router. Securing this plane usually involves using access control lists (ACLs).

There are recommended steps for securing a Cisco router and routing protocols. This chapter starts by discussing how to secure the management plane of Cisco routers using recommended practices. Next we discuss control plane security by discussing the benefits of routing protocol authentication and how to configure routing authentication for Enhanced Interior Gateway Routing Protocol (EIGRP), Open Shortest Path First (OSPF), and Border Gateway Protocol (BGP) to prevent routers from accepting false route updates. Finally, we configure VRF-lite and have a look at Cisco Easy Virtual Network (EVN) feature.

Securing the Management Plane on Cisco Routers

Securing the network infrastructure is critical to overall network security. The network infrastructure includes routers, switches, servers, endpoints, and other devices.

To prevent unauthorized access to all infrastructure devices, appropriate security policies and controls must be implemented. Although all infrastructure devices are at risk, routers are a primary target for network attackers. This is because routers act as traffic police, directing traffic into, out of, and between networks.

A compromised router can cause the network to be compromised on a larger scale. Consider a disgruntled employee casually looking over the shoulder of a network administrator while the administrator is logging in to an edge router. This is known as shoulder surfing, and it is a surprisingly easy way for an attacker to gain unauthorized access.

If an attacker gained access to a router, the security and management of the entire network can be compromised, leaving servers and endpoints at risk. For example, the attacker could cause a network disruption by erasing the startup configuration and reloading the router. When the router reboots, it will not have a startup configuration and, therefore, will not boot properly. The administrator should be able to restore the configuration within a reasonable time; however, the disruption could be longer if there is no backup copy or if the copy is outdated.

Routers must be hardened so that any attempts to disable a router, gain unauthorized access, or otherwise impair the functionality of the router can be stopped.

This section discusses device hardening tasks related to securing the management plane of a Cisco router, including the following:

- Following the router security policies
- Securing management access
- Using SSH and ACLs to restrict access to a Cisco router
- Implement logging
- Securing SNMP
- Backup configurations
- Using network monitoring
- Disabling unneeded services

Securing the Management Plane

The management plane handles the traffic that is sent to the Cisco IOS device and is used for device management. To secure the management plane a Cisco IOS router and provide basic protection from various attacks, implement the following recommended steps:

Step 1. **Follow the written router security policy:** The policy should specify who is allowed to log in to a router and how, who is allowed to configure and update the router, or who is allowed to perform logging and monitoring actions. The policy should also specify the requirements for passwords that are used to access the router.

Step 2. **Secure physical access:** Place the router and physical devices that connect to it in a secure locked room that is accessible only to authorized personnel. The room should also be free of electrostatic or magnetic interference, have fire suppression, and controls for temperature and humidity. Install an uninterruptible power supply (UPS) and keep spare components available. This reduces the possibility of a network outage from power loss.

Step 3. **Use strong encrypted passwords:** Use a complex password with a minimum of eight characters. Enforce a minimum length using the **security password min-length** global configuration command. Strong passwords should generally be maintained and controlled by a centralized authentication, authorization, and accounting (AAA) server; however, the Cisco IOS and other infrastructure devices generally store some sensitive information locally. Some local passwords and secret information may be required, for local fallback in case AAA servers become unavailable, such as special-use usernames, secret keys, and other password information. Such local passwords should be properly encrypted to secure them from prying eyes.

Step 4. **Control the access to a router:** Routers can be accessed for management purposes using the following:

- **Console and auxiliary ports:** These ports are used to gain access when a physical connection to the router is available in the form of a terminal.

- **vty lines:** Access to a router using SSH or Telnet is by far the most common administrative tool. For this reason, vty access should be protected using only SSH from authorized IP addresses identified in an ACL.

Step 5. **Secure management access:** Only authorized individuals should have access to infrastructure devices. For this reason, configure authentication, authorization, and accounting (AAA) to control who is permitted to access a network (authenticate), what they can do on that network (authorize), and audit what they did while accessing the network (accounting). Authentication can be performed locally or by using a AAA authentication server.

Step 6.   **Use secure management protocols:** Always use secure management protocols including SSH, HTTPS, and SNMPv3. If unsecure management protocols such as Telnet, HTTP, or SNMP must be used, then protect the traffic using an IPsec virtual private network (VPN). Also protect management access to the router by configuring ACLs that specify authorized hosts that can access the router. For example, SNMP is the most commonly used network management protocol. It is important to restrict SNMP access to the routers on which SNMP is enabled.

Step 7.   **Implement system logging:** System logging provides traffic telemetry, which helps detect unusual network activity and network device failures. Traffic telemetry is implemented by using various mechanisms such as syslog logging, SNMP traps, and NetFlow exports. Use the **service timestamps log datetime** global configuration command to include date and time in the log messages. When implementing network telemetry, it is important that the date and time is both accurate and synchronized across all network infrastructure devices. This is achieved using Network Time Protocol (NTP). Without time synchronization, it is very difficult to correlate different sources of telemetry.

Step 8.   **Periodically back up configurations:** A backed-up configuration allows a disrupted network to recover very quickly. This can be achieved by copying a configuration to an FTP (or TFTP) server at regular intervals or whenever a configuration change is made.

Step 9.   **Disable unneeded services:** Routers support many services. Some of these services are enabled for historical reasons, but are no longer required today. Services that are not needed on the router can be used as back doors to gain access to it and should therefore be disabled.

All of these steps must be completed to effectively help secure a router and make it much harder for it to be compromised.

Router Security Policy

The first step to protect a router is to create and maintain a router security policy, which defines the security posture of routers.

The router security policy should help answer the following questions:

■ **Password encryption and complexity settings:** Do passwords appear in encrypted form when viewed at the configuration file? According to policy, how often do router passwords (Telnet, username, enable) have to be changed? Do the router passwords meet the required complexity as defined by the policy?

■ **Authentication settings:** Is a message of the day (MOTD) banner defined? Is authentication on the router done through locally configured usernames and passwords, or through external AAA servers? Are login and logout tracking and command accounting for the router administrators through the external AAA server enabled?

- **Management access settings:** Is Telnet access allowed for router management? Is the HTTP or HTTPS server used for router management? Which version of SNMP is used to manage the router? Is the SNMP process restricted to a certain range of IP addresses only? How often is the SNMP community string changed?

- **Securing management access using SSH:** Is management access secure? Do we still have to support Telnet? Are we using SSH for management access? If Telnet support is required, how are we securing it?

- **Unneeded services settings:** Are the unneeded services and interfaces disabled? Which services are unneeded?

- **Ingress/egress filtering settings:** Is filtering of RFC 1918 IP addresses enabled? Are antispoofing ACLs in place? Is Unicast RPF filtering enabled?

- **Routing protocol security settings:** Is routing protocol message authentication enabled?

- **Configuration maintenance:** How often are the router configurations backed up? Is the backup moved to an offsite (disaster recovery) site? Is there a documented procedure for the backup of router configurations? Is TFTP used to transfer the configuration or the image files to and from the router? On the system where the configuration files are stored, is the local operating system's security mechanism used for restricting the access to the files?

- **Change management:** Are all the router changes and the updates documented in a manner suitable for a review according to the change management procedure?

- **Router redundancy:** Do we have a first-hop redundancy protocol (FHRP) configured?

- **Monitoring and incident handling:** Are all the attempts to access any port, protocol, or service that is denied logged? Is the CPU utilization/memory of the router monitored? Is logging to a syslog server enabled on the router? What is the course of action to be followed if any malicious incident is noticed?

- **Security updates:** Is the network engineer aware of the latest vulnerabilities that could affect the router? Are the procedures and documentation in place on how to upgrade a router with vulnerable software?

Encrypted Passwords

Attackers deploy various methods of discovering administrative passwords. They can shoulder surf, attempt to guess passwords based on the user's personal information, or sniff for packets containing plain-text files. Attackers can also use legitimate network management software such as a password auditing tool, like L0phtCrack or Cain & Abel to discover passwords.

Use Strong Passwords

Administrators should ensure that strong passwords are used across the network. To protect assets, such as routers and switches, follow these common guidelines for choosing strong passwords. These guidelines are designed to make passwords more difficult to discover through the use of intelligent guessing and password-cracking tools:

- Use a password length of ten or more characters. A longer password is a better password.

- Make passwords complex. Include a mix of uppercase and lowercase letters, numbers, symbols, and spaces.

- Avoid passwords based on repetition, dictionary words, letter or number sequences, usernames, relative or pet names, biographical information, such as birthdates, ID numbers, ancestor names, or other easily identifiable pieces of information.

- Deliberately misspell a password (for example, Smith = Smyth = 5mYth or Security = 5ecur1ty).

- Change passwords often. If a password is unknowingly compromised, the window of opportunity for the attacker to use the password is limited.

- Do not write passwords down and leave them in obvious places, such as on the desk or monitor.

On Cisco routers and many other systems, password-leading spaces are ignored, but spaces after the first character are not ignored; therefore, one method to create a strong password is to use the spacebar in the password and create a phrase made of many words. This is called a *passphrase*. A passphrase is often easier to remember than a simple password. It is also longer and harder to guess.

Encrypting Passwords

Typically routers require passwords for consoles access, remote vty access, and privileged EXEC access, as shown in Figure 8-1.

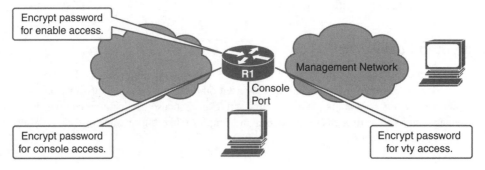

Figure 8-1 *Management Passwords*

The recommended security solution for password management in a network with multiple devices is to authenticate against a central external AAA server. However, some passwords still might need to be configured on the router itself. Therefore, it is important to ensure that these passwords are properly encrypted to be secure from prying eyes.

Global password encryption and **enable secret** are the features available in the Cisco IOS to help secure locally stored sensitive information.

Encrypting Privileged EXEC Password

Define a local enable privileged EXEC password using the **enable secret** *password* global configuration command. The command is stored in the router configuration using a hashing algorithm. IOS 15.0(1)S and later default to the SHA256 hashing algorithm. SHA256, which is considered to be a very strong hashing algorithm, is extremely difficult to reverse. Earlier IOS versions use the weaker message digest 5 (MD5) hashing algorithm.

Note If the **enable secret** *password* command is lost or forgotten, it must be replaced using the Cisco router password recovery procedure. Refer to Cisco.com for more information.

Encrypting Console and vty Passwords

When defining a console or vty line password using the **password line** command, the passwords are stored in clear text in the configuration.

Passwords can be encrypted globally using the **service password-encryption** global configuration command. Password encryption is applied to all the passwords, including the **username** passwords, the authentication key passwords, the privileged command password, the console and the virtual terminal line access passwords, and the BGP neighbor passwords. Passwords that are protected using the automatic password encryption are shown as type 7 passwords in the router configuration.

Note Type 7 passwords are encrypted using a Vigenère cipher, which can be easily reversed. Therefore, this command primarily protects from shoulder surfing attacks.

Example 8-1 configures the privileged EXEC mode, console, vty passwords.

Example 8-1 *Configure and Encrypt Passwords*

```
R1(config)# enable secret class123
R1(config)# line console 0
R1(config-line)# password cisco123
R1(config-line)# login
R1(config-line)# exit
```

```
R1(config)# line vty 0 4
R1(config-line)# password cisco123
R1(config-line)# login
R1(config-line)# exit
R1(config)# service password-encryption
R1(config)# exit
R1#
```

Example 8-2 verifies whether the passwords are encrypted in the running configuration.

Example 8-2 *Verify Encrypted Passwords*

```
R1# show run
Building configuration...

<Output omitted>

service password-encryption

<Output omitted>

enable secret 4 JpAg4vBxn6wTb6NE3N1p0wfUUZzR6eOcVUKUFftxEyA

<Output omitted>

line con 0
 password 7 070C285F4D06485744
 login
line aux 0
line vty 0 4
 password 7 070C285F4D06485744
 login
 transport input all
!
end

R1#
```

Notice in the output how the **enable secret** command indicates that the password is encrypted using level 4 encryption, which is SHA256. The line console and line vty lines are encrypted using level 7 encryption. However, level 7 encryption is considered weak.

Therefore, to increase the encryption level of console and vty lines, it is recommended to enable authentication using the local database. The local database consists of usernames and password combinations that are created locally on each device. The local and vty lines are configured to refer to the local database when authenticating a user.

To create local database entry encrypted to level 4 (SHA256), use the **username** *name* **secret** *password* global configuration command.

Example 8-3 configures console and vty authentication using the local database entries.

Example 8-3   *Configure and Encrypt Passwords*

```
R1(config)# username ADMIN secret class12345
R1(config)# username JR-ADMIN secret class123
R1(config)# line console 0
R1(config-line)# login local
R1(config-line)# exit
R1(config)# line vty 0 4
R1(config-line)# login local
R1(config-line)# end
R1#
```

Notice how the **login local** command is now used. The command makes the line authenticate using the credentials configured in the local database.

Example 8-4 verifies the configuration.

Example 8-4   *Verify Local Authentication*

```
R1# show running-config | include username
username ADMIN secret 4 VYlArd0J6s2X4dZwZ42oTpLQ5Zog8wZDgZKHMP2SHEw
username JR-ADMIN secret 4 JpAg4vBxn6wTb6NE3N1p0wfUUZzR6eOcVUKUFftxEyA
R1#
R1# show running-config | section line
line con 0
 login local
line aux 0
line vty 0 4
 login local
 transport input all
R1# exit


<Output omitted>


R1 con0 is now available


Press RETURN to get started.


User Access Verification


Username: ADMIN
Password:
R1>
```

Notice how the username passwords are encrypted to level 4 indicating that SHA256 was used for the encryption. The lines are also now configured to use the local database for authentication. Finally, authentication is verified by login using the ADMIN username and passwords.

Authentication, Authorization, Accounting

Securing management access to the infrastructure network consists of authenticating users before they access the network, identifying what they are capable of doing and what restrictions apply to them, and logging the information about user activities for accounting purposes.

Authentication, authorization, and accounting (AAA) is a standards-based framework that can be implemented to control who is permitted to access a network (authenticate), what they can do on that network (authorize), and to audit what they did while accessing the network (accounting).

Implementation of the AAA model provides the following advantages:

- **Increased flexibility and control of access configuration:** AAA offers additional authorization flexibility on a per-command or per-interface level.

- **Scalability:** Local authentication is appropriate for a small network with few administrative users. However, it does not scale well beyond that. AAA provides a very scalable solution that is required when managing large networks.

- **Multiple backup systems:** Multiple AAA servers can be identified for redundancy reasons. If a AAA server fails, the next server on the list would provide AAA services.

- **Standardized authentication methods:** AAA supports the RADIUS protocol open standard to ensure interoperability and flexibility with other vendor devices.

Users must authenticate against an authentication database, which can be stored:

- **Locally:** Users are authenticated against the local device database, which is created using the **username secret** command (sometimes referred to self-contained AAA).

- **Centrally:** A client/server model where users are authenticated against AAA servers. This provides improved scalability, manageability, and control. Communication between the device and AAA servers is secured using either the RADIUS or TACACS+ protocols.

RADIUS and TACACS+ Overview

When users attempt to authenticate to a device, the device communicates with a AAA server using either the

- **RADIUS protocol:** An open standard protocol described in RFCs 2865 (authentication and authorization) and 2866 (accounting). It combines authentication and authorization into one service using UDP port 1812 (or UDP 1645), and the accounting service uses UDP port 1813 (or UDP 1646). RADIUS does not encrypt the entire message exchanged between device and server. Only the password portion of the RADIUS packet header is encrypted, thereby identifying the AAA server as an authoritative source to authenticate against.

■ **TACACS+:** A Cisco proprietary protocol that separates all three AAA services using the more reliable TCP port 49. TACACS+ encrypts the entire message exchanged therefore communication between the device and the TACACS+ server is completely secure.

Refer to Figure 8-2 to see how RADIUS is used between a AAA server and a device to exchange authentication credentials.

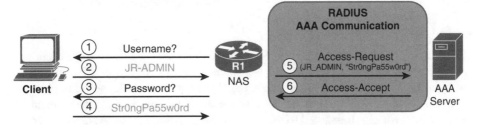

Figure 8-2 *RADIUS Message Exchange*

In the figure, the client attempts to authenticate to R1. The router is called a network access server (NAS) or remote-access server (RAS). Typically, NAS is a router, switch, firewall, or access point. Steps 1 through 4 illustrate how the client is queried by the NAS for their credentials. In Step 5, the NAS sends the client's login request in the form of an Access-Request packet, which contains the username, encrypted password, NAS IP address, and NAS port number.

To ensure that the NAS is authorized to communicate with, the server compares the shared secret key sent in the request packet with the value configured on the server. If the shared secrets do not match, the server drops the packet. If shared secrets match, the credentials in the packet are compared to the username and password in the AAA server database.

If a match is found, the RADIUS server returns an Access-Accept packet with list of attributes to be used with this session. If a match is not found, the RADIUS server returns Access-Reject packet.

Accounting phase is realized separately after authentication and authorization phases, using Accounting-Request and Accounting-Response messages.

Figure 8-3 shows how TACACS+ is used between a AAA server and a device to exchange authentication credentials.

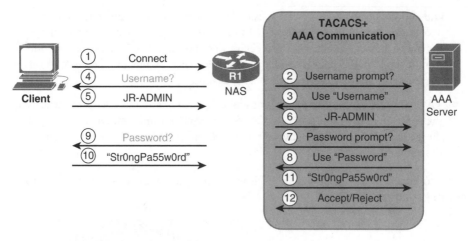

Figure 8-3 *TACACS+ Message Exchange*

In the figure, the client attempts to authenticate to the NAS, R1. In Step 1, the client initiates a connection to the NAS, and the NAS immediately establishes a TCP connection with the AAA server. In Steps 2 through 4, the NAS contacts the AAA server to obtain a username prompt, which is then displayed to the client. In Steps 5 and 6, the username entered by the user is forwarded to the server, In Steps 7 through 9, the NAS contacts the AAA server to obtain the password prompt, which is then displayed to the client. Steps 10 and 11 forward the client's password to the AAA server to be validated against the database.

If a match is found, the server will send an Accept message to the client, and authorization phase may begin (if configured on the NAS). If a match is not found, however, the server will respond with the Reject message, and any further access will be denied.

Enabling AAA and Local Authentication

The following are the configuration steps required to enable AAA local authentication:

Step 1. Create local user accounts using the **username** *name* **secret** *password* global configuration command.

Step 2. Enable AAA by using the **aaa new-model** global configuration command. This command is required to enable all other AAA-related commands. Until this command is enabled, all other AAA commands are hidden. The command also immediately applies local authentication to all lines and interfaces except the console line.

Step 3. Configure the security protocol parameters including the server IP address and secret key. The actual commands will vary depending on whether RADIUS or TACACS+ is used and whether multiple servers are being implemented.

Step 4. Define the authentication method lists using the **aaa authentication login** {default | *list-name*} *method1* [...[*method4*]]. The **default** method list applies to any interface, line, or service unless a *list-name* method list is defined. The **default** keyword is typically used in smaller environments with a single shared AAA infrastructure. Alternatively, a *list-name* method list must be explicitly applied to an interface, line, or service. The *list-name* method list overrides the default method list.

Multiple authentication methods can be defined for fault tolerance. The most commonly used **aaa authentication** command methods include **group radius**, **group tacacs+**, **local**, **local-case**. When multiple authentication methods are configured, the additional methods of authentication are used only if the previous method returns an error, not if it fails.

Step 5.   If required, apply the method lists to the console, vty, or aux lines. If a default authentication method was defined, the console, vty, and aux lines are automatically configured for AAA authentication. If a *list-name* was configured, the lines require the **login** *list-name* line configuration command.

Step 6.   (Optional) Configure authorization using the **aaa authorization** global configuration command.

Step 7.   (Optional) Configure accounting using the **aaa accounting** global configuration command.

Enabling AAA RADIUS Authentication with Local User for Backup

RADIUS is commonly implemented to provide AAA authentication. For fallback purposes, it is a good idea to configure a few local accounts on each device to serve as a backup, should external servers fail.

Example 8-5 configures line console and vty to use to authenticate against RADIUS servers, and if they are not reachable, then authenticate against the local user database as a backup.

Example 8-5   *Configure RADIUS Authentication with Local User for Fallback*

```
R1(config)# username JR-ADMIN secret Str0ngPa55w0rd
R1(config)# username ADMIN secret Str0ng5rPa55w0rd
R1(config)#
R1(config)# aaa new-model
R1(config)#
R1(config)# radius server RADIUS-1
R1(config-radius-server)# address ipv4 192.168.1.101
R1(config-radius-server)# key RADIUS-1-pa55w0rd
R1(config-radius-server)# exit
R1(config)#
R1(config)# radius server RADIUS-2
R1(config-radius-server)# address ipv4 192.168.1.102
R1(config-radius-server)# key RADIUS-2-pa55w0rd
```

```
R1(config-radius-server)# exit
R1(config)#
R1(config)# aaa group server radius RADIUS-GROUP
R1(config-sg-radius)# server name RADIUS-1
R1(config-sg-radius)# server name RADIUS-2
R1(config-sg-radius)# exit
R1(config)#
R1(config)# aaa authentication login default group RADIUS-GROUP local
R1(config)# aaa authentication login TELNET-LOGIN group RADIUS-GROUP local-case
R1(config)# line vty 0 4
R1(config-line)# login authentication TELNET-LOGIN
R1(config-line)# exit
R1(config)#
```

In the example, the **username** *username* **secret** *password* is used to create two local user database accounts. Next the **aaa new-model** command is used to enable AAA. It's important to note that the command immediately applies local authentication to all lines except the console. Therefore, to avoid being locked out, the local database accounts should be created first.

The RADIUS servers are individually configured using the **radius server** *server-name* global configuration command. The **address ipv4** {*hostname* | *server-ip-address*} [**auth-port** *integer*] [**acct-port** *integer*] command is used to configure the server IP address. Optionally, a custom UDP port number can be specified if the RADIUS server is listening on nondefault ports. Port numbers for authentication and accounting differ. The **key** *string* specifies the authentication and encryption key used between access device and RADIUS server. This value must match on both devices.

Note   IPv6 RADIUS servers could be added using the **address ipv6** {*hostname* | *server-ip-address*} command.

The RADIUS servers are then added to a server group using the **aaa group server radius** *group-name* global configuration command. Individual servers are added using the **server name** *server-name* command. Multiple RADIUS servers can be added to the group, as long as they were previously defined using the **radius server** command.

Next, AAA login authentication is configured using the **aaa authentication login** command. The default authentication method applies to all lines. In our example, the default method authenticates against the RADIUS servers identified in the RADIUS-GROUP. AAA will attempt to authenticate using the first server in the group. If it does not respond, the AAA will attempt to authenticate against the second server in the group. If it does not respond, authentication will be done using the local database.

A second AAA login authentication method is specified using a named method list called TELNET-LOGIN. This method authenticates like the default list, except that the

local-case keyword also makes the username case sensitive. The **local** keyword only makes the password case sensitive.

Finally, the TELNET-LOGIN method is applied to the vty lines using the **login authentication** *named-list* command. This command overrides the default authentication method.

Enabling AAA TACACS+ Authentication with Local User for Backup

TACACS+ is commonly implemented in Cisco networks to provide AAA authentication. Example 8-6 configures line console and vty to use authenticate against TACACS+ servers, and if they are not reachable, then authenticate against the local user database as a backup.

Example 8-6 *Configure TACACS+ Authentication with Local User for Fallback*

```
R1(config)# username JR-ADMIN secret Str0ngPa55w0rd
R1(config)# username ADMIN secret Str0ng5rPa55w0rd
R1(config)#
R1(config)# aaa new-model
R1(config)#
R1(config)# tacacs server TACACS-1
R1(config-server-tacacs)# address ipv4 192.168.1.201
R1(config-server-tacacs)# key TACACS-1-pa55w0rd
R1(config-server-tacacs)# exit
R1(config)#
R1(config)# tacacs server TACACS-2
R1(config-server-tacacs)# address ipv4 192.168.1.202
R1(config-server-tacacs)# key TACACS-2-pa55w0rd
R1(config-server-tacacs)# exit
R1(config)#
R1(config)# aaa group server tacacs TACACS-GROUP
R1(config-sg-tacacs+)# server name TACACS-1
R1(config-sg-tacacs+)# server name TACACS-2
R1(config-sg-tacacs+)# exit
R1(config)#
R1(config)# aaa authentication login default group TACACS-GROUP local
R1(config)# aaa authentication login TELNET-LOGIN group TACACS-GROUP local-case
R1(config)# line vty 0 4
R1(config-line)# login authentication TELNET-LOGIN
R1(config-line)# exit
R1(config)#
```

Configuring authentication using TACACS+ is nearly identical to the RADIUS configuration. Use the **tacacs server** *server-name* global configuration command to identify available TACACS+ servers. The **address ipv4** {*hostname* | *server-ip-address*} command is used to configure the server IP address.

Optionally, a custom TCP port number can be specified using the **port** *integer* command if the TACACS+ server is listening on nondefault ports. The **key** *string* specifies the authentication and encryption key used between access device and TACACS+ server. This value must match on both devices.

> **Note**   IPv6 TACACS+ servers could be added using the **address ipv6** {*hostname* | *server-ip-address*} command.

The TACACS+ servers are then added to a server group using the **aaa group server tacacs** *group-name* global configuration command. Individual servers are added using the **server name** *server-name* command. Multiple TACACS+ servers can be added to the group, as long as they were previously defined using the **tacacs server** command.

The remainder of the configuration is the same as the RADIUS example.

Configuring Authorization and Accounting

After the AAA authentication has been configured on a Cisco IOS device, AAA authorization and accounting can be enabled if required.

To configure authorization, follow these steps:

Step 1.   Define a method list for an authorization service with the **aaa authorization** command. Authorization can be implemented for various services such as executing EXEC commands, entering configuration commands, and more. The authorization feature is not valid without a previously configured authentication.

Step 2.   Apply authorization method list to a corresponding interface or line with the **authorization** global configuration command. This does not apply if authorization component is not configured in Step 1.

To configure accounting, follow these steps:

Step 1.   Define a method list for an accounting service with the **aaa accounting** global configuration command. Accounting is not valid without a previously configured authentication method.

Step 2.   Apply an accounting method list to a corresponding interface or line using the **accounting** command. This does not apply if the accounting component is not configured in Step 1.

Limitations of TACACS+ and RADIUS

RADIUS is not suitable to be used in the following situations:

■ **Multiprotocol access environments:** RADIUS does not support older protocols such as ARA, NBFCP, NASI, and X.25 PAD connections.

- **Device-to-device situations:** RADIUS operates in a client/server mode, where authentication can only be initiated by a client and where the server always authenticates the client. RADIUS does not offer two-way authentication. Therefore, if two devices need mutual authentication, RADIUS is not an appropriate solution.

- **Networks using multiple services:** RADIUS authentication can be used for character mode service or PPP mode service. Character mode is authenticating the user for administrative access to the device using Telnet service. PPP mode is used to authenticate the user to provide access to network resources behind the NAS. RADIUS can bind a user to a single service model only. Therefore, RADIUS cannot bind a user simultaneously to character and PPP mode.

TACACS+ is not suitable to be used in the following situations:

- **Multivendor environment:** TACACS+ is a Cisco proprietary protocol. Some vendors may not support it although Cisco has published TACACS+ specification in a form of a draft RFC.

- **When speed of response from the AAA services is of concern:** TACACS+ is a little slower at responding than RADIUS. The reason is because RADIUS uses the UDP transport protocol, which is faster than TACACS+, which uses the TCP transport protocol. TCP is a connection-oriented protocol, which means that a connection between two endpoints has to be established before the data can start to flow. This mechanism consumes precious time, and therefore TACACS+ might not be the best option if a fast response from the AAA services is required.

Use SSH Instead of Telnet

When enabling remote administrative access, consider the security implications of sending information across the network. Traditionally, remote access on routers was configured using Telnet on TCP port 23. However, Telnet was developed in the days when security was not an issue; therefore, all Telnet traffic is forwarded in plain text.

An attacker could capture Telnet frames originating from an administrator's computer using a protocol analyzer such as Wireshark to discover administrative password or device configuration.

Secure Shell (SSH) provides an encrypted mechanism for accessing a router. It has replaced Telnet as the recommended practice for providing remote router administration with connections that support confidentiality and session integrity. It provides functionality that is similar to an outbound Telnet connection, except that the connection is encrypted and operates on port 22. With authentication and encryption, SSH allows for secure communication over a nonsecure network. Therefore, it is advisable to set up SSH access on a router and then disable Telnet access to it.

Before enabling SSH on a router, ensure that the target routers are running a Cisco IOS release that supports SSH. The target routers must also have a unique hostnames and use the same domain name of the network. Finally, the target routers must be configured for local authentication or AAA services for username and password authentication. This is mandatory for a router-to-router SSH connection.

Complete the following steps to enable the SSH access instead of Telnet:

Step 1. **Enable the use of SSH protocol:** Ensure that the target routers are running a Cisco IOS release that supports SSH.

Step 2. **Enable local authentication for SSH access:** This is because SSH access requires login using username and password.

Step 3. **Allows SSH from authorized hosts:** Optionally allow SSH access only from authorized hosts by specifying an ACL.

For example, consider the topology in Figure 8-4.

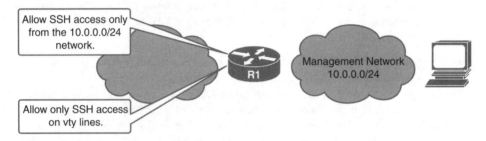

Figure 8-4 *SSH Topology*

In this scenario, the network security policy states that R1 must be configured to only allow incoming SSH Version 2 access on the vty lines. Furthermore, only hosts on the management LAN can be granted access.

Example 8-7 configures the required hostname, domain name, and local user account.

Example 8-7 *Configure Hostname, Domain Name, and Local User Account*

```
Router(config)# hostname R1
R1(config)# ip domain-name cisco.com
R1(config)# username ADMIN privilege 15 secret class12345
```

In the example, the router hostname and domain name are configured. Both are required to create a name for the RSA key pair created in the next example. A local user account is created with the name ADMIN, privilege level 15, and password class12345.

Example 8-8 creates the RSA key pair that will be used to encrypt SSH traffic.

Example 8-8 *Create RSA Keys*

```
R1(config)# crypto key generate rsa modulus 2048
The name for the keys will be: R1.cisco.com
```

```
% The key modulus size is 2048 bits
% Generating 2048 bit RSA keys, keys will be non-exportable...
[OK] (elapsed time was 8 seconds)

R1(config)#
*Aug 13 17:22:58.625: %SSH-5-ENABLED: SSH 1.99 has been enabled
```

One-way secret keys must be generated for a router to encrypt the SSH traffic. These keys are referred to as asymmetric keys. Cisco IOS Software uses the Rivest, Shamir, and Adleman (RSA) algorithm to generate keys.

The RSA key is created using the **crypto key generate rsa general-keys modulus** *modulus-size* global configuration command. The **modulus-size** determines the size of the RSA key and can be configured from 360 bits to 2048 bits. The larger the modulus, the more secure the RSA key; however, keys with large modulus values take slightly longer to generate and longer to encrypt and decrypt. The minimum recommended modulus key length is 1024 bits.

> **Note**   SSHv.199 is automatically enabled after the RSA keys are generated.

Cisco routers support two versions of SSH:

- **SSH Version 1 (SSHv1):** Original version but has known vulnerabilities

- **SSH Version 2 (SSHv2):** Provides better security using the Diffie-Hellman key exchange and the strong integrity-checking message authentication code (MAC)

The default setting for SSH is SSH version 1.99. This is also known as compatibility mode and is merely an indication that the server supports both SSH Version 2 and SSH Version 1. However, best practice is to enable Version 2 only. To change from compatibility mode to a specific version, use the **ip ssh version** {1 | 2} global configuration mode command.

Example 8-9 enables SSHv2 on R1.

Example 8-9   *Enable SSHv2 on R1*

```
R1(config)# ip ssh version 2
```

Example 8-10 creates a service-specific ACL that limits the access to users on the management LAN.

Example 8-10   *Create a Management LAN ACL*

```
R1(config)# ip access-list standard PERMIT-SSH
R1(config-std-nacl)# remark ACL permitting SSH to hosts on the Management LAN
R1(config-std-nacl)# permit 10.0.0.0 0.0.0.255
R1(config-std-nacl)# deny any log
R1(config-std-nacl)# exit
```

The **permit** statement only allows traffic from the specified network of trusted management LAN. Although there is an implicit **deny any** statement automatically created, the command is still entered with the **log** keyword, which will keep track on the number of attempts from unauthorized sources.

Example 8-11 enters the vty line configuration mode, enables local authentication for incoming SSH access, and permits only access to users on the management LAN.

Example 8-11   *Create a Management LAN ACL*

```
R1(config)# line vty 0 4
R1(config-line)# login local
R1(config-line)# transport input ssh
R1(config-line)# access-class PERMIT-SSH in
R1(config-line)# end
R1#
```

Example 8-12 verifies the SSH version configured and displays the generated keys.

Example 8-12   *Verify the SSH Configuration*

```
R1# show ip ssh
SSH Enabled - version 2.0
Authentication timeout: 120 secs; Authentication retries: 3
Minimum expected Diffie Hellman key size : 1024 bits
IOS Keys in SECSH format(ssh-rsa, base64 encoded):
ssh-rsa AAAAB3NzaC1yc2EAAAADAQABAAABAQDSYRdGaX5NesMnkkgCF5JYoREFTMzaUEbjhRMP/Mn/
7zhBtaNAnDlPTmY01A8ymtBMXr2LW/NrX/FuNJqTZMWDVy0Hm9rYs0P6aZCsRn+8EzMzjZgMQCM8A9rO
gDgRnRVEyAm9VORaZN4hx9F7JBug1cnCjghSzbfo0fBeypE3NzJlI/ekCKMO1zXvoWAGjqV+ArtyADwb
kNnw4tmEz1OkP0GXzua/IrHUZRTKNMhd3YTZgkki0GpUowmXBfF2s4Hhy4w/I1twtEr+/sVKkU9wqs2W
UDhZD2ZUxmJKo0GuFxIPNSpMJkn6fRte2MuALGs1a8QUCGzuibVz/Gua7P9R
R1# show crypto key mypubkey rsa
% Key pair was generated at: 09:46:39 PST Aug 13 2014
Key name: R1.cisco.com
Key type: RSA KEYS
 Storage Device: not specified
 Usage: General Purpose Key
 Key is not exportable.
 Key Data:
  30820122 300D0609 2A864886 F70D0101 01050003 82010F00 3082010A 02820101
  00D26117 46697E4D 7AC32792 48021792 58A11105 4CCCDA50 46E38513 0FFCC9FF
  EF3841B5 A3409C39 4F4E6634 D40F329A D04C5EBD 8B5BF36B 5FF16E34 9A9364C5
  83572D07 9BDAD8B3 43FA6990 AC467FBC 1333338D 980C4023 3C03DACE 8038119D
  1544C809 BD54E45A 64DE21C7 D17B241B A0D5C9C2 8E0852CD B7E8D1F0 5ECA9137
  37326523 F7A408A3 0ED735EF A160068E A57E02BB 72003C1B 90D9F0E2 D984CF53
  A43F4197 CEE6BF22 B1D46514 CA34C85D DD84D982 4922D06A 54A30997 05F176B3
  81E1CB8C 3F235B70 B44AFEFE C54A914F 70AACD96 5038590F 6654C662 4AA341AE
```

```
   17120F35 2A4C2649 FA7D1B5E D8CB802C 6B356BC4 14086CEE 89B573FC 6B9AECFF
   51020301 0001
% Key pair was generated at: 09:46:40 PST Aug 13 2014
Key name: R1.cisco.com.server
Key type: RSA KEYS
Temporary key
 Usage: Encryption Key
 Key is not exportable.
 Key Data:
   307C300D 06092A86 4886F70D 01010105 00036B00 30680261 00F2F560 34C0D7F2
   009D1E3C 61EE2919 2412B516 A5DC89BF 4D6426E8 A3CC0F54 206B1058 F54041B5
   0F8C55A1 34AD23C1 FEC1A6DE 63217F8B 23D75B7F 89B79B5A A80CF342 99C429DA
   D274F66B 7D4C196D 1A8DAB20 A722A0BC 7137ABC9 49665130 D7020301 0001
R1#
```

Note   To replace existing key pairs, it is recommended that they are overwritten using
the **crypto key zeroize rsa** command.

Securing Access to the Infrastructure Using Router ACLs

Infrastructure ACLs are typically applied in the input direction on the interface that connects to the network users or external networks with the following policies:

■ All the traffic to the IP addresses of the network infrastructure devices is dropped
and logged. This rule prevents the network users from sending the routing protocol
or the management traffic to network devices. Include the destination addresses
that encompass all the device IP addresses as a condition. Note that this approach
does not prevent users from sending malicious transit traffic that would require
processing in the CPU-intensive slow data plane paths on the network devices. Such
transit traffic may include packets with IP options or packets that require processing
that is not supported in the efficient fast data plane path.

■ All the other traffic is permitted and allows all the transit traffic over the network.

The first rule may need to be relaxed to permit some network signaling exceptions,
such as BGP sessions from trusted external peers, internal routing protocol sessions, and
ICMP, SSH, and SNMP traffic from management stations.

An infrastructure ACL is constructed and applied to specify connections from hosts or
networks that need to be allowed to the network devices. Common examples of these
types of connections are EBGP, SSH, and SNMP. After the required connections have
been permitted, all the other traffic to the infrastructure is explicitly denied. All the
transit traffic that crosses the network and is not destined to the infrastructure devices is
then explicitly permitted.

Example 8-13 configures an inbound infrastructure ACL on the Ethernet 0/0 LAN interface.

Example 8-13   *Enable an Infrastructure ACL*

```
R1(config)# ip access-list extended ACL-INFRASTRUCTURE-IN
R1(config-ext-nacl)# remark Deny IP fragments
R1(config-ext-nacl)# deny tcp any any fragments
R1(config-ext-nacl)# deny udp any any fragments
R1(config-ext-nacl)# deny icmp any any fragments
R1(config-ext-nacl)# deny ip any any fragments
R1(config-ext-nacl)# remark permit required connections for management traffic
R1(config-ext-nacl)# permit tcp host 10.10.12.2 host 10.10.12.1 eq 179
R1(config-ext-nacl)# permit tcp host 10.10.12.2 eq 179 host 10.10.12.1
R1(config-ext-nacl)# permit tcp host 10.0.0.10 any eq 22
R1(config-ext-nacl)# remark Permit ICMP Echo from management station
R1(config-ext-nacl)# permit icmp host 10.0.0.10 any echo
R1(config-ext-nacl)# remark Deny all other IP traffic to any network device
R1(config-ext-nacl)# deny ip any 10.0.0.0 0.0.0.255
R1(config-ext-nacl)# remark permit transit traffic
R1(config-ext-nacl)# permit ip any any
R1(config-ext-nacl)# exit
R1(config)# interface ethernet 0/0
R1(config-if)# ip access-group ACL-INFRASTRUCTURE-IN in
R1(config-if)#^Z
R1#
*Aug 13 18:19:57.308: %SYS-5-CONFIG_I: Configured from console by console
```

The infrastructure ACL configuration in the example illustrates the structure that can be used as a starting point:

- The ACL denies IP fragments. Fragmentation is often used in attempts to evade detection by intrusion detection systems. It is for these reasons that IP fragments are often used in attacks, and why they must be explicitly filtered at the top of any configured infrastructure ACLs.

- The ACL permits BGP sessions from trusted hosts to local IP addresses, and allows the SSH management traffic from a trusted management station. Similar entries should also be configured to allow internal routing protocols if any are used inside the network.

- The ACL also permits ICMP echo (ping) traffic from the trusted management station.

- The ACL then denies all the other traffic to the infrastructure IP addresses.

- The ACL finally permits all the transit traffic across the router.

Once created, the infrastructure ACL must be applied to all the interfaces that face noninfrastructure devices. This includes interfaces that connect to other organizations, remote-access segments, user segments, and segments in data centers. In the example, the ACL is applied to the Ethernet 0/0 interface in the inbound direction.

Implement Unicast Reverse Path Forwarding

Network administrators can use Unicast Reverse Path Forwarding (uRPF) to help limit the malicious traffic on an enterprise network. This security feature works with Cisco Express Forwarding (CEF) by enabling the router to verify that the source of any IP packets received is in the CEF table and reachable via the routing table. If the source IP address is not valid, the packet is discarded.

The uRPF feature is commonly used to prevent common spoofing attacks and follows RFC 2827 for ingress filtering to defeat denial-of-service (DoS) attacks, which employ IP source address spoofing. RFC 2827 recommends that service providers filter their customers' traffic and drop any traffic entering their networks that is coming from an illegitimate source address.

The uRPF feature works in one of two modes:

- **Strict mode:** The packet must be received on the interface that the router would use to forward the return packet. uRPF configured in strict mode may drop legitimate traffic that is received on an interface that was not the router's choice for sending return traffic. Dropping this legitimate traffic could occur when asymmetric routing paths are present in the network.

- **Loose mode:** The source address must appear in the routing table. Administrators can change this behavior using the **allow-default** option, which allows the use of the default route in the source verification process. In addition, a packet that contains a source address for which the return route points to the Null 0 interface will be dropped. An access list may also be specified that permits or denies certain source addresses in uRPF loose mode.

Note Another uRPF mode called Unicast in VRF mode is available but beyond the scope of this course.

Care must be taken to ensure that the appropriate uRPF mode (loose or strict) is con-figured during the deployment of this feature because it can drop legitimate traffic. Although asymmetric traffic flows may be of concern when deploying this feature, uRPF loose mode is a scalable option for networks that contain asymmetric routing paths.

uRPF in an Enterprise Network

In many enterprise environments, it is necessary to use a combination of strict mode and loose mode uRPF. The choice of the uRPF mode to use depends on the design of the network segment connected to the interface on which uRPF is deployed.

Administrators should use uRPF in strict mode on network interfaces for which all packets received on an interface are guaranteed to originate from the subnet assigned to the interface. A subnet composed of end stations or network resources fulfills this requirement. Such a design would be in place for an access layer network or a branch office where there is only one path into and out of the branch network. No other traffic originating from the subnet is allowed and no other routes are available past the subnet.

uRPF loose mode can be used on an uplink network interface that has a default route associated with it.

uRPF Examples

An important consideration for deployment is that CEF switching must be enabled for uRPF to function. CEF is enabled by default on IOS Version 12.2 and later.

Note   If disabled, it can be reenabled using the **ip cef** global configuration command.

The uRPF feature is enabled on a per-interface basis using the **ip verify unicast source reachable-via** {**rx** | **any**} [**allow-default**] [**allow-self-ping**] [*list*] interface configuration command.

Note   The **ip verify unicast source reachable-via** command replaces the older **ip verify unicast reverse-path** [*list*].

To configure

- **Strict mode:** Use the **ip verify unicast source reachable-via rx** command.

- **Loose mode:** Use the **ip verify unicast source reachable-via any** option to enforce the requirement that the source IP address for a packet must appear in the routing table.

The **allow-default** option may be used with either the **rx** or **any** option to include IP addresses not specifically contained in the routing table. The **allow-self-ping** option should not be used because it could create a DoS condition. A numbered access list can also be configured to specifically permit or deny a list of addresses through uRPF.

Note   Named ACLs are not supported by uRPF.

Enabling uRPF

Example 8-14 configures the Gigabit Ethernet 0/0 interface for uRPF loose mode, and Gigabit Ethernet 0/1 is configured for uRPF strict mode.

Example 8-14   *Enabling uRPF Loose and Strict Mode*

```
R1(config)# interface GigabitEthernet 0/0
R1(config-if)# ip verify unicast source reachable-via any
R1(config-if)# exit
R1(config)#
R1(config)# interface GigabitEthernet 0/1
R1(config-if)# ip verify unicast source reachable-via rx
R1(config-if)# exit
R1(config)#
```

Configuring loose mode makes sure the router can reach the source of any IP packet received on interface Gigabit Ethernet 0/0 using any interface on the router. Strict mode makes the router verify that the source of any IP packet received on interface Gigabit Ethernet 0/1 should be reachable by the interface and not any other interface on the router. The router verifies connectivity by looking at the CEF table, and if CEF points to an interface that the packet was not received on, that packet will get dropped.

Implement Logging

Network administrators need to implement logging to get insight into what is happening in their network. These logs and reports can include content flow, configuration changes, and new software installs, to name a few. Logging helps to detect unusual network traffic, network device failures, or just to monitor what kind of traffic traverses the network.

Although logging can be implemented locally on a router, this method is not scalable. As well, if a router reloads then all the logs stored on it will be lost. Therefore, it is important to implement logging to external destination. As shown in Figure 8-5, logging to external destinations can be implemented using various mechanisms, such as syslog logging, SNMP traps, and NetFlow exports.

Figure 8-5   *Logging Mechanisms*

In the figure, the router is logging syslog, SNMP, and NetFlow information to a Security Information & Event Management (SIEM) server.

To implement accurate logging, it is important that all network infrastructure devices have their dates and times synchronized. Without time synchronization, it would be difficult tracking a problem from one device to another. As shown in the figure, the Network Time Protocol (NTP) can be used to synchronize network devices to the correct time.

It is also important that syslog entries be stamped with the correct time and date. Time stamps are configured using the **service timestamps** [debug | log] [uptime | datetime [*msec*]] [localtime] [show-timezone] [year] global configuration command.

Implementing Network Time Protocol

An NTP network usually gets its time from an authoritative time source, such as a radio clock or an atomic clock attached to a time server. NTP then distributes this time across the network using UDP port 123.

NTP uses the concept of a stratum to describe how many NTP hops away a machine is from an authoritative time source. For example, a stratum 1 time server has a radio or atomic clock that is directly attached to it. It then sends its time to a stratum 2 time server through NTP, and so on. A machine running NTP automatically chooses the machine with the lowest stratum number that it is configured to communicate with using NTP as its time source.

NTP Modes

NTP devices can operate in one of four different modes to provide flexibility when enabling time synchronization in a network:

- **Server:** Also called the NTP master because it provides accurate time information to clients. An NTP server is configured using the using the **ntp master** [*stratum*] global configuration command. The server should also have its local clock accurately set using the **clock set** privileged EXEC command.

- **Client:** Synchronizes its time with the NTP server. A client sends a request to (that is, polls) the server and expects a reply at some future time. An NTP client is enabled with the **ntp server** {*ntp-master-hostname* | *ntp-master-ip-address*} command.

- **Peers:** Also called symmetric mode, peers exchange time synchronization information. Symmetric modes are most often used between two or more servers operating as a mutually redundant group. Peers are configured using the **ntp peer** {*ntp-peer-hostname* | *ntp-peer-ip-address*} command.

- **Broadcast/multicast:** Special "push" mode of NTP server that provides one-way time announcements to receptive NTP clients. Typically used when time accuracy is not a big concern. Clients only need to be configured with the **ntp broadcast client** interface configuration command.

Figure 8-6 displays a sample enterprise campus topology highlighting the various NTP modes.

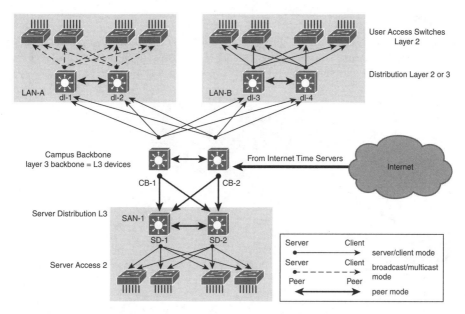

Figure 8-6   *NTP Design Hierarchy*

In the topology, the two multilayer campus backbone switches

■ Receive their time from external time sources on the Internet

■ Are NTP servers to the distribution layer switches in LAN-A, LAN-B, and SAN-1

■ Are NTP peers

In LAN-A, the two distribution layer switches are

■ NTP clients of the backbone campus NTP servers

■ NTP servers for the access layer switches, which are configured as NTP broadcast clients

■ NTP peers

In LAN-B, the two distribution layer switches are

■ NTP clients of the backbone campus NTP servers

■ NTP masters for the access layer switches

■ NTP peers

In SAN-1, the two distribution layer switches are

■ NTP clients of the backbone campus NTP servers

■ NTP masters for the access layer switches

■ NTP peers

Enabling NTP

In the reference NTP topology in Figure 8-7, R1 will be synchronizing its system clock with an external NTP time source and become an NTP master for the two access layer switches. Switches S1 and S2 will be NTP clients of R1 and NTP peers to each other.

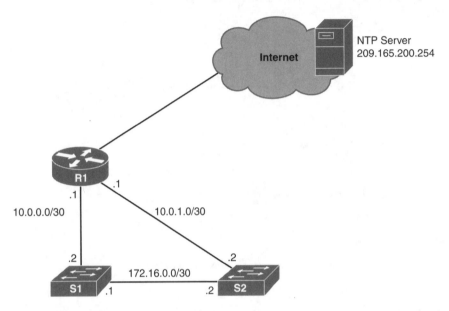

Figure 8-7 *Reference NTP Topology*

Example 8-15 configures R1 as an NTP client to an external time source. It also adjusts the time.

Example 8-15 *Configuring NTP on R1*

```
R1(config)# ntp server 209.165.200.254
R1(config)# clock timezone EST -5
R1(config)# clock summer-time EST recurring
R1(config)#
```

In this example, the time zone is set to EST and summer-time is enabled. The –5 is the actual offset from UTC.

Note EST is not a command keyword. It is a descriptive label for the time zone.

When a device is synchronized to an NTP source, all of its interfaces in turn serve as NTP servers, providing time to any system that requests synchronization. Use the **ntp disable** interface configuration command on interfaces that should not provide clock services.

An organization may not want to synchronize with an external time source. In this situation, a device must be chosen and configured as the authoritative time source for the network using the **ntp master** [*stratum*] global configuration command. It is recommended to have multiple NTP servers for devices to synchronize to.

Example 8-16 configures NTP on S1.

Example 8-16 *Configuring NTP on S1*

```
S1(config)# ntp server 10.0.0.1
S1(config)# clock timezone EDT -5
S1(config)# clock summer-time EDT recurring
S1(config)# ntp peer 172.16.0.2
S1(config)#
```

NTP clients identify the NTP server using the **ntp server** {*ntp-master-hostname* | *ntp-master-ip-address*} [**prefer**] global configuration command. Use the **prefer** keyword to identify a central NTP server.

S1 is also configured to adjust the time and to identify S2 as its NTP peer. NTP peers exchange time information with each other and help prevent a single point of failure.

Example 8-17 configures NTP on S2.

Example 8-17 *Configuring NTP on S2*

```
S2(config)# ntp server 10.0.1.1
S2(config)# clock timezone EST -5
S2(config)# clock summer-time EST recurring
S2(config)# ntp peer 172.16.0.1
S2(config)#
```

Note   NTP is slow to synchronize and can take up to 5 minutes for a device to synchronize with an upstream server.

Securing NTP

NTP can be an easy target in a network because many services such as device certificates rely on accurate time. The NTP operation can be secured using the following:

- **Authentication:** NTP authenticates the source of the information, so it only benefits the NTP client. Cisco devices support only MD5 authentication for NTP.

- **Access control lists:** Configure access lists on devices that provide time synchronization to others. ACLs are applied to NTP using the **ntp access-group** {**peer** | **query-only** | **serve** | **serve-only**} *ACL-#* global configuration command.

To configure NTP authentication, follow these steps:

Step 1.   Define NTP authentication key or keys with the **ntp authentication-key** *key_ number* **md5** key global configuration command. Every number specifies a unique NTP key.

Step 2.   Enable NTP authentication using the **ntp authenticate** global configuration command.

Step 3.   Tell the device which keys are valid for NTP authentication using the **ntp trusted-key** *key* global configuration command. The *key* argument should be the key defined in Step 1.

Step 4.   Specify the NTP server that requires authentication using the **ntp server** *ip_address* **key** *key_number* global configuration command. The command can also be used to secure NTP peers.

Example 8-18 configures NTP MD5 authentication on R1 and applies an NTP ACL to only answer synchronization requests from 10.0.0.0/16.

Example 8-18   *Configuring NTP Authentication on R1*

```
R1(config)# ntp authentication-key 1 md5 NTP-pa55w0rd
R1(config)# ntp authenticate
R1(config)# ntp trusted-key 1
R1(config)#
R1(config)# access 10 permit 10.0.0.0 0.0.255.255
R1(config)# ntp access-group serve-only 10
R1(config)#
```

Example 8-19 configures NTP MD5 authentication on S1.

Example 8-19   *Configuring NTP Authentication on S1*

```
S1(config)# ntp authentication-key 1 md5 NTP-pa55w0rd
S1(config)# ntp authenticate
S1(config)# ntp trusted-key 1
S1(config)# ntp server 10.0.0.1 key 1
S1(config)#
```

NTP Versions

Currently NTP Versions 3 and 4 are used in production networks. NTPv4 is an extension of NTP Version 3 and provides the following capabilities:

- Supports both IPv4 and IPv6 and is backward-compatible with NTPv3. NTPv3 does not support IPv6.

- Uses IPv6 multicast messages instead of IPv4 broadcast messages to send and receive clock updates.

- Improved security over NTPv3 as NTPv4 provides a whole security framework based on public key cryptography and standard X509 certificates.

- Improved time synchronization and efficiency as NTPv4 can automatically discover the hierarchy of NTP servers to achieve the best time accuracy for the lowest bandwidth cost. It does so by using multicast groups to automatically calculate the time-distribution hierarchy through an entire network.

- NTPv4 access group functionality accepts IPv6 named access lists as well as IPv4 numbered access lists. NTPv3 only accepts numbered IPv4 ACLs.

NTP in IPv6 Environment

NTPv4 enables IPv6 enabled device to obtain time information on a network by:

- **Polling NTP servers:** Also called client mode, this is configured on NTP clients using the **ntp server** *ipv6_address* **version 4** global configuration command.

- **Synchronizing with NTP peers:** Also called asymmetric active mode, this is configured on peers using the **ntp peer** *ipv6_address* **version 4** global configuration command.

- **Listening to NTPv4 multicasts:** To configure multicast-based NTPv4 associations, use the **ntp multicast** *ipv6_address* global configuration command. The device interface must also be configured to receive NTPv4 multicast packets by using the **ntp multicast client** [*ipv6_address*] interface configuration command. The IPv6 address of the multicast group which could be the all-nodes IPv6 address (FF02::1) or any other selected IPv6 multicast address.

Simple NTP

Simple NTP (SNTP) is a client-only version of NTP that can only receive the time from NTP servers. SNTP cannot be used to provide time services to other systems. SNTP typically provides time within 100 milliseconds of the accurate time, but it does not provide the complex filtering and statistical mechanisms of NTP.

SNTP and NTP cannot coexist on the same machine as they use the same port. If configured, informational messages such as "Cannot configure SNTP as NTP is already running." and "Unable to start SNTP process" will appear.

SNTP configuration commands simply replace the **ntp** portion of NTP commands with **sntp**. For instance, the client is configured using the **sntp server** *server_ip* global configuration command (and not the **ntp server** *server_ip* command).

To enable SNTP authentication, use the **sntp authenticate** global configuration command. To define an authentication key, use the **sntp authentication-key** *number* **md5** *key* global configuration command. To mark keys as trusted for SNTP, use the **sntp trusted-key** *key* command.

To verify whether a device has synchronized its time via SNTP use the **show sntp** command. The output will show you what the IP address is of the SNTP server or servers it uses, what the stratum number is, SNTP version number, when the last synchronization cycle was done, and whether time is synchronized.

To troubleshoot SNTP server selection, use the **debug sntp select** command to display IPv4 and IPv6 NTP output messages. To troubleshoot the SNTP process, use the **debug sntp packets [detail]** command.

Implementing SNMP

SNMP is the most commonly used network management protocol. Therefore, it is important to restrict SNMP access to the routers on which it is enabled.

SNMP was developed to allow administrators to manage nodes, such as servers, workstations, routers, switches, and security appliances, on an IP network. It enables network administrators to manage network performance, find and solve network problems, and plan for network growth.

There are three elements in an SNMP-enabled network, as shown in Figure 8-8.

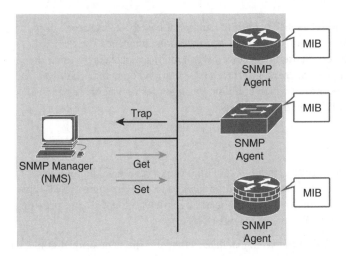

Figure 8-8   *SNMP Elements*

Note   A Get action provides the SNMP manager with read access to the SNMP agent's Management Information Base (MIB), and a Set action provides read-write access to the SNMP device.

SNMP defines management information between these three elements:

- **SNMP manager:** The SNMP manager is part of a network management system (NMS). The SNMP manager collects information from an SNMP agent using the Get action and can change configurations on an agent using the Set action.

- **SNMP agents (managed node):** Resides on the SNMP-managed networking client and responds to the SNMP manager's Set and Get requests to the local MIB. SNMP agents can be configured to forward real-time information directly to an SNMP manager using traps (or notifications). Devices supporting SNMP include routers, switches, firewalls, and servers running SNMP agent software.

- **Management Information Base (MIB):** Resides on the SNMP-managed networking client and stores data about the device operation including resources and activity. The MIB data is available to authenticated SNMP managers.

Note   SNMP uses UDP, port number 161; UDP port 162 is also used, for sending traps.

SNMP has evolved over the years, and currently there are three versions of SNMP. Each version has more features than the next:

- **SNMPv1:** Original version, which uses community strings for authentication. These community strings are exchanged in clear text and therefore very unsecure. SNMPv1 is considered to be obsolete.

- **SNMPv2:** Update to SNMPv1 that improved performance, security, confidentiality, and SNMP communications. There are several variations of SNMPv2, but SNMPv2c is the de facto standard and uses the same community string authentication format of SNMPv1.

- **SNMPv3:** Update to SNMPv2 that adds security and remote configuration enhancements. Specifically, SNMPv3 provides authentication, message integrity, and encryption.

These SNMP versions support three different security models. The SNMP security level defines the cryptographic security services that are applied to an SNMP session. The three security SNMP levels are as follows:

- **noAuthNoPriv:** Authenticates SNMP messages using a clear-text community string

- **authNoPriv:** Authenticates SNMP messages using either HMAC with MD5 (RFC 2104) or HMAC with SHA-1

- **authPriv:** Authenticates SNMP messages by using either HMAC-MD5 or SHA usernames and encrypts SNMP messages using DES, 3DES, or AES

Table 8-1 identifies differences between SNMP versions:

Table 8-1 *Differences Between SNMP Security Levels*

SNMP Version	Security Level	Authentication	Encryption
SNMPv1	noAuthNoPriv	Community string	No
SNMPv2	noAuthNoPriv	Community string	No
SNMPv3	noAuthNoPriv	Username	No
	authNoPriv	MD5 or SHA-1	No
	authPriv	MD5 or SHA-1	DES, 3DES, or AES

Note   If SNMP is required, it should be adequately protected. If SNMP is not required, the SNMP service should be disabled using the **no snmp-server** global configuration command.

SNMPv1 and SNMPv2 are by their very nature not secure protocols. The only authentication mechanism available in SNMPv1 and SNMPv2 are clear-text community strings. There are two types of community strings in SNMPv2:

- **Read-only (RO):** Provides access to the MIB variables, but does not allow these variables to be changed, only read. Because security is so weak in SNMPv2, many organizations only use SNMP in this read-only mode.

- **Read-write (RW):** Provides read and write access to all objects in the MIB.

If SNMPv2 is used, it should be secured by

- Using an uncommon, complex, long community string.

- Changing the community strings at regular intervals.

- Enabling read-only access only. If read write access is required, limit the read write access to the authorized SNMP manager.

- SNMP trap community names must be different than Get and Set community strings. This is considered best practice, and it also avoids unrelated issues in the Cisco IOS Software.

Example 8-20 creates a named ACL identifying the NMS host and then configures a difficult-to-guess community string (for example, R1-5ecret-5tr1ng), allowing access from only the NMS host at address 10.1.2.3.

Example 8-20 *Sample SNMPv2 Configuration*

```
R1(config)# ip access-list standard PROTECT-SNMP
R1(config-std-nacl)# remark Identify SNMP manager host
R1(config-std-nacl)# permit host 10.1.2.3
R1(config-std-nacl)# exit
R1(config)# snmp-server community R1-5ecret-5tr1ng ro PROTECT-SNMP
```

SNMPv3

SNMPv3 should be used whenever possible because it provides authenticity, integrity, and confidentiality. However, the added security makes SNMPv3 a little more complex to implement than SNMPv2.

Configuring SNMPv3 involves the following steps:

Step 1. Configure an ACL to limit who has access SNMP access to the device.

Step 2. Configure an SNMPv3 view using the **snmp-server view** *view-name* global configuration command.

Step 3. Configure an SNMPv3 group using the **snmp-server group** *group-name* global configuration command.

Step 4. Configure an SNMPv3 user using the **snmp-server user** *username group-name* global configuration command.

Step 5. Configure an SNMPv3 trap receiver using the **snmp-server host** global configuration command.

Step 6. Configure interface index persistence using the **snmp-server ifindex persist** global configuration command.

Enabling SNMPv3

Refer to the sample SNMPv3 configuration in Example 8-21.

Example 8-21 *Sample SNMPv3 Configuration*

```
R1(config)# ip access-list standard SNMPv3-ACL
R1(config-std-nacl)# remark ACL limits SNMP access to management network
R1(config-std-nacl)# permit 10.1.1.0 0.0.0.255
R1(config-std-nacl)# exit
R1(config)#
R1(config)# snmp-server view OPS sysUpTime included
R1(config)# snmp-server view OPS ifOperStatus included
R1(config)# snmp-server view OPS ifAdminStatus included
R1(config)# snmp-server view OPS ifDescr included
R1(config)#
R1(config)# snmp-server group MY-GROUP v3 priv read OPS write OPS access SNMPv3-ACL
R1(config)# snmp-server user ADMIN MY-GROUP v3 auth sha SNMP-Secret1 priv aes 256
SNMP-Secret2
*Nov  3 21:12:10.863: Configuring snmpv3 USM user, persisting snmpEngineBoots.
Please Wait...
R1(config)#
R1(config)# snmp-server enable traps
NHRP MIB is not enabled: Trap generation suppressed
```

```
However, configuration changes effective
R1(config)#
R1(config)# snmp-server host 10.1.1.254 traps version 3 priv ADMIN cpu
R1(config)#
R1(config)# snmp-server ifindex persist
R1(config)#
```

In the example, the SNMPv3-ACL is created and will be used to limit SNMP access to the local device to users in the management subnet (that is, 10.1.1.0/24).

Next a view called OPS is created that will be used as both read and write view for the group MY-GROUP. Specific MIB object IDs (OIDs) can be included or excluded from the view. In the example, the OIDs for system uptime, interface status, and description were added.

The security policy binding users and groups is configured next. The SNMPv3 group MY-GROUP is configured with authPriv security level (**snmp-server group MY-GROUP v3 priv**) and the user ADMIN (**snmp-server ADMIN MY-GROUP**) with passwords for both authentication (**auth sha SNMP-Secret1**) and encryption (**priv aes 256 SNMP-Secret2**).

SNMP traps are then enabled with the **snmp-server enable traps** command. SNMPv3 traps will be sent by R1 to the 10.1.1.254 IP address (**snmp-server host 10.1.1.254 traps**) using authPriv security level (**priv**) for the user ADMIN. Events for which traps are sent can also be limited, and in the example, only CPU-related events (**cpu**) will be sent.

SNMP identifies object instances, such as network interfaces, by their numeric indexes. This may cause problems when the number of instances changes. For example, if a new loopback interface is configured, index numbers would shuffle. As a consequence, NMS may mismatch data from different interfaces. To prevent index shuffle, the **snmp-server ifindex persist** command should be used to guarantee index persistence over device reboots and minor software upgrades.

Verifying SNMPv3

Verification of administrative and operational state of SNMP is a very important step in the overall process of setting up SNMPv3 in your network.

The **show snmp** command provides basic information about the SNMP configuration. You can use it to display SNMP traffic statistics, see whether the SNMP agent is enabled, or verify whether the device is configured to send traps, and if so, to which SNMP managers.

The **show snmp** *view* command provides information about configured SNMP views to verify for each group, see which OIDs are included, and more. There is a default read view (v1default), which can be used if a custom read view was not created.

The **show snmp group** command provides information about the configured SNMP groups. The most important parameters are the security model and levels.

The **show snmp user** command displays information about the configured SNMP users. The most important parameters are the user name and group name to which the user belongs. If authentication and encryption algorithms are displayed, the group that the user belongs to is configured with authPriv security level.

Configuration Backups

Infrastructure devices are crucial to the operation of any network. Having a current backup of the configuration file of a device is crucial if the device configuration file becomes corrupted and is inadvertently changed. Having access to a recent backup of the configuration will enable an administrator to quickly recover and restore the network to normal operation.

A backup of the configuration file can be created by manually copying the router configurations to an FTP server using the **copy** command. Although TFTP can be used, as well, FTP is a more secure means of transporting router configuration files.

Another method is to use the Cisco IOS **archive** global configuration command. The advantage of this command is that it can be used to automate the saving process. In the event that the configuration of the device becomes corrupt or is deleted, the **archive** command can then be used to restore configuration on the device.

As illustrated in Figure 8-9, an archive can be saved to a FTP server every time the running configuration is saved to NVRAM. An archive can also be configured to save the configuration periodically at a predefined length of time.

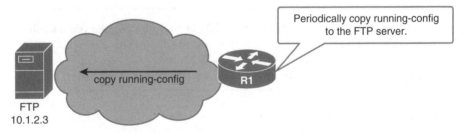

Figure 8-9   *Periodically Archiving the Configuration*

The **archive** Command

When the **archive** global configuration command is used, it prompts a change to archive configuration mode. From this mode, the administrator can configure the base file path to store and retrieve the configuration using the **path** archive configuration mode command. This is a required parameter that is specified by using URL notation form. It can denote either a local or a network path.

You can use two variables with the **path** command:

- **$h** will be replaced with device hostname.

- **$t** will be replaced with date and time of the archive.

If the **$t** variable is not used, the names of the new files will have the version number appended to differentiate it from the previous configurations of the same device.

Example 8-22 enters archive configuration mode and sets the path to an FTP server at 10.1.2.3. The username to access the FTP server is admin and the password is cisco123.

Example 8-22   *Sample Archive Configuration*

```
R1(config)# archive
R1(config-archive)# path ftp://admin:cisco123@10.1.2.3/$h.cfg
R1(config-archive)# ^Z
R1#
```

This is the only required parameter to configure and enable the archiving feature. Other optional archive parameters are used to enable automatic archiving.

After specifying the location of the archive, an archive copy of the configuration can be created either manually or automatically.

To manually archive the configuration file, use the **archive config** privileged EXEC command, as shown in Example 8-23.

Example 8-23   *Manually Archiving the Configuration File*

```
R1# archive config
Writing R1.cfg-Sep-20-13-05-09.868-0
R1#
```

To automate the archiving process and have the IOS periodically save the configuration file, use the **write-memory** archive configuration command, as shown in Example 8-24.

Example 8-24   *Automatically Archiving the Configuration File*

```
R1(config)# archive
R1(config-archive)# write-memory
R1(config-archive)# time-period 10080
R1(config-archive)# end
R1#
R1# copy running-config startup-config
Destination filename [startup-config]?
Building configuration...
[OK]
Writing R1.cfg-Sep-20-13-15-09.496-1
R1#
```

This **write-memory** archive command triggers the archive feature to copy the configuration each time the running configuration is copied into NVRAM. Notice how the action of saving the running configuration created an archive as highlighted in the figure.

The optional **time-period** archive command specifies a periodic interval time that the configuration is automatically saved. In the example, the archive will automatically save the configuration every week (10,080 minutes).

Use the **show archive** command to list the existing archives, as shown in Example 8-25.

Example 8-25 *Verifying Archives*

```
R1# show archive
The maximum archive configurations allowed is 10.
The next archive will be named ftp://admin:cisco123@10.1.2.3/R1-5
Archive #    Name
0
1            ftp://admin:cisco123@10.1.2.3/R1-1
2            ftp://admin:cisco123@10.1.2.3/R1-2
3            ftp://admin:cisco123@10.1.2.3/R1-3
4            ftp://admin:cisco123@10.1.2.3/R1-4
```

Notice how the version number is automatically appended.

Using SCP

The Secure Copy (SCP) feature provides a secure and authenticated method for copying router configuration or router image files.

The behavior of SCP is similar to that of Remote Copy (RCP), which comes from the Berkeley R-tools suite, except that SCP relies on SSH for security. Therefore, before enabling SCP, SSH must be enabled, and the router must have an RSA key pair. In addition, SCP requires that AAA authorization be configured so that the router can determine whether the user has the correct privilege level.

SCP allows a user who has appropriate authorization to copy any file that exists in the Cisco IOS File System (IFS) to and from a router by using the **copy** command. An authorized administrator may also perform this action from a workstation.

Enabling SCP on a Router

To configure the router for server-side SCP, perform these steps:

Step 1.   Use the **username name [privilege** *level*] {**secret** *password*} command to configure a username and password to use for local authentication. This step is optional if using network-based authentication, such as TACACS+ or RADIUS.

Step 2.   Enable SSH. Configure a domain name using the **ip domain-name** and generating the crypto keys using the **crypto key generate rsa general key** global configuration commands.

Step 3.   AAA with the **aaa new-model** global configuration mode command.

Step 4.   Use the **aaa authentication login** {default | *list-name*} *method1* [*method2*...] command to define a named list of authentication methods.

Step 5.   Use the **aaa authorization** {**network** | **exec** | **commands** *level*} {**default** | *list-name*} *method1*...[*method4*] command to configure command authorization.

Step 6.   Enable SCP server-side functionality with the **ip scp server enable** command.

Example 8-26 shows an SCP configuration.

Example 8-26   *Sample SCP Configuration on R1*

```
R1(config)# username ADMIN privilege 15 secret SCP-Secret
R1(config)# ip domain-name scp.cisco.com
R1(config)# crypto key generate rsa general-keys modulus 1024
The name for the keys will be: R1.scp.cisco.com

% The key modulus size is 1024 bits
% Generating 1024 bit RSA keys, keys will be non-exportable...
[OK] (elapsed time was 2 seconds)

R1(config)#
*Nov  3 22:25:28.135: %SSH-5-ENABLED: SSH 1.99 has been enabled
R1(config)# aaa new-model
R1(config)# aaa authentication login default group radius local-case
R1(config)# aaa authorization exec default group radius local
R1(config)# ip scp server enable
```

A workstation running a command-line SCP client can authenticate to the SCP server on the router to securely transfer files from the router flash memory. This allows a network administrator to store backup copies of a router's configuration and IOS files to any secure network location.

Example 8-27 displays the command line to copy a file from the router flash memory to the local computer and name it R1.cfg. The SCP client in the example (that is, pscp) is the PuTTY Secure Copy client included in the PuTTY suite of utilities.

Example 8-27   *Using an SCP Client on a PC to Copy Files*

```
C:\> pscp -l ADMIN -pw SCP-Secret ADMIN@10.1.1.1:flash:backup.cfg R1.cfg
C:\>
```

When transferring files between routers, one router acts as the SCP client. As shown in Example 8-28, the router can authenticate to and copy files from the SCP server–enabled router.

Example 8-28 *Using SCP on Router to Copy a File*

```
R2# copy scp: flash:
Address or name of remote host []? 10.1.1.1
Source username [ADMIN]? ADMIN
Source filename []? R2backup.cfg
Destination filename [R2backup.cfg]?
Password:
!
982 bytes copied in 13.916 secs (71 bytes/sec)
R2#
```

Disabling Unused Services

Many services are offered by the Cisco IOS Software. Although each service carries a useful function, it could present a potential security risk. For example, many of these services are enabled for legacy purposes and should be disabled.

All services that are not required should be disabled; otherwise, they are a security liability that an attacker could exploit. Keep in mind that different Cisco IOS Software releases maintain different services that are on or off by default. If a service is off by default, disabling it does not appear in the running configuration. It is best, however, not to make any assumptions and to explicitly disable all unneeded services, even if you think they are already disabled.

Table 8-2 describes the potential security risk of several services and the recommended commands to disable them.

Table 8-2 *Services and Recommended Commands*

Service	Description of Service	Commands Used to Disable Service
DNS Name Resolution	If no DNS server is specifically mentioned in the router configuration, all the name queries are sent to the broadcast address of 255.255.255.255 by default.	Router(config)# **no ip domain-lookup**
CDP	The CDP is a proprietary protocol that Cisco devices use to identify their directly connected neighbors. CDP, like any other unnecessary local service, is considered potentially harmful to security.	Router(config)# **no cdp run** Router(config-if)# **no cdp enable**
NTP	If NTP is not used in the network, it should be disabled. You can disable the processing of NTP packets on a specific interface.	Router(config-if)# **ntp disable**

Service	Description of Service	Commands Used to Disable Service
BOOTP Server	BOOTP uses UDP to formulate a network request to allow a device to obtain and configure its own IP information, such as IP address and subnet mask. However, the BOOTP protocol is seldom used, and it gives a hacker an opportunity to steal an IOS image.	Router(config)# no ip bootp server
DHCP	DHCP is essentially an extension of BOOTP.	Router(config)# no ip dhcp-server
Proxy ARP	Proxy ARP replies are sent to an ARP request destined for another device. When an intermediate Cisco device knows the MAC address of the destination device, it can act as a proxy. When an ARP request is destined for another Layer 3 network, a proxy ARP device extends a LAN perimeter by enabling transparent access between multiple LAN segments. This presents a security problem. An attacker can issue multiple ARP requests and use up the proxy ARP device's resources when it tries to respond to these requests in a DoS attack. Proxy ARP is enabled on Cisco router interfaces.	Router(config-if)# no ip proxy-arp
IP Source Routing	An option is found in the header of every IP packet. The Cisco IOS Software examines the option and acts accordingly. Sometimes an option indicates source routing. This means that the packet is specifying its own route. This feature poses a known security risk, such as a hacker taking control of a packet's route and directing it through the network. So, if source routing is not necessary in your network, you should disable it on all routers.	Router(config)# no ip source-route
IP Redirects	ICMP messages that are automatically sent by Cisco routers in response to various actions can give away a lot of information, such as routes, paths, and network conditions, to an unauthorized individual.	Router(config-if)# no ip redirects
HTTP Service	The Cisco IOS Software includes a web browser user interface from which you can issue Cisco IOS commands. You should disable HTTP server if it is not used.	Router(config)# no ip http server

Conditional Debugging

Debugging can generate a great deal of output and sometimes filtering through the output can be tedious. For this reason, it is practical to know how to limit debug output:

- Use an ACL
- Enable conditional debugging

The **debug ip packet** [*access-list*] command displays general IP debugging and is useful for analyzing messages traveling between local and remote hosts and to narrow down the scope of debugging.

Conditional debugging is sometimes called "conditionally triggered debugging." It can be used to

- Limit output based on the interface. Debugging output is turned off for all interfaces except the specified interface.

- Enable debugging output for conditional debugging events. Messages are displayed as different interfaces meet specific conditions.

To enable, define the condition with the **debug condition interface** *interface* command. The condition remains defined and applied until it is removed.

Enabling Conditional Debugging

Example 8-29 displays the commands required to debug NAT and IP packet details and limit to output for interface Fa0/0 only.

Example 8-29   *Debugging for Only Fast Ethernet 0/0*

```
R1# debug condition interface fa0/0
Condition 1 set
R1# debug ip packet detail
IP packet debugging is on (detailed)
R1#
R1# debug ip nat detailed
IP NAT detailed debugging is on
R1#
```

Check the active debug conditions using the **show debug condition** command.

Example 8-30 displays how to disable the debug condition when done.

Example 8-30   *Disabling Debugging for Fast Ethernet 0/0*

```
R1# no debug condition interface fa0/0
This condition is the last interface condition set.
Removing all conditions may cause a flood of debugging messages to result, unless
specific debugging flags are first removed.
Proceed with removal? [yes/no]: y
Condition 1 has been removed
R1# undebug all
All possible debugging has been turned off
R1#
```

Routing Protocol Authentication Options

The routing protocol is also susceptible to an attack. For example, a router could be receiving false route updates from an attacker to nefarious destinations. The solution is to enable routing protocol authentication.

This section describes neighbor router authentication as part of a total security plan and addresses the following topics:

- The purpose of routing protocol authentication
- Increasing the security of routing protocol authentication with time-based key chains
- Authentication options with different routing protocols

At the end of this section, you should know what neighbor router authentication is, how it works, and why you should use it to increase your overall network security.

The Purpose of Routing Protocol Authentication

The falsification of routing information is a more subtle class of attack that targets the information carried within the routing protocol. The consequences of falsifying routing information are as follows:

- Redirect traffic to create routing loops
- Redirect traffic to monitor on an insecure line
- Redirect traffic to discard it

A security compromise could occur if an attacker interferes with the network. For example, an unauthorized router might launch a fictitious routing update to convince the corporate router to send traffic to an incorrect destination, causing a DoS attack.

Neighbor authentication can be enabled so that routers only exchange routing updates with authorized neighbors based on predefined password. Without neighbor authentication, unauthorized or deliberately malicious routing protocol packets can compromise the security of the network traffic.

When neighbor authentication has been configured on routers, those routers authenticate the source of each routing protocol packet that they receive. The routers do so by exchanging an authentication key that is known to both the sending and the receiving router.

Two types of neighbor authentication can be used:

- Plain-text authentication (also referred to as simple password authentication)
- Hashing authentication

Each method requires the use of a key to be used in the authentication process.

Plain-Text Authentication

With plain-text authentication, a password (key) is configured on a router. Each participating neighbor router must be configured with the same key.

Refer to the example in Figure 8-10.

Figure 8-10 *Routing Update Using Plain-Text Authentication*

When a routing update packet is sent from R1 to R2, it also contains the plain-text key. R2 checks the received key against the same key stored in its memory. If the two keys match, R2 accepts the routing update. If the two keys do not match, the routing update is rejected.

Routing protocols that support plain-text authentication include RIPv2, OSPFv2, and IS-IS.

Example 8-31 provides an example of an OSPFv2 plain-text configuration in OSPFv2 on R1.

Example 8-31 *Sample Plain-Text Configuration on R1*

```
R1(config)# interface ethernet 0/1
R1(config-if)# ip ospf authentication
R1(config-if)# ip ospf authentication-key PLAINTEXT
% OSPF: Warning: The password/key will be truncated to 8 characters
R1(config-if)# ip ospf authentication-key PLAINTEX
R1(config-if)#
*Sep 21 11:45:53.670: %OSPF-5-ADJCHG: Process 1, Nbr 2.2.2.2 on Ethernet0/1 from
FULL to DOWN, Neighbor Down: Dead timer expired
R1(config-if)#
```

Notice how Cisco IOS software displays a warning message if a password is longer than eight characters. Only the first eight characters will be used.

Also notice the informational message that states that the OSPF adjacency is down. Enabling the authentication on one side causes the neighborship to time out. This is because only R2 is still not configured with plain-text authentication, and therefore R1 disregards the R2 updates. When the configuration on both routers is complete, the adjacency will be reestablished.

All neighboring routers on the same network must have the same password to be able to exchange OSPF information. Therefore, Example 8-32 provides the complimentary OSPFv2 plain-text authentication on R2.

Example 8-32   *Sample Plain-Text Configuration on R2*

```
R2(config)# interface ethernet 0/0
R2(config-if)# ip ospf authentication
R2(config-if)# ip ospf authentication-key PLAINTEX
R2(config-if)#
*Sep 21 11:46:38.709: %OSPF-5-ADJCHG: Process 1, Nbr 1.1.1.1 on Ethernet0/0 from
LOADING to FULL, Loading Done
R2(config-if)# exit
```

Notice how the adjacency was reestablished. This is because the routers are authenticating each other's updates.

Example 8-33 verifies the plain-text authentication configuration.

Example 8-33   *Verify Plain-Text Configuration on R2*

```
R2# show ip ospf interface e0/0 | include authentication
  Simple password authentication enabled
R2#
R2# show ip ospf neighbor

Neighbor ID     Pri   State        Dead Time   Address        Interface
1.1.1.1          1    FULL/BDR     00:00:31    172.16.12.1    Ethernet0/0
R2#
```

The **show ip ospf interface** command confirms that plain-text configuration is configured, and the output of the **show ip ospf neighbor** command shows that R1 has an adjacency with R1 (1.1.1.1).

Plain-text authentication should no longer be used because it is vulnerable to passive attacks. It is considered unsecure because the routing update uses a very small key string (eight characters or less) in plain text. An attacker could use a brute-force method to guess the key or intercept a routing update that contains the key in plain text.

The primary use of simple password authentication is to avoid accidental changes to the routing infrastructure. Using MD5 or SHA authentication is a recommended security practice.

Hashing Authentication

With hashing authentication, the routing protocol update does not contain the plain-text key. Instead, it contains a hash value that is used by the receiving router to validate the authenticity of the routing update. The hash value is often referred to as a signature.

Refer to the example in Figure 8-11.

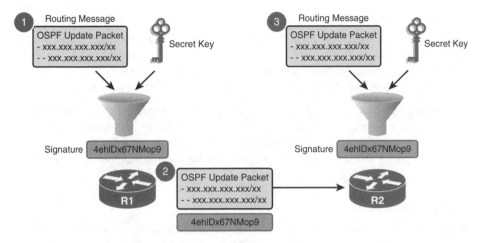

Figure 8-11 *Routing Update Using Hashing Authentication*

The process can be explained in three steps:

Step 1.   When R1 sends a routing update to R2, it uses a hashing algorithm such as MD5 or SHA. The hashing algorithm is essentially a complex mathematical formula that uses the data in the OSPF update and a predefined secret key to generate a unique hash value (signature). The resulting signature can be derived only by using the OSPF update and the secret key that is only known to the sender and receiver.

Step 2.   The resulting signature is appended to the routing update and sent to R2.

Step 3.   When R2 receives the routing update and uses the same hashing algorithm as R1 to calculate a hash value. Specifically, it uses the data from the received OSPF update and its predefined secret key.

In the example, the resulting hash value matches the hash value in the update, proving the authenticity of the sender. Therefore, it is accepted and processed by OSPFv2. If the hash values did not match, R2 would simply ignore and drop the update.

> **Note** To protect against replay attacks, the OSPF update also contains a nondecreasing sequence number. The sequence numbers identify each OSPF packet in the exchange.

It is important to understand that MD5 or SHA only provide authentication. They do not provide confidentiality. This means that the content of the routing protocol packet is not encrypted. If the update was intercepted, attackers could still see the content of the update.

The hashing algorithm used depends on the routing protocol. All routing protocols support MD5, but only OSPFv2, OSPFv3, and named EIGRP support the more secure SHA hashing algorithm.

Time-Based Key Chains

The security of routing protocol authentication can be increased by changing the secret keys often. However, routing between neighbors can be interrupted during the key rollover process. For instance, when a router is reconfigured with a new key, it will lose its neighbor adjacency until the other neighbors are configured with the same new key.

Some routing protocols support a time-based key chain management feature that provides a secure mechanism to maintain stable communications while handling this key rollover period. These routing protocols can use more than one key at a time to authenticate the update. Transitioning between the keys using timed-based key chains provides a nondisruptive exchange of routing updates.

Key Chain Specifics

A key chain is created using the **key chain** *key-name* global configuration command. Entering this command changes the prompt to key chain configuration mode. The key chain contains sets of keys (sometimes called shared secrets) that include

- **Key ID:** Configured using the **key** *key-id* key chain configuration mode command. Key IDs can range from 1 to 255. Entering this command changes the prompt to key chain key configuration mode.

- **Key string (password):** Configured using the **key-string** *password* key chain key configuration mode command.

- **Key lifetimes:** (Optional) Configured using the **send-lifetime** and **accept-lifetime** key chain key configuration mode commands.

Key-based routing protocols store and use more than one key for a feature at the same time. The key used will vary based on the send and accept lifetimes of a key. The device uses the lifetimes of keys to determine which keys in a key chain are active.

Each key in a keychain has two lifetimes, as follows:

- **Accept lifetime:** The time interval within which the device accepts the key during key exchange with another device

- **Send lifetime:** The time interval within which the device sends the key during key exchange with another device

The send and accept lifetimes of a key are specified using the start time and end time. During a key send lifetime, the device sends routing protocol packets with the key. The device does not accept communication from other devices when the key sent is not within the accept lifetime of the key on the device.

Each key definition within the key chain can specify a time duration for when that key will be activated (its lifetime). Then, during a given key's lifetime, routing protocol packets are sent with this activated key. Only one authentication packet is sent, regardless of how many valid keys exist. The software examines the key numbers in order from lowest to highest. It then uses the first valid key it encounters.

For example, to improve network security a network administrator wants to change the keys on all network routers every month with a key rollover time frame of one week. Example 8-34 provides an example to help illustrate this example.

Example 8-34 *Sample EIGRP Key Chain Configuration*

```
R1(config)# key chain R1-Chain
R1(config-keychain)# key 1
R1(config-keychain-key)# key-string firstkey
R1(config-keychain-key)# accept-lifetime 4:00:00 Jan 1 2015 4:00:00 Jan 31 2015
R1(config-keychain-key)# send-lifetime 4:00:00 Jan 1 2015 4:00:00 Jan 31 2015
R1(config-keychain-key)# exit
R1(config-keychain)# key 2
R1(config-keychain-key)# key-string secondkey
R1(config-keychain-key)# accept-lifetime 4:00:00 Jan 25 2015 4:00:00 Feb 28 2015
R1(config-keychain-key)# send-lifetime 4:00:00 Jan 25 2015 4:00:00 Feb 28 2015
R1(config-keychain-key)# end
R1#
```

In the example, R1 is configured with the key chain **R1-Chain**, which contains two keys. Each key has an authentication string and lifetime specified.

Key 1 will accept routing updates containing the key string **firstkey**. This key is acceptable from January 1, 2015 until the end of the month. Routing updates sent by R1 can use key 1 in the month of January only.

Key 2 will accept routing updates containing the key string **secondkey**. This key is acceptable from January 25, 2015, until the end of February. Routing updates sent by R1 can use key 2 from January 25 until the end of February.

When more than one key is configured such as in our example, the first key (key 1) will be used first until its lifetime expires.

Note The previous authentication configuration is incomplete. Authentication is not enabled until the key chain is applied to the routing protocol process.

In the example, key 1 specified an end time of January 31, 2015, and key 2 specified an end time of February 28, 2015. If an end time is not configured, the key send or accept lifetime defaults to *infinite*. The end time parameter can also be manually configured with the **infinite** keyword. When using the **infinite** parameter to configure the lifetime, the key is valid for use on received packets from the start-time value and never expires.

Authentication Options with Different Routing Protocols

Table 8-3 summarizes the different routing protocol authentication options.

Table 8-3 *Authentication Options with Different Routing Protocols*

Routing Protocol	Plain Text Authentication	MD5 Hashing Authentication	SHA Hashing Authentication	Key Chain Support
RIPv2	Yes	Yes	No	Yes
EIGRP	No	Yes	Yes, using named EIGRP	Yes
OSPFv2	Yes	Yes	Yes, using key chains	Yes
OSPFv3	No	Yes	Yes	No
BGP	No	Yes	No	No

Note EIGRP SHA does not support key chains.

Notice how all routing protocols support MD5 hashing authentication. Named EIGRP and OSPF support the newer, more secure SHA hashing authentication. Support for SHA was introduced in recent Cisco IOS 15 releases together with the named EIGRP configuration mode. Whenever possible, always use the SHA hashing authentication.

Both OSPFv2 and OSPFv3 support authentication. However, there is significant difference in authentication mechanisms in both protocols. OSPFv2 uses a built-in authentication mechanism and supports plain-text and hashing (MD5 and SHA) authentication. Authentication information (plain-text password or hash produced from a key and the routing protocol packet itself) in OSPFv2 is inserted into the OSPF header and checked by the other router.

OSPFv3 does not use a built-in authentication mechanism and relies on IPv6 native security capabilities and native security stack, which uses IPsec. Using an IPsec connection for OSPFv3 authentication requires you to define a security policy for every neighbor router. The security policy defines which protocol is used for communication (AH or ESP), hashing and encryption algorithm, keys, and the SPI value.

Configuring EIGRP Authentication

Implementing routing protocol authentication is one of the steps on how to harden routers and improve network security. Therefore, in networks running EIGRP, implement EIGRP neighbor authentication using a hashing algorithm and predefined passwords.

This section describes how to configure the following:

- Classic IPv4 and neighbor authentication using preshared passwords

- IPv6 EIGRP neighbor authentication using preshared passwords

- IPv4 and IPv6 EIGRP neighbor authentication using the named EIGRP method

EIGRP Authentication Configuration Checklist

The EIGRP MD5 authentication configuration steps are as follows:

Step 1.   **Configure the key chain:** The **key chain** global configuration command is used to define all the keys that are used for EIGRP MD5 authentication. Once in key chain configuration mode, use the **key** command to identify the key in the key chain. Each key is defined by the number, which defines the key ID. When the **key** command is used, the configuration enters the key chain key configuration mode, where the **key-string** *authentication-key* configuration command must be used to specify the authentication string (or password). The key ID and authentication string must be the same on all neighboring routers.

Step 2.   **Configure the authentication mode for EIGRP:** The only authentication type that is available in classic EIGRP configuration is MD5. The newer named EIGRP configuration method also supports the more secure SHA hashing algorithm.

Step 3.   **Enable authentication to use the key or keys in the key chain:** When an authentication type is selected and a key chain is configured, authentication of EIGRP packets must be enabled on all interfaces that are participating in the EIGRP domain as well. Authentication is enabled using the **ip authentication key-chain eigrp** interface command.

Configuring EIGRP Authentication

This section discusses how to configure EIGRP authentication using the topology in Figure 8-12.

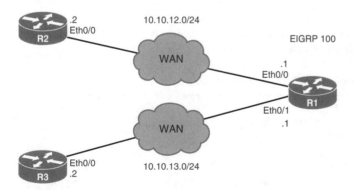

Figure 8-12   *EIGRP Routing Authentication Reference Topology*

In the example, you will

- Configure EIGRP MD5 authentication mode
- Configure EIGRP key-based routing authentication

Configure EIGRP MD5 Authentication Mode

Example 8-35 configures a key chain named **EIGRP-KEYS** with key string **secret-1** on R1.

Example 8-35 *Configuring the Key Chain on R1*

```
R1(config)# key chain EIGRP-KEYS
R1(config-keychain)# key 1
R1(config-keychain-key)# key-string secret-1
R1(config-keychain-key)# end
R1# show key chain
Key-chain EIGRP-KEYS:
    key 1 -- text "secret-1"
        accept lifetime (always valid) - (always valid) [valid now]
        send lifetime (always valid) - (always valid) [valid now]
R1#
```

Notice how the **show key chain** command is used to verify the key detail.

Example 8-36 configures a key chain named **EIGRP-KEYS** with key string **secret-1** on R2.

Example 8-36 *Configuring the Key Chain on R2*

```
R2(config)# key chain EIGRP-KEYS
R2(config-keychain)# key 1
R2(config-keychain-key)# key-string secret-1
R2(config-keychain-key)# end
R2#
```

Now that the key chain is created, the interfaces must be configured to support MD5 authentication.

Example 8-37 configures EIGRP MD5 authentication mode on R1's e0/0 interface and then binds the **EIGRP-KEYS** key chain with EIGRP autonomous system 100.

Example 8-37 *Configuring EIGRP MD5 Authentication on R1*

```
R1(config)# interface Ethernet 0/0
R1(config-if)# ip authentication mode eigrp 100 md5
R1(config-if)#
*Sep 20 19:47:43.654: %DUAL-5-NBRCHANGE: EIGRP-IPv4 100: Neighbor 10.10.12.2
(Ethernet0/0) is down: authentication mode changed
R1(config-if)# ip authentication key-chain eigrp 100 EIGRP-KEYS
R1(config-if)#
```

Notice how the adjacency with R2 was broken once the EIGRP authentication was enabled.

Example 8-38 configures EIGRP MD5 authentication mode on R2's e0/0 interface.

Example 8-38 *Configuring EIGRP MD5 Authentication on R2*

```
R2(config)# interface e0/0
R2(config-if)# ip authentication mode eigrp 100 md5
R2(config-if)# ip authentication key-chain eigrp 100 EIGRP-KEYS
R2(config-if)#
*Sep 20 19:49:56.127: %DUAL-5-NBRCHANGE: EIGRP-IPv4 100: Neighbor 10.10.12.1
(Ethernet0/0) is up: new adjacency
R2(config-if)#
```

Notice now how the adjacency with R1 was renewed once the key chain was identified.

Note   Although SHA authentication would be more secure, it is not supported in classic EIGRP. The MD5 is the only authentication type that is available for EIGRP.

Example 8-39 verifies the EIGRP neighbor relationships.

Example 8-39 *Verify the EIGRP Neighbor Adjacency with R2*

```
R1# show ip eigrp neighbors
EIGRP-IPv4 Neighbors for AS(100)
H   Address               Interface       Hold Uptime    SRTT   RTO  Q   Seq
                                          (sec)          (ms)        Cnt Num
0   10.10.12.2            Et0/0             13 00:24:32    15    100  0   7
1   10.10.13.2            Et0/1             13 01:03:32     9    100  0   3
R1#
```

The highlighted text confirms that R2 is an EIGRP neighbor confirming that the routing updates are being exchanged securely.

Configure EIGRP Key-Based Routing Authentication

The link between R1 and R3 will use key-based authentication.

Example 8-40 configures a key chain named **EIGRP-LIFETIME-KEYS** with two keys. Key 1 with the key string **secret-2** and key 2 with the key string **secret-3** on R1.

Example 8-40 *Key-Based Authentication Configuration on R1*

```
R1(config)# key chain EIGRP-LIFETIME-KEYS
R1(config-keychain)# key 1
R1(config-keychain-key)# key-string secret-2
R1(config-keychain-key)# accept-lifetime 00:00:00 Jan 1 2014 23:00:00 Mar 20 2015
R1(config-keychain-key)# send-lifetime 00:00:00 Jan 1 2014 23:00:00 Mar 20 2015
R1(config-keychain-key)# key 2
R1(config-keychain-key)# key-string secret-3
```

```
R1(config-keychain-key)# accept-lifetime 22:45:00 Mar 20 2015 infinite
R1(config-keychain-key)# send-lifetime 22:45:00 Mar 20 2015 infinite
R1(config-keychain-key)# exit
R1(config)# interface ethernet0/1
R1(config-if)# ip authentication mode eigrp 100 md5
R1(config-if)# ip authentication key-chain eigrp 100 EIGRP-LIFETIME-KEYS
R1(config-if)#
*Sep 20 20:35:13.837: %DUAL-5-NBRCHANGE: EIGRP-IPv4 100: Neighbor 10.10.13.2
(Ethernet0/1) is down: authentication mode changed
R1(config-if)#
```

Notice how the accept and send lifetimes of key 1 and key 2 overlap by 15 minutes.

Example 8-41 configures a complementary key chain on R3.

Example 8-41 *Key-Based Authentication Configuration on R3*

```
R3(config)# key chain EIGRP-LIFETIME-KEYS
R3(config-keychain)# key 1
R3(config-keychain-key)# key-string secret-2
R3(config-keychain-key)# accept-lifetime 00:00:00 Jan 1 2014 23:00:00 Mar 20 2015
R3(config-keychain-key)# send-lifetime 00:00:00 Jan 1 2014 23:00:00 Mar 20 2015
R3(config-keychain-key)# exit
R3(config-keychain)# key 2
R3(config-keychain-key)# key-string secret-3
R3(config-keychain-key)# accept-lifetime 22:45:00 Mar 20 2015 infinite
R3(config-keychain-key)# send-lifetime 22:45:00 Mar 20 2015 infinite
R3(config-keychain-key)# exit
R3(config-keychain)# exit
R3(config)# interface ethernet 0/0
R3(config-if)# ip authentication mode eigrp 100 md5
R3(config-if)# ip authentication key-chain eigrp 100 EIGRP-LIFETIME-KEYS
Sep 20 20:49:34.554: %DUAL-5-NBRCHANGE: EIGRP-IPv4 100: Neighbor 10.10.13.1
(Ethernet0/0) is up: new adjacency
R3(config-if)#
```

Example 8-42 verifies the EIGRP neighbor relationships.

Example 8-42 *Verify the EIGRP Neighbor Adjacency with R3*

```
R1# show ip eigrp neighbors
EIGRP-IPv4 Neighbors for AS(100)
H   Address              Interface       Hold Uptime   SRTT   RTO   Q   Seq
                                         (sec)         (ms)         Cnt  Num
1   10.10.12.2           Et0/0            14 01:59:15  2002   5000  0   10
0   10.10.13.2           Et0/1            14 02:00:28     1   4500  0   7
R1#
```

The highlighted text confirms that R2 is an EIGRP neighbor confirming that the routing updates are being exchanged securely.

Configuring EIGRP for IPv6 Authentication

This section discusses how to configure EIGRP for IPv6 authentication using the topology in Figure 8-13.

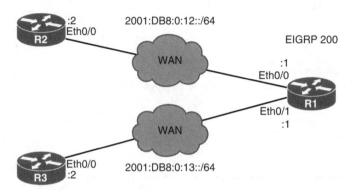

Figure 8-13 *EIGRP for IPv6 Routing Authentication Reference Topology*

In the example, you will configure EIGRP for IPv6 MD5 authentication mode.

Configure EIGRP for IPv6 MD5 Authentication Mode

Configuring EIGRP for IPv6 authentication is almost identical to the EIGRP method.

Example 8-43 configures a key chain named **R1-IPv6-Chain** with key string **secret-1** on R1.

> **Note** The **debug eigrp packet terse** command is useful when troubleshooting EIGRP authentication issues.

Example 8-43 *Configuring EIGRP for IPv6 Authentication on R1*

```
R1(config)# key chain R1-IPv6-Chain
R1(config-keychain)# key 1
R1(config-keychain-key)# key-string secret-1
R1(config-keychain-key)# exit
R1(config-keychain)# exit
R1(config)# interface ethernet 0/0
R1(config-if)# ipv6 authentication mode eigrp 200 md5
Sep 20 23:06:57.444: %DUAL-5-NBRCHANGE: EIGRP-IPv6 200: Neighbor
FE80::A8BB:CCFF:FE00:7400 (Ethernet0/0) is down: authentication mode changed
R1(config-if)# ipv6 authentication key-chain eigrp 200 R1-IPv6-Chain
R1(config-if)# end
R1#
```

Notice how the interface commands now use the **ipv6** keyword.

Example 8-44 configures a key chain named **R2-IPv6-Chain** with key string **secret-1** on R2.

Example 8-44   *Configuring EIGRP for IPv6 Authentication on R2*

```
R2(config)# key chain R2-IPv6-Chain
R2(config-keychain)# key 1
R2(config-keychain-key)# key-string secret-1
R2(config-keychain-key)# exit
R2(config-keychain)# exit
R2(config)# interface ethernet 0/0
R2(config-if)# ipv6 authentication mode eigrp 200 md5
R2(config-if)# ipv6 authentication key-chain eigrp 200 R2-IPv6-Chain
R2(config-if)# exit
R2(config)# exit
*Sep 20 23:13:09.602: %DUAL-5-NBRCHANGE: EIGRP-IPv6 200: Neighbor
FE80::A8BB:CCFF:FE00:5F00 (Ethernet0/0) is up: new adjacency
R2#
```

Notice now how the adjacency with R1 was renewed once the key chain was identified.

Configuring Named EIGRP Authentication

This section discusses how to configure authentication in named EIGRP.

Example 8-45 configures a key chain named **NAMED-R1-Chain** with key string **secret-1** on R1.

Example 8-45   *Configuring Authentication in Named EIGRP on R1*

```
R1(config)# key chain NAMED-R1-Chain
R1(config-keychain)# key 1
R1(config-keychain-key)# key-string secret-1
R1(config-keychain-key)# exit
R1(config-keychain)# exit
R1(config)# router eigrp ROUTE
R1(config-router)# address-family ipv4 autonomous-system 110
R1(config-router-af)# network 10.10.0.0 0.0.255.255
R1(config-router-af)# af-interface ethernet 0/0
R1(config-router-af-interface)# authentication key-chain NAMED-R1-Chain
R1(config-router-af-interface)# authentication mode md5
R1(config-router-af-interface)# end
R1#
```

Notice how in the named EIGRP method the interface authentication specifics are configured under the EIGRP process.

Example 8-46 configures a key chain named **NAMED-R2-Chain** with key string **secret-1** on R2.

Example 8-46 *Configuring Authentication in Named EIGRP on R2*

```
R2(config)# key chain NAMED-R2-Chain
R2(config-keychain)# key 1
R2(config-keychain-key)# key-string secret-1
R2(config-keychain-key)# exit
R2(config-keychain)# exit
R2(config)# router eigrp ROUTE
R2(config-router)# address-family ipv4 autonomous-system 110
R2(config-router-af)# network 10.10.0.0 0.0.255.255
R2(config-router-af)# af-interface ethernet 0/0
R2(config-router-af-interface)# authentication key-chain NAMED-R2-Chain
R2(config-router-af-interface)# authentication mode md5
R2(config-router-af-interface)# end
*Sep 20 23:37:12.032: %DUAL-5-NBRCHANGE: EIGRP-IPv4 110: Neighbor 10.10.12.1
(Ethernet0/0) is up: new adjacency
R2#
```

Notice now how the adjacency with R1 was renewed once the key chain was identified. Named EIGRP also supports the newer, more secure SHA256 authentication. This method simplifies the authentication configuration since it does not require key chains. To configure SHA256, use the authentication mode hmac-sha-256 encryption-type password address family interface configuration mode command.

Configuring OSPF Authentication

In networks running OSPF, you need to implement OSPF neighbor authentication using a hashing algorithm and predefined passwords.

This section describes how to do the following:

- Configure OSPFv2 neighbor authentication
- Configure OSPFv3 neighbor authentication

OSPF Authentication

When OSPFv2 neighbor authentication is enabled on a router, the router authenticates the source of each routing update packet that it receives. It performs this authentication by embedding an authentication data field in each OSPF packet. The authentication data is computed based on the authentication key, sometimes referred to as a password, which is known to both the sending and the receiving router.

By default, OSPF does not authenticate routing updates. This means that routing exchanges over a network are not authenticated. OSPFv2 supports

- **Plain-text authentication:** Simple password authentication. Least secure and not recommended for production environments.

- **MD5 authentication:** Secure and simple to configure using two commands. Should only be implemented if SHA authentication is not supported.

- **SHA authentication:** Most secure solution using key chains. Referred to as the OSPFv2 cryptographic authentication feature and only available since IOS 15.4(1)T.

OSPF MD5 Authentication

There are two tasks to enable MD5 hashing authentication:

Step 1.   Configure a key ID and keyword (password) using the **ip ospf message-digest-key** *key-id* **md5** *password* interface configuration command. The key ID and password are used to generate the hash value that is appended to the OSPF update. The password maximum length is 16 characters. Cisco IOS Software will display a warning if a password longer than 16 characters is entered.

Step 2.   Enable MD5 authentication using either the **ip ospf authentication message-digest** interface configuration command or the **area** *area-id* **authentication message-digest** OSPF router configuration command. The first command only enables MD5 authentication on a specific interface, and the second command enables authentication for all OSPFv2 interfaces.

Note   If you have conflicting key configuration on the interface and per area, the interface-specific setting takes precedence.

To provide seamless routing during key rollover an interface can be configured with multiple **ip ospf message-digest-key** commands using different key IDs.

Rollover allows neighboring routers to continue communication while the network administrator is updating them with the new key. When an interface is configured with two different keys, it sends two OSPF updates each authenticated by different keys. Rollover stops when the local system finds that all its neighbors know the new key. The system detects that a neighbor has the new key when it receives packets from the neighbor that are authenticated by the new key. After all neighbors have been updated with the new key, the old key must be manually removed using the **no ip ospf message-digest-key** command.

As well, note that different interfaces can be configured with different passwords. For example, an R1 to R2 link could use the password secret-1, and an R1 to R3 link could use the password secret-2.

Configure OSPF MD5 Authentication

This section discusses how to configure OSPF authentication using the topology in Figure 8-14.

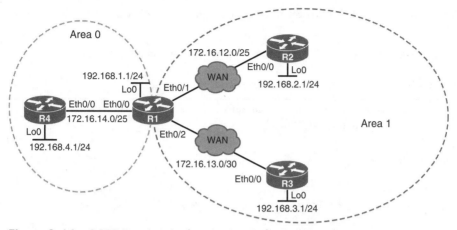

Figure 8-14 *OSPF Routing Authentication Reference Topology*

In the example, you will

- Configure MD5 authentication in the interfaces between R1 and R3

- Configure MD5 authentication in area 0

Configure OSPF MD5 Authentication on Interfaces

Example 8-47 configures OSPF MD5 authentication on the R1 interface connecting to R3.

Example 8-47 *Configuring OSPF MD5 Authentication on R1*

```
R1(config)# interface ethernet 0/2
R1(config-if)# ip ospf authentication message-digest
R1(config-if)# ip ospf message-digest-key 1 md5 secret-1
R1(config-if)#
*Sep 21 14:56:55.750: %OSPF-5-ADJCHG: Process 1, Nbr 3.3.3.3 on Ethernet0/2
from FULL to DOWN, Neighbor Down: Dead timer expired
R1(config-if)#
```

As expected, the neighbor adjacency changes to down because interface Ethernet 0/2 now only accepts MD5 authenticated updates.

Example 8-48 configures OSPF MD5 authentication on the R3 interface connecting to R1.

Example 8-48 *Configuring OSPF MD5 Authentication on R3*

```
R3(config)# interface ethernet 0/0
R3(config-if)# ip ospf authentication message-digest
R3(config-if)# ip ospf message-digest-key 1 md5 secret-1
R3(config-if)#
*Sep 21 14:57:41.473: %OSPF-5-ADJCHG: Process 1, Nbr 1.1.1.1 on Ethernet0/0
from LOADING to FULL, Loading Done
R3(config-if)#
```

Now R3 is also using OSPF MD5 authentication and therefore the adjacency is reestablished.

Example 8-49 verifies the MD5 authentication between R1 and R3.

Example 8-49   *Verifying the OSPF MD5 Authentication on R3*

```
R3# show ip ospf interface E0/0 | include authentication
   Message digest authentication enabled
R3#
R3# show ip ospf neighbor

Neighbor ID     Pri   State       Dead Time    Address        Interface
1.1.1.1           1   FULL/BDR    00:00:33     172.16.13.1    Ethernet0/0
R3#
```

As highlighted in the output, the **show ip ospf interface** command confirms that MD5 authentication is configured, and the output of the **show ip ospf neighbor** commands confirms the OSPF adjacency with R1 (1.1.1.1).

Configure OSPF MD5 Authentication in an Area

This first example enabled MD5 authentication on the interfaces. This next example will enable MD5 authentication on R1 and R4 for area 0.

Example 8-50 configures OSPF MD5 authentication on the R1.

Example 8-50   *Configuring OSPF MD5 Authentication for Area 0 on R1*

```
R1(config)# interface ethernet 0/0
R1(config-if)# ip ospf message-digest-key 1 md5 secret-2
R1(config-if)# exit
R1(config)#
R1(config)# router ospf 1
R1(config-router)# area 0 authentication message-digest
R1(config-router)#
*Sep 21 15:22:27.614: %OSPF-5-ADJCHG: Process 1, Nbr 4.4.4.4 on Ethernet0/0
from FULL to DOWN, Neighbor Down: Dead timer expired
R1(config-router)#
```

Example 8-51 configures OSPF MD5 authentication on the R4.

Example 8-51   *Configuring OSPF MD5 Authentication for Area 0 on R4*

```
R4(config)# interface ethernet 0/0
R4(config-if)# ip ospf message-digest-key 1 md5 secret-2
R4(config-if)# exit
R4(config)# router ospf 1
```

```
R4(config-router)# area 0 authentication message-digest
R4(config-router)#
*Sep 21 15:23:12.394: %OSPF-5-ADJCHG: Process 1, Nbr 1.1.1.1 on Ethernet0/0 from
LOADING to FULL, Loading Done
R4(config-router)#
```

Example 8-52 verifies the MD5 authentication between R1 and R4.

Example 8-52   *Verifying the OSPF MD5 Authentication on R4*

```
R4# show ip ospf interface E0/0 | include authentication
  Message digest authentication enabled
R4#
R4# show ip ospf neighbor

Neighbor ID     Pri   State         Dead Time    Address         Interface
1.1.1.1           1   FULL/BDR      00:00:32     172.16.14.1     Ethernet0/0
R4#
```

As highlighted in the output, the **show ip ospf interface** command confirms that MD5 authentication is configured, and the output of the **show ip ospf neighbor** commands confirms the OSPF adjacency with R1 (1.1.1.1).

OSPFv2 Cryptographic Authentication

Since Cisco IOS Software Release 15.4(1)T, OSPFv2 supports SHA hashing authentication using key chains. Cisco refers to this as the OSPFv2 Cryptographic Authentication feature. The feature prevents unauthorized or invalid routing updates in a network by authenticating OSPFv2 protocol packets using HMAC-SHA algorithms.

Note   SHA-256 or higher algorithms are expected to provide next-generation encryption (NGE) to meet the security and scalability requirements of the next two decades.

Configuring OSPFv2 Cryptographic Authentication

The configuration is a two-step process:

Step 1.   Configure a key chain using the **key chain** *key-name* global configuration command. The key chain contains the key ID and key string and enables the cryptographic authentication feature using the **cryptographic-algorithm** *auth-algo* key chain key configuration mode command.

Step 2.   Assign the key chain to the interface using the **ip ospf authentication key-chain** *key-name* interface configuration mode command. This also enables the feature.

> **Note**   An existing key chain name that is being used by another protocol can be used, or a new key chain specifically for OSPFv2 can be created.

> **Note**   If the **cryptographic-algorithm** *auth-algo* key chain key configuration mode command does not work, most likely the IOS does not support this feature.

As with other key chain configurations, the OSPFv2 cryptographic authentication can be configured with accept lifetime and a send lifetime.

> **Note**   If OSPFv2 is configured to use a key chain, all MD5 keys that were previously configured using the **ip ospf message-digest-key** command are ignored.

Configure OSPFv2 Cryptographic Authentication Example

Example 8-53 configures OSPFv2 cryptographic authentication on R1 using a key chain.

Example 8-53   *Configuring OSPF SHA Authentication on R1*

```
R1(config)# key chain SHA-CHAIN
R1(config-keychain)# key 1
R1(config-keychain-key)# key-string secret-1
R1(config-keychain-key)# cryptographic-algorithm ?
  hmac-sha-1     HMAC-SHA-1 authentication algorithm
  hmac-sha-256   HMAC-SHA-256 authentication algorithm
  hmac-sha-384   HMAC-SHA-384 authentication algorithm
  hmac-sha-512   HMAC-SHA-512 authentication algorithm
  md5            MD5 authentication algorithm

R1(config-keychain-key)# cryptographic-algorithm hmac-sha-256
R1(config-keychain-key)# exit
R1(config-keychain)# exit
R1(config)# interface s0/0/0
R1(config-if)# ip ospf authentication key-chain SHA-CHAIN
R1(config-if)#
*Sep 21 16:53:03.227: %OSPF-5-ADJCHG: Process 1, Nbr 2.2.2.2 on Serial0/0/0
from FULL to DOWN, Neighbor Down: Dead timer expired
R1(config-if)#
```

In the example, R1 is configured with a key chain named **SHA-CHAIN**, which contains key 1 with the password **secret-1**. The key is also enabled to support sha-hmac-256 encryption. Notice the other authentication algorithms listed including MD5.

Example 8-54 configures the complementary OSPFv2 cryptographic authentication on R2 using a key chain.

Example 8-54 *Configuring OSPF SHA Authentication on R2*

```
R2(config)# key chain SHA-CHAIN
R2(config-keychain)# key 1
R2(config-keychain-key)# key-string secret-1
R2(config-keychain-key)# cryptographic-algorithm hmac-sha-256
R2(config-keychain-key)# exit
R2(config-keychain)# exit
R2(config)# interface s0/0/0
R2(config-if)# ip ospf authentication key-chain SHA-CHAIN
R2(config-if)#
*Jul 21 16:13:32.555: %OSPF-5-ADJCHG: Process 1, Nbr 1.1.1.1 on Serial0/0/0 from
LOADING to FULL, Loading Done
R2(config-if)#
```

Notice how OSPF has now reestablished the adjacency.

Example 8-55 verifies the cryptographic authentication configuration on R1.

Example 8-55 *Verifying the OSPFv2 Cryptographic Authentication on R1*

```
R1# show key chain
Key-chain SHA-CHAIN:
    key 1 -- text "secret-1"
        accept lifetime (always valid) - (always valid) [valid now]
        send lifetime (always valid) - (always valid) [valid now]
R1#
R1# show ip ospf interface s0/0/0 | section Crypto
  Cryptographic authentication enabled
    Sending SA: Key 1, Algorithm HMAC-SHA-256 - key chain SHA-CHAIN

R1# show ip ospf neighbor

Neighbor ID     Pri   State         Dead Time   Address         Interface
2.2.2.2           0   FULL/  -      00:00:39    10.10.0.2       Serial0/0/0
R1#
```

As highlighted in the output, the **show ip ospf interface** command confirms that MD5 authentication is configured, and the output of the **show ip ospf neighbor** commands confirms the OSPF adjacency with R2 (2.2.2.2).

OSPFv3 Authentication

OSPFv3 requires the use of IPsec to enable authentication. Crypto images are required to use authentication because only crypto images include the IPsec application programming interfaces (APIs) needed for use with OSPFv3.

In OSPFv3, authentication fields have been removed from OSPFv3 packet headers. When OSPFv3 runs on IPv6, OSPFv3 requires the IPv6 Authentication Header (AH) or IPv6 Encapsulating Security Payload (ESP) header to ensure integrity, authentication, and confidentiality of routing exchanges. IPv6 AH and ESP extension headers can be used to provide authentication and confidentiality to OSPFv3.

To use the IPsec AH, use the **ipv6 ospf authentication** interface configuration command. To use the IPsec ESP header, use the **ipv6 ospf encryption** interface configuration command. The ESP header may be applied alone or in combination with the AH. When ESP is used, both encryption and authentication are provided. Security services can be provided between a pair of communicating hosts, between a pair of communicating security gateways, or between a security gateway and a host.

To configure IPsec, configure a security policy, which is a combination of the security policy index (SPI) and the key (the key is used to create and validate the hash value). IPsec for OSPFv3 can be configured on an interface or on an OSPFv3 area. For higher security, configure a different policy on each interface configured with IPsec. If IPsec for an OSPFv3 area is configured, the policy is applied to all the interfaces in that area, except for the interfaces that have IPsec configured directly.

Configuring OSPFv3 Authentication

To deploy OSPFv3 authentication, first define the security policy on each of the devices within the group. The security policy consists of the combination of the key and the security parameter index (SPI). The SPI is an identification tag added to the IPsec header.

The authentication policy can be configured either on an

- **Interface:** Can be configured using either the **ospfv3 authentication** {ipsec *spi*} {**md5** | **sha1**} {*key-encryption-type key*} | **null** interface configuration command or the **ipv6 ospf authentication** {**null** | **ipsec spi** *spi authentication-algorithm* [*key-encryption-type*] [*key*]} interface configuration commands. A *key* with the key length of exactly 40 hex characters must be specified.

- **Area:** Use the **area** *area-id* **authentication ipsec spi** *spi authentication-algorithm* [*key-encryption-type*] *key* router configuration mode. When configured for an area, the security policy is applied to all the interfaces in the area. For higher security, use a different policy on each interface.

This section discusses how to configure OSPFv3 authentication using the topology in Figure 8-15.

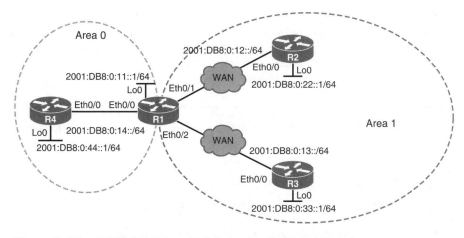

Figure 8-15 *OSPFv3 Routing Authentication Reference Topology*

In the example, you will

- Configure OSPFv3 authentication on interfaces between R1 and R2
- Configure OSPFv3 in area 0

Configuring OSPFv3 Authentication on an Interface Example

Example 8-56 configures OSPFv3 authentication on the R1 interface to R2.

Example 8-56 *Configuring OSPFv3 Authentication R1 E0/1 Interface*

```
R1(config)# interface Ethernet0/1
R1(config-if)# ipv6 ospf authentication ipsec spi 300 sha1
12345678901234567890123456789012345678901234567890
R1(config-if)#
*Sep 21 19:56:02.195: %CRYPTO-6-ISAKMP_ON_OFF: ISAKMP is ON
R1(config-if)#
*Sep 21 19:56:35.245: %OSPFv3-5-ADJCHG: Process 1, IPv6, Nbr 2.2.2.2 on
Ethernet0/1 from FULL to DOWN, Neighbor Down: Dead timer expired
R1(config-if)#
```

Notice the key argument in the **ipv6 ospf authentication** command must be exactly 40 hexadecimal digits.

Example 8-57 configures OSPFv3 authentication on the R2 interface to R1.

Example 8-57 *Configuring OSPFv3 Authentication R2 E0/1 Interface*

```
R2(config)# interface Ethernet 0/0
R2(config-if)# ipv6 ospf authentication ipsec spi 300 sha1 12345678901234567890012345
678901234567890
```

```
R2(config-if)#
*Sep 21 19:58:51.543: %CRYPTO-6-ISAKMP_ON_OFF: ISAKMP is ON
R2(config-if)#
*Sep 21 19:58:55.179: %OSPFv3-5-ADJCHG: Process 1, IPv6, Nbr 1.1.1.1
on Ethernet0/0 from LOADING to FULL, Loading Done
R2(config-if)#
```

Notice the information message informing us that the OSPFv3 adjacency has been reestablished.

Configuring OSPFv3 Authentication in an Area Example

Example 8-58 configures OSPFv3 authentication in an area 0 on R1.

Example 8-58 *Configuring OSPFv3 Authentication for Area 0 on R1*

```
R1(config)# router ospfv3 1
R1(config-router)# area 0 authentication ipsec spi 500 sha1 123456789012345678901234
5678901234567890
R1(config-router)#
*Sep 21 20:02:24.415: %OSPFv3-5-ADJCHG: Process 1, IPv6, Nbr 4.4.4.4 on
Ethernet0/0 from FULL to DOWN, Neighbor Down: Dead timer expired
R1(config-router)#
```

Example 8-59 configures OSPFv3 authentication in an area 0 on R4.

Example 8-59 *Configuring OSPFv3 Authentication for Area 0 on R4*

```
R4(config)# router ospfv3 1
R4(config-router)# area 0 authentication ipsec spi 500 sha1 123456789012345678901234
5678901234567890
R4(config-router)#
*Sep 21 20:02:29.367: %CRYPTO-6-ISAKMP_ON_OFF: ISAKMP is ON
R4(config-router)#
*Sep 21 20:02:31.186: %OSPFv3-5-ADJCHG: Process 1, IPv6, Nbr 1.1.1.1
on Ethernet0/0 from LOADING to FULL, Loading Done
R4(config-router)#
```

Notice the information message informing us that the OSPFv3 adjacency has been reestablished.

Example 8-60 verifies the OSPFv3 security association of Ethernet 0/0 on R1.

Example 8-60 *Verifying the OSPFv3 Security Associations*

```
R1# show crypto ipsec sa interface ethernet 0/0

interface: Ethernet0/0
```

```
      Crypto map tag: Ethernet0/0-OSPF-MAP, local addr FE80::A8BB:CCFF:FE00:5F00

   IPsecv6 policy name: OSPFv3-500

   protected vrf: (none)
   local  ident (addr/mask/prot/port): (FE80::/10/89/0)
   remote ident (addr/mask/prot/port): (::/0/89/0)
   current_peer FF02::5 port 500
     PERMIT, flags={origin_is_acl,}
   #pkts encaps: 21, #pkts encrypt: 21, #pkts digest: 21
   #pkts decaps: 0, #pkts decrypt: 0, #pkts verify: 0
   #pkts compressed: 0, #pkts decompressed: 0
   #pkts not compressed: 0, #pkts compr. failed: 0
   #pkts not decompressed: 0, #pkts decompress failed: 0
   #send errors 0, #recv errors 0

<Output omitted>
R1#
```

The command displays the IPsecv6 policy name OSPFv3-500. The protocol number of
OSPFv2 and OSPFv3 is 89. Notice how the protocol number of the protected protocol
in the local ident and remote ident is set to 89, designating the OSPF protocol. Also
highlighted are packet statistics, which track the number of encrypted and unencrypted
packets.

Configuring BGP Authentication

As enterprises increase their web presence and reliance on the Internet for revenue, the
need for reliable and geographically diverse Internet connectivity has become more
common. These needs are often met through multihome configurations that require BGP
for connectivity to a service provider's BGP-speaking routers.

However, introducing BGP routing into organizations introduces additional risks that are
present due to threats to BGP. One such threat is the advertisement of false BGP routing
updates that are sent from unauthorized BGP peers. To prevent receiving of false routing
updates, you can enable BGP authentication, which prevents establishment of BGP session with unauthorized BGP peers.

This section covers the following topics:

■ How BGP authentication using MD5 hashes works

■ Configuring and verifying BGP for IPv4 authentication

■ Configuring and verifying BGP for IPv6 authentication

BGP Authentication Configuration Checklist

BGP neighbor authentication can be configured on a router so that the router authenticates the source of each routing update packet that it receives. This authentication is accomplished by the exchange of an authentication key (password) that is shared between the source and destination routers.

Like EIGRP and OSPF, BGP also supports MD5 neighbor authentication. To generate an MD5 hash value, BGP uses the shared secret key and portions of the IP and TCP headers and the TCP payload. The MD5 hash is then stored in TCP option 19, which is created specifically for this purpose by RFC 2385.

The receiving BGP neighbor uses the same algorithm and shared secret to compute its own version of the MD5 hash. It then compares its own version with the one it received and either keeps the update or ignores it. If the shared secret is configured incorrectly, the BGP peering session will not be established.

Successful MD5 authentication requires the same password on both BGP peers. Configuring MD5 authentication causes Cisco IOS Software to generate and check the MD5 digest of every segment that is sent on the TCP connection.

BGP Authentication Configuration

This section discusses how to configure BGP authentication using the topology in Figure 8-16.

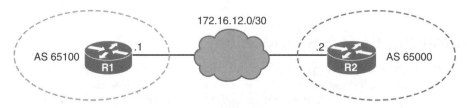

Figure 8-16 *BGP Authentication Reference Topology*

In the example, you will configure BGP authentication between BGP peers R1 and R2.

To enable MD5 authentication on a TCP connection between two BGP peers, use the **neighbor password** router configuration command with IP address to specify individual BGP peer, or use the peer group name to specify entire group of peers, followed by the shared password.

Example 8-61 configures BGP MD5 authentication on R1 for the BGP peering session to R2.

Example 8-61 *Configuring BGP Authentication on R1*

```
R1(config)# router bgp 65100
R1(config-router)# neighbor 172.16.12.2 remote-as 65000
R1(config-router)# neighbor 172.16.12.2 password secret-1
R1(config-router)#
```

The same password must be configured on the remote peer before the hold-down timer expires.

Example 8-62 configures BGP MD5 authentication on R2 for the BGP peering session to R1.

Example 8-62 *Configuring BGP Authentication on R2*

```
R2(config)# router bgp 65000
R2(config-router)# neighbor 172.16.12.1 remote-as 65100
R2(config-router)# neighbor 172.16.12.1 password secret-1
R2(config-router)#
```

Operationally, BGP neighbor authentication can be added to existing BGP sessions. The shared password may also be changed on existing sessions without terminating and reestablishing these sessions, as long as both sides of the BGP session are modified within the BGP session timeout window, which has a default of 180 seconds.

Example 8-63 verifies that the authenticated BGP session is up and that the BGP peers exchange information about prefixes.

Example 8-63 *Verifying the BGP Authentication on R1*

```
R1# show ip bgp summary
BGP router identifier 192.168.11.1, local AS number 65100
BGP table version is 4, main routing table version 4
3 network entries using 444 bytes of memory
3 path entries using 192 bytes of memory
3/3 BGP path/bestpath attribute entries using 408 bytes of memory
1 BGP AS-PATH entries using 24 bytes of memory
0 BGP route-map cache entries using 0 bytes of memory
0 BGP filter-list cache entries using 0 bytes of memory
BGP using 1068 total bytes of memory
BGP activity 6/0 prefixes, 6/0 paths, scan interval 60 secs


Neighbor        V    AS MsgRcvd   MsgSent   TblVer  InQ OutQ Up/Down    State/PfxRcd
172.16.12.2     4         65000        14        13    4    0 0 00:06:33           2
R1#
R1# show ip bgp neighbors 172.16.12.2 | include BGP
BGP neighbor is 172.16.12.2,  remote AS 65000, external link
  BGP version 4, remote router ID 192.168.22.1
  BGP state = Established, up for 00:07:27
  BGP table version 4, neighbor version 4/0
  BGP table version 4, neighbor version 4/0
R1#
```

The highlighted output of the **show ip bgp summary** command confirms R2 is a BGP neighbor. The highlighted output of the **show ip bgp neighbors** command confirms that we are actively exchanging BGP updates.

BGP for IPv6 Authentication Configuration

This section discusses how to configure BGP for IPv6 authentication using the topology in Figure 8-17.

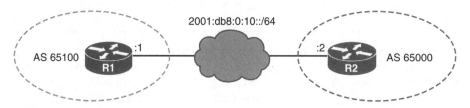

Figure 8-17 *BGP forIPv6 Authentication Reference Topology*

In the example, you will configure BGP for IPv6 authentication between BGP peers R1 and R2.

To enable MD5 authentication on a TCP connection between two BGP peers, use the **neighbor password** router configuration command with IP address to specify individual BGP peer, or use the peer group name to specify entire group of peers, followed by the shared password.

Example 8-64 configures BGP MD5 authentication on R1 for the BGP peering session to R2.

Example 8-64 *Configuring BGP Authentication on R1*

```
R1(config)# router bgp 65100
R1(config-router)# neighbor 2001:db8:0:10::2 remote-as 65000
R1(config-router)# neighbor 2001:db8:0:10::2 password secret-2
R1(config-router)#
```

The same password must be configured on the remote peer before the hold-down timer expires; otherwise, the session will drop.

Example 8-65 configures BGP MD5 authentication on R2 for the BGP peering session to R1.

Example 8-65 *Configuring BGP Authentication on R2*

```
R2(config)# router bgp 65000
R2(config-router)# neighbor 2001:db8:0:10::1 remote-as 65100
R2(config-router)# neighbor 2001:db8:0:10::1 password secret-2
R2(config-router)#
```

Implementing VRF-Lite

Virtual Routing and Forwarding (VRF) is a technology that allows the device to have multiple but separate instances of routing tables exist and work simultaneously. A VRF instance is essentially a logical router and consists of an IP routing table, a forwarding table, a set of interfaces that use the forwarding table, and a set of rules and routing protocols that determine what goes into the forwarding table.

A VRF increases

- Network functionality by allowing network paths to be completely segmented without using multiple devices.

- Network security because traffic is automatically segmented. VRF is conceptually similar to creating Layer 2 VLANs but operates at Layer 3.

Service providers (SPs) often take advantage of VRF to create separate virtual private networks (VPNs) for customers. Therefore, VRF is often referred to as *VPN routing and forwarding*.

VRF and VRF-Lite

VRF is usually associated with a service provider running Multiprotocol Label Switching (MPLS) because the two work well together. In a provider network, MPLS isolates each customer's network traffic, and a VRF is maintained for each customer. However, VRF can be used in other deployments without using MPLS.

VRF-lite is the deployment of VRF without MPLS. With the VRF-lite feature, the Catalyst switch supports multiple VPN routing/forwarding instances in customer-edge devices.

VRF-lite allows an SP to support two or more VPNs with overlapping IP addresses using one interface. VRF-lite uses input interfaces to distinguish routes for different VPNs and forms virtual packet-forwarding tables by associating one or more Layer 3 interfaces with each VRF.

Interfaces in a VRF can be either physical, such as Ethernet or serial ports, or logical, such as VLAN SVIs. However, a Layer 3 interface cannot belong to more than one VRF at any time.

Enabling VRF

Refer to the topology in Figure 8-18.

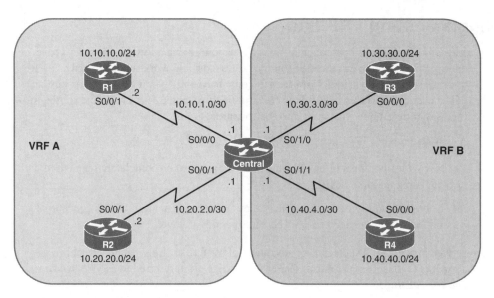

Figure 8-18 *VRF-Lite Reference Topology*

Example 8-66 displays a sample VRF-lite configuration for the indicated topology.

Example 8-66 *Sample VRF-Lite Configuration on Central*

```
Central(config)# ip vrf VRF-A
Central(config-vrf)# exit
Central(config)# ip vrf VRF-B
Central(config-vrf)# exit
Central(config)# interface Serial0/0/0
Central(config-if)# ip vrf forwarding VRF-A
Central(config-if)# ip address 10.10.1.1 255.255.255.252
Central(config-if)# clock rate 2000000
Central(config-if)# no shut
Central(config-if)# exit
Central(config)#
Central(config-if)# interface Serial0/0/1
Central(config-if)# ip vrf forwarding VRF-A
Central(config-if)# ip address 10.20.2.1 255.255.255.252
Central(config-if)# no shut
Central(config-if)# exit
Central(config)#
Central(config-if)# interface Serial0/1/0
Central(config-if)# ip vrf forwarding VRF-B
Central(config-if)# ip address 10.30.3.1 255.255.255.252
Central(config-if)# clock rate 2000000
Central(config-if)# no shut
```

```
Central(config-if)# exit
Central(config)#
Central(config-if)# interface Serial0/1/1
Central(config-if)# ip vrf forwarding VRF-B
Central(config-if)# ip address 10.40.4.1 255.255.255.252
Central(config-if)# no shut
Central(config-if)# exit
Central(config)#
```

Note The VRF instance must be configured on an interface first; otherwise, an error message will appear.

Example 8-67 verifies the routing table on Central.

Example 8-67 *Verify the Routing Table on Central*

```
Central# show ip route | begin Gateway
Gateway of last resort is not set


Central#
Central# show ip route vrf VRF-A | begin Gateway
Gateway of last resort is not set


      10.0.0.0/8 is variably subnetted, 4 subnets, 2 masks
C        10.10.1.0/30 is directly connected, Serial0/0/0
L        10.10.1.1/32 is directly connected, Serial0/0/0
C        10.20.2.0/30 is directly connected, Serial0/0/1
L        10.20.2.1/32 is directly connected, Serial0/0/1
Central#
Central# show ip route vrf VRF-B | begin Gateway
Gateway of last resort is not set


      10.0.0.0/8 is variably subnetted, 4 subnets, 2 masks
C        10.30.3.0/30 is directly connected, Serial0/1/0
L        10.30.3.1/32 is directly connected, Serial0/1/0
C        10.40.4.0/30 is directly connected, Serial0/1/1
L        10.40.4.1/32 is directly connected, Serial0/1/1
Central#
```

Notice how the first IP routing table is empty. That's because the directly connected interfaces now belong to the respective VRFs. The next two routing tables displayed in the example verify the content of each VRF.

Example 8-68 configures EIGRP for the VRF-A domain.

Example 8-68 *Enable EIGRP for VRF-A*

```
Central(config)# router eigrp 1
Central(config-router)# address-family ipv4 vrf VRF-A
Central(config-router-af)# network 10.10.1.0 0.0.0.3
Central(config-router-af)# network 10.20.2.0 0.0.0.3
Central(config-router-af)# autonomous-system 1
Central(config-router-af)# no auto-summary
Central(config-router-af)#
*Aug  5 04:45:35.879: %DUAL-5-NBRCHANGE: EIGRP-IPv4 1: Neighbor 10.20.2.2
(Serial0/0/1) is up: new adjacency
*Aug  5 04:45:35.883: %DUAL-5-NBRCHANGE: EIGRP-IPv4 1: Neighbor 10.10.1.2
(Serial0/0/0) is up: new adjacency
Central(config-router-af)# ^Z
Central#
```

Example 8-69 verifies the EIGRP routing table and neighbors for the VRF-A domain.

Example 8-69 *Verify the Routing Table of VRF-A*

```
Central# show ip route vrf VRF-A | begin Gateway
Gateway of last resort is not set


      10.0.0.0/8 is variably subnetted, 6 subnets, 3 masks
C        10.10.1.0/30 is directly connected, Serial0/0/0
L        10.10.1.1/32 is directly connected, Serial0/0/0
D        10.10.10.0/24 [90/2297856] via 10.10.1.2, 00:00:06, Serial0/0/0
C        10.20.2.0/30 is directly connected, Serial0/0/1
L        10.20.2.1/32 is directly connected, Serial0/0/1
D        10.20.20.0/24 [90/2297856] via 10.20.2.2, 00:05:41, Serial0/0/1
Central# show ip eigrp neighbors
EIGRP-IPv4 Neighbors for AS(1)
% No usable Router-ID found
Central#
Central# show ip eigrp vrf VRF-A neighbors
EIGRP-IPv4 Neighbors for AS(1) VRF(VRF-A)
H   Address              Interface       Hold Uptime   SRTT   RTO  Q  Seq
                                         (sec)         (ms)       Cnt Num
1   10.20.2.2            Se0/0/1          13 00:43:42     3    100  0  4
0   10.10.1.2            Se0/0/0          11 00:47:54     1    100  0  5
Central#
```

Notice that the R1 and R2 routes now appear in the routing table and that the two
EIGRP neighbors are listed as well. Also notice how we had to specify the VRF to display the EIGRP neighbors.

Example 8-70 configures OSPF for the VRF-B domain.

Example 8-70 *Enable OSPF for VRF-B*

```
Central(config)# router ospf 1 vrf VRF-B
Central(config-router)# router-id 5.5.5.5
Central(config-router)# network 10.30.3.0 0.0.0.3 area 0
Central(config-router)# network 10.40.4.0 0.0.0.3 area 0
Central(config-router)#
*Aug  5 04:47:22.327: %OSPF-5-ADJCHG: Process 1, Nbr 3.3.3.3 on Serial0/1/0 from
LOADING to FULL, Loading Done
*Aug  5 04:47:22.467: %OSPF-5-ADJCHG: Process 1, Nbr 4.4.4.4 on Serial0/1/1 from
LOADING to FULL, Loading Done
Central(config-router)# ^Z
Central#
```

Example 8-71 verifies OSPF for the VRF-B domain.

Example 8-71 *Verify the Routing Table of VRF-B*

```
Central# show ip route vrf VRF-B | begin Gateway
Gateway of last resort is not set

      10.0.0.0/8 is variably subnetted, 6 subnets, 3 masks
C        10.30.3.0/30 is directly connected, Serial0/1/0
L        10.30.3.1/32 is directly connected, Serial0/1/0
O        10.30.30.0/24 [110/65] via 10.30.3.2, 00:05:07, Serial0/1/0
C        10.40.4.0/30 is directly connected, Serial0/1/1
L        10.40.4.1/32 is directly connected, Serial0/1/1
O        10.40.40.0/24 [110/65] via 10.40.4.2, 00:07:30, Serial0/1/1
Central#
```

Notice that the R3 and R4 route now appears in the routing table.

Easy Virtual Network

For true path isolation, Cisco Easy Virtual Network (EVN) provides the simplicity of
Layer 2 with the controls of Layer 3. EVN provides traffic separation and path isolation
capabilities on a shared network infrastructure.

EVN is an IP-based network virtualization solution that takes advantage of existing VRF-
lite technology to

■ Simplify Layer 3 network virtualization

■ Improve support for shared services

■ Enhance management and troubleshooting

EVN reduces network virtualization configuration significantly across the entire network infrastructure by creating a virtual network trunk. The traditional VRF-lite solution requires creating one subinterface per VRF on all switches and routers involved in the data path, creating a lot of burden in configuration management.

EVN removes the need of per-VRF subinterface by using the **vnet trunk** interface command. This helps reduce the amount of provisioning across the network infrastructure, as shown in Figure 8-19.

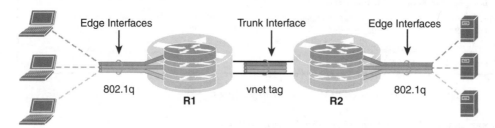

Figure 8-19   *EVN Reduces the Network Infrastructure*

EVN improves shared services support with route replication. Multiple EVN users may require common sets of services such as Internet connectivity, e-mail, video, Dynamic Host Configuration Protocol (DHCP), or Domain Name System (DNS). Traditionally, sharing common services can be achieved through importing and exporting routes between virtual networks using Border Gateway Protocol (BGP), which is complex.

EVN's route replication feature allows each virtual network to have direct access to the Routing Information Base (RIB) in each VRF, allowing the ability to

- Link routes from a Shared VRF to several segmented VRFs but still maintain separation where it is required

- Remove dependency on the BGP route target and route distinguisher, simplifying both configuration and complexity of importing and exporting routes

- Remove duplicate routing tables or routes, saving memory and CPU

EVN enhances network virtualization troubleshooting by making VRF-lite easier to deploy, operate, and scale. A routing context command mode allows network operators to perform troubleshooting issues that pertain specifically within a VRF without specifying the VRF name in every command.

Example 8-72 enters the red routing context.

Example 8-72   *Entering an EVN Routing Context*

```
R1# routing-context vrf red
R1%red#
```

Once in a routing context, the IOS commands do not have to be explicitly identified as VRF commands.

Summary

In this chapter, you learned about the following topics:

- Write and follow a security policy before securing a device.

- Passwords are stored in the configuration and should be protected from eavesdropping.

- Use SSH instead of Telnet, especially when using it over an unsecure network.

- Create router ALCs to protect the infrastructure by filtering traffic on the network edge.

- Secure SNMP if it is used on the network.

- Periodically save the configuration in case it gets corrupted or changed.

- Implement logging to an external destination to have insight into what is going on in a network.

- Disable unused services.

- Unauthorized routers might launch a fictitious routing update to convince a router to send traffic to an incorrect destination. Routers authenticate the source of each routing update that is received when routing authentication is enabled.

- There are two types of routing authentication: plain-text and hashing authentication.

- Avoid using plain-text authentication.

- A key chain is a set of keys that can be used with routing protocol authentications.

- Different routing protocols support different authentication options.

- When EIGRP authentication is configured, the router verifies every EIGRP packet.

- Classic EIGRP for IPv4 and IPv6 supports MD5 authentication, and named EIGRP supports SHA authentication.

- To configure classic MD5 authentication, define a key, enable EIGRP authentication mode on the interface, and associate the configured key with the interface.

- To configure SHA authentication, you need to use EIGRP named configuration mode.

- Verify the EIGRP authentication by verifying neighborship.

- When authentication is configured, the router generates and checks every OSPF packet and authenticates the source of each update packet that it receives.

- In OSPFv2 simple password authentication the routers send the key that is embedded in the OSPF packets.

- In OSPFv2 MD5 authentication the routers generate a hash of the key, key ID, and message. The message digest is sent with the packet.

- OSPFv3 uses native functionality offered by IPv6. All that is required for OSPFv3 authentication is IPsec AH. AH provides authentication and integrity check. IPsec ESP provides encryption for payloads, which is not required for authentication.

- BGP authentication uses MD5 authentication.

- Router generates and verifies MD5 digest of every segment sent over the BGP connection.

- Verify BGP authentication by verifying if BGP sessions are up.

References

For additional information, see these resources:

- **Cisco IOS Software Releases support page:** http://www.cisco.com/cisco/web/psa/default.html?mode=prod&level0=268438303

- **Cisco IOS Master Command List, All Releases:** http://www.cisco.com/c/en/us/td/docs/ios/mcl/allreleasemcl/all_book.html

- **The Cisco IOS IP SLAs Command Reference:** http://www.cisco.com/en/US/docs/ios/ipsla/command/reference/sla_book.html

Review Questions

Answer the following questions, and then see Appendix A, "Answers to Review Questions," for the answers.

1. Which routing protocol enables authentication by default?
   a. EIGRP
   b. Named EIGRP
   c. OSPFv2
   d. OSPFv2 with key chains
   e. No routing protocol enables authentication by default.

2. Which statement about plain-text authentication is true?
   a. Plain-text authentication is supported by RIPv2, EIGRP, and OSPFv2.
   b. Plain-text authentication uses the MD5 algorithm to encrypt routing updates.
   c. Plain-text authentication is considered to be insecure and should not be used.
   d. Plain-text authentication uses the key and hashing algorithm to produce a signature.
   e. Plain-text authentication peers require different passwords to authenticate the routing updates.

3. Which two authentication methods does EIGRP support?

   a. Plain text

   b. MD5

   c. SHA

   d. IPsec encryption

   e. None of these answers

4. The output of the **show running-configuration** command displays the following line:

   ```
   enable secret 4 JpAg4vBxn6wTb6NE3Nlp0wfUUZzR6eOcVUKUFftxEyA
   ```

   Based on the output, which statement is true regarding the enable password?

   a. It was encrypted using the **service password-encryption** command.

   b. It was encrypted using the **password service-encryption** command.

   c. It is encrypted using MD5.

   d. It is encrypted using SHA256.

   e. It is encrypted using IPsec.

5. The output of the **show ip ssh** command displays **SSH Enabled - version 2**. Based on this output, which statement is true?

   a. When SSH is enabled, this is the default SSH version.

   b. This is the original version but has known vulnerabilities.

   c. This is also known as compatibility mode because it supports both SSHv1 and SSHv2.

   d. The device was configured with the **ip ssh version 2** command.

   e. None of these answers.

6. When implementing logging, it is also important that dates and times are accurate and synchronized across all the network infrastructure devices using

   _____.

7. Which statement about SNMP is true?

   a. SNMPv1 uses community strings to encrypt SNMP messages.

   b. SNMPv1 is the most secure version to use.

   c. SNMPv2 supports the use of read-write community strings to encrypt SNMP messages.

   d. SNMPv3 can provide authenticity, integrity, and confidentiality.

   e. SNMPv1, SNMPv2, and SNMPv3 use community strings.

8. Refer to the following configuration:

```
R1(config)# archive
R1(config-archive)# path ftp://admin:cisco123@10.1.2.3/$h.cfg
R1(config-archive)# write-memory
R1(config-archive)# time-period 1440
R1(config-archive)# end
R1#
```

Based on the configuration, which statements are true?

a. The FTP path specified has a folder named admin:cisco on a server located at 10.1.2.3.

b. The only required parameter is the **path** archive configuration command.

c. To save the configuration, the administrator needs to use the **config archive** privileged EXEC command.

d. The startup configuration file is automatically saved every 24 hours.

e. The **write-memory** archive configuration command saves the archive every time the running configuration is saved to NVRAM.

9. Fill in the blank: The _____ _____ privileged EXEC command can be used to manually create an archive of the running configuration file.

Answers to End of Chapter Review Questions

Chapter 1

1. A converged network describes the state of the network in which all routers have the same view of the network topology.

2. A and D

3. A and B

4. B

5. A

6. B

7. When a router is performing autosummarization and it needs to send an update about a subnet of a network across an interface belonging to a different network, the router does not include the subnet, but rather sends the major (classful) network address instead. If the routing protocol is a classful routing protocol the (classful) subnet mask is not included and is assumed by the receiving router. If the routing protocol is a classless routing protocol, then the (classful) subnet mask is included with the update.

8. D

9.

distance-vector protocols	e
link-state protocols	f
convergence time	c
scalability	d
EGP	b
IGP	a

10. A, D, and E

11. A, B, and C

12. B

13. A

14.

IPsec	c
mGRE	a
NHRP	b

15. B

Chapter 2

1. E

2. B

3. A and E

4. D

5. C

6. D

7. E

8. C and E

9. EIGRP operational traffic is multicast (and unicast).

10. The four key technologies are neighbor discovery/recovery mechanism, Reliable Transport Protocol (RTP), diffusing update algorithm (DUAL) finite-state machine, and protocol-dependent modules.

11. B

12. EIGRP uses the following five types of packets:

Hello: Hello packets are used for neighbor discovery. They are sent as multicasts and do not require an acknowledgment. (They carry an acknowledgment number of 0.)

Update: Update packets contain route change information. An update is sent to communicate the routes a particular router has used to converge. An update is sent only to affected routers. Update packets are sent as multicasts when a new route is discovered and when convergence is completed (in other words, when a route becomes passive). To synchronize topology tables, update packets are sent as unicasts to neighbors during their EIGRP startup sequence. Update packets are sent reliably.

Query: When a router is performing route computation and does not find an FS, it sends a query packet to its neighbors asking whether they have a successor to the destination. Queries are normally multicast, but can be retransmitted as unicast packets in certain cases. They are sent reliably.

Reply: A reply packet is sent in response to a query packet. Replies are unicast to the originator of the query and are sent reliably. A router must reply to all queries.

Acknowledge (ack): The ack is used to acknowledge updates, queries, and replies. Ack packets are unicast hello packets and contain a nonzero acknowledgment number. (Note that hello and ack packets do not require acknowledgment.)

13. EIGRP hello packets are sent every 5 seconds on LAN links.

14. The hello interval determines how often hello packets are sent. It is 5 or 60 seconds by default, depending on the media type.

The hold time is the amount of time a router considers a neighbor up without receiving a hello or some other EIGRP packet from that neighbor. Hello packets include the hold time. The hold time interval is set by default to three times the hello interval.

15. A, C, and E

16. A and C

17. One EIGRP configuration for router A is as follows:

RouterA(config)# **router eigrp 100**

RouterA(config-router)# **network 172.16.2.0 0.0.0.255**

RouterA(config-router)# **network 172.16.5.0 0.0.0.255**

18. The **passive-interface** command prevents a routing protocol's routing updates from being sent through the specified router interface. When you use the **passive-interface** command with EIGRP, hello messages are not sent out of the specified interface. Neighboring router relationships do not form with other routers that can be reached through that interface (because the hello protocol is used to verify bidirectional communication between routers). Because no neighbors are found on an interface, no other EIGRP traffic is sent.

19. Stub routers are not queried. Instead, hub routers connected to the stub router answer the query on behalf of the stub router.

20. This command makes the router an EIGRP stub. The **receive-only** keyword restricts the router from sharing any of its routes with any other router within the EIGRP autonomous system.

Chapter 3

1. C

2. B

3. A and C

4. C

5. D and E

6. A

7. B and C

8. C and D

9. A

10. A

11. E

12. B

13. B

14. A and C

15. D

16. B

17. C

18. B

19. A

20. B

21. B

Chapter 4

1. C and E

2. A and C

3. B and E

4. B and C

5. D

6. A and F

7. D

8. A and C

9. A

10. E

11. C

12. A

13. B

14. B

15. F

Chapter 5

1. C

2. A

3. D

4. A, C, and E

5. PBR is applied to incoming packets on an interface

6. B, D, and E

7. A, B, and E

8. The Cisco IOS IP SLAs use active traffic monitoring, generating traffic in a continuous, reliable, and predictable manner, to measure network performance.

9. track 2 ip sla 100 reachability

10. ip sla schedule 100 life forever start-time now

Chapter 6

1. C
2. D
3. B
4. B
5. D
6. A
7. B
8. B
9. A
10. C
11. A
12. B
13. B
14. C
15. B
16. A
17. C
18. B
19. D

Chapter 7

1. B
2. B and C
3. A and C
4. A and C
5. C
6. D
7. A
8. A
9. B
10. A
11. A, C, and D
12. B
13. B and D
14. C and D
15. B

16.

Attribute	Order Preferred In	Highest or Lowest Value Preferred?	Sent to Which Other Routers?
Local preference	2	Highest	Internal BGP neighbors only.
MED	3	Lowest	External BGP neighbors. Those routers propagate the MED within their autonomous system, and the routers within the autonomous system use the MED, but do not pass it on to the next autonomous system.
Weight	1	Highest	Not sent to any BGP neighbors; local to the router only.

17. __10__ Prefer the path with the lowest neighbor BGP router ID

__6__ Prefer the lowest MED

__4__ Prefer the shortest AS-path

__9__ Prefer the oldest route for eBGP paths

__5__ Prefer the lowest origin code

__1__ Prefer the highest weight

__8__ Prefer the path through the closest IGP neighbor

__2__ Prefer the highest local preference

__3__ Prefer the route originated by the local router

__11__ Prefer the route with the lowest neighbor IP address

__7__ Prefer the eBGP path over the iBGP path

Chapter 8

1. E

2. C

3. B and C

4. D

5. D

6. Network Time Protocol (NTP)

7. D

8. B, D, E

9. archive config

IPv4 Supplement

This appendix covers the following topics:

- IPv4 Addresses and Subnetting Job Aid
- Decimal-to-Binary Conversion Chart
- IPv4 Addressing Review
- IPv4 Access Lists
- IPv4 Address Planning
- Hierarchical Addressing Using Variable-Length Subnet Masks
- Route Summarization
- Classless Interdomain Routing

This Internet Protocol Version 4 (IPv4) supplement provides job aids and supplementary information intended for your use when working with IPv4 addresses.

> **Note** In this appendix, the term *IP* refers to IPv4.

This appendix includes an IP addressing and subnetting job aid and a decimal-to-binary conversion chart. The information in the sections "IPv4 Addressing Review" and "IPv4 Access Lists" should serve as a review of the fundamentals of IP addressing and of the concepts and configuration of access lists, respectively.

The remainder of the sections relate to IP address planning. Scalable, well-behaved networks are not accidental. They are the result of good network design and effective implementation planning. A key element for effective scalable network implementation is a well-conceived and scalable IP addressing plan, as described in the "IPv4 Address Planning" section. Variable-length subnet masking (VLSM), route summarization, and classless interdomain routing (CIDR) are then explored. VLSM allows the network administrator to subnet a previously subnetted address to make the best use of the available address space. Summarization and CIDR are advanced IP addressing techniques that keep the size of the routing tables from increasing as networks grow.

IPv4 Addresses and Subnetting Job Aid

Figure B-1 is a job aid to help you with various aspects of IP addressing, including how to distinguish address classes, the number of subnets and hosts available with various subnet masks, and how to interpret IP addresses.

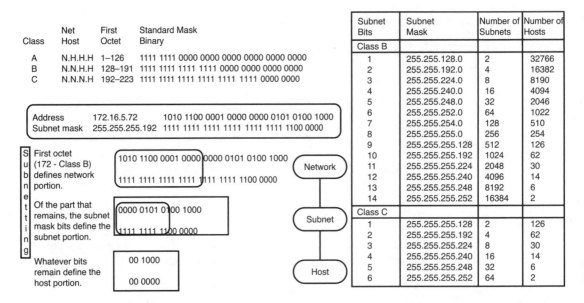

Figure B-1   *IP Addresses and Subnetting Job Aid*

Decimal-to-Binary Conversion Chart

Table B-1 can be used to convert from decimal to binary and from binary to decimal.

Decimal	Binary	Decimal	Binary	Decimal	Binary
0	00000000	28	00011100	56	00111000
1	00000001	29	00011101	57	00111001
2	00000010	30	00011110	58	00111010
3	00000011	31	00011111	59	00111011
4	00000100	32	00100000	60	00111100
5	00000101	33	00100001	61	00111101
6	00000110	34	00100010	62	00111110
7	00000111	35	00100011	63	00111111
8	00001000	36	00100100	64	01000000
9	00001001	37	00100101	65	01000001
10	00001010	38	00100110	66	01000010
11	00001011	39	00100111	67	01000011
12	00001100	40	00101000	68	01000100
13	00001101	41	00101001	69	01000101
14	00001110	42	00101010	70	01000110
15	00001111	43	00101011	71	01000111
16	00010000	44	00101100	72	01001000
17	00010001	45	00101101	73	01001001
18	00010010	46	00101110	74	01001010
19	00010011	47	00101111	75	01001011
20	00010100	48	00110000	76	01001100
21	00010101	49	00110001	77	01001101
22	00010110	50	00110010	78	01001110
23	00010111	51	00110011	79	01001111
24	00011000	52	00110100	80	01010000
25	00011001	53	00110101	81	01010001
26	00011010	54	00110110	82	01010010
27	00011011	55	00110111	83	01010011

Decimal	Binary	Decimal	Binary	Decimal	Binary
84	01010100	112	01110000	140	10001100
85	01010101	113	01110001	141	10001101
86	01010110	114	01110010	142	10001110
87	01010111	115	01110011	143	10001111
88	01011000	116	01110100	144	10010000
89	01011001	117	01110101	145	10010001
90	01011010	118	01110110	146	10010010
91	01011011	119	01110111	147	10010011
92	01011100	120	01111000	148	10010100
93	01011101	121	01111001	149	10010101
94	01011110	122	01111010	150	10010110
95	01011111	123	01111011	151	10010111
96	01100000	124	01111100	152	10011000
97	01100001	125	01111101	153	10011001
98	01100010	126	01111110	154	10011010
99	01100011	127	01111111	155	10011011
100	01100100	128	10000000	156	10011100
101	01100101	129	10000001	157	10011101
102	01100110	130	10000010	158	10011110
103	01100111	131	10000011	159	10011111
104	01101000	132	10000100	160	10100000
105	01101001	133	10000101	161	10100001
106	01101010	134	10000110	162	10100010
107	01101011	135	10000111	163	10100011
108	01101100	136	10001000	164	10100100
109	01101101	137	10001001	165	10100101
110	01101110	138	10001010	166	10100110
111	01101111	139	10001011	167	10100111

Decimal	Binary	Decimal	Binary	Decimal	Binary
168	10101000	198	11000110	228	11100100
169	10101001	199	11000111	229	11100101
170	10101010	200	11001000	230	11100110
171	10101011	201	11001001	231	11100111
172	10101100	202	11001010	232	11101000
173	10101101	203	11001011	233	11101001
174	10101110	204	11001100	234	11101010
175	10101111	205	11001101	235	11101011
176	10110000	206	11001110	236	11101100
177	10110001	207	11001111	237	11101101
178	10110010	208	11010000	238	11101110
179	10110011	209	11010001	239	11101111
180	10110100	210	11010010	240	11110000
181	10110101	211	11010011	241	11110001
182	10110110	212	11010100	242	11110010
183	10110111	213	11010101	243	11110011
184	10111000	214	11010110	244	11110100
185	10111001	215	11010111	245	11110101
186	10111010	216	11011000	246	11110110
187	10111011	217	11011001	247	11110111
188	10111100	218	11011010	248	11111000
189	10111101	219	11011011	249	11111001
190	10111110	220	11011100	250	11111010
191	10111111	221	11011101	251	11111011
192	11000000	222	11011110	252	11111100
193	11000001	223	11011111	253	11111101
194	11000010	224	11100000	254	11111110
195	11000011	225	11100001	255	11111111
196	11000100	226	11100010		
197	11000101	227	11100011		

IPv4 Addressing Review

This section reviews the basics of IPv4 addresses:

■ Converting IP addresses between decimal and binary

■ Determining an IP address class

■ Private addresses

■ Extending an IP classful address using a subnet mask

■ Calculating a subnet mask

■ Calculating the networks for a subnet mask

■ Using prefixes to represent a subnet mask

Converting IP Addresses Between Decimal and Binary

An *IP address* is a 32-bit two-level hierarchical number. It is hierarchical because the first portion of the address represents the network, and the second portion of the address represents the node (or host).

The 32 bits are grouped into 4 octets, with 8 bits per octet. The value of each octet ranges from 0 to 255 decimal, or 00000000 to 11111111 binary. IP addresses are usually written in dotted-decimal notation, which means that each octet is written in decimal notation and dots are placed between the octets. Figure B-2 shows how you convert an octet of an IP address in binary-to-decimal notation.

Value for Each Bit

2^7	2^6	2^5	2^4	2^3	2^2	2^1	2^0
128	64	32	16	8	4	2	1

Converting From Binary to Decimal

0	1	0	0	0	0	0	1
128	64	32	16	8	4	2	1

0 + 64 + 0 + 0 + 0 + 0 + 0 + 1 = 65

Figure B-2 *Converting an Octet of an IP Address from Binary to Decimal*

It is important that you understand how this conversion is done because it is used when calculating subnet masks, a topic discussed later in this section.

Figure B-3 shows three examples of converting IP addresses between binary and decimal.

Binary
Address: 00001010.00000001.00010111.00010011

Decimal
Address: ___10___ . ___1___ . ___23___ . ___19___

Binary
Address: 10101100 . 00010010 . 01000001 . 10101010

Decimal
Address: 172 ▪ 18 ▪ 65 ▪ 170

Binary
Address: 11000000.10101000.00001110.00000110

Decimal
Address: ___192___ ▪ ___168___ ▪ ___14___ ▪ ___6___

Figure B-3   *Converting IP Addresses Between Binary and Decimal*

Now that you understand the decimal-to-binary and binary-to-decimal conversion processes, use the following sections to review address classes and the uses of subnet masks.

Determining an IP Address Class

To accommodate large and small networks, the 32-bit IP addresses are segregated into Classes A through E. The first few bits of the first octet determine the class of an address. This then determines how many network bits and host bits are in the address. Figure B-4 illustrates the bits for Class A, B, and C addresses. Each address class allows for a certain number of network addresses and a certain number of host addresses within a network. Table B-2 shows the address range, the number of networks, and the number of hosts for each of the classes. (Note that Class D and E addresses are used for purposes other than addressing hosts.)

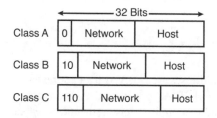

Figure B-4   *Determining an IP Address Class from the First Few Bits of an Address*

Table B-2   *IP Address Classes*

Class	Address Range	Number of Networks	Number of Hosts
A[1]	1.0.0.0 to 126.0.0.0	126 ($2^7 - 2$ that are reserved)	16,777,214
B	128.0.0.0 to 191.255.0.0	16,386 (2^{14})	65,532
C	192.0.0.0 to 223.255.255.0	Approximately 2 million (2^{21})	254
D	224.0.0.0 to 239.255.255.255	Reserved for multicast addresses	—
E	240.0.0.0 to 254.255.255.255	Reserved for research	—

[1] The network 127.0.0.0 (any address starting with decimal 127) is reserved for loopback. Network 0.0.0.0 is also reserved and cannot be used to address devices.

Using classes to denote which portion of the address represents the network number and which portion represents the node or host address is called classful addressing. Several issues exist with classful addressing. First, the number of available Class A, B, and C addresses is finite. Another problem is that not all classes are useful for a midsize organization, as illustrated in Table B-2. Subnet masks, as described later in this appendix, in the "Extending an IP Classful Address Using a Subnet Mask" section, were introduced to maximize the use of the IP addresses an organization receives, regardless of the class.

Private Addresses

Requests For Comments (RFC) 1918, *Address Allocation for Private Internets*, has set aside the following IPv4 address space for private use:

- **Class A network:** 10.0.0.0 to 10.255.255.255

- **Class B network:** 172.16.0.0 to 172.31.255.255

- **Class C network:** 192.168.0.0 to 192.168.255.255

Note   RFCs are available at http://tools.ietf.org/html/.

Addresses that are not private are public. Private addresses are reserved IPv4 addresses to be used only internally within a company's network. These private addresses are not to be used on the Internet, so they must be mapped to a public (registered) address when anything is sent to a recipient on the Internet.

Extending an IP Classful Address Using a Subnet Mask

RFC 950, *Internet Standard Subnetting Procedure*, was written to tackle the IP address shortage. It proposed a procedure, called *subnet masking*, for dividing Class A, B, and C addresses into smaller pieces, thereby increasing the number of possible networks.

A subnet mask is a 32-bit value that identifies which address bits represent network bits and which represent host bits. In other words, the router does not determine the network portion of the address by looking at the value of the first octet. Instead, it looks at the subnet mask that is associated with the address. In this way, subnet masks let you extend the usage of an IP address. This is one way of making an IP address a three-level hierarchy, as shown in Figure B-5.

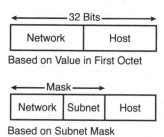

Figure B-5 *A Subnet Mask Determines How an IP Address Is Interpreted*

To create a subnet mask for an address, use a binary 1 for each bit that you want to represent the network or subnet portion of the address, and use a binary 0 for each bit that you want to represent the node portion of the address. Note that the 1s in the mask are contiguous. The default subnet masks for Class A, B, and C addresses are as shown Table B-3.

Table B-3 *IP Address Default Subnet Masks*

Class	Default Mask in Binary	Default Mask in Decimal
A	11111111.00000000.00000000.00000000	255.0.0.0
B	11111111.11111111.00000000.00000000	255.255.0.0
C	11111111.11111111.11111111.00000000	255.255.255.0

Calculating a Subnet Mask

When contiguous 1s are added to the default mask, making the all-1s field in the mask longer, the definition of the network part of an IP address is extended to include subnets. However, adding bits to the network part of an address decreases the number of bits in the host part. Therefore, creating additional networks (subnets) is done at the expense of the number of host devices that can occupy each network segment.

The number of subnets created is calculated by the formula 2^s, where s is the number of bits by which the default mask was extended.

Note   Subnet 0 (where all the subnet bits are 0) is allowed by default (since Cisco IOS Release 12.0) with the **ip subnet-zero** global configuration command being configured by default.

The number of hosts available is calculated by the formula $2^h - 2$, where h is the number of bits in the host portion. The two addresses subtracted in this host formula are for the addresses with all 0s and all 1s in the host field. In the host field, the all-0s bit pattern is reserved as the subnet identifier (sometimes called *the wire*), and the all-1s bit pattern is reserved as a directed broadcast address, to reach all hosts on that subnet.

Because subnet masks extend the number of network addresses you can use by using bits from the host portion, you do not want to randomly decide how many additional bits to use for the network portion. Instead, you want to do some research to determine how many network addresses you need to derive from your given IP address. For example, suppose that you have the IP address 172.16.0.0 and that you want to configure the network shown in Figure B-6. To establish your subnet mask, do the following:

IP Address = 172.16.0.0

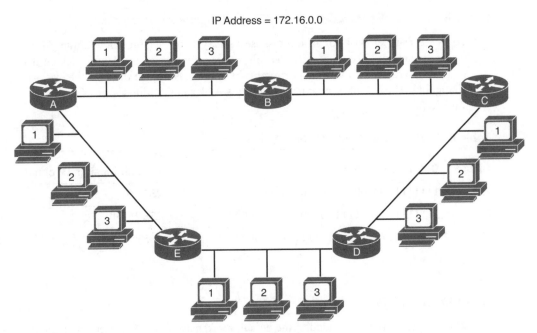

Figure B-6   *Network Used in the Subnet Mask Example*

Step 1.   Determine the number of networks (subnets) needed. Figure B-6, for example, has five networks.

Step 2.   Determine how many nodes per subnet must be defined. This example has five nodes (two routers and three workstations) on each subnet.

Step 3.   Determine future network and node requirements. For example, assume 100 percent growth.

Step 4.   Given the information gathered in Steps 1 to 3, determine the total number of subnets required. For this example, ten subnets are required. See the earlier section "IPv4 Addresses and Subnetting Job Aid" to select the appropriate subnet mask value that can accommodate 10 networks.

No mask accommodates exactly 10 subnets. Depending on your network growth trends, you might select 4 subnet bits, resulting in a subnet mask of 255.255.240.0. The binary representation of this subnet mask is as follows:

```
11111111.11111111.11110000.00000000
```

The additional 4 subnet bits would result in $2^s = 2^4 = 16$ subnets.

Calculating the Networks for a Subnet Mask

Continuing with the network in Figure B-6, after you identify your subnet mask, you must calculate the ten subnetted network addresses to use with 172.16.0.0 255.255.240.0. One way to do this is as follows:

Step 1.   Write the subnetted address in binary format, as shown at the top of Figure B-7. If necessary, use the decimal-to-binary conversion chart provided in Table B-1.

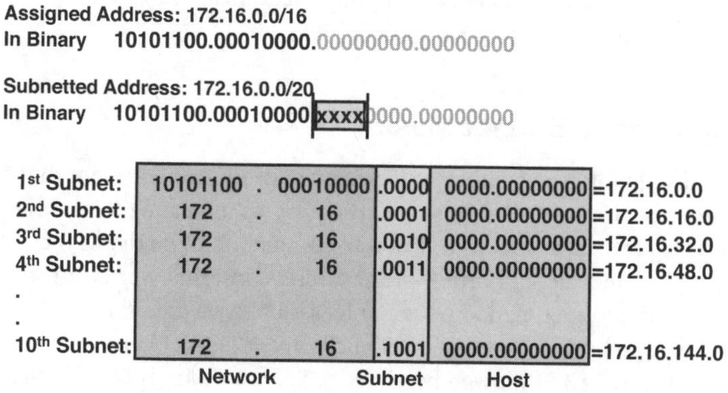

Assigned Address: 172.16.0.0/16
In Binary   **10101100.00010000**.00000000.00000000

Subnetted Address: 172.16.0.0/20
In Binary   **10101100.00010000**|xxxx|0000.00000000

1st Subnet:	10101100 . 00010000	.0000	0000.00000000	=172.16.0.0
2nd Subnet:	172 . 16	.0001	0000.00000000	=172.16.16.0
3rd Subnet:	172 . 16	.0010	0000.00000000	=172.16.32.0
4th Subnet:	172 . 16	.0011	0000.00000000	=172.16.48.0
.				
.				
10th Subnet:	172 . 16	.1001	0000.00000000	=172.16.144.0
	Network	Subnet	Host	

Figure B-7   *Calculating the Subnets for the Network in Figure B-6*

Step 2.   On the binary address, draw a line between the 16th and 17th bits, as shown in Figure B-7. This is the transition point between the network bits and the subnet bits. Then draw a line between the 20th and 21st bits. This is the transition point between the subnet bits and the host bits, and is the transition point between 1s and 0s in the subnet mask. Now you can focus on the target subnet bits.

Step 3.   Historically, it was recommended that you begin choosing subnets from highest (from the far left bit) to lowest, so that you could leave bits available in case you need more host bits later on. However, this strategy does not allow you to adequately summarize subnet addresses, so the present recommendation is to choose subnets from lowest to highest (right to left).

When you calculate the subnet address, all host bits are set to 0. Therefore, for the first subnet, the subnet bits are 0000, and the rest of this third octet (all host bits) is 0000. To convert back to decimal, it is important to note that you must always convert an entire octet, 8 bits.

If necessary, use the decimal-to-binary conversion chart provided in Table B-1, and locate this first number. The third octet of the first subnet number is 00000000, or decimal 0. Do not forget the other 8 host bits in the fourth octet. This fourth octet is also 00000000, or decimal 0.

Step 4.   (Optional) List each subnet in binary form to reduce the number of errors. This way, you will not forget where you left off in your subnet address selection.

Step 5.   Calculate the second-lowest subnet number. In this case, it is 0001. When combined with the next 4 bits (the host bits) of 0000, this is binary 00010000, or decimal 16. Again, don't forget the other 8 host bits in the fourth octet. This fourth octet is again 00000000, or decimal 0.

Step 6.   Continue calculating subnet numbers until you have as many as you need—in this case, ten subnets, as shown in Figure B-7.

Using Prefixes to Represent a Subnet Mask

As discussed, subnet masks identify the number of bits in an address that represent the network, subnet, and host portions of the address. Another way of indicating this information is to use a *prefix*. A prefix is a slash (/) followed by a numeric value that is the number of bits in the network and subnet portion of the address. In other words, it is the number of contiguous 1s in the subnet mask. For example, assume you are using a subnet mask of 255.255.255.0. The binary representation of this mask is 11111111.1111111 1.11111111.00000000, which is 24 1s followed by eight 0s. So, the prefix is /24, for the 24 bits of network and subnet information, the number of 1s in the mask.

Table B-4 shows some examples of the different ways you can represent a prefix and subnet mask.

Table B-4   *Representing Subnet Masks*

IP Address/Prefix	Subnet Mask in Decimal	Subnet Mask in Binary
192.168.112.0/21	255.255.248.0	11111111.11111111.11111000.00000000
172.16.0.0/16	255.255.0.0	11111111.11111111.00000000.00000000
10.1.1.0/27	255.255.255.224	11111111.11111111.11111111.11100000

It is important to know how to write subnet masks and prefixes because Cisco routers use both, as shown in Example B-1. You will typically be asked to input a subnet mask when configuring an IP address, but the output generated using **show** commands typically displays an IP address with a prefix.

Example B-1 *Examples of Subnet Mask and Prefix Use on Cisco Routers*

```
p1r3#show run
<Output omitted>
interface Ethernet0
 ip address 10.64.4.1 255.255.255.0
!
interface Serial0
 ip address 10.1.3.2 255.255.255.0
<Output omitted>

p1r3#show interface ethernet0
Ethernet0 is administratively down, line protocol is down
  Hardware is Lance, address is 00e0.b05a.d504 (bia 00e0.b05a.d504)
   Internet address is 10.64.4.1/24
<Output omitted>

p1r3#show interface serial0
Serial0 is down, line protocol is down
  Hardware is HD64570
   Internet address is 10.1.3.2/24
<Output omitted>
```

IPv4 Access Lists

This section reviews IPv4 access lists. It includes the following topics:

- IP access list overview
- IP standard access lists
- IP extended access lists
- Restricting virtual terminal access
- Verifying access list configuration

IP Access List Overview

An IP access list is a sequential collection of permit and deny conditions that apply to IP addresses or upper-layer IP protocols. IP access lists identify traffic, and can be used for many applications, including filtering packets coming into or going out of an interface, or restricting packets to and from virtual terminal lines.

Packet filtering helps control packet movement through the network, as shown in Figure B-8. Such control can help limit network traffic and restrict network use by certain users or devices.

Table B-5 shows the available types of IP access lists on a Cisco router and their access list numbers. Named access lists are also available for IP.

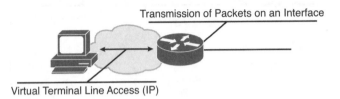

Transmission of Packets on an Interface

Virtual Terminal Line Access (IP)

Figure B-8   *Access Lists Can Control Packet Movement Through a Network*

Table B-5   *IP Access List Numbers*

Type of Access List	Range of Access List Numbers
IP standard	1 to 99 or from 1300 to 1999
IP extended	100 to 199 or from 2000 to 2699

This section covers IP standard and extended access lists, used for filtering. For information on other types of access lists, see the technical documentation on the Cisco website at http://www.cisco.com.

IP Standard Access Lists

Standard access lists permit or deny packets based only on the packet's source IP address, as shown in Figure B-9. The access list number range for standard IP access lists is 1 to 99 or from 1300 to 1999. Standard access lists are easier to configure than their more robust counterparts, extended access lists, but do not provide the granularity available with extended access lists.

A standard access list is a sequential collection of permit and deny conditions that apply to source IP addresses. The router tests addresses against the conditions in an access list one by one. The first match determines whether the router permits or denies the packet. Because the router stops testing conditions after the first match, the order of the conditions is critical. If no conditions match, and the access list is being used for filtering, the router rejects the packet. (Note that when access lists are used for reasons other than filtering, the meaning of "permit" and "deny" is different.)

Figure B-10 shows the processing of inbound standard access lists used for filtering. After receiving a packet, the router checks the packet's source address against the access list. If the access list permits the address, the router exits the access list and continues to process the packet. If the access list rejects the address, the router discards the packet and returns an Internet Control Message Protocol (ICMP) administratively prohibited message.

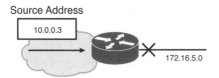

Figure B-9   *Standard IP Access Lists Filter Based Only on the Source Address*

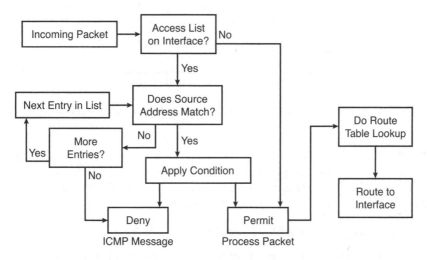

Figure B-10   *Processing of an Inbound Standard IP Access List Used for Filtering*

Note that the action taken if no more entries are found in the access list is to deny the packet. This illustrates an important rule to remember when creating access lists: The last entry in an access list is known as an implicit **deny any**; all traffic not explicitly permitted is implicitly denied. For example, consider what will happen if you create a list that just denies traffic that you do not want to let into your network, and you configure this to filter on an interface. If you forget about this rule, *all* of your traffic is denied—the traffic explicitly denied by your list, and the rest of the traffic that is implicitly denied because the access list is applied to the interface.

Another important point to remember when configuring access lists is that order is important. Make sure that you list the entries in order, from specific to general. For example, if you want to deny a specific host address and permit all other addresses, make sure that your entry about the specific host appears first.

Figure B-11 illustrates the processing of outbound standard IP access lists used for filtering. After receiving and routing a packet to a controlled interface, the router checks the packet's source address against the access list. If the access list permits the address, the router sends the packet. If the access list denies the address, the router discards the packet and returns an ICMP administratively prohibited message.

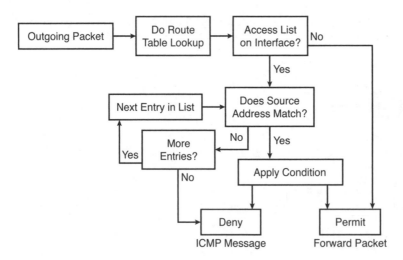

Figure B-11   *Processing of an Outbound Standard IP Access List Used for Filtering*

Wildcard Masks

Both standard and extended IP access lists use a wildcard mask. Like an IP address, a *wildcard mask* is a 32-bit quantity written in dotted-decimal format. The wildcard mask tells the router which bits of the address to use in comparisons:

- Address bits corresponding to wildcard mask bits set to 1 are ignored in comparisons.

- Address bits corresponding to wildcard mask bits set to 0 are used in comparisons.

An alternative way to think of the wildcard mask is as follows. If a 0 bit appears in the wildcard mask, the corresponding bit location in the access list address and the same bit location in the packet address must match. (Both must be 0 or both must be 1.) If a 1 bit appears in the wildcard mask, the corresponding bit location in the packet matches (whether it is 0 or 1), and that bit location in the access list address is ignored. For this reason, bits set to 1 in the wildcard mask are sometimes called *don't care bits*.

Remember that the order of the access list statements is important because the access list is not processed further after a match is found.

Wildcard Masks

The concept of a wildcard mask is similar to the wildcard character used in command-line interface on computers. For example, to delete all files on your computer that begin with the letter *f*, you would enter this:

delete f*.*

The * character is the wildcard. Any files that start with f, followed by any other characters, and then a dot, and then any other characters, are deleted.

Instead of using wildcard characters, routers use wildcard masks to implement this concept.

Examples of addresses and wildcard masks, and what they match, are shown in Table B-6.

Table B-6 *Access List Wildcard Mask Examples*

Address	Wildcard Mask	What It Matches
0.0.0.0	255.255.255.255	Any address
172.16.0.0/16	0.0.255.255	Any host on network 172.16.0.0
172.16.7.11/16	0.0.0.0	Host address 172.16.7.11
255.255.255.255	0.0.0.0	Local broadcast address 255.255.255.255
172.16.8.0/21	0.0.7.255	Any host on subnet 172.16.8.0/21

Access List Configuration Tasks

Whether you are using a standard or extended access list for filtering, you need to complete the following two tasks:

Step 1.   Create an access list in global configuration mode by specifying an access list number and access conditions.

Define a standard IP access list using a source address and wildcard, as shown later in this section.

Define an extended access list using source and destination addresses, and optional protocol-type information for finer granularity of control, as discussed in the "IP Extended Access Lists" section, later in this appendix.

Step 2.   Apply the access list in interface configuration mode to interfaces (or in line configuration mode to terminal lines).

After creating an access list, you can apply it to one or more interfaces. Access lists can be applied either outbound or inbound on interfaces.

IP Standard Access List Configuration

Use the **access-list** *access-list-number* {**permit** | **deny**} {*source* [*source-wildcard*] | **any**} [**log**] global configuration command to create an entry in a standard access list, as detailed in Table B-7.

Table B-7 *Standard IP* **access-list** *Command Description*

Parameter	Description
access-list-number	Identifies the list to which the entry belongs. A number from 1 to 99 or from 1300 to 1999.
permit | **deny**	Indicates whether this entry allows or blocks traffic from the specified address.

Parameter	Description
source	Identifies the source IP address.
source-wildcard	(Optional) Identifies which bits in the address field must match. A 1 in any bit position indicates don't care bits, and a 0 in any bit position indicates that the bit must strictly match. If this field is omitted, the wildcard mask 0.0.0.0 is assumed.
any	Use this keyword as an abbreviation for a source and source wildcard of 0.0.0.0 255.255.255.255.
log	(Optional) Causes an informational logging message about the packet that matches the entry to be sent to the console. Exercise caution when using this keyword, because it consumes CPU cycles. The message is generated for the first packet that matches, and then at 5-minute intervals, including the number of packets permitted or denied in the prior 5-minute interval.

When a packet does not match any of the configured lines in an access list, the packet is denied by default because there is an invisible line at the end of the access list that is equivalent to **deny any**. (Using **deny any** is the same as denying an address of 0.0.0.0 with a wildcard mask of 255.255.255.255.)

The keyword **host** can also be used in an access list. It causes the address that immediately follows it to be treated as if it were specified with a mask of 0.0.0.0. For example, configuring **host 10.1.1.1** in an access list is equivalent to configuring **10.1.1.1 0.0.0.0**.

Use the **ip access-group** *access-list-number* {**in** | **out**} interface configuration command to link an existing access list to an interface, as shown in Table B-8. Each interface can have both an inbound and an outbound IP access list.

Table B-8   ip access-group *Command Description*

Parameter	Description
access-list-number	Indicates the number of the access list to be linked to this interface
in	**out**	Processes packets arriving on or leaving from this interface

Eliminate the entire list by entering the **no access-list** *access-list-number* global configuration command. Remove an access list from an interface with the **no ip access-group** *access-list-number* {**in** | **out**} interface configuration command.

Implicit Wildcard Masks

Implicit, or default, wildcard masks reduce typing and simplify configuration, but you must take care when relying on the default mask.

The access list line shown in Example B-2 is an example of a specific host configuration. For standard access lists, if no wildcard mask is specified, the wildcard mask is assumed to be 0.0.0.0. The implicit mask makes it easier to enter a large number of individual addresses.

Example B-2   *Standard Access List Using the Default Wildcard Mask*

```
access-list 1 permit 172.16.5.17
```

Example B-3 shows some common errors found in access list lines.

Example B-3   *Common Errors Found in Access Lists*

```
access-list 1 permit 0.0.0.0
access-list 2 permit 172.16.0.0
access-list 3 deny any
access-list 3 deny 0.0.0.0 255.255.255.255
```

The first list in Example B-3—**permit 0.0.0.0**—would exactly match the address 0.0.0.0 and then permit it. Because you would never receive a packet from 0.0.0.0, this list would prevent all traffic from getting through (because of the implicit **deny any** at the end of the list).

The second list in Example B-3—**permit 172.16.0.0**—is probably a configuration error. The intention was probably 172.16.0.0 0.0.255.255. The exact address 172.16.0.0 refers to the network and would never be assigned to a host. As a result, nothing would get through with this list, again because of the implicit **deny any** at the end of the list. To filter networks or subnets, use an explicit wildcard mask.

The next two lines in Example B-3—**deny any** and **deny 0.0.0.0 255.255.255.255**—are unnecessary to configure because they duplicate the function of the implicit **deny** that occurs when a packet fails to match all the configured lines in an access list. Although they are not necessary, you might want to add one of these entries so that you can see any matches on these lines for record-keeping purposes.

Configuration Principles

The following general principles help ensure that the access lists you create have the intended results:

- Top-down processing.

    - Organize your access list so that more specific references in a network or subnet appear before more general ones.

    - Place more frequently occurring conditions before less-frequent conditions.

- Implicit **deny any**.

    - Unless you end your access list with an explicit **permit any**, it denies all traffic that fails to match any of the access list lines by default.

- New lines added to the end by default.

    - Subsequent additions are always added to the end of the access list by default.

    - Cisco IOS Release 12.2(14)S introduced a feature called IP Access List Entry Sequence Numbering that enables network administrators to apply sequence numbers to **permit** or **deny** statements in a named IP access list and also reorder, add, or remove such statements. Before this feature, network administrators could only add access list entries to the end of an access list (which is the case for numbered access lists), meaning that if statements need to be added anywhere except the end of the access list, the entire access list must be reconfigured. You can selectively add or remove lines when using numbered access lists only by editing the numbered access list as though it is a named access list with the name equal to the number and using the sequence numbers that are automatically assigned to the lines.

- An undefined access list equals **permit any**.

    - If you apply an access list with the **ip access-group** command to an interface before any access list lines have been created, the result is **permit any**. However, the list is live, so if you enter only one line, it goes from a **permit any** to a **deny** *most* (because of the implicit **deny any**) as soon as you press **Enter**. For this reason, you should create your access list before applying it to an interface.

Standard Access List Example

Figure B-12 shows a sample network, and Example B-4 shows the configuration on Router X in that figure.

Example B-4   *Standard Access List Configuration of Router X in Figure B-12*

```
RouterX(config)# access-list 2 permit 10.48.0.3
RouterX(config)# access-list 2 deny 10.48.0.0 0.0.255.255
RouterX(config)# access-list 2 permit 10.0.0.0 0.255.255.255
RouterX(config)# !(Note: all other access implicitly denied)
RouterX(config)# interface ethernet 0
RouterX(config-if)# ip access-group 2 in
```

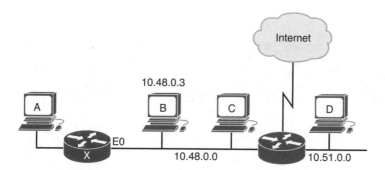

Figure B-12 *Network Used for the Standard IP Access List Example*

Consider which devices can communicate with Host A in this example:

- Host B can communicate with Host A. It is permitted by the first line of the access list, which uses an implicit host mask.

- Host C cannot communicate with Host A. Host C is in the subnet that is denied by the second line in the access list.

- Host D can communicate with Host A. Host D is on a subnet that is explicitly permitted by the third line of the access list.

- Users on the Internet cannot communicate with Host A. Users outside this network are not explicitly permitted, so they are denied by default with the implicit **deny any** at the end of the access list.

Location of Standard Access Lists

Access list location can be more of an art than a science. Consider the network in Figure B-13 and the access list configuration in Example B-5 to illustrate some general guidelines. If the policy goal is to deny Host Z access to Host V on another network, and not to change any other access policy, determine on which interface of which router this access list should be configured.

Example B-5 *Standard Access List to Be Configured on a Router in Figure B-13*

```
access-list 3 deny 10.3.0.1
access-list 3 permit any
```

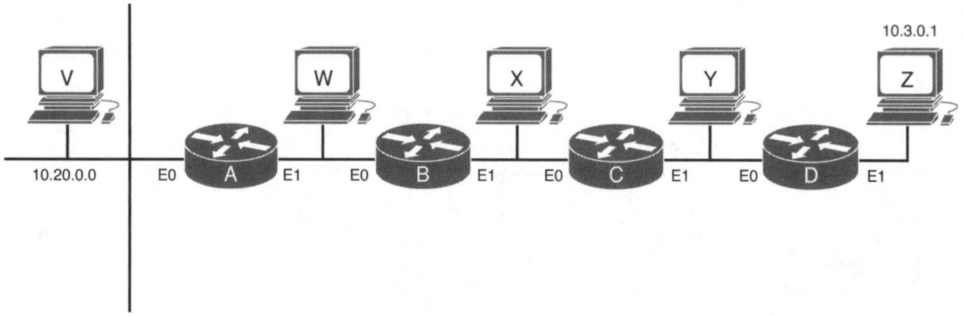

Figure B-13   *Location of the Standard IP Access List Example*

The access list should be placed on Router A because a standard access list can specify only a source address. No hosts beyond the point in the path where the traffic is denied can connect.

The access list could be configured as an outbound list on E0 of Router A. However, it would most likely be configured as an inbound list on E1 so that packets to be denied would not have to be routed through Router A first.

Consider the effect of placing the access list on other routers:

- **Router B:** Host Z could not connect with Host W (and Host V).

- **Router C:** Host Z could not connect with Hosts W and X (and Host V).

- **Router D:** Host Z could not connect with Hosts W, X, and Y (and Host V).

Therefore, for standard access lists, the rule is to place them as close to the *destination* as possible to exercise the most control. Note, however, that this means that traffic is routed through the network, only to be denied close to its destination.

IP Extended Access Lists

Standard access lists offer quick configuration and low overhead in limiting traffic based on source addresses in a network. *Extended access lists* provide a higher degree of control by enabling filtering based on the source and destination addresses, transport layer protocol, and application port number. These features make it possible to limit traffic based on the uses of the network.

Extended Access List Processing

As shown in Figure B-14, every condition tested in a line of an extended access list must match for the line of the access list to match and for the permit or deny condition to be applied. As soon as one parameter or condition fails, the next line in the access list is compared.

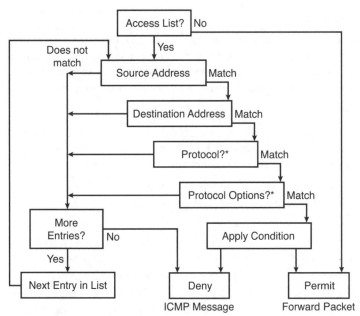

* If Present in Access List

Figure B-14 *Processing Flow of an Extended IP Access List Used for Filtering*

The extended access list checks source address, destination address, and protocol. Depending on the configured protocol, more protocol-dependent options might be tested. For example, a TCP port might be checked, which allows routers to filter at the application layer.

Extended IP Access List Configuration

Use the **access-list** *access-list-number* {**permit** | **deny**} *protocol* {*source source-wildcard* | **any**} {*destination destination-wildcard* | **any**} [*protocol-specific-options*] [**log**] global configuration command to create an entry in an extended-traffic filter list. Table B-9 describes this command.

Table B-9 *Extended IP* access-list *Command Description*

Parameter	Description
access-list-number	Identifies the list to which the entry belongs (a number from 100 to 199 or from 2000 to 2699).
permit | **deny**	Indicates whether this entry allows or blocks traffic.

Parameter	Description
protocol	**ip, tcp, udp, icmp, igmp, gre, eigrp, ospf, nos, ipinip, pim,** or a number from 0 to 255. To match any Internet protocol, use the keyword **ip.** As shown later in this section, some protocols allow more options that are supported by an alternative syntax for this command.
source and *destination*	Identifies the source and destination IP addresses.
source-wildcard and *destination-wildcard*	Identifies which bits in the address field must match. A 1 in any bit position indicates don't care bits, and a 0 in any bit position indicates that the bit must strictly match.
any	Use this keyword as an abbreviation for a source and source wildcard or destination and destination wildcard of 0.0.0.0 255.255.255.255.
log	(Optional) Causes informational logging messages about a packet that matches the entry to be sent to the console. Exercise caution when using this keyword, because it consumes CPU cycles. The message is generated for the first packet that matches, and then at 5-minute intervals, including the number of packets permitted or denied in the prior 5-minute interval.

The wildcard masks in an extended access list operate the same way as they do in standard access lists, but note that they are not optional in extended access lists. The keyword **any** in either the source or the destination position matches any address and is equivalent to configuring an address of 0.0.0.0 with a wildcard mask of 255.255.255.255. Example B-6 shows an example of an extended access list.

Example B-6   *Use of the Keyword* any

```
access-list 101 permit ip  0.0.0.0  255.255.255.255  0.0.0.0  255.255.255.255
! (alternative configuration)
access-list 101 permit ip any any
```

The keyword **host** can be used in either the source or the destination position. It causes the address that immediately follows it to be treated as if it were specified with a mask of 0.0.0.0. Example B-7 shows an example.

Example B-7   *Use of the Keyword* host

```
access-list 101 permit ip  0.0.0.0  255.255.255.255  172.16.5.17  0.0.0.0
! (alternative configuration)
access-list 101 permit ip any host 172.16.5.17
```

Use the **access-list** *access-list-number* {**permit** | **deny**} **icmp** {*source source-wildcard* | **any**} {*destination destination-wildcard* | *any*} [*icmp-type* [*icmp-code*] | *icmp-message*] global configuration command to filter ICMP traffic. The protocol keyword **icmp** indicates that an alternative syntax is being used for this command and that protocol-specific options are available, as described in Table B-10.

Table B-10 *Extended IP **access-list icmp** Command Description*

Parameter	Description
access-list-number	Identifies the list to which the entry belongs (a number from 100 to 199 or from 2000 to 2699).
permit	**deny**	Indicates whether this entry allows or blocks traffic.
source and *destination*	Identifies the source and destination IP addresses.
source-wildcard and *destination-wildcard*	Identifies which bits in the address field must match. A 1 in any bit position indicates don't care bits, and a 0 in any bit position indicates that the bit must strictly match.
any	Use this keyword as an abbreviation for a source and source wildcard or destination and destination wildcard of 0.0.0.0 255.255.255.255.
icmp-type	(Optional) Packets can be filtered by ICMP message type. The type is a number from 0 to 255.
icmp-code	(Optional) Packets that have been filtered by ICMP message type can also be filtered by ICMP message code. The code is a number from 0 to 255.
icmp-message	(Optional) Packets can be filtered by a symbolic name representing an ICMP message type or a combination of ICMP message type and ICMP message code. These names are listed in Table B-11.

Cisco IOS Release 10.3 and later versions provide symbolic names that make configuring and reading complex access lists easier. With symbolic names, it is no longer critical to understand the meaning of the ICMP message type and code. (For example, message 8 and message 0 can be used to filter the **ping** command.) Instead, the configuration can use symbolic names, as shown in Table B-11. For example, the **echo** and **echo-reply** symbolic names can be used to filter the **ping** command. (You can use the Cisco IOS context-sensitive help feature by entering **?** when entering the **access-list** command to verify the available names and proper command syntax.)

Table B-11   *ICMP Message and Type Names*

administratively-prohibited	information-reply	precedence-unreachable
alternate-address	information-request	protocol-unreachable
conversion-error	mask-reply	reassembly-timeout
dod-host-prohibited	mask-request	redirect
dod-net-prohibited	mobile-redirect	router-advertisement
echo	net-redirect	router-solicitation
echo-reply	net-tos-redirect	source-quench
general-parameter-problem	net-tos-unreachable	source-route-failed
host-isolated	net-unreachable	time-exceeded
host-precedence-unreachable	network-unknown	timestamp-reply
host-redirect	no-room-for-option	timestamp-request
host-tos-redirect	option-missing	traceroute
host-tos-unreachable	packet-too-big	ttl-exceeded
host-unknown	parameter-problem	unreachable
host-unreachable	port-unreachable	

Use the **access-list** *access-list-number* {**permit** | **deny**} **tcp** {*source source-wildcard* | **any**} [*operator source-port* | *source-port*] {*destination destination-wildcard* | **any**} [*operator destination-port* | *destination-port*] [**established**] global configuration command to filter TCP traffic. The protocol keyword **tcp** indicates that an alternative syntax is being used for this command and that protocol-specific options are available, as described in Table B-12.

Table B-12   *Extended IP* **access-list tcp** *Command Description*

Parameter	Description
access-list-number	Identifies the list to which the entry belongs (a number from 100 to 199 or from 2000 to 2699).
permit	**deny**	Indicates whether this entry allows or blocks traffic.
source and *destination*	Identifies the source and destination IP addresses.
source-wildcard and *destination-wildcard*	Identifies which bits in the address field must match. A 1 in any bit position indicates don't care bits, and a 0 in any bit position indicates that the bit must strictly match.
any	Use this keyword as an abbreviation for a source and source wildcard or destination and destination wildcard of 0.0.0.0 255.255.255.255.
operator	(Optional) A qualifying condition. Can be **lt**, **gt**, **eq**, or **neq**.

Parameter	Description
source-port and *destination-port*	(Optional) A decimal number from 0 to 65535 or a name that represents a TCP port number.
established	(Optional) A match occurs if the TCP segment has the ACK or RST bits set. Use this if you want a Telnet or other activity to be established in one direction only.

established Keyword in Extended Access Lists

When a TCP session is started between two devices, the first segment that is sent has the synchronize (SYN) code bit set but does not have the acknowledge (ACK) code bit set in the segment header, because it is not acknowledging any other segments. All subsequent segments sent do have the ACK code bit set, because they are acknowledging previous segments sent by the other device. This is how a router can distinguish between a segment from a device that is attempting to *start* a TCP session and a segment of an ongoing *established* session. The RST code bit is set when an established session is being terminated.

When you configure the **established** keyword in a TCP extended access list, it indicates that that access list statement should match only TCP segments in which the ACK or RST code bit is set. In other words, only segments that are part of an established session are matched. Segments that are attempting to start a session do not match the access list statement.

Table B-13 lists some of the TCP port names that can be used instead of port numbers. You can find the port numbers corresponding to these protocols by entering a **?** in place of a port number or by looking at the port numbers on http://www.iana.org/assignments/port-numbers.

Table B-13   *TCP Port Names*

bgp	echo	irc	pop3	telnet
chargen	finger	klogin	smtp	time
daytime	ftp	kshell	sunrpc	uucp
discard	ftp-data	lpd	syslog	whois
domain	gopher	nntp	tacacs-ds	www
drip	hostname	pop2	talk	

You can find other port numbers at http://www.iana.org/assignments/port-numbers. A partial list of the assigned TCP port numbers is shown in Table B-14.

Table B-14   *Some Reserved TCP Port Numbers*

Port Number (Decimal)	Keyword	Description
7	ECHO	Echo
9	DISCARD	Discard
13	DAYTIME	Daytime
19	CHARGEN	Character generator
20	FTP-DATA	File Transfer Protocol (data)
21	FTP-CONTROL	File Transfer Protocol
23	TELNET	Terminal connection
25	SMTP	Simple Mail Transfer Protocol
37	TIME	Time of day
43	WHOIS	Who is
53	DOMAIN	Domain name server
79	FINGER	Finger
80	WWW	World Wide Web HTTP
101	HOSTNAME	NIC hostname server

Use the **access-list** *access-list-number* {**permit** | **deny**} **udp** {*source source-wildcard* | **any**} [*operator source-port* | *source-port*] {*destination destination-wildcard* | **any**} [*operator destination-port* | *destination-port*] global configuration command to filter User Datagram Protocol (UDP) traffic. The protocol keyword **udp** indicates that an alternative syntax is being used for this command and that protocol-specific options are available, as described in Table B-15.

Table B-15   *Extended IP* access-list *udp Command Description*

Parameter	Description
access-list-number	Identifies the list to which the entry belongs (a number from 100 to 199 or from 2000 to 2699).
permit	**deny**	Indicates whether this entry allows or blocks traffic.
source and *destination*	Identifies the source and destination IP addresses.
source-wildcard and *destination-wildcard*	Identifies which bits in the address field must match. A 1 in any bit position indicates don't care bits, and a 0 in any bit position indicates that the bit must strictly match.

Parameter	Description
any	Use this keyword as an abbreviation for a source and source wildcard or destination and destination wildcard of 0.0.0.0 255.255.255.255.
operator	(Optional) A qualifying condition. Can be **lt**, **gt**, **eq**, or **neq**.
source-port and *destination-port*	(Optional) A decimal number from 0 to 65535 or a name that represents a UDP port number.

Table B-16 lists some of the UDP port names that can be used instead of port numbers. You can find port numbers corresponding to these protocols by entering a ? in place of a port number or by looking at http://www.iana.org/assignments/port-numbers.

Table B-16   *UDP Port Names*

biff	domain	netbios-ns	snmptrap	tftp
bootpc	echo	non500-isakmp	sunrpc	time
bootps	mobile-ip	ntp	syslog	who
discard	nameserver	rip	tacacs-ds	xdmcp
dnsix	netbios-dgm	snmp	talk	

You can find other port numbers at http://www.iana.org/assignments/port-numbers. Table B-17 shows a partial list of the assigned UDP port numbers.

Table B-17   *Some Reserved UDP Port Numbers*

Port Number (Decimal)	Keyword	Description
7	ECHO	Echo
9	DISCARD	Discard
37	TIME	Time of day
42	NAMESERVER	Host name server
43	WHOIS	Who is
53	DNS	Domain name server
67	BOOTPS	Bootstrap protocol server
68	BOOTPC	Bootstrap protocol client
69	TFTP	Trivial File Transfer Protocol
123	NTP	Network Time Protocol
137	NetBios-ns	NetBIOS name service

Port Number (Decimal)	Keyword	Description
138	NetBios-dgm	NetBIOS datagram service
161	SNMP	SNMP
162	SNMPTrap	SNMP traps
520	RIP	RIP

Extended Access List Examples

In Figure B-15, Router A's interface Ethernet 1 is part of a Class B subnet with the address 172.22.3.0, Router A's interface Serial 0 is connected to the Internet, and the e-mail server's address is 172.22.1.2. The access list configuration applied to Router A is shown in Example B-8.

Example B-8   *Configuration on Router A in Figure B-15*

```
access-list 104 permit tcp any 172.22.0.0 0.0.255.255 established
access-list 104 permit tcp any host 172.22.1.2 eq smtp
access-list 104 permit udp any any eq dns
access-list 104 permit icmp any any echo
access-list 104 permit icmp any any echo-reply
!
interface serial 0
 ip access-group 104 in
```

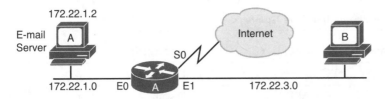

Figure B-15   *Network Used for the Extended IP Access List Example*

In Example B-8, access list 104 is applied inbound on Router A's Serial 0 interface. The keyword **established** is used only for the TCP protocol to indicate an established connection. A match occurs if the TCP segment has the ACK or RST bits set, which indicate that the packet belongs to an existing connection. If the session is not already established (the ACK bit is not set and the SYN bit is set), this means that someone on the Internet is attempting to initialize a session, in which case the packet is denied. This configuration also permits Simple Mail Transfer Protocol (SMTP) traffic from any address to the e-mail server. UDP domain name server packets and ICMP echo and echo-reply packets are also permitted from any address to any other address.

Another example is shown in Figure B-16. Example B-9 shows the access list configuration applied to Router A.

Example B-9   *Configuration on Router A in Figure B-16*

```
access-list 118 permit tcp any 172.22.0.0  0.0.255.255 eq www established
access-list 118 permit tcp any host 172.22.1.2 eq smtp
access-list 118 permit udp any any eq dns
access-list 118 permit udp 172.22.3.0  0.0.0.255 172.22.1.0 0.0.0.255 eq snmp
access-list 118 deny icmp any 172.22.0.0  0.0.255.255 echo
access-list 118 permit icmp any any echo-reply
!
interface ethernet 0
 ip access-group 118 out
```

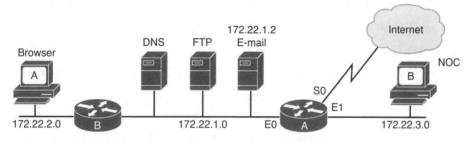

Figure B-16   *Extended IP Access List Example with Many Servers*

In Example B-9, access list 118 is applied outbound on Router A's Ethernet 0 interface. With the configuration shown in Example B-9, *replies* to queries from the Client A browser (or any other host on the corporate network) to the Internet are allowed back into the corporate network (because they are established sessions). Browser queries *from* external sources are not explicitly allowed and are discarded by the implicit **deny any** at the end of the access list.

The access list in Example B-9 also allows e-mail (SMTP) to be delivered exclusively to the mail server. The name server is permitted to resolve Domain Name Service (DNS) requests. The 172.22.1.0 subnet is controlled by the network management group located at the NOC server (Client B), so network-management queries (Simple Network Management Protocol [SNMP]) will be allowed to reach these devices in the server farm. Attempts to ping the corporate network from the outside or from subnet 172.22.3.0 will fail because the access list blocks the echo requests. However, replies to echo requests generated from within the corporate network are allowed to reenter the network.

Location of Extended Access Lists

Because extended access lists can filter on more than a source address, location is no longer the constraint it was when considering the location of a standard access list. Policy decisions and goals are frequently the driving forces behind extended access list placement.

If your goal is to minimize traffic congestion and maximize performance, you might want to push the access lists close to the source to minimize cross-network traffic and administratively prohibited ICMP messages. If your goal is to maintain tight control over access lists as part of your network security strategy, you might want them to be more centrally located. Notice how changing network goals affects access list configuration.

Here are some things to consider when placing extended access lists:

- Minimize distance traveled by traffic that will be denied (and ICMP unreachable messages).

- Keep denied traffic off the backbone.

- Select the router that will have the CPU overhead from processing the access lists.

- Consider the number of interfaces affected.

- Consider access list management and security.

- Consider network growth impacts on access list maintenance.

Time-Based Access Lists

Time-based access lists were introduced in Cisco IOS Software Release 12.0.1.T, with the **time-range** *time-range-name* option for extended access lists.

The time range uses the router's system clock; it is advisable to use the Network Time Protocol (NTP) on all routers.

To define the time range, use the **time-range** *time-range-name* command; this command enters time-range configuration mode for the specified time range name. To specify a recurring time range, use the **periodic** *days-of-the-week hh:mm* **to** [*days-of-the-week*] *hh:mm* time-range configuration command. Table B-18 describes this command.

Table B-18   periodic *Command Description*

Parameter	Description
days-of-the-week	The first occurrence of this argument is the starting day, and the second occurrence is the ending day that the time range is in effect. This argument can be any single day (**Monday, Tuesday, Wednesday, Thursday, Friday, Saturday,** or **Sunday**), or the values: **daily** (Monday through Sunday), **weekdays** (Monday through Friday), or **weekend** (Saturday and Sunday).
hh:mm	The first occurrence of this argument (expressed in a 24-hour clock) is the starting hours and minutes, and the second occurrence is the ending hours and minutes, that the time range is in effect.

To specify an absolute time range, use the **absolute** [**start** *time date*] [**end** *time date*] *time-range configuration* command. Table B-19 describes this command.

Table B-19   absolute *Command Description*

Parameter	Description
start *time date*	(Optional) Absolute time and date that the time range is in effect. The time is expressed in 24-hour notation, in the form of *hours:minutes*, and the date is expressed in the format *day month year*.
end *time date*	(Optional) Absolute time and date that the time range is no longer in effect. The time and date are in the same format as the start time and date. The end time and date must be after the start time and date.

Restricting Virtual Terminal Access

This section discusses how you can use standard access lists to limit virtual terminal access. Standard and extended access lists applied to interfaces block packets from going *through* the router. They are not designed to block packets that originate within the router. For example, an outbound Telnet extended access list does not prevent router-initiated Telnet sessions by default.

For security purposes, users can be denied virtual terminal (vty) access to the router, or they can be permitted vty access to the router but denied access to destinations from that router. Restricting vty access is less of a traffic-control mechanism than one technique for increasing network security.

Vty access is accomplished using the Telnet or Secure Shell (SSH) protocol. There is only one type of vty access list.

How to Control vty Access

Just as a router has physical ports or interfaces such as Ethernet 0 and Ethernet 1, it also has virtual ports. These virtual ports are called virtual terminal lines. By default, there are five such virtual terminal lines on a router, numbered vty 0 to 4, as shown in Figure B-17. The number of virtual terminal lines can be increased.

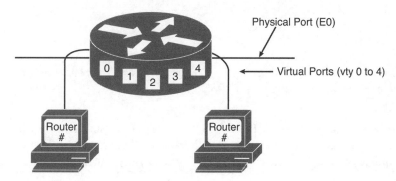

Figure B-17   *A Router Has Five Virtual Terminal Lines (Virtual Ports) by Default*

You should set identical restrictions on all virtual terminal lines, because you cannot control on which virtual terminal line a user will connect.

Virtual Terminal Line Access Configuration

Use the **line vty** {*vty-number* | *vty-range*} global configuration command to place the router in line configuration mode, as described in Table B-20.

Table B-20   line vty *Command Description*

Parameter	Description
vty-number	Indicates the number of the vty line to be configured
vty-range	Indicates the range of vty lines to which the configuration applies

Use the **access-class** *access-list-number* {**in** | **out**} line configuration command to link an existing access list to a terminal line or range of lines, as described in Table B-21.

Table B-21   access-class *Command Description*

Parameter	Description
access-list-number	Indicates the number of the standard access list to be linked to a terminal line. This is a decimal number from 1 to 99 or from 1300 to 1999.
in	Prevents the router from receiving incoming connections from the addresses defined in the access list.
out	Prevents someone from initiating a Telnet to the addresses defined in the access list.

Note   When you use the **out** keyword in the **access-class** command, the addresses in the specified standard access list are actually treated as *destination* addresses, rather than as source addresses.

Note   You can also refer to an extended access-list in the **access-class** command, but the destination address must be **any**, so it is not useful to do this.

In Example B-10, any device on network 192.168.55.0 is permitted to establish a virtual terminal session (for example, a Telnet session) with the router. Of course, the user must know the appropriate passwords for entering user mode and privileged mode.

Example B-10   *Configuration to Restrict Telnet Access to a Router*

```
access-list 12 permit 192.168.55.0 0.0.0.255
!
line vty 0 4
 access-class 12 in
```

Notice that in this example, identical restrictions have been set on all virtual terminal lines (0 to 4), because you cannot control on which virtual terminal line a user will connect. Note that the implicit **deny any** still applies to this alternative application of access lists.

Verifying Access List Configuration

Use the **show access-lists** [*access-list-number | name*] privileged EXEC command to display access lists from all protocols, as described in Table B-22. If no parameters are specified, all access lists are displayed.

Table B-22   show access-lists *Command Description*

Parameter	Description
access-list-number	(Optional) Number of the access list to display
name	(Optional) Name of the access list to display

The system counts how many packets match each line of an access list. The counters are displayed by the **show access-lists** command.

Example B-11 illustrates sample output from the **show access-lists** command. In this example, the first line of the access list has been matched three times, and the last line has been matched 629 times. The second line has not been matched.

Example B-11   *Output of the* show access-lists *Command*

```
p1r1# show access-lists
Extended IP access list 100
    deny tcp host 10.1.1.2 host 10.1.1.1 eq telnet (3 matches)
    deny tcp host 10.1.2.2 host 10.1.2.1 eq telnet
    permit ip any any (629 matches)
```

Use the **show ip access-list** [*access-list-number | name*] EXEC command to display IP access lists, as described in Table B-23. If no parameters are specified, all IP access lists are displayed.

Table B-23   show ip access-list *Command Description*

Parameter	Description
access-list-number	(Optional) Number of the IP access list to display
name	(Optional) Name of the IP access list to display

Use the **clear access-list counters** [*access-list-number* | *name*] EXEC command to clear the counters for the number of matches in an extended access list, as described in Table B-24. If no parameters are specified, the counters are cleared for all access lists.

Table B-24   clear access-list counters *Command Description*

Parameter	Description
access-list-number	(Optional) Number of the access list for which to clear the counters
name	(Optional) Name of the access list for which to clear the counters

Use the **show line** [*line-number*] EXEC command to display information about terminal lines. The *line-number* is optional and indicates the absolute line number of the line for which you want to list parameters. If a line number is not specified, all lines are displayed.

IPv4 Address Planning

A well-designed large-scale internetwork with an effective IP addressing plan has many benefits, as described in this section.

Benefits of an Optimized IP Addressing Plan

An optimized IP addressing plan uses hierarchical addressing.

Perhaps the best-known addressing hierarchy is the telephone network. The telephone network uses a hierarchical numbering scheme that includes country codes, area codes, and local exchange numbers. For example, if you are in San Jose, California, and you call someone else in San Jose, you dial the San Jose prefix, 528, and the person's four-digit line number. Upon seeing the number 528, the central office recognizes that the destination telephone is within its area, so it looks up the four-digit number and transfers the call.

Note   In many places in North America now, the area code must also be dialed for local calls. This is because of changes in the use of specific digits for area codes and local exchange numbers. The telephone network is suffering from *address exhaustion*, just like the IPv4 network. Changes in how telephone numbers are used is one solution being implemented to solve this problem.

In another example (see Figure B-18), to call Aunt Judy in Alexandria, Virginia, from San Jose, you dial 1, and then the area code 703, and then the Alexandria prefix 555, and then Aunt Judy's local line number, 1212. The central office first sees the number 1, indicating a remote call, and then looks up the number 703. The central office immediately routes the call to a central office in Alexandria. The San Jose central office does not know exactly where 555-1212 is in Alexandria, nor does it have to. It needs to know only the area codes, which summarize the local telephone numbers within an area.

Note   As you might have noticed, the telephone number used in this example is the number for international directory assistance. It is used for illustration purposes to ensure that Aunt Judy's personal number is not published.

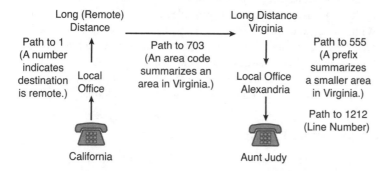

Figure B-18   *The Telephone Network Uses an Addressing Hierarchy*

If there were no hierarchical structure, every central office would need to have every telephone number worldwide in its locator table. Instead, the central offices have summary numbers, such as area codes and country codes. A summary number (address) represents a group of numbers. For example, an area code such as 408 is a summary number for the San Jose area. In other words, if you dial 1-408 from anywhere in the United States or Canada, followed by a seven-digit telephone number, the central office routes the call to a San Jose central office. Similarly, a routed network can employ a hierarchical addressing scheme to take advantage of those same benefits.

One of the benefits of hierarchical addressing is a reduced number of routing table entries. Whether it is with your Internet routers or your internal routers, you should try to keep your routing tables as small as possible by using route summarization.

Summarization (also called *aggregation*, *supernetting*, or *information hiding*) is not a new concept. When a router announces a route to a given network, the route is a summarization of all the host and device individual addresses that reside on that network. Route summarization is a way of having a single IP address represent a collection of IP addresses. This is most easily accomplished when you employ a hierarchical addressing plan. By summarizing routes, you can keep your routing table entries (on the routers that receive the summarized routes) manageable, which offers the following benefits:

- More efficient routing.

- A reduced number of CPU cycles when recalculating a routing table or sorting through the routing table entries to find a match.

- Reduced router memory requirements.

- Reduced bandwidth required to send the fewer, smaller routing updates.

- Faster convergence after a change in the network.

- Easier troubleshooting.

- Increased network stability. Because summarization limits the propagation of detailed routes, it also reduces the impact to the network when these detailed routes fail.

Another benefit of hierarchical addressing is the efficient allocation of addresses. Hierarchical addressing lets you take advantage of all possible addresses because you group them contiguously. With random address assignment, you might end up wasting groups of addresses because of addressing conflicts. For example, classful routing protocols (discussed in the later section "Implementing VLSM in a Scalable Network") automatically create summary routes at a network boundary. Therefore, these protocols do not support discontiguous addressing, so some addresses would be unusable if not assigned contiguously.

Scalable Network Addressing Example

The network illustrated in Figure B-19 shows an example of scalable addressing. In this example, a U.S. national drugstore chain plans to have a retail outlet in every city in the country with a population greater than 10,000. Each of the 50 states has up to 100 stores, with two Ethernet LANs in each store, as follows:

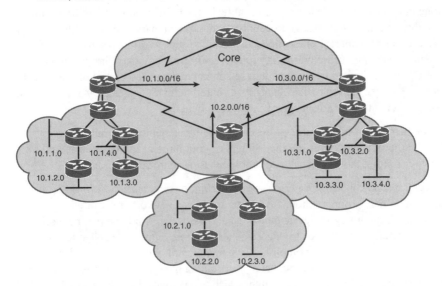

Figure B-19   *Scalable Addressing Allows Summarization*

- One LAN is used to track customer prescriptions, pharmacy inventory, and reorder stock.

- The second LAN is used to stock the rest of the store and connect the cash registers to a corporate-wide, instantaneous point-of-sale evaluation tool.

The total number of Ethernet LAN networks is 50 states * 100 stores per state * 2 LANs per store = 10,000. (An equal number of serial links interconnects these stores.)

Using a scalable design and creating 51 divisions (one for each state and one for the backbone interconnecting the divisions), the corporation can assign each division a block of IP addresses 10.x.0.0 /16. Each LAN is assigned a /24 subnet of network 10.0.0.0, and each division has 200 such subnets (two for each of the 100 stores). The network will have 10,000 subnets; without summarization, each of the 5000 routers will have all these networks in their routing tables. If each division router summarizes its block of networks 10.x.0.0 /16 at the entry point to the core network, any router in a division has only the 200 /24 subnets within that division, plus the 49 10.x.0.0 /16 summarizations that represent the other divisions, in its routing table. This results in a total of 249 networks in each IP routing table.

Nonscalable Network Addressing

In contrast to the previous example, if a hierarchical addressing plan is not used, summarization is not possible, as is the case in Figure B-20. Problems can occur in this network related to the frequency and size of routing table updates and how topology changes are processed in summarized and unsummarized networks. These problems are described next.

Update Size

Routing protocols such as the Routing Information Protocol (RIP), which sends a periodic update every 30 seconds, use valuable bandwidth to maintain a table without summarization. A single RIP update packet is limited to carrying 25 routes. Therefore, 10,000 routes means that RIP on every router must create and send 400 packets every 30 seconds. With summarized routes, the 249 routes means that only 10 packets need to be sent every 30 seconds.

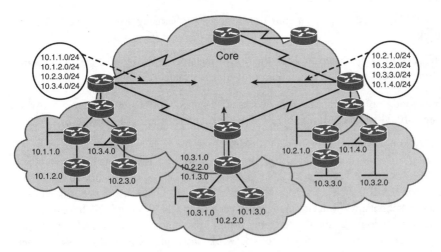

Figure B-20 *Nonscalable Addressing Results in Large Routing Tables*

Unsummarized Internetwork Topology Changes

A routing table with 10,000 entries constantly changes. To illustrate this constant change, consider the sample network with a router at each of 5000 different sites. A power outage occurs at site A, a backhoe digs a trench at site B, a newly hired system administrator begins work at site C, a Cisco IOS Software upgrade is in progress at site D, and a newly added router is being installed at site E.

Every time a route changes, all the routing tables must be updated. For example, when using a routing protocol such as Open Shortest Path First (OSPF) Protocol, an upgrade or topology change on the internetwork causes a shortest path first (SPF) calculation. The SPF calculations are large because each router needs to calculate all known pathways to each of the 10,000 networks. Each change a router receives requires time and CPU resources to process.

Summarized Network Topology Changes

In contrast to an unsummarized network, a summarized network responds efficiently to network changes. For example, in the sample drugstore network with 200 routes for each division, the routers within the division see all the subnets for that division. When a change occurs on one of the 200 routes in the division, all other routers in the division recalculate to reflect the topology change of those affected networks. However, the core router of that division passes a summarized /16 route and suppresses the /24 networks from advertisement to the core routers of other divisions. The summarized route is announced as long as any portion of the summarized block can be reached from that core router. The more specific routes are suppressed so that changes from this division are not propagated to other divisions.

In this scenario, each router has only 200 /24 networks, compared to the 10,000 /24 networks in an unsummarized environment. Obviously, the amount of CPU resources, memory, and bandwidth required for the 200 networks is less than the 10,000 networks. With summarization, each division hides more-specific information from the other divisions and passes only the summarized route that represents that overall division.

Hierarchical Addressing Using Variable-Length Subnet Masks

VLSM is a crucial component of an effective IP addressing plan for a scalable network. This section introduces VLSM, provides examples, and discusses methods of determining the best subnet mask for a given address requirement.

Subnet Mask

This section discusses the purpose of the subnet mask and its use within a network.

Use of the Subnet Mask

If a PC has an IP address of 192.168.1.67 with a mask of 255.255.255.240 (or a prefix length of /28), it uses this mask to determine the valid host addresses for devices on its local connection. These devices have the first 28 bits in their IP address in common (the range of these local devices is 192.168.1.65 through 192.168.1.78). If communication with any of these devices is necessary, the PC uses Address Resolution Protocol (ARP) to find the device's corresponding Media Access Control (MAC) address (assuming that it does not already have a destination MAC address for the IP address in its ARP table). If a PC needs to send information to an IP device that is not in the local range, the PC instead forwards the information to its default gateway. (The PC also uses ARP to discover the MAC address of the default gateway.)

A router behaves in a similar manner when it makes a routing decision. A packet arrives on the router and is passed to the routing table. The router compares the packet's destination IP address to the entries in the routing table. These entries have a prefix length associated with them.

The router uses the prefix length as the minimum number of destination address bits that must match to use the corresponding outbound interface that is associated with a network entry in the routing table.

Subnet Mask Example

Consider a scenario in which an IP packet with a destination address of 192.168.1.67 is sent to a router. Example B-12 shows the router's IP routing table.

Example B-12 *IP Routing Table for Subnet Mask Example*

```
192.168.1.0 is subnetted, 4 subnets
O 192.168.1.16/28 [110/1800] via 172.16.1.1, 00:05:17, Serial 0
C 192.168.1.32/28 is directly connected, Ethernet 0
O 192.168.1.64/28 [110/10] via 192.168.1.33, 00:05:17, Ethernet 0
O 192.168.1.80/28 [110/1800] via 172.16.2.1, 00:05:17, Serial 1
```

In this scenario, the router determines where to send a packet that is destined for 192.168.1.67 by looking at the routing table. The routing table has four entries for network 192.168.1.0. The router compares the destination address to each of the four entries for this network.

The destination address of 192.168.1.67 has the first three octets in common with all four entries in the routing table, but it is not clear by looking at the decimal representation which of those entries is the best match to route this packet. A router handles all packets in binary, not dotted-decimal, notation.

Following is the binary representation of the last octet for destination address 192.168.1.67 and the binary representation of the last octet for the four entries in the IP routing table. Because the prefix length is 28 and all four entries match at least the first 24 bits of 192.168.1, the router must find the routing table entry that matches the first 4 bits (bits 25 to 28) of the number 67. It is not important if the last 4 bits match (because they are host bits), so the target is 0100*xxxx*. The routing entry 64, which has a value of 0100 in the first 4 bits, is the only one that matches the requirement:

- **67:** 01000011
- **16:** 00010000
- **32:** 00100000
- **64:** 01000000
- **80:** 01010000

The router therefore uses the 192.168.1.64 entry in the routing table and forwards this packet out of its Ethernet 0 interface to the next router (192.168.1.33).

Implementing VLSM in a Scalable Network

A major network (also known as a classful network) is a Class A, B, or C network.

With classful routing, routing updates do not carry the subnet mask. Therefore, only one subnet mask can be used within a major network. This is known as fixed-length subnet masking (FLSM). An example of a classful routing protocol is RIP Version 1 (RIPv1).

With classless routing, routing updates do carry the subnet mask. Therefore, different masks may be used for different subnets within a major network. This is known as VLSM. Examples of classless routing protocols are RIP Version 2 (RIPv2), OSPF

Protocol, Intermediate System-to-Intermediate System (IS-IS) Protocol, and Enhanced Interior Gateway Routing Protocol (EIGRP).

VLSM allows more than one subnet mask within a major network and enables the subnetting of a previously subnetted network address.

The network shown in Figure B-21 is used to illustrate how VLSM works.

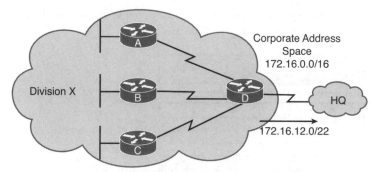

172.16.12.0/22 has been assigned to Division X.
Range of Addresses: 172.16.12.0 to 171.16.15.255

Figure B-21   *Network for the VLSM Example*

The following are some characteristics that permit VLSMs to conserve IP addresses:

- **Efficient use of IP addresses:** Without the use of VLSMs, companies are locked into implementing a single subnet mask within an entire Class A, B, or C network number.

  - For example, suppose a network architect decides to use the 172.16.0.0/16 address space to design a corporate network. The architect determines that 64 blocks of addresses with up to 1022 hosts in each are required. Therefore, 10 host bits ($2^{10} - 2 = 1022$) and 6 subnet bits ($2^6 = 64$) are required for each block. The mask is therefore 255.255.252.0. The prefix is /22.

  - The network architect assigns address block 172.16.12.0/22 to Division X, as shown in Figure B-21. The prefix mask of /22 indicates that all addresses within that range have the first 22 bits in common (when reading from left to right). The prefix mask provides Division X with a range of addresses from 172.16.12.0 through 172.16.15.255. The details of the range of addresses available to Division X are shown in the center block of Figure B-22. Within Division X, the networks are assigned addresses in this range, with varying subnet masks. Details of these address assignments are provided in the next section.

- **Greater capability to use route summarization:** VLSMs allow for more hierarchical levels within an addressing plan and thus allow better route summarization within routing tables. For example, in Figure B-21, address 172.16.12.0/22 summarizes all the subnets that are further subnets of 172.16.12.0/22.

■ **Reduced number of routing table entries:** In a hierarchical addressing plan, route summarization allows a single IP address to represent a collection of IP addresses. When VLSM is used in a hierarchical network, it allows summarized routes, which keeps routing table entries (on the routers that receive the summarized routes) manageable and provides the benefits described earlier in the "IPv4 Address Planning" section.

Because of the reduced router requirements, it also might be possible to use some less-powerful (and therefore less-expensive) routers in the network.

Dotted Decimal Notation	Binary Notation
172.16.11.0	10101100. 00010000.0000101 1.00000000
(Text Omitted for Continuation of Bit/Number Pattern)	
172.16.12.0	10101100. 00010000.0000110 0.00000000
172.16.12.1	10101100. 00010000.0000110 0.00000001
172.16.12.255	10101100. 00010000.0000110 0.11111111
172.16.13.0	10101100. 00010000.0000110 1.00000000
172.16.13.1	10101100. 00010000.0000110 1.00000001
172.16.13.255	10101100. 00010000.0000110 1.11111111
172.16.14.0	10101100. 00010000.0000111 0.00000000
172.16.14.1	10101100. 00010000.0000111 0.00000001
172.16.14.255	10101100. 00010000.0000111 0.11111111
172.16.15.0	10101100. 00010000.0000111 1.00000000
172.16.15.1	10101100. 00010000.0000111 1.00000001
172.16.15.255	10101100. 00010000.0000111 1.11111111
(Text Omitted for Continuation of Bit/Number Pattern)	
172.16.16.0	10101100. 00010000.000100 00.00000000

Figure B-22 *Center Block Shows Range of Addresses for VLSM for Division X in Figure B-21*

The address 172.16.12.0/22 represents all the addresses that have the same first 22 bits as 172.16.12.0. Figure B-22 displays the binary representation of networks 172.16.11.0 through 172.16.16.0. Notice that 172.16.12.0 through 172.12.15.255 all have the first 22 bits in common, whereas 172.16.11.0 and 172.16.16.0 do not have the same first 22 bits. Therefore, the address 172.16.12.0/22 represents the range of addresses 172.16.12.0 through 172.16.15.255.

VLSM Calculation Example

You can best understand the design and implementation of a scalable IP address plan if you study a detailed example of how a VLSM network is laid out.

Figure B-23 shows a detailed view of the same Division X shown in Figure B-21.

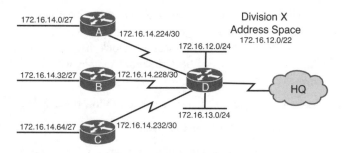

Figure B-23 *Detailed IP Addressing of Division X in Figure B-21*

In Division X, the following exist:

- One LAN on each of the two Ethernet ports of Router D, each with 200 users.

- Three remote sites, at Routers A, B, and C, each with a 24-port Cisco switch. The number of users at each remote site does not exceed 20.

- Three serial links to the remote sites. The serial links are point-to-point Frame Relay and require an address on each side.

VLSM allows you to further subnet the 172.16.12.0/22 address space, using variable masks, to accommodate the network requirements. For example, because point-to-point serial lines require only two host addresses, you can use a subnetted address that has only two host addresses and therefore does not waste scarce subnet numbers.

To start the VLSM process, determine the number of subnets necessary for the networks to which you need to assign IP addresses, and determine the number of hosts necessary per subnet. You can determine the number of hosts by checking corporate policy to see whether a limit is set per segment or virtual LAN (VLAN), checking the physical number of ports on a switch, and checking the current size of the network or networks at other sites that fulfill the same role.

Note   The decimal-to-binary conversion chart earlier in this appendix might be helpful when you are calculating VLSMs.

LAN Addresses

Because IP addresses are binary, they are used in blocks of powers of 2. A block of addresses contains 2, 4, 8, 16, 32, 64, 128, 256, 512, 1024, 2048, and so on addresses. Two addresses are lost each time you create a subnet: one for the network (wire) address and the other for the directed broadcast address.

The lowest address of the range, where the host bits are all 0s, is known as the network number or the wire address. The top of the address range, where the host bits are all 1s, is the directed broadcast address. The number of addresses in a block that can be assigned to devices is $2^h - 2$, where h is the number of host bits. For example, with 3 host bits, $2^3 - 2 = 8 - 2 = 6$ addresses can be assigned.

To determine the size of the block of addresses needed for a subnet, follow these steps:

Step 1.   Calculate the maximum number of hosts on that subnet.

Step 2.   Add 2 to that number for the broadcast and subnet numbers.

Step 3.   Round up to the next higher power of 2.

In this example, the LANs on Router D each have 200 users. Therefore, the number of addresses required is 200 + 2 = 202. Rounding up to the next power of 2 gives you 256. Thus, 8 ($2^8 = 256$) host bits are required for these LANs. Therefore, the prefix is /24 (32 bits – 8 bits for the host = 24 bits). The network administrator subnets the 172.16.12.0/22 into four /24 subnets on Router D.

172.16.12.0/24 is assigned to LAN 1, and 172.16.13.0/24 is assigned to LAN 2. This leaves two /24 subnets, 172.16.14.0/24 and 172.16.15.0/24, to use for the switches at the three remote sites and the three serial point-to-point links.

The number of addresses required for the LANs at each remote site is 20 + 2 = 22. Rounding this up to the next power of 2 gives you 32. So, 5 host bits ($2^5 = 32$) are required to address the remote users at each site. Therefore, the prefix to use is /27 (32 bits – 5 bits for the host = 27).

You cannot use the 172.16.12.0/24 or 172.16.13.0/24 networks because they are assigned to LANs 1 and 2 on Router D. The process to further subnet 172.16.14.0/24 into /27 subnets is shown in Figure B-24. The first three subnets calculated in Figure B-24 are used on the LANs in Figure B-23.

Serial Line Addresses

After you establish the addresses for the LANs at the remote sites, you must address the serial links between the remote sites and Router D. Because the serial links require two addresses, the number of addresses required is 2 + 2 = 4. (The two additional addresses are for the network number and the directed broadcast address.)

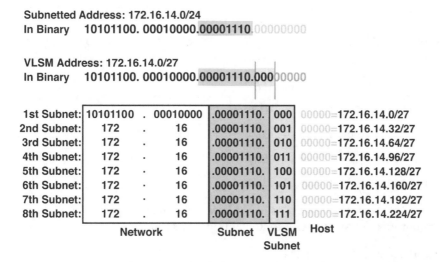

Figure B-24 *Calculating Subnet Addresses for the Remote Site LANs in Figure B-23*

> **Note** Because only two devices exist on point-to-point links, a specification has been developed (as documented in RFC 3021, *Using 31-Bit Prefixes on IPv4 Point-to-Point Links*) to allow the use of only 1 host bit on such links, resulting in a /31 mask. The two addresses created—with the host bit equal to 0 and with the host bit equal to 1—are interpreted as the addresses of the interfaces on either end of the link rather than as the subnet address and the directed broadcast address. Support for /31 masks requires the **ip classless** command, which is on by default on Cisco devices running IOS Release 12.2 and later. In the example in this section, however, we do not assume the use of this feature.

In this case, there is no need to round up, because 4 is a power of 2. Therefore, 2 host bits will allow for two hosts per subnet. A subnet mask of /30 (32 bits – 2 host bits = 30 bits) is used. This prefix allows for only two hosts—just enough hosts for a point-to-point connection between a pair of routers.

To calculate the subnet addresses for the WAN links, further subnet one of the unused /27 subnets. In this example, 172.16.14.224/27 is further subnetted with a prefix of /30. The three additional subnet bits result in $2^3 = 8$ subnets for the WAN links.

It is important to remember that only *unused* subnets should be further subnetted. In other words, if you use any addresses from a subnet, that subnet should not be further subnetted. In Figure B-23, three subnet numbers are used on the LANs. Another, as-yet-unused subnet, 172.16.14.224/27, is further subnetted for use on the WANs.

The WAN addresses derived from 172.16.14.224/27 are as follows. The shaded bits are the three additional subnet bits:

- 172.16.14.11100000 = 172.16.14.224/30
- 172.16.14.11100100 = 172.16.14.228/30
- 172.16.14.11101000 = 172.16.14.232/30
- 172.16.14.11101100 = 172.16.14.236/30
- 172.16.14.11110000 = 172.16.14.240/30
- 172.16.14.11110100 = 172.16.14.244/30
- 172.16.14.11111000 = 172.16.14.248/30
- 172.16.14.11111100 = 172.16.14.252/30

The first three of these subnets are used on the WANs shown in Figure B-23. The address information for the Router A to Router D link is as follows:

- **Network number: 172.16.14.224**
- **Router A serial interface: 172.16.14.225**
- **Router D serial interface: 172.16.14.226**
- **Broadcast address: 172.16.14.227**

The address information for the Router B to Router D link is as follows:

- **Network number: 172.16.14.228**
- **Router B serial interface: 172.16.14.229**
- **Router D serial interface: 172.16.14.230**
- **Broadcast address: 172.16.14.231**

The address information for the Router C to Router D link is as follows:

- **Network number: 172.16.14.232**
- **Router C serial interface: 172.16.14.233**
- **Router D serial interface: 172.16.14.234**
- **Broadcast address: 172.16.14.235**

Note that to provide the most flexibility for future growth, the 172.16.14.224/27 subnet was selected for the WANs instead of using the next available subnet, 172.16.14.96/27. For example, if the company purchases more switches, the next IP segment could be assigned the 172.16.14.96/27 subnet, and the new remote site would be connected to Router D with the 172.16.14.236/30 serial subnet.

The 172.16.15.0/24 block could have been used for these /30 subnets, but only three subnets are currently needed, so a lot of the address space would be unused. The 172.16.15.0/24 block is now available to use on another LAN in the future.

Summary of Addresses Used in the VLSM Example

Figure B-25 summarizes the addresses, in binary, used in this example.

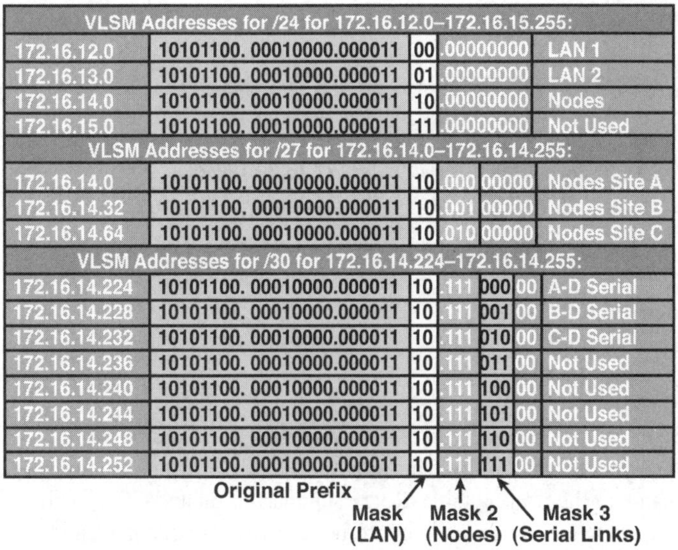

VLSM Addresses for /24 for 172.16.12.0–172.16.15.255:			
172.16.12.0	10101100. 00010000.000011	00 .00000000	LAN 1
172.16.13.0	10101100. 00010000.000011	01 .00000000	LAN 2
172.16.14.0	10101100. 00010000.000011	10 .00000000	Nodes
172.16.15.0	10101100. 00010000.000011	11 .00000000	Not Used
VLSM Addresses for /27 for 172.16.14.0–172.16.14.255:			
172.16.14.0	10101100. 00010000.000011	10 .000 00000	Nodes Site A
172.16.14.32	10101100. 00010000.000011	10 .001 00000	Nodes Site B
172.16.14.64	10101100. 00010000.000011	10 .010 00000	Nodes Site C
VLSM Addresses for /30 for 172.16.14.224–172.16.14.255:			
172.16.14.224	10101100. 00010000.000011	10 .111 000 00	A-D Serial
172.16.14.228	10101100. 00010000.000011	10 .111 001 00	B-D Serial
172.16.14.232	10101100. 00010000.000011	10 .111 010 00	C-D Serial
172.16.14.236	10101100. 00010000.000011	10 .111 011 00	Not Used
172.16.14.240	10101100. 00010000.000011	10 .111 100 00	Not Used
172.16.14.244	10101100. 00010000.000011	10 .111 101 00	Not Used
172.16.14.248	10101100. 00010000.000011	10 .111 110 00	Not Used
172.16.14.252	10101100. 00010000.000011	10 .111 111 00	Not Used

Original Prefix

Mask   Mask 2   Mask 3
(LAN) (Nodes) (Serial Links)

Figure B-25   *Binary Representation of the Addresses Used in Figure B-23*

Another VLSM Example

This section illustrates another example of calculating VLSM addresses. In this example, you have a subnet address 172.16.32.0/20, and you need to assign addresses to a network that has 50 hosts. With this subnet address, however, you have $2^{12} - 2 = 4,094$ host addresses, so you would be wasting more than 4,000 IP addresses. With VLSM, you can further subnet the address 172.16.32.0/20 to give you more subnet addresses and fewer hosts per subnet, which would work better in this network topology. For example, if you subnet 172.16.32.0/20 to 172.16.32.0/26, you gain 64 (2^6) subnets, each of which can support 62 ($2^6 - 2$) hosts.

To further subnet 172.16.32.0/20 to 172.16.32.0/26, do the following, as illustrated in Figure B-26:

Step 1.   Write 172.16.32.0 in binary.

Step 2.   Draw a vertical line between the 20th and 21st bits, as shown in Figure B-26. This is the transition point between the original subnet bits and the VLSM subnet bits.

Step 3.   Draw a vertical line between the 26th and 27th bits, as shown in Figure B-26. This is the transition point between the VLSM subnet bits and the host bits.

Step 4.   Calculate the 64 subnet addresses using the bits between the two vertical lines, from lowest to highest. Figure B-26 shows the first five subnets available.

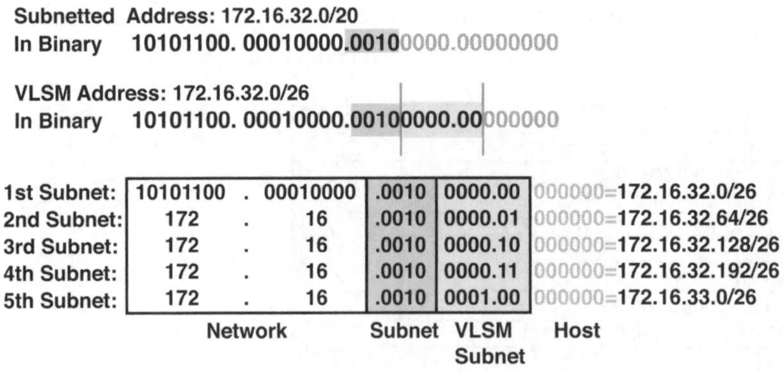

Subnetted Address: 172.16.32.0/20
In Binary   10101100. 00010000.**0010**0000.00000000

VLSM Address: 172.16.32.0/26
In Binary   10101100. 00010000.**0010**0000.00000000

1st Subnet:	10101100 . 00010000	.0010	0000.00	000000=172.16.32.0/26
2nd Subnet:	172 . 16	.0010	0000.01	000000=172.16.32.64/26
3rd Subnet:	172 . 16	.0010	0000.10	000000=172.16.32.128/26
4th Subnet:	172 . 16	.0010	0000.11	000000=172.16.32.192/26
5th Subnet:	172 . 16	.0010	0001.00	000000=172.16.33.0/26

Network   Subnet   VLSM   Host
Subnet

Figure B-26   *Further Subnetting a Subnetted Address*

Route Summarization

As the result of corporate expansion and mergers, the number of subnet and network addresses in routing tables is increasing rapidly. This growth taxes CPU resources, memory, and bandwidth used to maintain the routing table. Route summarization and CIDR techniques can manage this corporate growth much like Internet growth has been managed. With a thorough understanding of route summarization and CIDR, you can implement a scalable network. This section describes summarization. (CIDR is covered in the later section "Classless Interdomain Routing.") The relationship between summarization and VLSM is also examined. With VLSM, you break a block of addresses into smaller subnets. In route summarization, a group of subnets is rolled up into a summarized routing table entry.

Route Summarization Overview

In large internetworks, hundreds, or even thousands, of network addresses can exist. It is often problematic for routers to maintain this volume of routes in their routing tables. As mentioned in the "IPv4 Address Planning" section earlier, route summarization can reduce the number of routes that a router must maintain, because it is a method of representing a series of network numbers in a single summary address.

For example, in Figure B-27, Router D can either send four routing update entries or summarize the four addresses into a single network number. If Router D summarizes the information into a single network number entry, the following things happen:

- Bandwidth is saved on the link between Routers D and E.

- Router E needs to maintain only one route and therefore saves memory.

- Router E also saves CPU resources because it evaluates packets against fewer entries in its routing table.

A summary route is announced by the summarizing router as long as at least one specific route in its routing table matches the summary route.

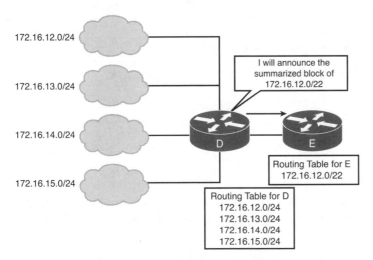

Figure B-27 *Routers Can Summarize to Reduce the Number of Routes*

Another advantage of using route summarization in a large, complex network is that it can isolate topology changes from other routers. For example, in Figure B-27, if a specific subnet (such as 172.16.13.0/24) is *flapping* (going up and down rapidly), the summary route (172.16.12.0/22) does not change. Therefore, Router E does not need to continually modify its routing table as a result of this flapping activity.

Note *Flapping* is a common term used to describe intermittent interface or link failures.

Route summarization is possible only when a proper addressing plan is in place. Route summarization is most effective within a subnetted environment when the network addresses are in contiguous blocks in powers of 2. For example, 4, 16, or 512 addresses can be represented by a single routing entry because summary masks are binary masks—just like subnet masks—so summarization must take place on binary boundaries (powers of 2). If the number of network addresses is not contiguous or not a power of 2, you can divide the addresses into groups and try to summarize the groups separately.

Routing protocols summarize or aggregate routes based on shared network numbers within the network. Classless routing protocols (such as RIPv2, OSPF, IS-IS, and EIGRP) support route summarization based on subnet addresses, including VLSM addressing. Classful routing protocols (such as RIPv1) automatically summarize routes on the classful network boundary and do not support summarization on any other bit boundaries. Classless routing protocols support summarization on any bit boundary.

> **Note**   Summarization is described in RFC 1518, *An Architecture for IP Address Allocation with CIDR.*

Route Summarization Calculation Example

Router D in Figure B-27 has the following networks in its routing table:

- 172.16.12.0/24
- 172.16.13.0/24
- 172.16.14.0/24
- 172.16.15.0/24

To determine the summary route on Router D, determine the number of highest-order (leftmost) bits that match in all the addresses. To calculate the summary route, follow these steps:

Step 1.   Convert the addresses to binary format and align them in a list.

Step 2.   Locate the bit where the common pattern of digits ends. (It might be helpful to draw a vertical line marking the last matching bit in the common pattern.)

Step 3.   Count the number of common bits. The summary route number is represented by the first IP address in the block, followed by a slash, followed by the number of common bits. As Figure B-28 illustrates, the first 22 bits of the IP addresses from 172.16.12.0 through 172.16.15.255 are the same. Therefore, the best summary route is 172.16.12.0/22.

> **Note**   In this network, the four subnets are contiguous, and the summary route covers all the addresses in the four subnets and only those addresses. Consider, for example, what would happen if 172.16.13.0/24 were not behind Router D, but instead were used elsewhere in the network, and only the other three subnets were behind Router D. The summary route 172.16.12.0/22 should no longer be used on Router D, because it includes 172.16.13.0/24 and might result in confusing routing tables. (However, this depends on how other routers in the network summarize. If the 172.16.13.0/24 route is propagated to all routers, they choose the route with the most bits that match the destination address and should route properly. This is further described in the section "Route Summarization Operation in Cisco Routers.")

> **Note**   In Figure B-28, the subnets before and after the subnets to be summarized are also shown. Observe that they do not have the same first 22 bits in common and therefore are not covered by the 172.16.12.0/22 summary route.

172.16.11.0/24 =	10101100	.	00010000	. 000010	11	. 00000000
172.16.12.0/24 =	**172**	.	**16**	**. 000011**	**00**	**. 00000000**
172.16.13.0/24 =	**172**	.	**16**	**. 000011**	**01**	**. 00000000**
172.16.14.0/24 =	**172**	.	**16**	**. 000011**	**10**	**. 00000000**
172.16.15.0/24 =	**172**	.	**16**	**. 000011**	**11**	**. 00000000**
172.16.15.255/24 =	**172**	.	**16**	**. 000011**	**11**	**. 11111111**
172.16.16.0/24 =	172	.	16	. 000100	00	. 00000000

Number of Common Bits = 22
Summary: 172.16.12.0/22

Number of Noncommon Bits = 10

Figure B-28 *Summarizing Within an Octet, for Router D in Figure B-27*

Summarizing Addresses in a VLSM-Designed Network

A VLSM design allows for maximum use of IP addresses and more-efficient routing update communication when using hierarchical IP addressing. In Figure B-29, route summarization occurs at the following two levels:

■ Router C summarizes two routing updates from networks 10.1.32.64/26 and 10.1.32.128/26 into a single update: 10.1.32.0/24.

■ Router A receives three different routing updates. However, Router A summarizes them into a single routing update, 10.1.0.0/16, before propagating it to the corporate network.

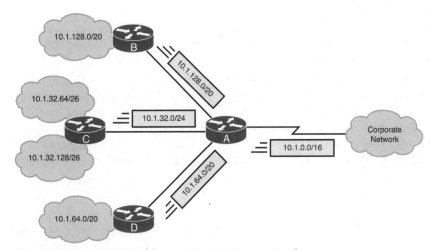

Figure B-29 *VLSM Addresses Can Be Summarized*

Route Summarization Implementation

Route summarization reduces memory use on routers and routing protocol network traffic, because it results in fewer entries in the routing table (on the routers that receive the summarized routes). For summarization to work correctly, the following requirements must be met:

- Multiple IP addresses must share the same highest-order bits.

- Routing protocols must base their routing decisions on a 32-bit IP address and a prefix length that can be up to 32 bits.

- Routing updates must carry the prefix length (the subnet mask) along with the 32-bit IP address.

Route Summarization Operation in Cisco Routers

This section discusses generalities of how Cisco routers handle route summarization. Details about how route summarization operates with a specific protocol are discussed in the corresponding protocol chapter of this book.

Cisco routers manage route summarization in two ways:

- **Sending route summaries:** Routing information advertised out an interface is automatically summarized at major (classful) network address boundaries by RIPv1 and RIPv2. EIGRP can be configured to do this automatic summarization (starting in Cisco IOS version 15 this automatic summarization is off by default). When using RIPv2, you can disable this automatic summarization. When enabled, this automatic summarization occurs for routes whose classful network address differs from the major network address of the interface to which the advertisement is being sent.

  For OSPF and IS-IS, you must configure summarization; it is not done by default. Route summarization is not always a solution.

  You would not want to use route summarization (especially classful route summarization) if you needed to advertise all networks across a boundary, such as when you have discontiguous networks.

- **Selecting routes from route summaries:** If more than one entry in the routing table matches a particular destination, the longest prefix match in the routing table is used. Several routes might match one destination, but the longest matching prefix is used. For example, if a routing table has the paths shown in Figure B-30, packets addressed to destination 172.16.5.99 are routed through the 172.16.5.0/24 path, because that address has the longest match with the destination address.

> **Note** When running classful protocols (for example, RIPv1), the **ip classless** command is required if you want the router to select a default route when it must route to an unknown subnet of a network for which it knows some subnets. As mentioned earlier, this command is on by default.

```
172.16.5.33    /32    host
172.16.5.32    /27    subnet
172.16.5.0     /24    network
172.16.0.0     /16    block of networks
0.0.0.0        /0     default
```

Figure B-30   *Routers Use the Longest Match When Selecting a Route*

Route Summarization in IP Routing Protocols

Table B-25 summarizes the route summarization support available in the various IP routing protocols.

Table B-25   *Routing Protocol Route Summarization Support*

Protocol	Automatic Summarization at Classful Network Boundary?	Capability to Turn Off Automatic Summarization?	Capability to Summarize at Other Than a Classful Network Boundary?
RIPv1	Yes	No	No
RIPv2	Yes	Yes	Yes
EIGRP[1]	No	—	Yes
OSPF	No	—	Yes
IS-IS	No	—	Yes

[1] EIGRP does automatic summarization by default in Cisco IOS versions before 15, but you can turn this off.

Classless Interdomain Routing

CIDR is a mechanism developed to help alleviate the problem of exhaustion of IP addresses and growth of routing tables. The idea behind CIDR is that blocks of multiple addresses (for example, blocks of Class C address) can be combined, or aggregated, to create a larger classless set of IP addresses, with more hosts allowed. Blocks of Class C network numbers are allocated to each network service provider. Organizations using the network service provider for Internet connectivity are allocated subsets of the service provider's address space as required. These multiple Class C addresses can then be summarized in routing tables, resulting in fewer route advertisements. (Note that the CIDR mechanism can be applied to blocks of Class A, B, and C addresses. It is not restricted to Class C.)

> **Note**   CIDR is described further in RFC 1518, *An Architecture for IP Address Allocation with CIDR*, and RFC 4632, *Classless Inter-domain Routing (CIDR): The Internet Address Assignment and Aggregation Plan*. RFC 2050, *Internet Registry IP Allocation Guidelines*, specifies guidelines for the allocation of IP addresses.

Note that the difference between CIDR and route summarization is that route summarization is generally done within, or up to, a classful boundary, whereas CIDR combines several classful networks.

CIDR Example

Figure B-31 shows an example of CIDR and route summarization. The Class C network addresses 192.168.8.0/24 through 192.168.15.0/24 are being used and are being advertised to Router X. When Router X advertises the available networks, it can summarize these into one route instead of separately advertising the eight Class C networks. By advertising 192.168.8.0/21, Router X indicates that it can get to all destination addresses whose first 21 bits are the same as the first 21 bits of the address 192.168.8.0.

The mechanism used to calculate the summary route to advertise is the same as shown in the earlier "Route Summarization" section. The Class C network addresses 192.168.8.0/24 through 192.168.15.0/24 are being used and are being advertised to Router X. To summarize these addresses, find the common bits, as shown here (in bold):

```
192.168.8.0       192.168.00001000.00000000
192.168.9.0       192.168.00001001.00000000
192.168.10.0      192.168.00001010.00000000
 . . .
192.168.14.0      192.168.00001110.00000000
192.168.15.0      192.168.00001111.00000000
```

The route 192.168.00001*xxx.xxxxxxxx* or 192.168.8.0/21 (also written as 192.168.8.0 255.255.248.0) summarizes these eight routes.

In this example, the first octet is 192, which identifies the networks as Class C networks. Combining these Class C networks into a block of addresses with a mask of less than /24 (the default Class C mask) indicates that CIDR, not route summarization, is being performed.

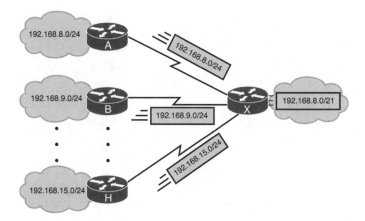

Figure B-31 *CIDR Allows a Router to Summarize Multiple Class C Addresses*

In this example, the eight separate 192.168.*x*.0 Class C networks that have the prefix /24 are combined into a single summarized block of 192.168.8.0/21. (At some other point in the network, this summarized block may be further combined into 192.168.0.0/16, and so on.)

Consider another example. A company that uses four Class B networks has the IP addresses 172.16.0.0/16 for Division A, 172.17.0.0/16 for Division B, 172.18.0.0/16 for Division C, and 172.19.0.0/16 for Division D. They can all be summarized as a single block: 172.16.0.0/14. This one entry represents the whole block of four Class B networks. This process is CIDR because the summarization goes beyond the Class B boundaries.

BGP Supplement

This appendix contains supplementary Border Gateway Protocol (BGP) information and covers the following topics:

- BGP Route Summarization
- Redistribution with IGPs
- Communities
- Route Reflectors
- Advertising a Default Route
- Not Advertising Private Autonomous System Numbers

This appendix provides you with some additional information about the Border Gateway Protocol (BGP).

BGP Route Summarization

This section reviews classless interdomain routing (CIDR) and describes how BGP supports CIDR and summarization of addresses. Both the **network** and **aggregate-address** commands are described.

CIDR and Aggregate Addresses

As discussed in Appendix B, "IPv4 Supplement," CIDR is a mechanism developed to help alleviate the problem of exhaustion of IP addresses and the growth of routing tables. The idea behind CIDR is that blocks of multiple addresses (for example, blocks of Class C address) can be combined, or aggregated, to create a larger classless set of IP addresses. These multiple addresses can then be summarized in routing tables, resulting in fewer route advertisements.

Earlier versions of BGP did not support CIDR. BGP Version 4 (BGP-4) does. BGP-4 support includes the following:

■ The BGP update message includes both the prefix and the prefix length. Previous versions included only the prefix. The length was assumed from the address class.

■ Addresses can be aggregated when advertised by a BGP router.

■ The autonomous system (AS)-Path attribute can include a combined unordered list of all autonomous systems that all the aggregated routes have passed through. This combined list should be considered to ensure that the route is loop-free.

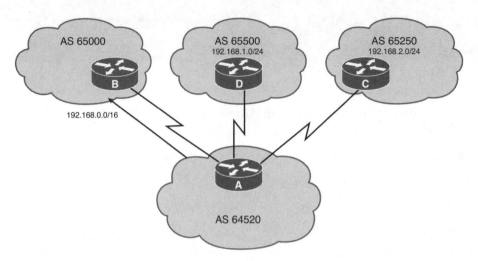

Figure C-1   *Using CIDR with BGP*

For example, in Figure C-1, Router C is advertising network 192.168.2.0/24, and Router D is advertising network 192.168.1.0/24. Router A could pass those advertisements to Router B. However, Router A could reduce the size of the routing tables by aggregating the two routes into one (for example, 192.168.0.0/16).

Note   In Figure C-1, the aggregate route that Router A is sending covers more than the two routes from Routers C and D. The example assumes that Router A also has jurisdiction over all the other routes covered by this aggregate route.

Two BGP attributes are related to aggregate addressing:

■ **Atomic aggregate:** A well-known discretionary attribute that informs the neighbor autonomous system that the originating router has aggregated the routes

■ **Aggregator:** An optional transitive attribute that specifies the BGP router ID and autonomous system number of the router that performed the route aggregation

By default, the aggregate route is advertised as coming from the autonomous system that did the aggregation and has the atomic aggregate attribute set to show that information might be missing. The autonomous system numbers from the nonaggregated routes are not listed.

You can configure the router to include the unordered list of all autonomous systems contained in all paths that are being summarized.

Note Indications are that aggregate addresses are not used in the Internet as much as they could be because autonomous systems that are multihomed (connected to more than one Internet service provider [ISP]) want to make sure that their routes are advertised without being aggregated into a summarized route.

In Figure C-1, by default the aggregated route 192.168.0.0/16 has an AS-Path attribute of (64520). If Router A were configured to include the combined unordered list, it would include the set {65250 65500} and (64520) in the AS-Path attribute. The AS-Path would be the unordered set {64520 65250 65500}.

Network Boundary Summarization

BGP was originally not intended to be used to advertise subnets. Its intended purpose was to advertise classful, or better, networks. *Better* in this case means that BGP can summarize blocks of individual classful networks into a few large blocks that represent the same address space as the individual network blocks (in other words, CIDR blocks). For example, 32 contiguous Class C networks can be advertised individually as 32 separate entries, with each having a network mask of /24. Or it might be possible to announce these same networks as a single entry with a /19 mask.

Consider how other protocols handle summarization. The Routing Information Protocol Version 1 (RIPv1) and Routing Information Protocol Version 2 (RIPv2) protocols summarize routes on the classful network boundary by default. In contrast, Open Shortest Path First (OSPF), Enhanced Interior Gateway Routing Protocol (EIGRP), and Intermediate System-to-Intermediate System (IS-IS) do not summarize by default, but you can configure summarization manually. (EIGRP can be configured to do auto summarization on the classful boundary.)

You can turn off autosummarization for RIPv2 (and EIGRP if it is on). For example, if you are assigned a portion of a Class A, B, or C address, summarization needs to be turned off. Otherwise, you risk claiming ownership of the whole Class A, B, or C address.

Note The Internet Assigned Numbers Authority (IANA) is reclaiming Class A addresses from organizations that no longer need them. IANA breaks these Class A addresses into blocks of /19 address space, which are assigned to various ISPs to be given out in place of Class C addresses. This process has helped make the Internet a classless environment.

BGP works differently than the other protocols. As discussed in Chapter 7, "BGP Implementation," the **network** *network-number* [**mask** *network-mask*] router configuration command for BGP permits BGP to advertise a network if it is present in the IP routing table. This command allows classless prefixes. The router can advertise individual subnets, networks, or supernets. The default mask is the classful mask and results in only the classful network number being announced. Note that at least one subnet of the specified major network must be present in the IP routing table for BGP to start announcing the classful network. However, if you specify the **mask** *network-mask*, an exact match to the network (both address and mask) must exist in the routing table for the network to be advertised.

The BGP **auto-summary** command determines how BGP handles redistributed routes. The **no auto-summary** router configuration command turns off BGP autosummarization. When summarization is enabled (with **auto-summary**), all redistributed subnets are summarized to their classful boundaries in the BGP table. When summarization is disabled (with **no auto-summary**), all redistributed subnets are present in their original form in the BGP table. For example, if an ISP assigns a network of 209.165.200.224/27 to an autonomous system, and that autonomous system then uses the **redistribute connected** command to introduce this network into BGP, BGP announces that the autonomous system owns 209.165.200.0/24 if the **auto-summary** command is on. To the Internet, it appears as if this autonomous system owns the entire Class C network 209.165.200.0/24, which is not true. Other organizations that own a portion of the 209.165.200.0/24 address space might have connectivity problems because of this autonomous system claiming ownership for the whole block of addresses. This outcome is undesirable if the autonomous system does not own the entire address space. Using the **network 209.165.200.224 mask 255.255.255.224** command rather than the **redistributed connected** command ensures that this assigned network is announced correctly.

> **Caution**   In Cisco IOS Release 12.2(8)T, the default behavior of the **auto-summary** command was changed to disabled. In other words
>
> ■ Before 12.2(8)T, the default is **auto-summary**.
>
> ■ Starting in 12.2(8)T, the default is **no auto-summary**.

BGP Route Summarization Using the network Command

To advertise a simple classful network number, use the **network** *network-number* router configuration command without the **mask** option. To advertise an aggregate of prefixes that originate in this autonomous system, use the **network** *network-number* [**mask** *network-mask*] router configuration command with the **mask** option (but remember that the prefix must exactly match [both address and mask] an entry in the IP routing table for the network to be advertised).

When BGP has a **network** command for a classful address and it has at least one subnet of that classful address space in its routing table, it announces the classful network and not the subnet. For example, if a BGP router has network 172.16.22.0/24 in the routing table as a directly connected network, and a BGP **network 172.16.0.0** command, BGP announces the 172.16.0.0/16 network to all neighbors. If 172.16.22.0 is the only subnet for this network in the routing table and it becomes unavailable, BGP will withdraw 172.16.0.0/16 from all neighbors. If instead the command **network 172.16.22.0 mask 255.255.255.0** is used, BGP will announce 172.16.22.0/24 and not 172.16.0.0/16.

For BGP, the **network** command requires that there be an exact match in the routing table for the prefix or mask that is specified. This exact match can be accomplished by using a static route with a null 0 interface, or it might already exist in the routing table, such as because of the Interior Gateway Protocol (IGP) performing the summarization.

Cautions When Using the **network** Command for Summarization

The **network** command tells BGP what to advertise but not how to advertise it. When using the BGP **network** command, the network number specified must also be in the IP routing table before BGP can announce it.

For example, consider Router C in Figure C-2. It has the group of addresses 192.168.24.0/24, 192.168.25.0/24, 192.168.26.0/24, and 192.168.27.0/24 already in its routing table. The configuration in Example C-1 is put on Router C.

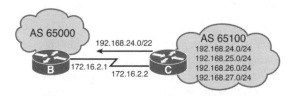

Figure C-2   *BGP Network for Summarization Examples*

Example C-1   *Sample BGP Configuration for Router C in Figure C-2*

```
router bgp 65100
 network 192.168.24.0
 network 192.168.25.0
 network 192.168.26.0
 network 192.168.27.0
 network 192.168.24.0 mask 255.255.252.0
 neighbor 172.16.2.1 remote-as 65000
```

Each of the four Class C networks is announced because each already exists in the routing table. These networks are summarized with the **network 192.168.24.0 mask 255.255.252.0** command on Router C. However, with this command the 192.168.24.0/22 route is *not* announced by default because that route is not in the routing table. If the IGP supports manual summarization (as EIGRP or OSPF do), and the same summarization is performed by the IGP command, BGP announces that summarized route. If route summarization is not performed with the IGP, and BGP is required to announce this route, a static route should be created that allows this network to be installed in the routing table.

The static route should point to the null 0 interface (using the command **ip route 192.168.24.0 255.255.252.0 null0**). Remember that 192.168.24.0/24, 192.168.25.0/24, 192.168.26.0/24, and 192.168.27.0/24 addresses are already in the routing table. This command creates an additional entry of 192.168.24.0/22 as a static route to null 0. If a network, such as 192.168.25.0/24, becomes unreachable, and packets arrive for 192.168.25.1, the destination address is compared to the current entries in the routing table using the longest-match criteria. Because 192.168.25.0/24 no longer exists in the routing table, the best match is 192.168.24.0/22, which points to the null 0 interface. The packet is sent to the null 0 interface, and an Internet Control Message Protocol (ICMP) unreachable message is generated and sent to the packet's originator. Dropping these packets prevents traffic from using up bandwidth following a default route that is either deeper into your autonomous system or (in a worst-case scenario) back out to the ISP (when the ISP would route it back to the autonomous system because of the summarized route advertised to the ISP, causing a routing loop).

In this example, five networks are announced using **network** commands: the four Class C networks plus the summary route. The purpose of summarization is to reduce the advertisement's size, and the size of the Internet routing table. Announcing these more specific networks along with the summarized route actually increases the table's size.

Example C-2 shows a more efficient configuration. A single entry represents all four networks, and a static route to null 0 installs the summarized route in the IP routing table so that BGP can find a match. By using this **network** command, the autonomous system 65100 router advertises a summarized route for the four Class C addresses (192.168.24.0/24, 192.168.25.0/24, 192.168.26.0/24, and 192.168.27.0/24) assigned to the autonomous system. For this new **network** command (192.168.24.0/22) to be advertised, it must first appear in the local routing table. Because only the more specific networks exist in the IP routing table, a static route pointing to null 0 has been created to allow BGP to announce this network (192.168.24.0/22) to autonomous system 65000.

Example C-2   *More-Efficient BGP Configuration for Router C in Figure C-2*

```
router bgp 65100
  network 192.168.24.0 mask 255.255.252.0
  neighbor 172.16.2.1 remote-as 65000
ip route 192.168.24.0 255.255.252.0 null 0
```

Although this configuration works, the **network** command itself was not designed to perform summarization. The **aggregate-address** command, described in the next section, was designed to perform summarization.

Creating a Summary Address in the BGP Table Using the aggregate-address **Command**

The **aggregate-address** *ip-address mask* [**summary-only**] [**as-set**] router configuration command is used to create an aggregate, or summary, entry in the BGP table. The parameters of this command are described in Table C-1.

Table C-1   aggregate-address *Command Description*

Parameter	Description
ip-address	Identifies the aggregate address to be created.
mask	Identifies the mask of the aggregate address to be created.
summary-only	(Optional) Causes the router to advertise only the aggregated route. The default is to advertise both the aggregate and the more specific routes.
as-set	(Optional) Generates AS-Path information with the aggregate route to include all the autonomous system numbers listed in all the paths of the more specific routes. The default for the aggregate route is to list only the autonomous system number of the router that generated the aggregate route.

Notice the difference between the **aggregate-address** and the **network** command:

- The **aggregate-address** command aggregates only networks that are already in the *BGP table*.

- With the BGP **network** command, the network must exist in the *IP routing table* for the summary network to be advertised.

When you use the **aggregate-address** command without the **as-set** keyword, the aggregate route is advertised as coming from your autonomous system, and the atomic aggregate attribute is set to show that information might be missing. The atomic aggregate attribute is set unless you specify the **as-set** keyword.

Without the **summary-only** keyword, the router still advertises the individual networks. This can be useful for redundant ISP links. For example, if one ISP is advertising only summaries, and the other is advertising a summary plus the more specific routes, the more specific routes are followed. However, if the ISP advertising the more specific routes becomes inaccessible, the other ISP advertising only the summary is followed.

When the **aggregate-address** command is used, a BGP route to null 0 is automatically installed in the IP routing table for the summarized route.

If any route already in the BGP table is within the range indicated by the **aggregate-address**, the summary route is inserted into the BGP table and is advertised to other routers. This process creates more information in the BGP table. To get any benefits from the aggregation, the more-specific routes covered by the route summary should be suppressed using the **summary-only** option. When the more specific routes are suppressed, they are still present in the BGP table of the router doing the aggregation. However, because the routes are marked as suppressed, they are never advertised to any other router.

For BGP to announce a summary route using the **aggregate-address** command, at least one of the more specific routes must be in the BGP table. This is usually a result of having **network** commands for those routes.

If you use only the **summary-only** keyword on the **aggregate-address** command, the summary route is advertised, and the path indicates only the autonomous system that did the summarization (all other path information is missing). If you use only the **as-set** keyword on the **aggregate-address** command, the set of autonomous system numbers is included in the path information (and the command with the **summary-only** keyword is deleted if it existed). However, you may use *both* keywords on one command. This causes only the summary address to be sent and all the autonomous systems to be listed in the path information.

Figure C-3 illustrates a sample network (it is the same network as in Figure C-2, repeated here for your convenience). Example C-3 shows the configuration of Router C using the **aggregate-address**.

Example C-3   *Configuration for Router C in Figure C-3 Using the* **aggregate-address** *Command*

```
router bgp 65100
  network 192.168.24.0
  network 192.168.25.0
  network 192.168.26.0
  network 192.168.27.0
  neighbor 172.16.2.1 remote-as 65000
  aggregate-address 192.168.24.0 255.255.252.0 summary-only
```

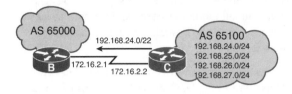

Figure C-3   *BGP Network for Summarization Examples*

This configuration on Router C shows the following:

■ **router bgp 65100:** Configures a BGP process for autonomous system 65100.

■ **network commands:** Configure BGP to advertise the four Class C networks in autonomous system 65100. This part of the configuration describes *what* to advertise.

■ **neighbor 172.16.2.1 remote-as 65000:** Specifies the router at this address (Router B) as a neighbor in autonomous system 65000. This part of the configuration describes *where* to send the advertisements.

■ **aggregate-address 192.168.24.0 255.255.252.0 summary-only:** Specifies the aggregate route to be created but suppresses advertisements of more specific routes to all neighbors. This part of the configuration describes *how* to advertise. Without the **summary-only** option, the new summarized route would be advertised along with the more specific routes. In this example, however, Router B receives only one route (192.168.24.0/22) from Router C. The **aggregate-address** command tells the BGP process to perform route summarization and automatically installs the null route representing the new summarized route.

The following summarizes the differences between the main BGP commands:

■ The **network** command tells BGP *what* to advertise.

■ The **neighbor** command tells BGP *where* to advertise.

■ The **aggregate-address** command tells BGP *how* to advertise the networks.

The **aggregate-address** command does not replace the **network** command. At least one of the more specific routes to be summarized must be in the BGP table. In some situations, the more-specific routes are injected into the BGP table by other routers, and the aggregation is done in another router or even in another autonomous system. This approach is called *proxy aggregation*. In this case, the aggregation router needs only the proper **aggregate-address** command, not the **network** commands, to advertise the more specific routes.

The **show ip bgp** command provides information about route summarization and displays the local router ID, the networks recognized by the BGP process, the accessibility to remote networks, and autonomous system path information. In Example C-4, notice the *s* in the first column for the lower four networks. These networks are being suppressed. They were learned from a **network** command on this router. The next-hop address is 0.0.0.0, which indicates that this router created these entries in BGP. Notice that this router also created the summarized route 192.168.24.0/22 in BGP (this route also has a next hop of 0.0.0.0, indicating that this router created it). The more-specific routes are suppressed, and only the summarized route is announced.

Example C-4   show ip bgp *Command Output with Routes Suppressed*

```
RouterC# show ip bgp
BGP table version is 28, local router ID is 172.16.2.1
Status codes: s = suppressed, * = valid, > = best, and i = internal
Origin codes : i = IGP, e = EGP, and ? = incomplete
Network            Next Hop         Metric  LocPrf  Weight  Path
*>192.168.24.0/22  0.0.0.0             0             32768  i
s>192.168.24.0     0.0.0.0             0             32768  i
s>192.168.25.0     0.0.0.0             0             32768  i
s>192.168.26.0     0.0.0.0             0             32768  i
s>192.168.27.0     0.0.0.0             0             32768  i
```

Redistribution with IGPs

Chapter 4, "Manipulating Routing Updates," discusses route redistribution and how it is configured. This section examines the specifics of when redistribution between BGP and IGPs is appropriate. As noted in Chapter 7, and as shown in Figure C-4, a router running BGP keeps a table of BGP information, separate from the IP routing table. The router offers the best routes from the BGP table to the IP routing table and can be configured to share information between the two tables (by redistribution).

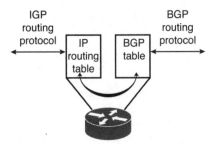

Figure C-4　*A Router Running BGP Keeps a BGP Table, Separate from the IP Routing Table*

Advertising Networks into BGP

Route information is sent from an autonomous system into BGP in one of the following ways:

- **Using the network command:** As discussed, the **network** command allows BGP to advertise a network that is already in the IP table. The list of **network** commands must include all the networks in the autonomous system you want to advertise.

- **By redistributing static routes to interface null 0 into BGP:** Redistribution occurs when a router running different protocols advertises routing information received by one protocol to the other protocol. Static routes in this case are considered a protocol, and static information is advertised to BGP. (The use of the null 0 interface is discussed in the earlier section "Cautions When Using the **network** Command for Summarization.")

- **By redistributing dynamic IGP routes into BGP:** This solution is not recommended in general, because it might cause instability.

Redistributing from an IGP into BGP is not recommended in general because any change in the IGP routes (for example, if a link goes down) might cause a BGP update. This method could result in unstable BGP tables.

If redistribution is used, care must be taken that only local routes are redistributed. For example, routes learned from other autonomous systems (that were learned by redistributing BGP into the IGP) must not be sent out again from the IGP. Otherwise, routing loops could result. Configuring this filtering can be complex.

Using a **redistribute** command into BGP results in an incomplete origin attribute for the route, as indicated by the **?** in the **show ip bgp** command output.

Advertising from BGP into an IGP

Route information may be sent from BGP into an autonomous system by redistributing the BGP routes into the IGP.

Because BGP is an external routing protocol, care must be taken when exchanging information with internal protocols because of the amount of information in BGP tables.

For ISP autonomous systems, redistributing from BGP normally is not required. Other autonomous systems may use redistribution, but the number of routes means that filtering normally is required. Each of these situations is examined in the following sections.

ISP: No Redistribution from BGP into IGP Is Required

An ISP typically has all routers in the autonomous system (or at least all routers in the transit path within the autonomous system) running BGP. Of course, this would be a full-mesh internal BGP (iBGP) environment, and iBGP would be used to carry the external BGP (eBGP) routes across the autonomous system. The BGP information would not need to be redistributed into the IGP. The IGP would need to route only information local to the autonomous system and routes to the next-hop addresses of the BGP routes.

One advantage of this approach is that the IGP protocol does not have to be concerned with all the BGP routes. BGP takes care of them. BGP also converges faster in this environment because it does not have to wait for the IGP to advertise the routes.

Non-ISP: Redistribution from BGP into IGP Might Be Required

A non-ISP autonomous system typically does not have all routers in the autonomous system running BGP, and it might not have a full-mesh iBGP environment. If this is the case, and if knowledge of external routes is required inside the autonomous system, redistributing BGP into the IGP is necessary. However, because of the number of routes that would be in the BGP tables, filtering normally is required.

As discussed in the "Multihomed Internet Connectivity" section in Chapter 6, "Enterprise Internet Connectivity," an alternative to receiving full routes from BGP is that the ISP could send only default routes, or default routes and some external routes, to the autonomous system.

Note An example of when redistributing into an IGP might be necessary is in an autonomous system that is running BGP only on its border routers and that has other routers in the autonomous system that do not run BGP but that require knowledge of external routes.

Communities

As discussed in Chapter 7, BGP communities are another way to filter incoming or outgoing BGP routes. Distribute lists and prefix lists are cumbersome to configure for a large network with a complex routing policy. For example, individual **neighbor** statements and access lists or prefix lists have to be configured for each neighbor on each router involved in the policy.

The BGP communities function allows routers to tag routes with an indicator (the *community*) and allows other routers to make decisions (filter) based on that tag. BGP communities are used for destinations (routes) that share some common properties and that, therefore, share common policies. Routers, therefore, act on the community, rather than on individual routes. Communities are not restricted to one network or autonomous system, and they have no physical boundaries.

Community Attribute

The community attribute is an optional transitive attribute. If a router does not understand the concept of communities, it passes it on to the next router. However, if the router does understand the concept, it must be configured to propagate the community. Otherwise, communities are dropped by default.

Each network can be a member of more than one community.

The community attribute is a 32-bit number. It can have a value in the range 0 to 4,294,967,200. The upper 16 bits indicate the autonomous system number of the autonomous system that defined the community. The lower 16 bits are the community number and have local significance. The community value can be entered as one decimal number or in the format *AS:nn*, where *AS* is the autonomous system number, and *nn* is the lower 16-bit local number. The community value is displayed as one decimal number by default.

Setting and Sending the Communities Configuration

Route maps can be used to set the community attributes.

The **set community** {[*community-number*] [*well-known-community*] [**additive**]} | **none** route map configuration command is used within a route map to set the BGP community attribute. The parameters of this command are described in Table C-2.

Table C-2   set community *Command Description*

Parameter	Description
community-number	The community number. Values are 1 to 4,294,967,200.
well-known-community	The following are predefined, well-known communities: ■ **internet:** Advertises this route to the Internet community and any router that belongs to it ■ **no-export:** Does not advertise to eBGP peers ■ **no-advertise:** Does not advertise this route to any peer ■ **local-AS:** Does not send outside the local autonomous system
additive	(Optional) Specifies that the community is to be added to the existing communities.
none	Removes the community attribute from the prefixes that pass the route map.

The **set community** command is used along with the **neighbor route-map** command to apply the route map to updates.

The **neighbor** {*ip-address* | *peer-group-name*} **send-community** router configuration command is used to specify that the BGP communities attribute should be sent to a BGP neighbor. Table C-3 explains the parameters of this command.

Table C-3   neighbor send-community *Command Description*

Parameter	Description
ip-address	The IP address of the BGP neighbor to which the communities attribute is sent
peer-group-name	The name of a BGP peer group

By default, the communities attribute is not sent to any neighbor. (Communities are stripped in outgoing BGP updates.)

In Figure C-5, Router C is sending BGP updates to Router A, but it does not want Router A to propagate these routes to Router B.

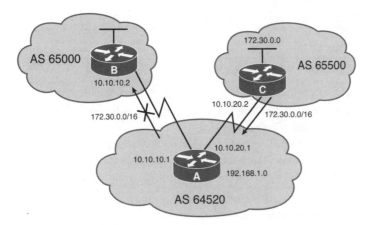

Figure C-5 *Network for BGP Communities Example*

Example C-5 shows the configuration for Router C in this example. Router C sets the community attribute in the BGP routes that it is advertising to Router A. The **no-export** community attribute is used to indicate that Router A should not send the routes to its external BGP peers.

Example C-5 *Configuration of Router C in Figure C-5*

```
router bgp 65500
  network 172.30.0.0
  neighbor 10.10.20.1 remote-as 64520
  neighbor 10.10.20.1 send-community
  neighbor 10.10.20.1 route-map SETCOMM out
!
route-map SETCOMM permit 10
  match ip address 1
  set community no-export
!
access-list 1 permit 0.0.0.0 255.255.255.255
```

In this example, Router C has one neighbor, 10.10.20.1 (Router A). When communicating with Router A, the community attribute is sent, as specified by the **neighbor send-community** command. The route map SETCOMM is used when sending routes to Router A to set the community attribute. Any route that matches **access-list 1** has the community attribute set to **no-export**. Access list 1 permits any routes. Therefore, all routes have the community attribute set to **no-export.**

In this example, Router A receives all of Router C's routes but does not pass them to Router B.

Using the Communities Configuration

The **ip community-list** *community-list-number* {**permit** | **deny**} *community-number* global configuration command is used to create a community list for BGP and to control access to it. The parameters of this command are described in Table C-4.

Table C-4 ip community-list *Command Description*

Parameter	Description
community-list-number	The community list number, in the range of 1 to 99
permit	**deny**	Permits or denies access for a matching condition
community-number	The community number or well-known-community configured by a **set community** command

The **match community** *community-list-number* [**exact**] route map configuration command enables you to match a BGP community attribute to a value in a community list. The parameters of this command are described in Table C-5.

Table C-5 match community *Command Description*

Parameter	Description
community-list-number	The community list number, in the range of 1 to 99, that is used to compare the community attribute.
exact	(Optional) Indicates that an exact match is required. All the communities and only those communities in the community list must be present in the community attribute.

In Figure C-6, Router C is sending BGP updates to Router A. Router A sets the weight of these routes based on the community value set by router C.

Example C-6 shows the configuration of Router C in Figure C-6. Router C has one neighbor, 10.10.20.1 (Router A).

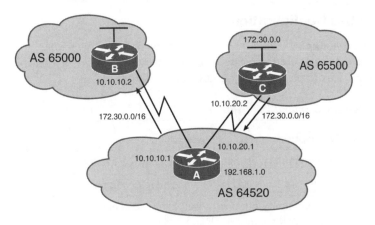

Figure C-6   *Network for BGP Communities Example Using Weight*

Example C-6   *Configuration of Router C in Figure C-6*

```
router bgp 65500
  network 172.30.0.0
  neighbor 10.10.20.1 remote-as 64520
  neighbor 10.10.20.1 send-community
  neighbor 10.10.20.1 route-map SETCOMM out
!
route-map SETCOMM permit 10
  match ip address 1
  set community 100 additive
!
access-list 1 permit 0.0.0.0 255.255.255.255
```

In this example, the community attribute is sent to Router A, as specified by the **neighbor send-community** command. The route map SETCOMM is used when sending routes to Router A to set the community attribute. Any route that matches access list 1 has community 100 added to the existing communities in the route's community attribute. In this example, access list 1 permits any routes. Therefore, all routes have 100 added to the list of communities. If the **additive** keyword in the **set community** command is not set, 100 replaces any old community that already exists. Because the keyword **additive** is used, the 100 is added to the list of communities that the route is part of.

Example C-7 shows the configuration of Router A in Figure C-6.

Example C-7   *Configuration of Router A in Figure C-6*

```
router bgp 64520
  neighbor 10.10.20.2 remote-as 65500
  neighbor 10.10.20.2 route-map CHKCOMM in
!
route-map CHKCOMM permit 10
```

```
    match community 1
    set weight 20
route-map CHKCOMM permit 20
    match community 2
!
ip community-list 1 permit 100
ip community-list 2 permit internet
```

Note   Other **router bgp** configuration commands for Router A are not shown in Example C-9.

In this example, Router A has a neighbor, 10.10.20.2 (Router C). The route map CHKCOMM is used when receiving routes from Router C to check the community attribute. Any route whose community attribute matches community list 1 has its weight attribute set to 20. Community list 1 permits routes with a community attribute of 100. Therefore, all routes from Router C (which all have 100 in their list of communities) have their weight set to 20.

In this example, any route that does not match community list 1 is checked against community list 2. Any route matching community list 2 is permitted but does not have any of its attributes changed. Community list 2 specifies the **internet** keyword, which means all routes.

The sample output shown in Example C-8 is from Router A in Figure C-6. The output shows the details about the route 172.30.0.0 from Router C, including that its community attribute is 100 and that its weight attribute is now 20.

Example C-8   show ip bgp *Output from Router A in Figure C-6*

```
RtrA # show ip bgp 172.30.0.0/16
BGP routing Table entry for 172.30.0.0/16, version 2
Paths: (1 available, best #1)
  Advertised to non peer-group peers:
    10.10.10.2
  65500
    10.10.20.2 from 10.10.20.2 (172.30.0.1)
      Origin IGP, metric 0, localpref 100, weight 20, valid, external, best, ref 2
Community: 100
```

Route Reflectors

BGP specifies that routes learned via iBGP are never propagated to other iBGP peers (this is sometimes referred to as the BGP split-horizon rule). The result is that a full mesh of iBGP peers is required within an autonomous system. As Figure C-7 illustrates, however, a full mesh of iBGP is not scalable. With only 13 routers, 78 iBGP sessions would need to be maintained. As the number of routers increases, so does the number of sessions required, governed by the following formula, in which *n* is the number of routers:

Number of iBGP sessions = $n(n - 1) / 2$

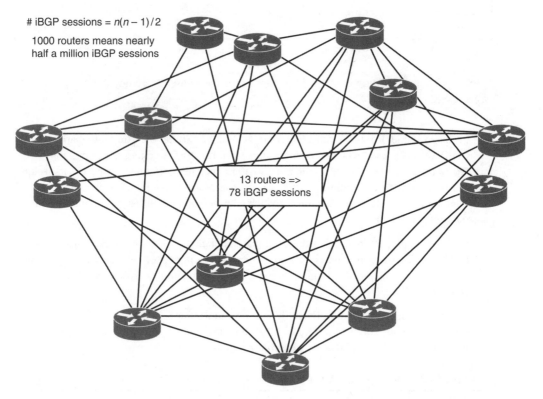

iBGP sessions = $n(n - 1)/2$

1000 routers means nearly half a million iBGP sessions

13 routers =>
78 iBGP sessions

Figure C-7   *Full-Mesh iBGP Requires Many Sessions and, Therefore, Is Not Scalable*

In addition to the number of BGP TCP sessions that must be created and maintained, the amount of routing traffic might also be a problem. Depending on the autonomous system topology, traffic might be replicated many times on some links as it travels to each iBGP peer. For example, if the physical topology of a large autonomous system includes some WAN links, the iBGP sessions running over those links might consume a significant amount of bandwidth.

A solution to this problem is the use of route reflectors (RRs). This section describes what an RR is, how it works, and how to configure it.

RRs modify the BGP rule by allowing the router configured as the RR to propagate routes learned by iBGP to other iBGP peers, as illustrated in Figure C-8.

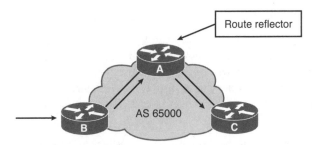

Figure C-8   *When Router A Is a Route Reflector, It Can Propagate Routes Learned via iBGP from Router B to Router C*

This saves on the number of BGP TCP sessions that must be maintained and also reduces the BGP routing traffic.

Route Reflector Benefits

With a BGP RR configured, a full mesh of iBGP peers is no longer required. The RR is allowed to propagate iBGP routes to other iBGP peers. RRs are used mainly by ISPs when the number of internal **neighbor** statements becomes excessive. Route reflectors reduce the number of BGP neighbor relationships in an autonomous system (thus, saving on TCP connections) by having key routers replicate updates to their RR clients.

Route reflectors do not affect the paths that IP packets follow. Only the path that routing information is distributed on is affected. However, if RRs are configured incorrectly, routing loops might result, as shown in the example later in this appendix in the "Route Reflector Migration Tips" section.

An autonomous system can have multiple RRs, both for redundancy and for grouping to further reduce the number of iBGP sessions required.

Migrating to RRs involves a minimal configuration and does not have to be done all at one time, because routers that are not RRs can coexist with RRs within an autonomous system.

Route Reflector Terminology

A *route reflector* is a router that is configured to be the router allowed to advertise (or reflect) routes it learned via iBGP to other iBGP peers. The RR has a partial iBGP peering with other routers, which are called *clients*. Peering between the clients is not needed, because the route reflector passes advertisements between the clients.

The combination of the RR and its clients is called a *cluster*.

Other iBGP peers of the RR that are not clients are called *nonclients*.

The *originator ID* is an optional, nontransitive BGP attribute that is created by the RR. This attribute carries the router ID of the route's originator in the local autonomous system. If the update comes back to the originator because of poor configuration, the originator ignores it.

Usually a cluster has a single RR, in which case the cluster is identified by the RR's router ID. To increase redundancy and avoid single points of failure, a cluster might have more than one RR. When this occurs, all the RRs in the cluster need to be configured with a *cluster ID*. The cluster ID allows route reflectors to recognize updates from other RRs in the same cluster.

A *cluster list* is a sequence of cluster IDs that the route has passed. When an RR reflects a route from its clients to nonclients outside the cluster, it appends the local cluster ID to the cluster list. If the update has an empty cluster list, the RR creates one. Using this attribute, an RR can tell whether the routing information is looped back to the same cluster because of poor configuration. If the local cluster ID is found in an advertisement's cluster list, the advertisement is ignored.

The originator ID, cluster ID, and cluster list help prevent routing loops in RR configurations.

Route Reflector Design

When using RRs in an autonomous system, you can divide the autonomous system into multiple clusters, each having at least one RR and a few clients. Multiple RRs can exist in one cluster for redundancy.

The RRs must be fully meshed with iBGP to ensure that all routes learned are propagated throughout the autonomous system.

An IGP is still used, just as it was before RRs were introduced, to carry local routes and next-hop addresses.

Normal split-horizon rules still apply between an RR and its clients. Thus an RR that receives a route from a client does not advertise that route back to that client.

Note   No defined limit applies to the number of clients an RR might have. It is constrained by the amount of router memory.

Route Reflector Design Example

Figure C-9 provides an example of a BGP RR design.

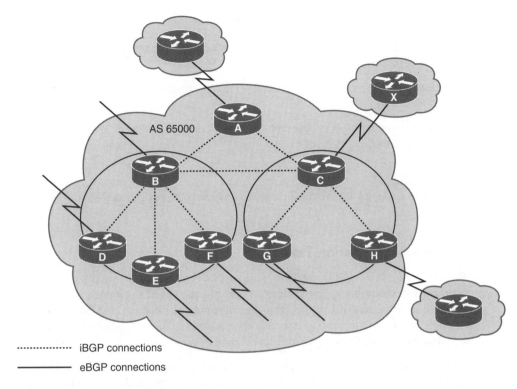

Figure C-9 *Example of a Route Reflector Design*

Note The physical connections within autonomous system 65000 are not shown in Figure C-9.

In Figure C-9, Routers B, D, E, and F form one cluster. Routers C, G, and H form another cluster. Routers B and C are RRs. Routers A, B, and C are fully meshed with iBGP. Note that the routers within a cluster are not fully meshed.

Route Reflector Operation

When an RR receives an update, it takes the following actions, depending on the type of peer that sent the update:

- If the update is from a client peer, it sends the update to all nonclient peers and to all client peers (except the route's originator).

- If the update is from a nonclient peer, it sends the update to all clients in the cluster.

- If the update is from an eBGP peer, it sends the update to all nonclient peers and to all client peers.

For example, in Figure C-9, the following happens:

- If Router C receives an update from Router H (a client), it sends it to Router G, and to Routers A and B.

- If Router C receives an update from Router A (a nonclient), it sends it to Routers G and H.

- If Router C receives an update from Router X (via eBGP), it sends it to Routers G and H, and to Routers A and B.

Note   Routers also send updates to their eBGP neighbors as appropriate.

Route Reflector Migration Tips

When migrating to using RRs, the first consideration is which routers should be the reflectors and which should be the clients. Following the physical topology in this design decision ensures that the packet-forwarding paths are not affected. Not following the physical topology (for example, configuring RR clients that are not physically connected to the route reflector) might result in routing loops.

Figure C-10 demonstrates what can happen if RRs are configured without following the physical topology. In this figure, the lower router, Router E, is an RR client for both RRs, Routers C and D. Note that Router A is an RR client of Router D, but Router A is not physically connected to Router D. Similarly, Router B is an RR client of Router C, but Router B is not physically connected to Router C.

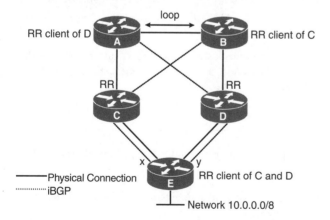

Figure C-10   *Bad Route Reflector Design That Does Not Follow the Physical Topology*

In this *bad design*, which does not follow the physical topology, the following happens:

- Router B knows that the next hop to get to 10.0.0.0 is x (because it learns this from its RR, Router C).

- Router A knows that the next hop to get to 10.0.0.0 is y (because it learns this from its RR, Router D).

- For Router B to get to x, the best route might be through Router A, so Router B sends a packet destined for 10.0.0.0 to Router A.

- For Router A to get to y, the best route might be through Router B, so Router A sends a packet destined for 10.0.0.0 to Router B.

- This is a routing loop.

Figure C-11 shows a better design (better because it follows the physical topology). Again, in this figure, the lower router, Router E, is an RR client for both route reflectors.

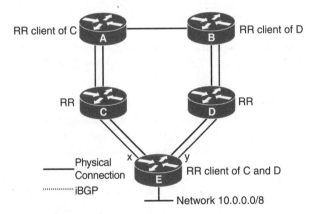

Figure C-11   *Good Route Reflector Design That Does Follow the Physical Topology*

In this *good design*, which follows the physical topology, the following are true:

- Router B knows that the next hop to get to 10.0.0.0 is y (because it learns this from its RR, Router D).

- Router A knows that the next hop to get to 10.0.0.0 is x (because it learns this from its RR, Router C).

- For Router A to get to x, the best route is through Router C, so Router A sends a packet destined for 10.0.0.0 to Router C, and Router C sends it to Router E.

- For Router B to get to y, the best route is through Router D, so Router B sends a packet destined for 10.0.0.0 to Router D, and Router D sends it to Router E.

- There is no routing loop.

When migrating to using RRs, configure one RR at a time, and then delete the redundant iBGP sessions between the clients. It is recommended that you configure one RR per cluster.

Route Reflector Configuration

The **neighbor** *ip-address* **route-reflector-client** router configuration command enables you to configure the router as a BGP RR and to configure the specified neighbor as its client. The *ip-address* is the IP address of the BGP neighbor being identified as a client.

Configuring the Cluster ID

To configure the cluster ID if the BGP cluster has more than one RR, use the **bgp cluster-id** *cluster-id* router configuration command on all the RRs in a cluster. You cannot change the cluster ID after the RR clients have been configured.

RRs cause some restrictions on other commands, including the following:

- When used on RRs, the **neighbor next-hop-self** command affects only the next hop of eBGP learned routes because the next hop of reflected iBGP routes should not be changed.

- RR clients are incompatible with peer groups. This is because a router configured with a peer group must send any update to *all* members of the peer group. If an RR has all of its clients in a peer group and then one of those clients sends an update, the RR is responsible for sharing that update with all *other* clients. The RR must not send the update to the originating client because of the split-horizon rule.

Route Reflector Example

Figure C-12 illustrates a network, with Router A configured as an RR in autonomous system 65000. Example C-9 shows the configuration for Router A, the RR.

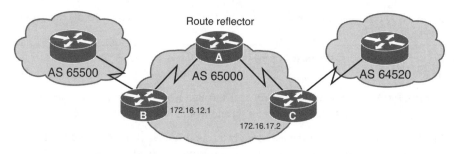

Figure C-12   *Router A Is a Route Reflector*

Example C-9   *Configuration of Router A in Figure C-12*

```
RTRA(config)# router bgp 65000
RTRA(config-router)# neighbor 172.16.12.1 remote-as 65000
RTRA(config-router)# neighbor 172.16.12.1 route-reflector-client
RTRA(config-router)# neighbor 172.16.17.2 remote-as 65000
RTRA(config-router)# neighbor 172.16.17.2 route-reflector-client
```

The **neighbor route-reflector-client** commands define which neighbors are RR clients. In this example, both Routers B and C are RR clients of Router A, the RR.

Verifying Route Reflectors

The **show ip bgp neighbors** command output indicates that a particular neighbor is an RR client. The sample partial output for this command, shown in Example C-10, is from Router A in Figure C-12 and shows that 172.16.12.1 (Router B) is an RR client of Router A.

Example C-10   show ip bgp neighbors *Output from Router A in Figure C-12*

```
RTRA# show ip bgp neighbors
BGP neighbor is 172.16.12.1, remote AS 65000, internal link
 Index 1, Offset 0, Mask 0x2
 Route-Reflector Client
 BGP version 4, remote router ID 192.168.101.101
 BGP state = Established, table version = 1, up for 00:05:42
 Last read 00:00:42, hold time is 180, keepalive interval is 60 seconds
 Minimum time between advertisement runs is 5 seconds
 Received 14 messages, 0 notifications, 0 in queue
 Sent 12 messages, 0 notifications, 0 in queue
 Prefix advertised 0, suppressed 0, withdrawn 0
 Connections established 2; dropped 1
 Last reset 00:05:44, because of User reset
 1 accepted prefixes consume 32 bytes
 0 history paths consume 0 bytes
--More--
```

Advertising a Default Route

The **neighbor** {*ip-address* | *peer-group-name*} **default-originate** [**route-map** *map-name*] router configuration command can be used for a BGP router to send the default route 0.0.0.0 to a neighbor, for its use as a default route. Table C-6 describes the parameters of this command.

Table C-6   neighbor default-originate *Command Description*

Parameter	Description
ip-address	The IP address of the BGP neighbor
peer-group-name	The name of a BGP peer group
route-map *map-name*	(Optional) Identifies a route map, to allow the default route to be sent to the neighbor conditionally

Not Advertising Private Autonomous System Numbers

As mentioned in Chapter 6, the IANA defines private autonomous system numbers 64512 through 65534 to be used for private purposes, much like the private IPv4 addresses.

Only public autonomous system numbers should be sent to eBGP neighbors on the Internet. Use the **neighbor** {*ip-address* | *peer-group-name*} **remove-private-as** [**all** [**replace-as**]] router configuration command to remove private autonomous system numbers from the AS-Path attribute; this command is available only for eBGP neighbors.

Table C-7 describes the parameters of this command.

Table C-7   neighbor remove-private-as *Command Description*

Parameter	Description
ip-address	The IP address of the BGP neighbor.
peer-group-name	The name of a BGP peer group.
all	(Optional) Removes all private autonomous system numbers from the autonomous system path in outgoing updates.
replace-as	(Optional) Only valid with the **all** keyword, the **replace-as** keyword causes all private autonomous system numbers in the autonomous system path to be replaced with the router's local autonomous system number. This ensures that the length of the AS-path attribute (used in the BGP path selection process) remains the same as it was before the autonomous system numbers were replaced.

Note   The command syntax documentation indicates that the **all** keyword can be used alone; in testing, this produced the same results as when the command was used without the **all** keyword.

Appendix D

Acronyms and Abbreviations

This appendix identifies abbreviations, acronyms, and initialisms used in this book and in the internetworking industry.

Acronym	Expanded Term
3DES	Triple DES
6-to-4	IPv6-to-IPv4
AAA	authentication, authorization, accounting
ABR	Area Border Router
ACK	1. acknowledge
	2. acknowledgment
	3. acknowledgment bit in a TCP segment
ACL	access control list
AD	advertised distance
AES	Advanced Encryption Standard
AfriNIC	African Network Information Centre
AH	Authentication Header
APNIC	Asia Pacific Network Information Center
ARIN	American Registry for Internet Numbers
ARP	Address Resolution Protocol
AS	autonomous system

Acronym	Expanded Term
ASBR	Autonomous System Boundary Router
ASN	AS number
BDR	backup designated router
BGP	Border Gateway Protocol
BGPv4 or BGP-4	BGP Version 4
bps	bits per second
BSCI	Building Scalable Cisco Internetworks
CCDP	Cisco Certified Design Professional
CCNA	Cisco Certified Network Associate
CCNP	Cisco Certified Network Professional
CCSP	Cisco Certified Security Professional
CDP	Cisco Discovery Protocol
CE	customer edge
CEF	Cisco Express Forwarding
CEFv6	Cisco Express Forwarding for IPv6

Acronym	Expanded Term
CIDR	classless interdomain routing
CoS	class of service
CPE	customer provider edge customer premise equipment
CPU	central processing unit
DAD	duplicate address detection
DBD	database description packets
DES	Data Encryption Standard
DESGN	Designing for Cisco Internetwork Solutions
DHCP	Dynamic Host Configuration Protocol
DHCPv6	DHCP for IPv6
DHCPv6-PD	DHCPv6 Prefix Delegation
DLCI	data-link connection identifier
DMVPN	Dynamic Multipoint VPN
DNA	DoNotAge
DNS	Domain Name Service or Domain Name System
DR	designated router
DUAL	diffusing update algorithm
E1	external type 1
E2	external type 2
eBGP	external BGP
EGP	Exterior Gateway Protocol
EIGRP	Enhanced Interior Gateway Routing Protocol
ESP	Encapsulating Security Payload
EUI-64	extended universal identifier 64-bit
FD	feasible distance
FHRP	first-hop redundancy protocol
FIB	Forwarding Information Base
FLSM	fixed-length subnet mask
FS	feasible successor
FTP	File Transfer Protocol
Gbps	gigabits per second

Acronym	Expanded Term
GE	Gigabit Ethernet
GLBP	Gateway Load Balancing Protocol
GRE	generic routing encapsulation
HMAC	hash message authentication code
HSRP	Hot Standby Router Protocol
HTTP	Hypertext Transfer Protocol
HTTPS	Secure HTTP
Hz	hertz
IANA	Internet Assigned Numbers Authority
iBGP	Internal BGP
ICANN	Internet Corporation for Assigned Names and Numbers
ICMP	Internet Control Message Protocol
ICMPv4	ICMP for IPv4
ICMPv6	ICMP for IPv6
ID	identifier
IDRP	Interdomain Routing Protocol
IEEE	Institute of Electrical and Electronics Engineers
IETF	Internet Engineering Task Force
IGMP	Internet Group Management Protocol
IGP	Interior Gateway Protocol
IGRP	Interior Gateway Routing Protocol
IKE	Internet Key Exchange
INARP	Inverse Address Resolution Protocol
IND	Inverse Neighbor Discovery
IOS	Internet Operating System
IP	Internet Protocol
IPsec	IP Security
IPv4	IP Version 4
IPv6	IP Version 6

Acronym	Expanded Term
IPX	Internetwork Packet Exchange
IS	1. information systems
	2. intermediate system
IS-IS	Intermediate System-to-Intermediate System
IS-ISv6	IS-IS for IPv6
ISP	Internet service provider
ISR	integrated services router
ITU-T	International Telecommunication Union Telecommunication Standardization Sector
Kbps	kilobits per second
LACNIC	Latin American and Caribbean IP Address Regional Registry
LAN	local-area network
LS	link state
LSA	link-state advertisement
LSAck	link-state acknowledgment
LSDB	link-state database
LSR	link-state request
LSU	link-state update
M	metric
MAC	1. Media Access Control
	2. message authentication code
MB	megabyte
Mbps	megabits per second
MD5	message digest algorithm 5
MED	multi-exit-discriminator
MIB	Management Information Base
MOTD	message of the day
MP-BGP	Multiprotocol extensions for BGP-4
MP-BGP4	Multiprotocol Border Gateway Protocol Version 4
MPLS	Multiprotocol Label Switching
ms	millisecond
MTU	maximum transmission unit
NA	Neighbor advertisement

Acronym	Expanded Term
NAT	Network Address Translation
NAT64	NAT IPv6 to IPv4
NAT-PT	NAT-Protocol Translation
NBMA	nonbroadcast multiaccess
ND	Neighbor discovery
NGE	next-generation encryption
NHRP	Next Hop Resolution Protocol
NLRI	network layer reachability information
NMS	network management system
NPTv6	IPv6-to-IPv6 Network Prefix Translation
NS	Neighbor solicitation
NSSA	not-so-stubby area
NTP	Network Time Protocol
NVI	NAT virtual interface
OS	operating system
OSI	Open System Interconnection
OSPF	Open Shortest Path First
OSPFv2	OSPF Version 2
OSPFv3	OSPF Version 3
OUI	organizationally unique identifier
P	propagate
PA	provider aggregatable
PAT	Port Address Translation
PBR	policy-based routing
PDM	protocol-dependent module
PDU	protocol data unit
PE	provider edge
PI	provider independent
PPP	Point-to-Point Protocol
pps	packets per second
QoS	quality of service
RA	router advertisement
RD	reported distance
RFC	Request For Comments
RIB	Routing Information Base

Acronym	Expanded Term
RIP	Routing Information Protocol
RIPE-NCC	Réseaux IP Européens-Network Coordination Center
RIPng	Routing Information Protocol new generation
RIPv1	Routing Information Protocol Version 1
RIPv2	Routing Information Protocol Version 2
RIRs	regional Internet registries
RO	read-only
RR	route reflector
RS	router solicitation
RTO	retransmit timeout
RTP	Reliable Transport Protocol
RTT	round-trip time
RTTMON	Round-Trip Time Monitor
RW	read-write
SA	security association
SHA	Secure Hash Algorithm
SHA256	SHA 256 bit
SIA	stuck in active
SIEM	Security Information & Event Management
SLAAC	stateless address autoconfiguration
SLAs	service-level agreements
SM	source metric
SMTP	Simple Mail Transfer Protocol
SNMP	Simple Network Management Protocol
SNMPv1	SNMP Version 1
SNMPv2	SNMP Version 2
SNMPv3	SNMP Version 3
SP	service provider
SPF	shortest path first
SPI	Security Parameter Index
SRTT	smooth round-trip time

Acronym	Expanded Term
SSH	secure shell
SSHv1	SSH version 1
SSHv2	SSH version 2
SSL	Secure socket layer
STP	1. shielded twisted-pair
	2. Spanning Tree Protocol
SYN	synchronize
TCP	Transmission Control Protocol
TCP/IP	Transmission Control Protocol/Internet Protocol
TFTP	Trivial File Transfer Protocol
TLV	Type, Length, Value
ToS	type of service
TTL	Time To Live
UDP	User Datagram Protocol
U/L	universal/local
UPS	uninterruptible power supply
URL	Uniform Resource Locator
uRPF	Unicast Reverse Path Forwarding
UTP	unshielded twisted-pair
VC	virtual circuit
VLAN	virtual LAN
VLSM	variable-length subnet mask
VoIP	Voice over IP
VPN	virtual private network
VRF	VPN routing and forwarding
VRRP	Virtual Router Redundancy Protocol
vty	virtual terminal
WAN	wide-area network
WWW	World Wide Web

Index

Numerics

A

D

data plane, 328, 527

databases

LSDB, 189-206

contents, displaying, 192

synchronizing, 204-205

OSPF exchange process, 169-170

RIPng, verifying, 53-54

DBD (Database Description) packets, 160

dead timer, manipulating, 179-182

debug eigrp packets hello command, 70-72

debugging

conditional debugging, 568-569

decimal-to-binary conversion, 618-619

default interface costs, OSPF, 211-214

default metrics, 272-273

default routes

cost of in stub areas, 236-238

obtaining, 120-123

propagating, 50-53

default seed metrics, 273-275

defining

BGP neighbor relationships, 443-444

route redistribution, 270-271

delay, EIGRP composite metric, 89

DHCP (Dynamic Host Configuration Protocol), 382-383

configuring, 384-385

provider-assigned IPv4 address, obtaining, 383-384

DHCPv6, 402-405

DHCPv6-PD, 405

stateful DHCPv6, 404

stateless DHCPv6, 403-404

Dijkstra's algorithm, 156

disabling

automatic summarization, 115-116

CEF, 341-343

unused services, 567

disadvantages

of single-homed connections, 410

of static routing, 20

displaying

EIGRP for IPv6 routing table, 133

LSDB contents, 192

distance vector protocols, 7

EIGRP

active timer, 108

authentication, configuring, 581-583

best path selection, 80-87

composite metric, 88-89

default routes, obtaining, 120-123

default seed metric, 274

DUAL, 76

feasibility condition, 91

features, 60-62

hello packets, 70-72

hello timer, 71

hold timers, 71

for IPv4, 64-72

load balancing, 123-128

multiple network layer support, 61

neighbor relationships, 63-64, 66-69

neighbor table, 63

over Frame Relay, 74

over Layer 2 MPLS VPN, 75-76

over Layer 3 MPLS VPN, 74-75

partial updates, 61

passive interfaces, 69-70

query packets, 79, 95-96

reply packets, 79

route summarization, 109

RTP, 62

SIA state, 108-109

topology table, 63

unequal metric load balancing, 62

VLSM, 61

wide metric, 90

I

J-K

L

M

O

Q-R

S

T

W-X-Y-Z

cisco

ciscopress.com: Your Cisco Certification and Networking Learning Resource

Subscribe to the monthly Cisco Press newsletter to be the first to learn about new releases and special promotions.

Visit **ciscopress.com/newsletters.**

While you are visiting, check out the offerings available at your finger tips.

–Free Podcasts from experts:
  · OnNetworking
  · OnCertification
  · OnSecurity

Podcasts

View them at **ciscopress.com/podcasts.**

–Read the latest author **articles** and **sample chapters** at **ciscopress.com/articles.**

–Bookmark the Certification Reference Guide available through our partner site at **informit.com/certguide.**

Connect with Cisco Press authors and editors via Facebook and Twitter, visit **informit.com/socialconnect.**